OS/2 2.1 Unleashed *should be read cover to cover. I highly recommend this book to OS/2 users of all experience levels, from beginner to advanced.*

—John Hoffman
NBC

As an experienced user of OS/2 and PCs in general, it's my opinion that users new to OS/2 will not be left confused by nor will advanced users be left disappointed by OS/2 2.1 Unleashed. *Recommended without reservation. And I can't wait to get hold of the second edition!*

—Bob Weeks

OS/2 2.1 Unleashed *is by far and away the best and most complete authority on OS/2 2.1. The text is useful for both the novice and the experienced user.*

—Ray Theiss, Team OS/2

This is far and above the best book about OS/2 that I've ever seen. In fact, it's probably the best book on any operating system I've read in the past 15 years!

—Chip Rabinowitz
Chief Technical Officer, Innovative Data Concepts, Inc.

It's the book I would have written if I had the technical knowledge, the editorial sophistication, and the dedication to the dissemination of knowledge so thoroughly demonstrated by Moskowitz and Kerr, et al.

—Adrian Brancato
Technical Services, N.C. Department of Corrections

In my opinion, OS/2 2.1 Unleashed *is the most comprehensive (read best!) book about OS/2 available anywhere. The book gets into all aspects of OS/2 and will likely become the premier reference for everyone that has a question about OS/2.*

—Steven Hoagland

If you need a reference work on 2.1 (and who doesn't) and need it written in a clear, concise manner by the foremost experts in their fields, bundled with a diskette of utilitiess that would cost you twice the price of the book alone, OS/2 2.1 Unleashed *is the way to go.*

—Paolo Pignatelli
The Corner Store

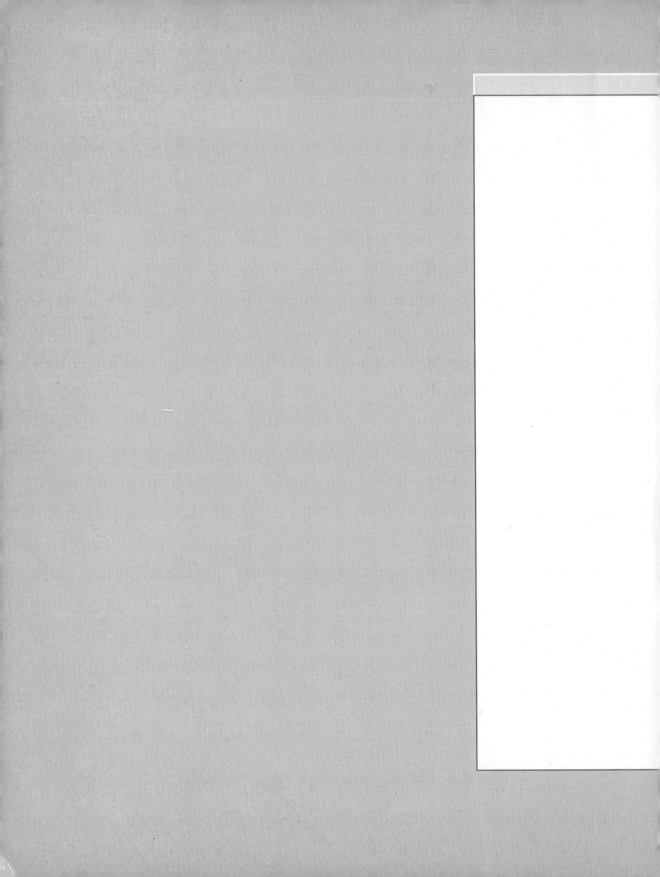

OS/2 2.1 Unleashed

David Moskowitz and David Kerr

A Division of Prentice Hall Computer Publishing
11711 North College, Carmel, Indiana 46032 USA

Copyright © 1993 by Sams Publishing

FIRST EDITION

International Standard Book Number: 0-672-30240-3

Library of Congress Catalog Card Number: 92-62682

96 95 94 93 5 4 3

Interpretation of the printing code: the rightmost double-digit number is the year of the book's printing; the rightmost single-digit, the number of the book's printing. For example, a printing code of 93-1 shows that the first printing of the book occurred in 1993.

Trademarks

Composed in Garamond and MCPdigital by Prentice Hall Computer Publishing

Printed in the United States of America

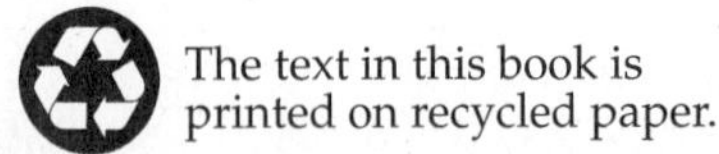

Publisher
Richard K. Swadley

Acquisitions Manager
Jordan Gold

Acquisitions Editor
Gregg Bushyeager

Development Editors
Gregg Bushyeager
Ella M. Davis
David Moskowitz

Senior Editor
Grant Fairchild

Editors
Susan Christophersen
Sandra Doell
Hugh Vandivier

Editorial Coordinator
Rebecca S. Freeman

Formatter
Bill Whitmer

Editorial Assistant
Rosemarie Graham

Technical Editor
Scott Kliger

Cover Designer
Jean Bisesi

Director of Production and Manufacturing
Jeff Valler

Production Manager
Corinne Walls

Imprint Manager
Matthew Morrill

Book Designer
Michele Laseau

Production Analyst
Mary Beth Wakefield

Proofreading/Indexing Coordinator
Joelynn Gifford

Graphics Image Specialists
Aaron Davis
Jerry Ellis
Dennis Sheehan
Sue VandeWalle

Production
Jeff Baker, Katy Bodenmiller, Julie Brown, Christine Cook, Lisa Daugherty, Mark Enochs, Tim Groeling, Dennis Clay Hager, Carla Hall-Batton, Howard Jones, John Kane, Heather Kaufman, Sean Medlock, Tim Montgomery, Roger Morgan, Juli Pavey, Angela Pozdol, Caroline Roop, Michelle Self, Susan Shepard, Greg Simsic, Phil Worthington, Alyssa Yesh

Indexers
Loren Malloy
Tina Trettin

Overview

Contents

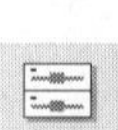

Video

Printer

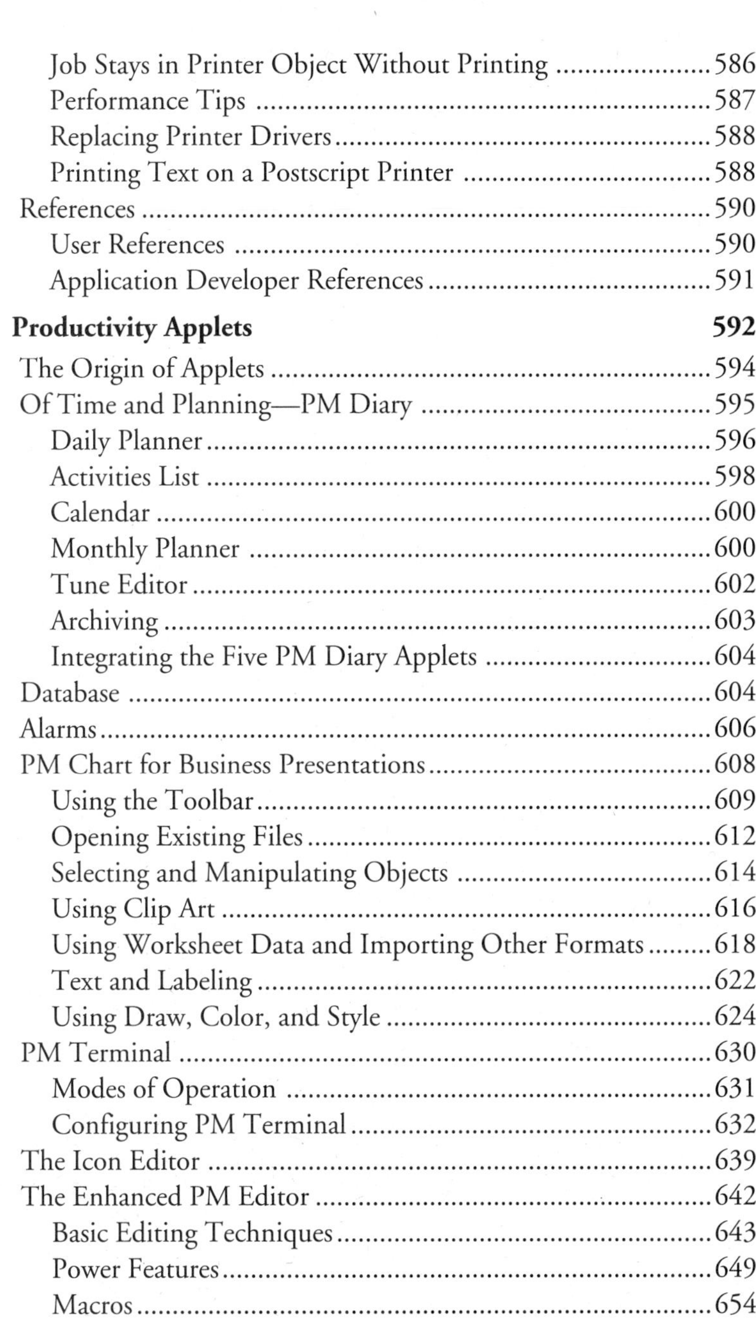

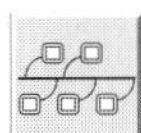

Foreward

Late in the evening of March 31, 1992, a dedicated team of designers and programmers in Boca Raton, Florida, completed the final testing of the OS/2 2.0 operating system. Their efforts have been rewarded with the success of the OS/2 2.0 product.

More than 2 million copies of OS/2 2.0 have been shipped, greatly exceeding industry and analyst expectations. More than 1,300 applications are available for OS/2, including major products from industry-leading software corporations. As each month passes, more and more OS/2 applications are launched.

The achievement of the OS/2 operating system has not gone unnoticed within the industry. To date, OS/2 2.0 has received 12 industry awards, including the following:

PC Magazine, Technical Excellence
Information Week, 1992 Top Products—the 10 most likely to succeed
PC Week Labs, Top Product 1992
Corporate Computing, Best Buy
Datamation, Product of the Year, PC Software category

1993 marks the availability of OS/2 2.1. We have incorporated many improvements to the operating system, including performance enhancements, support for Windows 3.1 applications, compatibility with many more printer and video devices, power management for portable computers, and MMPM/2, the multimedia extension for OS/2.

It is my pleasure to introduce *OS/2 2.1 Unleashed*, an excellent companion book to the OS/2 2.1 product. Within these pages you will find many valuable tips and techniques that you can use to improve your productivity and enhance the value of OS/2. With each chapter, you will learn how you can get the most from OS/2, how to tune your DOS applications, and how to integrate your Windows 3.1 applications with the Workplace Shell.

The authors span our industry and possess years of experience with the OS/2 operating system. Several of the authors are members of the original OS/2 design and development team, bringing an unequalled level of OS/2 knowledge to a single book.

The OS/2 development team is dedicated to providing you with a quality operating system product. We value learning from your experiences, and I welcome you to the family of OS/2 users. You can exchange ideas with other OS/2 users, the OS/2 development and support team, and the authors of *OS/2 2.1 Unleashed* by participating in the OS/2 forums on CompuServe.

Welcome to *OS/2 2.1 Unleashed.*

James A. Cannavino
Senior Vice President, IBM
General Manager, IBM Personal Systems

Introduction

In This Chapter

"The power of OS/2 2.0 is waiting for your direction. Take charge, and get ready for new and interesting experiences."

The preceding quotation was used in the first panel of the OS/2 2.0 Start Here object that appeared on your desktop every time the OS/2 2.1 operating system started. This is a bold statement that conveys the power that IBM believes lies within the OS/2 product. The message is still there for OS/2 2.1, but for many of you, the power is still unrealized and the new and interesting experiences await to be discovered.

OS/2 2.1 Unleashed will help you discover the potential that awaits you in the OS/2 operating system. There are other books available that offer guidance for users of the OS/2 operating system. *OS/2 2.1 Unleashed* is unlike any of those other books.

We do not attempt to repeat information in this book that you can find in the command reference or users' guides available from IBM. Instead, we dig under the covers of OS/2 2.1 and offer an unequaled level of information on the most important features and functions in the OS/2 2.1 product.

OS/2 2.1 Unleashed is not the product of a single author, or even two or three authors. No single individual has the depth of knowledge or experience to do justice to the capabilities of the OS/2 operating system. We sought knowledgeable authors, each experts in their own fields, to contribute to this work. To ensure that the material is accurate and up-to-date, we checked our material against the OS/2 2.1 product, incorporating changes from the OS/2 2.0 product as necessary.

To provide in-depth information on the Workplace Shell user interface, we obtained an author who works in the same IBM development organization responsible for creating the Workplace Shell. The level of knowledge and access to the development team available to this author are evident in the three chapters (Chapter 4, "The Workplace Shell," Chapter 5, "Workplace Shell Objects," and Chapter 6, "Configuring the Workplace Shell") devoted to a discussion of the Workplace Shell—these chapters reveal the inner structure that gives the shell its power and enable you to exploit it to its fullest.

This author is also responsible for the most detailed discussion of the OS/2 video subsystem that you will find in any OS/2 book or technical publication. The introduction of the 32-bit graphics subsystem with OS/2 2.1 changes the way video display drivers are installed. You will find information on this, together with an unparalleled discussion of video issues such as color and fonts selection, in Chapter 11, "The Video Subsystem."

An often under-realized feature of the OS/2 operating system is the REXX command and macro language. Although other OS/2 users' books touch on the surface of REXX, none describe the potential that it offers to average users. Again, *OS/2 2.1 Unleashed* differs from the average user book. You will find a complete introduction to the REXX language, its features and the control that it gives you over operating system features such as the Workplace Shell, the Enhanced Editor and its role as a macro language for other applications in Chapter 15, "REXX Programming," and other sections of chapters in this book. Our authors for this subject are none other than senior developers and architects from IBM's SAA/REXX project office.

Printing from OS/2 applications is an area where many OS/2 users do not realize the potential and the power in the operating system. Early versions of the OS/2 operating system suffered from unreliable and inconsistent printer device drivers. You may remember this if you ever tried to use OS/2 1.1 or OS/2 1.2. The story for OS/2 2.1 is quite different, thanks to a dedicated team of developers at IBM, the most senior of which authors our chapter on printing in OS/2 2.1 (Chapter 12, "Printing"). Our author is none other than one of the original architects of the OS/2 print subsystem.

Audience

When we set out to write this book, we chose to write it for the typical OS/2 user. You will quickly discover, however, that the depth to which we cover some of the material will also attract experienced users of the OS/2 operating system, system administrators, and even OS/2 application developers.

Don't worry, however, if you have no desire to understand all the internal workings of the Workplace Shell or the printing subsystem. We will not leave you out of your depth—we cover each topic from introduction to conclusion. The REXX chapter, for example, guides you from simple basics to sophisticated use of the REXX command language and the Workplace Shell.

Single OS/2 Users

If you use your computer as a productivity tool, perhaps with a communications adapter and a single printer, you will find *OS/2 2.1 Unleashed* particularly useful for installation, setup, and configuration of the OS/2 operating system.

If you are a new computer user, you will find the chapters on installation and setup particularly useful. As you become familiar with OS/2 2.1, you will learn more about the Workplace Shell from the first two of our Workplace Shell chapters in this book (Chapters 4 and 5).

If you have a lot of DOS and Windows applications and you wish to use OS/2 2.1, you will learn how to migrate your applications onto the OS/2 desktop. For some DOS applications you may have to modify special DOS settings that OS/2 2.1 uses to control how your DOS applications run. You may wish, for example, to reduce or increase the amount of memory allocated for a specific application. You can learn how to set these options (and more) in Chapter 8, "Virtual DOS Machines," and Chapter 9, "WIN-OS/2—Windows in OS/2," focuses on running your Windows 3.1 applications.

Things never go as expected with computers! You can learn how to recover from errors with our troubleshooting chapters and an appendix on system error messages. Chapters 4, 5, 6, and 12 also provide further assistance with specific problems you may encounter in the areas of the Workplace Shell and printing.

OS/2 Users on a Network

As OS/2 users, you will benefit from everything highlighted in the previous section. For more information, our chapters on networking (Chapter 17, "Networking"), the Workplace Shell, and printing guide you through working with OS/2 2.1 on a local area network (LAN). OS/2 2.1 is well equipped for network use, and it is considered by many to be the premium client and server network environment.

Chapter 5 guides you through the features available within OS/2 to link to your network and access data both on your network and other networks. Many of you may have access to printers connected to a server on your network, and you can learn how these work in Chapter 12.

Systems Administrators

The depth of coverage of many topics in *OS/2 2.1 Unleashed* gives you the knowledge and experience to tackle any problem you may encounter—from installing OS/2 2.1 on multiple machines and setting up custom configurations for the Workplace Shell, to diagnosing problems with DOS or Windows applications.

For installation problems with printers, video display drivers, or general problems with OS/2 2.1 both on single computers or on a network, you will find invaluable guidance in this book. Look for the less-well-known CONFIG.SYS and OS2.INI entries that you can use to improve the OS/2 operating system. You will find many tips for using these as we document and explain them in our chapters.

Systems Managers

In *OS/2 2.1 Unleashed* you will learn about the capabilities of the OS/2 operating system so you can understand and realize the enhancements to individual productivity it can offer. All the features of OS/2 2.1 are described clearly and in depth within *OS/2 2.1 Unleashed.* You can use the knowledge you gain from this book to make educated and considered strategic decisions for your computing environments.

Application Developers

Even application developers will benefit from reading *OS/2 2.1 Unleashed.* Unlike typical user guide books, *OS/2 2.1 Unleashed* uncovers the details of

many OS/2 2.1 features, such as the internal object hierarchy in the Workplace Shell and how your printers and spooler queues can be linked to provide pooling and sharing. Understanding these details will enable you to create more useful and complete applications.

Our chapters on a programming overview (Chapter 14, "Learning to Program OS/2—Tools, Tips, and Techniques"), REXX, and the Workplace Shell objects will give you guidance and, hopefully, ideas that you will want to incorporate within your own application design. Incorporating the REXX language as a macro language and allowing drag-and-drop capability are examples that the OS/2 Enhanced Editor adopts and which you may wish to copy or duplicate.

How to Use This Book

OS/2 2.1 Unleashed is written by several contributing authors. Although you will find it easy to read through each chapter in sequence, you may find it more useful to jump into one of the chapters immediately. We rarely assume that you have read a previous chapter, and each can stand alone, although we may reference material in other chapters. You may want to read the three Workplace Shell chapters in sequence (if you are an experienced OS/2 2.1 user, however, you might want to skip the first Workplace Shell chapter).

If you use OS/2 2.1 as an integrating platform for different types of applications (DOS, Windows, and OS/2), you will want to pay close attention to Chapters 1, 3 ("System Configuration, Setup, and Tuning"), 8, and 9. Chapter 3 is also a tuning guide to help you get the most out of OS/2 2.1.

Organization of This Book

We have organized *OS/2 2.1 Unleashed* so the chapters you are likely to want to read first are toward the front of the book. After installing OS/2 2.1, you will want to learn how to configure it for the best performance and how to work with the OS/2 2.1 user interface: the Workplace Shell.

These first chapters are of general interest to all users. After these chapters we inserted chapters that cover specific areas or features of OS/2 2.1. Again, we placed those topics of interest to most users toward the front of the book: the Workplace Shell, DOS and OS/2 command lines, and WIN-OS/2, the environment in which you run your Windows 3.1 applications.

We've tried to put things where you are likely to look. We've also tried to avoid needless duplication. If a given subject is covered in depth in another section or chapter, we've tried to make it easy for you to find what you need.

- Chapter 1 provides information about OS/2 2.1 installation. It provides recommendations, caveats, and options that may not be obvious. It also describes the procedure used to install the OS/2 Boot Manager and create a single boot disk.
- If you are moving to OS/2 2.1 from another comfortable environment and you'd like to preserve the look and feel of either the OS/2 1.3 desktopor the Windows 3.1 Program Manager, take a look at Chapter 2, which describes the various possible setups andconfigurations of OS/2 2.1.
- If you're into trying to get the most out of the system, consult Chapter 3. This chapter provides detailed information on the various settings and CONFIG.SYS parameters that can help you get the best performance from OS/2 2.1. It also describes some of the pitfalls associated with the various options.
- Chapters 4, 5, and 6 are the definitive treatises on the Workplace Shell. Everything you want to know about using the shell for end-users, administrators and developers can be found in these three chapters.
- Chapter 7 provides detailed information about the OS/2 command line. It covers both full-screen and windowed sessions, as well as information about replacement command processors.
- Chapters 8 and 9 cover various aspects of the DOS and Windows emulation that is part of OS/2 2.1. These chapters provide detailed information that will enable you to get the most out of these environments.
- Chapter 10 covers the OS/2 file system. Everything you want to know about the high performance file system (HPFS) and the file allocation table (FAT) can be found in this chapter, which also covers the drive objects on the Workplace Shell.

- Chapter 11 provides an in-depth look at the video subsystem. It provides information that will enable you to understand how the OS/2 video system works, how to install display drivers, as well information that will help you select the best adapter.
- Chapter 12 covers printing—often one of the most frustrating operations for an end-user. This chapter demystifies printing from OS/2 and details everything from printer objects, queues, and printer drivers to troubleshooting and printing with a network printer.
- Chapter 13 covers the productivity applets that are shipped with OS/2 2.1. You can use this chapter as both a tutorial and a reference manual.
- If you've thought about programming for OS/2 2.1, you will want to review Chapter 14, which covers the basic vocabulary and mindset changes needed to successfully write OS/2 applications. It isn't intended to be the definitive work in this area (there are *books* written about OS/2 programming). Instead it provides a good introduction to what you'll need and what is available.
- REXX is the command and macro language for the OS/2 operating system. Chapter 15 is required reading for anyone interested in becoming more than a casual OS/2 user. It starts with the basics, although it provides some extraordinary useful information on using REXX to enhance your working environment.
- If you've had trouble with the operating system, Chapter 16 should prove to be interesting. We've tried to make sure it covers most of the common problems, as well as some that are a bit more obscure.
- From the first release of OS/2 1.0, the operating system has been designed to be part of a networked environment. Chapter 17 provides information about configuration and management of OS/2 networks.
- Chapter 18 introduces you to the multimedia capabilities of OS/2. The power and versatility of OS/2 as an operating system make it an ideal multimedia platform.
- A description of the contents of the disk that accompanies this book can be found in Appendix A. Appendix B is a "where to find it" compendium of useful information about OS/2. Appendix C provides information on

system and fatal error messages that OS/2 2.1 can display. (Bill Wolff, founder and president of Wolff Data Systems, and Rob Keiser and Stan Spotts, consultants for Wolff Data Systems, contributed material to the Appendix sections.)

Conventions Used in This Book

Through the text we use the term *mouse button 1* to refer to what is commonly called the left mouse button and the term mouse button 2 to refer to what is commonly called the right mouse button. Mouse button 1 is the mouse button under your index finger (left-handed or right-handed). Mouse button 2 (sometimes called the manipulation button) refers to the mouse button under your middle finger (left-handed or right-handed). The OS/2 operating system permits you to change the assignment of the left and right mouse buttons (see Chapter 5); this is why we prefer to use mouse button 1 and 2 rather than the left and right mouse buttons.

In code lines that should be typed as one line, we use a continuation character (➡) for code lines that had to be broken into two lines. Remember that these lines must be typed as one line in order to function properly.

Acknowledgments

All chapters in this book, not just those authored by members of the IBM development team, have been reviewed by experienced OS/2 users and developers, both within and outside of IBM, to ensure the accuracy and timeliness of all the information.

You will see the contributing authors credited at the end of the chapters they authored. We would like to thank them for all the time and effort they put in to ensure that *OS/2 2.1 Unleashed* isn't just an average user's guide. We would also like to acknowledge the invaluable contribution from those who reviewed our text and offered information or guidance:

Chris Andrew
Bill Bodin
Larry Davis
Hank Henderson
Marilyn Johnson
Scott Kliger
Kelvin Lawrence
Darren Miclette
Kim Shepard
Pat Nogay
Mindy Pollack
David Reich
Irv Spalten
Andrea Westerinen
Steve Woodward

Thanks to the entire editorial staff at Sams Publishing, especially Wayne Blankenbeckler, Grant Fairchild, Susan Christophersen, Sandy Doell, and Hugh Vandivier.

To Gregg Bushyeager at Sams publishing we would like to offer our special thanks for cracking the whip and applying the pressure that ensured that *OS/2 2.1 Unleashed* was published on time, and for managing the contributing authors to ensure that they delivered complete and accurate material. This was a short-duration, high-intensity project, and he had the patience of Job. Thanks, Gregg.

Of course, we would be remiss if we did not give credit where credit is due: to the entire OS/2 development team at IBM.

Finally, we'd like to thank all of the families and friends of all the contributors for their support and tolerance.

As OS/2 changes, we'll consider writing another edition of the book. If you discover something we've omitted, or have ideas you would like to see us cover, let us know. If you have access to Internet or CompuServe, David Moskowitz can be reached at 76701.100@compuserve.com. David Kerr can be reached at dkerr@vnet.ibm.com.

For James Andrews, 1893-1992

David Kerr
Boca Raton, FL
January 26, 1993

To anyone who has ever asked me a question, especially Sharon and Ruth.

David Moskowitz
Norristown, PA
January 27, 1993

Installation Issues

In This Chapter

OS/2 2.1 is a big, reasonably complex operating system. Before you install the system it is a good idea to take a bit of time to plan the installation process. If you rush ahead, you may create potential problems or miss an opportunity to tune the system.

Hardware Considerations

In order to run OS/2 2.1 you need the following hardware:

- a computer with at least an Intel 80386sx processor
- 6M of random-access memory (RAM)
- a hard disk with at least 20M to 50M of free space
- a floppy disk (either 3.5-inch or 5.25-inch drive)
- a VGA monitor and adapter
- a mouse or equivalent pointing device

The preceding list is a bit more than the IBM suggested minimums. What you get by adding resources to your system is performance, not capability. You will see a significant performance improvement, for example, using OS/2 2.1 with 6M of memory versus the IBM recommended minimum of 4M of memory.

If your equipment doesn't meet the preceding criteria and you either intend to buy a new computer or upgrade some components, there are some things you should consider.

OS/2 2.1 is a virtual memory operating system—it is capable of managing and using more memory than is physically installed in the computer. It accomplishes this feat with a bit of sleight of hand using the hard disk to provide additional memory. Programs can only execute if they are in physical memory. OS/2 2.1, however, can use space on the hard disk to hold portions of programs that are not currently executing or data that is not currently in active use. When the piece of memory is needed (either program or data) the operating system recognizes it and copies the section of memory (the hard disk) into memory.

Any hard disk is always going to be slower than RAM. Anytime OS/2 2.1 has to use the hard disk to overcommit memory, system performance suffers. There are two things that you can do to minimize this performance penalty.

The most improvement in performance is accomplished by adding additional memory to your system. I recommend 6M to 8M of RAM for a casual end-user and 12M to 16M of memory for a power-user or a developer. Of course, you can always add more. Similarly, given the size of applications, the more application disk space you have the more you will be able to do. One popular Windows word processor, for example, takes 15M of disk space before you create a single document; the trend is for applications to grow in size. This makes it extremely likely that, over time, applications will take significantly more disk space than the operating system.

If you elect to acquire a hard disk, make it a fast hard disk. You must look at more than "access time" to determine how the disk will perform when used with OS/2 2.1. You should also look at the data transfer rate. A disk that can position the heads (access time) quickly (10 milliseconds, for example) but transfers data slowly (5 to 6 megabits per second, for example) may not have the overall throughput of a disk that moves the heads slower (12 to 15 milliseconds) but transfers data two to three times faster.

There are other hard disk considerations besides speed. OS/2 2.1 is a large operating system that is shipped on more than 25 disks. A full installation of OS/2 2.1 can take about 40M of disk space, which doesn't leave much room for applications on a small hard disk. In addition, there is overhead associated with system operation (depending upon installed devices and other factors); it is possible that an 80M disk may have only 30M of space available for applications. A more comfortable hard disk size is 100M to 120M. Developers or power-users may want to consider a disk in the 200M to 300M range, as the minimum.

> TIP: Consider the disk size of the applications you plan to use, and be sure you leave room for growth.

Preliminary Planning

It is a good idea to back up your system before you begin the installation. Depending upon the installation options, you may not strictly need this step. However, if you are going to either change the partitions or reformat the hard disk and you want to keep any of the files on the hard disk, then a backup is required.

OS/2 2.1 supports three different configurations that you should know about before you start the process: you can elect to install OS/2 2.1 as the only operating system on the hard disk; you can elect to have both OS/2 2.1 and DOS coexist on the same disk in a configuration called dual boot; and OS/2 2.1 provides a facility to support multiple operating systems installed on the same hard disk, called Boot Manager.

OS/2 2.1 Installed as the Only Operating System

If you decide to have OS/2 2.1 as the only operating system on the hard disk, you have two choices. You can either install OS/2 2.1 yourself or buy a preloaded system. There is something to be said for installing OS/2 2.1 this way (as the sole operating system on the hard disk). The only time I need to boot DOS is for certain maintenance functions (including disk defragmentation). Many of these utilities are now available for OS/2 2.1. As a consequence, many people may be able to remove DOS and Microsoft Windows from their disks and reclaim the disk space occupied by these systems.

Further, if this is either your first computer or a stand-alone system, you may not care about older software. The reality, however, is that most people feel more comfortable if they maintain the ability to run their older systems and software until they develop confidence in the new system.

Dual Boot

When OS/2 2.1 is installed for dual boot there is a copy of DOS and OS/2 2.1 on the same hard drive. A special command that comes with OS/2 2.1 (BOOT) allows you to switch between booting OS/2 and DOS. This is the most common installation option. However, it requires a previously installed version of DOS. The OS/2 2.1 installation program automatically sets up dual boot if it detects an installed version of DOS (3.3 or later).

If you want to install dual boot on a new computer, you must be sure that DOS is installed first. Once you have installed OS/2 2.1 you cannot install dual boot afterward without reinstalling OS/2 2.1.

Boot Manager

Some people may need to run multiple operating systems (for example, OS/2 1.3, a version of UNIX, or multiple DOS configurations). Boot Manager is installed into a separate partition. Consequently, you have to repartition and reformat at least part of the hard disk.

If you have the disk space and either support multiple configurations or are responsible for testing new operating systems, Boot Manager can make your life significantly easier. Install the new version into a separate Boot Manager-aware partition. Test the new version with confidence that the production version remains intact.

Installing OS/2 2.1

Before you can run OS/2 2.1, someone has to install it. This sounds simple enough. However, if you're about to install the operating system from disks, the prospect of dealing with more than 25 disks can be a bit intimidating. IBM ships OS/2 2.1 on high-density disks (either 3.5-inch or 5.25-inch) and CD-ROM. If you install OS/2 2.1 from disks, it takes anywhere between 20 to 45 minutes depending upon the speed of the components (CPU, hard disk, and disk drive), the amount of memory in your system, and the options you select. The fastest way to install OS/2 2.1 is either from CD-ROM or a network (15 to 25 minutes).

Disk Install

The OS/2 installation is a two-step process. Phase 1 is character-based and installs enough of the system to set up the second graphical phase. You need the installation disk and Disks 1 through 5 for the first Phase; you will be prompted for the remaining system disks during Phase 2 of the OS/2 installation. Optionally, you may also need the printer driver disks and the display driver disks if you elect to install these components.

During Phase 1, you need to make only a limited number of decisions to do the following:

install Boot Manager

install dual boot

change the disk partition where OS/2 2.1 will be installed

format the partition where OS/2 2.1 will be installed

If you intend to install OS/2 2.1 with dual boot, DOS must already be installed on the computer. If it is already there, you can continue with the OS/2 2.1 installation. If not, you should install a copy of DOS.

Review your DOS CONFIG.SYS and AUTOEXEC.BAT files to make sure they contain the following lines:

CONFIG.SYS: `SHELL=path\COMMAND.COM`

where `path` is a valid path on drive C:.

AUTOEXEC.BAT: `SET COMSPEC=path\COMMAND.COM`

(This is the same information as the `SHELL` statement in CONFIG.SYS and the valid `PATH` statement).

Be sure that both the `SHELL` and `COMSPEC` point to a subdirectory, not the root directory. This helps to avoid an "Incorrect COMMAND.COM version" error (if you use the `BOOT` command).

To install OS/2 2.1, put the installation disk into drive A and reboot the computer (either cycle the power, press the reset button if your computer has one, or use the three-finger salute: Ctrl-Alt-Del). The first thing you'll see is the IBM 8-bar logo screen that instructs you to "Insert the Operating System/2 Diskette 1 into drive A. Then, press Enter."

After about 1 to 2 minutes you should see a screen titled "Welcome to OS/2." If you don't, refer to the troubleshooting section at the end of this chapter. Press Enter to continue through the next few screens (you might want to take a bit of time to read them) until you get to the screen titled "Installation Drive Selection."

Installing Boot Manager

Boot Manager is an optional feature that you can install with OS/2 2.1. It allows you to install different operating systems and choose between them at boot time. After you install Boot Manager, each time you start the computer you will see a menu of choices of the installed bootable systems. Boot Manager

allows you to set up a separate partition for each operating system using the OS/2 FDISK utility. You can also establish a default selection and a time-out value to allow for unattended operation.

If you want to install the OS/2 2.1 Boot Manager or change the boot disk partition size or location, this is the decision point. If not, you can select choice 1 (Accept the drive) to install OS/2 2.1 on drive C and continue with the next section in this chapter, "Format the Boot Volume."

If your disk drive is larger than 60M to 80M, set up at least two partitions (not including the partition for Boot Manager). Place OS/2 2.1 in one partition and programs and data in the other.

Again, if you partition your hard disk you will lose all of the files on the volume. Back up your hard disk first!

To install Boot Manager select choice 2, "Specify a different drive or partition." The next screen is an "are you sure" screen. If you're positive you want to either change the partitions or install Boot Manager, press Enter. If not, press Esc to cancel or F3 to exit.

The next screen is the character mode version of FDISK (see Figure 1.1). There is also a corresponding Presentation Manager utility that you can use after you install OS/2 2.1 if you want to make additional partition changes.

You can install Boot Manager after you've installed OS/2 2.1. However, because Boot Manager always resides in its own partition, you always have to reformat part of the drive. Be sure you have a backup of the files you want to preserve.

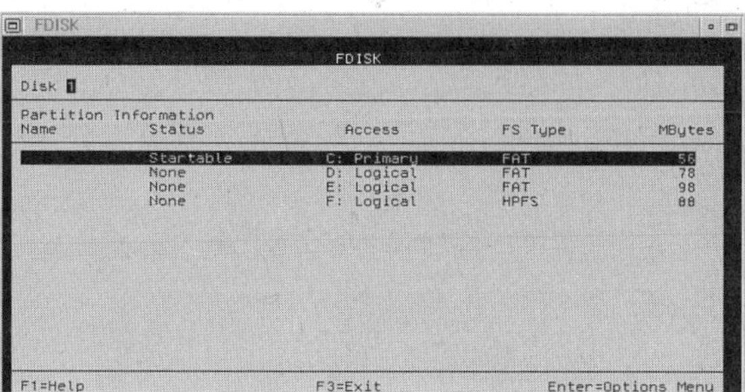

Figure 1.1. A sample initial FDISK screen.

You should see either a list of the current disk partitions or a single line with the word *None* in the status column. In order to change partitions (Boot Manager is installed in its own partition), press Enter with the highlight bar on the line you want to change. When you do you'll see a menu of options (see Figure 1.2).

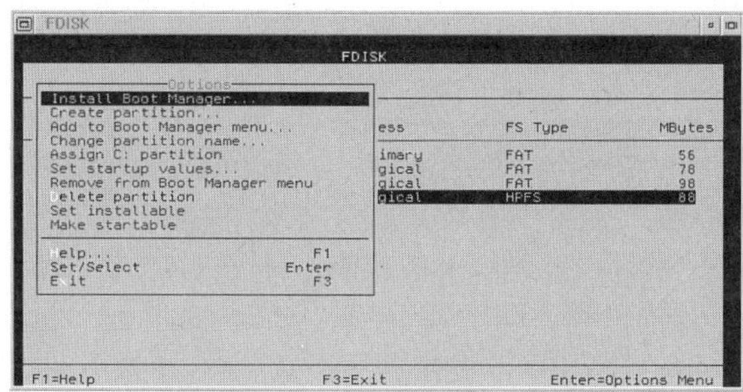

Figure 1.2. The FDISK Options menu.

When you create a partition in OS/2 2.1 you will be given the choice to place it at the beginning or end of the current free space. If you currently have multiple partitions on the disks, you have to remove something to make a place for Boot Manager. Given the size of the system, you may want to deal with different partition sizes for OS/2 2.1. If you have enough disk space (e.g., at least 100M free), consider putting OS/2 2.1 in its own partition.

If you're going to install a minimum OS/2 2.1 installation, you can get by with a 25M partition. If you install more than the minimum, intend to set up a dual boot system, or install components of OS/2 Extended Services, the space requirement goes up to as much as 50M to 60M.

Within limits, it is a good idea to consider the impact of your decision when you select a partition size. If it is possible that you will want (or need) to make the partition larger, it is better to do it now, before you have files on the disk.

Be sure you have a backup of any file you want to preserve before you continue. You can exit FDISK without making any changes if you want to back up your system.

Install Boot Manager at the end of free space (at the end of the hard disk), not the beginning. Some other operating systems make assumptions about the boot block and may wipe out Boot Manager. Placing Boot Manager at the end of the disk can minimize the conflicts.

The granularity of FDISK only allows you to establish partitions in 1M increments. As a consequence, even though Boot Manager is not that big, it will cost 1M of disk space to install.

Once Boot Manager is installed, you have to mark the partition that has Boot Manager as startable. Press Enter with the highlight bar on the Boot Manager partition and select Make startable from the menu.

Now you have to set up the other partitions on your hard disk. One of them will be used to house OS/2 2.1. Starting with OS/2 2.0, you can elect to place the OS/2 operating system into any partition; it does not have to be on drive C (i.e., if you want you can install OS/2 2.1 on drive D and so on). With the highlight bar on the empty free space, press Enter and select Create partition from the Options menu.

Once you've entered the Create partition dialogs, you can set up multiple primary partitions (up to four), determine where you want the partitions relative to the start of the current free space, and assign logical drives in the extended partition.

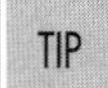

If you want to have either DOS or OS/2 1.x on the disk, you must install OS/2 2.1 in either a separate primary partition or drive D (preferred) or above. Some components of OS/2 Extended Services (ES) must be installed on the OS/2 2.1 boot drive. Check the ES documentation for the components you want to install. To that value add 20M to 40M for OS/2 2.1.

Press Enter with the highlight mark on the partition you just created for OS/2 2.1 and select Set installable from the Options menu. Once this much is done, you can add other partitions and logical drives to fit your needs.

After you have established all of the partitions, the next step is to add the bootable partitions to the Boot Manager Startup menu. Select the partition to be added and press Enter to display the Options menu. Select Add to Boot Manager menu and supply a name for the partition.

If you make a mistake or change your mind, you can remove any item using the Remove from Boot Manager menu option. Similarly, you can also select Change partition name. Figure 1.3 shows the FDISK screen with Boot Manager installed at the end of the drive and bootable partitions for OS/2 1.3 and OS/2 2.1.

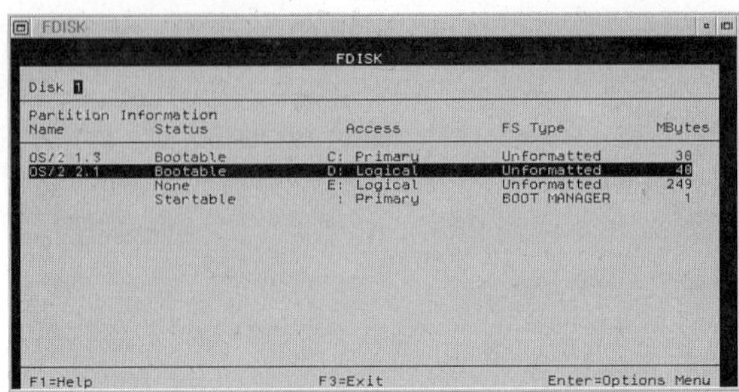

Figure 1.3. Boot Manager partition information.

You can establish more than one primary partition (for example, if you want to have separate partitions for DOS and OS/2 1.x). However, you should note that only one of the primary partitions will be "visible" when you boot the system—all of the other primary partitions are inaccessible. When you assign a drive C using Assign C: partition, you are selecting the default. If you pick a different one when you boot the system (from the resulting Boot Manager menu), it becomes the active drive C.

Logical drives exist in the extended partition; all logical drives are accessible.

Before you leave FDISK you should define Boot Manager default actions. Highlight the Boot Manager partition and select Set startup values. Identify the name of the partition you want to start at the end of the specified time-out period. Figure 1.4 shows this menu selection.

You can use the `SETBOOT` command to change these values after you install OS/2.

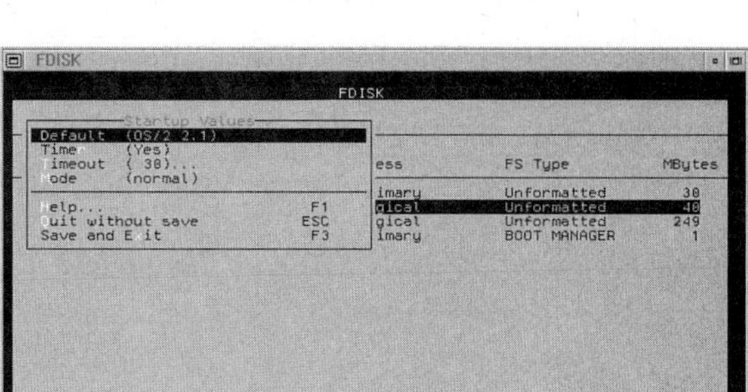

Figure 1.4. Set Boot Manager startup values.

Once you have completed all of the changes you want to make in FDISK, press F3 to accept the changes. If you change your mind and want to skip all of the changes, select Quit without saving.

The changes you make to the hard disk partitions only take effect if you exit by pressing F3. The Esc key causes an abort, preserving the status quo, if you change your mind.

Format the Boot Volume

At this point you have selected the drive to install OS/2 2.1, and you're ready for Disk 2. Whether or not you've installed Boot Manager, you will be given the choice to format the installation partition.

If you want to install dual boot or keep existing files, select Option 1 (do not format the partition); otherwise, select Option 2. If you elect to format the partition, you will be given a choice to use either the file allocation table (FAT) or the high performance file system (HPFS).

Select a File System

There has to be some way to organize data stored on a disk in order for any operating system to find it. The file system used by DOS is called FAT. DOS and the FAT file system had their origins on floppy disks. Although both have been updated to work with hard disks, FAT is not the optimal method to manage a hard disk.

FAT was originally designed to handle small floppy disks. As personal computer technology improved, disk capacities increased; Microsoft modified (some might suggest kluged) DOS to handle the larger sizes. OS/2 2.1 offers an alternative to FAT called HPFS.

HPFS was designed to work with large, fast hard disks. It supports long filenames (up to 255 characters), fast access, and relative freedom from fragmentation. On large volumes with large block I/O, HPFS offers performance improvements over FAT. On the down side, real DOS doesn't understand HPFS, so files stored on an HPFS volume are invisible to DOS; the whole HPFS volume is invisible to DOS, not just the files.

When I say, "real DOS," I mean DOS as supplied in its own shrink-wrapped package. The DOS emulation that comes with OS/2 2.1 can access HPFS files. However, DOS emulation sessions only see DOS-style filenames (sometimes called 8.3 names). In other words, DOS sessions cannot use long filenames, but they can use HPFS volumes.

For several reasons, HPFS is not the best choice for small hard disks (less than 60M to 80M). The OS/2 2.1 FAT file system is just as fast as HPFS on disks of this size. HPFS was designed to work with large hard disks—it can provide high performance, but at a cost. HPFS uses significantly more disk space overhead than FAT (on large hard disks the percentage of lost space is smaller). Without including a disk cache that is required to get maximum performance, HPFS takes almost 350K to 400K of memory. On a system with a limited amount of memory (less than 8M of RAM), you will see better system performance if you use the memory for operation versus supporting a file system.

If you intend to use dual boot, drive C must be FAT-based. If you intend to use DOS in a Boot Manager partition it will not be able to use or access HPFS volumes. In a mixed environment, place HPFS volumes at the end of your drive list.

If you elect to format a disk drive during installation, be aware that it only touches the boot volume. If you changed or modified partitions, you have to format the other partitions after you have completed the installation of the operating system.

You May Ignore This Warning

If you select dual boot and you used a replacement command-line processor for DOS's COMMAND.COM (for example, JP Software's 4DOS utility), you will see a "Dual Boot Installation Warning" screen. The screen says that OS/2 2.1 is unable to complete the dual boot feature because the `SHELL` statement in DOS CONFIG.SYS file is incorrect or missing. In the case of 4DOS, the line that OS/2 installation objects to looks something like this:

```
SHELL=C:\4DOS\4DOS.COM C:\4DOS /P
```

OS/2 installation doesn't recognize the replacement shell. It sets up both a `SHELL` and a `COMSPEC` statement in the OS/2 CONFIG.SYS that assumes you were using the original DOS command-line processor versus the replacement. You have to modify the OS/2 2.1 CONFIG.SYS statement to correct the `SHELL` and `COMSPEC` lines, in order to use your DOS command-line processor of choice.

In actuality, dual boot is installed. You have to change the OS/2 CONFIG.SYS file to use your replacement command-line processor (see the preceding command line).

The Rest of Phase 1

Once you get this far, you'll see prompts to insert Disks 2 through 5 and then to reinsert the installation disk and Disk 1 to complete the rest of the Phase 1 installation. Depending on how fast your system is, this takes no more than another 5 to 6 minutes. Follow the prompts and progress indicators to complete Phase 1.

The last thing you will be asked to do to complete Phase 1 is remove the installation disk from drive A and press Enter. The core of the operating system is now installed on the hard disk. Phase 2 is the graphical portion of the installation process that allows you to pick the components and utilities you want to install to customize the system to meet your needs.

Phase 2: Pick the Options and Complete the Install

After the system reboots to start Phase 2, you will see a screen that allows you to learn about the mouse, perform a full install, a minimal installation, or a custom installation. If you have limited experience with a mouse, review the minitutorial to help you feel more comfortable with the hand-eye coordination necessary to use the mouse.

Pick the custom option even if you want a full installation. There are some changes you should make to the CONFIG.SYS file that are easier to do if you select this path.

If you select either full or minimal install, edit the CONFIG.SYS manually and make the changes suggested in the following sections.

After you make your choice, you will see the screen shown in Figure 1.5, which shows the various elements you can configure. During Phase 1, the OS/2 installation program tried to determine the items installed in the computer.

The left side lists the mouse, serial, and display options OS/2 2.1 installs if you do not make changes.

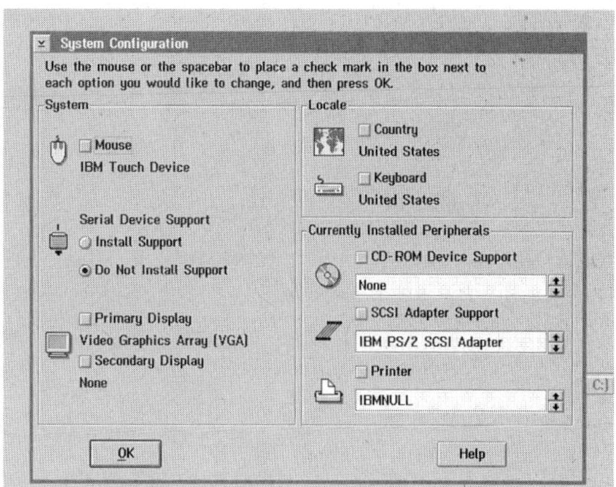

Figure 1.5. The System Configuration screen.

If you intend to use a modem or serial port, you should allow the installation program to install serial device support. If you have a high-resolution adapter and a monitor that supports higher resolution, you should consider installing a driver that supports your adapter. If you have two monitors in your system and you want to be able to use them, check the appropriate boxes.

Figure 1.6 shows the screen you will see if you check the Primary Display checkbox shown in Figure 1.4. If you want to change the default configuration, select the appropriate radio button, select the OK button, and follow the instructions to install the appropriate driver files.

OS/2 2.1 needs to execute the `SVGA ON` command in a full-screen DOS session to install a display driver for some SVGA video adapters. DOS support is not available during OS/2 installation, so you may have to use the Selective install feature after completing OS/2 2.1 installation. In this case, the initial configuration will be for a regular VGA video adapter. (See Chapter 11, "The Video Subsystem," for guidance on installing display drivers for your SVGA adapter.)

The right side of the screen allows you to change the country and keyboard information. You can also choose to install support for SCSI adapters,

CD-ROM drives, and a printer. Check the appropriate boxes, and the OK button at the bottom of the screen.

Figure 1.7 shows the resulting screen if you elect to install a CD-ROM drive. Select the line that corresponds to your drive and then click the OK button. See the CD-ROM Install section in this chapter for more information about CD-ROM.

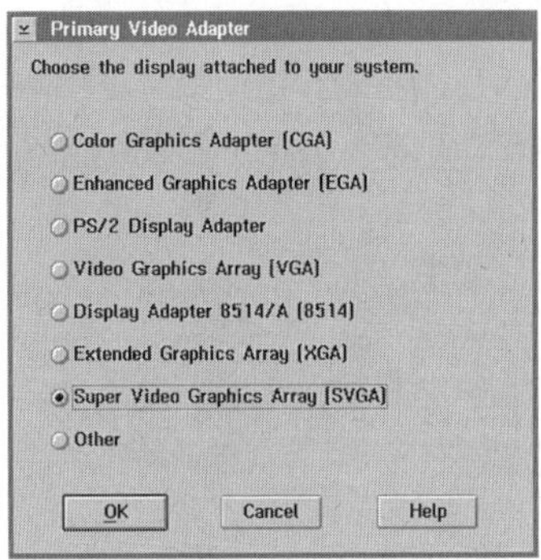

Figure 1.6. The Primary Video Adapter.

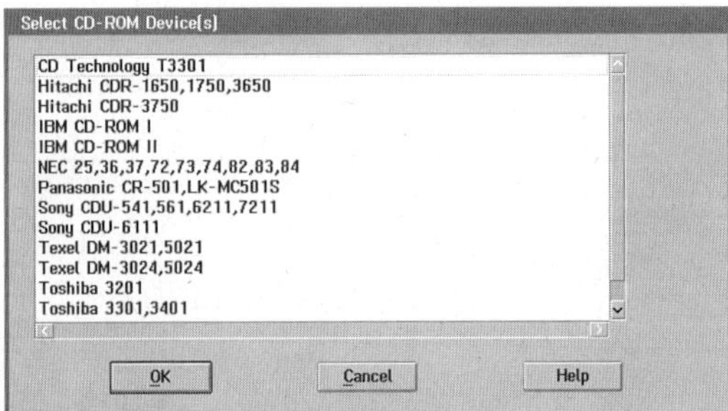

Figure 1.7. The CD-ROM device screen.

In order to use a CD-ROM drive with OS/2 2.1 you must also install support for a SCSI adapter. Figure 1.8 shows the screen that results if you elected to install a SCSI adapter. Like the CD-ROM drive installation, pick the line that corresponds to your adapter and then click the OK button.

If you elect to install a prin… …e a screen similar to Figure 1.9. Pick the printer driver and i… …he list of printers is quite long and is presented in alpha… …ght any printer and press the first letter of the nam… …nter, you can speed the search a bit. How… …a few printers from some manufac… …ter that matches.

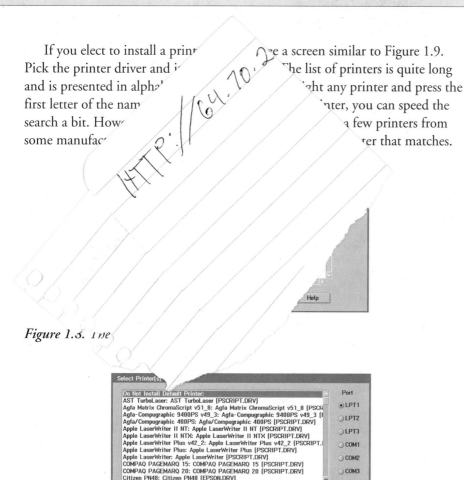

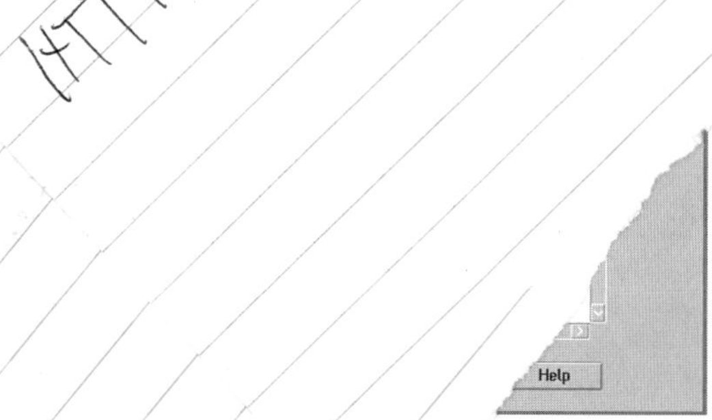

Help

Figure 1.8. The

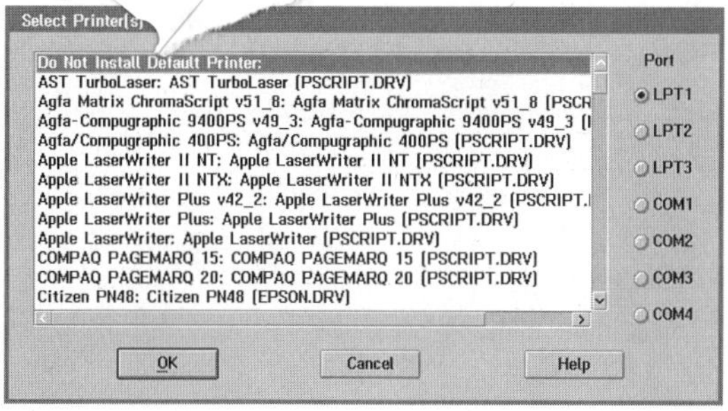

Select Printer(s)

Do Not Install Default Printer:
AST TurboLaser: AST TurboLaser (PSCRIPT.DRV)
Agfa Matrix ChromaScript v51_8: Agfa Matrix ChromaScript v51_8 (PSCR
Agfa-Compugraphic 9400PS v49_3: Agfa-Compugraphic 9400PS v49_3 (I
Agfa/Compugraphic 400PS: Agfa/Compugraphic 400PS (PSCRIPT.DRV)
Apple LaserWriter II NT: Apple LaserWriter II NT (PSCRIPT.DRV)
Apple LaserWriter II NTX: Apple LaserWriter II NTX (PSCRIPT.DRV)
Apple LaserWriter Plus v42_2: Apple LaserWriter Plus v42_2 (PSCRIPT.I
Apple LaserWriter Plus: Apple LaserWriter Plus (PSCRIPT.DRV)
Apple LaserWriter: Apple LaserWriter (PSCRIPT.DRV)
COMPAQ PAGEMARQ 15: COMPAQ PAGEMARQ 15 (PSCRIPT.DRV)
COMPAQ PAGEMARQ 20: COMPAQ PAGEMARQ 20 (PSCRIPT.DRV)
Citizen PN48: Citizen PN48 (EPSON.DRV)

Port: LPT1, LPT2, LPT3, COM1, COM2, COM3, COM4

OK | Cancel | Help

Figure 1.9. The Select Printer screen.

If you install a printer from this screen, OS/2 2.1 also installs the corresponding Win-OS/2 printer driver, provided you also elect to install DOS and Win-OS/2 support.

If you check any of the boxes on the system configuration screen, the installation program provides a series of dialogs to allow you to select features to install. Following installation, you have the opportunity to make changes and additions. When you select OK with no boxes checked, you will see the OS/2 Setup and Installation screen (see Figure 1.10).

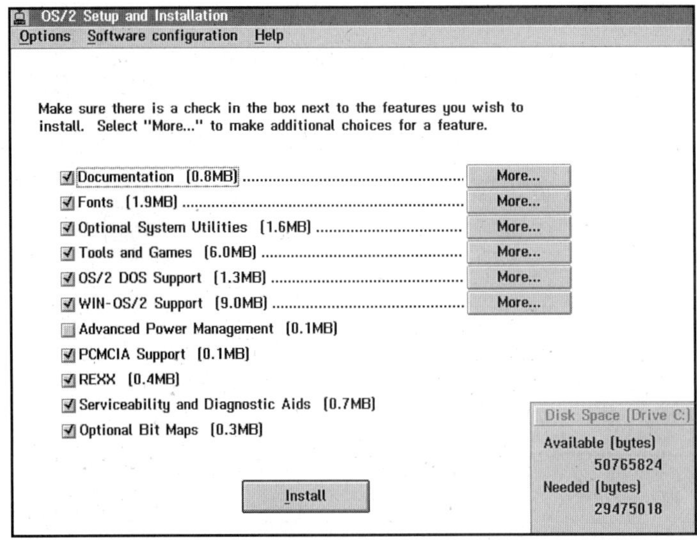

Figure 1.10. System Setup and Installation screen.

This screen allows you to pick the full features you want to install. Next to each feature is the amount of disk space the feature consumes if installed. Some of the features allow you to select a subset (the ones with the More button). The following sections cover each of these options.

Documentation

Figure 1.11 shows the components you can selectively install. Although the tutorial is on the list as an option, it really should not be. The first time OS/2 2.1 boots after installation it automatically runs the OS/2 tutorial. At the same time, the operating system also completes the final stages of installation and setup. The tutorial provides a convenient diversion while the system completes its initialization. Even if you are familiar with the system, it is a good idea to review the tutorial to see if anything has changed.

TIP Always install the OS/2 tutorial.

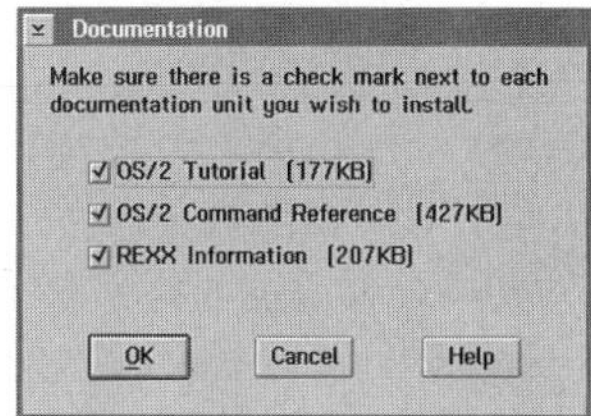

Figure 1.11. The install documentation.

The OS/2 *Command Reference* and the REXX information are online reference books that you can elect to install. If you have no plans to use REXX, you may decide to save the disk space for the online reference manual. Similarly, you may also elect to skip installation of the online *Command Reference.*

These selections control the online references, not the actual products. You are still able to use all of the commands even if you elect to skip installation of the reference material.

The online REXX information is separate from REXX support. Even if you elect to save the disk space for the reference manual, you should still install REXX.

A minimal installation only copies the tutorial to the hard disk.

Fonts

Figure 1.12 shows the fonts that can be installed with OS/2 2.1. OS/2 2.1 includes the Adobe Type Manager (for both Win-OS/2 and the OS/2 Presentation Manager). The Type Manager works with Adobe Type I or outline fonts. As you can see from the figure, Type I fonts take up less disk space than their bitmap counterparts. Type I fonts provide more flexibility than bitmap fonts and can be used on your printer as well as the display screen.

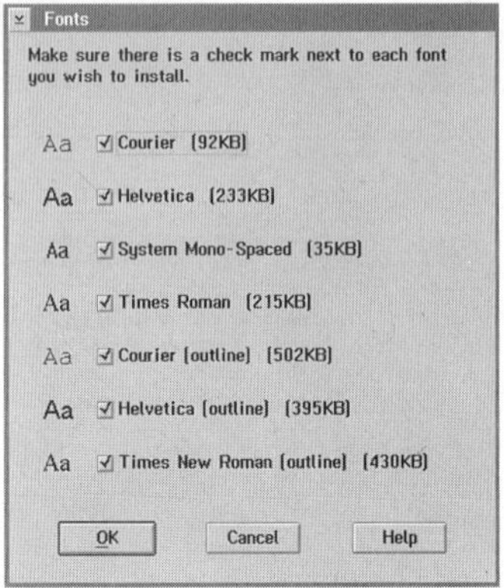

Figure 1.12. Font installation.

To install True Type fonts for use with Win-OS/2, wait until the OS/2 2.1 is installed and then install the True Type fonts from a Win-OS/2 session. You can install additional Adobe Type I fonts from the Workplace Shell's font palette object and the WIN-OS/2 ATM control panel. A minimal installation only copies the System Proportional and Helvetica bitmap fonts.

Optional System Utilities

Other than the OS/2 2.1 Installation Aid, the tools listed in Figure 1.13 are small, useful utilities. However, if you intend to use tape backup, you may not need the Backup and Restore tools.

You might also be able to save some additional disk space if you don't install the Link Object Modules tools. If you have an OS/2 developers' toolkit (for Version 2.1), use the linker in the kit to build OS/2 2.1 applications.

It is a good idea to install the Installation Aid. Some applications assume that it is available and will not install without it. Select

Manage Partitions from the optional features list to install the FDISK tools you need to change either the partitions or Boot Manager information after you've installed OS/2.

The minimal installation copies the Backup Hard Disk, Change File Attributes, Manage Partitions, Restore Backed-up Files, the Sort Filter and the Installation Aid utilities.

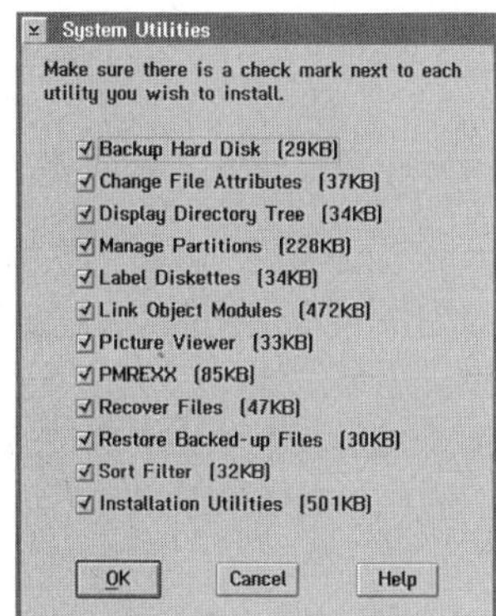

Figure 1.13. Optional system utilities.

Tools and Games

This collection of applets is documented in Chapter 13, "Productivity Applets." You might want to glance through that chapter to check the features and capabilities of some of these tools. If you aren't going to play games, you can save some disk space. If you plan to install the OS/2 Communications Manager or another communications program, you don't need the Terminal Emulator.

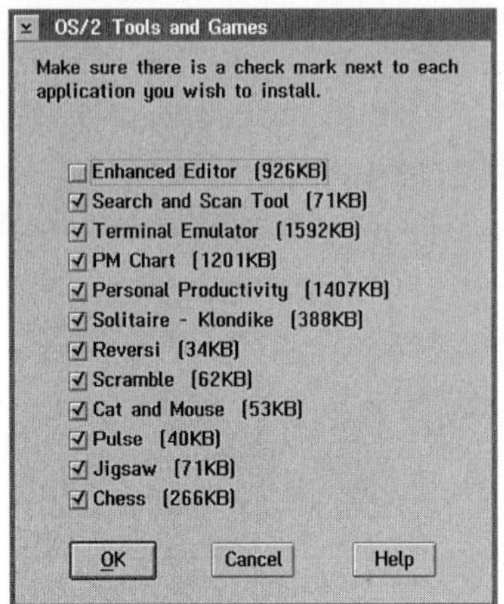

Figure 1.14. Tools and games.

The minimal installation only copies the Scan and Search Tool and the personal productivity tools.

OS/2 DOS and Win-OS/2 Support

You must install DOS support if you intend to run Microsoft Windows applications under Win-OS/2. DOS and Win-OS/2 do take a bit of disk space. However, because you are able to remove Windows 3.1 from your hard disk (if it is installed), the net additional increase is minimal. The OS/2 Installation program installs a full set of Win-OS/2 support for Windows 3.1.

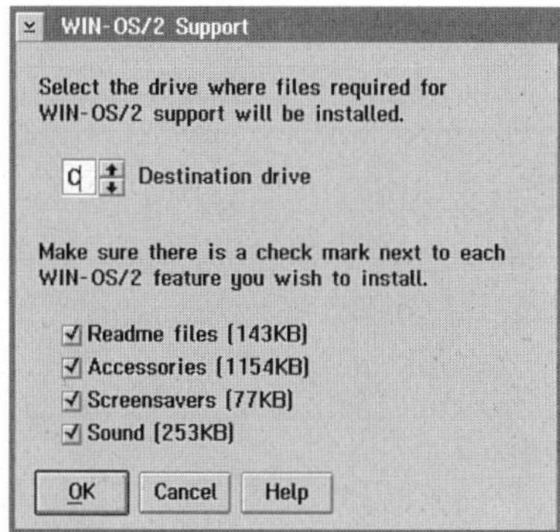

Figure 1.15. The DOS and Win-OS/2 selection.

Notebook Support

If you have one of the popular notebook computers, you should consider installing advanced power management (APM) if the computer supports it. If the OS/2 installation program detects a PC Memory Card International Association (PCMCIA) adapter, this feature should be checked (you can check it yourself, if needed). The two do not take much space, but they can help you when you assume the role of road warrior.

A minimal installation only copies the APM tools. If the OS/2 installation program detects APM BIOS support, the feature is automatically installed.

The BIOS on some desktop (nonportable) systems may have support for APM. The install program, when it sees the BIOS support, adds APM to the minimal installation list. If this is the case, you can deselect the feature without fear.

REXX

REXX is the macro language of OS/2 2.1. Many applications assume that REXX support is available. The installation procedures for quite a few applications are written in REXX (including the one for the companion disk to this book). REXX is always installed by default—you have to specifically deselect it. Don't do it!

Always install REXX! I'm not really convinced it should even be an option.

Serviceability and Diagnostic Aids

The tools in this category are designed to gather information that can be used to try to identify, isolate, and correct problems that might occur during the normal operation of the system. The information is used primarily by either a technical coordinator, consultant, or IBM support people.

These tools are always installed, even for a minimal installation.

Optional Bitmaps

If you want to change the desktop background, install the optional bitmaps. If you don't care, you can skip their installation and save the corresponding disk space.

A minimal installation does not install the optional bitmaps.

Software Configuration

There is a menu that is often overlooked. Specifically, you should focus on the Software configuration selection. If you select this menu item you will see a drop-down menu that enables you to change certain OS/2 2.1 and DOS settings. These changes show up in the OS/2 2.1 CONFIG.SYS file.

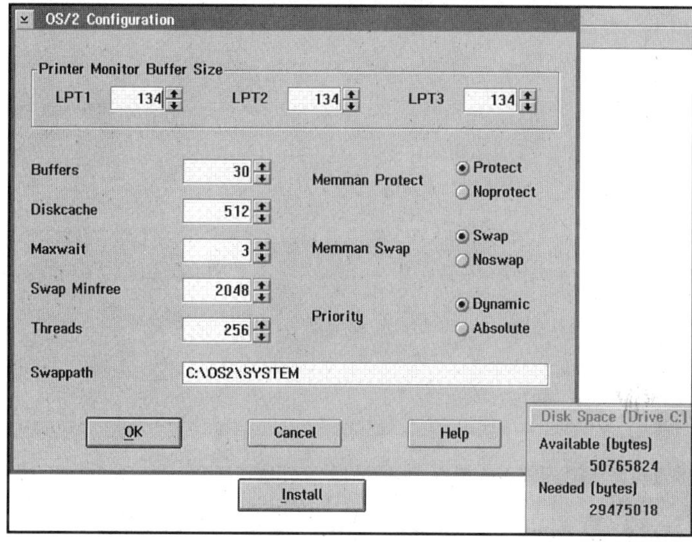

Figure 1.16. OS/2 configuration.

OS/2 Configuration

You should make changes to the OS/2 settings. Specifically, you should change the following value for SWAPPATH. In addition, developers may want to also change DISKCACHE, THREADS, and MAXWAIT. The suggested changes and some reasons are shown below.

Some of the tuning details and additional information can be found in Chapter 3, "Configuration and Setup."

SWAPPATH: this setting is used to control the location of the OS/2 2.1 swap file. The swap file is used by the operating system as a part of its virtual memory management. Without intervention, OS/2 installation places the swap file in the \OS2\SYSTEM directory. This is not the optimal location for the file.

The swap file should be moved to the root directory of the most frequently used partition of the least frequently used hard disk drive. If you only have one drive or you have two drives that have widely different speeds, you have limited choices.

With one hard drive, move the swap file to the root directory of the most active partition. With two hard drives that have very different performance characteristics, consider placing the swap file in the root directory of the most frequently used partition of the fastest drive.

As noted, disks are much slower than RAM. If the operating system has to swap information to disk, you should do everything possible to minimize the time it takes OS/2 2.1 to access the swap file.

- It takes less time to get a file from the root directory of a drive than it does to get it from the subdirectory.
- If the disk head is in constant use in another partition, it takes time to reposition the heads to the swap file partition. (This is one reason that can mitigate against a separate swap file partition.)
- If you have more than one hard disk drive and one is in constant use and the other isn't, the head movement of the infrequently used drive is likely to be minimal and may already be positioned within the swap file.

DISKCACHE: a disk cache helps to improve performance of the system by minimizing the number and frequency of hard disk access. The cache is a buffer that holds the most recently accessed data; it helps reduce the need to wait for the hard disk. When you select a disk cache size, you have to balance the potential performance gain against the loss of resources (memory). On a small system (4M) set the cache at 100K; on a 6M system set the cache at 256K to 300K; on larger systems you can set the value as high as 600K to 800K. (Disk caching is covered in more detail in Chapter 3.)

THREADS: if you are an applications developer, you may want to consider increasing the system-wide limit from 256 threads to some higher value. Similarly, some network server software may suggest that you increase this number to accommodate multiple network clients.

There is a system-wide maximum of 4,096 threads. Most of the time the default value (256) is sufficient. It takes internal system resources to support a thread. Do not blindly increase this value as a precaution. If you do, you may discover that it has a negative impact on performance in some systems with limited memory.

MAXWAIT: this parameter describes the maximum time that a thread is allowed to wait before it gets a priority boost from the operating system. A thread is the unit of execution in OS/2. This parameter helps to keep threads from starving for CPU access. The default value is 3 (seconds). If you're a software developer, you may want to consider setting this parameter to 2. I've found that this setting improves performance on my system.

DOS Configuration

There are only a limited number of options that you can change in the DOS configuration. If you had BREAK OFF set in you DOS environment, you may want to disable it here, too.

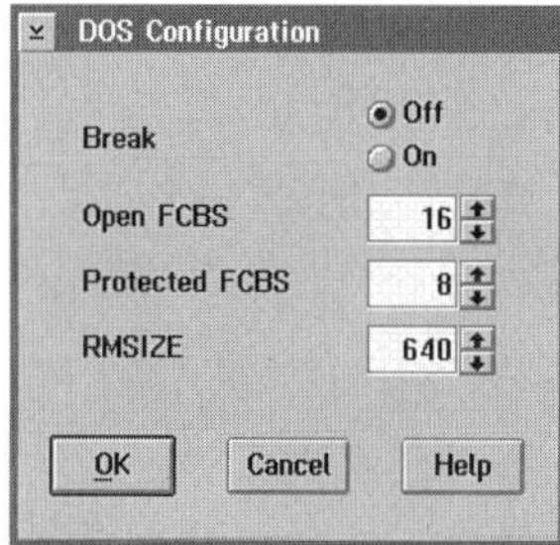

Figure 1.17. DOS configuration.

The DOS environment emulates DOS 5.0. The OS/2 installation program installs the following line in the OS/2 CONFIG.SYS file:

```
DOS=LOW,NOUMB
```

If you want to change this, you have to edit the CONFIG.SYS file after OS/2 2.1 is installed.

`RMSIZE`: set the default size for DOS or Real Mode sessions. The default value depends upon the amount of installed RAM in your computer. If you have a minimum system, the default is 512K (otherwise, it is 640K).

Any change you make to these parameters will show up in the OS/2 2.1 CONFIG.SYS file. They become global changes for all DOS sessions.

Disk Feeding

After you finish making changes to the selected items shown in Figure 1.4, press Enter (or select OK with the mouse) to move on to the next step. The OS/2 installation program posts a message box that asks you to confirm that you are ready to copy OS/2 2.1 from disks. If you respond by selecting OK, you will be asked to insert the remaining disks to complete the installation process (see Figure 1.18). After OS/2 has verified that the proper disk is in the drive, you'll see a progress screen that shows the current disk you are copying and the percentage of information transferred to the hard disk.

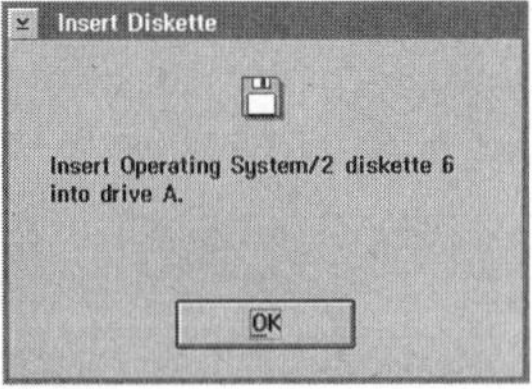

Figure 1.18. The insert disk screen.

No matter how much or how little of OS/2 2.1 you select, it still asks for all the disks.

Migration

After the OS/2 Installation program has completed copying files from the hard disk, you will see a screen that asks you about migrating existing applications. It is a good idea to let the OS/2 installation program do the migration for you. If you do, it reads the hard disks you select and looks for DOS, Windows, and OS/2 applications. The first window shows you a list of the applications OS/2 finds that it knows about from the migration database (refer to Chapter 3 and Chapter 8, "Virtual DOS Machines," for more information).

If you have additional applications other than the ones shown in the list, select Add before you make any selections from the list after the first step of migration. You will lose your selections if you make them before you add the others.

Let the installation program migrate your Microsoft Windows applications. The migration tool reads the Windows INI files and sets up OS/2 folders that correspond to your Windows groups.

You can also elect to migrate your existing Windows Desktop to OS/2 2.1.

After the migration is completed the system prompts you to insert the appropriate disks for any special drivers you specified on the screen that

matches Figure 1.5. Once those are loaded, the system provides you with a final prompt to remove the disk in drive A and then boots OS/2 2.1. The long process is almost complete.

The Last Word on Installation

You should always install the OS/2 tutorial even if you don't need it. When the system boots for the first time, after installation, you will see the tutorial while the system completes its setup. Spend a couple of minutes reviewing the tutorial to see if anything has changed. Do not try to use OS/2 2.1 immediately. Wait for OS/2 2.1 to complete the setup process and then click mouse button 2 (usually the right mouse button) anywhere on the blank desktop and select shutdown to save the position and setup information. The next time you start OS/2 2.1 it will be ready for use.

CD-ROM Install

As systems get bigger, manufacturers and users look for ways to shorten the installation time or reduce media handling. During the beta cycle for OS/2 2.1, IBM introduced the capability to install from CD-ROM in addition to other options.

In order to install OS/2 2.1 from a CD-ROM, you need the special installation disks that are shipped in the package. Insert the installation disk followed by Disk 1 and follow the prompts to install the rest of OS/2 directly from the CD-ROM.

Supported CD-ROMs

Before you can install OS/2 from a CD-ROM, you should be sure that both your CD-ROM and associated small computer system interface (SCSI) adapter are supported by OS/2 2.1. Table 1.1 lists the supported CD-ROM drives and Table 1.2 provides information about supported SCSI adapters.

Table 1.1. Supported CD-ROM drives.

Manufacturer	*CD-ROM Models*
Hitachi	CDR-1650S, CDR-1750S, CDR-3650, CDR-3750
IBM	CD-ROM I, CD-ROM II
NEC	CDR-36, CDR-37, CDR-72, CDR-73, CDR-74, CDR-82, CDR-83, CDR-84
Panasonic	CR-501, LK-MC501S
Sony	CDU-541, CDU-561, CDU-6111, CDU-6211, CDU-7211
Texel	DM-3021, DM-3024, DM-5021, DM-5024
Toshiba	XM-3201, XM-3301

There are a few integrators that distribute CD-ROM drives under their own name. In many cases they obtain their equipment from one of the manufacturers listed above.

Table 1.2. Supported SCSI adapters.

Manufacturer	*Adapter*
Adaptec	AIC 6260, AHA 1510/1512/1520/1522, AHA 1540/1542/1544, AHA 1640/1642/1644, AHA 1740/1742/1744
DPT	PM2011/2012

continues

Table 1.2. continued

Manufacturer	*Adapter*
Future Domain	TMC-850/860/875/885, TMC-1660/1670/1680, MCS-600/700, TMC-7000EX, TMC-850IBM
IBM	PS/2 SCSI Adapter, PS/2 SCSI Adapter with cache

Creating Disk from the CD-ROM

If you have difficulty installing OS/2 2.1 from the CD-ROM, you aren't lost. If your CD-ROM drive is supported in DOS, you can install OS/2, but you'll have to create the disks first.

IBM provides a utility (LOADDSKF.EXE) to create the necessary disks. You'll find it located in the \DISKIMGS directory of the CD-ROM drive. The following batch file works with JP Software's 4DOS and can be adapted as needed. You will need 23, 3.5-inch disks for the system (28, 5.25-inch disks) and 2 more (3, 5.25-inch disks) for MMPM/2 (the multimedia extensions):

```
cdromdrive:
cd \DISKIMGS\OS2\appropriate_diskette_size
for %%i in (0 1 2 3 4 5 6 7 8 9 10 11 12 13 14 15 16 17) do (
Pause make sure system diskette %%i is in the drive and hit enter.
\DISKIMGS\loaddskf disk%i.dsk floppy_drive:
)
for %%i in (1 2 3) do (
Pause make sure printer disk %%i is in the drive and hit enter.
\DISKIMGS\loaddskf pmdd%i.dsk floppy_drive:
)
for %%i in (1 2) do (
Pause make sure display disk %%i is in the drive and hit enter.
\DISKIMGS\loaddskf disp%i.dsk floppy_drive:
)
```

Network and Response File Install

There is one other method you can use to install OS/2 2.1, which is only likely to be of interest to system administrators. If you need to embark on the task of installing the OS/2 operating system on a number of computers, installing OS/2 2.1 across a network will be of interest to you.

Installing from a network combines everything that has been covered in this chapter, but instead of disks or CD-ROM as the source, the OS/2 installation program copies all the files from another computer on a local area network. You still have the choice of selecting installation options from the exact same dialogs and windows described in this chapter, or you can use a response file method.

Response files allow you to automate the selection of OS/2 features that you would like to install. Instead of you selecting each option from a dialog window, the OS/2 installation program determines what features to install based on the contents of a file you provide. This can be a significant time-saver when you need to install OS/2 2.1 on multiple computers.

If you look in the \OS2\INSTALL directory of a computer with a complete OS/2 2.1 installation, you will see two files:

SAMPLE.RSP
USER.RSP

The sample file contains all the valid keywords for a response file, together with comments explaining each one and the acceptable parameter settings. The second (user) file contains the keywords and settings that were actually used by the OS/2 2.1 installation program for the computer you are looking at, even if OS/2 2.1 was installed using the regular installation process from disk, CD-ROM, or across a network.

To use a response file you need to modify the OS/2 installation Disk 1. Make a copy of this disk and modify the copy, not the original. Using the SAMPLE.RSP file as a template, modify it so that only the options you want are included. To save space on the disk, you might want to delete all the comments from the working version of this file. When you copy your final response file to Disk 1, name it OS2SE20.RSP.

Now copy the file RSPINST.EXE onto your copy of Disk 1; you will find this file in the \OS2\INSTALL directory. For a 3.5-inch disk this is all you have to do. For a 5.25-inch disk there is insufficient space to accommodate the

RSPINST.EXE file without first deleting other files to make room. Delete the files MOUSE.SYS and SYSINST2.EXE and then edit the CONFIG.SYS file on Disk 1. Change the following line:

```
set os2_shell=sysinst2.exe
```

to:

```
set os2_shell=rspinst.exe a:\os2se20.rsp
```

and delete the following line:

```
device=\mouse.sys
```

Now you can use the modified Disk 1 to install the OS/2 operating system without the dialog windows appearing.

Installing OS/2 2.1 across a network is beyond the scope of this chapter. The number of configurations covered, the type of network you operate, and your own environment all contribute to how you should proceed with this type of installation. You can find full documentation for these in the Red Book publications from the IBM International Technical Support Centers. The *Remote Installation and Maintenance* volume, IBM publication number GG24-3780, describes how to prepare for installing the OS/2 operating system on a number of computers from a network.

Multimedia

Install the OS/2 2.1 multimedia extensions after you allow OS/2 2.1 to complete its initialization and setup after installation. Insert the first of the two disks into a floppy drive (what follows assumes drive A), and from the drive A object or a command-line window start the multimedia install program, MINSTALL.EXE (from an OS/2 command-line window type `START /N A:MINSTALL`). Figure 1.19 shows the selection from the drive A object.

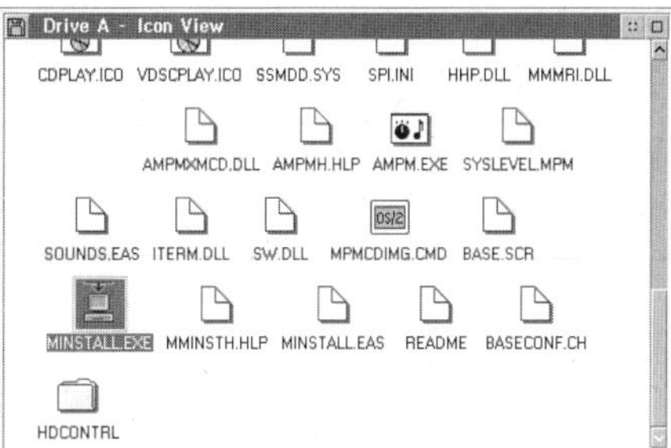

Figure 1.19. Starting the Multimedia installation routine.

After the logo screen you should see the screen shown in Figure 1.20. You can elect to install any of the multimedia subsystems shown. The total amount of disk space required is shown in the Code to install field on the right side. If you deselect any of the subsystems, this field (as well as the Subsystems to install) automatically updates to show the required space and number.

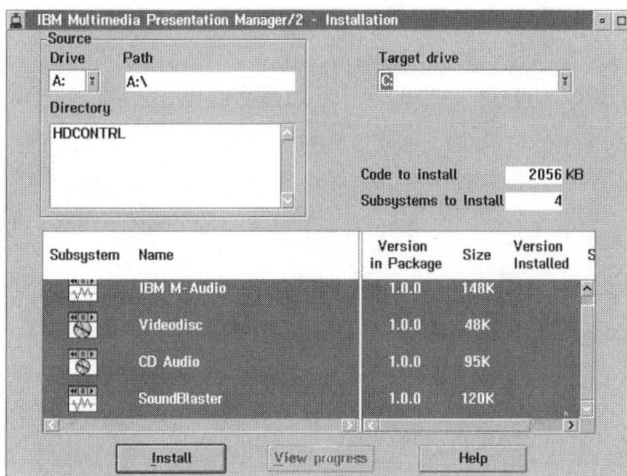

Figure 1.20. The IBM Multimedia Presentation Manager/2 installation screen.

When you finish editing this screen click the Install button to see the screen shown in Figure 1.21. The multimedia extensions require changes be made to the CONFIG.SYS file. It is a good idea to let the installation program make the

changes to CONFIG.SYS for you. The installation program displays a progress screen (Figure 1.21) while it copies the files from disks to the MMOS2 directory on the target drive.

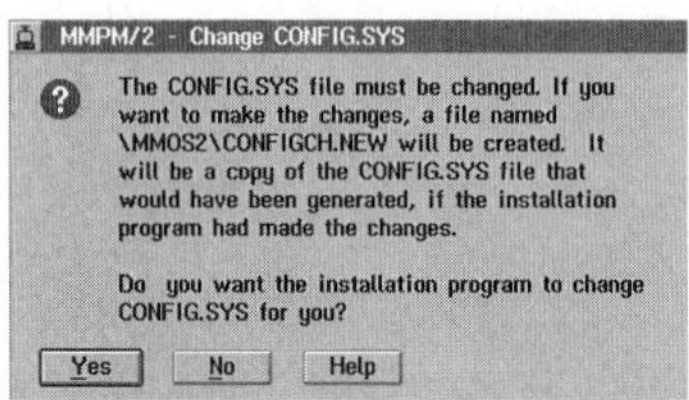

Figure 1.21. MMPM/2 CONFIG.SYS update warning.

After all of the files are copied, the installation program prompts you for information about the adapters of each type (corresponding to the subsystems you selected). You should respond with either the number of installed adapters or type or version information as appropriate.

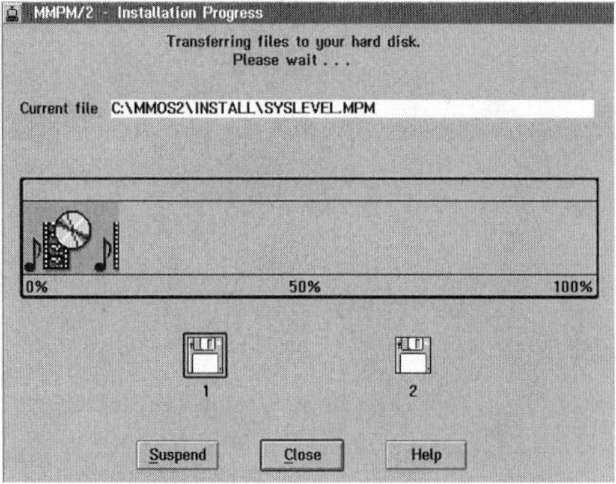

Figure 1.22. The MMPM/2 Installation Progress screen.

After you specify all of the information, the installation program updates various system files. Do not interrupt this process. Once this is complete, the MMPM/2 install program posts a screen that directs you to shut down the system and reboot in order for the changes to take effect.

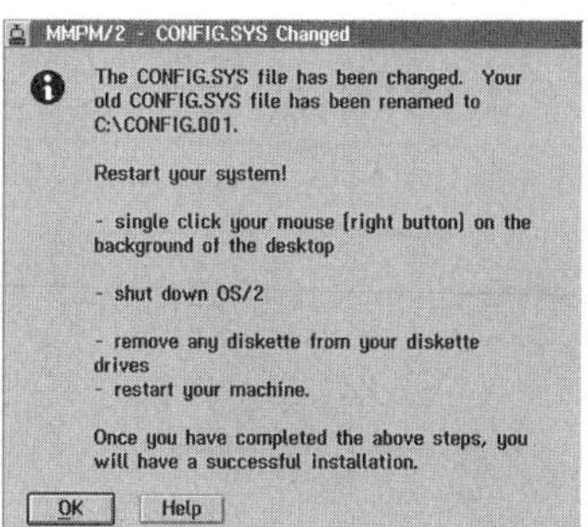

Figure 1.23. Completing the installation process.

The long process is complete. OS/2 2.1 should be successfully installed on your hard disk. Consult the troubleshooting section that follows for some installation-specific problems. If you were successful, you may want to read through Chapter 2, "Multiple Configurations," if you want to change your desktop, or Chapter 3 if you want to do a bit of tuning. Of course, there is the rest of the book to browse through at your leisure.

Troubleshooting

This is the best-laid-plans department. Although IBM has made every effort to try to minimize problems, I've seen some. The sections that follow describe some common problems and remedies.

Some of the following correction procedures tell you to get to an OS/2 command prompt. To do this, insert the installation disk in drive A and press Ctrl-Alt-Del. When prompted, insert Disk 1 in the drive and press Enter. When you see the opening screen for Disk 1, press Esc to get an OS/2 command prompt.

Disk 1 Doesn't Seem to Work!

If the installation stops while it is trying to read from Disk 1, you may have a problem with your hard disk controller. If you have a caching controller, turn off the feature and start the installation again.

If you have an ESDI, MFM, or RLL hard disk controller you may have a compatibility problem. Use the following steps to solve the problem:

- Make a copy of Disk 1.
- Edit the CONFIG.SYS file on the copy and `REM` out the line that reads: `BASEDEV=IBMS506.ADD`.
- Reboot the installation disk and try the new Disk 1.
- After you finish with the Phase 1 boot, you will be instructed to remove the installation disk from drive A and press Enter. Do *not* do this. Instead, eject the installation disk and press Enter. As soon as the screen blanks, place the installation disk back into the drive. Follow it immediately with the modified Disk 1. As soon as you see the Welcome screen, press Esc to get to an OS/2 command prompt.
- At the OS/2 command prompt, change the active drive to the location where you have installed OS/2 2.1 (usually C:). Change the current directory to be the OS2 directory (issue the command `CD \OS2`).
- Copy the IBMINT13.I13 file on top of the IBM1S506.ADD file (`copy IBMINT13.I13 IBM1S506.ADD`).
- Remove Disk 1 from drive A and press Ctrl-Alt-Del to restart the computer and resume installation.

Phase 2 Boot Produces White or Blank Screens

If the installation process appears to stop after you start the second stage boot, you may have a problem with your video adapter. Use the following steps to try to remedy this situation:

1. If the adapter has an auto-sense feature, turn it off.
2. Be sure a VGA adapter is operating in standard mode (640x480 with 16 colors).
3. Either force the card into 8-bit mode or temporarily move it to an 8-bit slot.

It is also possible that OS/2 2.1 thinks you have one adapter type when, in fact, you have another. To check if this is the case, go to an OS/2 command prompt and check the installation log (in the \OS2\INSTALL directory). If the adapter type agrees with the installed driver, you have another problem. If it doesn't agree, then you may have to create a response file to force the installation program to install a driver for the adapter you have versus what OS/2 2.1 thinks it detected.

Can't Find COUNTRY.SYS

If you see this message, try to remove any tape backup units or similar devices (even if they are attached to either the floppy disk or the hard disk controller). If the device is on a separate controller, try removing the controller, too.

ROM BIOS Problems

If you see either a SYS2025 or SYS2027 error message and your computer has an AMI BIOS, check the BIOS date. The BIOS must have been built after May 9, 1991. AMI BIOS have a serial/version number that ends with a version number similar to "mmddyy-Kv." If the BIOS is acceptable, it is possible you may have a problem with the keyboard controller. The *v* above must be at least level F (i.e., 050991KF). The version identifier is usually the last character of the number. (The Phoenix BIOS must be at least level 1.02.05D.) Contact either your computer system vendor or AMI or Phoenix for a replacement.

Trap 2 Problems

OS/2 2.1 often discovers RAM problems that the power on self test (POST) misses. OS/2 2.1 doesn't like bad RAM or RAM with different speeds. Before you replace the memory (particularly if you have SIMS) try to clean the contacts with a fresh pencil eraser and replace them.

Nonsupported SCSI Adapters

OS/2 2.1 supports SCSI adapters from Adaptec, DPT, Future Domain, and IBM. If your hard disk is attached to an adapter from another manufacturer, you need to contact them to get an OS/2 adapter device driver (.ADD) file. After you receive the .ADD file, perform the following steps to install OS/2 2.1:

1. Make a copy of installation Disk 1.
2. Copy the new .ADD file to this duplicate.
3. Edit the CONFIG.SYS file to add the appropriate `BASEDEV` statement. For example, if the .ADD file that accompanies the device is called DBM1SCSI.ADD, add the following statement: `BASEDEV=DBM1SCSI.ADD` (no path information).
4. Restart the installation from the install disk and follow the prompts to complete the first phase of the install process.
5. Before you go to the second installation phase, get to an OS/2 command prompt (see "Disk 1 Doesn't Seem to Work!" for the procedure).
6. Copy the new .ADD file to the OS2 directory on the hard drive.
7. Edit the CONFIG.SYS file on the hard disk to add the proper filename with the path information.

If you can't get an .ADD file and your SCSI controller can emulate a Western Digital controller, you can try the generic INT 13 driver (IBMINT13.I13). If none of the preceding suggestions work, you can yell and scream or get one of the supported cards.

Creating a Single Disk Boot

Once OS/2 2.1 starts to run, it opens a few files. If you want to change the system files or run CHKDSK /F on any volume that has open files, the system will deny the request. One of the solutions is to boot OS/2 2.1 from floppies. Normally, this procedure requires two disks: the installation disk and Disk 1. When you get to the first screen, press Esc to get a command prompt.

This is a long and cumbersome process. The following steps enable you to reduce this to a single disk. You will need the install disk and Disk 1 to create the single-disk boot. You also need a blank formatted disk.

1. Insert the installation disk into drive A: and copy the file SYSINSTX.COM to the OS2 directory.
2. Insert Disk 1 into drive A: and copy KEYBOARD.DCP and SYSINST1.EXE to a temporary directory. Be careful not to overwrite the KEYBOARD.DCP file in the OS2 directory. You must use the DCP file from Disk 1; it is smaller than the one used for normal operation.
3. Use the `ATTRIB` command to reveal OS2KRNL, OS2LDR, and OS2LDR.MSG; if they are already visible you can skip this step (for example, `ATTRIB -H -R -S OS2KRNL`).
4. Insert the blank disk into drive A and from an OS/2 command prompt issue the following command: `SYSINSTX A:` (to transfer the OS/2 boot block to the disk). From this point on I'll call this the target disk.
5. Transfer the OS2KRNL, OS2LDR, and OS2LDR.MSG files to the target disk (use the `COPY` command). Afterward, use the `ATTRIB` command to hide the files (for example, `ATTRIB +H +R +S OS2LDR`).
6. Transfer the saved KEYBOARD.DCP and SYSINST1.EXE files from the temporary directory created in Step 2 to the target disk.
7. Transfer the following dynamic link libraries from the \OS2\DLL directory to the target disk:

   ANSICALL.DLL
   DOSCALL1.DLL
   NLS.DLL

BKSCALLS.DLL
KBDCALLS.DLL
OS2CHAR.DLL
BMSCALLS.DLL
MOUCALLS.DLL
QUECALLS.DLL
BVHINIT.DLL
NPXEMLTR.DLL
MSG.DLL
SESMGR.DLL
BVSCALLS.DLL
NAMPIPES.DLL
VIOCALLS.DLL

8. From the \OS2\SYSTEM directory, transfer HARDERR.EXE and COUNTRY.SYS to the target disk.

9. From the \OS2\INSTALL directory, transfer SYSLEVEL.OS2 to the target disk.

10. From the \OS2 directory, transfer CMD.EXE, DOS.SYS IBMINT13.I13, and OS2DASD.DMD to the target disk. If you have plans to use HPFS, copy HPFS.IFS to the target disk.

11. The rest of the files depend upon the type of system bus and hard disk you have in your system. The rest of the files have different names depending upon your system type. The files CLOCK0x.SYS, KBD0x.SYS, PRINT0x.SYS, , SCREEN0x.SYS, and IBMxFLPY.ADD are supplied in two versions. The value "x" is a "1" for ISA and EISA type systems and "2" for Microchannel PS/2-based systems. Transfer the appropriate files from the \OS2 directory to the target disk.

    If you have an ISA system, copy CLOCK01.SYS, KBD01.SYS, PRINT01.SYS, SCREEN01.SYS, and IBM1FLPY.ADD to the target disk.

    If you have a Microchannel PS/2, copy CLOCK02.SYS, KBD02.SYS, PRINT02.SYS, SCREEN02.SYS, and IBM2FLPY.ADD. In addition, for a PS/2 system, use the following command to create a dummy ABIOS.SYS file on the target disk: `ECHO . > A:ABIOS.SYS`

12. One last file remains, which depends upon your hard disk type. If you have a SCSI drive, copy IBM2SCSI.ADD (or the .ADD file from your manufacturer). If you have another hard disk, copy IBM1S506.ADD to the target disk.

13. Finally, using the Enhanced Editor, create the following CONFIG.SYS file with the following lines:

```
IFS=HPFS.IFS /CACHE:64
BUFFERS=32
IOPL=YES
MEMMAN=NOSWAP
PROTSHELL=SYSINST1.EXE
SET OS2_SHELL=CMD.EXE
DISKCACHE=64,LW
PROTECTONLY=YES
LIBPATH=.;\;
PAUSEONERROR=NO
CODEPAGE=850
DEVINFO=KBD,US,KEYBOARD.DCP
DEVICE=\DOS.SYS
SET PATH=.;\
SET DPATH=\;
SET KEYS=ON
BASEDEV=PRINT0x.SYS
BASEDEV=IBMxFLPY.ADD
BASEDEV=IBMINT13.I13
BASEDEV=OS2DASD.DMD
```

If you have a SCSI hard disk, add the following line:

```
BASEDEV=IBM2SCSI.ADD
```

If you do not have a SCSI, add the following line:

```
BASEDEV=IBM1S506.ADD
```

The single disk boot is now ready. If you have room, you can also copy CHKDSK.COM from the \OS2 directory to the target disk.

Author Bio

David Moskowitz, president of Productivity Solutions, was the original developer and instructor of the IBM OS/2 Conversion Workshops. Moskowitz developed a set of workshops presented by IBM to members of their Develop Assistance Program to help them migrate their applications to OS/2. He is a

frequent speaker at conferences and symposiums, including Miller Freeman's Software Development Conferences. He is the author of a book about DOS to OS/2 migration, Converting Applications to OS/2 *(1989, Brady Books). He has written many articles about OS/2 and object-oriented development for various publications including* OS/2 Monthly, VAR Herald, *and* IBM's OS/2 Developer.

2

Multiple Desktop Views

In This Chapter

This chapter focuses on the different ways in which you can configure your OS/2 2.1 system, describes the major configuration options that are available, discusses and contrasts the advantages and disavdantages of each, and details their setup on an individual basis. This chapter also covers different methods to maintain your individual configurations and highlights some unique configurations for use in special circumstances.

The Major Configurations

This section describes each of the major configurations available under OS/2 2.1 and the Workplace Shell, provides a high-level overview of each available configuration, and discusses some of the reasons for considering each of the different alternatives. This section also discusses the setup of multiple configurations and methods for navigating between them.

OS/2 2.1—The Workplace Shell

The Workplace Shell is the standard desktop that is set up when you install OS/2 2.1. It is both the simplest configuration to use and the most powerful in terms of its capabilities. If you are a novice or an advanced user, the Workplace Shell is an environment that is highly adaptable to your needs.

Objects and the Workplace Shell

The main feature that differentiates the Workplace Shell from the other environments supported under OS/2 2.1 is its object orientation. In the Workplace Shell environment, applications are no longer presented on your desktop. You are given objects that can represent many different things: spreadsheets, word processing documents, or file folders. The advantage to this approach is that it presents things to you visually in the way that you normally think of them. Instead of a word processing application, you see the letter you want to work on.

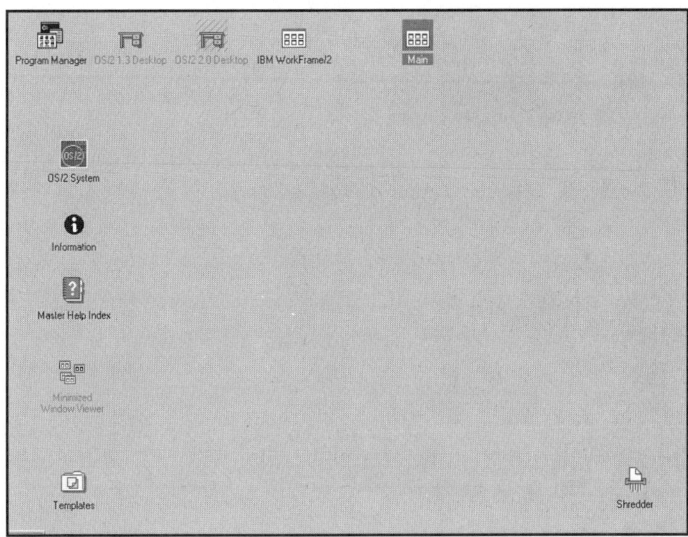

Figure 2.1. *The OS/2 2.1 Workplace Shell.*

Object orientation makes the shell very attractive whether you are a new computer user or a seasoned pro. New users find it very easy to work with the shell because it can be made to model work environments. You are able to see the file cabinet, letters, and documents that you normally work with on your computer screen. More advanced users appreciate the Workplace Shell because it is a highly customizable environment.

Changing to an Object Orientation

If you are an experienced Windows or OS/2 user, you may find the shell's object orientation to be a little strange at first. Your desktop will look different because it is now populated with objects instead of applications—familiar file managers and system trees are replaced with drive icons and folders.

Take the time to become familiar with the shell and its underlying capabilities. Once you get used to its new method of presenting information, I think you'll find it to be a much quicker and more intuitive interface than the traditional application desktops provided by OS/2 1.3 and Windows.

Existing Applications and the Workplace Shell

One of the great advantages of OS/2 2.1 and the Workplace Shell is that it enables you to easily migrate all of your existing applications to your new environment. You can run all of your DOS, Windows, and OS/2 1.x applications directly from your desktop. This feature makes it simple to upgrade your existing system to OS/2 2.1, and you don't have to worry that your existing applications won't run within your new environment.

The actual details of installing applications within the Workplace Shell are covered in a subsequent chapter. At this point, it is sufficient to realize that OS/2 2.1 understands the requirements of your applications and tailors itself to run them in the correct manner.

OS/2 1.3—The Original Desktop

The second major configuration supported by OS/2 2.1 is the OS/2 1.3 desktop, which provides a familiar environment if you are a current OS/2 user upgrading to OS/2 2.1.

One of the advantages of OS/2 2.1's implementation of the 1.3 desktop over its native implementation is that you can maintain a familiar environment and still have access to OS/2 2.1's advanced features. The shell's local menus, drag/drop features, and notebook controls are all accessible from the 1.3 environment. In fact, the only thing that has really changed is the look of the desktop; its underlying capabilities and concepts remain intact.

OS/2 2.1 is capable of running all your OS/2 1.3 applications (as well as native 2.1 applications). This capability enables you to use all your current programs on your new desktop. In effect, you are able to structure your new OS/2 2.1 system to be identical to your OS/2 1.3 desktop.

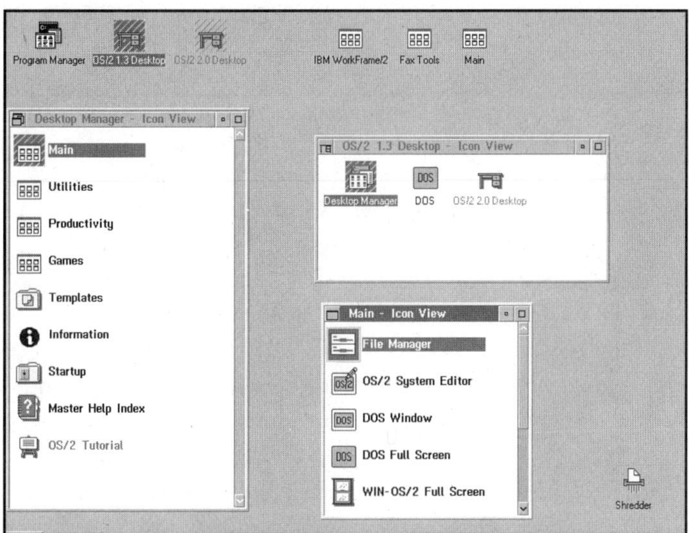

Figure 2.2. *The OS/2 1.3 desktop.*

OS/2 1.3 System Programs

One difference between the OS/2 1.3 desktop supplied by OS/2 2.1 and the native 1.3 desktop is that the OS/2 1.3 system programs have been removed. You will not, for example, find the OS/2 1.3 file manager anywhere on the desktop or the 1.3 control panel.

These programs were removed because OS/2 2.1 supplies its own equivalent system programs that have improved functionality and ease of use. The 1.3 file manager, for example, was replaced with customizable drive icons that contain additional functions. The control panel is no longer used because OS/2 2.1 supplies a system folder that contains tools to enable you to customize many aspects of your desktop.

If you wish to transfer some of your old 1.3 system programs, such as the file manager, to your new system, you can copy the appropriate files to a subdirectory and set up an icon for the program. It is a good idea, however, to avoid copying most of your 1.3 system setup programs such as the print manager or control panel programs. These programs do not work well with an OS/2 2.1 environment and certainly do not support all of its capabilities.

Copying 1.3 Programs from Disk

If you have already installed OS/2 2.1 on your system and wish to retrieve some of the original OS/2 1.3 system programs, you can obtain them from the original OS/2 1.3 installation disks. All of the OS/2 1.3 system programs are available on the original OS/2 1.3 installation in a specialized, compressed format. Because they are compressed, you cannot simply copy the files to your hard disk. You can, however, retrieve these files by using the `UNPACK` program that is provided with OS/2. `UNPACK` reads the compressed files on the disks and copies them in a usable format to your hard disk.

In order to use `UNPACK` to install programs from your OS/2 1.3 installation disks, you must first locate the particular files you wish to copy. The files for the OS/2 1.3 file manager, for example, can be found on Disk 3 of the 1.3 installation disks. Three files are needed for the proper operation of the file manager, and they all begin with the PMFILE prefix. You should note that all these files have suffixes that end with an @ sign; the file manager executable program, for example, is named PMFILE.EX@. OS/2 uses the @ sign at the end of the file extension to indicate that the file has been compressed.

Once you have located the files you wish to copy, you should create a target directory for your new files and set it as the default directory for your command-line session. Using the previous example, you would create a new subdirectory for the file manager programs and then use OS/2's change directory command to move to the new subdirectory. You now can use the use `UNPACK` command to decompress the 1.3 programs using the following format:

```
UNPACK <filename>
```

The `<filename>` parameter can be any valid OS/2 filename. Multiple files can also be specified by using wildcards such as the asterisk (`*`). The three file manager programs, for example, can be decompressed by using the following statement:

```
UNPACK A:\PMFILE*.*
```

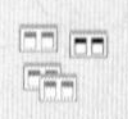

This statement finds all of the files with a PMFILE prefix on the disk and copies them in a decompressed format to your hard disk. It is important that you execute this command from within your target subdirectory, or your files will be copied to the wrong place. Once the `UNPACK` has been completed, your 1.3 programs will be ready for use.

Windows 3.1—Windows Compatibility

The third major configuration that is supported under OS/2 2.1 is the Windows 3.1 desktop. This configuration enables you to model your OS/2 2.1 desktop after the Microsoft Windows desktop to include such things as the Program Manager, application icons, and Windows menus.

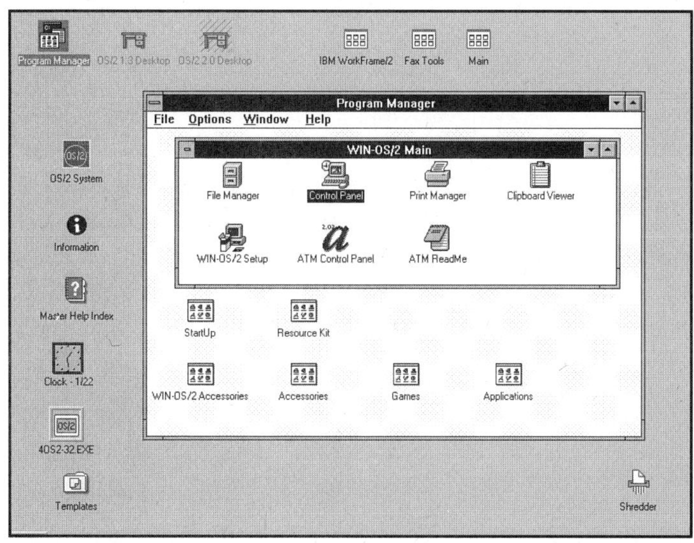

Figure 2.3. *The Windows desktop.*

The Windows 3.1 configuration is very useful if you are a current Microsoft Windows 3.1 user who is upgrading to OS/2 2.1. You are presented with a familiar desktop, and you are still able to take advantage of many of the advanced features of OS/2 2.1 such as full multitasking. It is important to remember, however, that OS/2 2.1 is just simulating the look and feel of Windows 3.1; the full power of OS/2 2.1 is still available.

Windows Groups and Applets

One difference that you should note between OS/2 2.1's implementation of the Windows desktop and the native Windows desktop is the fact that the OS/2 version does not contain some of the groups and icons that come with Microsoft Windows 3.1. This difference is due to the fact that the additional icons and groups provided by the Windows environment are not necessary in an OS/2 2.1 environment.

The groups and icons that are different between the OS/2 Windows implementation and the native Windows desktop fall into two main categories: system setup and applets. The system setup programs are no longer necessary because all of the system setup is handled directly by OS/2 2.1. These programs are accessed by double clicking on the OS/2 System folder. The applet programs supplied with Windows have been replaced by OS/2 2.1's own productivity applets. These applets are accessed by opening the OS/2 System folder and then opening the Productivity folder.

The Windows Desktop Versus Win-OS2

One area of possible confusion is the difference that exists between the Windows desktop configuration and the Win-OS2 desktop. As discussed, the Windows 3.1 desktop is simply a reconfiguration of the Workplace Shell; it is not a separately running program.

The Win-OS2 desktop, however, is a completely different matter. This desktop is actually started in a DOS session in the background. The DOS operating system is first started, and then a special OS/2 version of Windows 3.1 is loaded on top of it. It looks very similiar to the Windows 3.1 desktop configuration of the Workplace Shell, but it possesses its own unique environment and has many of the limitations of the DOS operating system that it is using.

Accessibility of the Workplace Shell

One of the major points brought up in this chapter that deserves further discussion is the fact that each of the major configurations previously described is actually just a reconfiguration of the Workplace Shell. Though they all have a very different look and feel, they are also all identical in that they are simply different setups of the shell that is running beneath them.

One of the consequences of this fact is that the native Workplace Shell configuration is always accessible regardless of the current desktop setup. If you set up either the OS/2 1.3 or Windows 3.1 desktop configurations, an OS/2 desktop icon is created on the screen. This icon represents the native OS/2 2.1 desktop. Double clicking on the icon brings you directly to the Workplace Shell.

Another consequence of the fact that each configuration is just another view of the Workplace Shell is that multiple configurations can be created and made accessible on the desktop. Executing both of the procedures for setting up the OS/2 1.3 and Windows 3.1 environments makes each of these configuration options available from the shell in the form of a 1.3 desktop icon and a Windows 3.1 icon.

The actual appearance of your desktop is a matter of personal choice. Accessing each of these configurations simply becomes a matter of double clicking on the appropriate icon—the OS/2 1.3 desktop icon if you want it to look like the 1.3 desktop or the Windows icon if you want the Windows 3.1 desktop. If you are currently in the 1.3 or Windows desktops you can switch back to the Workplace Shell by double clicking the OS/2 desktop icon.

> TIP
>
> Do not confuse the Windows 3.1 desktop icon with the Win-OS2 Window icon. The Windows 3.1 desktop icon changes your view of the desktop shell, and the Win-OS2 Window icon actually starts a special OS/2 version of Windows 3.1 in a background DOS session and brings that session to the foreground of the screen.

Configuring the System

This section discusses the actual mechanics of the system configuration process. It describes the different files involved in the configuration process along with their specific purposes, and it details the actual steps involved in the configuration process.

INI and RC Files

OS/2 2.1 uses two distinct types of files in the system configuration process: INI files and RC files. OS/2 files that have an INI extension are binary files that the system and certain applications use when they start up. They usually contain encoded information about the state of the desktop that can be read by your application programs during their initialization.

INI Files

The two main INI files used by OS/2 are OS2.INI and OS2SYS.INI. OS2SYS.INI is the OS/2 system file. It contains technical details about your system (information about printers, hardware details, communications parameters, and so on). This file is for the use of application programs and the OS/2 system itself. It does not contain any information that you should update directly.

The OS2.INI file is usually called the User INI file. It contains information about your desktop configuration (the colors you have selected, the icons on the screen, the size of various windows, and so on). OS2.INI is the file that gets updated when you customize screen options. Color changes, font selection, and various other options are all stored in this INI file when you are setting up your screen.

OS2.INI is also the file that you should change when you are ready to customize your desktop. Normally, all of your changes to OS2.INI are indirect;

they are made by the system while you are adjusting your desktop. System reconfiguration to a new desktop environment, however, requires you to directly update the OS2.INI file using a system-supplied utility. The actual steps required to perfrom this update are detailed in the following sections.

RC Files

RC files are system configuration files that are used to create the system-readable INI files. These files are in ASCII format and can be read into the OS/2 system editor if you wish to view their contents. Typically, the system configuration RC files are made up of many `PMInstallObject` statements, which are used to place items and groups on the desktop and to identify their associated programs.

OS/2 2.1 comes with three preconfigured RC files that are installed in the \OS2 subdirectory. Each of these three preconfigured files corresponds to one of the three major desktop configurations. The actual filenames and their corresponding desktops are as follows:

OS2_20.RC	OS/2 2.1 desktop
OS2_13.RC	OS/2 1.3 desktop
WIN_30.RC	Windows 3.1 desktop

You should not try to alter these RC files directly using the system editor. If you wish to make a change to one of them, you should first make a copy of the appropriate file and then alter the copy, leaving the original file intact. It is very easy to make a mistake when changing an RC file, and it is very difficult to re-create the original file after a number of changes have been made. The best approach is to use the original RC files to set up one of the OS/2 desktop configurations and then use the system facilities available on each desktop to change the various screen options.

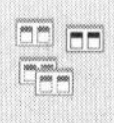

Booting from a Disk

In order to successfully reconfigure your system, you must boot OS/2 from a disk. This procedure is necessary because OS/2 locks the INI files that it uses while displaying your desktop. If you tried to create a new INI file while the system is running, you would get a "File in use" error and the procedure would be unsuccessful.

There are two different ways in which your system can be started from a disk. The first way, using the OS/2 installation disks, is the simplest but more time consuming way to boot from a disk. The second method is to create a separate boot disk for use in the boot procedure. Creating a separate boot disk is a much more complicated process under OS/2 than it is under DOS.

You will find that booting from a separate boot disk is noticeably faster than booting from the installation disks. It also has the advantage that you do not have to be available to switch disks and enter some keystrokes during the startup process.

Boot Disks

Most of the recovery methods discussed so far require you to boot the system using disks. As shipped, you can use the OS/2 2.1 disks by booting with the installation disk, swapping it with Disk 1 when prompted, and pressing Esc at the next OS/2 logo screen. At this point, the OS/2 2.1 command prompt, [A:\], is displayed. You can access CHKDSK by swapping Disk 1 with Disk 2.

This procedure works fine if you only need to boot OS/2 2.1 from disk occasionally. If you are part of a support network for a corporation, however, the extra time expended booting with two disks is time wasted. Chapter 1, "Installation," includes instructions on creating a single boot disk.

Using the MAKEINI Utility

MAKEINI is the utility that transforms an RC file into a system-readable INI file. The simplest way to use MAKEINI is to change to the OS/2 system directory (\OS2) and type the following command:

```
MAKEINI <filename.INI> <filename.RC>
```

The first parameter (`filename.INI`) is the name of the target INI file that you wish to create. In most cases, you should use the name of the standard OS/2 INI file: OS2.INI. The second parameter (`filename.RC`) is the name of the source RC file that is used to create the INI file. This parameter typically is one of the standard RC files that comes with OS/2: OS2_20.RC, WIN_30.RC, or OS2_13.RC.

It is important to realize that the parameters of the MAKEINI utility are not in the standard order. Most of OS/2's command-line programs have the source file as the first parameter and the target file as the second. MAKEINI, however, switches the order of its arguments. This swapping is a frequent source of error with the MAKEINI program.

MAKEINI typically produces some very cryptic error messages. If you get the message "File not in standard RC format," the chances are very good that you have accidentally swapped the program arguments when you typed your command.

OS/2 1.3

The OS/2 1.3 desktop can be set up under OS/2 2.1 by following the previously described boot procedure and running the MAKEINI utility with the system-supplied OS2_13.RC file. The actual command appears as follows:

```
MAKEINI OS2.INI OS2_13.RC
```

It is important to remember to change your current directory to the \OS2 subdirectory. The INI file will be created in the wrong place and the

reconfiguration will fail if you don't make this change. This situation is not obvious because no error message is generated. Your only indication that something went wrong is the reappearance of the standard Workplace Shell desktop the next time you restart your system.

After you have completed the MAKEINI procedure and have received a successful message, remove the OS/2 boot disk from your disk drive and press Ctrl-Alt-Delete to restart your system. When the system starts up, you should see the OS/2 1.3 desktop.

Windows 3.x

The setup for the Windows 3.x desktop is similar to the procedure used for the OS/2 1.3 desktop. Begin the procedure by booting OS/2 2.1 from a disk and running the MAKEINI utility with the preconfigured WIN_30.RC file. The MAKEINI statement for the Windows desktop configuration appears as follows:

```
MAKEINI OS2.INI WIN_30.RC
```

Again, you must ensure that you are currently in the \OS2 subdirectory when you execute this command or the reconfiguration procedure will fail.

After you are finished running the MAKEINI facility and have received a successful message, remove the boot disk and restart the system by pressing Ctrl-Alt-Delete. The next time your system starts, you will see it configured as the Windows 3.1 desktop.

OS/2 2.1

The OS/2 2.1 desktop configuration can be accomplished in two ways. The first configuration method is identical to the procedure that was outlined for installing the 1.3 and Windows desktops—reboot your machine from disks and run the MAKEINI utility with the following statement:

```
MAKEINI OS2.INI OS2_20.RC
```

OS/2 re-creates the original Workplace Shell configuration and places the appropriate system icons on your desktop. Remember that the first reboot of a Workplace Shell configuration takes a significantly longer amount of time than the normal system bootup, so do not worry if the system takes a long time to start.

The original Workplace Shell configuration can also be reinitialized by hitting a special key sequence when starting up your system. This method is detailed in the "Configuration Maintenance" section of this chapter.

Multiple Configurations

The setup of multiple configurations is accomplished by running both the OS/2 1.3 configuration and the Windows 3.1 configuration in sequence. It makes no difference which order you pick for the configuration sequence, but for the sake of this discussion, I will assume that you first run the 1.3 configuration and then the Windows configuration.

The first step is to run the 1.3 configuration using the procedure described in the preceding sections. Reboot the system to ensure that you completed the procedure correctly and run the Windows 3.1 configuration procedure. Reboot the system again. If you perform this sequence correctly, you are presented with the Windows 3.1 desktop when you are finished. If you wish to access the Workplace Shell at this point, click on the OS/2 desktop icon.

After you have accessed the shell, two additional icons appear on-screen: an OS/2 1.3 desktop icon and a Windows 3.1 desktop icon. Picking the configuration you wish is now simply a matter of double clicking on the appropriate icon. You can always return to the Workplace Shell from either desktop configuration by double clicking on the OS/2 desktop icon.

Configuration Maintenance

Chapter 16, "Troubleshooting," describes procedures that help you to maintain and easily re-create your system configuration in the event that a system problem, such as file corruption or hardware failure, ever occurs. These procedures show you how to save copies of your current configuration and detail quick processes for re-creating the standard desktop from scratch.

Unique Configurations

This section discusses some of the unique configurations that are available in OS/2 2.1. It provides a description of each of these unique configuration options, describes its uses, and details the specific steps needed for its creation.

The CMD.EXE Configuration

OS/2 2.1 allows you to set up a "barebones" configuration in which you can completely bypass the loading of the Workplace Shell and move directly to a command prompt when the operating system is initially loaded. This configuration produces an effect similar to the loading of the DOS command prompt when you boot the DOS operating system; the only visible difference here is the presence of brackets ([C:]) around the prompt as opposed to the traditional DOS "greater than" sign (C:>).

The main reason for bypassing the loading of the Workplace Shell and setting up this barebones configuration is the conservation of system resources. The shell can take up a large amount of memory and processing time while it is running; bypassing the loading of the Workplace Shell can free these resources for other uses.

You might consider setting up this particular configuration when you are loading OS/2 2.1 on a server machine. Many server applications, such as database servers or mail gateways, are designed to run without user interaction; they do not provide a graphical interface, and they consume large amounts of system resources. Bypassing the load of the Workplace Shell on such a machine reserves valuable resources for the server application without hampering any of its basic functionality.

TIP

OS/2 developers of full screen or server applications will also find this configuration to be very useful. The system initializes much more quickly when the OS/2 command-line processor is loaded in place of the Workplace Shell. This time conservation can be very valuable in a development environment where the system is constantly being restarted.

Setting Up the Configuration

The Workplace Shell is initially loaded by a combination of the `RUNWORKPLACE` and `PROTSHELL` statement in the OS/2 2.1 CONFIG.SYS file. In order to bypass this process and go directly to the OS/2 command line, you have to use the system editor or any other text editor to edit CONFIG.SYS and change one of these statements. The actual statements in the CONFIG.SYS file appear as follows:

```
PROTSHELL=C:\OS2\PMSHELL.EXE
SET RUNWORKPLACE=C:\OS2\PMSHELL.EXE
```

Chapter 6, "Configuring the Workplace Shell," describes how each of these statements are used. You will find that you have a choice of either one of these statements to load the CMD.EXE command processor.

Replacing the Command Processor

This section describes the OS/2 command processor and its alternatives. It discusses the usage of the various command-line interfaces and details the steps needed to replace the default command line with an alternative product.

Alternative Command Processors

The default command processor for OS/2 2.1 is a powerful tool that is similar in appearance to the basic DOS command processor (COMMAND.COM),

although it contains additional functionality. OS/2 also provides you, however, with the capability to substitute an alternative command processor for the one supplied by OS/2.

There are a number of different circumstances under which you might consider substituting a new command processor for the one supplied by OS/2. You may, for example, be very comfortable with a command processor supplied by a different system. If an OS/2 version of this command-line interface is also available, you will be able to use it in place of OS/2's native command-line interface.

You may want to use a command-line interface supplied by a third-party vendor. Third-party vendors offer "add-on" programs that contain functionality not found in the command interface supplied by OS/2. OS/2 easily enables you to substitute the vendor's product in place of its own default interface.

You may also need to use a different command-line interface because you work in a unique environment. A financial institution, for example, might need a command line that processes numeric values in a particular way. This requirement can be met by acquiring or writing a command-line interface designed to meet these financial requirments and using it in place of OS/2's native command processor.

Setting Up a New Default Command Processor

OS/2 enables you to change its default command processor by altering two statements in the CONFIG.SYS file: the `OS2_SHELL` and `COMSPEC` statements. To change these statements, you must start the OS/2 system editor or any other text editor and load the CONFIG.SYS file. After you have completed this step, find the `OS2_SHELL` and `COMSPEC` statements; the default setup procedure does not place these statements together, but they should be relatively close to each other in the file. The actual `OS2_SHELL` and `COMSPEC` commands appear as follows:

```
OS2_SHELL=C:\OS2\CMD.EXE
SET COMSPEC=C:\OS2\CMD.EXE
```

The OS2_SHELL command identifies, for the Workplace Shell, the actual program to use as the default command processor. This example shows the command loading OS/2's default command processor, CMD.EXE. The COMSPEC statement is used by the command processor, while it is running, to identify the location of its executable file. It is possible to load a new command processor by only changing one of the statements, the OS2_SHELL statement, but the system may not operate correctly while it is running, unless you also change the COMSPEC statement.

The loading of a new command processor is simply a matter of changing the path and filenames on the right side of each statement to point to your alternative command-line program. If you wish to substitute a new command-line program called NEWCOM, for example, whose file was named NEWCOM.EXE and located in the NEWC subdirectory, change the statements to appear as follows:

```
OS2_SHELL=C:\NEWC\NEWCOM.EXE
SET COMSPEC=C:\NEWC\NEWCOM.EXE
```

After you have changed the statements in the CONFIG.SYS file, you must save the file and reboot the system; your changes will not take affect until the system is rebooted. After your system is booted, start an OS/2 command session—your new command-line program is now being loaded.

Setting Up Multiple Command Processors

OS/2 also provides you with the capability to keep your default command processor and set up alternative command-line programs to be loaded when needed. This feature gives you the capability to use the normal command-line shell for your everyday work and yet gives you alternatives available for specialized uses. You might wish to use this feature, for example, if you are sharing a machine with another person. If both of you want to use different command-line processors, you can easily set up the system to make your command-line processor the default, but still give the other person the ability to invoke a command program whenever he or she wishes to use it.

The actual setup of an alternative command-line processor is accomplished using the Workplace Shell. One approach is to create a new program from the

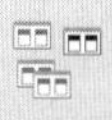

Templates folder, another is to copy the icon of an existing command-line processor and tailor it to accept the alternative program. (See chapter 4, "The Workplace Shell," to learn how you can copy or create a program.)

When you create your new object by copying from an existing command processor icon, you must change the settings for your new program. Click on the icon with mouse button 2, and a menu will appear. Go to the top of the menu, select the small right arrow next to Open, and a second menu will appear. Choose Settings from the second menu, and a notebook will appear. Go to the program name field in the notebook and you will find that it contains an "*." Erase the asterisk and type in the full path and filename of your new command-line processor, then tab down to the Working directory field and enter the path (not the filename) of your command-line processor. When you are done, close the notebook by double clicking on its system icon in the upper-left corner.

You are now ready to invoke the new command-line processor. Simply double click on the icon you just created, and it will start. Note that only this new icon will start up the alternative command-line program; you have not changed the default used by OS/2. If you wish to add more command-line icons, simply repeat this procedure as many times as necessary. You can create additional copies of your alternative command-line icon, or you can produce new icons that use different command-line programs.

Author Bio

John Campbell is a project manager at a large insurance company working on the development of LAN-based, Client/Server application systems. He has worked in the computer industry since 1982 when he first started developing systems for the analysis of commodities futures. He subsequently worked on the development of large computer-integrated manufacturing systems and applications for the insurance industry. Campbell received a B.S. degree in Computer Science from Duke University and an M.S. in Computer Science from NYU.

System Configuration, Setup, and Tuning

In This Chapter

"I know engineers, they love to change things."
—*Dr L. McCoy,* USS Enterprise

It is more than likely that at some point you will want to make changes to your OS/2 installation. It may be to install new features, to change some operational characteristics, or remove something that you've discovered you aren't really using. This chapter covers the basic issues that you will have to address as you customize OS/2 2.1 to fit the way you work.

Everyone is likely to use the system in slightly different ways. Some people are more comfortable using a command-line interface, others prefer the Workplace Shell, and a different group may prefer to use both interfaces. Many of the recommendations you'll find in this chapter are based on personal experience and experimentation. This is an important point when I talk about tuning and configuration.

Treat some of what follows as a jump start on your own experimentation process instead of gospel. Tuning a personal computer (operating system and hardware) can be a personal issue based on your patterns of use and budget for both money and time. If you do a lot of communications, you may want to seek out third-party serial port drivers that let you deal with potentially higher throughput. If you depend on graphical applications, you may want to get a video adapter with an accelerator and a large monitor; you may want to get local-bus adapters versus ISA or EISA, and so on. The configuration possibilities are extraordinarily varied.

There are a couple of areas that make sense to investigate as you tune the performance of the operating system to match the hardware and your needs. In order to do that you have to understand a little bit about what the operating system does "under the covers." The sections that follow cover some of the things you need to know to tune your system. I'll start with a brief introduction to multitasking, followed by an overview of disk operations. With this information as background, I'll examine the CONFIG.SYS file and highlight the parameters that you may want to tune.

A Brief Introduction to Multitasking

Since OS/2 1.1 there have been three major benefits touted for the operating system: freedom from the 640K barrier, an integral graphical user interface, and powerful multitasking. Once you know that OS/2 2.1 is a virtual memory operating system (covered briefly in Chapter 1, "Installation") that allows applications to access 512M of memory, the issues of constrained memory disappear. You can see the graphical user interface that is called the Workplace Shell; with a bit of practice, you can manipulate the environment. The one area that isn't obvious is multitasking. What is it? What makes it work? Why is it of interest?

All versions of the OS/2 operating system have been designed to work with the Intel 80x86 family of microprocessors. Regardless of the power of OS/2, most personal computers today have only a single microprocessor that can really only perform one function at a time. Multitasking is a sleight of hand that makes it appear that the computer is doing more than one thing at a time. In actuality, the operating system executes one portion of code (or thread) for a specified period of time, then it preempts (or interrupts) the execution and switches to another.

Multitasking works because of the extreme mismatch in speed between the microprocessor and the attached devices. Even the world's fastest hard disk is slower than today's microprocessors. With rare exceptions, most applications spend a great deal of time waiting for something to happen besides computation (e.g., user input, disk I/O, mouse movement, information from a communications port or network). If you can find a way to use the time the computer spends waiting for this external information productively, you can improve overall system throughput.

The following sections provide a brief introduction to the OS/2 multitasking and disk-caching vocabulary. Where appropriate, I've also included the relevant CONFIG.SYS parameters (covered in detail a bit later in this chapter).

Sessions and Processes and Threads, Oh My!

In a multitasking environment, you need some way to prevent the output of one program from being confused with the output of another program. A session (often called a screen group, the terms are sometimes used interchangeably), is a logical grouping of screen, keyboard, and mouse. To see an example, open a full-screen OS/2 Command Prompt and issue the `DIR` command to see a directory of the current directory (it doesn't make any difference which one you choose).

Use the Ctrl-Esc key sequence to get back to the Workplace Shell and open another full-screen session. In this second session run the CHKDSK utility to put something on the screen. If you switch back to the Workplace Shell, you can select between the two full-screen sessions. Notice that each one has something different on the screen. The operating system does not mix the output of one with the output of the other.

The application that would receive keystrokes (if you typed something) is called the foreground application; all of the others are background. Even on the OS/2 desktop, the active window (see Figure 3.1) is considered to be the foreground task, and everything else (even other windows you can see) is considered to be executing in the background.

OS/2 2.1 starts a couple of sessions when the system boots. The most obvious of these is the OS/2 desktop. The others are used to handle errors and other functions that you don't normally see. You can have one or more processes within a screen group.

Process: Under DOS, a process is a program that accesses memory and files directly. The OS/2 operating system distinguishes between resource ownership and execution. The OS/2 process is identified by its file extension (either COM or EXE). The term *process* defines the resource owner; execution is accomplished by threads.

Threads: All programs have one thing in common: they're composed of a sequence of instructions that are loaded into RAM, read by the CPU, and executed. As the CPU moves through each instruction, it is executing a thread. The OS/2 operating system (unlike DOS) permits multiple threads of execution within a single process. To put it another way, an

OS/2 application can execute in more than one part of the code at the same time. Each process has at least one thread and may start other threads or processes as appropriate for the particular problem.

Figure 3.1. The active window.

Integral to the OS/2 operating system is its capability to control and direct. Remember, regardless of the multitasking power of the system, the computer only has one CPU that can really only perform one task at a time. The operating system executes one thread for a maximum interval then it switches to another thread. This interval of execution is called a time slice.

Each time the system switches from one thread to another, it remembers the state of the one it just left behind. When it is time for the first thread to have its turn again, the operating system restores everything so that it appears as if there had been no interruption. Threads are affected by the following CONFIG.SYS parameters: `THREADS` and `MAXWAIT`, `TIMESLICE`, `PRIORITY`.

Scheduling: The mechanism that all versions of the OS/2 operating system have used to determine which thread executes next is called round-robin scheduling. The system provides four classes of priority (each class has 32 levels).

The system schedules threads that are ready to run from the highest class before threads in the next highest class. Threads that are ready to run in this second highest class are scheduled before threads in the third and so on. A thread in a higher priority class in a higher class that becomes ready to run is given a time slice before a thread in a lower priority class.

Scheduling is affected by the following parameters in CONFIG.SYS: MAXWAIT, PRIORITY_DISK_IO, PRIORITY, TIMESLICE, and THREADS (if more threads are allowed and running there is additional scheduling overhead to manage them).

Memory: OS/2 2.1 manages memory through a technique called virtual memory. An application must be loaded into the computer's physical memory to execute. In the DOS world, as many programs as will fit into 640K of available memory can be loaded, and the application directly accesses all of the memory available.

In OS/2 2.1, as in other operating systems, the program must still be loaded into physical memory before it can execute. However, the operating system allows overcommitment of memory, so the total of all currently executing applications may exceed the amount of physical memory installed. OS/2 2.1 can address 4 gigabytes of memory, and individual programs are "limited" to 512 megabytes of memory.

As OS/2 2.1 runs programs, it first uses RAM memory, the actual physical memory of your system. Because it is unlikely that your system has 4 gigabytes of RAM memory, the operating system needs to be able to get the additional memory from somewhere else. This additional memory is the "virtual" memory portion of your system. This virtual memory is obtained by reserving space on your hard disk and storing the same data that would be stored in RAM in a file on your hard drive. This file is called SWAPPER.DAT and is pointed to by the SWAPFILE setting in your OS/2 CONFIG.SYS file. If data is needed by the system that isn't already in RAM memory and there is no additional available RAM memory, a portion of RAM is "swapped" out to disk in order to make room for the needed portion. The required memory piece is then loaded from disk into the place left by the swapped memory.

This new memory may come from either the application program file itself or from the swap file if it had been previously loaded and swapped out. Under OS/2 2.1, memory is "swapped" in chunks of 4K at a time. This 4K unit of memory is called a page; the system has a very efficient algorithm for page management. The algorithm ensures that the least recently used pages (the oldest pages) will be swapped to disk prior to any other page. The reason for this is that the time required to access memory is much longer if the system needs to swap the memory in from disk rather than accessing it from RAM. It wouldn't make much sense to have to constantly swap memory in order to get a piece of memory that was being used frequently. Therefore, the actual amount of usable memory is limited by your physical memory (RAM) plus your available hard disk space for your SWAPFILE. It is likely that this number is something less than the 4 gigabyte limit that OS/2 2.1 is able to address.

The easiest way to get performance is to throw hardware at the problem. Adding more memory is the most obvious way to get performance. Adding a larger, faster hard disk can also help.

Memory is affected by the following CONFIG.SYS parameters: `MEMMAN`, `SWAPPATH`, `PROTECTONLY`, `PROTOSHELL`, `RMSIZE`, and all of the `DEVICE` statements.

If you can afford to dedicate a single physical hard disk drive (not a logical drive) for the use of just the SWAPFILE, you will get optimal swapping performance. This allows the "arm," which reads data off the hard disk in a manner similar to a phonograph, to stay positioned in the swap file and not race back and forth across the surface of the disk like it would if your SWAPFILE and your application were on the same drive.

Cache: HPFS and FAT

OS/2 2.1 provides a way to improve the performance of hard disks. Specifically, the system supports a special form of buffer called a cache. A cache uses RAM memory as a hard disk buffer. It keeps the most frequently read disk sectors in memory to minimize disk access. When a request for data normally stored on the hard disk occurs, the system checks the cache first. If the requested data is already in the cache from a previous read it is returned to the requester without the need for an additional disk operation.

The cache also optimizes disk writes. It collects data written to the disk and tries to schedule the output when the disk is idle to cause minimal impact to system performance.

Although it is hard to estimate the overall performance improvement that results from using a cache, there are some guidelines you can follow to determine the size and operational characteristics of the cache. On some systems there is a tradeoff between the amount of memory dedicated to disk caching and the amount of memory available for applications. I'll cover this in detail when I describe the `IFS` and `DISKCACHE` statements (in CONFIG.SYS).

CONFIG.SYS

The OS/2 CONFIG.SYS file controls some of the basic operational characteristics of the system. If you install a new file system (including a network), modify this file. If you want to tune the system, change this file. If you install an application that changes any of the path information, it changes this file. If you want to change the command-line prompt for all sessions, change this file.

Unfortunately, many times users either don't make a backup copy or the application doesn't. Make sure you make a backup copy of the CONFIG.SYS file before you install a program that modifies the file.

OS/2 is, after all, a multitasking system. If you start an installation you can usually open a window and make a copy of the CONFIG.SYS file while the installation of the program is running.

You can use any ASCII text editor to make changes to the CONFIG.SYS file. If you try to use the OS/2 System Editor (this is not the same thing as the Enhanced Editor, EPM), you will be prompted for a file type before you can save the file. The file type is not necessary for operation, but there is no way around it in the OS/2 System Editor.

Making Changes

There is a lot about OS/2 that is dependent on the CONFIG.SYS file and very little that is really known about the impact of the changes. Although the commands are documented in the IBM documentation, optimal settings or tuning information is lacking. In the sections that follow, I'll try to cover how these parameters relate to each other and what types of changes you should consider.

Installable File Systems

```
IFS=C:\OS2\HPFS.IFS /CACHE:512 /CRECL:4 /AUTOCHECK:F
RUN=C:\OS2\CACHE.EXE /LAZY:state /DISKIDLE:time
                     ➥/MAXAGE:time /BUFFERIDLE:time
```

The first line installs the HPFS as an installable file system. The installation program places this line in CONFIG.SYS to make it easier for users to use HPFS. If you have no plans to ever use HPFS, you can `REM` this line out and save almost 500K of memory that would normally be used for the executable

code as well as the cache. However, if you change your mind, you have to reinstate the line and reboot the system before you'll be able to format a drive to use the HPFS.

The `CACHE` statement is not automatically added to CONFIG.SYS. HPFS has a set of defaults that you can override with this command. If you want to change the defaults you have to add the `RUN` line manually. In addition, you can issue the `CACHE` command in an OS/2 window while the system is running (see Chapter 6, "Configuring the Workplace Shell").

```
IFS=full_path_of_the_installable_file_system
```

/CACHE defines the size of a cache (in kilobytes) to use with HPFS. The installation program sets the initial value based on the amount of RAM in the computer. If this parameter is omitted, the default is 10 percent of the installed RAM.

/CRECL defines the size of the maximum record size that will be cached (range: 2K to 64K with 4K as the default if you don't specify it).

/AUTOCHECK is automatically updated whenever you format an HPFS drive. If the file system is not properly shutdown the system automatically runs CHKDSK and all HPFS drives listed (the sample line would only check drive F). You may have to add this parameter if you formatted your boot volume for HPFS during the installation; check the CONFIG.SYS—if it isn't there, add it for the boot volume.

On a large HPFS volume, an `AUTOCHECK` can take some time. The best way to avoid it is to either use Shutdown from the Workplace Shell desktop menu or use Ctrl-Alt-Del and wait until the beep before you shut the computer off. Ctrl-Alt-Del does go through part of an internal mechanism that properly closes the file system. It does not allow applications to save their state the way Shutdown does, but it does close the file system and flush the buffers.

/LAZY can be set to On or Off, for all HPFS volumes (default is On).

A LAZY write cache is used to improve system performance. It allows the operating system to schedule disk writes when the disk is idle. There is a trade off, however. If your system crashes before the data is written, the files could be in an unpredictable state. The solution to this problem is noted in the following sections.

The following parameters are designed to minimize the exposure:

/DISKIDLE determines the length of time (in milliseconds) the disk must be idle before lazy writer tries to write cached data (default: 1,000—1 second).

/BUFFERIDLE determines how long the buffer should be idle (in milliseconds) before its contents must be written to disk (default: 500—0.5 seconds).

/MAXAGE sets the amount of time (in milliseconds) that data read into the cache should be considered current. Once this time expires, the cache considers the memory used by the data to be available for reuse (default: 5,000).

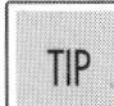

HPFS is designed to work with a LAZY write cache. Do not turn this parameter off. If you do, system performance will suffer.

Application developers should open individual critical files to be sure data actually gets to the hard disk (this is called write-through). In other words, if you have critical information that must be written to the disk, the way to do it is on an individual file basis, not for the entire volume. For example, if the system swap file is on an HPFS volume, you take a significant performance hit if you disable the lazy writer.

As mentioned, the default cache size is 10 percent of available RAM. You can change this value based on usage. Don't try to set it larger than 2M—the result won't be worth the lost system memory. Optimal settings for /C and /CRECL depend upon the way you use the hard disk. For the cache size (/C) use the 10 percent as a starting point for adjustment to fit your specific usage patterns. Adjust the CRECL parameter upward if you read large block files.

I have not found a need to adjust any of the time parameters for the cache. The default settings work quite well.

HPFS is designed to work with a cache. Do not disable it or set the value so small that it minimizes cache impact. The file system information comprises a small but important part of the CONFIG.SYS file.

The OS/2 Desktop and Command-Line Processor

```
PROTSHELL=C:\OS2\PMSHELL.EXE
SET USER_INI=C:\OS2\OS2.INI
SET SYSTEM_INI=C:\OS2\OS2SYS.INI
SET OS2_SHELL=C:\OS2\CMD.EXE
SET AUTOSTART=PROGRAMS,TASKLIST,FOLDERS,CONNECTIONS
SET RUNWORKPLACE=C:\OS2\PMSHELL.EXE
SET COMSPEC=C:\OS2\CMD.EXE
```

An inspection of these lines shows that `PMSHELL.EXE` appears in two places. On the `PROTSEHLL` line it defines the program that OS/2 uses for session management. Session management provides the capability to select (or switch) between applications. Its placement on the `RUNWORKPLACE` line cause the Workplace Shell dynamic link libraries to load to run the OS/2 desktop. For detailed information see Chapter 6.

The `SET` statements in the CONFIG.SYS file set up environment variables for the entire system (for more information about the command see Chapter 7, "The OS/2 Command Line"). In this case, it defines the USER_INI file as OS/2.INI and the SYSTEM_INI file as OS2SYS.INI. (See Chapter 6 for a discussion of .INI files and their importance, especially to the Workplace Shell.)

`OS2_SHELL` defines the application to use as the command-line interface program. The `COMSPEC` line defines the environment variable used by older programs to determine the name and location of the OS/2 command-line processor. If you have a replacement for CMD.EXE, you should place the filename (including the full path) on both lines. For example, to install 4OS2 as the command-line processor change these lines to read as follows:

```
SET OS2_SHELL=C:\4OS2\4OS2-32.EXE
SET COMSPEC=C:\4OS2\4OS2-32.EXE
```

If you delete the AUTOSTART line, you disable the Workplace Shell. For a complete reference to all of the CONFIG.SYS parameters that affect the Workplace Shell, consult Chapter 6.

Paths and Environment

```
LIBPATH=.;C:\OS2\DLL;C:\OS2\MDOS;C:\;C:\OS2\APPS\DLL;
SET PATH=C:\OS2;C:\OS2\SYSTEM;C:\OS2\MDOS\WINOS2;C:\OS2\INSTALL;
➥C:\;C:\OS2\MDOS;C:\OS2\APPS;
SET DPATH=C:\OS2;C:\OS2\SYSTEM;C:\OS2\MDOS\WINOS2;C:\OS2\INSTALL;
➥C:\;C:\OS2\BITMAP;C:\OS2\MDOS;C:\OS2\APPS;
SET PROMPT=$i[$p]
SET HELP=C:\OS2\HELP;C:\OS2\HELP\TUTORIAL;
SET GLOSSARY=C:\OS2\HELP\GLOSS;
SET IPF_KEYS=SBCS
SET KEYS=ON
SET BOOKSHELF=C:\OS2\BOOK;E:\OS2APPS\BOOK;
SET EPMPATH=C:\OS2\APPS
```

The lines in this group help determine the operating environment of OS/2 2.1. With the exception of one line, each of these lines has a couple of things in common. First, they all begin with the word SET. Second, the symbol between the SET and the equal sign (=) is called the environment variable. Environment variables influence the way a session looks and acts. The SET command enables you to control these variables.

SET commands in the CONFIG.SYS file establish environment variables that become global to every protected-mode session. You can override or change any of these settings for a specific protected-mode session either from a batch file or the command line, directly. However, if you want to permanently change a setting, you must edit CONFIG.SYS and reboot your system before the changes will "stick."

There is one exception: the LIBPATH environment variable can be changed only from within the CONFIG.SYS file. It controls the search order for special runtime libraries called dynamic link libraries (DLLs). Under normal conditions,

when the operating system searches for files, it looks at the current directory first, then starts with the first directory in the PATH statement (DPATH for data files); if the system doesn't find the file, it searches the next one, and so on. If the search fails, the "Bad command of file name" message appears (for programs, each application that uses DPATH issues its message if it can't find necessary data files). LIBPATH does not automatically search the current directory first. The OS/2 Installation Program places .; as the first directory to search for dynamic link libraries. The semicolon (;) separates directories on any PATH statement.

The PROMPT environment variable controls the OS/2 protected-mode prompt string. The string in this example turns on the online help at the top of an OS/2 Command Window ($i) and places the current drive and path within brackets [$p]. See Chapter 7 for a complete description of the PROMPT command.

The HELP environment variable identifies a path the system uses to find application specific "help" with the file extension HLP. The GLOSSARY environment variable identifies the location of the Workplace Shell glossary file.

The KEYS variable enables a recall list in the command processor. It allows you to retrieve previously issued commands that can be edited and reused. With KEYS set ON (the default) the Up arrow key cycles through the previously issued commands. To enable the same behavior for a DOS command session, remove REM from the following line in the AUTOEXEC.BAT:

```
REM LOADHIGH DOSKEY FINDFILE=DIR /A /S /B $*
```

The BOOKSHELF variable does for online documentation files (.INF extension) what the HELP variable does for HLP files. Files with the INF extension can be viewed using the OS/2 VIEW command (for example, the command VIEW CMDREF would run the Presentation Manager View utility to browse through the command processor online reference manual).

The EPMPATH variable is application specific. It points to the directory that contains files and/or subdirectories used by one of the productivity applications (in this case, the Enhanced Editor—EPM).

Disk Parameters

```
PRIORITY_DISK_IO=YES
FILES=20
BUFFERS=30
DISKCACHE=512,32,LW,ac:c
```

The variables in this category are related to hard disk operation. Since the first release of OS/2 1.0 and in all subsequent versions, the operating system is optimized to give preference to the foreground task. `PRIORITY_DISK_IO` toggles similar behavior for disk activity. If the parameter is set to `YES` (the default), disk I/O associated with the foreground task gets a priority boost over background processes. If the parameter is `NO`, the priority is assigned without regard to foreground or background status.

If you set this parameter to `NO`, you boost the performance of long, disk-intensive background tasks at the expense of the foreground process.

Don't change this parameter unless you must.

- `FILES` and `BUFFERS` affect the way the DOS sessions operate. They correspond to the same parameters in the DOS CONFIG.SYS file. The `FILES` statement only affects DOS sessions.
- The `BUFFERS` statement affects both DOS sessions and OS/2 applications. The value is the number of 512-byte blocks to reserve for buffers. In the example shown, this amounts to 30, 512-byte blocks for a total of 15K of memory. A cache is significantly more effective as an aid to performance than buffers.
- `DISKCACHE` sets the size of the disk cache used for FAT-based disks. It corresponds to the `/CACHE` parameter on the `IFS` line documented above.

  `512` is the size of the FAT cache in K that I use on a system with 16M of RAM.

32 is the size threshold for caching. Disk I/O blocks less than the threshold value are not cached.

LW enables the lazy write option for FAT. Its functions are similar to the LAZY parameter for HPFS. The recommendations for the DISKCACHE LW parameter are identical to HPFS.

AC:C enables auto-checking similar to the /AUTOCHECK parameter for HPFS. It specifies the disks to check at boot time for problems. This parameter has to be added manually to CONFIG.SYS.

Operation and Configuration

```
IOPL=YES
SWAPPATH=F:\ 2048
BREAK=OFF
THREADS=511
PRINTMONBUFSIZE=134,134,134
SET DELDIR=C:\DELETE,512;D:\DELETE,512;E:\DELETE,512;F:\DELETE,512;
PROTECTONLY=NO
MAXWAIT=2
MEMMAN=SWAP,PROTECT
DEVICE=C:\OS2\TESTCFG.SYS
PAUSEONEROR=YES
```

The parameters in this section determine some of the operational characteristics of the system. Some of the items are used for performance and tuning, others are used during installation.

IOPL stands for I/O privilege level. Under most circumstances, OS/2 does not allow applications to gain access to the hardware. Instead, applications must access devices through the interface provided by a device driver. In some cases an application may need limited access to some hardware. For example, some FAX software requires that IOPL be set to YES. The old Microsoft CodeView debugger also required this parameter. The default is YES. If you change it, some applications may refuse to work properly.

SWAPPATH defines the location of the OS/2 2.1 virtual memory swap file. The system uses the swap file for virtual memory. The first parameter specifies the location for the swap file. If you didn't change the location of this file according the guidelines in Chapter 1, consider doing it now. (The complete

rationale can be found in Chapter 1.) For now, the swap file should be located in the root directory of the most frequently used partition on the least frequently used drive (if you have more than one spindle—if you only have one drive, place the swap file in the root directory of the most frequently used partition).

The second parameter sets a warning threshold level (in M). OS/2 2.1 warns you when the amount of free space on the swap drive reaches this level. The system, however, will continue to allocate space. If you see the warning, you should either close some applications or erase some files on the drive.

Table 3.1. Initial swap file size.

Memory size	*Initial swap file size*
4	6M (6144)
5 to 6	5M (5120)
7 to 8	4M (4096)
9 to 10	3M (3072)
11 to 12	2M (2048)
more than 12	1M (1024)

The third parameter (not set in a default CONFIG.SYS) specifies the starting size (in M) of the swap file at boot time. Each time OS/2 boots it allocates a fresh swap file in the specified location.

When OS/2 boots it resets the swap file size to initial value; the swap file is not preserved across reboots.

BREAK determines if DOS VDMs check for the Ctrl-Break key sequence. The value in CONFIG.SYS determines the global default for the system. You can override it with the DOS settings (DOS_BREAK)—see Chapter 7.

THREADS was covered in Chapter 1. Remember, however, that the maximum system-wide number is 4096. Do not increase this from the default value on a non-networked system unless you are a developer and need the extra capacity. It is also possible that network servers may want to increase this value to handle thread-per-client requests. Check the network software for details.

PRINTMONBUF exists more for compatibility with prior versions of OS/2 than anything else. Some applications may use the values if they install a device monitor. In a small system you have to balance buffer versus system memory. The default size is 134 bytes, the maximum size is 2K (2048 bytes). For some fax drivers, I've seen an improvement in performance if this value is set to 1024.

When the OS/2 installation program establishes the original CONFIG.SYS, DELDIR is disabled; it is initially a REM (or comment) statement. If you want a certain amount of protection against accidental erasure, remove the REM as shown to enable delete protection. The general pattern is as follows:

```
X:\D S;
```

Each time you delete a file on drive X the system copies the file to directory D. The size S parameter defines the total size of files that can be stored in the directory. The system automatically purges files from the directory (first in first out) until the combined total of all files in the directory is less than S.

To restore deleted files use the UNDELETE command. In order for UNDELETE to work, the path must exist and DELDIR must be enabled. This means that if you have renamed or removed the original source directory, you must recreate the full path before UNDELETE has a chance to be successful.

The statement in CONFIG.SYS only works for OS/2 sessions. You can enable DELDIR protection for DOS sessions by modifying a similar line in the OS/2 AUTOEXEC.BAT file located in the root directory of the OS/2 boot drive.

If you elect to enable this feature, system performance will be affected. It will take longer for most file system operations.

> **TIP** If DELDIR is enabled, you can force a file to be deleted and not copied to the DELDIR directory if you use the /F or Force option on the command-line DELETE or ERASE command (for example, DEL JUNK.TXT /F).

PROTECTONLY set to YES disables DOS and Win-OS/2 sessions. Otherwise, OS/2 2.1 reserves memory for DOS sessions. If you don't need VDM capability, set this parameter to YES to save memory.

MAXWAIT defines the maximum amount of time that OS/2 2.1 allows a thread to "starve" for CPU attention before it gives the thread a priority boost within its class.

MEMMAN is used to control the swapping in the system. The default value (shown above) enables memory swapping to the path specified in the SWAPPATH variable. PROTECT allows application programs to allocate protected memory.

If you have at least 16M of memory you can consider setting the NOSWAP option to turn off swapping.

If you are a software developer you may want to add the COMMIT parameter to the MEMMAN line. It forces the OS/2 Memory Manager to allocate space in the swap file whenever the program commits memory. This enables an error code if there is not enough room in the swap file. If you use COMMIT, increase the minimum swap file size (on the SWAPPATH line) by the amount you are likely to use.

TESTCFG.SYS is a special device driver (see the next section for an explanation of device drivers) that is used by OS/2 2.1 to determine system configuration. It is used on non-IBM hardware to identify the bus type (e.g., ISA or EISA), BIOS information, and so on. It is also used by the install programs for some applications and during device drive installation. It is documented in the OS/2 Device Driver Kit.

PAUSEONEERROR is not normally included in the CONFIG.SYS file. (See the following default setting.) The impact of this parameter is to pause the boot process if the system detects an error processing the CONFIG.SYS file. For unattended operation where you do not care about the error condition, add a line to your CONFIG file:

```
PAUSEONERROR=NO
```

Base Devices

```
BASEDEV=PRINT01.SYS
BASEDEV=IBM1FLPY.ADD
BASEDEV=IBM1S506.ADD
BASEDEV=OS2DASD.DMD
```

A device driver is a special software program that the OS/2 operating system uses to access a device. The device driver is specific to a particular device type. A base device driver (BASEDEV) is needed to get the operating system started. Notice that the BASEDEV commands contain neither drive nor path information; the system does not "know" enough to process that information at the time these commands are processed. Instead, the operating system searches the root directory of the startup drive; if the file is found, it is loaded and executed—if not, the only other directory that is searched is the \OS2 directory on the same drive.

Table 3.2. Base device drivers.

Base device driver	*Comments*
IBM1FLPY.ADD	Supports disk drives on ISA and EISA computers
IBM2FLPY.ADD	Supports disk drives on Microchannel computers
IBM1S506.ADD	Supports non-SCSI hard disk drives on ISA and EISA systems
IBM2ADSK.ADD	Supports non-SCSI hard disks on Microchannel systems
IBM2SCSI.ADD	Supports SCSI hard disk on Microchannel systems
IBMINT13.I13	Generic int 13 support for ISA and EISA systems
OS2DASD.DMD	General-purpose hard disk support
OS2SCSI.DMD	Supports non-disk SCSI devices
PRINT01.SYS	Supports local printers on ISA and EISA systems
PRINT02.SYS	Supports local printers on Microchannel systems

DOS Settings

```
SHELL=C:\OS2\MDOS\COMMAND.COM C:\OS2\MDOS /P
FCBS=16,8
RMSIZE=640
DEVICE=C:\OS2\DOS.SYS
DEVICE=C:\OS2\MDOS\VEMM.SYS
rem DOS=LOW,NOUMB
DOS=high,UMB
DEVICE=C:\OS2\MDOS\VDPX.SYS
DEVICE=C:\OS2\MDOS\VXMS.SYS /UMB
DEVICE=C:\OS2\MDOS\VDPMI.SYS
DEVICE=C:\OS2\MDOS\VWIN.SYS
DEVICE=C:\OS2\MDOS\VCDROM.SYS
DEVICE=C:\OS2\MDOS\VMOUSE.SYS
```

This part of the CONFIG.SYS file controls the operation of the DOS sessions. `SHELL` is the name and location of the DOS command-line processor. It is similar to `OS2_SHELL`. If you want to replace the command processor for all DOS sessions, change this line. For example, to support JP Software's 4DOS utility, it should read as follows (change the drive and path information as appropriate):

```
SHELL=C:\4dos\4dos.com C:\4dos /P
```

`FCBS` defines the number of file control blocks allowed and protected. Most DOS applications today use file handles instead of control blocks. If you have an old DOS application you may have to fiddle with this parameter (check with the manufacturer of the software, if they are still around, to determine the proper numbers).

`RMSIZE` is the amount of RAM available to each DOS session. The default value is based on the amount of installed RAM in your system. If you have 6M or less, the default value is 512K, otherwise, it is 640K.

DOS.SYS is a device driver used to communicate between DOS and OS/2 applications running in the same machine. It provides support for named pipes and so on.

The next two lines show the default and suggested configuration for the DOS line. The default is to load DOS in the lower `RMSIZE` bytes and no upper memory blocks (UMB). To make more memory available for DOS sessions, change this as shown on the next line (load `DOS HIGH` and use UMB).

The lines that take the form `DEVICE=...Vsomething.SYS` load virtual device drivers that are identified in the following table. The VXMS.SYS line is installed in CONFIG.SYS as shown. If UMBs are not enabled, the `/UMB` parameter is ignored.

Table 3.3. Virtual device drivers.

Virtual Device Driver	*Comments*
VEMM.SYS	Provides DOS EMM support
VXMS.SYS	Provides DOS Extended Memory support
VDPMI.SYS	Provides DOS Protected Mode Interface (DPMI) support
VWIN.SYS	Provides support for Win-OS/2 sessions on the OS/2 desktop (sometimes called seamless). It also provides DDE and clipboard communications between the Win-OS/2 session and their OS/2 counterparts
VCDROM.SYS	Provides CD-ROM support for DOS sessions
VMOUSE.SYS	Provides DOS sessions with mouse support
VDPX.SYS	Is the protected mode to real mode device driver for DPMI applications
VCOM.SYS	Provides DOS access to the communications ports (serial ports)

The values in the CONFIG.SYS file affect the DOS settings notebook pages. Specifically, the DOS settings in Table 3.4 can be set in CONFIG.SYS for all DOS sessions; you can override the global settings on a per-session basis.

Table 3.4. Equivalence between DOS settings and CONFIG.SYS.

DOS setting	*CONFIG.SYS parameter*
`DOS_BREAK`	`BREAK=` `ON` or `OFF`
`DOS_DEVICE`	`DEVICE=device driver`
`DOS_FCBS`	`FCBS=count`
`DOS_FCBS_KEEP`	`FCBS=count,keep`
`DOS_FILES`	`FILES=number`
`DOS_HIGH`	`DOS=LOW` or `HIGH`
`DOS_LASTDRIVE`	`LASTDRIVE=letter`
`DOS_RMSIZE`	`RMSIZE=number`
`DOS_SHELL`	`SHELL=command processor`
`DOS_UMB`	`DOS=HIGH,UMB`

Mouse and Other Serial Ports

```
DEVICE=C:\OS2\PMDD.SYS
DEVICE=C:\OS2\POINTDD.SYS
DEVICE=C:\OS2\MOUSE.SYS SERIAL=COM1
DEVICE=C:\OS2\COM.SYS
DEVICE=C:\OS2\MDOS\VCOM.SYS
```

There are quite a few device drivers supplied with OS/2 2.1 (see Table 3.6). In this group you have both an OS/2 device driver (COM.SYS) and a DOS virtual device driver (VCOM.SYS). The OS/2 driver must be loaded before the corresponding virtual device driver.

It is possible that you may not be able to get to all of the serial ports installed on your system. It is possible that some of the internal interrupt settings will have to be set because your system is a bit different than COM.SYS expects. Specifically, if you have a COM3 or 4 you can modify the COM.SYS line as follows:

```
COM.SYS (n, addr, IRQ,s) (n,addr,IRQ,s)...
```

`n` is the port number (1,2,3 or 4)

`addr` is the port address (for COM3 try 3,3e8,10; for COM4 4,2e8,11)

`IRQ` is the IRQ level where (see Table 3.5)

`s` is the interrupt handling option (`D` deinstalls the driver after more than 1,000 unexpected interrupts and `I` says to ignore unexpected interrupts. The default, if not specified, is `D`.

Table 3.5. IRQ values.

IRQ	*description*	*IRQ*	*description*
0	system timer	8	real-time clock
1	keyboard	9	unused
2	secondary interrupt controller	10	unused
3	COM2	11	unused
4	COM1	12	unused
5	LPT2	13	math coprocessor
6	disk	14	hard disk
7	LPT1	15	unused

Table 3.6. OS/2 device drivers.

Device driver	*Comments*
ANSI.SYS	Provides extended keyboard and video support for DOS sessions
COM.SYS	Provides serial device support
EGA.SYS	Supports DOS sessions that require an enhanced graphics adapter (EGA)
EXTDSKDD.SYS	Provides a logical drive letter to an external disk drive
LOG.SYS	Provides support for the system error-logging facility (SYSLOG)
MOUSE.SYS	Provides mouse support (and similar pointing devices)
PMDD.SYS	Startup pointer draw driver
POINTDD.SYS	Draws the mouse pointer (works with MOUSE.SYS)
TOUCH.SYS	Supports touch devices (e.g., touch screen)
VDISK.SYS	Installs a virtual DISK also known as a RAM disk

Keyboard and Screen

```
SET VIDEO_DEVICES=VIO_SVGA
SET VIO_SVGA=DEVICE(BVHVGA,BVHSVGA)
COUNTRY=001,C:\OS2\SYSTEM\COUNTRY.SYS
CODEPAGE=437,850
DEVINFO=KBD,US,C:\OS2\KEYBOARD.DCP
DEVICE=C:\OS2\MDOS\VSVGA.SYS
DEVINFO=SCR,VGA,C:\OS2\VIOTBL.DCP
```

These commands setup the proper drivers for the screen and keyboard. Chapter 11, "The Video Subsystem," goes into the video settings in detail.

CODEPAGE and COUNTRY.SYS work together. COUNTRY.SYS defines the set of CODEPAGES that can be used for code-page switching. The code page defines the valid character sets that can be used. Related to this is the DEVINFO settings for the keyboard (KBD), screen (SCR), and printer (PRN). The example shows DEVINFO settings for the keyboard and screen.

The DEVINFO lines specify the keyboard layout, the character table to use to display information on the screen. You may not need a DEVINFO for your printer.

How to Setup a RAM Disk—When and Why

In DOS, you set up a RAM disk to get faster processing for some disk activities. When you established the RAM disk you knew that if you had to reboot the system, anything in the RAM disk would be lost. In this regard, nothing changes when you move to OS/2 2.1. However, in the DOS world, if you had extra memory (above the 640K limit) you could be secure in the knowledge that you would lose only a minimal amount of precious RAM below the 640K line.

In OS/2 2.1 that is no longer the case. Like a cache, the RAM disk uses memory that could be used by the system for applications. If you have a limited system (less than 12M to 16M of RAM) you may lose more than you gain by installing a RAM disk. To setup a RAM disk add the following line to your CONFIG.SYS:

```
DEVICE=C:\OS2\VDISK.SYS K,S,D
```

K is the size of the RAM disk in K (default: 64)

S is the number of sectors

D is the number of subdirectories allowed in the root (default: 128)

Sample Configurations

The preceding sections described some of the changes you could make to your system. In many cases I said there were trade-offs for a small system, but I really didn't go into details. The following sections are specific recommendations for some of the parameters based on experimentation. In addition, all of the systems include room for real-world applications, including at least a character-based word processor, a character-based spreadsheet (on the minimum system the word processor and spreadsheet were part of an integrated package), a personal finance package, and a communication package to allow you to get to CompuServe.

The Minimum System

Systems in this category have a slow 386sx processor (16 to 20 MHz) and a 60M hard disk. Partition the system with two partitions, a 20M boot partition (this means there isn't room for a full installation of OS/2 2.1 and a 40M data partition). In addition, also assume that neither dual boot nor Boot Manager is installed.

With a minimum system you have to be able to separate needs from *thneeds* (from Dr Seuss's *The Lorax*, something you think you need). If you don't need an applet, don't install it. For example, if you intend to use another communication package (or have no need for communications), skip the terminal emulator. If your software comes in an OS/2 version (or doesn't require Windows 3.1 compatibility), skip Win-OS/2 and possibly DOS. The key with this minimum system is that you have to skip something if you want room for applications and operation.

Equipment summary: 16 MHz 386sx, 4M RAM, 60M hard disk

To get an acceptable level of performance, I did not install Win-OS/2 support. I then set the following parameters:

```
BUFFERS=20
DISKCACHE=64,LW,AC:C
```

```
SWAPPATH=D:\ 2048 8096
RMSIZE=384
THREADS=64
```

If you don't install DOS support, add the following:

```
PROTECTONLY=YES
```

If the CONFIG.SYS has an `IFS` line, remove it to save the additional memory.

With this configuration I was able to load the following applications:

Lotus Works (word processor and spreadsheet)
Quicken (personal finance)
TAPCIS (communications with CompuServe)
The OS/2 System Editor

I could have added a small desktop publisher (PFS: First Publisher) and some other applications if I wanted. However, with only 4M of memory, the system starts to swap almost immediately. It didn't take long before I wished for more memory and a bigger, faster hard disk.

With this system you really can't expect to run more than a few concurrent applications (three is about the limit of acceptability).

I increased the amount of space for the initial swap file size from the default of 6M to 8M. Experience proved that the swap file grows. By starting with a larger value, I was less worried about the impact of disk fragmentation on the swap file.

Recommended Minimum System

To the minimum system add 2M of memory and 20M of hard disk space. With the additional memory, system performance (with the same installed software) is significantly better. I could almost double the number of concurrent tasks.

I still removed the IFS line, but I increased the amount of memory for the FAT-based disk cache. In addition, I could use stand-alone packages versus the integrated package. Substitute WordPerfect 5.1 and Lotus 1-2-3 (Version 2) instead of Lotus Works, the OS/2 Enhanced Editor instead of the System Editor, and a fax application and I still had room. I changed the partition to allow a 30M partition for OS/2 and a 50M data partition.

Equipment summary: 20 MHz 386sx, 6M RAM, 80M hard disk

I changed the CONFIG.SYS as follows:

```
BUFFERS=30
DISKCACHE=128,32,LW,AC:C
SWAPPATH=D:\ 2048
```

This system, with the same processor and comparable speed in the hard disk was almost 40 to 50 percent faster than the 4M minimum system. Although this is better, there is room for improvement.

A Better System

If you add another 2M of RAM, 40M to the hard disk, and change the processor to at least a 25 MHz 386 DX, you get a very comfortable system. I partitioned the disk with a 40M OS/2 boot partition and an 80M program and data partition. This allowed me to install all of OS/2 2.1, the applications in the minimum system, plus Relish (a 32-bit OS/2 personal information manager), Golden CommPass (as 16-bit CompuServe access utility), and FAXWORKS For OS/2. I could also have installed both a Postscript and HP LaserJet III printer driver.

Equipment summary: 25 MHz 386DX, 8M RAM, 120M hard disk

I changed CONFIG.SYS to the following (I left the rest at their installation defaults):

```
DISKCACHE=512,32,LW,AC:c
SWAPPATH=d:\ 2048
```

On a whim I also decided to install the IBM C-Set/2 compiler and toolkit (I removed some applications for this test) and tried to build an application. It took close to 5 hours to build the whole thing with a tremendous amount of disk space.

A Power-User System

This time I added 8M of RAM and took the disk size to 340M on a 33 MHz 486DX. This system, while still not top of the line by today's standards, is acceptably fast. With this configuration, I have a 60M OS/2 system partition with room for the complete system plus OS/2 Extended Services, dual boot, a 40M system test partition. This leaves 240M for programs and data. I split this into two 120M partitions—one formatted as FAT (so that it was available if I used dual boot to get back to real DOS) and the other 120M HPFS partition.

Equipment summary: 33 MHz 486DX, 16M memory, 340M hard disk

Note the following CONFIG.SYS changes:

```
IFS=C:\OS2\HPFS.IFS /CACHE=1024 /CRECL:64 /AUTOCHECK:E
DISKCACHE=512,32,LW,AC:C
SWAPPATH=E:\ 4096 10240
MAXWAIT=2
```

With this much memory I added HPFS and a 1M cache. I could take the cache up to 2M, but that begins to impact swapping when I make heavy use of the system. This is also one of the reasons I initially allocate 10M to the swap file. It can make a difference under heavy use.

To make a point about memory and swapping and the impact on performance, one of my clients called to complain that it was taking almost 5 hours to build an application on an IBM PS/2 Model 95 0KD with 8M of memory. I suggested they check the size of the swap file during the build. They reported that it was almost 12M. I suggested that they add more memory to decrease the requirement to swap. The following day I got a call; they added 8M of memory to take the total to 16M of RAM. The build time dropped from just under 5 hours to 45 minutes!

Performance Tuning

When it comes to tuning your system, there isn't a magic formula that will produce the guaranteed best results for everybody. I've talked about using a disk cache to improve disk performance. I've also mentioned the trade-off:

cache memory is not available to run applications. Although disk performance could improve, overall system performance could suffer because of the increased need for swapping.

Similarly, some of the tuning you may do will be to compensate for a slow processor, limited memory, limited hard disk space, and so on. The trick is to understand that tuning is a balancing act between using resources and acceptable throughput. Don't be afraid to play with your system to see what works and what doesn't. However, before you play, be sure you have a backup so that you can get back to a workable condition if you find something that degrades performance.

Change Boot Manager Operation

In Chapter 1 I described the process to install the OS/2 Boot Manager. I also suggested that there was a way to change the behavior of Boot Manager from the command-line using the `SETBOOT` command.

The syntax of the `SETBOOT` command includes the parameters contained in Table 3.7.

Table 3.7. *SETBOOT* parameters.

Parameter	*Meaning*
`/T:x`	Sets the time-out value in seconds. A value of 0 bypasses the display and starts the default partition immediately.
`/T:NO`	Disables the time-out value thereby forcing manual intervention.
`/M:m`	Sets the mode for the Boot Manager menu. `N` sets normal mode that shows only the alias (or name) for each partition. `A` sets advanced mode that displays additional information.

continues

Table 3.7. continued

Parameter	*Meaning*
`/Q`	Provides a query mode to determine the current set defaults.
`/B`	Performs an orderly shutdown (simulating a Ctrl-Alt -Del).
`/X:x`	Changes the default startup for the next reboot.
`/n:name`	Assigns a name to system index `n`. The name assigned to system index `0` becomes the new default. Numbers greater then 0 change the name associated with partition `n`.
`/IBA:name`	Shutdown and reboot the system from the named partition.
`/IBD:d`	Shutdown and reboot from logical drive `d`.
`/H`	Provides the help shown in the following listing.

You can combine the `/n:name` and `/X` parameter.

Listing 3.1. The contents of the */H* help screen.

```
1 d:\unleash>setboot /h
h is not a valid parameter.


Help for SETBOOT

SetBoot [/Parameters[:Value] ... ]
```

```
Parameters:
  T[IMEOUT]:nnn       Set TimeOut Value to nnn seconds (Default 30)
  T[IMEOUT]:NO        No TimeOut will occur
  M[ODE]:m            Set mode. m = n sets normal mode (Default)
                                m = a sets advance mode
  Q[UERY]             Query boot information
  B[OOT]              Restart the system
  [INDE]X:n           Sets the system index to n (0-3)
  n:cccccccc          Assigns the logical disk named cccccccc as the
                      boot system assigned to the index number n
```

If you setup a time-out value during installation, Boot Manager runs in unattended mode. It displays a list of bootable partitions and indicates the default if no action is taken within the specified time period.

Migration

In Chapter 1 the OS/2 migration facility is discussed. After you've installed OS/2 2,1 you can migrate additional DOS or Windows applications to work in OS/2 2.1. The migration facility creates program objects for 16-bit OS/2 applications as well as DOS and Windows programs. It places the program objects in folders on the desktop. If the application is in the migration database the migration tool also establishes the correct DOS settings for each program.

Check the migration database located in the \OS2\INSTALL directory of the boot drive to find DATABASE.TXT, an ASCII text file that contains an entry per program. Each program entry is preceded by a comment that names the application followed by the program information (see Listing 3.2).

Listing 3.2. A sample migration database text entry.

```
REM ----------------------------------------------
REM Lotus 123 3.1 by Lotus
REM ----------------------------------------------
    NAME                          123.EXE
    TITLE                         Lotus 123
    TYPE                          DOS
    ASSOC_FILE                    123DOS.EXE
```

continues

Listing 3.2. continued

```
DEF_DIR                    \123R3
DOS_UMB                    ON
DOS_HIGH                   ON
DPMI_MEMORY_LIMIT          4
DOS_VERSION                123DOS.EXE,3,00,255
DOS_VERSION                INSTALL.EXE,3,40,255
DOS_VERSION                LOTUS.EXE,3,40,255
DOS_VERSION                ZAP.EXE,3,40,255
DOS_VERSION                INS.EXE,3,40,255
DOS_VERSION                123.EXE,3,40,255
```

NAME is the name of the executable file.

TITLE is the icon (window) title.

TYPE is either DOS, WINDOWS, OS/2, or CUSTOM (for MS-Windows applications that must run full screen).

ASSOC_FILE is the name of an associated file or NULL.

DEF_DIR is the default directory or NULL.

You can change any of the values in the database as well as add additional programs that aren't there. The fields are required for each program entry. To get full information about all of the settings check the DBTAGS.DAT file in the \OS2\INSTALL directory.

Before you make changes, copy the file DATABASE.TXT and work with the copy.

The DBTAGS file lists the defaults. You do not have to create an entry in the text database if the default conditions are sufficient.

The DEF_DIR directory in the DATABASE.TXT file assumes that you've used the installation suggested default location. You can change this if you've changed directory names.

COMMON_SESSION allows you to specify either a common WIN-OS/2 session or a separate WIN-OS/2 session. If the application, running in

Windows, does not allow more than one instance in execution you can set this parameter to Off (default is On). This creates a separate WIN-OS/2 session for each instance of the program; this allows you to bypass the single copy-running problem.

Once you made the appropriate changes, the following command creates the migration database (DATABASE.DAT):

```
PARSEDB DBTAGS.DAT DBCOPY.TXT DATABASE.DAT.
```

You can get help for the PARSEDB utility in the Master Help (see Figure 3.2).

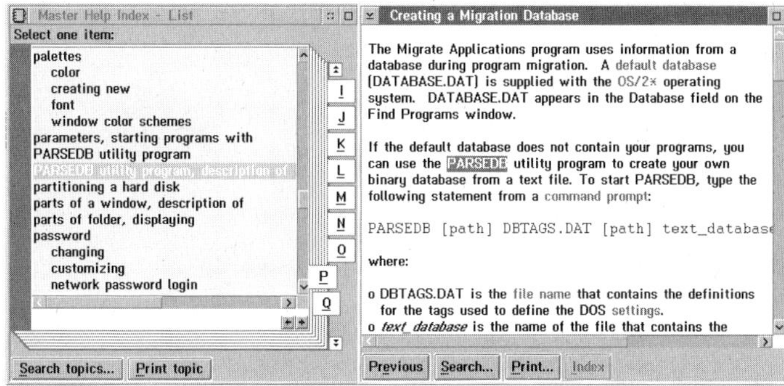

Figure 3.2 *Help for PARSEDB.*

Author Bio

David Moskowitz, president of Productivity Solutions, was the original developer and instructor of the IBM OS/2 Conversion Workshops. Moskowitz developed a set of workshops presented by IBM to members of their Developer Assistance Program to help them migrate their applications to OS/2. He is a frequent speaker at conferences and symposiums including Miller Freeman's Software Development Conferences. He is the author of a book about DOS to OS/2 migration, Converting Applications to OS/2 *(1989, Brady Books). He has written many articles about OS/2 and object-oriented development for various publications including* OS/2 Monthly, VAR Herald, *and IBM's* OS/2 Developer.

The Workplace Shell

In This Chapter

With the release of OS/2 2.0, IBM introduced the first of a new generation of user interfaces built around an object-oriented design. Extensive usability and human-factor studies by IBM indicated that first-time users of computer systems had trouble learning to use existing computer-user interfaces. Early in 1991, the OS/2 development team made the most significant decision affecting the OS/2 2.0 product. Based on a prototype created by a small group of programmers, IBM made the Workplace Shell a component of the operating system.

During the ensuing 12 months, the Workplace Shell team grew from that small group of programmers to include many other areas of IBM's research and development community, including usability testing, human-factor research, object-oriented programming technology, compiler research and development, information development, graphics design, and, of course, the tens of thousands of beta testers both inside IBM and in the industry who provided invaluable guidance, advice, and feedback.

The goals behind the Workplace Shell were to provide a user interface more powerful than the one it replaced, at the same time being much easier to learn and use. The shell needed to satisfy two, sometimes conflicting, audiences:

1. Application developers: programmers require interfaces in the shell to allow their applications to integrate and exploit some of the power behind the user interface (for example, drag-and-drop techniques).

2. Computer users: OS/2 users need easy-to-learn interfaces that they can customize and enhance to meet growing requirements and knowledge.

The OS/2 Workplace Shell succeeds in meeting both of these demands extremely well. Credit for this goes to the designers and programmers who had the courage and foresight to adopt object-oriented programming techniques (using IBM's System Object Model) and carry this object design into the user interface.

This chapter (and Chapter 5, "Workplace Shell Objects," and Chapter 6, "Configuring the Workplace Shell") gives you, a user of the Workplace Shell, some insight into the power behind the user interface, how the shell works, and information on how you can customize it to create your own simple drag-and-drop objects. In short, you'll find out how to get the most from your computer.

> TIP
>
> Like the rest of this book, the discussion of the Workplace Shell covers the OS/2 2.1 product. There are few differences in the Workplace Shell from the OS/2 2.0 release (other than a noticeable performance improvement).

Getting Started

When you use the Workplace Shell you need to become familiar with the mouse and the keyboard. This section shows you some of the basic operations of the Workplace Shell.

This book refers to the buttons on your mouse as button 1 and button 2 (not the right or left button) because the positions change depending on whether you are right- or left-handed. The Workplace Shell allows you to set up whichever you prefer. Once set up, mouse button 1 is the one you press with your forefinger and button 2 is the one you press with your middle finger.

Unless you choose a different configuration, you normally use mouse button 1 for selection and mouse button 2 for direct manipulation to perform drag-and-drop operations or request the pop-up menu.

The word *desktop* refers to the background of the screen on which all your application windows are running. Also, the word *object* in this chapter refers to any application program, data file, or device that you can work with in the Workplace Shell. The Workplace Shell represents these objects as icons and text on the desktop screen and in folder windows that appear on the desktop.

Some objects in the Workplace Shell represent files on your hard disk; these objects can be data files, executable programs, or directories. You can generally move or copy these types of objects anywhere. Other objects in the Workplace Shell do not have a corresponding file on your hard disk. For these objects, the shell holds information in a special system file on your hard disk, and you cannot move or copy these objects onto disks or network drives. Chapter 5 discusses the differences between these and other object types.

There are several keys on the keyboard that you can use instead of the mouse or at the same time as you use the mouse. These keys are discussed in the following sections.

Pop-Up Context Menus

With the mouse, the primary user interface element of the Workplace Shell is the pop-up menu. The term *context menu* is sometimes used because the contents of the menu can vary depending upon the current operation or selection. Pop-up menus are important in the Workplace Shell for two reasons:

1. They provide a quick and easy method of accessing functions for objects with which you are currently working, wherever the mouse pointer is located or wherever the keyboard is focused.
2. They provide a method of performing functions with the keyboard which would otherwise be possible only by drag-and-drop operations and mouse usage.

You obtain the pop-up menu by clicking mouse button 2 on the object with which you want to work. If the object is currently highlighted, you can also use the Shift-F10. If you select multiple objects, the menu contains only options available for all these objects, and any action you request applies to all the selected objects.

If you click on an object that is not selected, the pop-up menu applies to that object only. It does not matter if other objects are selected.

If you click within a window, but not directly on an object, the action you select from the pop-up menu applies to the object that owns the window.

The shell provides visual feedback so you can identify the objects affected by any action from a pop-up menu. If the menu applies to the window object, a

dotted line appears around the interior of the window frame (see Figure 4.1); if it applies to a single object, the dotted line appears around the single object's icon or text.

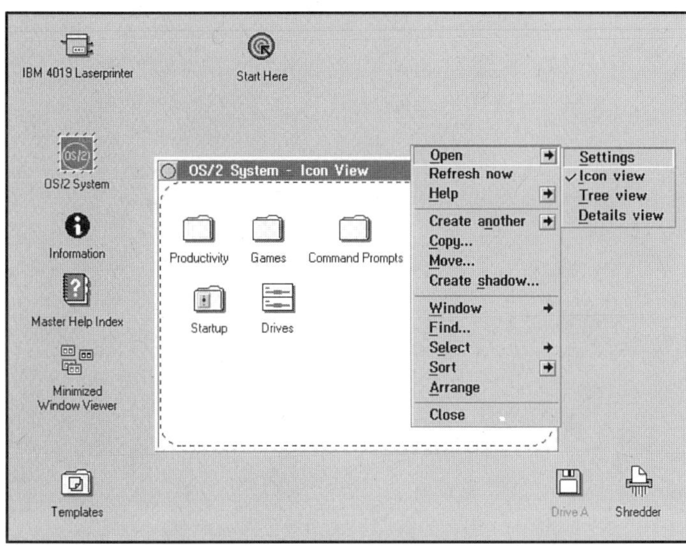

Figure 4.1. *A pop-up menu for the System folder with an open submenu.*

It is possible to add items to many of the pop-up menus provided by objects in the Workplace Shell. In "The Menu Page" in Chapter 5 you will learn how to do this.

To the right of some menu items you will see a right-pointing arrow. This indicates that there are submenus, or cascade menus. If the arrow is on a raised button, the submenu is a conditional cascade menu. Conditional menus appear only when you select the arrow button; if you select a menu item with a conditional menu attached, without going into the submenu, a default action applies. A check mark to the left of an item on the conditional menu identifies the default and, for objects that represent files, you can change the default in the Menu settings page. For example, a folder's Open submenu marks the icon view as the default.

Feedback

When you request the pop-up menu, the dotted line drawn around your object's icon is one example of the visual feedback that the Workplace Shell gives you during drag-and-drop and mouse operations. Many other types of visual signals are used as well. The complete list of visual signals is contained in Table 4.1 (each signal is discussed later in this chapter).

Table 4.1. Examples of Workplace Shell visual feedback.

Action	*Visual Signal*
Copy	Halftone (gray) icon
Move	Solid icon
Create shadow	Elastic line back to original
Multiple move/copy	Cascading icons
Illegal drop	No entry sign
Target	Solid box or line around or between objects
In-use	Hatched pattern background
Pop-up focus	Dotted box around objects
Selected	Solid gray background

Where to Find Help

OS/2 2.1 includes a large amount of online help information and documentation. The complete set takes up about 2.5 megabytes of your hard disk. This is compressed data that you read with the OS/2 Information Presentation Facility using the `VIEW` or `HELP` commands, by selecting Help from any menu or pushbutton, or from the Master Help Index.

If you printed all the online information included with OS/2 2.1 in a book, it would be approximately twice the size of this book! With such a vast library of information available, where do you start to look if you need help? The answer, of course, is to simply select Help. OS/2 2.1 searches the online database and displays only those pages relevant to the action you are trying to complete. Using the keyboard you can press the F1 key at any time to access a help window.

Many commands can display abbreviated help if you use the `/?` parameter. `DIR /?`, for example, displays the information shown in Listing 4.1.

Listing 4.1. Output from the *DIR /?* command.

```
[C:\]dir /?
Use the DIR command to list the files and subdirectories.

SYNTAX:  DIR [drive:][filename]  [/A[adshr]] [/B] [/F]
         [/L] [/N] [/O[nedsg]] [/P] [/S] [/W] [/R]
Where:
  [drive:][filename] Specifies the directories and
            files to list.
  /A[adshr] Displays only specified attributes.
  /B        Displays only filename and extension.
  /F        Displays only fully-qualified files and directories.
  /L        Displays directory information in lowercase letters.
  /N        Displays the listing in the new OS/2 format.
  /O[nedsg] Orders the display by specified fields.
  /P        Pauses after each screen of information.
  /S        Displays all subdirectories.
  /W        Displays the directory listing horizontally.
  /R        Displays .LONGNAME extended attributes.
```

Chapter 7, "Command-Line Interface," includes more information on obtaining help for system commands and the `HELP` command.

Using the Master Help Index

One of the more powerful tools OS/2 2.1 provides is the Master Help Index. This object is a single point of entry to all the online help information provided with OS/2 2.1. When you open this object it searches selected directories on

your hard disk and reads the contents sections of each online help file (.HLP) that it finds. After reading all files, the contents are sorted by topic and subtopic and displayed in a notebook list box.

Because of the large number of files that the Master Help Index has to read, it can take several seconds to open the index for the first time.

From this list box you can select any help topic. For example, if you want to learn how to install a printer device driver, you can look for either Installing or Printing. Under either topic you will find a subtopic on how to install a printer driver. When looking for a topic, you can jump to sections of the alphabet by pressing a single letter key on the keyboard, scrolling down with the scroll bar, or selecting any of the tabs on the right side of the notebook.

Once you have found a topic in the index, select it by double-clicking mouse button 1 or pressing Enter. A window appears to the right of the index list with your requested information (see Figure 4.2).

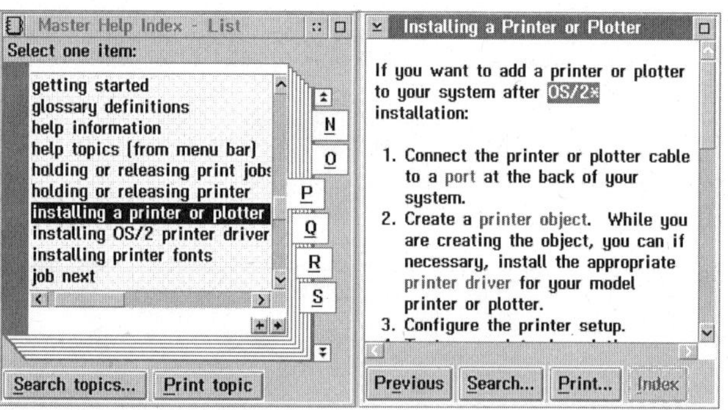

Figure 4.2. *The Master Help Index with printer installation help.*

From this one page you will often find references to other related topics. You can jump to these by selecting the highlighted key words in the text.

Pushbuttons at the bottom of the text window allow you to search for other topics, backtrack to pages you previously viewed (since opening the Master Help Index), and print the page you are viewing.

The Glossary is similar to the help index and provides definitions of terms you may come across in any of the online information that OS/2 2.1 provides.

Adding to the Master Help Index

Normally the Master Help Index includes online information only for OS/2 2.1, the Workplace Shell, and applets provided with OS/2 2.1. It does not contain information for any other application. However, you can add online information for any application into the Master Help Index. You can do this in one of two ways:

1. Move the application's online help file into the \OS2\HELP directory.
2. Add the name of the directory containing the application's online help file to the HELP path specified in CONFIG.SYS. The online help files for applications usually have the same name as the executable file (with an extension of .HLP).

Either method works but you should try to use the first so you don't have to edit your CONFIG.SYS file. The first method also reduces the number of directories that the Master Help Index has to search.

Think about whether you want to move, or copy, the .HLP files for your applications. Moving the file means that you don't waste hard disk space by having extra files you don't need. It also means, however, that you risk losing the file if you ever install a new copy of OS/2 2.1 onto your computer (some applications only look in the same directory as the executable program file, so moving the .HLP file may cause the application to fail).

You can also change the locations that the Master Help Index and Glossary search for in each object's settings notebook. On the Properties page you can

enter either the name of an environment variable (that is set in your CONFIG.SYS file) or a list of help files, complete with directory path. If you want to include multiple files, you must separate them with + symbols.

You can create your own specialized help index objects by copying either the Master Help Index or Glossary and changing the properties to search in a location that you specify.

Online Manuals and Tutorials

Apart from the context-sensitive help information, OS/2 2.1 also includes tutorials to teach you how to use the system, reference manuals for commands, and the REXX command language. REXX is an extremely powerful tool in OS/2 2.1 that you can use to control many aspects of the operating system. Later, in Chapter 5, small REXX utilities that can create Workplace Shell objects are discussed. Chapter 15, "REXX Programming," shows some of the other tasks that REXX can perform.

Start Here and Tutorial Objects

You will most likely use the Start Here and tutorial objects only when you first start to use OS/2 2.1. They contain information for users who are not familiar with the OS/2 operating system or the Workplace Shell.

The tutorial starts automatically the first time you install OS/2 2.1, while the system performs its initial configuration and setup. Because OS/2 2.1 can multitask, you can read the tutorial while this initial set up takes place.

If your computer system arrived with OS/2 2.1 preloaded, the tutorial starts every time you restart your computer, not just the first time. Once you have learned about using OS/2 2.1, you can

delete the shadow of the tutorial from the Startup folder. This stops the tutorial from running every time your computer starts.

The tutorial guides you through using OS/2 2.1 with the mouse and keyboard, informs you about the icons on the desktop, and shows you how to move, copy, and work with them. Once you have used the tutorial, you are unlikely to ever need to return to it.

It is a good idea to walk through the tutorial once, regardless of your experience with software—you will probably learn something new and useful!

The Start Here object is a very short list of common actions that you might need to perform in the first few days of working with OS/2 2.1. There are only 13 topics in the list but many more pages of information. Figure 4.3 shows the topic list and the first page of information. Again, once you become familiar with OS/2 2.1, you are unlikely to need to return here—the Master Help Index will become your main source of information.

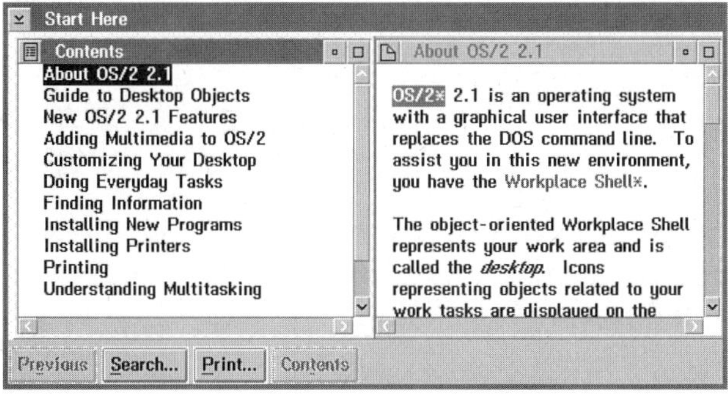

Figure 4.3. *The first page of the Start Here object.*

Inside the Information Folder

Within the Information folder you can find the online reference manuals for the OS/2 2.1 commands and REXX. Access the reference manuals by opening the one you are interested in (double-click mouse button 1, or select it and press Enter). This uses the OS/2 Information Presentation Facility (IPF) that provides you with a number of features including full index and contents, search, and an option to print a page or more on your default printer. Figure 4.4 shows an example page from the REXX command reference.

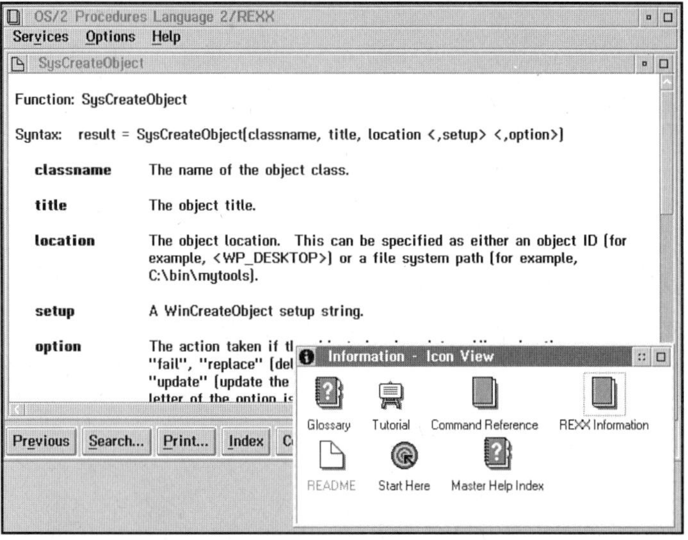

Figure 4.4. *An online REXX command reference page.*

Also in the Information folder is a shadow of the OS/2 2.1 README file. Most software products include such a file for information in addition to the printed manuals that accompany the product.

The Information folder contains a shadow of README because OS/2 2.1 keeps the file in the root directory of your boot drive, not the directory corresponding to the Information folder. (Shadows of objects are discussed in Chapter 5.)

The README file contains latest information concerning OS/2 2.1 compatibility with applications and computer hardware, known problems, and the results of some of IBM's own testing of OS/2 2.1 with many DOS, OS/2, and Windows applications. If you are an administrator for a number of OS/2 2.1 installations, it is a good idea to review the contents of the README file. Even if you are not responsible for other installations, you may want to search the file should you experience any problems running an application on OS/2 2.1 or with any hardware device.

Learning to Use the Shell

Now that you have started to use OS/2 2.1, it is time to learn some of the basic features of the Workplace Shell and some of the characteristics of the shell that may be different from the interfaces that you have used up to this point.

Copying, Moving, and Deleting

The Workplace Shell allows you to copy, move, delete, and print any of your objects using drag-and-drop techniques.

Moving an object is just a matter of picking it up and placing it where you want it. Move the mouse pointer over the object and depress and hold mouse button 2. Moving the mouse slightly with this button pressed picks up the object. You can now move the mouse pointer to a target and release the button. This drops the object. If you drop it into another folder, the object moves to this folder. Drop it on the desktop and it moves to the desktop. While you drag, the object icon appears on the end of the mouse pointer, as shown in Figure 4.5.

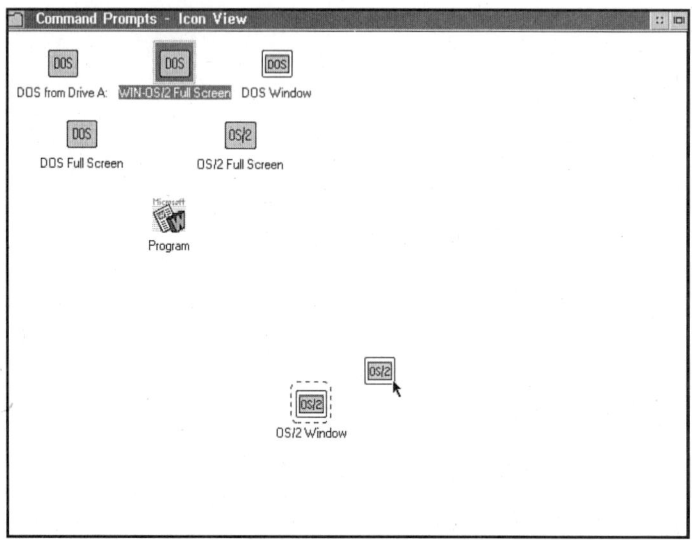

Figure 4.5. *Move operation feedback.*

Drop it on the shredder to delete it. Drop it on the printer and, if the object supports printing, it prints. If it is a single object, it moves, but if it is a folder, the folder and its contents move.

Normally, the default action is to move the object. To copy an object instead of moving it, press and hold the Ctrl key on the keyboard while you do the drag-and-drop operation and release the mouse button before releasing the Ctrl key.

You need to hold only the Ctrl key as you drop the object if you want the operation to be a copy. How do you know that a copy is occurring instead of a move? When the operation is a move, the icon looks just like it did before you picked it up. When it is a copy, however, the icon appears somewhat fuzzier than before (see Figure 4.6). This tells you that the original is intact and that what you are carrying is a copy of the original.

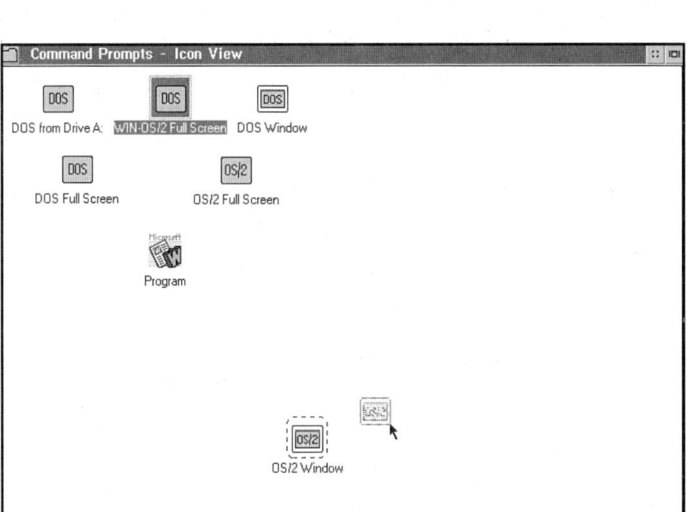

Figure 4.6. *Copy operation feedback.*

In some cases the default action is a copy and not a move. Workplace Shell chooses to copy instead of move when the move action could result in the unintentional deletion of the object. This feature protects inexperienced users from accidentally deleting data.

For example, if you drag an object onto a disk and the operation is a move, OS/2 2.1 deletes the object from your hard disk—not exactly what you might expect! The same is true if you drag-and-drop between your hard disk and a folder on a network or drop on a printer.

If you want to enforce a move rather than a copy, you can hold down the Shift key while performing the drag and then release the mouse button before you release the Shift key. You are free to change your mind at any time during the drag by releasing the Shift key first; you can even cancel the drag operation completely. To cancel a drag operation before you drop the object, press Esc on the keyboard before you let go of mouse button 2.

Selecting with the Mouse

To select an item on the Workplace Shell, press mouse button 1 when the pointer is over the object of interest. Simply clicking button 1 selects the new object and deselects all previous objects. If you want to select more than one item, you have three choices:

1. You can hold down the Ctrl key on your keyboard before clicking mouse button 1. When you hold this key, previously selected objects are not deselected.
2. When the objects appear as an ordered list, you can hold down the Shift key before clicking mouse button 1. When you hold this key, every object from the currently selected one up to the object under the mouse pointer is selected.
3. Use a marquee or swipe selection.

You select objects by clicking the mouse button. This means that you must press and release the mouse button within a short period of time without moving the mouse more than a very short distance. Moving the mouse starts a swipe selection.

To start a marquee selection, press and hold mouse button 1 when the pointer is not directly over any object icon. Move the mouse and you will see an elastic box drawn around all the icons as you move the mouse (see Figure 4.7). Releasing the mouse button selects all object icons within the box.

To start a swipe selection, press and hold mouse button 1 when the pointer is directly over any object icon. Move the mouse to select every object icon that you move over with the pointer. All these objects remain selected when you release the mouse button.

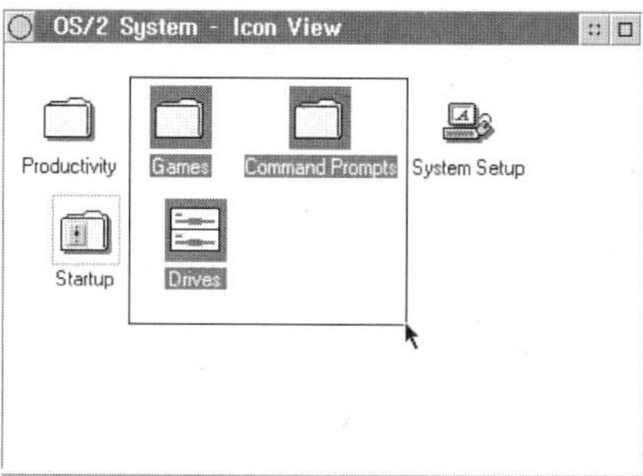

Figure 4.7. *Marquee selection of multiple objects.*

If some objects are out of view, you have to scroll them into view and then use the Ctrl key while continuing your selection. Folder windows do not automatically scroll for you when you perform a swipe or marquee selection.

If you want to drag-and-drop or display the pop-up menu for a single object, you do not need to select it first; just press mouse button 2. If you want to work with multiple objects, you need to select them all first.

Augmentation Keys

The Ctrl and Shift keys you learned to use in the previous sections are known as augmentation keys—keys that you can press during a drag-and-drop. You use these to modify the behavior of the operation. The Workplace Shell uses the following augmentation keys:

Ctrl	Force copy
Shift	Force move

Ctrl-Shift	Create Shadow
Esc	Cancel drag

You should press the augmentation keys after you pick up an object with mouse button 2. Some keys perform differently if you hold them down before pressing a mouse button. For example, holding down the Ctrl key and then pressing mouse button 1 allows you to select another object without deselecting any already selected object.

The default drag-and-drop operation is a move for all objects except templates. You must use an augmentation key to move, copy, or create a shadow of a template with drag-and-drop (see Chapter 5). A shadow of an object is an important feature of the Workplace Shell (Chapter 5 also discusses this feature).

No Entry Here

While you are dragging an object you may notice that as you pass over other objects or windows various forms of highlighting appear. The two common forms are a solid black line drawn around the target and a No Entry symbol that appears next to the object you are dragging. The solid black line tells you exactly where you are about to drop the object (perhaps on a single object or into a folder containing many objects). The No Entry symbol, shown in Figure 4.8, tells you that, for whatever reason, you can't drop the object onto this window.

When you try to drag a file marked read-only to the shredder you'll see the "Do Not Enter" sign. The shredder recognizes the read-only flag and responds by saying that it cannot delete the file. Sometimes, however, it might not know that it can't delete the file, in which case the shredder accepts the drop, then displays a message saying that the delete failed. This can also happen if another program is currently using the file.

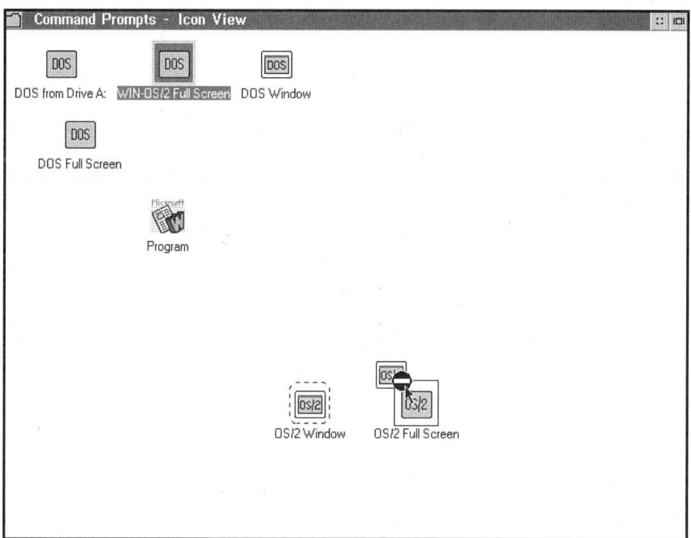

Figure 4.8. *Feedback indicating that you cannot drop the object here.*

TIP

Because of the drag-and-drop interaction that takes place when you drag an object over a window, there is potential for performance degradation. If the window is swapped out, it has to be swapped back in so that it can react to the drag-and-drop inquiry. One way to avoid the problem is by adding memory to your system. Another way is to reduce the number of open windows and icons on the desktop.

If You Don't Have a Mouse . . .

You don't have to use drag-and-drop to move, copy, delete, or print objects. Each object that supports these operations has a menu option on its pop-up menu.

For example, you can move an object by bringing up the folder's pop-up menu and selecting the Move option. Selecting this option brings up a window that queries you about the move. The notebook in this window has options that help you to tell the Workplace Shell where to move the object. The Workplace Shell uses this notebook in several places (see "Using Find to Search for Objects" later in this chapter).

To delete an object or print an object, select the appropriate menu selection from the object's pop-up menu.

Not all objects have all the Move, Copy, Delete, and Print selections available on the pop-up menu—they may not have any of them available. Menus display only those actions that are valid for the object. If your object is a read-only file, for example, no Delete option is available.

Selecting with the Keyboard

It may sound easy, but if you don't have a mouse, how do you move your object icons, select them, and request the pop-up menu?

The answer is to use the cursor movement keys on your keyboard. As you press the cursor keys you move the selection between all the objects in the current window. The current window is known as the focus window, and everything you type on the keyboard goes to this window, except for four special keys known as hot keys. Use these hot keys to tell the Workplace Shell to move between windows or applications on the screen:

Alt-Esc	Move to the next application window or full-screen program
Alt-Tab	Move to the next application window (this combination skips full-screen programs)

Ctrl-Esc	Display the Window List of all open applications or windows
Alt-Shift-Tab	Move the focus to the desktop window

Some DOS applications use these special hot keys themselves. To allow applications like this to work, you may need to set the KBD_CTRL_BYPASS DOS setting.

If you want to select an object in a window, you must first ensure that this window has the focus.

OS/2 2.1 treats the desktop window just like any other object window, and you can select it like any other, using one of the hot keys or with the Window List described in "Using the Window List" later in this chapter. It remains locked to the back of your screen, however, and does not come to the front.

When you select object icons or text, their background color changes to the current selection highlight color (by default this color is dark gray). After you arrive at the desired object, you can request the pop-up menu by pressing Shift-F10.

Inside the pop-up menu, select actions with the cursor keys. To execute an action, press Enter. If you change your mind and want to cancel the pop-up menu, press Esc.

Selecting Multiple Objects with the Keyboard

When you move between icons with the cursor keys, you are automatically selecting the next object and deselecting the previous one. Selecting multiple objects with your mouse is easy (see "Selecting with the Mouse" earlier in this chapter). Using the keyboard, however, is a little more difficult. If you want to select more than one object, you must switch the Workplace Shell into multiple-selection mode by pressing Shift-F8.

Now when you move between object icons with the keyboard, the object selection does not change. You can select or deselect objects using the cursor keys and pressing the spacebar. The spacebar toggles the selection on or off, depending on the current state. A very light dotted line appears around each object as you move between them; the dark-gray selection background highlight appears when you select the object.

Two keyboard keys make it easier for you to select or deselect all of your objects in the window:

Ctrl-/	(Ctrl-slash) selects all objects
Ctrl-\	(Ctrl-backslash) deselects all objects

Multiple-selection mode is active only for as long as you continue to work in the same window. If you switch away from this window, you go back to single-selection mode and remain in this mode until you press Shift-F8 again, even if you return to the same window.

Rearranging Your Desktop

Now that you know how to move and copy icons around the desktop, you might want to rearrange the default desktop. When you first install OS/2 2.1, the desktop has a number of icons placed around the edges of the screen. The icons placed here include all the objects that you are likely to need the first time you use OS/2 2.1. After a few hours of use, however, you are unlikely to ever want to access some of them again. Figure 4.9 shows the desktop as it appears after you have completed the installation.

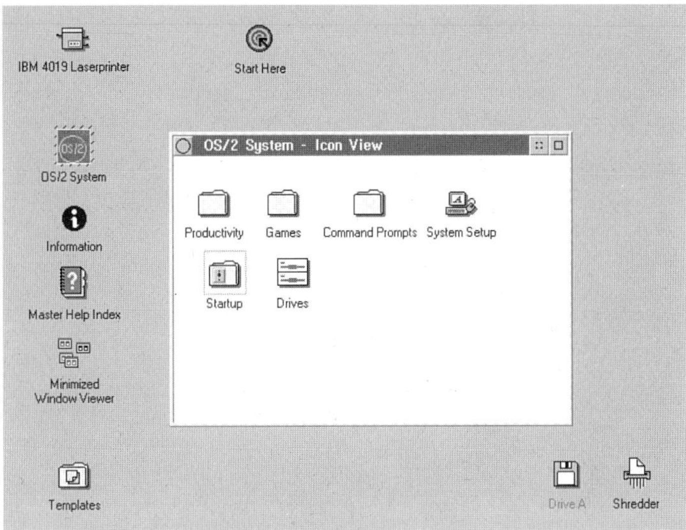

Figure 4.9. *The default OS/2 2.1 desktop.*

The following suggestions might help you to rearrange your desktop:

- Move the Master Help Index and Start Here objects into the Information folder. These are online documentation objects which, if you don't access them frequently, can be placed into the Information folder.
- Move the Information and Templates folders into the OS/2 System folder. You will probably have the OS/2 System folder open all the time, and you may find it easier to access objects from here than on the desktop. The Desktop folder is always in the background, and you can bring the OS/2 System folder to the front easily.
- After moving the objects, you will probably want to rearrange the position of those icons remaining on the desktop. You can do this with the Arrange action on the desktop pop-up menu or move the icons yourself.

If you move icons around in a folder, or use Arrange, the Workplace Shell does not save these positions until you close the folder object. The only way to close the Desktop folder is to shutdown OS/2 2.1 from its pop-up menu; this also causes all other folder to close. (In Chapter 5 you will learn how to change the appearance and format of object icons in your folders—see "The View Pages" in that chapter.)

If you rearrange your desktop as described previously and use the flowed icon view in the OS/2 System folder and move the command prompts out of their folders and into the OS/2 System folder, the screen should look like the one shown in Figure 4.10.

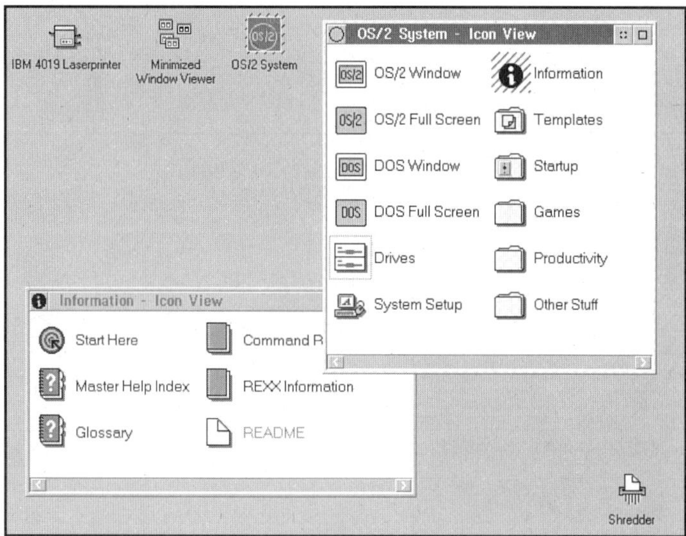

Figure 4.10. A rearranged OS/2 2.1 desktop.

Using Find to Search for Objects

From the desktop pop-up menu, or any other folder pop-up menu, you can search for Workplace Shell objects. When you select the Find option from a folder's menu, or from a pushbutton on several other dialog boxes, a window similar to that shown in Figure 4.11 appears. The search capability provided by the Workplace Shell is extremely powerful.

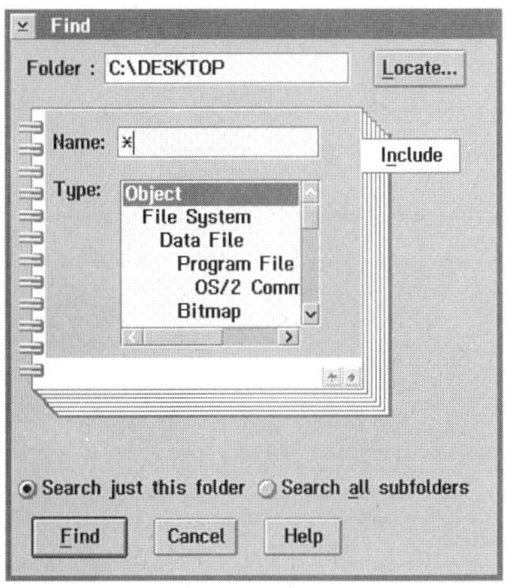

Figure 4.11. *The Find dialog window.*

You use the list box in the center to select which types of Workplace objects you want to include in the search. The shell may already have selected a default for you. For example, if you access this dialog through a Find program pushbutton, the shell selects Program type. You can select multiple types of objects for inclusion in your search.

> NOTE
>
> Workplace objects exist in a hierarchy (see Chapter 5). If you select an object type that is the parent of another type, OS/2 2.1 includes all its children in the search. For example, if you select Program File, you also include the OS/2 Command File.

The entry field above the list box allows you to further restrict the search by specifying a name to search for. Wild cards like * and ? can be included here. If you want to search for all .EXE program files and exclude .COM and .CMD files, you can give *.EXE as the search name.

The Workplace Shell searches for the object types you select starting in the current folder—for example, the OS/2 Desktop—and normally includes this folder only. You can ask the shell to include all subfolders in the search, and you can change the starting location of the search.

The Locate pushbutton allows you to specify the starting location. When you press this pushbutton, a window appears with a notebook containing several pages (see Figure 4.12). This is a general-purpose notebook that you will use in several places when you need to identify a folder or directory location on your hard disk.

You can directly edit the entry field to the left of the Locate pushbutton and avoid the need to use the locate notebook. You must enter a full drive and path name here if you do not use the locate notebook.

The locate notebook is the same as the one you use if you select Move, Copy, Create another, or Create shadow from an object's pop-up menu.

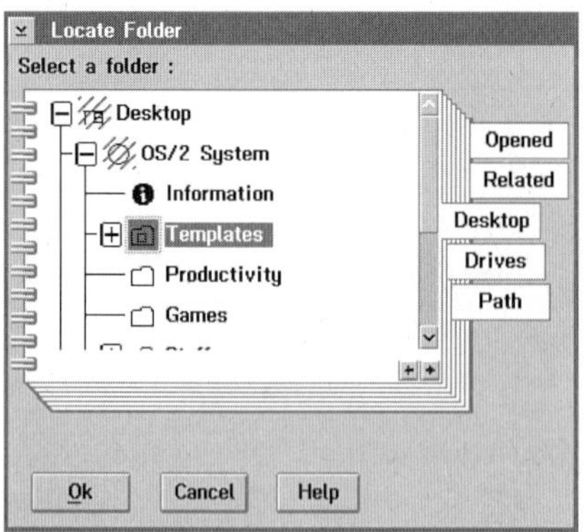

Figure 4.12. *The Locate Folder dialog window.*

There are five pages in the locate notebook. Each gives you a different selection of locations, divided in a logical manner:

Opened	Lists all the currently open folders. Because this is a common choice, it is the default when you open the notebook.
Related	Lists locations that are near the currently selected location. For example, if the current location is a directory on a hard drive, it lists all directories one level above and one level below the current location. You can expand or collapse any branch of your directory tree by clicking mouse button 1 on the + / - symbols.
Desktop	Lists all folders on your desktop, whether they are open or not. You can expand or collapse any branch of the tree by clicking mouse button 1 on the + / - symbols.
Drives	Lists all locations that are in your Drives folder, including network directories that have an assigned drive letter. This page is similar to the Related page but includes every drive and directory that you can access. You can expand or collapse any branch of the tree.
Path	Here you can enter the full path name of a directory for the location you want to use.

Once you select a location from any of these pages, simply press the OK pushbutton. In the Find dialog window your choice appears in the field to the left of the Locate pushbutton. It appears as a full drive and path name.

Opening Objects

You can open objects or application program windows in one of three ways:

1. Double-click mouse button 1 on the icon representing the object.
2. Select the object and press Enter. You can select the object with either the mouse or the keyboard. If you select more than one object, OS/2 2.1 opens them all.
3. Open them with the Open item on each object's pop-up menu. You can obtain this menu with either mouse button 2 or the Shift-F10 key.

Using option 1 or 2 opens the object or application in its default view. Most objects have at least two possible open views. Use the settings view to change object properties—other views depend on the object type. Application objects, for example, always have a program view that starts the application program execution, and folder objects have icon, tree, and detail views.

You can change the default open view for object types that represent a file on your hard disk in the Menu settings page (see "The Menu Page" in Chapter 5).

Resurfacing an Open Object

Because the default behavior of the Minimize or Hide buttons removes your application from the desktop (by placing it in the minimized window viewer or hiding it) the behavior of opening objects is different from that in OS/2 1.3 and Microsoft Windows.

If the object icon you select to open is already open or executing, instead of opening a new copy of the object or application program, OS/2 2.1 again displays the currently executing copy. This is most useful for objects that hide when you minimize them.

You can find out whether an object is currently open by looking for in-use emphasis highlighting on the icon. In-use emphasis appears as a diagonal hatch pattern on the icon background whenever an object is open.

For most purposes, this resurfacing action is the most useful and preferred behavior. It is seldom necessary to execute more than one copy of an application program or Workplace object or folder that is open at the same time. (Exceptions to this are command-line prompts.)

Opening a Second View of an Object

The Workplace Shell does allow you to change the open action to resemble that of OS/2 1.3 or Microsoft Windows by always opening a new copy of the program or window. You can change the behavior of the open action for all application windows and most Workplace objects, and you can do this system-wide or for each application or object. To change the behavior for a single object, use the settings notebook for the object:

1. From the pop-up menu select Open followed by Settings to display settings notebook.
2. Select the Window page in the notebook.
3. Select the Create new window button to cause a new copy of the object to start; use Display existing window to cause an already open copy to reappear.

In Step 2, if there is no notebook section called Window, the object does not allow you to open multiple copies.

Figure 4.13 shows the Window settings page for the Workplace Color Palette. To change the behavior for all windows and objects in OS/2 2.1, you must use the settings notebook for the System object in the System Setup folder, as shown in Figure 4.16.

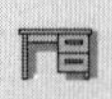

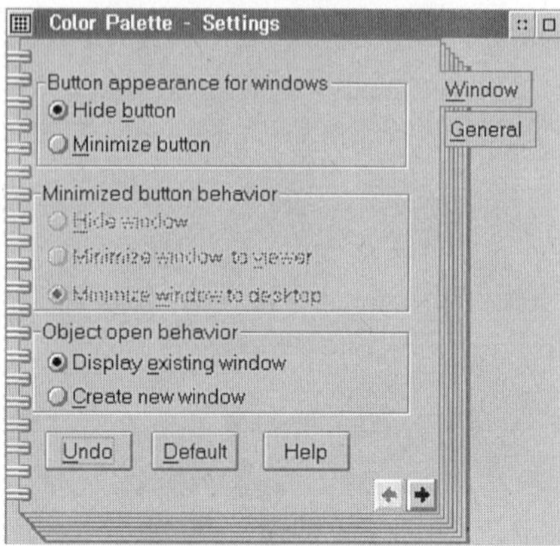

Figure 4.13. *Changing object open behavior.*

It is not a good idea to change the object open behavior system-wide. Because most objects hide rather than minimize, it becomes difficult to ensure that you resurface the existing copy rather than start a new one. Starting new copies when you could use an already open view uses more system resources and degrades system performance.

You can change the object open behavior setting at any time—the change takes place immediately, even when applications are executing. This is useful if you discover that you need another copy of an application that is already open.

Settings notebooks never open multiple windows of themselves, regardless of the settings for the actual object.

Opening Multiple Command Lines

Although the resurface behavior is appropriate for most applications, it is not ideal for DOS and OS/2 command-line prompts. It is very likely that you will want to open multiple copies of these. In this case the recommended approach is to change the object open setting for the four objects individually. The ones that you may want to change are as follows:

- OS/2 Window
- OS/2 Full-Screen
- DOS Window
- DOS Full-screen

You have to open the settings notebook for each of these—you cannot change them all through a single notebook.

An alternative way to open multiple command lines, or other frequently started applications, is to add it to the desktop system pop-up menu. (See "The Menu Page" in Chapter 5 to learn how to edit a pop-up menu.)

If you want a command line to be slightly different from the default, you can make a copy of one of the command-line objects, or create new ones from a template. Then you can edit the object's settings, for example, to give each its own title and working directory. This gives you multiple icons all representing command-line prompts.

Where Has My Window Gone?

You minimize or hide windows in OS/2 2.1 by clicking mouse button 1 on the Minimize or Hide button (the left button in the upper-right corner of every window) or through the system menu of every window.

In OS/2 2.1 the behavior of the Minimize button on application windows is different from both OS/2 1.3 and Microsoft Windows. Instead of causing the window to minimize to an icon at the bottom of the screen, the default action is for the window to disappear, to become hidden.

This behavior is a result of the object-oriented design of the Workplace Shell user interface. Because the user interface encourages you to work with data objects, the original icon from which you open the window is almost always still visible on the screen when you hide the window. It therefore becomes unnecessary and possibly confusing to have a second icon representing a view of the same data object visible on the screen.

For application programs and most Workplace Shell objects it is possible to change the default behavior of the Minimize button to one of three supported selections:

1. Hide window
2. Place window icon into the Minimized Window Viewer folder
3. Minimize window to desktop

All application programs have a Minimize button. Workplace Shell objects have a Hide button and most of them let you change it to a Minimize button. You cannot change the behavior of the Hide button. Settings notebooks always have a Hide button, and you cannot change this to a Minimize button.

Hidden Windows

The default action for all Workplace Shell objects (folders, system settings, and so on) is to have a Hide button. You can change this to a Minimize button for most objects so the window is placed into the minimized window viewer.

When a window is hidden, the only way to return to it is from the OS/2 Window List by pressing Ctrl-Esc, or by opening it again from the original object icon.

Hiding windows is not a substitute for closing them. Hidden windows still use system memory and other resources.

The Minimized Window Viewer

The default action for executable programs is to place their icon into the Minimized Window Viewer folder. You cannot delete this folder from the Workplace Shell desktop. To restore an application window, you must either select it from the OS/2 Window List or open the Minimized Window Viewer and select the icon representing the application window.

Although you cannot delete the Minimized Window Viewer from the desktop, you can delete it by removing the Minimize Directory from your hard disk. You must do this from a command line. This, however, is not recommended because you cannot simply re-create it by making a new directory of the same name.

While the icon is in the minimized window viewer, the Workplace Shell provides a pop-up menu for it. This allows you to close or restore the application window. This menu is not the same as the application's system menu, which is not available from the Minimized Window Viewer.

To access the application system menu, you either have to restore the application window or change the settings to have the application minimized to the desktop. To access the DOS settings for a full-screen DOS application while it is executing, you must change the program object's settings to minimize the application icon onto the desktop.

Figure 4.14 shows the Minimized Window Viewer with a DOS Window and the pop-up menu for this window. Contrast the contents of this pop-up menu with Figure 4.15.

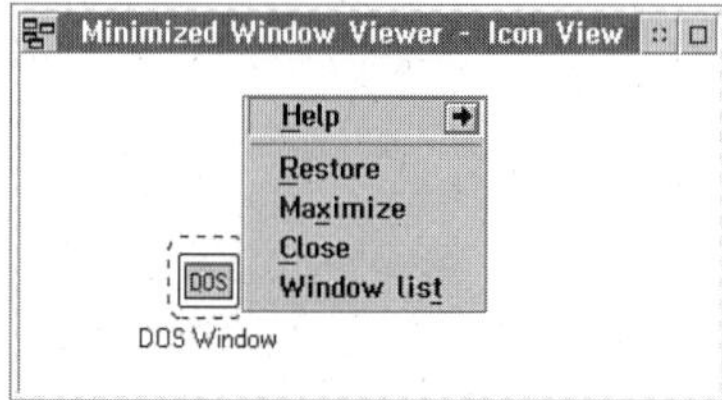

Figure 4.14. *The DOS Window placed in a Minimized Window Viewer.*

Minimizing to the Desktop

If an executable program does not hide or appear in the Minimized Window Viewer, then its icon is placed on the screen desktop. The shell arranges minimized application icons from the lower-left of the screen and progresses across and up.

Workplace does not attempt to prevent collision between object icons and minimized application icons placed on the desktop. Sometimes you may see a minimized application icon on top of a Workplace object icon.

When placed on the desktop, a border appears around the application's icon in the current window frame color. This additional frame makes it easier to tell the difference between Workplace object icons and minimized application icons. Figure 4.15 shows a DOS Window command line minimized to the desktop. Notice the added window frame border and contrast the contents of the pop-up system menu with Figure 4.14.

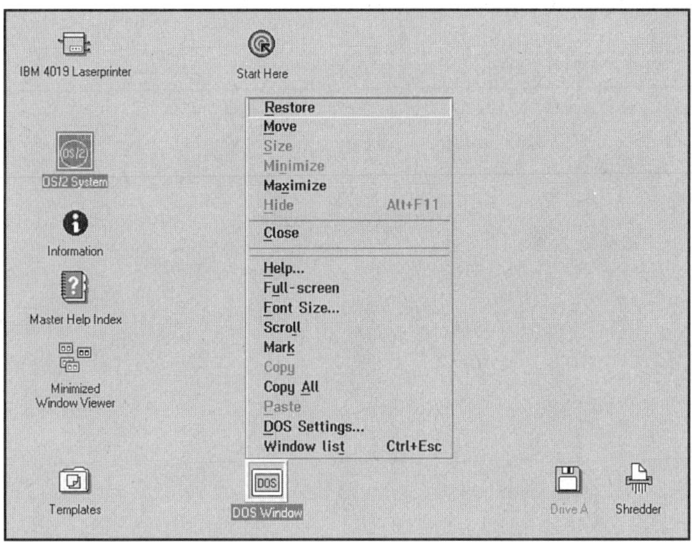

Figure 4.15. *A DOS Window minimized on-screen desktop.*

Minimized WIN-OS/2 windowed applications do not have a frame border drawn around their icons.

Changing the Minimize Behavior

You can change the behavior of the Minimize button for all application windows and most Workplace objects. You can do this system-wide or for each application or object.

To change the behavior for all windows and objects in OS/2 2.1, you must use the settings notebook for the System object in the System Setup folder (see Figure 4.16).

1. From the pop-up menu select Open followed by Settings to display a settings notebook.
2. Select the Window page in the notebook.
3. Select the minimize behavior you want from the list of radio buttons.

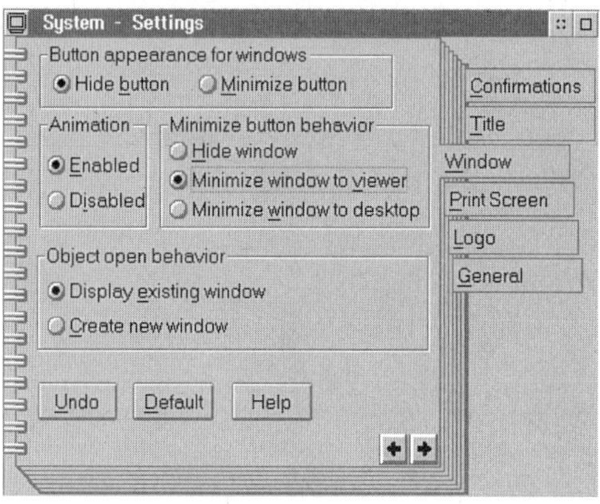

Figure 4.16. *Changing minimize behavior.*

Most Workplace Shell objects have their own Window settings page where you can change individual object behavior. By default they have a Hide button and disable the list of available minimize choices. If you want to select from one of the minimize behaviors, you must first select the Minimize button to change the appearance and action.

In Steps 2 and 3, if there is no notebook section called Window or if the button appearance choices are all disabled, the object does not allow its minimize behavior to change.

TIP

If you change the setting for individual objects, it overrides the system-wide setting. Subsequent changes to the system-wide setting do not affect the individual object. You can reset an object to use the system-wide settings by selecting the Default push-button on its Window settings page.

You can change the minimize behavior setting at any time and the change takes place immediately, even when applications are executing. Changing the appearance of the button, however, only takes effect the next time you open the object.

Using the Window List

The Workplace Shell keeps track of all objects or application programs that you open. The shell keeps this information in a Window List that you can access at any time using Ctrl-Esc on the keyboard or by clicking mouse buttons 1 and 2 together on the desktop background. Clicking both buttons simultaneously is known as chording. Figure 4.17 shows a typical Window List, also known as the Task List in OS/2 1.3 and Microsoft Windows.

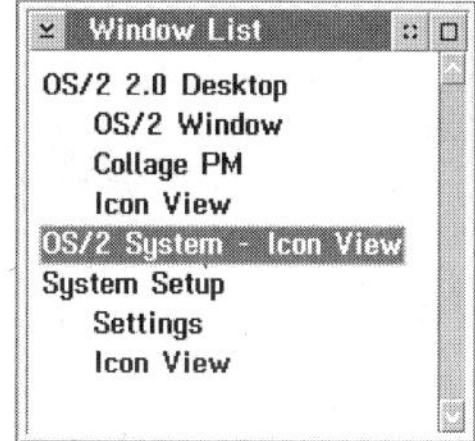

Figure 4.17. *The OS/2 Window List.*

In the Window List you can use the keyboard cursor keys or the mouse to select any one of the listed windows. For any of them you can display a pop-up menu that contains options like Show to take you to the selected window or application, and Close to shut the window or terminate the application.

Tile and Cascade

Two interesting options available on some of the pop-up menus within the Window List are the Tile and Cascade actions. These allow you to organize your desktop by moving and sizing the selected windows into either a tiled or a cascaded fashion.

TIP

Remember that the tile or cascade applies only to the windows that you select from the list, not to all windows on the desktop. Therefore, you don't have to rearrange everything—you can just select a few windows, request the pop-up menu, and select Tile or Cascade.

Figures 4.18 and 4.19 show examples of four tiled windows and the same four windows in cascade formation.

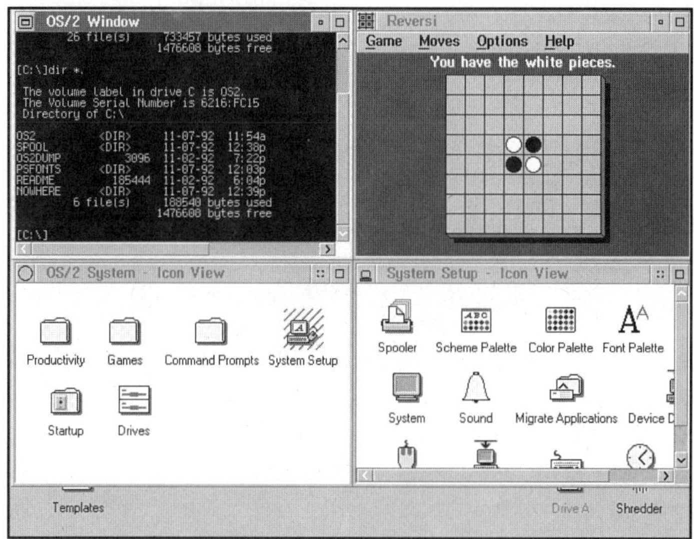

Figure 4.18. *Four windows tiled on the desktop.*

Obtaining the Desktop Pop-Up Menu

It is important for you to learn how to obtain the pop-up menu for the desktop because you must perform a shutdown from this menu before switching off your system. Most of the time you will probably have a mouse, and you can press mouse button 2 on the desktop background. For those rare occasions when you don't have a mouse, use the following step-by-step guide:

1. Bring the desktop into focus using the Alt-Shift-Tab. Alternatively, you can press Ctrl-Esc to obtain the Window List, use the cursor keys to select desktop, and press Enter.
2. Deselect all objects on the desktop. Use Ctrl-\ or simply press the spacebar.
3. Bring up the Desktop pop-up menu. Press Shift-F10, use the cursor keys to select Shutdown, and press Enter.

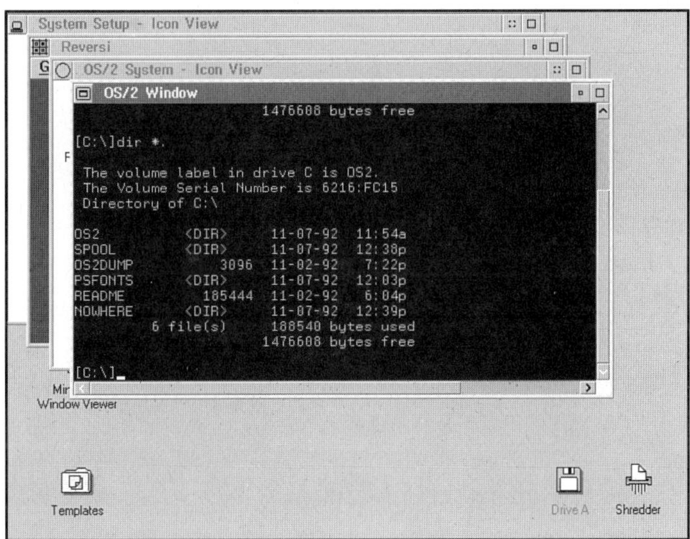

Figure 4.19. Four windows cascaded on the desktop.

Shutdown and Lockup

It is important that you shutdown OS/2 2.1 from the Desktop pop-up menu before you switch off your computer or restart the operating system. OS/2 2.1

is not unique in requiring this step; many other systems require it for similar reasons. The principle reasons are as follows:

- To ensure that the file system lazy write cache is empty.
- The Workplace Shell saves information such as size and position of folder windows and icons, lists of applications that are currently running, and so on. Use Shutdown so that when you restart OS/2 2.1, all these can be reopened and repositioned correctly.

When you ask to shutdown OS/2 2.1, the shell sends a message to all open applications asking them to close. Some of these applications may prompt you if they have data that may need saving. You may notice a lot of disk activity during the shutdown process; it is important that you wait until all this activity is complete before switching off your computer.

The Workplace Shell also saves all information except icon positions (see "Rearranging Your Desktop" earlier in this chapter) when you press Ctrl-Alt-Del on the keyboard.

The Shutdown action is available only through the desktop pop-up menu. Also on this menu is a Lockup now option. This allows you to lock the keyboard so that no one else can use your computer while you are absent. In addition, the screen blanks out so that no one can read whatever you have currently displayed, and it can optionally provide a screen-saver function known as Auto-dim. To return to your normal desktop you must enter a password that you previously selected.

There are a number of options available for lockup from the desktop settings notebook. The Lockup page is available only for the Desktop folder and is not present on any other folder's settings notebook. This is a three-page settings section. The first page lets you select whether the lockup feature is to automatically activate after a period of inactivity. If you select Automatic Lockup, you can specify a time period from 1 minute to 99 minutes.

OS/2 2.1 does not automatically lock if a full-screen OS/2, DOS or WIN-OS/2 application is currently using the display. Automatic Lockup does work from the Workplace Shell, any Presentation Manager application, any WIN-OS/2 window application, or any OS/2 or DOS program running in a window.

Figure 4.20 shows page 2 of the Lockup settings page (obtained by selecting the right arrow in the lower-left portion of the notebook).

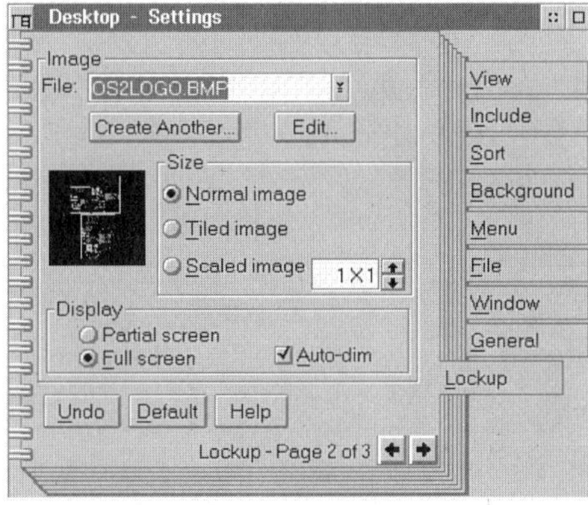

Figure 4.20. *The Lockup settings page.*

This second page is the most interesting as it lets you tell the Workplace Shell what you want your screen to look like when it locks. The default is to display the OS/2 logo, but you can use any bitmap that you may have if it is in the correct file format. OS/2 2.1 accepts bitmaps in the OS/2 1.3, OS/2 2.0, and Microsoft Windows formats. These types of bitmaps are readily available; you can find many at little or no cost on bulletin board systems (BBS). OS/2 2.1 includes a picture of a lighthouse, as an example.

You can also choose to scale and tile the bitmap. This option is useful if your bitmap can make up a larger pattern. If you select Partial screen, your screen does not blank out and it is not replaced by a bitmap; instead, your applications remain visible. The Auto-dim feature is not available for partial screen lockup.

OS/2 2.1 selects the Auto-dim check box for you by default. This completely blanks out your computer screen after a further period of inactivity. All that is visible on your screen is a mouse pointer bouncing around in a random pattern. The purpose of this is to avoid phosphor burn-in on your computer screen and to prolong the life of your display monitor. Auto-dim automatically activates two minutes after your system locks; you cannot change this time period.

The third page of the lockup settings allows you to change the password. If you have not set a password the first time you use lockup, the shell prompts you to provide one. You must enter it twice to ensure that you don't make a mistake.

If You Forget Your Password . . .

If you forget your lockup password, you must switch off your machine. Doing this may cause you to lose data in applications that you did not save before locking the system. Be sure to protect your system using whatever other methods your computer provides—for example, a key lock or a power-on password.

If you selected the option to lock your system each time OS/2 2.1 starts, even turning off the power and restarting your computer will not unlock your system. In this situation, you must restart OS/2 2.1 from disk (see Chapter 1) and run a command to tell the Workplace Shell not to lock the keyboard. You can restart OS/2 2.1 from disk by using the installation disk followed by Disk 1. When you see the first panel you should press Esc to exit to an OS/2 command prompt. From the OS/2 command prompt, change to the hard drive that you normally start OS/2 2.1 from, and enter the OS/2 directory. From here, execute the following command:

```
MAKEINI OS2.INI LOCK.RC
```

Now you can restart the OS/2 operating system from your hard disk and the Workplace Shell will not lock the keyboard and mouse.

Author Bio

David A. Kerr is an Advisory Programmer with the OS/2 development team in Boca Raton, Florida. He joined IBM in 1985 at the Hursley Laboratories, England, where he worked on the design and implementation of the GDDM-OS/2 Link product. In 1989 he joined the Presentation Manager Team in the technical planning office and moved into the OS/2 planning department in Boca Raton the following year. His broad knowledge of all aspects of the internals of OS/2 has earned him the recognition as an expert on the Presentation Manager and a position as a key member in the OS/2 design team. He frequently speaks at conferences and seminars for OS/2 customers and developers in Europe, Australia, the Far East, and America. David holds a BSc in Computer Science and Electronics from the University of Edinburgh, Scotland.

5

Workplace Shell Objects

In This Chapter

In the previous chapter you learned some of the basic techniques of working with the OS/2 2.1 Workplace Shell. There is a great deal of power within the shell that you can learn to use, or adapt to your own requirements. This chapter introduces you to the objects that are available and all of the features and functions that they offer.

Before describing each of the objects, however, you should learn a little about the internal structure of the Workplace Shell. This will help you understand why the Workplace Shell operates the way it does, and you will realize the huge potential that lies under the user interface. The first sections of this chapter will be of most interest if you want to start creating your own working environment around the Workplace Shell. Whether this interests you or not, I encourage you to read them.

The Workplace Object Hierarchy

There are several places in the Workplace Shell where it is useful to understand a little about its internal structure, particularly how the shell holds your desktop icons in a dual hierarchy of type and location. For example, in the Find dialog window, shown in Figure 4.11, there is a list of object types that directly corresponds to the internal hierarchy of object classes in the Workplace Shell. This hierarchy defines the type of information held within each object and the functions that you can perform on the object's data.

One of the features of Workplace Shell objects is that the information held within them is permanently saved. Any change that you make to an object's data is effective immediately and remains in the state that you assign until you change it. This applies even if you restart OS/2 2.1 or switch off your system. When you change object settings through any object's settings notebook, there is no need to explicitly save the information, a behavior known as perfect save.

For many settings, you have to close the notebook for OS/2 2.1 to permanently save your changes, even though you can see the change take effect immediately.

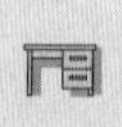

There are three main object classes within the Workplace Shell, called base classes. The Workplace Shell derives these three base classes from the top-level object class. Only base classes can be immediate children of the top-level class; all other object classes within the Workplace Shell inherit their characteristics from one of these three. The names assigned to the base classes are as follows:

```
WPFileSystem
WPAbstract
WPTransient
```

Table 5.1 shows a hierarchy of object classes within the Workplace Shell inherited from the base classes.

Table 5.1. The Workplace Shell internal class hierarchy.

```
WPObject
  WPFileSystem        WPAbstract             WPTransient
    WPDataFile           WPClock                WPCnrView
      WPBitmap           WPCountry                 WPDiskCV
      WPIcon             WPDisk                    WPFolderCV
      WPPointer          WPKeyboard             WPFilter
      WPProgramFile      WPMouse                   WPFinder
        WPCommandFile    WPPalette              WPMinWindow
      WPMet                 WPSchemePalette     WPJob
      WPPif                 WPColorPalette      WPPort
    WPFolder                WPFontPalette       WPPrinterDriver
      WPDesktop          WPProgram              WPQueueDriver
      WPStartup          WPPrinter
      WPDrives              WPRPrinter
      WPMinWinViewer     WPShadow
      WPFindFolder          WPNetLink
      WPNetgrp           WPShredder
      WPNetwork          WPSound
      WPServer           WPSpecialNeeds
      WPSharedDir        WPSpool
      WPTemplates        WPSystem
      WPRootFolder       WPPower
```

The table shows each class as the Workplace Shell knows them internally. Each class has a `WP` two-letter prefix. Classes created by other programs, or even by other components of OS/2 2.1, will have a different prefix.

Classes also have a name that the Workplace Shell displays to you—for example, in the Find dialog notebook. This name usually corresponds closely to the internal name. The class `WPCommandFile`, for example, appears as "OS/2 Command File" in the Find dialog.

The Root Object Class

The top-level object class in the Workplace Shell is `WPObject`, known as the root class. This is responsible for the characteristics common to all other object classes; for example, the title, icon, and styles (such as whether the object is a template). The root class provides the two settings pages common to almost all objects: General and Window. All Workplace Shell objects are children of this class, although only base classes are immediate descendants.

The main purpose of a base class is to define where an object saves its instance data so that it is permanent, a location known as the persistent storage for an object class. In addition, base classes are responsible for allocating a unique handle as you create each object. These handles are permanent and, for objects that are not temporary, valid even after restarting OS/2 2.1 or switching your system off and on again.

Table 5.2 summarizes the location of the persistent storage for some common object types in the Workplace Shell and lists the base classes that define the storage location.

Table 5.2. Persistent storage examples.

Type	*Base class*	*Object location*	*Persistent settings*
Data File	`WPFileSystem`	File	Extended attributes
Program File	`WPFileSystem`	File	Extended attributes
Program	`WPAbstract`	OS2.INI	OS2.INI
Folder	`WPFileSystem`	File	Extended attributes
Shadow	`WPAbstract`	OS2.INI	Original object

The File System Base Class

Objects inherited from the `WPFileSystem` base class save their properties and data on your hard disk in extended attributes attached to the object file. The extended attributes used by Workplace Shell are as follows:

```
.CLASSINFO
.ICON
.TYPE
.LONGNAME
```

Because a file system object saves all its instance data in extended attributes, objects of this type are portable and you may move them between systems, on disk, or any other media that support extended attributes on files.

Files on your hard disk typically represent `WPFileSystem` class objects. Directories represent Workplace Shell folder windows. Other files usually represent objects of `WPDataFile` class or one of its subclasses. For example, bitmap files are `WPBitmap` class objects and executable program files are `WPProgramFile` class objects.

To identify whether an object is a `WPFileSystem` type, look in the settings notebook for the object. If there is a File page, the object is a representation of a file on your hard disk.

The Abstract Base Class

Objects inherited from the `WPAbstract` base class save their properties and data in the OS/2 2.1 user initialization files, OS2.INI, and OS2SYS.INI. The information is saved as a block of object state data keyed by the object's handle.

Accessing the INI files is usually a slow process in OS/2 2.1. To improve system responsiveness, the Workplace Shell implements a lazy write scheme that significantly improves the performance of the user interface when creating or modifying `WPAbstract`-based classes. This is one of the reasons why it is so important for you to perform a shutdown from the desktop pop-up menu before switching off your computer.

The Workplace Shell uses the `WPAbstract` class for all objects that do not represent files on your hard disk. `WPAbstract` object types typically represent devices available on your system, system setup, and other objects internal to the Workplace Shell. Program references and shadows to other types of objects (which may represent files on your hard disk) are also of the `WPAbstract` type.

Because `WPAbstract` class objects are specific to each machine and often represent devices with no associated file on your hard disk, they are not portable between machines and you cannot copy them onto disk or other media.

If a folder object contains any `WPAbstract` objects, or anything else that is not a child of `WPFileSystem`, you cannot copy the folder onto a disk. Even though the folder itself is a file system object, you cannot copy it unless all its contents are also file system objects.

The Transient Base Class

The Workplace Shell provides no way to save persistent data for objects inherited from the `WPTransient` base class. Classes that you create inherited from this class either manage their own storage or have no properties that need to be persistent.

Icons in the minimized window viewer representing your executing programs are examples of objects that have no persistent storage. They exist only for as long as your application program is executing. If you shutdown OS/2 2.1 or switch off your system, the application no longer executes and the icon in the minimized window viewer no longer exists.

Print jobs in your spooler queue, however, do exist after you shutdown OS/2 2.1 or switch off your computer. The print subsystem does not use a Workplace Shell base class to save any information about print jobs in the OS2.INI file or on extended attributes in the file system. Instead, the print subsystem takes responsibility for saving all necessary information in .SPL and .SHD files in your spool directory. Spooler print jobs are therefore `WPJob` class objects, a subclass of the `WPTransient` base class.

Dormant and Awakened Objects

Workplace Shell objects exist in one of two states: dormant or awakened. Objects that are open or executing on your system are awake. You can work with awakened objects and change their properties, and the object can be accessed by other application programs or objects.

If the object is not in your system's memory, it exists only on your hard disk in the form of the object's persistent storage. Objects like this are dormant.

All the Workplace Shell objects become dormant when you switch your system off. The Workplace Shell automatically awakens objects as they are accessed after you switch your system on. Only those objects with which you work are awake at any time. You may rarely work with some objects, and these objects remain dormant until you later open them or until another application or object tries to access them.

The Workplace Shell automatically handles the process of awakening an object from its dormant state. Because the process involves accessing the persistent data of an object from your hard disk, it can be slow. This is the main reason for the delays you experience when opening objects or folders for the first time.

When you close a folder or some other object, it does not immediately become dormant. Instead, the object remains in your system memory for a short time, known as snooze time. This means that if you go back and open the folder or object, the Workplace Shell does not have to go back to your hard disk to retrieve all the persistent data. This is why you see faster response when opening an object for the second time. This scheme only works for `WPFileSystem` and `WPAbstract` objects. Objects that manage their own persistent storage, printer objects, for example, that are members of the `WPTransient` class, do not benefit from this feature of the shell.

An object is still awake when you hide or minimize it and whenever it is in an open folder. It enters snooze time and later becomes dormant only when you close both it and the folder that contains it.

After the period of snooze time expires for an object, it immediately becomes dormant and the Workplace Shell discards all information in the object from system memory. This allows the Workplace Shell to reduce the amount of memory it uses.

The object snooze time defaults to 90 seconds but you can change this. (See "CONFIG.SYS Settings" in Chapter 6, "Configuring the Workplace Shell.")

Shadows of Objects

Shadows are a special type of object, based on the `WPAbstract` type, that does not hold any information itself but instead points to another object in the Workplace Shell. The only information that the shadow object holds is the location of the other object. If you view the settings notebook for a shadow object, you see (and edit) the settings of the actual object, not the shadow.

To create a shadow, hold the Ctrl-Shift keys as you drag the original object. You will see visual feedback (a line connecting the original and the new shadow as shown in Figure 5.1) to confirm that you are creating a shadow. Alternately, you can use the pop-up menu for the object and pick Create Shadow.

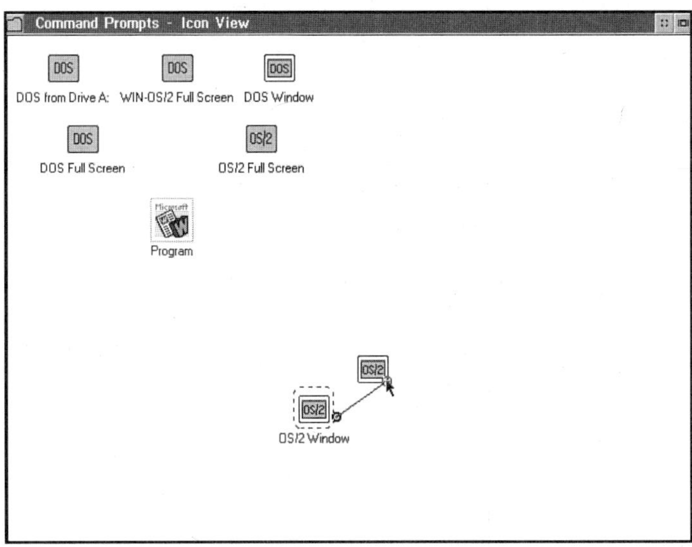

Figure 5.1. The feedback displayed when creating a shadow.

You can identify a shadow by the color of its title text. Instead of the default color black, the text is gray. Shadow objects have their own pop-up menus. They contain one additional action item: a submenu called Original. You can use this to Delete, Copy, or Locate the original object.

The Locate option on the Original submenu is the most useful because it allows you to find the original object and work with it. When you select this action, the folder window containing the original object opens and keyboard focus transfers to the original object. This is very useful if the original object is on a remote network disk or several levels deep in your folder window hierarchy.

A shadow can point to any type of object, data files, program objects, the shredder, and so on. Shadows are useful because they let you place a pointer to a data file, for example, in a location that is convenient for you. You can create a shadow of a file that is somewhere on drive D and put it on a folder on your desktop. You don't have to open the drive D folder and then open the folders that contain the file to get at it—just open the folder on your desktop and access the shadow of the file.

Changes that you make to shadow settings are changes to the original object. You can delete, move, or copy the shadow, however, without affecting the original object.

All other changes that you make on a shadow are changes to the original object. For example, if you change the name of the shadow, the original object's name changes at the same time.

It is not a good idea to create a shadow of a program file object. As you will learn, there is a significant difference between a program reference object and a program file object. Shadows of program files are dangerous because you could accidentally edit the name of the program executable file from the shadow when you mean to edit the name of the program reference, not the name of the actual file. You should use a program reference object instead of a shadow.

Folders and data files are good candidates for shadows. If you add a file to the shadow of a folder, the file really gets added to the folder. If you delete a file from the shadow of a folder, you are deleting the actual file from the original folder. If, however, you delete the shadow of the folder, the folder remains intact. If you delete a shadow of a data file, the original data remains intact.

To delete a shadow, drop it on the shredder. Remember, you are deleting the shadow, not the original object. Alternately, use the pop-up menu for the shadow and select Delete. Shadows give you great power to organize your data. You can have files located on as many disk drives, partitions, and logical drives as you want, yet still organize your data on your desktop.

Object Identifiers

In addition to the class of an object, Workplace Shell can assign unique identifiers (IDs) to an instance of each object class. These IDs are unique to each object instance, and the shell uses them to identify the location of objects and the parent-child relationship between objects.

You need to use object IDs if you want to use REXX commands to create objects or to modify existing objects. You also need to use these if you want to create your own custom desktop, a process you will learn in "Creating Your Own Desktop" in Chapter 6.

When you create an object, you need to specify a location. This has to be either an object identifier or a file system path. You can use any object ID that you may create for your own folders, or one of the IDs that the Workplace Shell creates during its initialization. Table 5.3 lists all the folders and their object IDs in a default OS/2 2.1 installation.

Table 5.3. Object identifiers for default Workplace Shell folders.

Object Identifier	*Object Name*	*Class of Object*
<WP_NOWHERE>	Nowhere	WPFolder
<WP_DESKTOP>	Desktop	WPDesktop
<WP_INFO>	Information	WPFolder
<WP_NETWORK>	Network	WPNetwork
<WP_OS2SYS>	OS/2 System	WPFolder
<WP_CONFIG>	System Setup	WPFolder
<WP_DRIVES>	Drives	WPDrives
<WP_GAMES>	Games	WPFolder
<WP_PROMPTS>	Command Prompts	WPFolder
<WP_START>	Startup	WPStartup
<WP_TOOLS>	Productivity	WPFolder
<WP_TEMPS>	Templates	WPTemplates
<WP_VIEWER>	Minimized Window Viewer	WPMinWinViewer

The Workplace Shell places all other objects that it creates during its initialization into one of these folders. If you plan to create your own custom desktop, you may want to remove some of these, or place them in a different folder. Table 5.4 lists all the object identifiers for a default OS/2 2.1 installation.

If you use REXX commands to change the settings for any of these objects, you also need to know the identifier assigned by the Workplace Shell during its initialization. Later in this chapter you will learn the process that OS/2 2.1 goes through to create these objects from a file called INI.RC. In Chapter 15, "REXX Programming," you will learn how to change the settings of any object from a REXX command.

Table 5.4. Object identifiers for default non-folder Workplace Shell objects.

Object Identifier	*Object Name*	*Class of Object*
	On the desktop:	
<WP_GLOSS>	Glossary	Mindex
<WP_MINDEX>	Master Help Index	Mindex
<WP_PDVIEW>	Printer	PDView
<WP_SHRED>	Shredder	WPShredder
<WP_STHR>	Start Here	WPProgram
	In the Information folder:	
<WP_TUTOR>	Tutorial	WPProgram
<WP_CMDREF>	Command Reference	WPProgram
<WP_REXREF>	REXX Information	WPProgram
<WP_RDME>	ReadMe	WPShadow

Object Identifier	*Object Name*	*Class of Object*
	In the System Setup folder:	
<WP_CLOCK>	System Clock	WPClock
<WP_CLRPAL>	Color Palette	WPColorPalette
<WP_CNTRY>	Country	WPCountry
<WP_DDINST>	Device Driver Install	WPProgram
<WP_FNTPAL>	Font Palette	WPFontPalette
<WP_INST>	Selective Install	WPProgram
<WP_KEYB>	Keyboard	WPKeyboard
<WP_MIGAPP>	Migrate Applications	WPProgram
<WP_MOUSE>	Mouse	WPMouse
<WP_POWER>	Power Management	WPPower
<WP_SCHPAL>	Scheme Palette	WPSchemePalette
<WP_SOUND>	Sound	WPSound
<WP_SPOOL>	Spooler	WPSpool
<WP_SYSTEM>	System	WPSystem
<WP_TOUCH>	Touch	WPTouch
<WP_WINCFA>	WIN-OS2 Setup	WPWinConfig
	In the Games folder:	
<WP_CHESS>	OS/2 Chess	WPProgram
<WP_JIGSAW>	Jigsaw	WPProgram
<WP_KLDK>	Solitaire - Klondike	WPProgram
<WP_NEKO>	Cat and Mouse	WPProgram
<WP_RVRSI>	Reversi	WPProgram
<WP_SCRBL>	Scramble	WPProgram

continues

Table 5.4. continued

Object Identifier	*Object Name*	*Class of Object*
	In the Command Prompts folder:	
<WP_DBOOT>	Dual Boot	WPProgram
<WP_DOSFS>	DOS Full Screen	WPProgram
<WP_DOSWIN>	DOS Window	WPProgram
<WP_DOS_DRV_A>	DOS from Drive A:	WPProgram
<WP_OS2FS>	OS/2 Full Screen	WPProgram
<WP_OS2WIN>	OS/2 Window	WPProgram
<WP_WINFS>	WIN-OS/2 Full Screen	WPProgram
	In the Productivity Folder:	
<WP_CHART>	PM Chart	WPProgram
<WP_CLIPV>	Clipboard Viewer	WPProgram
<WP_DALARM>	Alarms	WPProgram
<WP_DBASE>	Database	WPProgram
<WP_DCALC>	Calculator	WPProgram
<WP_DCALEM>	Calendar	WPProgram
<WP_DDARC>	Planner Archive	WPProgram
<WP_DDIARY>	Daily Planner	WPProgram
<WP_DLIST>	Activities List	WPProgram
<WP_DMNTH>	Monthly Planner	WPProgram
<WP_DNOTE>	Notepad	WPProgram
<WP_DTARC>	To-Do List Archive	WPProgram
<WP_EPM>	Enhanced Editor	WPProgram

Object Identifier	*Object Name*	*Class of Object*
<WP_ICON>	Icon Editor	WPProgram
<WP_PICV>	Picture Viewer	WPProgram
<WP_PULSE>	Pulse	WPProgram
<WP_SEEK>	Seek and Scan Files	WPProgram
<WP_SPREAD>	Spreadsheet	WPProgram
<WP_STICKY>	Sticky Pad	WPProgram
<WP_SYSED>	OS/2 System Editor	WPProgram
<WP_TERM>	PM Terminal	WPProgram
<WP_TODO>	To-Do List	WPProgram
<WP_TUNE>	Tune Editor	WPProgram

All object identifiers are enclosed with angle brackets. For the default Workplace Shell objects, the IDs have a prefix of `WP`. You should try to avoid using these prefix letters for any objects you create.

When you create an object, you do not need to assign an object identifier to it. If you don't assign an ID, however, you will not be able to modify it or delete it in any way other than with the mouse or keyboard. For this reason it is always a good idea to specifically set an object identifier.

Creating Objects

There are several ways for you to create new objects in the Workplace Shell. One method is to copy an existing object of the same type that you want to create and then change its settings (see "Copying, Moving, and Deleting" in Chapter 4). Other methods you can use include dragging an object from a template or using the Create another item from an object's pop-up menu.

Using Templates

The Workplace Shell encourages you to work with data objects rather than with application programs. For example, rather than executing a program and then loading and saving data files, click on the data object to execute an associated program. You can use a similar method to create new objects. Rather than starting a program and creating a data file from it, simply take an existing object and copy a new one from it. The Workplace Shell provides templates for the specific purpose of creating new objects from it.

Templates resemble a pad of yellow sticky notes: each time you want to use another, you peel one from the top of the pad. Templates exhibit a special behavior when you try to drag one. Instead of moving or copying the template object, you cause the shell to create a new object of the same type as the template.

If you want to actually move, copy, or create a shadow of the template, you must use one of the augmentation keys—Shift, Ctrl, or Shift+Ctrl, respectively.

OS/2 2.1 includes a number of templates for frequently used object types such as program, printer, and data file. Figure 5.2 shows the standard Templates folder.

An important characteristic of a template is that when you create a new object from it, all the settings are set to match those in the template. This can be particularly valuable if you need to frequently create new files that have some data preloaded into them—for example, a word processor file with company letterhead. Some objects display a dialog settings notebook as part of the creation process. For example, creating a program object will prompt you for the name of the executable file and let you change other object settings.

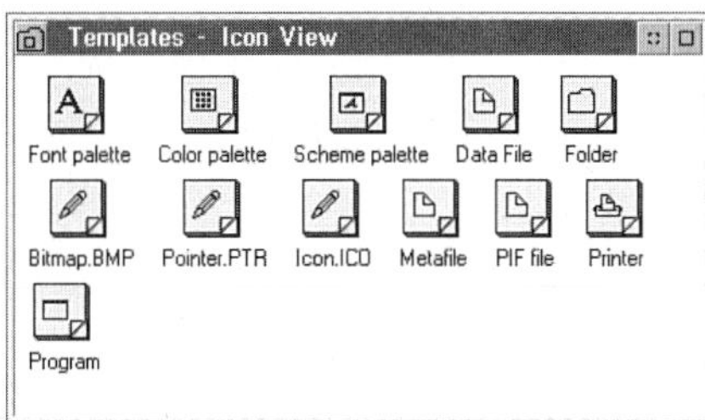

Figure 5.2. The standard Templates folder.

You can change the settings associated with any template through the object's settings notebook in the same way as any other type of object. Any objects you later create from this template inherit all the changes you make in the template object.

Creating Your Own Template

You can create your own templates very simply. First, you need to create an object of the type on which you are going to base the new one. For example, if you want to create a word processor document associated with WordPerfect for Windows, you first need to create a data file by dragging from the data file template, use WordPerfect to enter some information like a company letterhead, and save it in the WordPerfect file format. In the General settings page for the object you then mark it as a template. Use the following step-by-step process for this example:

1. Ensure that you have a program reference object for WordPerfect.
2. Create a new Data File object. Drag it from a template or use Create another from a data file's pop-up menu.
3. Open the settings notebook for this new object and select the Menu page. Create a new item on the Open submenu for WordPerfect and mark it as the default. The section in this chapter called "The Menu Page" describes how to do this. You can use the Find dialog to locate the program reference that you created in Step 1.
4. Close the settings notebook and double-click mouse button 1 to open the data file. At this point, WordPerfect starts and reads the data file.

5. You can now enter any information you want and set up your company letterhead. When you finish, be sure to save the file in WordPerfect's file format, not plain text.

6. Open the settings notebook for the object, and on the General page, select the Template check box. You can also use this opportunity to create a nice icon for the object!

Every time you drag from this template the Workplace Shell creates a new WordPerfect format file. If you double-click on this object, WordPerfect opens and reads the new file containing your letterhead.

You can follow a similar process for any application you want. As this example shows, the application does not have to be specially written for the Workplace Shell; any OS/2, DOS, Windows, or Presentation Manager application works. The only requirement is that the application must be able to accept a filename as a command-line parameter.

DOS and Windows applications do not accept long filenames. If you are using the high performance file system (HPFS), you must keep your data file object names less than 8.3 characters.

Create Another Menu Item

If you select the Create another menu item, a submenu appears with a list of all the types of objects that you can create. This list always starts with Default, which creates an object of the same type with default settings. Next in the list is an action to create an object of the same type and the same settings. For example, a program object has two items on its submenu, Default and Program, as shown in Figure 5.3.

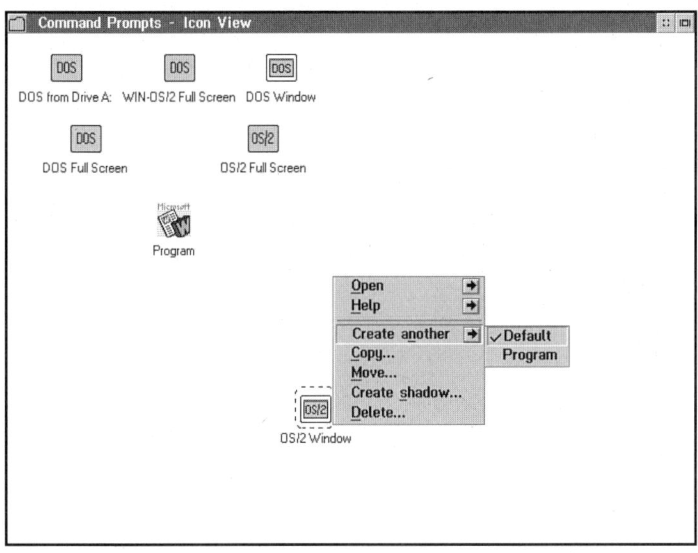

Figure 5.3. Create another menu for a program object.

> **NOTE** Using Create another, default action is exactly the same as dragging from a template object for the same type of object.

Other options follow the Default option. The list includes all objects for which there is a template and that are of the same type as your selected object. For example, if you create new templates of your own that are of the `WPDataFile` type, then for all data file objects the Create another submenu includes the name of your object templates. Figure 5.4 shows an example of the menu after a Spreadsheet File template was created, based on the `WPDataFile` type.

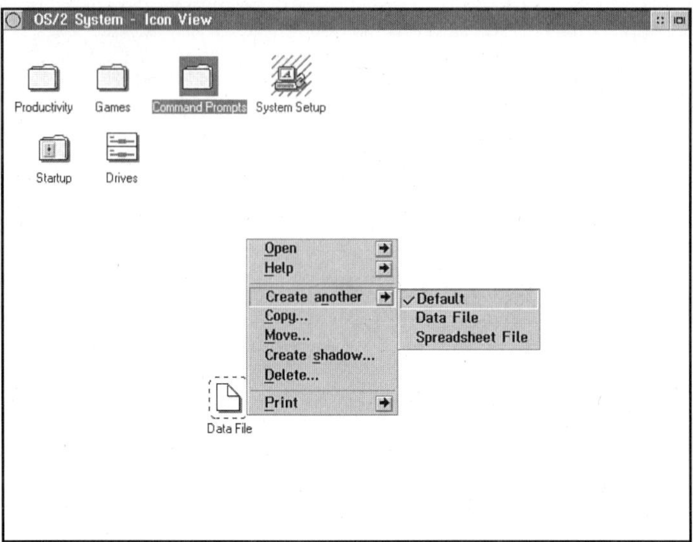

Figure 5.4. Create another menu for a data file object.

If you use Create another from a program file (`WPProgramFile` object class), you do not create another file. Instead, you create a program reference (`WPProgram` object class) object that points back to this original file.

From a REXX Command

Creating a lot of objects on several different computers can be time-consuming with drag-and-drop. This is a common task if you are an administrator for a network of computers and you want to install applications or configure the desktop in some special way.

This is where the power of REXX becomes useful. You can use REXX commands to create, delete, or change any Workplace Shell object. Chapter 15 includes information on all the features in the shell that you can access. REXX

becomes particularly powerful when you learn how to attach object settings or even DOS settings such as device drivers and memory limits to program reference objects.

Listing 5.1 shows a simple REXX command, CRTOBJ.CMD, which first creates a folder on your desktop and then creates a program and a plain text data file inside it.

Listing 5.1. A REXX command to create folder and data object.

```
/* CRTOBJ.CMD Create folder on Desktop and include data file */
/* (c) Copyright IBM Corp. 1992, All rights reserved */
Call RxFuncAdd 'SysCreateObject', 'RexxUtil', 'SysCreateObject'
Rc=SysCreateObject('WPFolder', 'My Folder', '<WP_DESKTOP>',,
                   'OBJECTID=<MY_FLDR>');
If Rc = 1 Then Do
  Rc=SysCreateObject('WPProgram', 'My Editor', '<MY_FLDR>',,
                     'EXENAME=E.EXE;ASSOCTYPE=Plain Text;');
  Rc=SysCreateObject('WPDataFile', 'My Data', '<MY_FLDR>');
End
Else Say 'Error creating folder'
Exit
```

This command fails if a folder with an object ID of <MY_FLDR> already exists on your desktop. The double commas (,,) at the end of lines 4 and 7 are intentional. The second comma allows a single statement to break into two lines.

You can create objects of any type shown in Table 5.1, or of any other type available on your computer.

Creating Your Own Drag-and-Drop Object

You can use the techniques described previously to create powerful objects that respond to your drag-and-drop operations. Listing 5.2 shows a simple REXX

command to count words in a plain text file and display the result in a Presentation Manager message box (because of this, it must be run with the PMREXX utility). You can create an icon on your desktop from this command file, on to which you can drop any file.

Listing 5.2. A REXX command to count words in a file.

```
/* WCOUNT.CMD Count words in file */
/* (c) Copyright IBM Corp. 1992, All rights reserved */
Call RxFuncAdd 'RxMessageBox', 'RexxUtil', 'RxMessageBox'
Parse Arg Filename
Count=0
Do Until Lines(Filename) = 0
  Line = Linein(Filename)
  Count = Count + Words(Line)
End
Ok = RxMessageBox(Count 'Words in file:' Filename,'Result')
Say Count
Exit
```

The following steps present the process to create your own drag-and-drop object (you will see the object on the open submenu of every file object with a type of plain text):

1. Create a program reference object on your desktop by dragging from the Program template. The settings notebook for this object opens automatically.
2. In the Program page, type the following two lines into the first two entry fields:

   ```
   PMREXX.EXE
   WCOUNT.CMD %*
   ```

   This causes the program to execute in the Presentation Manager program PMREXX so it can display the result in a message box on your screen.
3. In the Association page, add plain text to the currently associated types list. This allows you to execute the word count program from any plain-text object's pop-up menu.

4. In the Window page, select Create new window. This ensures that you can count the words in more than one file at the same time.
5. In the General page, give your object a name like "Count Words" and edit the icon so that it looks more appropriate.

This example uses some techniques that you will learn about later in this chapter.

You can use a REXX command to do all this! Listing 5.3 shows everything described in Steps 1 through 5, although it doesn't set the icon—not because it isn't possible but because it requires an .ICO file, which you must create with the icon editor.

Listing 5.3. A REXX command to install WCOUNT.CMD.

```
/* INSTWC.CMD Create Count Words object */
/* (c) Copyright IBM Corp. 1992, All rights reserved */
Call RxFuncAdd 'SysCreateObject', 'RexxUtil', 'SysCreateObject'

Settings = 'EXENAME=PMREXX.EXE;ASSOCTYPE=Plain Text;'
Settings = Settings¦¦'PARAMETERS=C:\WCOUNT.CMD %*;'
Settings = Settings¦¦'PROGTYPE=PM;MINIMIZED=YES;'
Settings = Settings¦¦'CCVIEW=YES;OBJECTID=<MY_WCOUNT>;'

Rc=SysCreateObject('WPProgram', 'Count Words',,
                   '<WP_DESKTOP>',Settings);
Say Rc
Exit
```

This is an example that you can adapt for your own purposes. The Workplace Shell, in combination with the REXX command language, creates a powerful environment that you can quickly and easily customize.

Object Settings

You can access an object's settings by selecting the Settings action from the pop-up menu's Open submenu. This displays a notebook that may have one or more sections to it. Each section has a tab at the right side of the notebook. Using a mouse you can easily move around the sections and pages within a notebook.

You can jump straight to a section by clicking mouse button 1 on the appropriate tab. To access the next page, which may be part of the same section or the next section, click mouse button 1 on the right arrow in the lower-left portion of the notebook.

If you need to use a keyboard, the main keys are Alt-Page Down and Tab. The Tab key moves the input focus around sections of the notebook page. You can also use the Alt-Up and Alt-Down cursor keys to move keyboard focus between the notebook page contents and the section tabs. You can jump straight to a notebook section when the focus is on the section tabs by pressing the letter key that corresponds to the underlined letter on the tab.

Some object settings in a notebook are multiple page. You can access only the first page from the tabs to the right of the notebook. You can see subsequent pages by selecting the right arrow in the lower-right portion or by pressing Alt-Page Down. A statement like "page 1 of 3" helps to identify multipage setting.

You may notice that on the settings notebook pages you will hardly ever find a pushbutton marked Save or OK. The Workplace Shell always remembers any changes that you make as you enter them—there is no need explicitly to tell the shell to save it. This behavior of the shell is called perfect save. Rather than a Save or OK button, you will find an Undo, which returns the settings to the values they had when you opened the notebook page.

To close a notebook settings window, you need to double-click mouse button 1 on the system menu icon (the upper-left area), select Close from the system menu, or press Alt-F4 on the keyboard.

All objects have basic settings provided for them by the Workplace Shell. The following sections describe these basic settings. Each object class may provide other settings that other objects can inherit. In this section you will learn the most important objects and their settings:

- folder objects
- file objects
- program objects

There are additional objects that you can use to set up and configure your system. These all have their own special settings. You will learn about these later in this chapter. Other chapters describe several more object types, such as the printer object and the drives object.

The General Settings Page

Use the General settings page to give a title to your object, edit or create an icon, and mark it as a template. Figure 5.5 shows the General settings page for a typical object.

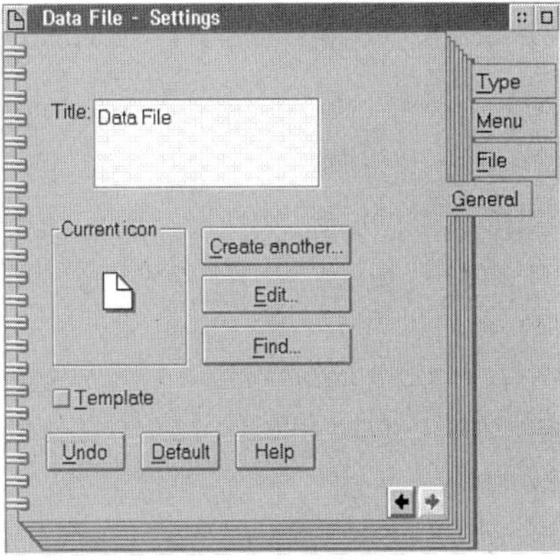

Figure 5.5. The General settings page for an object.

Renaming an Object

You can rename your object from the General settings page by typing into the multiline entry field to the right of Title, and you can use multiple lines. The Workplace Shell saves the name that you enter here in either the OS2.INI file or as the name of the object file on your hard disk. If you are using HPFS, whatever you enter here is the actual filename; if you are using a file allocation table (FAT) file system, the name is held in the .LONGNAME extended attribute and the shell truncates the actual filename at 8.3 characters, avoiding duplicate names by appending numericals if necessary.

If you rename an object file from a command line, the OS/2 2.1 file system tells Workplace Shell of your changes, a process known as file system notification. This is done to ensure that the shell can still access the object file even if you rename or move it.

You can use an alternative method of renaming your objects without first opening the settings notebook: from the object's icon or name in the Window List, select the object title text using mouse button 1 while holding the Alt key. You can then edit the object name, as shown in Figure 5.6. When complete, click mouse button 1 anywhere away from the text box. From the keyboard you can use Shift-F9 to start editing the icon text for the currently selected object.

Be careful when renaming programs. If you rename a program file object, you are renaming the actual executable file. This is not the same as renaming a program reference object, which just changes the name that you see for your installed program objects and leaves the physical filename and .LONGNAME extended attribute unchanged.

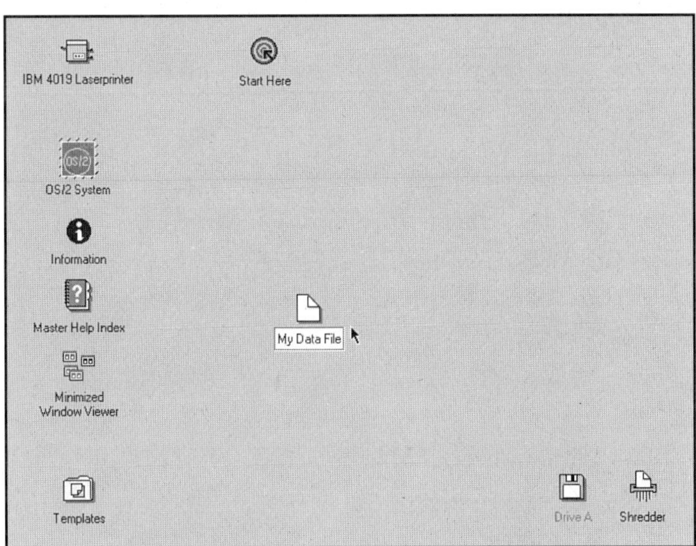

Figure 5.6. Renaming an object.

Editing the Icon

You can edit, create new icons, or use an existing icon file on your hard disk for any object. If you select the Create another pushbutton, the icon editor starts and you can create your own new icon. It is usually easier to edit the existing icon; to do this select the Edit pushbutton.

When editing an icon, be sure to check that you are modifying the correct version of it. Every icon in the Workplace Shell has five different versions of itself—all held in the same icon file! Each version of the icon has a specific purpose:

32 x 32 color	Used as the standard icon on 640-by-480 and 800-by-600 display systems
32 x 32 black and white	Hardly ever used; intended for 640-by-480, black-and-white display systems (not gray scale)

40 x 40 color	Used as the standard icon on 1024-by-768 and higher resolution display systems
16 x 16 black and transparent	Used as the mini-icon and title bar icon on 640-by-480 and 800-by-600 display systems
20 x 20 black and transparent	Used as the mini-icon and title bar icon on 1024-by-768 and higher resolution display systems

When the icon editor starts, it always shows the 32 x 32 color version of the icon, no matter what type of display you are using. Use the Device submenu in the icon editor to ensure that you edit the right versions of the icon for your display system. If you plan to use the object on other systems, be sure to edit all five versions of the icon! The copy and paste features of the editor can help you do this.

If you are creating a new object, it can be quicker to create its icon by editing an existing icon used by another object. To do this you can open the icon editor for both objects and then use cut-and-paste to copy the icon from one object to another.

For `WPFileSystem` classes of objects, the Workplace Shell saves the icon in the .ICON extended attribute. For `WPAbstract` classes, it saves the icon in the OS2.INI file. If the Workplace Shell cannot find the object's icon, it looks for the icon in one of three other locations:

1. If it is an executable file (.EXE or .DLL) for Presentation Manager or Microsoft Windows, it looks for the icon from the file's internal icon resource.

2. It looks for the icon from an icon file (.ICO) of the same name as the object file in the same directory.
3. It looks for the icon from Workplace Shell's internal collection of icons, based on the file object type.

As soon as you edit an object's icon, the shell places a copy into the .ICON extended attribute or OS2.INI file, depending on the object's class. You can also use a REXX command to attach a .ICO file to an object.

The Find pushbutton causes the Find dialog window to appear; you can use this to locate icon files. The shell preselects the `WPIcon` object type for you in this dialog. For more information, see "Using Find To Search For Objects" in Chapter 4.

You can set an object's icon to match any other icon you may have by simply dragging the new icon onto the current icon displayed in the General Settings page.

The Window Settings Page

Use the Window settings page to change the hide or minimize behavior of each object or, when used from the system setup object, for all objects in the system.

You can also turn window animation on or off when you are in system setup object. When animation is turned on, a zoom animation effect appears every time you open, close, minimize, or restore an icon. This can help you identify where the object icon is when you open or close the window. When turned on it causes windows to appear to be noticeably slower in opening because of the time to draw the animation.

Folder Objects

Workplace Shell folders are one of the most important object types that you can use in OS/2 2.1. They give you the power to organize your work and the information that you use in your everyday tasks.

You can think of folders as directories on your hard file, and you can use them in much the same way that you formerly used directories to hold data and program files. In fact, folders are directories on your hard disk, plus a whole lot more as well. In addition to data and program files, you can place any other type of Workplace Shell object into a folder, including a shadow of an object that has its real data held somewhere else. As well as holding more types of data, you have great control over how you view the contents of your folders.

Folders as Directories on Your Hard Disk

Every folder on your desktop represents a directory on your hard disk. This is an important feature of the Workplace Shell because it identifies where an object's data is located. Many objects save information in extended attributes. The location of the folder's directory on your hard disk determines where the shell saves the extended attributes.

Even the desktop is a directory on your hard disk. This is the top-level directory; the shell places all other folders under this. If you look at the root of your OS/2 2.1 boot drive you will find a directory called DESKTOP.

The FAT file system restricts all filenames to 8 characters with a 3-character extension, and Workplace Shell must abbreviate the names of all folders to fit within this requirement. The .LONGNAME extended attribute holds the full name of the folder.

If you are using HPFS on your boot drive, Workplace Shell does not need to abbreviate the name and you will see the actual names of your folders on the hard disk. For example, your OS/2 System folder's directory name is "OS!2 System" complete with spaces and mixed case. Table 5.5 shows the default directory layout on your boot drive for both a FAT and an HPFS hard disk—these are the Workplace Shell's default folders. Note the difference that FAT and HPFS file systems make to the names of the directories. Even the HPFS file system cannot accept some characters. In the table you can see that the / symbol is replaced by an ! and that new lines are represented by a ^ symbol.

Table 5.5. Folder directories on FAT and HPFS file systems.

FAT filename	*HPFS filename*
NOWHERE	Nowhere
DESKTOP	Desktop
INFORMAT	Information
MINIMIZE	Minimized^Window Viewer
NETWORK	Network
OS!2_SYS	OS!2 System
COMMAND_	Command Prompts
DRIVES	Drives
GAMES	Games
PRODUCTI	Productivity
STARTUP	Startup
SYSTEM_S	System Setup
TEMPLATE	Templates

If you move or copy a folder object to a different folder, the corresponding directory on your hard disk and all files and directories held in it move to the new location. You can even move the deskt op directory itself from a tree view of the boot drive!

The View Pages

You can view the contents of your folders in three different basic forms known as views. Some of these views allow you to further customize how they appear (for example, as small or large icons). The three basic contents views are as follows:

1. icon
2. tree
3. details

The view you are likely to use most often is the icon view, and this is the default when you simply double-click on a folder. Even in icon view you can further customize the look. Figure 5.7 shows the first View setting page for a folder from which you can select the icon size, a font, and how you would like the icons arranged.

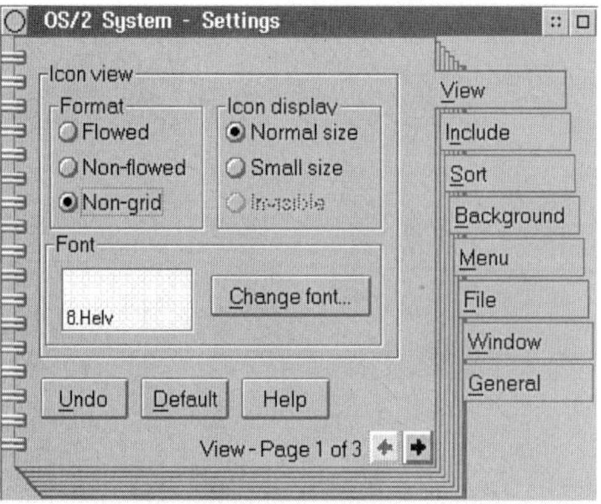

Figure 5.7. *The View settings page.*

There are three methods of arranging your icons inside your folder. In non-grid, the folder places your icons anywhere you want them. You can move them and they do not have to slot into any imaginary grid.

In flowed view, your icons are arranged as an orderly list, with icons on the left and text on the right. When the list reaches the bottom of the window, it starts a second column, and so on for as many columns as may be required. Non-flowed is similar although does not create a second column; instead, the icons flow off the bottom of the window.

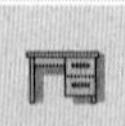

TIP

Using the flowed icon view gives the most organized view of your folder's contents. Unlike non-grid view, the flowed view automatically arranges itself when you change the folder window's size.

Figure 5.8 shows an example of some different views on folders. You can customize each folder to suit your needs. The shell considers each one separately; changing one does not affect any other folder.

NOTE

In many cases it is desirable for folders to inherit the view of their parent—for example, in the drives object. Unfortunately, the Workplace Shell in OS/2 2.1 does not support this.

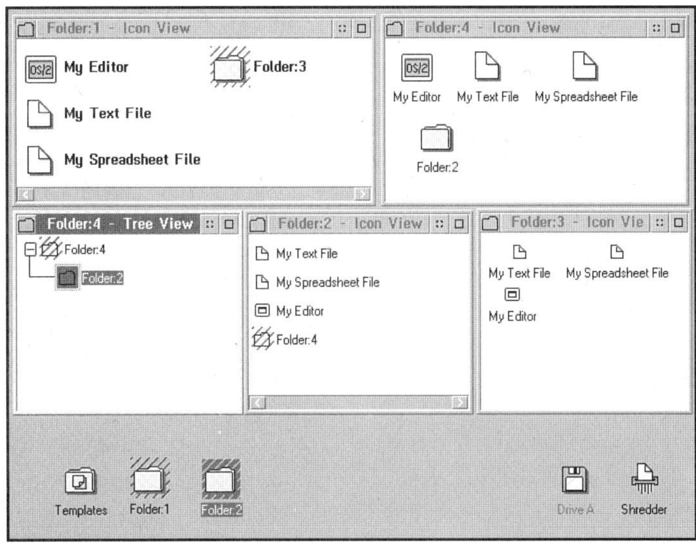

Figure 5.8. Some different types of icon view.

The folder View settings are on multiple pages (note the "Page 1 of 3" cue in the lower-right portion of Figure 5.7). The other two pages control the tree view and the details view.

You can open up a tree view of a folder by selecting the Open item on the folder's context menu, followed by the tree view item that appears on the submenu. Tree view is most useful when you are looking at your hard disk drives, perhaps from the drives object, because it allows you to see the layout of your hard disk directories. The second View settings page for a folder gives you further control over this view. Like the icon view, you can change fonts and select icon sizes.

When you first open a tree view, the folder displays the first level of your hard disk directories only. This improves folder open performance while a background thread scans all the lower directories. You may see plus or minus symbols appear in the tree after it initially opens. These symbols indicate that there are subfolders within the tree. You can click on the plus or minus symbols to expand or collapse a branch of the tree.

The details view of a folder, like the tree view, is most useful when looking at files or data on your hard disk. In details view the folder arranges all your objects in a single list with the icon and name to the left and all relevant information in columns to the right. Common details shown are the date and time that you created each object. As many different details are possible for each object type, the information usually extends beyond the size of your window. You can scroll to the extra information or you can use page 3 of the View settings to select which details the folder displays. Figure 5.9 shows a folder in details view alongside the settings page that controls how it appears.

Folder:1 - Details View

Icon	Title	Real name	Size	Last write date	Last write time	Flags
	My Editor					
	My Text File	My_Text_	0	11-7-92	12:39:38 PM	-A--
	My Spreadsheet File	My_Sprea	0	11-7-92	12:39:38 PM	-A--
	Folder:3	Folderl3	0	11-7-92	3:12:02 PM	----

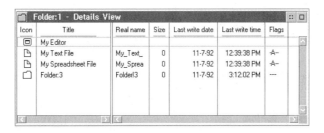

Figure 5.9. A details view of a folder.

Arrange, Sort, and Refresh

The pop-up menu of most folders contains three actions that assist you in maintaining the contents of your folders and ensuring that the view you see is accurate.

The Arrange action is useful in icon non-grid view. When you select this action, the Workplace Shell moves all your icons in the folder into an orderly arrangement.

The Sort action allows you to change the order of your object icons in the folder. The section of this chapter called "The Sort Page" describes this in more detail.

There is no way to undo an arrange or sort action, so be careful not to do this unintentionally!

If you select the Refresh action, the Workplace Shell updates the contents of the folder by reading all the information from the OS2.INI file and your hard disk. You may find it useful to use this when viewing the contents of network drives that other network users may update, or after putting a new disk in your disk drive.

The Include Pages

You control what types of objects a folder can display in the Include settings for a folder, which is a multiple-page setting. There is no "page 1 of" cue to indicate the number of pages; the exact number of pages is unknown to the Workplace Shell because it can vary by object type. On the first page you select which types of objects you want to include; on the second page you have further control over these types—for example, date and time. If you want to see all data files only, select Data file from this list. If you want to see only those matching a certain filename mask, enter the mask in the Name field above the list box. The default setting is to include all object types in the folder view. Figure 5.10 shows an example of including only data files matching *.TXT as the filename.

Figure 5.10. The first Include settings page.

TIP

In "The Workplace Object Hierarchy" earlier in this chapter you learned that the Workplace Shell arranges object types in a hierarchy. The hierarchy is important in this settings page because the shell also includes everything inherited from the selected object type. Selecting Data file, for example, also includes Bitmap,

Icon, Pointer, Program file, and OS/2 Command file. These are all objects inherited from the data file type (see Table 5.1).

The second page of the Include settings allows you to add more criteria to further restrict what objects the folder displays. You have control over such parameters as the size of the object, date and time, and file attribute flags. You can apply various comparisons such as less than, greater than, equal to, and so on. Multiple criteria may apply to the inclusion algorithm, and you can use these in either an AND or OR fashion. Figure 5.11 shows this second page of the Include settings together with the dialog box used to add or change inclusion criteria.

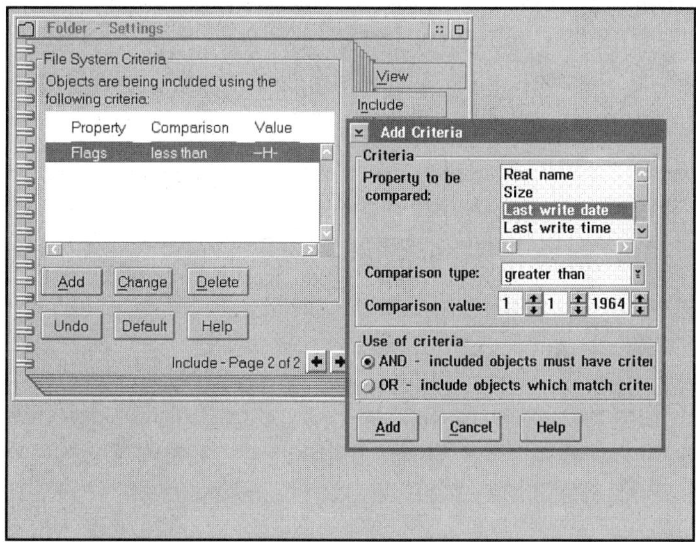

Figure 5.11. Setting inclusion criteria.

Although it is somewhat complex to set up the first time, this process of selectively displaying object types in a folder represents an extremely powerful feature of the Workplace Shell. It is particularly useful when viewing directories or folders on a network when there might be many different objects that do not interest you.

The Include settings control only what objects a folder window displays. It does not restrict the folder from containing other types of objects. Although they are present in the folder, they are not displayed.

The Sort Page

You can sort the contents of a folder using the folder's pop-up menu. The Sort item is a submenu containing a number of different attributes—for example, name, size, date, or time. You can control what sort attributes this menu displays with the Sort settings page for the folder.

The Sort page, shown in Figure 5.12, has two list boxes. The left list box allows you to select what type of objects to include when you select the Sort action from the pop-up menu. Remember that, just like the include criteria, the shell holds object types in a hierarchy. If you want to include every object type in the sort, you must select the highest-level object. The default is to apply the sort to all file system objects.

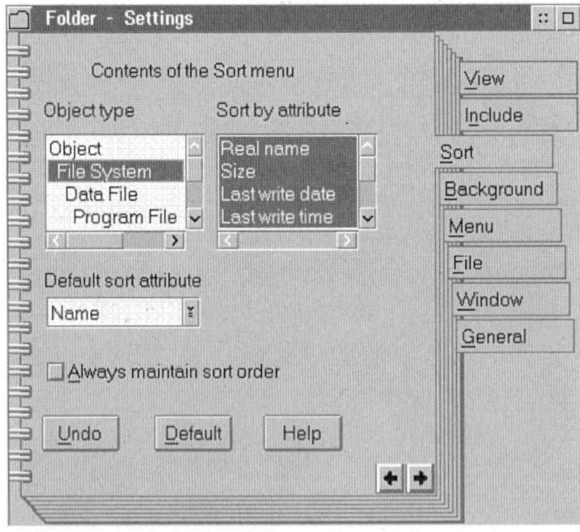

Figure 5.12. The Sort settings page for folders.

If you see unexpected results from a sort—for example, the objects did not sort correctly by size—check to see that you included all object types in the sort.

Once you have selected what types of objects to include in any sort operation, the right list box contains all the valid attributes against which you can sort. Every object type allows you to sort by name. Objects that represent a file on your hard disk also allow the use of file attributes such as date or time. You can select from this list box those options that you would like the shell to list on the folder's pop-up menu.

The final drop-down list box lets you choose which of the sort criteria is to be the default (should you choose to click on the Sort menu item without picking from the submenu).

Workplace Shell allows you to sort by date or time. For some reason you cannot sort by date and time. If you sort first by date and then by time, you lose the order, so you cannot use this two-stage approach to solve this shortcoming. This problem with the Workplace Shell makes the sort feature almost useless for date and time.

Besides sorting the order of your objects, you can manually move them around using drag-and-drop. In icon non-grid view you can place the icons anywhere in the folder window. In details view, or in one of the icon flowed or non-flowed views, you can change the order in which the icons appear, again using drag-and-drop. When you drag an object, look for the visual feedback known as target emphasis. This indicates the new position for the icon. In one of the ordered list views you will see a horizontal line to indicate between which two icons you are moving the object to (see Figure 5.13).

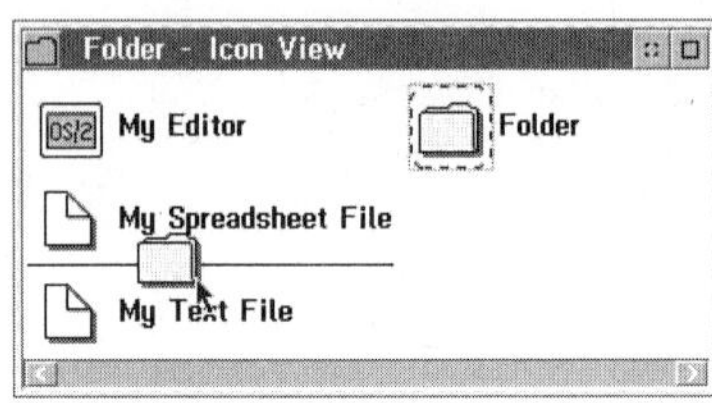

Figure 5.13. Inserting an icon between two others.

The Background Page

The Background page (see Figure 5.14) lets you change the color or select a picture for the background of any folder, including the desktop. If you want, you can have a different color or image for every folder, or perhaps color-code folders by the type of objects they contain.

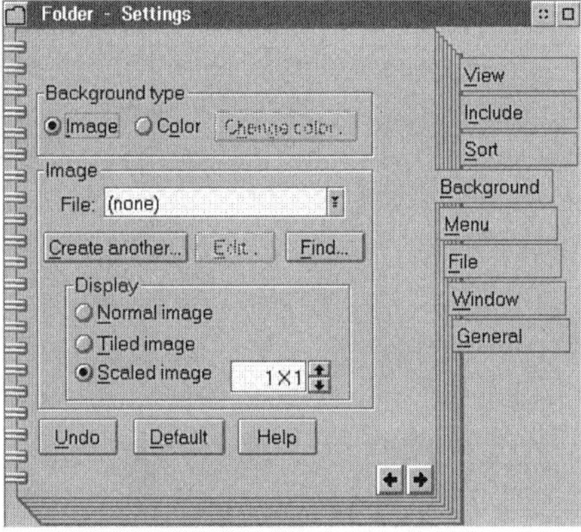

Figure 5.14. The Background settings page.

You use the Background page in the same way as the second page of the Lockup settings, described in "Shutdown and Lockup" in Chapter 4. If you select the Change color pushbutton, the color wheel described in the section called "Colors and Fonts" appears, from which you choose the color.

If you select Image, you can choose any bitmap file in one of the formats recognized by Presentation Manager. These are OS/2 1.3, OS/2 2.0, and Microsoft Windows formats. You can display these in any folder window either full size, scaled, or tiled. As you change color or image, any open view of the folder changes immediately.

If you want to create your own bitmap, or edit an existing one, select the appropriate pushbutton. It is usually easier to create a small bitmap and then tile it instead of trying to create one the size of your screen. It is also more memory-efficient to do this, and the icon editor is more efficient with small bitmaps.

Bitmaps can take up a lot of memory and consequently may affect the overall performance of your system. The list of available bitmaps on the background settings page initially includes only those that are physically in the \OS2\BITMAP directory on your boot drive. If you want to use a bitmap from another directory, you must use the Find pushbutton to locate it so it may be added to the list of available bitmaps.

Work Area Folders

On the first page of the File settings for a folder there is a check box marked Work area. You can use this to give you greater control in grouping applications and data together.

If you have a number of applications and data files that you use for a particular task, you can group them all in one folder. By marking this folder as a work area, you can take advantage of the following features:

- When you minimize or hide your folder, all applications and data files opened from this folder are minimized or hidden at the same time.
- When you close your folder, all applications and data files opened from this folder are closed at the same time.

- If you later open this folder again, all applications and data files that were open the last time you used the folder are opened at the same time.

The work area feature is very useful to group multiple applications or data together in the same location, and it provides an easy way to open and close these applications. You can of course place shadows of objects into the Work Area folder.

Currently, most applications do not exploit this feature of the Workplace Shell. It is very likely that when an application restarts it does not restore you to the last position in the data on which you were working, and its window does not appear at the same size or location.

Creating Another View of the Desktop

The Desktop folder is a special case of a work area. It is special because it is the first folder that opens when the Workplace Shell initializes and the shell fixes it to the background of your screen. All other windows appear on top of the desktop. Additional features like Shutdown and Lockup are also available only from the Desktop folder.

However, like a Work Area folder, all applications executing when you shutdown OS/2 2.1 restart every time you open the desktop—in other words, every time you start the operating system. You can change this behavior. "CONFIG.SYS Settings" in Chapter 6 describes what you need to do.

Because the shell always fixes the Desktop folder to the background, it can often be difficult to find an object icon on it without first having to minimize, hide, or move currently open windows. You can open either a tree view or a details view of the desktop and position it like any other window. If, however, you want to open another icon view of the desktop, you need to allow multiple copies of the desktop to be open.

Use the procedure explained in "Opening a Second View of an Object" in Chapter 4, "The Workplace Shell," to change the object open behavior in the Window page of the desktop's settings notebook. If you set this to Create a new window, you can open another icon view of the desktop from the Open choice on the desktop pop-up menu.

You can also create a shadow of the desktop so that you can open this second view from an icon. If you want, you can even place a shadow of the desktop in the Startup folder to automatically open every time OS/2 2.1 restarts.

This method creates another view of your current desktop. It is also possible for you to create different desktops to look, for example, like the Microsoft Windows desktop. To do this you need to place special entries into the OS2.INI file (see "The OS2.INI and OS2SYS Files" in Chapter 6).

The Startup Folder

The Startup folder is another special case of a folder. Every time you start OS/2 2.1, all objects held in this folder automatically start, whether or not they were executing the last time you used your computer.

You can place shadows of objects into the Startup folder so that it does not contain the actual data or program reference objects.

It is possible to control the order in which objects in the Startup folder start. To do this you must open the Startup folder in a flowed or non-flowed icon view (you cannot use non-grid), and then drag the objects (or shadows of objects) into the folder in the order in which you want them to start.

As an example of how you might use the Startup folder, consider the following configuration. The Startup folder contains two objects: one is the OS/2 Extended Services Communications Manager, itself configured to automatically start a 3270 emulation session; the other is a command file that performs a number of NET USE operations to link network drives.

OS/2 2.1 continues to support the STARTUP.CMD command file mechanism that earlier versions of the OS/2 operating system used. Every time OS/2 2.1 restarts, this command file executes, and it can contain any OS/2 command or REXX commands. There are two significant differences between this command file and using the Workplace Shell Startup folder.

STARTUP.CMD starts to execute before the Workplace Shell initializes, and all the commands in this file execute serially. The Startup folder opens after the Workplace Shell initializes, and opens its objects synchronously and in parallel with each other. In other words, each object is started one after the other, but the Workplace Shell does not wait for an object to complete executing before starting the next object. If you do not need to execute programs serially, it is better to use the Workplace Shell's Startup folder.

OS/2 2.1 also supports the AUTOEXEC.BAT command file used by DOS. This executes every time you start a DOS session on your computer. Both this file and STARTUP.CMD have to be in the root of your boot drive for OS/2 2.1 to read them.

OS/2 2.1 lets you specify a different location and name for an AUTOEXEC.BAT file in the DOS settings for a DOS program object. Different programs can be set up with different AUTOEXEC.BAT files.

Combining the use of the Startup folder, STARTUP.CMD, AUTOEXEC.BAT, restarting previously executing applications and the `SET RESTARTOBJECTS=` setting (described in "CONFIG.SYS Settings" in Chapter 6), gives you a great deal of flexibility in configuring your Workplace Shell startup environment.

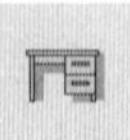

It is possible to create multiple Startup folders by copying from the original.

File Objects

The Workplace Shell uses file objects to represent data files on your hard disk as icons on your desktop. Most of the files with which you work on your hard disk are either of the class `WPDataFile` or one of the classes inherited from this class. From Table 5.1 you can see that these are `WPBitmap`, `WPIcon`, `WPPointer`, `WPMet`, `WPPif`, `WPProgramFile`, and `WPCommandFile`.

Be careful how you use the program file and OS/2 command file objects. Because of the danger of accidentally renaming or deleting these object's files, it is better if you use program reference type objects. The section in this chapter called "Program Objects" describes program references.

When you install an application that uses features of the Workplace Shell, it may create data file object classes of its own. These are usually children of the `WPDataFile` object class. You can only create new object classes of your own by programming with the Workplace Shell object interface.

The Type Page

In addition to the object class, the Workplace Shell also uses the .TYPE extended attribute feature provided by the OS/2 file system. This is particularly important when you set up association links between applications and data files. Because associations are useful, try to mark all your data files with a specific type as you use them.

Extended attributes (EAs) are a feature of the OS/2 operating system, and consequently, DOS and Windows applications do not understand them. Chapter 10, "Drive Objects and File Systems," explains how this can cause you to lose EAs.

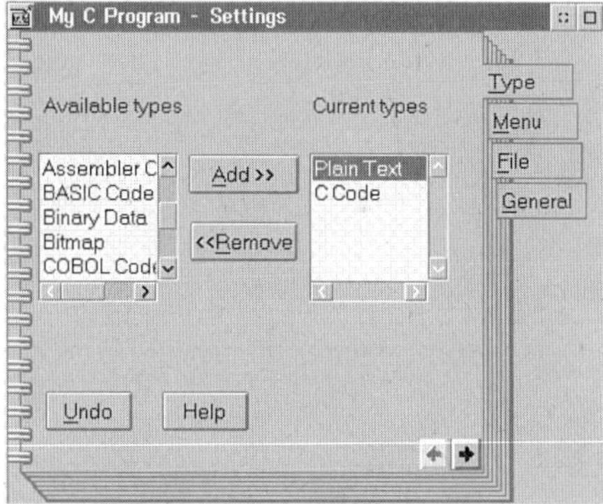

Figure 5.15. The Type page for a data file object.

If you want to change the type of a file, you can use the Type page shown in Figure 5.15. The two list boxes show all the file types recognized by the Workplace Shell. The list box on the right shows all the types currently set for the file; the list box on the left shows all other types understood by the shell. You can move types between the list boxes by marking a type and using the Add or Remove pushbuttons. If no file type information is attached to the data file, the Workplace Shell assumes that the file is plain text.

TIP

You can have more than one type for a file. For example, a C program source file can have types of Plain Text and C Code, it might then have associations for both an editor and a C compiler.

As you add or remove types, you affect any associations that may be set up in application programs. The Open submenu on a file's pop-up menu lists all application programs that have associations for data files of the selected types.

The list boxes include only file types known to the Workplace Shell. If you want to create new types of your own, you can do this by creating a REXX command file that creates a new program object with associations for your new types of file. Listing 5.1 includes the ASSOCTYPE keyword for Plain Text, but if you specify a type that does not already exist, the shell creates it for you. Deleting the program object does not delete your new file type.

The Menu Page

In the previous section you learned about file types. In later sections you will learn how associating applications with types of files modifies the pop-up menu for these files. In addition to application association, you can modify pop-up menus directly.

You can only change the menus for file and folder object types. You cannot change the pop-up menu for program, device, or any other type of object.

On the Menu setting page you can add an item to the primary pop-up menu or to any of the submenus on the pop-up menu. Figure 5.16 shows the menu page for a data file. The first list box shows all the menus that you can edit for the selected object. You can add to the primary pop-up menu and to the Open submenu. Sometimes there may be other menus, too, or you can create new menus of your own. The second list box shows all the items on the menu that you selected from the first list box. Characters on the menu preceded by a tilde (~) character appear with an underline and indicate the keyboard accelerator key.

NOTE

You cannot delete items from the primary pop-up menu (other than those you create yourself). It is possible only to remove items that OS/2 2.1 provides by programming your own Workplace Shell object.

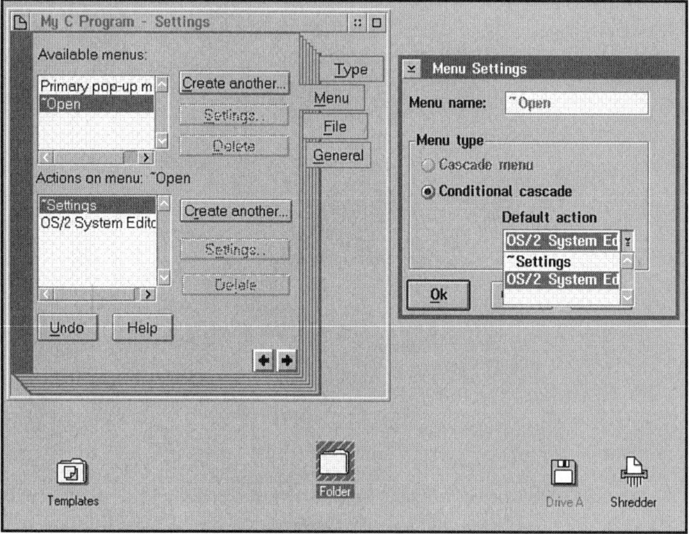

Figure 5.16. The Menu settings page for a data file.

If you want to add a new submenu to the pop-up menu, select the Create another option that is alongside the first list box. You can enter any name you like for it and choose between an ordinary cascade menu or a conditional cascade. Conditional cascade menus require you to select the small pushbutton to the right of their text before the menu appears.

To add a menu item to any of the available menus, first select the menu from the first list box, then select the Create another pushbutton next to the second (Actions on menu) list box. You then have an option of entering the full path and filename for an application or searching for one using the Find program pushbutton.

You should use the Find program dialog, rather than entering the filename. This allows the Workplace Shell to use any settings that you entered in the program reference for the application. This is particularly important for DOS and WIN-OS/2 applications that may require special settings to operate correctly!

To change an existing menu item, use the Settings pushbutton next to the second list box. You can use the same method you just learned to add a new item.

An easy way to add a specific program object to a menu is to drag its icon and drop it onto the Actions on Menu list box.

When you select one of your new actions from a pop-up menu, the program that executes receives the name of the object as a parameter, using the rules for parameter substitution described in "The Program Page" later in this chapter. This happens for folder and file objects and can cause the application to issue a warning message if it does not know how to cope with only a directory name.

If you encounter an application that fails to work if only a directory name is provided, create a program reference object specifically for use on folder pop-up menus. On the program settings page, if you enter `%` in the Parameters entry field, no parameter will be passed to the program. Alternatively, you can enter `[prompt]` and the shell will prompt you for a filename.

Once you have more than one item on a conditional cascade submenu, you can choose one of them to be the default. OS2 2.1 chooses this default action if you simply click on the submenu name and do not specifically select any of the action items. To change the default, use the Settings pushbutton that is next to

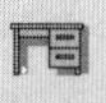

the first list box and choose the default action from the list of items in the drop-down list box shown in Figure 5.16.

Adding a Command Prompt to the Desktop Menu

As an example, the following steps describe how you can add a command prompt to the pop-up menu for the desktop using the method described previously.

1. Open the settings notebook for the desktop and select the Menu page.
2. Be sure that Primary pop-up menu is selected in the first list box and then select the Create another pushbutton to the right of the second list box.
3. Use the Find program pushbutton to search for all programs. Using the Locate pushbutton, it is faster to search only in the folder that you know contains a command line.
4. Select the OS/2 command-line prompt that you want to add to the menu.

As an alternative to Steps 3 and 4, you could enter the name of the executable, \OS2\CMD.EXE, and the shell would start a command-line window. If, however, you want it to start full-screen or you want to use a DOS command line with specific settings, you need to use Steps 3 and 4.

When you start a program from a menu, the program receives the name of the current directory or file as a parameter. Starting a command line from the desktop menu causes CMD.EXE to receive a parameter of C:\DESKTOP. The command processor tries to open this file and process its contents. This fails because it is a directory, and a warning message appears at the top of the command screen or window.

You can avoid this by using a program reference type object in your pop-up menu (using Steps 3 and 4). In the Parameters field of the program settings, enter a single % sign and the command-line processor will not receive any parameter.

The File Pages

The File settings page is only present on object types that represent physical files on your hard disk. The settings let you view and change the file attributes, other than the .TYPE extended attribute.

You use the first page of the file settings to specify the subject and view the physical filename for the object. It is important to understand that the physical name of a file is not the same as the logical name that you assign on the General settings page. This is particularly important on hard disks with the FAT file system because the Workplace Shell always truncates the physical name to 8.3 characters.

You cannot change the physical filename of an object from this settings page; you change the object's name from the General page. If the name you give the object here is valid as a filename on your physical hard disk, then the shell uses it; otherwise the .LONGNAME extended attribute holds this name and the shell generates a physical name for you.

If you rename or copy a file from a command line, the Workplace Shell updates the physical filename. It does not update the logical name, however, even if it used to match the physical name.

The Subject entry field enables you to assign a topic to the file that the shell saves in the file's extended attributes. You can set and view other attributes on the second and third pages of the file settings (see Chapter 10 for more information).

Printing File Objects

Pop-up menus for a file object have an additional Print submenu. This submenu contains a list of all the printer objects available to you, with your default printer already selected. The Workplace Shell knows how to print certain types of data when you drag-and-drop a data file onto a printer object or select the Print action on the pop-up menu. Note the following data types:

- plain text files
- graphics metafile (*.MET)
- graphics picture interchange file (*.PIF)
- printer-specific text or graphics files

If you print a file that is either a metafile or a picture interchange file, the Workplace Shell uses a special utility to read the data and format it for your printer using the Presentation Manager printer drivers.

If you try to print a text file, the Workplace Shell asks you whether the file is plain text or is in printer-specific format. You should select plain text if your data file has not been formatted already for your target printer. If your data file has been formatted as a PostScript file, for example, and you are printing it on a PostScript printer, you should select the printer-specific pushbutton.

If the file type extended attribute is already set to either plain text or printer-specific, the shell does not display this dialog and assumes that the file type information is accurate.

If you select printer-specific, OS/2 2.1 sends the data from your file directly to the print spool queue with no further formatting. If you select plain text, the data file is printed by the Workplace Shell using the Presentation Manager printer drivers, formatting it as appropriate for your target printer.

Program Objects

The Workplace Shell uses a special type of object to represent all your executable programs. These objects are program references and are not the same as program files. A program file object represents the actual file on your hard disk; if you rename the program file object, you rename the actual file on your hard disk also. A program reference, however, is a pointer to the filename of the executable program, somewhat like an object shadow. Unlike shadows, however, there are a number of settings held by a program reference object that tell the Workplace Shell, and in some cases the program itself, how the application should execute.

There are three types of settings unique to programs: program information that identifies the application executable; session types that tell the Workplace Shell what type of application it is; and association links that tell the Workplace Shell what types of data file the application can work with. The session and association settings are also available from program file type objects. You can access these object settings in the same way as any other type of setting—through the notebook obtained from the pop-up context menu.

The Program Page

When you create a program reference object, the shell asks you to give the full filename of the executable program, including drive and path. If you know the name and location of the executable, simply enter it. If you do not, you can use the Find pushbutton to locate it from any of your folders or disk drives.

Like other areas of OS/2 2.1, the Workplace Shell accepts universal naming convention (UNC) filenames for a program, or anywhere else that you may have to provide a filename. UNC names allow you to specify the name of a file on a network without first assigning a drive letter, and they always start with a double backslash—for example, \\Server\Share\Filename. Some applications, however, may not work without a drive letter.

You can optionally provide parameters for your application and a working directory. The working directory is important because it tells OS/2 2.1 which directory to look in first when it tries to load files like the online help and dynamic link libraries. Think of this as performing a change directory before executing the application.

It is better to specify the name of the directory that contains all the applications DLL's here rather than update the `LIBPATH` in CONFIG.SYS. Updating the `LIBPATH` slows performance for all applications, especially if the path becomes long.

The Parameters field is very powerful. Here you can enter the actual parameter to pass, special key strings, or nothing at all. If you do not type any parameters, what the program receives depends on how you start it. If you start the program by double-clicking on it, it receives no parameters; if you start the program by dragging another file onto it, it receives the name of the file being dragged.

If you specify a parameter in this field, the name of the file being dragged is added to the end of your parameter list, unless you use the `%*` substitution.

You can enter special substitution strings into the Parameters field:

`[ ]` (square brackets around one space) The shell prompts you to provide a parameter when the program executes.

`[prompt]` If you place text within the square brackets, it appears as the prompt string.

`%` The application program receives no parameters at all. This may be useful for programs you start from a folder's pop-up menu.

`%*`	Similar to leaving the Parameter field empty, although it allows you to insert the filename of the dragged object somewhere other than at the end of the parameter list.
`%**P`	Insert drive and path information without the last backslash (\).
`%**D`	Insert drive with `':'` or UNC name.
`%**N`	Insert filename without extension.
`%**F`	Insert filename with extension.
`%**E`	Insert extension without leading dot.

The Session Page

The Workplace Shell automatically determines what type of application a particular program is by examining the header information in the executable file. The shell recognizes the following types of applications:

- Presentation Manager
- OS/2 Text
- DOS
- Microsoft Windows

You have no control over Presentation Manager applications from the session notebook page. OS/2 2.1 expects these types of applications to provide their own mechanisms for you to configure them. For these applications, the shell disables the entire session page; although you can see it, you can make no changes on it.

For OS/2 text applications, you have a choice of running these in a full-screen session or in an OS/2 Window on your Workplace Shell desktop. A few applications do not work in a window because they use some of the programming interfaces that are not valid in this environment. An example of such an application is the OS/2 Extended Services Communications Manager and the

LAN Server's NET.EXE program. Most applications, however, do work perfectly well in a window. If you try to run an application in a window and it won't run, it automatically switches to full-screen.

DOS programs also give you a choice of running them in a full-screen session or in a DOS Window on your Workplace Shell desktop. All text-based DOS applications run either in full-screen or in a window; performance is better, however, in full-screen. It is not easy to determine whether a graphics-based DOS applications will run in a window. The issue is complex because of the large number of video adapters available and the number of different graphics modes that they support. Determining whether your DOS graphics program will run in a window is often a case of trying it to find out. (See Chapter 11, "The Video Subsystem," for more information.)

When the Workplace Shell opens an OS/2 or DOS window on the desktop, the shell determines its size, position, and font. The font chosen is the one that you last saved from the windowed command-line font selection dialog. The shell calculates the window size unless you have overridden it by holding down the Shift key the last time you resized a command-line window.

If you always want your windowed command lines to open with a size of your choice, hold down the Shift key when you resize a windowed command line. Command-line windows save this size and use it every time a new one opens. You need to do this only once for it to be remembered.

You can switch a DOS application between full-screen and a window at any time while it is executing using the Alt-Home keys. This is useful if you want to use the Clipboard. However, you cannot do this for OS/2 applications (see Chapter 11).

For OS/2 and DOS applications, you can select Start minimized and the application starts in the background, either as an icon on your desktop in the Minimized Window Viewer, or hidden, depending on your selected preference.

This is useful for running applications that have no user interface. The example used earlier of linking to network drives during OS/2 2.1 startup is one such case.

You cannot set a Presentation Manager to start minimized or maximized from this settings page, but you can set non-Presentation Manager applications to start minimized. You can, however, use the `START` command with the `/MAX` parameter, or create a REXX command file to do it. See Chapter 15 for more information.

If you run an application in a window and you want to prevent the window from disappearing when the program completes, you can deselect Close window on exit. This is useful if you want to run a lengthy task and see the results on the screen when it finishes. With the Close window on exit option selected, the window disappears as soon as the task completes!

Microsoft Windows applications execute in a WIN-OS/2 session, either full-screen or in a WIN-OS/2 window on your Workplace Shell desktop. You will find it much easier to work with the application and the Workplace Shell if you select to run it in a window. You can set the defaults for the WIN-OS/2 session page and WIN-OS/2 settings using the WIN-OS/2 object in the System Setup folder. Chapter 9, "WIN-OS/2," provides more information on WIN-OS/2 and how to configure it.

For both DOS and WIN-OS/2 type programs, there are many configuration settings available for you through the DOS settings and WIN-OS/2 settings pushbutton.

The Association Page

One of the more powerful and useful features of the Workplace Shell is the ability to associate different applications with different types of data files.

All data files in OS/2 2.1 can have extended attributes attached to them. (See Chapter 10 for a discussion of EAs.) One of these EAs is known as the .TYPE and identifies what kind of information the file contains. You can use the type information in program references to tell the Workplace Shell that this application works with certain types of data.

In addition to the .TYPE extended attribute, the Workplace Shell also lets you associate using a filename extension—for example, .TXT, .DOC, or any other extension you choose.

Use the Associations page of an application's settings notebook to establish the links between a program and data files. This page, shown in Figure 5.17, contains a list box, on the left, with all the file types that the Workplace Shell recognizes. On the right is a list box with all the file types to which the application is currently associated. You can move types between the two list boxes by selecting a type and pressing either the Add or the Remove pushbutton.

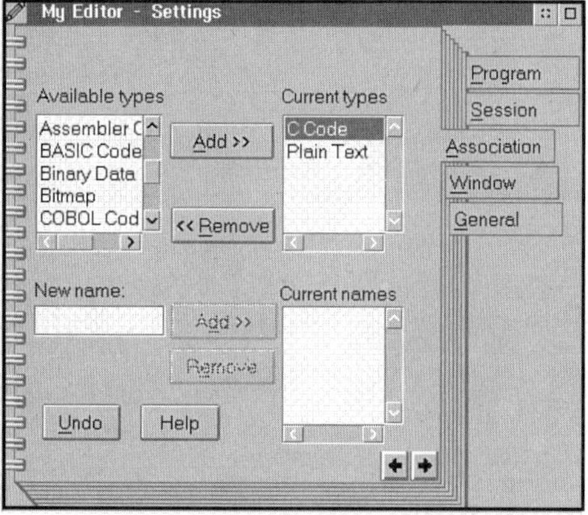

Figure 5.17. Associations settings for a program reference.

If you cannot find a type appropriate to your data in the list box, you can add new types to the Workplace Shell (see Chapter 10).

Below the list boxes for file types is an entry field and a third list box. In the entry field, enter the name of any file to which you want this application associated; the list box shows you the current associations.

In the filename field, you can enter specific filenames or use wild cards. For example, CONFIG.SYS is a text file that you could associate to an editor, but *.SYS includes this file and all other .SYS files that are not plain text.

Once you create a link between an application and files, the name of the application appears on the Open submenu of every pop-up menu for files of the associated type or filename. If your new association is the only application associated to the file, it is automatically the default. If there is more than one, however, the old association remains as the default; if you want to change the default, you have to do this from each file object's Menu setting page.

The Workplace Shell holds information on what application associations exist for each type of data file in your OS2.INI file.

Inside the System Setup Folder

Once you become familiar with the Workplace Shell, you may quickly want to change the way it looks or change any of the configuration options in OS/2 2.1. In previous sections you learned how to move icons and objects to any location and how you can change the way that the icons appear in your desktop folders. If you want to make any further changes to your OS/2 2.1 configuration, you can find all the tools you need in the System Setup folder.

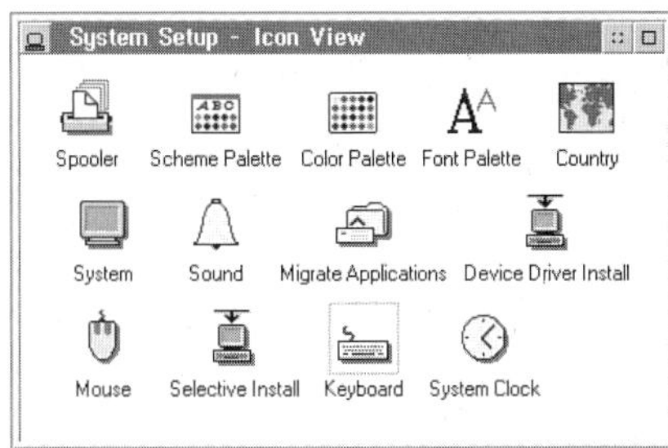

Figure 5.18. The System Setup folder.

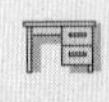

The System Setup folder, shown in Figure 5.18, is similar to the Control Panel with which you may be familiar from OS/2 1.3 or Microsoft Windows. Each provides a similar set of options for you to configure, but there are two significant differences:

1. The System Setup folder contains objects for each feature that you can configure. Like the rest of the Workplace Shell, it has an object-oriented design, and you can use drag-and-drop techniques.
2. All setup for printers, including parallel and serial port control, is performed from the printer object, not from the System Setup folder.

You will learn each of the major areas in the following sections. This section does not include all of the configuration objects. Some, like the WIN-OS/2 setup, selective install, and migrate applications, are covered in later chapters.

Colors and Fonts

One of the first things that everyone loves to do is to change the colors and fonts used by OS/2 2.1. This is easy to do using any one of three configuration objects:

1. Color palette
2. Font palette
3. Scheme palette

These objects enable you to pick from a wide variety of colors and fonts for you to drag-and-drop on any window on your desktop.

The Color, Font, and Scheme palettes affect only OS/2 Presentation Manager applications. To change colors and fonts used in WIN-OS/2 or for a WIN-OS/2 window, you must use the WIN-OS/2 Control Panel. You can create an object for this by dragging a program from the Templates folder and entering `\OS2\MDOS\WINOS2\CONTROL.EXE` as the program to execute.

Color Palette

When you open the Color palette, a window filled with a selection of color circles appears. You can pick up any of these colors and drag them onto any window visible on your desktop. When you release mouse button 2 with the pointer over any window item, the color changes in the window you drop on.

Normally the background color in the window you drop on changes color. If you want to change the foreground color—for example, title text—hold down the Ctrl key before you drop.

The Color palette holds 30 colors, but you can have multiple palettes, each with 30 colors. To do this, use Create another from the pop-up menu to create a second (or third) Color palette.

You can edit any one of the 30 color circles by double-clicking button 1 on it or by selecting the Edit color pushbutton. This may take a few seconds the first time you do this because OS/2 2.1 has to calculate all the possible colors it can display! What appears is the color wheel showing the full spectrum of available colors. You can select any shade color from the wheel and its intensity from the scale on the right. Figure 5.19 shows the color wheel alongside a Color palette.

If you want to prevent OS/2 2.1 from dithering colors, you can select the Solid color check box. You can see the effect immediately in the color scale; how significant this is depends on your video adapter. (Chapter 11 explains dithering and how your video adapter affects the range of colors available to you.)

In addition to selecting a shade of color by clicking mouse button 1 anywhere on the color wheel, you can also directly enter a color with a known value. You can enter this in Red, Green, and Blue (RGB) levels from 0 to 255, or Hue, Saturation, and Brightness (HSB) levels from 0 to 359 (for hue) and 0 to 100 (for saturation and brightness).

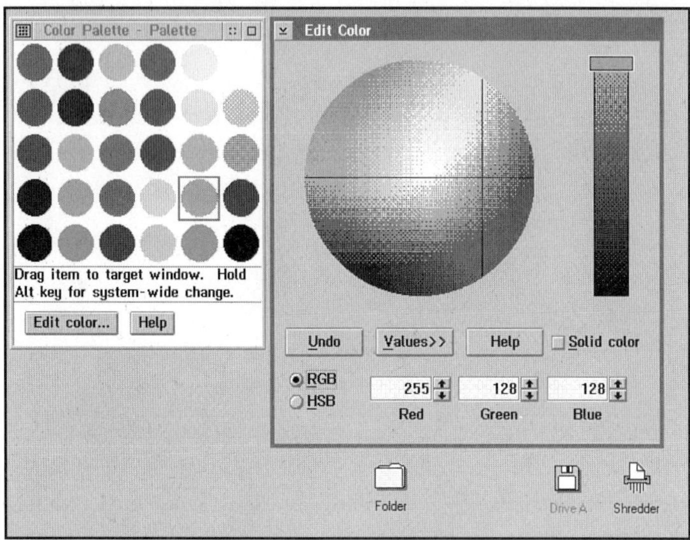

Figure 5.19. A color wheel and palette.

The Font Palette

The Font palette is similar to the Color palette. When you open it, a selection of fonts appears, each with its point size and face name displayed in the actual font. (See Chapter 11 for a description of font point sizes.) Like the Color palette, you can drag any one of the fonts onto a window, icon, or title bar and you can create multiple font palettes.

If you want to change the font used in one of the palette entries, or if you want to install a new font, you can double-click on a font name or use the Edit font pushbutton. The dialog shown in Figure 5.20 appears, from which you can select any of the fonts available, and you can change its style and size.

To install a new font onto your system, select the Add pushbutton. OS/2 2.1 asks you for a disk (or directory name) that holds the fonts and, after OS/2 2.1 scans all the font files, it asks you to choose which ones to install.

OS/2 2.1 recognizes fonts in the OS/2 .FON file format or the Adobe Type 1 file format. You will find the Adobe format of fonts much easier to obtain as

they are exactly the same as the fonts used by every PostScript printer. You can ask your software dealer for a font that you can download to a PostScript printer, and you will be able to use this font on OS/2 2.1 also. Any dealer that can supply PostScript printers should also be able to supply you with fonts. (Chapter 11 includes further information on fonts used by OS/2 2.1 and the effects of international standards on a font's design and use.)

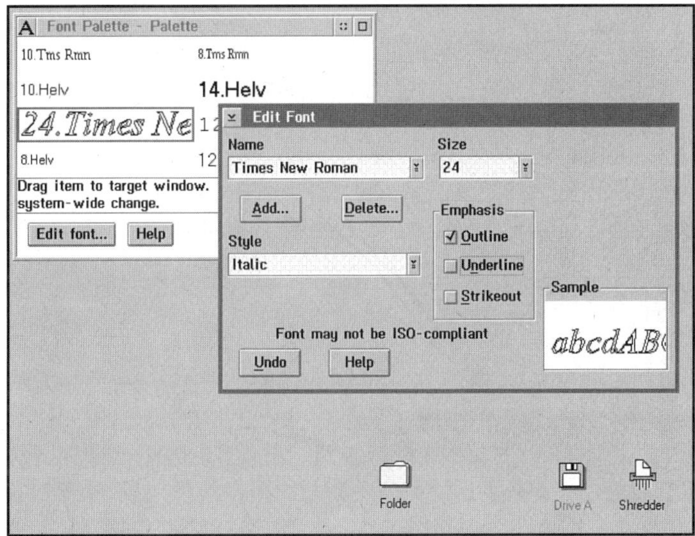

Figure 5.20. The Edit Font dialog and the Font palette.

Although you can change the fonts used by menus, icons, and window titles, it is not possible to change the default font used by all applications from the Font palette. Chapter 11 describes one method of overcoming this limitation.

Scheme Palette

The Scheme palette combines a number of fonts and colors into a single object that you can apply to a window or your entire desktop. Opening the Scheme palette displays a window with a selection of sample color schemes. From here

you can go on and select Edit scheme, which opens a window with a simulation of every other window element inside it (see Figure 5.21). Editing any color or font from this window uses the color wheel and Font palettes described in previous sections of this chapter.

Whether you choose to edit a scheme or not, you use the palette by dragging a scheme from it and dropping on whichever window you want to change.

Notice the two monochrome color schemes? The left scheme is truly black and white. The right scheme uses a selection of colors that produces a good result on black-and-white liquid crystal displays (LCD), and it is still acceptable for the occasional use in color.

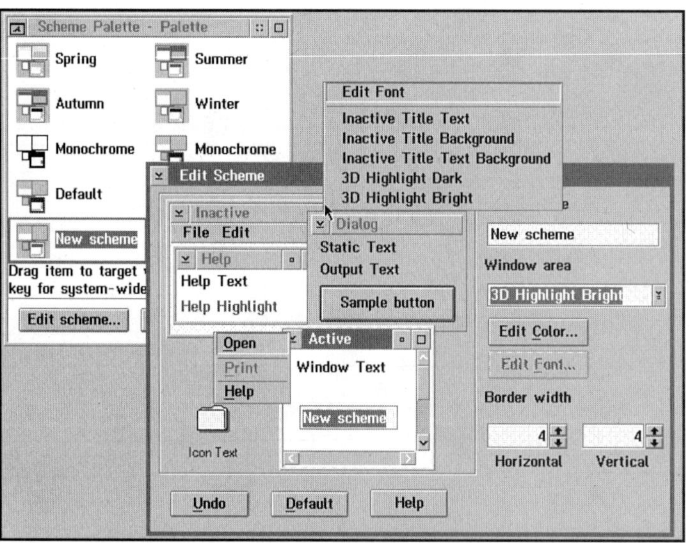

Figure 5.21. The Scheme palette.

To edit a particular color or font for a window element, you can either use the drop-down list box under the Window area prompt, or you can simply click mouse button 2 over the element you want to change to obtain a pop-up menu with all the available choices listed.

Changing Colors System-Wide

For each of the Color, Font, and Scheme palettes, when you drop onto a window the changes apply to that single window only. If you want to make any change to affect all windows in the system, including those that are not even open yet, you can hold down the Alt key just before dropping the color, font, or scheme.

Holding down the Alt key tells the Workplace Shell to apply the change everywhere. If you Alt-drop onto a window, however, other windows that you previously changed from default retain their current colors—system-wide changes do not override these.

To make a window forget your previous changes, drag the color scheme that you are trying to make system-wide onto the window and drop it while holding the Alt key. The window will forget its colors and use the ones being set for system-wide use. Any future changes you make to the system-wide colors will be picked up in this window, too.

Keyboard, Mouse, and Touch

OS/2 2.1 supports two primary input methods for users: the keyboard and mouse, and one optional method, a touch-sensitive display. Future versions of the OS/2 operating system may support other methods such as pens for use on notepad computers.

Keyboard

For the keyboard, you can change settings such as the repeat rate (how fast characters repeat when you hold down a key) and how long to delay before repeating. Figure 5.22 shows the settings notebook. Additionally, you can change the keys used to request the pop-up menu or edit an icon's title (Shift-F10 and Shift-F9 by default) on separate settings pages.

Take care if you change these keyboard keys. Your new selections must not conflict with any other key combinations used by OS/2 2.1 (Alt-F4, for example, is used to close an application window).

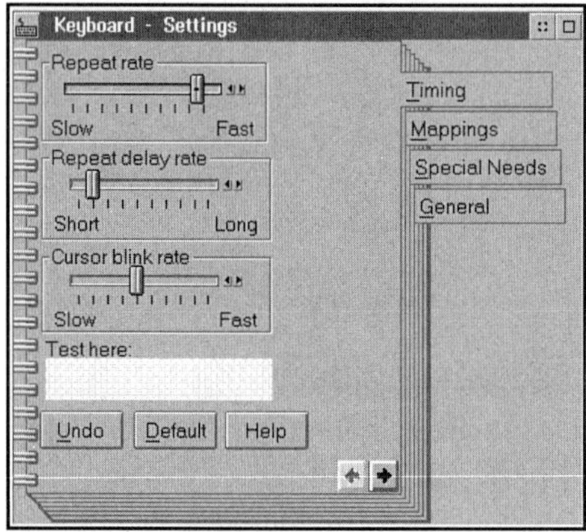

Figure 5.22. *The Timing settings page.*

Microsoft Windows sets the keyboard repeat rate slightly differently than OS/2 2.1. If you run a Windows application in WIN-OS/2, you may notice that the keyboard repeat rate changes, even after you finish the application and return to the Workplace Shell. You can avoid this by changing the KBD_RATE_LOCK setting to On for each WIN-OS/2 object.

The Special Needs page is for people who are perhaps not very nimble with their hands, or those who are unable to hold two keys down at the same time (Ctrl-Esc, for example). The online help information gives you information on how to use these special features. You should read this because it is not obvious from the settings notebook, shown in Figure 5.23, how to activate the features. For example, to activate the special needs feature, you must hold down the Shift key for 5 seconds and set the activation to "on."

You will hear a beep after the fourth second, not the fifth. Be sure to hold the key down for the full five seconds.

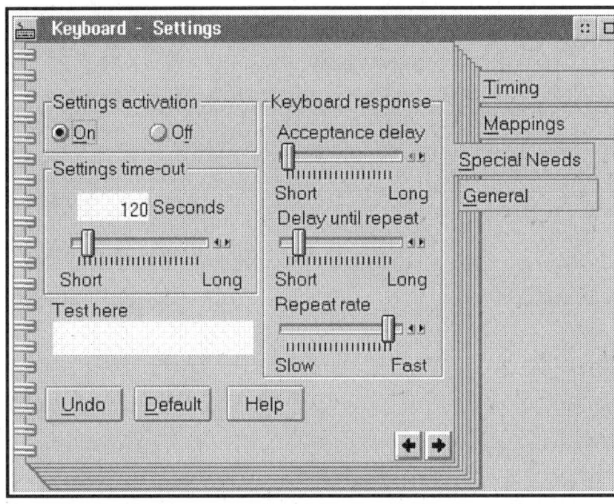

Figure 5.23. The Special Needs settings page.

When Special Needs is active, the keyboard repeat rate and repeat delay in effect are those set on the Special Needs page and not on the Timing page. With Special Needs turned on, a sticky key is set by pressing the Shift key three times, followed by the key you want to stick down. The key remains stuck down until you press it again. For example, to obtain the Window List without having to use two fingers:

1. Press the Shift key three times.
2. Press the Ctrl key once. This causes the Ctrl key to stick down.
3. Press the Esc key. Effectively, this is the Ctrl-Esc sequence.
4. Press the Ctrl key again. This causes the Ctrl key to release.

Mouse

You can use the Mouse settings object to change how the Workplace Shell responds to mouse buttons 1 and 2 and to change the mouse's sensitivity to movement.

The first page, Timing, lets you set the double-click interval and the tracking speed. Double-click time is the period after you press a mouse button during which a second press causes the shell to consider the two clicks as a single action. Tracking speed adjusts the mouse's sensitivity to movement. With a higher tracking speed, the mouse travels further across the screen each time you move the mouse.

The second page, Setup, lets you tell OS/2 2.1 whether you use the mouse in your left or right hand. This swaps the actions caused by each mouse button. For left-hand use, button 1 becomes the right-hand button.

The third page, Mappings, shown in Figure 5.24, lets you change the actions that the Workplace Shell takes when you press each mouse button or a combination of buttons and keyboard augmentation keys.

Figure 5.24. The Mouse Mappings settings page.

The Mappings page does not prevent you from assigning the same button(s) to different actions. Be careful that you don't do this! If you assign an action to both single-click and double-click, OS/2 2.1 carries out both actions when you double-click because OS/2 2.1 recognizes and acts on the first click before you go on and click the second time.

Touch

If you have a touch-sensitive display screen attached to your computer, OS/2 2.1 loads a device driver for it and places a new object into the System Setup folder. Currently, OS/2 2.1 only recognizes the IBM 8516 touch display.

To run the calibration program, select the Calibrate action from the object's pop-up menu. You should use this before performing any other touch screen setup; the calibration program adjusts the display's internal electronics so that it calculates the position of your touch correctly.

Once you calibrate the touch display, you can use the settings notebook to adjust the sensitivity of the display to your touch. Whenever you touch the display, the device driver converts this into mouse movement and button messages. This means that you can often use a touch screen for applications that do not have specific support for it, although in many cases it is not as easy as using a mouse or keyboard.

There are three distinct thresholds of touch pressure that you can adjust:

1. Touch and drag—the pressure needed for OS/2 2.1 to move the pointer to your finger position.
2. Button down—the pressure needed to record a mouse button down action.
3. Button up—the pressure needed to record a mouse button up action. This must be less than the button down pressure. It is often a lot less to allow you to easily move your finger over the display screen while OS/2 2.1 considers the button to be pressed down.

The other touch screen setting lets you set up an offset between your finger and the actual coordinate for the pointer. It is often desirable for this to be slightly above your finger so that you do not cover up the pointer. Figure 5.25 shows this settings page.

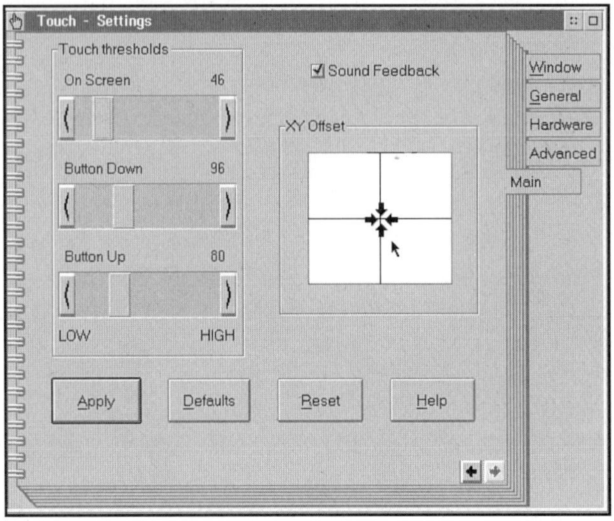

Figure 5.25. The Touch screen setup page.

System Settings

You learned about many of the settings available in the system setup object in Chapter 4—for example, the Window settings page in "Where Has My Window Gone?" This section covers only the other system settings.

Use the Confirmations settings page to tell the Workplace Shell how you would like it to act whenever you ask it to perform some type of destructive operation, such as delete, rename, or copy. The default settings, shown in Figure 5.26, cause a dialog window to appear whenever you try to do something that may result in the loss of some data.

You can change these settings so that the Workplace Shell does not interrupt you by asking whether you are really sure that you want to perform a given operation. Think very carefully before you remove the confirmations on Delete, especially Folder Delete!

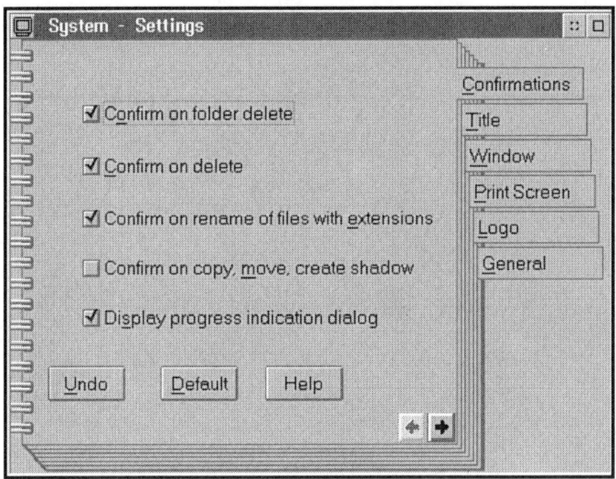

Figure 5.26. The Confirmations system setup page.

Use the Title settings page to tell the shell how to react when you try to copy or create a new object with the same name as an existing object in the same folder. Normally, the Workplace Shell does not allow this (although it can occur if you copy an object from a command-line prompt). Figure 5.27 shows the default settings.

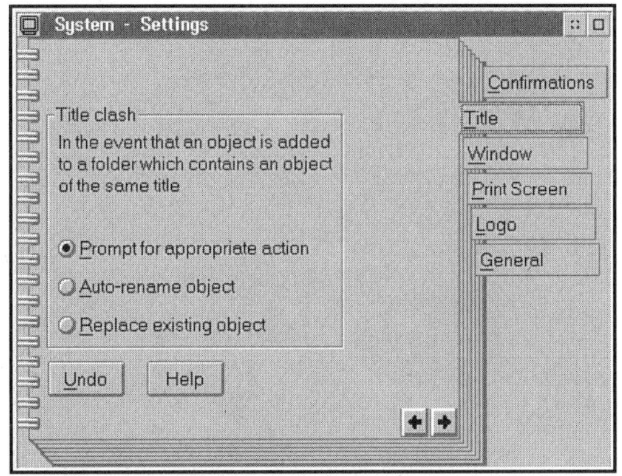

Figure 5.27. The Title settings page.

The Print screen settings page lets you switch on and off the Presentation Manager print screen key. This can be useful if you have an application that processes the Print Screen key. If you do not switch it off, OS/2 2.1 prints the screen and the application responds to the key as well, possibly causing the screen to be printed twice.

When you press the Print Screen key, OS/2 2.1 prints the window that the mouse pointer is currently over, providing that this window has the focus (responds to keyboard input). If you want to print the entire screen, place the mouse pointer over the desktop background. OS/2 2.1 scales the image to fit onto the default printer's paper size.

Printing a Presentation Manager screen can take some time. You can still work with OS/2 2.1 and perform other tasks but if you try to print the screen again, while the first print is still spooling into the print queue, OS/2 2.1 ignores your request and you will hear a beep.

The Logo settings page lets you set a time period for use by other application programs when they start. Often they will display a company logo and copyright statement, and many applications query OS/2 2.1 to see whether they should display this logo, and if so, for how long.

This has no effect on the OS/2 2.1 or the computer manufacturer's logo you see when the OS/2 operating system starts.

Country Settings

Different countries have different standards for the display of dates, numbers, and currency symbols. For example, some countries standardize on a date format of month, day, year whereas others prefer day, month, year.

OS/2 2.1 allows you to indicate your preference for these settings in the Country object. Figure 5.28 shows an example of the Numbers page.

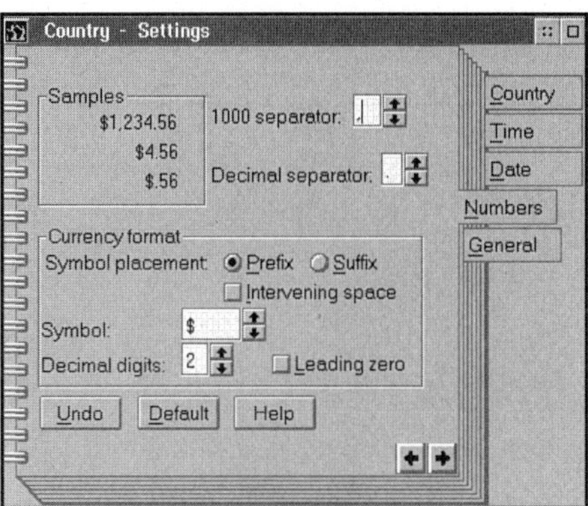

Figure 5.28. Country settings for Numbers.

Most OS/2 applications query this information before deciding how to display information that may need different formats in different countries. Some applications, however, are not as thorough at this, or they provide their own configuration.

The Workplace Shell and Networks

OS/2 2.1 activates the network independent shell extension to the Workplace Shell if you have an appropriate network requester installed. The network independent shell is also known as the LAN-independent shell or LAN-aware shell. The word *network* is used instead of *LAN* because these shell extensions can work with any suitably modified communications requester such as an AS/400 link or a TCP/IP link to a UNIX machine.

The network-independent shell has the following advantages:

- It is fully integrated with the Workplace Shell and only activates when a network requester is available.
- It lets you access multiple networks simultaneously.

- It uses common dialog windows to log in and log out to networks and servers and to assign drive letters to network directories and port names to network printers.
- You can browse available servers and resources on a network.
- You can create a shadow of any network object on your desktop or in any folder.
- It provides seamless access to network folders and files on the network.
- It provides seamless access to network printers on the network, and you can assign one of these as your default printer.

To make use of the network-independent shell, you need to install a network requester that supports network independence. Currently there are two available; IBM LAN Server and Novell NetWare. You can obtain programming details of how to write such a requester from IBM. Applications can also use a network-independent programming interface (API). The documentation for this API is available from IBM.

There are five types of network objects in the Workplace Shell:

- Network folder
- network group object
- server object
- network directory object
- network printer object

Network Folder

The Network folder appears on your desktop only when you are using a network requester that supports OS/2 network independence. You can choose to move the Network folder to another folder. You cannot delete the Network folder.

When you open the Network folder, OS/2 2.1 displays a window of network group objects. There is one network group object for each network requester that supports OS/2 network independence (see Figure 5.29).

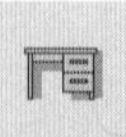

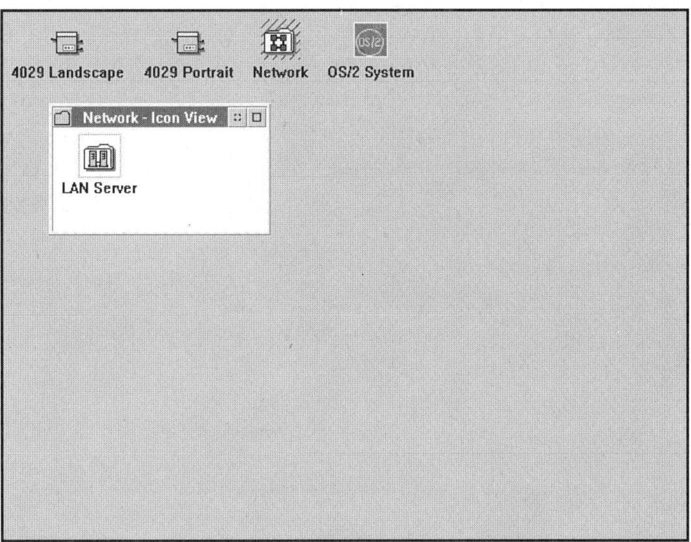

Figure 5.29. The Network folder and network group objects.

Network Group Object

The network group object represents a single network. It is your view into the network and all the objects available within that network. When you double-click on a network group object, a window opens showing an icon view of all the servers available within that network group (Figure 5.30 shows an example). OS/2 2.1 shows each server with a descriptive title that the network administrator determines when he or she configures the server for the network. If there is no server description, the name defaults to the server name (eight characters for IBM LAN Server).

You can open the network object in tree view. In the normal case, tree view shows only the first level of servers. If you open a server object, OS/2 2.1 expands the tree to include the expand (the plus symbol) pushbuttons. If you expand to the network directory objects, it is possible to traverse down the whole tree of folders beneath each network directory object (see Figure 5.31).

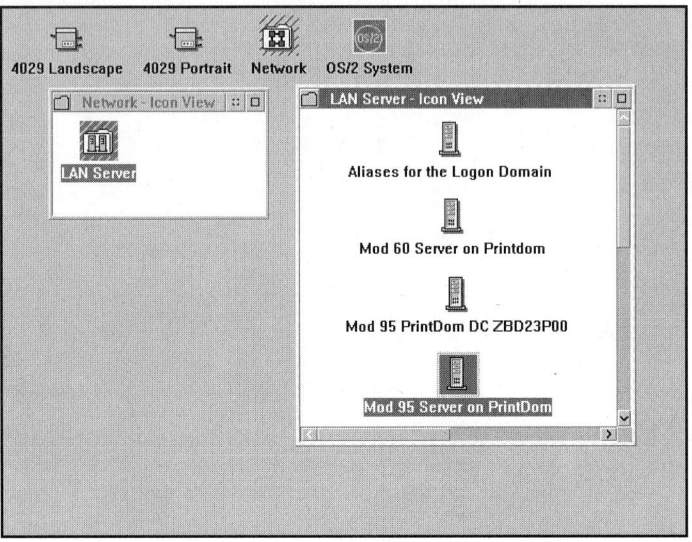

Figure 5.30. The Network group object icon view.

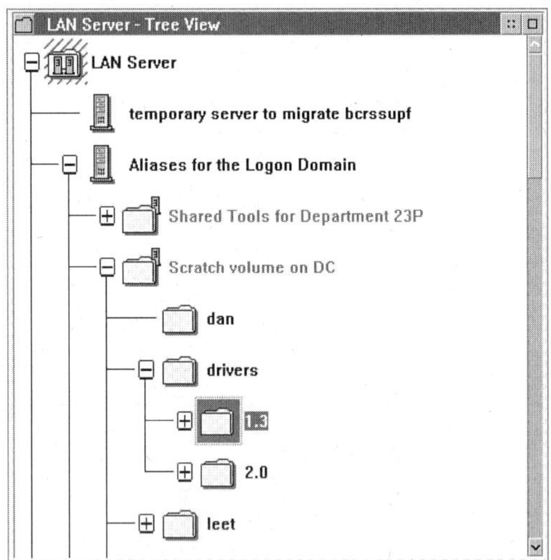

Figure 5.31. The Network group object tree view.

In the open view, a Refresh item is available on the object's pop-up menu. You can use this to see new servers that may become available in the network group.

A network group object has the same settings page as for a folder object. OS/2 2.1 adds a Network status page to describe the network name and status of the network.

If you open the network group object named Lan Server (for IBM LAN Server requesters), the shell prompts you to log in first before you can view the servers available.

For Novell NetWare, OS/2 2.1 shows all the servers on the network. For IBM Lan Server, OS/2 2.1 shows all the servers that are in your current domain. It also lists the servers in the domains listed in your `othdomain` statement in the IBMLAN.INI file.

OS/2 2.1 may show a network group object with a grayed icon. This indicates that the network group is not available. This is most likely to occur when you have uninstalled a network requester.

You can delete a network group object. This is especially useful when OS/2 2.1 indicates that the network group object is no longer available.

Server Object

You can shadow the server object into another folder. This allows you to use the server object without returning to the Network folder. You cannot move or copy a server object; you can only create a shadow.

When you double-click on a server object, a window opens showing the icon view of the server. The open view shows all the network resources available for that server regardless of whether the network allows you to access them. Network resources can be either directory objects or printer objects, as shown in Figure 5.32. OS/2 2.1 shows each network resource with a descriptive title that the network administrator determines when configuring the network resources. If there is no resource description, the name defaults to the resource name.

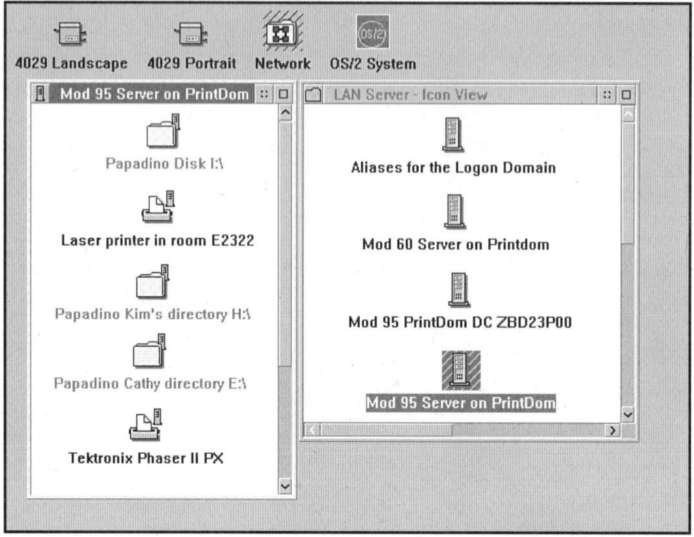

Figure 5.32. A server object and available network resources.

In the open view, a Refresh menu item is available. You can use this to see new resources that have become available for that server.

When you open the IBM LAN Server network group object, OS/2 2.1 shows a special server named Aliases for the Logon domain. This server object contains all the resource aliases that the network administrator has defined for this domain.

> **TIP** For IBM LAN Server, you should use resource objects (network directory and network printer objects), if they exist, from the server named Aliases for the Logon domain because it lists all the resources that you have permission to use on the network. If you are an administrator for IBM LAN Server, for each network printer or directory that you configure, you should also ensure that an alias is defined.

When you open a server object, the Workplace Shell prompts you to log in. You always have to log in for servers in a Novell NetWare network. For servers in an IBM LAN Server network, the shell prompts you to log in only if there is password protection on the resources contained within the server object. A server object has settings pages that are the same as a folder settings pages and has one extra settings page named Network Status, shown in Figure 5.33.

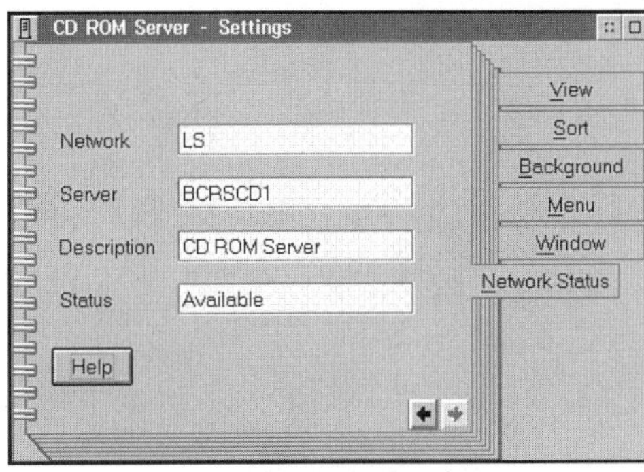

Figure 5.33. *Server object Network Status settings page.*

The Network Status page gives the name of the network group, server, and server description. The Status field shows one of the following:

Login required	You are not logged on or have not supplied sufficient authority to use this object. OS/2 2.1 prompts you to log in when you try to use this object. The only valid open action is to display the settings notebook.
Available	You have sufficient authority to use this object.
Not Available	The object is not available on the network. It was available at one time but is no longer available. OS/2 2.1 indicates this status by a grayed icon (see Figure 5.34).

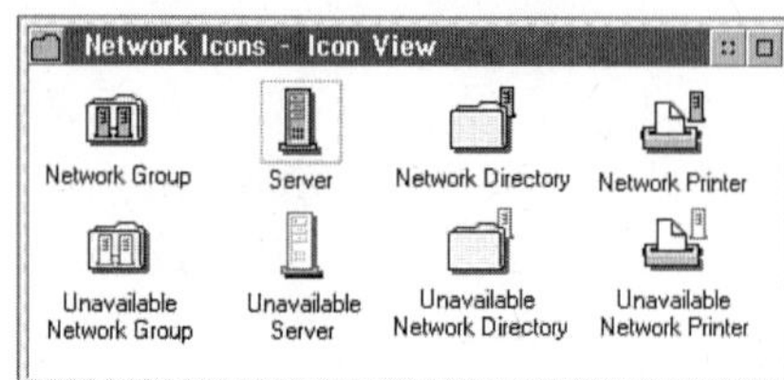

Figure 5.34. Available and unavailable network object icons.

You can delete a server object. This is especially useful when OS/2 2.1 indicates that the server is no longer available, using the grayed icon, and now you want to delete it.

OS/2 2.1 does not automatically delete unavailable network objects such as a network group, server, network directory, or network printer objects, but grays them instead. This indicates to you that it is unavailable at the current time. At some future time the object may become available again and the object will be ungrayed. OS/2 2.1 grays or ungrays a network object only when you try to access the object (opening it or displaying a pop-up menu).

For IBM LAN Server network objects, displaying a pop-up menu or performing some other operation may take some time because the network requester has to query across the network to ensure that the object is available. For objects that are not available, the network requester waits a specified time-out period that is dependent on the network configuration. In some cases this time-out could be 30 seconds or more. OS/2 2.1 displays an hourglass pointer during this time-out period and then displays the pop-up menu, or it may perform the requested action if appropriate.

An additional menu item for servers is Access another. You can use this option to access other servers that are either in another domain or are IBM PCLP servers that run DOS rather than the OS/2 operating system. The newly accessed server object is placed in the appropriate network group folder and a shadow appears on your desktop.

Network Directory Object

A network directory object represents a shared directory on a network server. The icon for a network directory is a modified folder icon. You can shadow a network directory object into another folder. This allows you to use the network directory object without returning to the Network folder. You cannot move or copy a network directory object; you can only create a shadow.

When you open a network directory object, OS/2 2.1 displays a multilevel tree view of the folders. This tree view, shown in Figure 5.35, is very similar to a drive object's tree view.

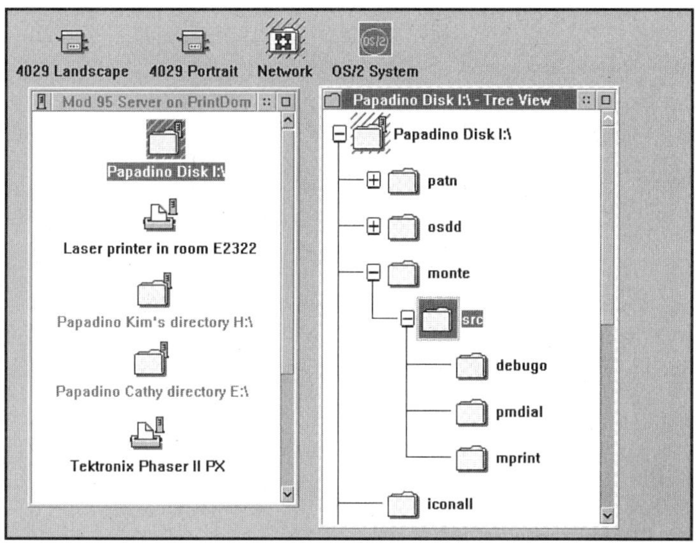

Figure 5.35. Tree view for a network directory object.

> TIP: The icon view is actually much faster than the tree view.

In the open view of a network directory, a Refresh menu item is available. You can use this to see new folders and files for that network directory.

If someone tells you that a new file has just become available on the network, you can use Refresh on the appropriate folder to see the new file.

The refresh operation is also available for every folder within the network directory tree.

You can move, copy, or shadow the folders in the network directory tree view to any other folder. The default operation is copy. These folders look like and operate just like folders on your local machine. For example, you can move a set of files from one server to another server in one operation; you may need read-write authority to write the files on the new server.

You can open one of the folders out on the network and see files on the network server. These look like and operate just like files on your local machine. You can move, copy, or shadow these files to any other folder in the same network directory, another server, or your local machine. The default operation is copy. For example, you can copy network files to your desktop or backup your local files to a network drive.

Application References and Network Data Files

Even more significant is that you can create a program reference object that points to an application stored on a network. Hence you can run applications that are stored on the network. This saves local disk space. OS/2 2.1 saves program references created this way across system restarts. You may occasionally see a network program reference object with a broken link icon. This indicates that the server, or network directory, is offline or the application no longer exists on the network.

You can also create a shadow of a data file on the network on your Desktop folder to save local disk space. Some operations on the file may be prohibited because the network directory is read-only. OS/2 2.1 displays an error message if there is a problem.

When you access any of these network objects such as folders, data files, or program references, OS/2 2.1 automatically prompts you to provide a login if required. This means that you can let the system worry about when you need to provide user ID and password authorizations.

Assigning Drive Letters

You can assign a drive letter, such as E: or Z:, to the network directory by selecting Assign drive from the pop-up menu. OS/2 2.1 displays another dialog window, shown in Figure 5.36, consisting of a list of available drive letters. This list does not include any drive letters already assigned to other network directory objects or local drives. The drive assignment is equivalent to doing an IBM LAN Server `NET USE` command, or a Novell NetWare `MAP` command. You can find the current drive assignment for a network directory object on the Network status settings page. When you assign a drive, OS/2 2.1 also adds a drives object to the Drives folder.

This drive assignment is important in two circumstances:

1. You are loading an application from a network directory. Some applications load extra files such as DLLs and expect to find them in a certain place. When OS/2 2.1 loads the application, it uses a universal naming convention (UNC) path. This may cause a problem. One solution is to assign a drive. Another solution is to store your applications in a few folders and add the UNC paths for these folders to the `LIBPATH` and `DPATH` statements in CONFIG.SYS.

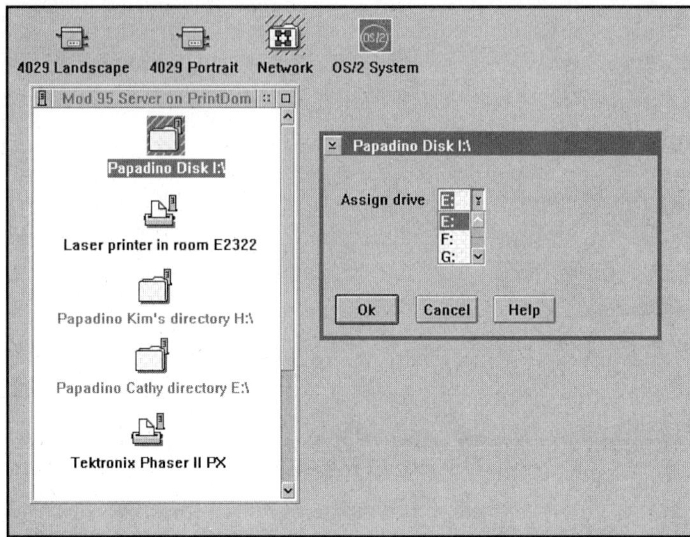

Figure 5.36. The Assign drive dialog.

For best performance, the UNC path should be added to the end of the `LIBPATH` or `DPATH` statement.

2. You are loading a data file into an application. Many applications understand UNC paths for data files. Some do not understand the UNC naming convention, however, and you need to assign a drive to the network directory object that contains the data file.

You can remove the drive assignment using the Unassign Drive option on the network directory object's pop-up menu. OS/2 2.1 also removes the appropriate drive object from the Drives folder.

You can use the `CONNECTIONS` option in the `AUTOSTART` statement in CONFIG.SYS to ensure that OS/2 2.1 maintains assigned drives each time you restart the system.

You can delete a network directory object. This is especially useful when OS/2 2.1 indicates that the network directory is no longer available using the grayed icon and you want to delete it.

A network directory has settings pages similar to a folder object. OS/2 2.1 adds a Network Status page, shown in Figure 5.37, to describe the status of the network directory. OS/2 2.1 uses the Assigned drive field to indicate the drive to which this network directory is assigned.

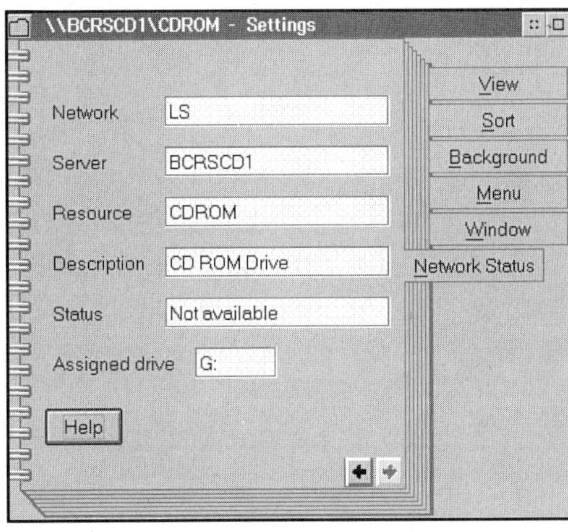

Figure 5.37. The Network Status settings page.

Accessing Network Directories on Other Domains or Networks

You can access network directory objects on other domains, or in other networks, in two different ways:

1. Add the IBM LAN Server domain names to the `othdomain` statement in your IBMLAN.INI file.
2. Select Access another on the pop-up menu of any network directory object.

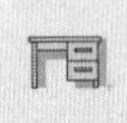

If you use the first method, the servers and network directory objects are accessible through the Network folder as usual.

The second method presents an Access another network directory dialog, shown in Figure 5.38. You can select the network and enter the name of the server and network directory you want to access. The dialog also provides drop-down list boxes that show objects that are accessible. You can use Access another to access a DOS server and network directory.

After you enter valid names and select OK, OS/2 2.1 adds the server object to the network group, if required, and adds the network directory object to the server. OS/2 2.1 puts a shadow of the network directory object on the desktop.

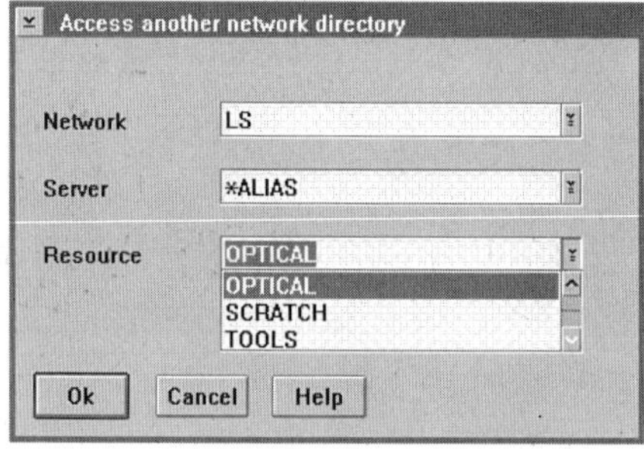

Figure 5.38. Accessing another network directory object.

Network Printer Object

A network printer object represents a network printer on a given server. Network printer objects are similar to local printer objects. You can learn more about network printers in Chapter 12, "The Printing Subsystem."

Login and Logout

You may need to log in for network groups, servers, network directory objects, and network printer objects. You may also need to log in for folder, data file, or program reference objects that reference objects held in a network directory.

The general term *login* includes IBM LAN Server's `LOGON` command and Novell NetWare's `LOGIN` command.

If an object requires login, OS/2 2.1 implicitly logs it in when you open or connect to the object. A login dialog, shown in Figure 5.39, prompts you for a user ID and password. The network may provide a default user ID that you can change. If the log in fails, OS/2 2.1 displays an error message and gives you another chance to log in. There is no limit to the number of times you may try to log in. When you have successfully logged in, OS/2 2.1 displays a confirmation dialog.

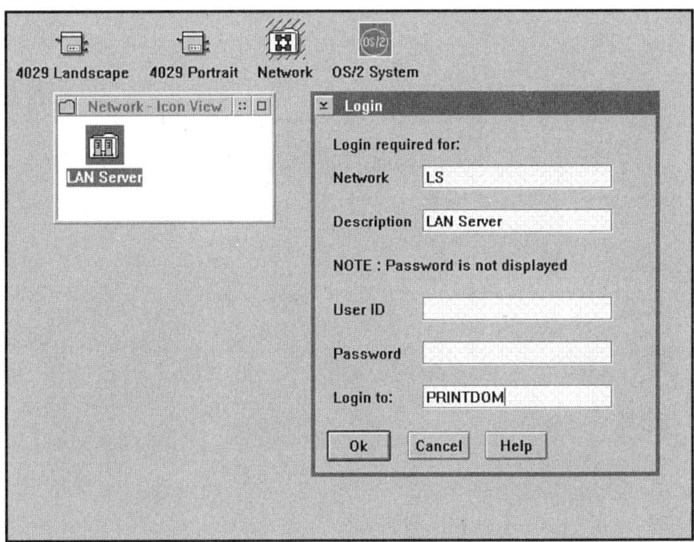

Figure 5.39. Login dialog for LAN Server network group object.

The network object provides three levels of login authorization:

network group	Normally used by IBM LAN Server.
server	Normally used by Novell NetWare. Also used by IBM LAN Server for password-protected resources on a server.
resource	Not currently used.

NOTE

When you log in to IBM LAN Server, it may also start the LAN Requester on your system and display some additional messages.

You can also explicitly log in using the Login item on the pop-up menu of any network object. You will not normally need to use this menu action. OS/2 2.1 provides the log in menu item for operations and programs outside the Workplace Shell and it is a convenient method of having a network-independent method for login.

You can also choose to log in by adding the appropriate network commands to a command file in your Startup folder or to the STARTUP.CMD command file.

You can log out from an object using the Logout item on the pop-up menu of a network object. OS/2 2.1 displays a confirmation dialog that shows the level of logout. This is useful because logging out from one object may imply that you have logged out from all levels of network objects. OS/2 2.1 displays the Logout menu item independent of the method you used to log in. For example, you could use the LAN Server `LOGON` command in STARTUP.CMD and then see the Logout menu item on the Lan Server network group object.

OS/2 2.1 shows either Login or Logout, but not both, on the pop-up menu of any network object.

Author Bio

David A. Kerr is an Advisory Programmer with the OS/2 development team in Boca Raton, Florida. He joined IBM in 1985 at the Hursley Laboratories, England, where he worked on the design and implementation of the GDDM-OS/2 Link product. In 1989 he joined the Presentation Manager Team in the technical planning office and moved into the OS/2 planning department in Boca Raton the following year. His broad knowledge of all aspects of the internals of OS/2 has earned him the recognition as an expert on the Presentation Manager and a position as a key member in the OS/2 design team. He frequently speaks at conferences and seminars for OS/2 customers and developers in Europe, Australia, the Far East, and America. David holds a BSc in Computer Science and Electronics from the University of Edinburgh, Scotland.

Configuring the Workplace Shell

In This Chapter

In Chapter 4, "The Workplace Shell," and Chapter 5, "Workplace Shell Objects," you learned the features of the Workplace Shell. There are also a number of configuration options that you can use to change the behavior of the shell. In this chapter you will learn each of them and how you can create new desktops with the `MAKEINI` command.

CONFIG.SYS Settings

When OS/2 2.1 initializes, it reads the system configuration file, CONFIG.SYS, in the root directory of your boot drive. The Workplace Shell uses statements in this file to control how it operates, what other files it may need to use, and in what directories to search for information.

In most cases you will already have a line in your CONFIG.SYS file that exactly matches each of the settings covered here. In one or two cases, the file does not include a statement and the Workplace Shell uses a built-in default.

This section assumes that you installed OS/2 2.1 on the C: drive. If you installed it on another drive, be sure to use the correct boot drive when you edit the CONFIG.SYS file.

The OS/2 Shell

The `PROTSHELL` statement tells OS/2 2.1 what program you want to use as the protect mode shell, the application that determines what your user interface looks like, and how it operates. The program that you specify here is the very first application started by OS/2 2.1, and it executes in a special process known as the shell process. Note the following default configuration statement:

```
PROTSHELL=C:\OS2\PMSHELL.EXE
```

The default, PMSHELL.EXE, does nothing other than initialize OS/2 Presentation Manager when it executes in the shell process. The Workplace Shell dynamic link library (DLL) contains all the code for the Workplace user interface, and this is called during Presentation Manager initialization. You could specify any application program as the protect mode shell because OS/2 2.1 automatically initializes the Workplace DLL when this program initializes. If you do change this statement, remember two rules for the program that you are using:

1. It should be a Presentation Manager program. If it is not, the Workplace Shell is not initialized and you will not be able to run any Presentation Manager or Workplace Shell applications.

2. It must never terminate. If the program ends, you will not be able to use your system until you restart OS/2 2.1.

You should not change this statement unless you are replacing it with a program designed to work as an OS/2 2.1 user interface shell. If you do choose to do this, you must also modify the AUTOSTART statement (described later in this chapter).

Following the name of the program, you can provide any parameters that you want to pass into the program. For example, you could give the name of a configuration file.

The Workplace Shell Process

When the program specified in the PROTSHELL statement initializes, OS/2 2.1 also starts another process in which to run the actual Workplace Shell. You specify what program runs in this process with the SET RUNWORKPLACE statement. If the program you specify in the PROTSHELL statement is a Presentation Manager program, OS/2 2.1 always starts up this second process known as the Workplace process. You can control what features of the shell start within the Workplace process using the AUTOSTART statement described in the following section. Note the following default configuration statement:

```
SET RUNWORKPLACE=C:\OS2\PMSHELL.EXE
```

The default program executed by OS/2 2.1 in the Workplace process is the same as that executed in the shell process, PMSHELL.EXE. This program, however, is smart: it can tell which process it is executed on and it behaves differently in each case. When executing on the Workplace process, it immediately calls a function in the Workplace Shell dynamic link library that causes the Workplace user interface to start.

If you change this statement so that it does not execute PMSHELL.EXE, the Workplace Shell will not start. Worse, the application programming interfaces provided by the Workplace dynamic link library will not be available to any other applications.

The only circumstances under which you may change this are when you are debugging a Workplace Shell object class that you are writing. In this case, put the name of a debugger, or CMD.EXE, on the `RUNWORKPLACE` statement. If you use CMD.EXE (the OS/2 command line), you should run a debugger only from there. The application to debug is always PMSHELL.EXE, and you can set a break point at the entry to your object's dynamic link library.

You should not change the `RUNWORKPLACE` statement for any other purpose.

Starting Workplace Shell Components

When the Workplace Shell initializes on the Workplace process, it examines the `AUTOSTART` statement to decide which components of the shell to initialize. Note the following default configuration statement:

```
SET AUTOSTART=PROGRAMS,TASKLIST,FOLDERS,CONNECTIONS
```

There are four possible parameters that you can specify:

`PROGRAMS` You can use this to control whether application programs that were executing when you last shutdown OS/2 2.1 are restarted for you

	automatically each time OS/2 2.1 starts. This setting only controls object classes of `WPProgram` or `WPProgramFile`.
`TASKLIST`	This parameter enables the OS/2 window list (sometimes also known as the task list) that appears when you press Ctrl-Esc on the keyboard or click both mouse buttons on the desktop.
`FOLDERS`	This parameter opens the desktop folder. Because the desktop is a work area, all other Workplace folders, objects, or applications (see `PROGRAMS`) that were running when you shutdown the desktop restart as well.
`CONNECTIONS`	This parameter restores any network connections in use the last time you shutdown OS/2 2.1.

Removing the `PROGRAMS` setting causes the shell to open every object type that was open when you shutdown OS/2 2.1 (except application programs). Contrast this with the `RESTARTOBJECTS` statement described in the next section.

You cannot set `PROGRAMS` without also setting `FOLDERS` because the Desktop folder must open before the Workplace Shell attempts to start any other object type. Also, any program in your Startup folder is not affected by the `PROGRAMS` setting—a program in this folder always executes unless you use the `RESTARTOBJECTS` statement to prevent the program from executing.

If you replace the OS/2 2.1 shell with another application program, using the `PROTSHELL` statement, you will probably also want to modify the `AUTOSTART` statement as well. If you do not remove the `FOLDERS` option, you will have all of the Workplace Shell as well as the application program you specified!

Restarting Applications and Objects

A feature of the Workplace Shell is to reopen all folders, objects, and application programs that you were using the last time you shutdown OS/2 2.1. This ensures that your system starts in the same state that it was in when you ended your last session. By default there is no statement in your configuration file; if there was, it would look like the following line:

```
SET RESTARTOBJECTS=YES
```

You may not like the default behavior, in which case you can add this statement to your CONFIG.SYS file to control how the Workplace Shell starts previously executing applications. Note the following recognized parameters:

`YES`	This parameter is the default. All application programs and objects restart when the Workplace Shell initializes, depending on the settings of the `AUTOSTART` statement.
`NO`	If you specify this parameter, nothing other than the Desktop folder starts when the Workplace Shell initializes.
`STARTUPFOLDERSONLY`	If you specify this parameter, only those folders, objects, or applications that are in the Startup folder restart. You can put shadows of objects into the Startup folder.
`REBOOTONLY`	You can include this parameter in addition to any of the preceding parameters. It causes objects and applications to restart only if the Workplace Shell is initializing after you

switched on your system, or reset the system with Ctrl-Alt-Del. The objects will not restart if the Workplace Shell restarts as a result of its own internal error correcting process (see "How the Workplace Shell Protects Itself—and You" later in this chapter).

If you dislike having all your applications restarted when OS/2 2.1 initializes, you can use this statement in your CONFIG.SYS file:

```
SET RESTARTOBJECTS= STARTUPFOLDERSONLY, REBOOTONLY
```

If you do not have the FOLDERS option set in the AUTOSTART statement, the Workplace Shell does not open the Desktop folder and therefore does not open anything else. In this case, the shell ignores the RESTARTOBJECTS statement.

Setting the Object Snooze Time

The object snooze time setting is useful if you are programming your own Workplace Shell objects. Because you cannot overwrite your object's DDL when it is in use by the Workplace Shell, you need a way to have the shell unload the DLL as quickly as possible. Setting the snooze value to a short time period causes the shell to quickly unload the DLL after you close your object. There is no default configuration statement; if there was, it would look like the following statement:

```
SET OBJECTSNOOZETIME=90
```

Because the process of awakening an object from its dormant state accesses the hard disk, it is better not to set this value to a short time period. The default setting for the snooze time is 90 seconds. Unless you are developing your own Workplace Shell objects, you should not change this.

Turning Off the Shell's Error Handler

This is useful only if you are writing your own Workplace Shell object and debugging or testing your object's DLL. You can add the following configuration statement:

```
SET SHELLEXCEPTIONHANDLER=OFF
```

Normally, the Workplace Shell has its own internal exception handler that deals with fatal errors that might cause the shell to terminate. This is useful for normal operation, but when you are developing and debugging your own objects, you want to see all the errors as they occur. When you turn the shell's exception handler off, OS/2 2.1 catches all fatal errors in its main hard error handler and you see them occur in the hard error pop up.

Debugging a Workplace Shell object is the only time you want to add this statement to CONFIG.SYS to turn off the Workplace Shell's exception handler.

Master Help Index and Glossary Database

You tell OS/2 2.1 the location of all online help and glossary files on your computer's hard disk with two configuration statements:

```
SET HELP=C:\OS2\HELP;C:\OS2\HELP\TUTORIAL;
SET GLOSSARY=C:\OS2\HELP\GLOSS;
```

These statements are the `HELP` path and `GLOSSARY` path that OS/2 2.1 uses for two purposes:

1. To locate your application's help file when it is loaded.
2. To locate all online information (used by the Master Help Index and Glossary).

When an application initializes, it may load an online help file. This file is usually the same name as your application's executable file but with an extension of .HLP. OS/2 2.1 first looks in the current directory for the help file; if the file is not there, it searches for it in all the directories specified in the HELP path.

When you install an application in the Workplace Shell, you can specify a Working directory. You should specify the name of the directory that contains all the application's DLLs and help files.

The second, and more important, use for the HELP path is for the Workplace Shell's Master Help Index. When you start the Master Help Index, it searches every directory included in the HELP path and reads the table of contents from every .HLP file that it finds. It then sorts everything alphabetically and you see the contents in a list box on your screen. This is the process that causes the Master Help Index to be so slow to open the first time you access it. The section "Adding to the Master Help Index" in Chapter 4 tells you how you can use this to add other applications' help to the Master Index.

The GLOSSARY path is very similar to the previous one. It tells OS/2 2.1 what directories to search when opening the OS/2 2.1 online glossary of terms. Like help files, online glossary files have a filename extension of .HLP.

User and System Initialization Files

These statements specify the name of the user initialization file and system initialization file that OS/2 2.1 uses as default. Note the following configuration statements:

```
SET USER_INI=C:\OS2\OS2.INI
SET SYSTEM_INI=C:\OS2\OS2SYS.INI
```

The user file contains information about all the fonts installed, colors that you are using, the default printer, and any other configuration information that the Workplace Shell, and other applications, may save there.

The system file contains information about your system configuration—for example, installed printer drivers, serial and parallel ports, and other machine-specific information.

The system initialization file holds information that is specific to your computer system—for example, installed hardware and files. The user initialization file holds information that is more personal and could change among users (such as colors and fonts).

You can change the `USER_INI` statement to point to a different file. This can be useful if a single machine is shared between multiple users.

Identifying the Command-Line Processor

This statement tells the Workplace Shell what program to execute as the OS/2 2.1 command-line processor. Note the following default configuration statement:

```
SET OS2_SHELL=C:\OS2\CMD.EXE
```

This is the program that the Workplace Shell starts each time you ask for an OS/2 command line. If you change this statement to another executable program, it starts each time instead.

Replacing the Workplace Shell

You can replace the Workplace Shell with any other application program of your choice. This is not a common requirement, but it is very useful if you

want to create a system that in some way restricts users to a limited set of functions.

Although it is unlikely that you will want to do this, if you are an administrator for a large number of OS/2 2.1 systems, you may have a need to replace the shell with one especially developed for you.

If you use applications in the banking or travel industry, for example, you may want to ensure that your users can run only your applications. This is useful because it can protect you from problems caused by users who are not familiar with computer systems. These users could accidentally start another application and not know how to get back to your application. From within your application you can start other applications.

There are three steps you need to take to replace the Workplace Shell with a program of your choice. Edit the CONFIG.SYS file as follows:

1. Change the `PROTSHELL` statement to specify the path and name of your program.
2. Change the `SET AUTOSTART=` statement to delete all the parameters except `TASKLIST`.

If you want to try this, you can use the OS/2 System Editor as an example. Change your CONFIG.SYS file to include the following statements. This causes only the OS/2 System Editor to execute.

```
PROTSHELL=C:\OS2\E.EXE C:\CONFIG.SYS
SET AUTOSTART=TASKLIST
```

The OS/2 System Editor is a good choice with which to experiment because the next thing that you have to do is edit the CONFIG.SYS file again! You need some way of resetting CONFIG.SYS back to using the PMSHELL.EXE program. Don't forget to change the `AUTOSTART` statement too.

It is also possible, using this method, to have an OS/2 command line started as the only executing process. To implement this, set the `PROTSHELL` statement to point at the command processor, CMD.EXE.

If you select the command processor as your primary shell process, the first Presentation Manager application that you execute becomes the shell process. If you run PMSHELL.EXE, the Workplace Shell starts.

The OS2.INI and OS2SYS.INI Files

The OS2.INI and OS2SYS.INI files are probably the most critical system files in OS/2 2.1. The Workplace Shell saves a great deal of object information in these files, as well as in extended attributes. OS2.INI holds most of the object information for the shell. The printer objects also hold some information in the OS2SYS.INI file. This section discusses some of the contents of the OS2.INI file, how OS/2 2.1 creates it, and how you can create your own.

Contents

The OS2.INI file contains information on all `WPAbstract` object types including their locations and icons. In addition, the Workplace Shell uses it to hold information on application associations, by file type and by filename filters, along with a list of all file types recognized by the Workplace Shell.

When OS/2 2.1 starts for the first time on your computer, it looks into the OS2.INI file for information on how to build your desktop, folders, and objects.

The OS2.INI file is not plain text, and you cannot view or edit it with a text editor. Instead, you need to use a special program to read and write from these files. Alternatively, you can use simple REXX commands to view or edit the contents. Chapter 15, "REXX Programming," discusses this in more detail.

You can index into the contents of an INI file with two keys: an application name and a key name within each of these. Under each application and key name pair is binary data representing the information being held there by the Workplace Shell, or any other Presentation Manager application.

The shell holds association filename filters under the application name of PMWP_ASSOC_FILTER. Each key name represents the filename filter—for example, *.TXT. The data held represents the handles of all program reference objects that have associations for the name filter.

In this section, when application and key names are given, upper- and lowercase is significant. Some application and key names are all uppercase, others are mixed case. It is important to use the names accurately.

The shell holds association file types under the application name PMWP_ASSOC_TYPE. Each key name represents the file type. Listing 6.1 shows an example REXX command to list all the types.

Listing 6.1. An example REXX command to list file types.

```
/* LISTINI.CMD List all keys for an application name */
/* (c) Copyright IBM Corp. 1992, All rights reserved */
Call RxFuncAdd 'SysIni', 'RexxUtil', 'SysIni'
AppName = 'PMWP_ASSOC_TYPE'
Call SysIni 'BOTH', AppName, 'ALL:', 'Keys'
if Result = 'ERROR:' then do
  say 'Error occurred reading INI files.'
end
Do i = 1 to Keys.0
  Say Keys.i
End
Exit
```

You can adapt this REXX program to read other entries in the OS2.INI file.

It is safe to view the contents of the OS2.INI files. Be very careful, however, about writing any changes to the file. OS/2 2.1 is highly dependent on the contents, and a corrupt OS2.INI file can cause the operating system to fail to start correctly.

The contents of the associations in the INI file change as you change program and file associations in a program reference's settings notebook.

There are many other application names used by the Workplace Shell. The following list includes some of the more interesting ones. This is by no means a complete list and only includes those that may be of interest to advanced or REXX users:

`FolderWorkareaRunningObjects`	Key names represent every Work Area folder, and data is the handle of all objects that are open. This is so that when you open, close, or minimize a Work Area folder, Workplace Shell knows which other windows to open, close, or minimize at the same time.
`PM_InstallObject`	This causes the shell to install a new object. It is used only the first time OS/2 2.1 starts on your computer or after you rebuild your INI files (see the following sections).
`PM_DefaultSetup`	This specifies defaults used when the OS/2 2.1 desktop is not the default (see the following sections).
`PM_Abstract:Icons`	Key names are handles of abstract objects on which you have edited the icon. Data is the binary representation of the icon.
`PM_Workplace:Location`	Key names are the identifiers of every object to which the Workplace Shell has assigned a unique

	ID. Note that not all objects may have an ID assigned to them. Knowing the ID for an object is useful when using REXX to create objects. (See Chapter 15 for more information.)
`PM_WorkPlace:Restart`	This holds information on what folders and applications to restart when you start OS/2 2.1.

The format of data held in the OS2.INI file for the preceding entries may be release-dependent. You cannot assume that it remains the same across releases of the OS/2 operating system, and you should not build dependencies on it into any application program you write.

The OS2.INI file also contains a list of all the object classes registered in the Workplace Shell. If you want to list all the classes you should use one of the programming interface calls and not read directly from the INI file (see Listing 6.2).

Listing 6.2. A REXX command to list Workplace object classes.

```
/* LSTCLASS.CMD List all Workplace object classes */
/* (c) Copyright IBM Corp. 1992, All rights reserved */
Call RxFuncAdd 'SysQueryClassList', 'RexxUtil', 'SysQueryClassList'
Call SysQueryClassList 'List'
Say List.0 'classes'
Do i = 1 to List.0
Say List.i
End
Exit
```

The INI.RC File

OS/2 2.1 determines the initial contents of your OS2.INI and OS2SYS.INI file when you first install it on your computer. OS/2 2.1 creates them from two source files, INI.RC and INISYS.RC, with the MAKEINI command. To help you recover from INI file corruption, OS/2 2.1 includes the source files used.

OS/2 2.1 also includes three others that you can use to make your desktop look like Microsoft Windows or OS/2 1.3. You can find the files located in the \OS2 directory on your boot drive:

INI.RC	Creates an original OS2.INI file
SYSINI.RC	Creates an original OS2SYS.INI
OS2_13.RC	Modifies OS2.INI to make your desktop look like OS/2 1.3
OS2_20.RC	Modifies OS2.INI to make your desktop look like OS/2 2.0 (this is the same for OS/2 2.1)
WIN_30.RC	Modifies OS2.INI to make your desktop look like Windows 3.0

These source files contain string tables with keywords to control the contents of the OS2.INI file. Each line in the file consists of three strings held within double quotations. The strings represent the application name, key name, and data for the INI file. OS/2 2.1 generates the INI files by executing the following commands:

```
MAKEINI OS2.INI INI.RC
MAKEINI OS2SYS.INI INISYS.RC
```

You can do this yourself if you need to rebuild OS2.INI, but you must do it after restarting OS/2 2.1 from a disk because the OS/2 operating system locks the INI files when you start OS/2 2.1 from your hard disk.

The MAKEINI command appends (or replaces entries) to your INI file—it does not destroy anything in the file that is not updated by the source .RC file. If you want to completely replace your OS2.INI file, you must create a new INI file and copy it:

```
MAKEINI NEW.INI INI.RC
COPY NEW.INI OS2.INI
```

An alternative to copying the INI file is to change the `SET USER_INI` statement in your CONFIG.SYS file (see "User and System Initialization Files" in this chapter) and restart OS/2 2.1. This is useful because it offers an alternative to restarting OS/2 2.1 from a disk to replace your INI files.

The interesting entries in the INI files are those starting with the string `"PM_InstallObject"`. Each time the Workplace Shell starts it looks for this application name in the INI file and installs all the objects identified by the key names. After installing the object, the shell deletes the entry from the INI file. The following are two examples from the INI.RC file.

```
"PM_InstallObject" "System Clock;WPClock;<WP_CONFIG>"
➥"OBJECTID=<WP_CLOCK>"
"PM_InstallObject" "Keyboard;WPKeyboard;<WP_CONFIG>"
➥"OBJECTID=<WP_KEYB>"
```

The key name identifies the name for the object being created, its object class (see Chapter 5, "Workplace Shell Objects," Table 5.1), and its location. The location can be either an object identifier (held within angle brackets) or a path name on your hard disk (a question mark represents your boot drive).

The preceding example creates the system clock and keyboard setup objects with classes of `WPClock` and `WPKeyboard`, respectively. They are located in the folder object with an identifier of `<WP_CONFIG>`. The third string, representing data being placed into the INI file, holds the setup string. The example simply sets the object's identity, but the string can contain any of the setup parameters recognized by the Workplace Shell. Chapter 15 describes all the setup strings. You can see some of them in use by looking at the OS2_20.RC file on your hard disk.

Making the Desktop Look Like Windows

If you have used Microsoft Windows, you may find it difficult to get used to the OS/2 2.1 default desktop. It is possible, however, to configure the desktop to look more like Windows or even like OS/2 1.3.

Although you can make the desktop look more familiar, this does not take away any of the functions available to you from the Workplace Shell.

To make your desktop look more familiar to you, rebuild the OS2.INI file with the `MAKEINI` command. To do this you must first restart OS/2 2.1 from the installation disk.

1. Restart OS/2 2.1 from the installation disk.
2. Enter Disk 1 and, when prompted, exit from the welcome screen by pressing Esc.
3. Change to the \OS2 directory on the normal boot drive and enter the following command:

   ```
   MAKEINI OS2.INI WIN_30.RC
   ```

4. Restart OS/2 2.1.

To return to the OS/2 desktop look, repeat this process and use the OS2_20.RC file. There is also an OS2_13.RC file that creates a desktop similar to the one offered by OS/2 1.3.

When you create either the OS/2 1.3 or the Windows desktop look, it becomes your default desktop but it does not erase the old one. The Workplace Shell creates a shadow icon on your new desktop so you can access the old one.

Creating Your Own Desktop

You can edit the .RC files used in the previous section to create your own customized desktop. This technique may be useful if you need to create a similar setup for a number of OS/2 2.1 users. You can, for example, remove objects from the desktop or any folder or change their locations and settings.

Use one of the three .RC files that OS/2 2.1 provides for the Windows, OS/2 desktop, and OS/2 1.3 looks and change them to suit your own needs. You can add or remove keywords from the settings strings.

OS/2 2.1 uses the identities <WP_DESKTOP>, <WP1.3_DESKTOP>, and <WPWIN_DESKTOP>. You can use these to create a shadow pointing back to one of the OS/2 desktops from your own desktop.

If you give your new desktop the identity <WP_DESKTOP>, it replaces the existing desktop. If you use any other identity, you need to ensure that the PM_DefaultSetup statement in the .RC file points to your desktop. The following series of commands from the .RC file may be used to set the default desktop:

```
"PM_DefaultSetup" "ACTIVEDESKTOP" "<WP1.3_DESKTOP>"
"PM_DefaultSetup" "GROUPFOLDER"   "<WP1.3_DSKMGR>"
"PM_DefaultSetup" "GROUPVIEW"     "ICONVIEW=NONFLOWED,NORMAL"
"PM_DefaultSetup" "ICONVIEW"      "FLOWED,MINI"
"PM_DefaultSetup" "TREEVIEW"      "MINI"
"PM_DefaultSetup" "OPEN"          "<WP1.3_DSKMGR>,<WP1.3_MAIN>"
"PM_DefaultSetup" "MINWIN"        "DESKTOP"
"PM_DefaultSetup" "HIDEBUTTON"    "NO"
```

If you have multiple desktops installed, ACTIVEDESKTOP identifies which one the Workplace Shell should start as the default. Other statements in this example set the default behavior for minimized windows, folder views, and objects that open automatically with the desktop.

The layout of the .RC files is critical. If you edit one for your own needs, don't remove any of the header information from the top of the file. It is safe to remove only lines from the blocks of PM_InstallObject.

Threads of the Workplace Shell

Like most well-written OS/2 Presentation Manager applications, the Workplace Shell includes a number of separate threads. The shell is structured to include a primary input thread, a number of tasking threads that carry out most

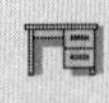

of the actual work, and some specialist threads responsible for managing specific areas of the shell.

User Input and Tasking Threads

Whenever you move your mouse, press a button, or type on the keyboard, OS/2 2.1 sends a message to the primary user input thread. This thread interprets the message and decides what course of action you are requesting. The shell sends the actual work to be performed to a tasking thread for completion. For example, when you try to move or copy many objects at once, a tasking thread performs the operation. This allows you to continue working with the Workplace Shell, or other applications, while the operation completes. You do not have to wait for the move or copy to finish.

In many cases you can even interrupt an operation that is in progress. You can do this from the progress indication dialog box that appears for lengthy operations.

The progress indication dialog appears by default. You can turn it off from the system settings object.

Specialist Threads

The Workplace Shell assigns specific housekeeping tasks to other threads. The file system notification thread receives messages from the OS/2 file systems whenever you copy, move, or rename a file on your hard disk that represents an object on your desktop or any other folder. This ensures that the Workplace Shell keeps up with any changes you make to a file from the command line. Workplace uses a separate thread to receive the message so that it is always ready to respond and, therefore, does not slow down file system operations.

The shell uses a lazy writer thread whenever it needs to write information to the OS2.INI or OS2SYS.INI files. These files are a simple database, and access

to them is very slow because of all the integrity-checking built into the INI file. Every time you move, copy, create, or delete objects, the shell may have to update information in the INI file. Because of the perfect save implementation of the settings notebooks, this can be a very frequent operation. So you do not have to wait for the information to write to the INI file, the shell asks this lazy writer thread to do it in the background. Normally, the thread saves this almost immediately but it can take up to ten seconds to complete. This is one of the reasons why it is important to shutdown OS/2 2.1 from the desktop pop-up menu before switching off your computer or restarting OS/2 2.1. The benefits in user responsiveness are very significant.

The Workplace Shell uses other threads to manage the object snooze time, to keep objects asleep for a short period of time after you close them before making them dormant. Again, this significantly improves the responsiveness of the shell to your requests. It is much quicker to obtain object information from system memory than from your hard disk (this happens if the object is dormant).

You may notice, when opening a tree view folder of your hard disk, network object, or the Find dialog, that OS/2 2.1 progressively updates the tree. You see the first level of directories, then the second level appears, or + and - symbols are added to branches of the tree. Again, a background thread reads in the directory structure from your hard disk so you do not have to wait for it to complete—although sometimes you cannot work with the tree, you can work with any other area of the Workplace Shell while the tree is being populated.

How the Workplace Shell Protects Itself—and You

IBM is advertising OS/2 crash protection. This term describes a number of features in OS/2 2.1 designed to ensure that any one application cannot cause an error to occur in OS/2 2.1 that affects any other application, or in any other application itself. The Workplace Shell uses two of these features to protect itself from other applications, and to protect any other application you may be executing from an error inside the shell. Note the following two features:

1. Process-level protection
2. Exception handlers

Process-Level Protection

In the simplest terms, process-level protection ensures that data used by one application is not available to any other application. Each application executes in its own process, and OS/2 2.1 ensures that if one process fails for any reason, its failure does not affect any other process.

By default, multiple WIN-OS/2 window applications all run in a single process, and OS/2 2.1 cannot protect them from other WIN-OS/2 window applications. This is similar to Microsoft Windows. You can ensure that OS/2 2.1 does protect them by selecting Separate session on the Session settings page for your WIN-OS/2 window applications.

OS/2 2.1 arranges processes in a hierarchy, so one process can own several child processes. If the parent process dies, all its children die! When OS/2 2.1 starts, it creates one process, from which all other processes are started. This is the Shell process discussed in "CONFIG.SYS Settings" in this chapter. As you can now see, it is important that this process never terminates for any reason; if it does, every application process executing on OS/2 2.1 terminates with it!

In OS/2 1.3 and Microsoft Windows, this shell process is the user interface application, sometimes known as the Desktop Manager. This can be a fairly complex application which, if it fails for any reason, causes every other application to terminate. On OS/2 2.1, however, the user interface application, the Workplace Shell, does not execute on this shell process. Instead, OS/2 2.1 isolates it in its own process known as the Workplace process, also discussed in "CONFIG.SYS Settings." When you ask the Workplace Shell to start an application, it sends a message to the shell process so that it owns all applications, including the Workplace Shell. If the Workplace Shell should die for any reason, it does not cause any other application to terminate because the Workplace process does not own any child processes.

As an added protection, OS/2 2.1 alerts the shell process should the Workplace process fail. It can then automatically restart it and restore your user interface, usually within 15 to 20 seconds. If the Workplace Shell process should fail, for whatever reason, all other applications—including time-critical and communications-intensive programs—continue unaffected.

It is extremely rare for the Workplace process to fail because of an error in the Workplace Shell. Other application objects, however, also execute on this same process; it is reassuring to know that process-level protection is present. If one of these other application objects causes the shell to terminate, it attempts to restore itself.

Exception Handlers

The Workplace Shell also uses an exception handler to protect itself from fatal errors caused by bad internal handlers or memory pointers. If the Workplace Shell tries to access an illegal memory location or perform any other illegal request, the shell includes its own error handler to respond and recover. Instead of causing the shell to fail and terminate, it records an error code and passes it back to the application, or Workplace object, causing the illegal request.

If you are developing your own Workplace objects, you should disable this internal error handler (see "CONFIG.SYS Settings") while you develop and test your object—this makes it easier to detect errors in your code.

Recovering from Errors

You can use a number of recovery procedures if the Workplace Shell fails for any reason. The most common symptom of failure you may see is that, when restarting OS/2 2.1, your desktop fails to appear and all you see is a blank screen. This is a clear case of failure within the Workplace Shell. This may be because the file system corrupted the extended attributes attached to object files, which can happen if you don't shutdown OS/2 before switching off your computer.

You may see other types of failure caused by an application being restarted automatically by the shell. As you have learned, every application that is running when you shutdown OS/2 2.1 restarts when OS/2 2.1 itself restarts. One of these applications may sometimes cause an error if it is dependent on other applications or network connections that may not be present.

There are three processes to try if you experience either of the symptoms described. Try restarting OS/2 2.1 without starting any of the applications that you were using when you shutdown OS/2 2.1. You can do this in one of two ways:

1. Press and hold the left Ctrl-Shift-F1 keys when you first see the gray screen appear after restarting OS/2 2.1.
2. Edit your CONFIG.SYS file to include the `RESTARTOBJECTS` statement described in "CONFIG.SYS Settings."

The first method is preferable if you only occasionally run into this problem. If it occurs frequently, you should consider the CONFIG.SYS setting.

If your Workplace Shell desktop never appears, your problem is probably a corrupt OS2.INI file. This may occur because you did not shutdown OS/2 2.1 before switching off your computer. There are two methods of recovering from this. One attempts to repair the damage in your OS2.INI file; the other completely replaces the file.

To repair the damage, you need to restart OS/2 2.1 from disk so that the OS2.INI file is not locked. Once you restart OS/2 2.1 from disk, change to the \OS2 directory on the normal boot drive and execute the following command:

```
MAKEINI OS2.INI INI.RC
```

This command reinitializes all Workplace Shell objects. When you restart OS/2 2.1, the Workplace Shell rebuilds all objects and places them into their

default locations. The `MAKEINI` command does not affect any other entries in the OS2.INI file for other applications. The online command reference documents the `MAKEINI` command.

If this fails to recover your Workplace Shell desktop, you need to try completely replacing the CONFIG.SYS, OS2.INI, and OS2SYS.INI files. Restart OS/2 2.1 and, before the first OS/2 2.1 logo appears, press Alt-F1. This causes backup copies of these two files to replace the ones currently in use.

OS/2 2.1 keeps the backup copies of the CONFIG.SYS and INI files in the \OS2\INSTALL directory on the boot drive. Pressing Alt-F1 simply causes OS/2 2.1 to copy from this directory into the root and \OS2 directory.

Because this copy destroys the existing files, you should consider Alt-F1 a last resort. It creates a new active desktop, and you will lose all abstract objects and associations.

You can place your own backup versions of these files into the \OS2\INSTALL directory. The default versions exactly match the files when you first install OS/2 2.1—you will lose all changes you have made if you ever need to recover with this method.

Restoring your own backup copy of OS2.INI may cause you to lose some program references and shadow objects. There may also be problems if there is a mismatch between information in the OS2.INI file and extended attributes. The degree of these problems depends on how much moving, copying, and creating of these object types you have done since backing up OS2.INI. You can usually recover by selecting Refresh from a folder's pop-up menu.

Author Bio

David A. Kerr is an Advisory Programmer with the OS/2 development team in Boca Raton, Florida. He joined IBM in 1985 at the Hursley Laboratories, England, where he worked on the design and implementation of the GDDM-OS/2 Link product. In 1989 he joined the Presentation Manager team in the technical planning office and moved into the OS/2 planning department in Boca Raton the following year. His broad knowledge of all aspects of the internals of OS/2 has earned him the recognition as an expert on the Presentation Manager and a position as a key member in the OS/2 design team. He frequently speaks at conferences and seminars for OS/2 customers and developers in Europe, Australia, the Far East, and America. David holds a BSc in Computer Science and Electronics from the University of Edinburgh, Scotland.

7

Command-Line Interface

In This Chapter

The command-line interface in OS/2 2.1 remains virtually unchanged from previous versions. It looks and feels much like the standard DOS interface. It is most useful for quick administrative tasks and command file programs. The command-line interface is consistent across many platforms including UNIX and Windows NT. The concepts are shared, but the syntax may differ. In any case, one or more text commands are entered and the results are displayed in a scrolling character window. This window can be the entire screen or a sizable window. Many commands are provided for system and disk administration, program control, problem determination, and user customization. Many network, development, system, and shareware utilities are coded as character applications and require knowledge of the command-line interface.

The default command processor in OS/2 is CMD.EXE. It is a small program located in the OS2 directory that knows several common commands, called internal commands, by heart. When a text line is entered at the command prompt, CMD.EXE accepts the input and parses the text. If the action verb (`DIR`, for example) matches an internal command, it is executed and passed any additional text on the line as parameters. These parameters are interpreted by the internal routine.

Other OS/2 system utilities are stored as .EXE files in the OS2 directory and are referred to as external commands. If the command is not internal, the specified or current directory is searched for a matching program with a .COM, .EXE, .CMD, or .BAT extension. If needed, this search continues for each directory listed in the environment `PATH` variable. If a matching program is found, it is started in the appropriate session type and the additional text passed as parameters. If no matches are found, an error message is displayed. The command processor can also parse multiple commands stored in a text file. These batch files are interpreted one line at a time and have simple conditional logic. Grouping often-used commands in this fashion can help automate repetitive tasks such as backup or file maintenance.

There are several special considerations that make command-line expertise valuable. System maintenance often requires booting with a floppy. Commands can be executed from the boot floppy or hard drive but are limited to the command line. Presentation Manager programs like the Workplace Shell are inoperable. Sometimes this type of configuration is useful for security or performance reasons. The `PROTSHELL` option in CONFIG.SYS can be changed to a command processor like CMD.EXE. The system then boots into a command line which requires fewer resources than the Workplace Shell. This helps optimize memory and thread resources for a file or database server. There are also boot options provided by the command line. Dual boot with DOS is initiated by the `BOOT` command and Multi-Boot is started with SETBOOT.

If you change the `PROTSHELL` to something other than a PM program, you won't have the PM interface. In addition, you will only have a single character base session.

Managing Command Windows

Most users prefer to start with the Workplace Shell. Inside the OS/2 System folder is another folder called Command Prompts shown in Figure 7.1. This typically includes objects for OS/2 and DOS command prompts, the full-screen WINOS2 session, DOS from drive A, and dual boot.

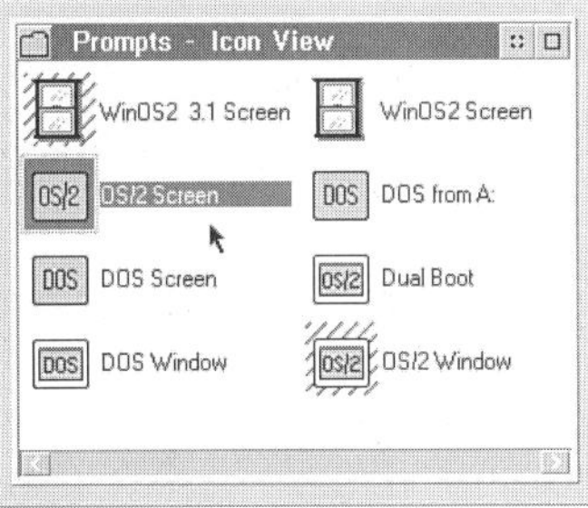

Figure 7.1. The Command Prompts folder.

The two objects of interest are OS/2 screen (full screen) and OS/2 Window. Both provide a command-line interface using the same commands; the full-screen option has faster video. The window option can be sized, positioned, minimized, and have its font changed. It can also partake in

cut-and-paste operations with the Workplace clipboard. The latter is preferred for most interactive operations because of its flexibility. The full-screen option is required by some programs that limit console activity.

Opening the full-screen object switches the display to character mode. A help line is printed on the top of the screen suggesting the method for returning to the Workplace Shell. The screen in Figure 7.2 is very familiar to a DOS user but limited in functionality.

```
 OS/2        Ctrl+Esc = Window List         Type HELP = help
 Directory of C:\

WINDOWS      <DIR>       9-26-92   2:41p
SPOOL        <DIR>       9-29-92   9:48p
DOS          <DIR>       9-26-92   2:56p
OS2LDR         32768     9-04-92   1:11p
OS2KRNL       715744     9-09-92   4:36p
CDROM        <DIR>       9-29-92   7:33p
OS2          <DIR>       9-29-92   9:13p
PSFONTS      <DIR>       9-29-92   9:24p
README        146144     8-14-92  12:50p
NOWHERE      <DIR>       9-29-92   9:48p
NOWHERE1     <DIR>       9-29-92   9:51p
WINOS231     <DIR>      10-04-92   8:06a
QE           <DIR>      10-04-92   5:04p
IBMCOM       <DIR>      10-04-92  12:13p
IBMLAN       <DIR>      10-04-92  12:23p
MUGLIB       <DIR>      10-04-92  12:26p
40S2         <DIR>      10-05-92   7:11a
MITNOR       <DIR>      10-22-92   9:41p
        18 file(s)      894656 bytes used
                      12980224 bytes free

[C:\]_
```

Figure 7.2. *The OS/2 full-screen command interface.*

Pressing Ctrl-Esc will switch back to the Workplace Shell with the OS/2 Screen session highlighted in the Window List. Selecting this Window List option will return again to the full-screen session. The other, less exact method is to press Alt-Esc, which switches to the next active program. This may be the Workplace Shell, a WINOS2 session, or another full-screen command-line session. Full-screen sessions are closed by typing `EXIT` on the command line, by selecting Close from the session pop-up Menu in the Window List, or by selecting Close from the minimized icon if you have selected minimized windows.

The Close option ends a session abruptly. If there is a program running in the window, it will not have a chance to save information or close files. Use this option with care.

With a few exceptions, OS/2 window sessions can run the same programs as a full-screen session, and they do this with enhanced functionality and control. The Workplace Shell presents the sizable window in Figure 7.3 with the command-line characters printed in a graphic font.

```
OS/2 Window
WINDOWS        <DIR>       9-26-92  14:41
WINOS231       <DIR>      10-04-92   8:06
autoexec.bak       230    10-04-92   8:24
autoexec.bat       305    10-04-92  14:38
autoexec.syd        74     9-29-92  19:37
config.lap        1968    10-04-92  12:16
config.new         131     9-29-92  20:00
config.ss         2662    10-04-92  16:30
config.sys        3032    10-11-92  16:19
ibmlvl.ini        1025    10-04-92  13:07
os2krnl         715744     9-09-92  16:36
os2ldr           32768     9-04-92  13:11
os2ldr.msg        8440     8-10-92  19:57
readme          146144     8-14-92  12:50
test.cmd            29    10-17-92  14:43
~ins3848.exe    164352    10-04-92  15:29
    1,076,904 bytes in 31 file(s)          1,095,680 bytes all
   12,961,792 bytes free

[c:\]
```

Figure 7.3. The OS/2 Window command interface.

The window usually starts with a title bar, border, system buttons, and horizontal and vertical scroll bars. The scroll bars indicate that some of the command-line information is hidden behind the window. Use these scroll bars to slide the text where appropriate. Maximizing the window as shown in Figure 7.4 removes these scroll bars and allows full viewing of all command-line characters. This can be achieved by clicking the Maximize button, double-clicking the title bar, selecting Maximize from the pop-up menu, or resizing the window to the maximum proportions.

> **TIP**
>
> Hold the Shift key and press the Maximize button or resize the window to maximize the window and all subsequent instances of this object. Position information is also saved.

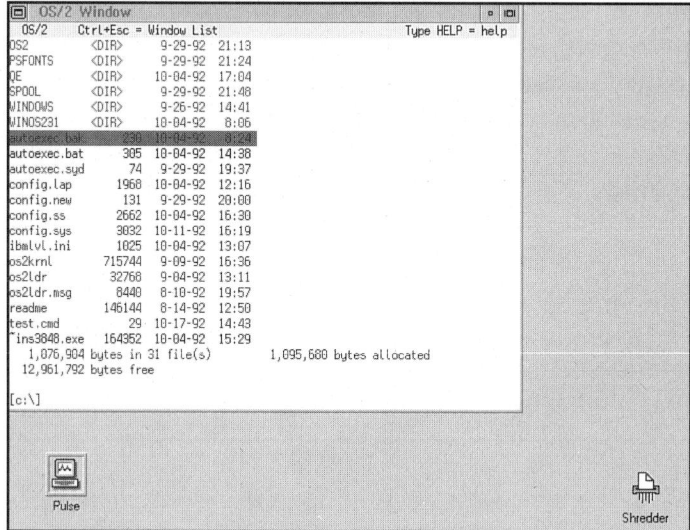

Figure 7.4. The maximized command window.

The window can be minimized by clicking the Minimize button or selecting Minimize from the pop-up menu. Once the window has been minimized, you can reactivate the window by selecting it from the Window List or selecting the original Workplace object. Depending on the settings, the minimized object will also be represented in the Minimized Viewer or on the bottom of the desktop.

> **NOTE**
>
> Depending on the setting of the Window Create New Setting, it is possible that selecting the original Workplace object may open a new instance instead of maximizing it.

Several keystrokes are used to control the command window. Most command activities are keyboard intensive, so these key techniques should be practiced. Ctrl-Esc activates the Window List and Alt-Esc switches to the next session just like the full-screen interface. Alt-Tab switches to the next active Workplace object, which may be a PM program, a folder, or another command window. The Alt key by itself (or F10) activates the pull-down menu for the command window shown in Figure 7.5. This can be tricky when running character-mode applications that rely on the Alt key for other functions. Perseverance and timing will get the desired result.

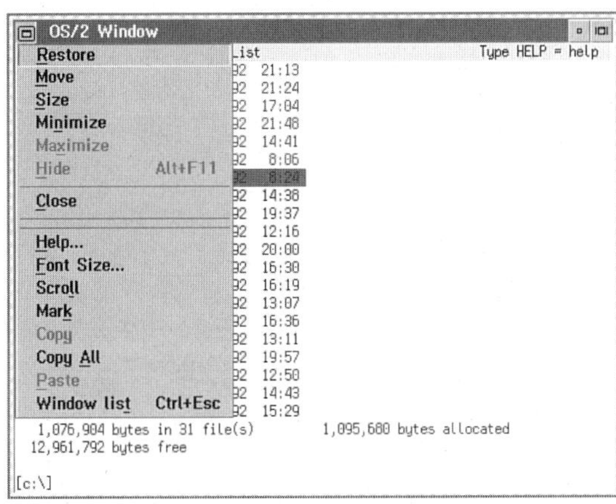

Figure 7.5. Command window pop-up menu.

Another important keyboard technique is scrolling. If the window has scroll bars and some of the text is hidden, press Alt for the pop-up menu and select Scroll. This changes the definition of the arrow keys in the window. The arrows scroll the text within the window instead of performing their normal application assignments. Other keys are unaffected by this setting. The title bar posts a reminder with the word *Scrolling* before the application name. Figure 7.6 shows that the pull-down menu also has a check mark next to the Scroll option. Simply select this option again to cancel scrolling. This scrolling technique is useful when larger fonts are required for presentations or poor video displays.

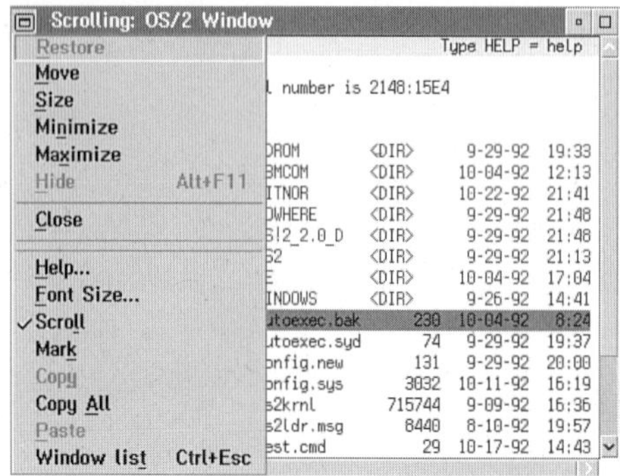

Figure 7.6. Scrolling a command window.

The mouse can handle many of these tasks more efficiently than the keyboard. Scrolling, sizing, minimizing, and maximizing are simple click events. The title bar is used for moving the window. Grab the title with either mouse key and drag to the desired location. Double-clicking the title has the same effect as using the Maximize button. Clicking the title bar icon displays the pop-up menu for the command window.

> NOTE
> This menu is for window control and does not have options for object settings. Those must be changed directly on the Workplace object.

> TIP
> If a command window is at the back of other windows, but its title bar is still visible, you can reposition it without bringing it to the foreground by holding the Ctrl key down while dragging the window.

Double-clicking the title bar icon will close the command window session abruptly. This is the same as selecting Close from the Window List pop-up or selecting Close from the title bar icon menu.

Clipboard interaction is another important advantage for the windowed interface. Any portion of the text window can be marked and copied to the Clipboard. The pop-up menu Mark option is used to initiate a copy. In Figure 7.7, the cursor changes to a reverse video block and the mouse pointer appears as a cropping symbol. Pressing the arrow keys while holding Shift expands the reverse video rectangle. Dragging the mouse while pressing mouse button 1 has the same effect. The operation is completed by pressing Enter or selecting Mark again from the pop-up menu. Cancel the operation by pressing Esc.

```
Marking: OS/2 Window
 OS/2     Ctrl+Esc = Window List                          Type HELP = help
[c:\]dir os2\*.sys

 Volume in drive C is BILL            Serial number is 2148:15E4
 Directory of  c:\os2\*.sys

cdrom.sys       21556   7-15-92  16:07
clock01.sys      3674   8-10-92  22:56
com.sys         24760   8-10-92  22:34
dos.sys          1142   8-10-92  23:11
extdskdd.sys     1634   8-10-92  23:12
kbd01.sys       29013   8-10-92  23:40
log.sys          9514   8-10-92  23:32
mouse.sys       12799   8-10-92  23:57
pclogic.sys      1739   8-11-92   0:01
pmdd.sys         4939   8-11-92   0:05
pointdd.sys      1787   8-10-92  23:53
print01.sys      9046   8-11-92   0:06
screen01.sys     1441   8-11-92   0:10
testcfg.sys      3216   8-11-92   0:47
vdisk.sys         260   8-11-92   0:27
     128,860 bytes in 15 file(s)          143,360 bytes allocated
  12,855,296 bytes free

[c:\]
```

Figure 7.7. Marking a rectangular window area.

Only one rectangular region can be marked at a time. The marked text is stored on the Clipboard and can be viewed or pasted into other applications, including DOS and WINOS2 sessions. A shortcut for copying the entire window contents is the pop-up menu Copy All option. This is equivalent to marking all text for copy. Try a mark or copy and call the system editor by entering `E` at the command prompt. Use the Edit menu Paste option to insert the marked text from the command window into a new document. The result is shown in Figure 7.8.

Figure 7.9 shows the windowed command-line object pop-up menu, which also includes options for Copy All and Paste. These work even when the object is minimized to the desktop. If minimized to the Minimized Window Viewer, these options don't exist.

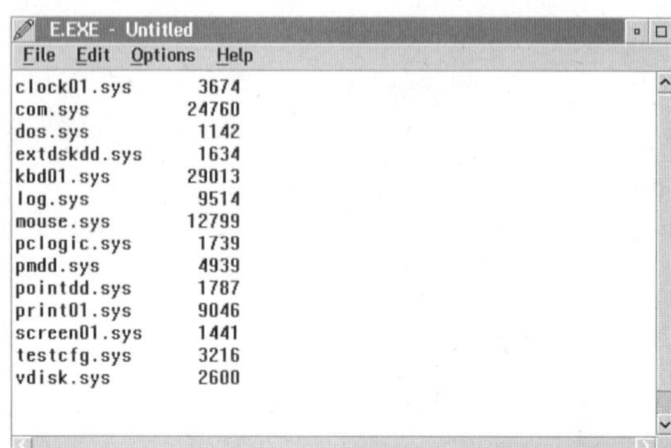

Figure 7.8. Marked command text pasted into an editor.

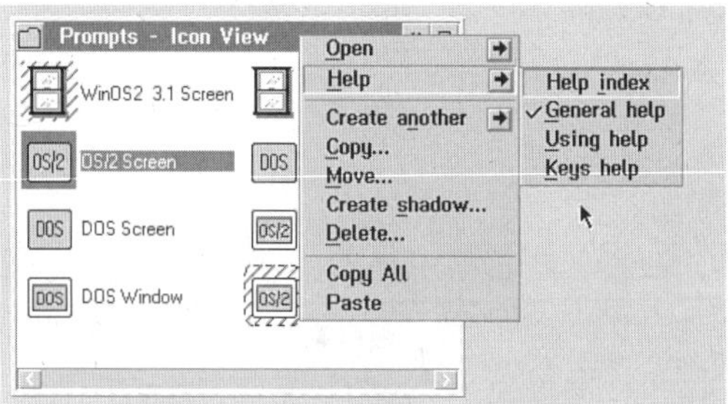

Figure 7.9. Pop-up menu help for command-line objects.

Command windows can accept character input but not bitmap images from other applications. This facility works by filling the keyboard buffer with the current Clipboard characters. These characters are entered into the current application as if they were typed. This is very useful for character applications that have no macro capability or command-line history.

> **NOTE** Full-screen command lines cannot copy or paste text.

Creating New Command Objects

The two command-line objects provided in the Command Prompts folder may not be sufficient. They can be moved to another folder or to the desktop by dragging with mouse button 2 or using the object pop-up menu Move option. They can be deleted by dragging to the shredder or using the pop-up menu option Delete. Shadows are useful for avid command-line users, especially when placed on the desktop. Shadows are created by dragging the object to the desktop while pressing Ctrl and Shift or using the pop-up menu option Create Shadow. Object copies are also a possibility. Several might be created with subtle differences in settings and environment. Copies are created by dragging the object while pressing the Ctrl key or using the pop-up menu option Copy. Once the copy is made, the settings notebook is used to tailor the object.

The default behavior of a command object window depends on the settings notebook option, Object open behavior. This is normally set to Display existing window, which limits you to one command window of each type. In Figure 7.10, change this to Create new window, which causes a new command session to start each time the object is opened.

Every time you open the object with Create new window, you get a new instance of it on the desktop and on the Window List. This can make locating the specific instance difficult.

Starting a new command session every time is not necessary for multiple sessions, however. To provide an extra command window for temporary use, simply copy the object and open it. After closing, shred the object to free desktop resources. The START command can also be used to initiate command sessions and will be discussed in detail later in this chapter.

If permanent copies are desired, use the copy options mentioned previously or the Program template in the Templates folder. This causes a settings notebook to open for program details. Enter an asterisk (*) in the Program page Path and file name. The Session page in Figure 7.11 presents a menu of command types, which includes OS/2 full screen or window.

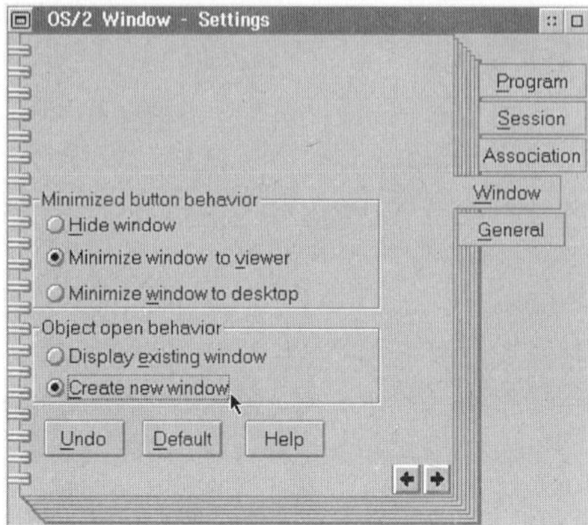

Figure 7.10. Setting the Create new window option.

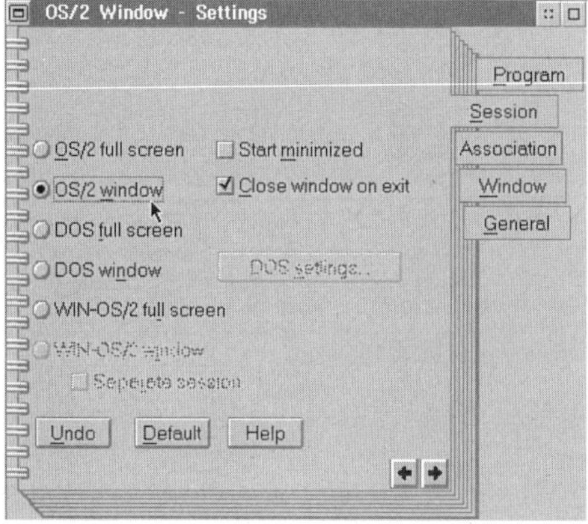

Figure 7.11. Setting the session type for a command object.

The initial path on the Program page can be set as needed. If an alternative command processor is available, enter the full path and filename on the Program page.

Templates can also be used when multiple command-line sessions are needed quickly. Make a copy of a command window object. Use the settings notebook General page Template option to change the object into a template. The object icon will now appear as a pad of paper. Whenever a copy of the template is dragged to a folder or the desktop, a command window starts. The windows in Figure 7.12 are sequentially numbered and inherit the settings of the template.

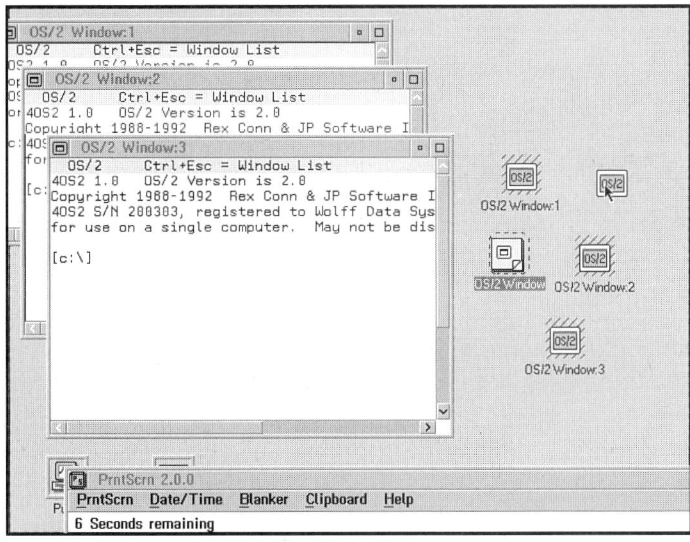

Figure 7.12. Creating multiple sessions from a template.

Customizing Settings

The command window position and size are remembered from one session to another. Whenever the position is changed, the new coordinates are written to the OS2.INI file. Maximized windows always move to the upper-left corner of the screen. A settings notebook option is provided to start a minimized command window. There are no settings to force a maximized command window. This can be achieved using the `START` command from a command session or the STARTUP.CMD file.

Fonts

The font size can be changed in a command window. Several sizes are provided with a dialog box for testing and selecting the appropriate style. Use the pop-up menu Font Size option to call the dialog in Figure 7.13. The Window preview graphic displays the approximate size of the current window on the screen and the Font preview shows a sample of the font.

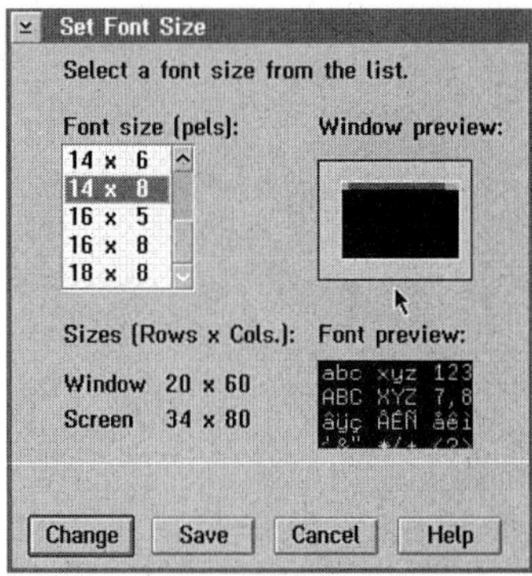

Figure 7.13. The command window Font dialog.

These are system-supplied bitmaps; the additional Adobe Type Manager fonts are not available.

The default Change option sets the font for the active window. Save sets the font for all command windows and writes to the OS2.INI file for use in subsequent sessions. This same font option is also provided for character-based DOS and OS/2 applications that run in windows on the Workplace Shell.

Mode Command

The number of characters in a window can also be set with the `MODE` command. MODE is a multipurpose command that controls device modes. It works with printer ports, serial ports, disks, and console displays. The display options affect the appearance of full-screen and command windows. The monitor can be switched between monochrome and color mode. The characters per line option can be 40, 80, or 132. The latter is available only for XGA adapters and for SVGA if you have the drivers. These numbers may be preceded by CO for color or MO for monochrome. MONO by itself forces an 80-character line. The number of rows can be 25, 43, or 50. These two options can be set independently. For example, to get the maximum text on a color VGA display, enter `MODE CO80, 50`. The result is shown in Figure 7.14.

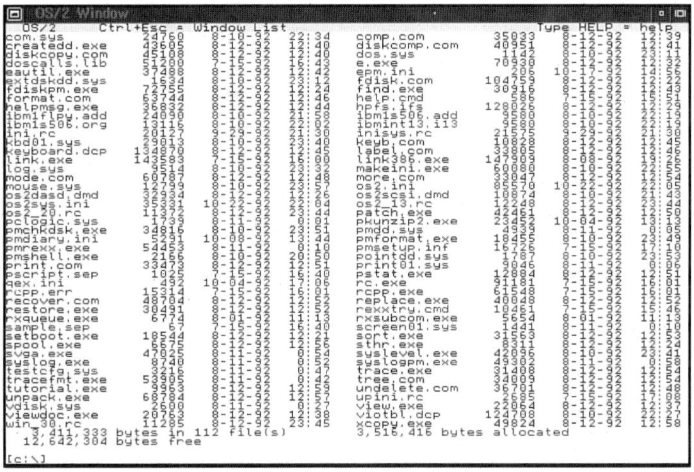

Figure 7.14. MODE CO80, 50 *displays 50 lines of text.*

On an XGA adapter, use `MODE CO132, 50`. MODE MONO is useful for black and white monitors attached to a color display.

Prompt

PROMPT is a key item in the environment table. It defines the characters that begin each command line and usually displays system information. The current drive letter or directory are popular for prompting. The date and time, color changes, nicknames, and other gimmicks are possible. The prompt string is built from ASCII text and several special characters in the form $?, where ? is described in Table 7.1.

Table 7.1. Special prompt characters.

Character	*Description*
`b`	The ¦ character
`c`	The open parenthesis (
`d`	Current date
`e`	The ASCII ESC character (decimal 27)
`f`	The close parenthesis)
`g`	The > character
`h`	BACKSPACE over the previous character
`i`	The default OS/2 line 0 prompt
`l`	The < character
`n`	Default drive letter
`p`	Current disk and directory
`q`	The = character
`r`	The numeric exit code from last command
`s`	The space character
`t`	Current time
`v`	OS/2 version number, in the format: 2.1
`$`	The $ character
`_`	CR/LF (go to beginning of new line)

The SET PROMPT or PROMPT commands can modify the contents of the prompt variable. SET is used to display the variable. Complex prompts are possible by combining the symbols above. A two-line prompt with time and date on top and the path on line 2 might look like this:

```
PROMPT $_$t$h$h$h$s$d$_[$p]$s
```

TIP Use the backspace and space symbols for proper formatting.

Command window colors and fonts can be set for the title bar and border using the Workplace Shell palettes. Oddly enough, these are not saved to the OS2.INI file and must be reset for each session. The color of text in the window is controlled by the built-in ANSI support. This can be set by a utility program or the prompt command. For example, white text on a blue background is set with the following:

```
PROMPT $e[37,44m$i[$p]
```

in which `$e` represents the escape character, `37` the foreground color, and `44` the background color. Note that the prompt command also changes the prompt text, so `$i` is added for the additional help line on the top of the screen and `$p` prints the current path. Table 7.2 lists some color and attribute options.

Table 7.2. ANSI escape attributes.

Code	*Attribute/Color*
0	All attributes off (normal white on black)
1	High intensity (bold)
2	Normal intensity
4	Underline (effective on monochrome displays)
5	Blinking

continues

Table 7.2. continued

Code	*Attribute/Color*
7	Reverse video
8	Invisible
30,40	Black foreground, background
31,41	Red
32,42	Green
33,43	Yellow
34,44	Blue
35,45	Magenta
36,46	Cyan
37,47	White

Settings are cumulative, so set all attributes off, and then set the color, and finally set bold for a bright green foreground:

```
PROMPT $e[0;32;1m$i[$p]
```

Environment

Many of the customization settings for the command line are stored in the session environment. This is an area of memory used to store text strings shared by various applications. These memory variables can be displayed and changed as needed. The `SET` command is used to view and change these strings. `SET` might return Listing 7.1 that follows.

Listing 7.1. Environment variables displayed with *SET*.

```
USER_INI=C:\OS2\OS2.INI
SYSTEM_INI=C:\OS2\OS2SYS.INI
OS2_SHELL=C:\4OS2\4OS2.EXE
AUTOSTART=PROGRAMS,TASKLIST,FOLDERS
RUNWORKPLACE=C:\OS2\PMSHELL.EXE
COMSPEC=C:\4OS2\4OS2.EXE
PATH=C:\OS2;C:\OS2\SYSTEM;C:\OS2\MDOS\WinOS2;C:\OS2\INSTALL;
C:\;C:\OS2\MDOS;C:\OS2\APPS;
DPATH=C:\OS2;C:\OS2\SYSTEM;C:\OS2\MDOS\WinOS2;C:\OS2\INSTALL;
C:\;C:\OS2\BITMAP;C:\OS2\MDOS;C:\OS2\APPS;C:\4OS2;
HELP=C:\OS2\HELP;C:\OS2\HELP\TUTORIAL;
GLOSSARY=C:\OS2\HELP\GLOSS;
KEYS=ON
BOOKSHELF=C:\IBMLAN\BOOK;C:\OS2\BOOK;C:\4OS2;
EPMPATH=C:\OS2\APPS
WORKPLACE__PROCESS=NO
CMDLINE=e
WP_OBJHANDLE=68279
PROMPT=[$p]
```

The USER_INI and SYSTEM_INI are used by the Workplace Shell. The OS2_SHELL item defines the default command processor for command-line sessions. COMSPEC is the command processor called by applications when they shell to the command line. This is rarely used because multiple concurrent sessions are supported in OS/2. BOOKSHELF, HELP, and GLOSSARY are used in the online help system. The PATH settings are important and indicate which directories are searched when an application is started from the command line or the Workplace Shell. New directories can be added to this easily by referencing the current value of PATH in the statement:

```
PATH %PATH%;D:\TEMP;
```

Any environment variable can be referenced in this fashion. This technique is often used in command files and REXX programs, which are discussed in "Programming with Command Files" later in this chapter.

Each command session keeps a separate environment table. Any variable defined in CONFIG.SYS is global to all sessions. Changes made once a session is started belong to that session only. This is useful for customizing sessions for a particular task.

Getting Help

There are several methods for access to help information on command-line procedures. The Information folder on the desktop contains the Command Reference book. This is a view document with help panels on most of the command-line utilities. These panels are organized alphabetically and by function in Figure 7.15. There are syntax diagrams, hot links between topics, and descriptive examples. Printing from this book will produce the command reference manual not included with the product release.

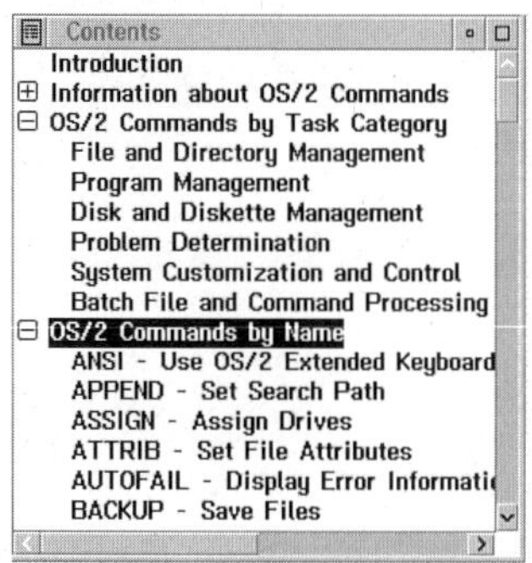

Figure 7.15. The Command Reference help book.

The Glossary object is also included in the Information folder. It consists of a tabbed alphabetical notebook with summary descriptions of important terms. Several of these reference command-line actions. The Master Index is similar to the Glossary but presents information in outline fashion. This object is initially placed on the desktop and is designed for quick and handy access to procedures. Each command-line object has Help as an option in the pop-up menu. This Help option (shown in Figure 7.16) cascades the following four choices: Index, General, Using, and Keys.

General is the default and provides concise instructions on managing command windows. It does not include command-line syntax; that information is found only in the Command Reference view guide mentioned previously.

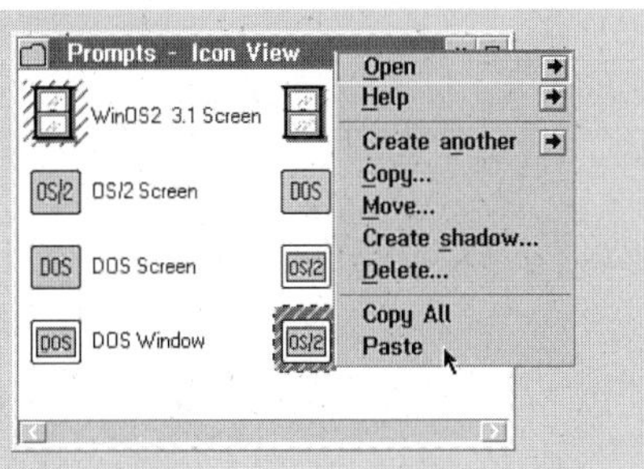

Figure 7.16. Command object pop-up menu help options.

There are several ways to access help directly from the command line. The keyword HELP is used to interface between the character session and the Presentation Manager viewer. HELP is actually a .CMD command file in the \OS2 directory. It parses the command line and checks for the parameters `ON` or `OFF`. These signal the system to toggle the prompt between a top screen banner and the default.

> TIP
>
> A custom prompt can be reset by using the HELP OFF option. To remedy this, edit HELP.CMD and add the desired customization.

If `ON` or `OFF` are not present, HELPMSG.EXE is called with one or two parameters. For one parameter, HELPMSG first checks for a valid error message. Message files come in pairs and have the extension .MSG. They are usually stored in the \OS2\SYSTEM directory and have a three-letter code. One file has the message header and the other has the detail text. Each item in a message file is assigned a number up to four digits. An example would be SYS0002, in which SYS is the file code and 0002 is the item number. Network messages use NET and REXX uses REX. A number by itself assumes a code of SYS. If found, the appropriate text is displayed from the message file.

If a message code is not found, HELPMSG opens the Command Reference view book with the focus on the parameter text topic. For example, to learn more about the `START` command, type `HELP START` at the prompt to see Figure 7.17.

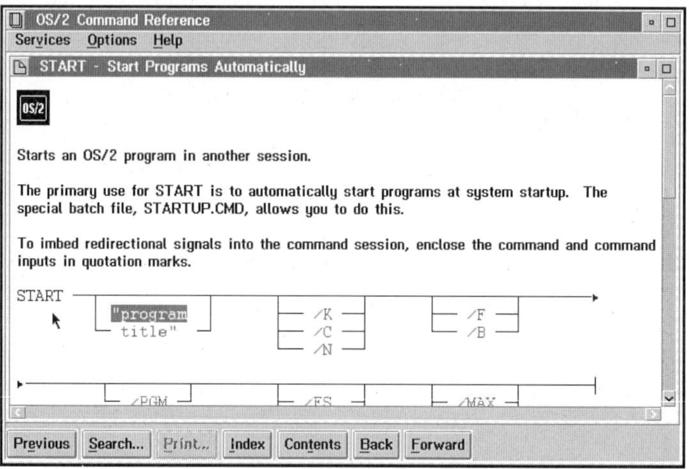

Figure 7.17. HELP START *at the command line opens a book.*

If two parameters are passed, the first is used as a book name and the second as a topic. `HELP REXX PMREXX` opens the REXX book to the PMREXX topic. The books can be browsed and printed as usual, and the program returns to the calling command session when the books are closed. Many OS/2 add-on products include documentation in view book format. Paths to all of these should be included in the `BOOKSHELF` environment variable to facilitate quick access from the command line.

Printing Options

Most application programs have their own facility for formatting and printing data. The command-line utilities rely on system resources for this function. The printer has a device name that represents the port, such as LPT1, COM1,

and so forth. The default print device is called PRN. Text and printer-ready files can be copied directly to the print device with the COPY command. Wildcards can be used to copy multiple files. If the file has special printer formatting characters or embedded graphics, use the /b (binary) option:

```
COPY GRAPH.PCL PRN: /b
```

Another important print option is the PRINT command. It is similar to COPY but queues the files and immediately returns control to the user. The queue can be listed and controlled. The /t option terminates all queued files, and /c cancels the current file. Wildcards and the /b option are available as they are with COPY.

Many command-line utilities direct their output in a standard way. This output can be redirected to a print device instead of the console.

Starting Sessions

Application programs can start from CONFIG.SYS or STARTUP.CMD at boot time, from direct manipulation of Workplace Shell objects, or from command-line sessions. There are three methods available for the command-line approach. The first is to call the executable directly. When a string is entered at the prompt, the command processor parses the string and determines the name and filespec of the program to run. The current directory and each directory listed in the PATH environment variable are searched until a match is found. The executable is opened and examined for the session type. This could be a PM, VIO, DOS, or WINOS2 session.

Presentation Manager applications switch the display to the Workplace Shell if necessary and proceed from there. The command-line session is suspended until the PM program terminates. Control is then returned to the original command-line session. This scenario applies to other application types. Most character-based OS/2 applications run directly in the current command window and inherit the environment and display characteristics of the calling window. Some older character applications, most notably network administration tools, force the display to full-screen mode for operation. The display is switched back to the window when these programs terminate.

The command processor will automatically initiate a DOS session by calling the DOS command processor and passing the name of the executable. For a WINOS2 session, the Windows code is also loaded even if other Winapps are already running. This can be confusing and tends to crowd memory. DOS and especially WINOS2 applications should be run from the Workplace Shell or existing DOS or WINOS2 sessions.

START

The second method for starting sessions is the `START` command. This is a very powerful option that derives its functionality from OS/2 1.0, which lacked a Presentation Manager. It is useful in command files like STARTUP.CMD. Many of the functions are also covered by Workplace Shell object settings and the Startup folder.

You can start any type of session and keep the current command-line session operational. The basic syntax includes several sets of options:

```
START "Name" /K¦C¦N /F¦B /FS¦WIN /PM¦DOS /MAX¦MIN
/I program options
```

in which the vertical bar (¦) indicates a choice between two or more options. `"Name"` is an optional title that will display in the window title bar and the Window List. `/K` and `/C` use a command processor to start the program; `/N` starts it directly without a command processor. `/C` closes the new session and the window when the program is completed; `/K` keeps it. `/F` starts a foreground session which has the console focus; `/B` runs in the background. `/FS` is full-screen DOS or OS/2; `/WIN` is windowed on the desktop (not WINOS2). `/PM` is Presentation Manager, and `/DOS` is a DOS session. The latter is useful for starting family applications in the DOS mode. `/MAX` maximizes a windowed session and `/MIN` minimizes any session. `/I` allows a new session to inherit the environment table from the current command line. `program` is the name and filespec of the executable, followed by the parameter options specific to the application.

This command takes some practice but a few examples will demonstrate the facility. A new maximized windowed DOS session would be:

```
START /MAX /DOS
```

Run CHKDSK on drive E in the background, save the results in a file, and close the session:

```
START /B /C CHKDSK E: > CHECK.E
```

Start the system editor, label the session in the Window List, skip the command processor for a quicker load:

```
START "Edit Config.Sys" /N E C:\CONFIG.SYS
```

DETACH

DETACH is the third option for starting applications. This is a very specialized version of START. It is used for programs that do not need keyboard, mouse, or video interaction. Programs that write to standard output can be redirected to a file or print device in this mode. This provides true background processing but requires a good understanding of what the program is intended to do. These programs are expected to run constantly, stop themselves, or be stopped by some other application that communicates via IPC. A detached process is not listed in the Window List but status information is available with the PSTAT utility. Database servers and daemon processes are good candidates. SQL Server can be started in this fashion:

```
DETACH SQLSERVR -DC:\SQL\DATA\MASTER.DAT -EC:\SQL\ERROR
```

The process ID number is returned to the command line. This number can be tracked with PSTAT. In the case of SQL Server, a front-end application issues a SHUTDOWN command through named pipes to close the detached session.

Syntax and Symbols

Commands are edited with the arrow, Backspace, and Delete keys. The Insert key toggles between Insert and Overtype. Ctrl with a left or right arrow moves the cursor one word at a time. F3 recalls the previous command and Esc cancels an entry. If the KEYS environment variable is set to ON, the up- and down-arrows recall the command history. This is the preferred method and should be set in

CONFIG.SYS. KEYS by itself outputs the status and `KEYS LIST` displays a numbered table of saved commands. This list can grow as large as 64K and older entries are discarded past that point.

Commands are entered as text strings at the current cursor position. This is usually the lowest prompt line. The line number may change as command results scroll the text off the screen and new prompts are displayed. The strings are composed of three major parts including the command, parameters, and options. In the following example:

```
C:\OS2\XCOPY D: E: /s
```

the command is `XCOPY`, which has an optional filespec indicating a directory location. `D:` and `E:` are parameters that are passed to `XCOPY` for processing. Options typically start with a slash "/" and consist of one or more letters. Some utilities that have roots in UNIX tend to use a dash "-" instead of a slash, although some use either one. The option symbol is determined by the utility and not the command processor.

The symbols in Table 7.3 are interpreted by OS/2 and DOS sessions as special operators. The items in bold are specific to OS/2 sessions.

Table 7.3. Command line special symbols.

Symbol	*Description*
>	Redirects output—replaces existing file
>>	Appends redirected output to existing data
<	Redirects input
¦	Pipes output
&&	Allows a command to run only if the preceding command succeeds (`AND` operator)
¦¦	Allows a command to run only if the preceding command fails (`OR` operator)
&	Separates multiple commands

Symbol	Description
( )	Groups commands
"	Encloses HPFS file names with spaces: "Budget Report"
^	Allows input of command symbols as text

Output and error messages are normally directed to the console screen. These are referred to as standard output and standard error. The redirection symbols can force output to another device or file. This directory listing will print instead of displaying to the screen:

```
DIR > PRN
```

A new file is created or an existing file overwritten with:

```
DIR > FILELIST.TXT
```

If the file does exist and the output should be appended, double the symbol:

```
CHKDSK >> FILELIST.TXT
```

Standard input comes from the keyboard. The input needed to complete an operation can be stored in a file. Make certain that all keystrokes are contained in the file:

```
UTILITY.EXE < KEYS.TXT
```

More advanced combinations are possible by numbering the input and output streams. Input, output, and error are 0, 1, and 2, respectively. Other files on the command line take the numbers 3 through 9. The output and error can be separated as follows:

```
DISKCOPY A: B: > OUTPUT.LOG 2>ERROR.LOG
```

Output and error messages can be combined in one file:

```
DIR *.SYS > FILE.LOG 2>&1
```

An extreme case would prevent all output and errors by redirecting them to the `NUL` device:

```
WHOKNOWS.EXE 1>NUL 2>NUL
```

You can also redirect the input of a file by filtering. A filter reads information from the input stream, changes the information, and writes the result to standard output. The OS/2 commands `FIND`, `MORE`, and `SORT` are filters that work with ASCII text files. These utilities are combined with the piping symbol. Pipes take the output of one program and use it as input to another program. Search for a string in a directory:

```
DIR C:\OS2 ¦ FIND "FDISK"
```

Sort the directory by the date column and output to the printer:

```
DIR C:\OS2 ¦ SORT /+24 > PRN
```

Sort a large directory and display the result one screen at a time:

```
DIR ¦ SORT ¦ MORE
```

Conditional operation of commands is provided with the `AND` operator (`&&`) and the `OR` operator (`¦¦`). Print the contents of a file only if it exists:

```
DIR C:\STARTUP.CMD && PRINT C:\STARTUP.CMD
```

The `OR` operator will perform the second command only if the first one fails. If the dual boot DOS autoexec is missing, display the OS/2 version:

```
TYPE C:\OS2\SYSTEM\AUTOEXEC.DOS ¦¦ TYPE C:\AUTOEXEC.BAT
```

The ampersand (`&`) separator permits multiple commands on one line. This can be used to combine several similar actions:

```
DIR C:\*.SYS & DIR C:\OS2\*.SYS
DEL *.BAK & DEL *.TMP & DEL ~*.*
```

The grouping `()` symbol ensures that conditional commands operate in the correct order. The first example sorts the contents of a file if it exists:

```
DIR CONFIG.SYS && (TYPE CONFIG.SYS ¦ SORT > CONFIG.SRT)
```

This version combines the directory listing with the sorted file:

```
(DIR CONFIG.SYS && TYPE CONFIG.SYS ¦ SORT) > CONFIG.SRT
```

Command Tables

Tables 7.4 through 7.8 list the commands provided in OS/2 sessions. Many of these will be familiar to DOS users. The OS/2-specific commands are in bold. Detailed help is available in the CMDREF view file. Several commands support the /? convention for listing options. Table 7.4 contains the commands used for file and directory operations. These are the most popular command utilities and work like their DOS counterparts.

HPFS file system names can be as long as 255 characters and might contain embedded spaces. Any reference to a filespec with spaces must be surrounded with quotation marks.

Table 7.4. Files and directories.

Commands	*Descriptions*
`ATTRIB`	Turns the read-only and archive attributes of a file `ON` or `OFF`
`BACKUP`	Saves one or more files from one disk to another
`CD` or `CHDIR`	Changes the current directory or displays its name
`COMP`	Compares the contents of the first set of specified files with the contents of the second set of specified files
`COPY`	Copies one or more files and combines files; the `/F` option protects extended attributes
`DEL` or `ERASE`	Deletes one or more files
`DIR`	Lists the files in a directory; the `/N` option forces display in the HPFS long filename format

continues

Table 7.4. continued

Commands	*Descriptions*
EAUTIL	Splits and joins extended file attributes, which is necessary when copying files to and from DOS file systems; /S splits the attributes to a separate file and /R replaces them
FIND	Searches a file for a specific string of text
MD or MKDIR	Creates a new directory
MORE	Sends output from a file to the screen, one full screen at a time
MOVE	Moves one or more files from one directory to another directory on the same drive
PICVIEW	Displays a picture file
PRINT	Prints or cancels printing of one or more files
RD or RMDIR	Removes a directory
RECOVER	Recovers files from a disk containing defective sectors
REN or RENAME	Changes the name of a file
REPLACE	Selectively replaces files
RESTORE	Restores one or more backup files from one disk to another
SORT	Sorts information by letter or number
TREE	Displays all the directory paths and optionally lists files
TYPE	Displays the contents of a file
UNDELETE	Recovers deleted or erased files

Commands	*Descriptions*
UNPACK	Decompresses and copies files that have been compressed; compressed files are designated by an @ in the file extension
VIEW	Displays online documents; this is called by the help command
XCOPY	Selectively copies groups of files, including those in subdirectories, from one disk to another

Table 7.5 focuses on disk management. Two of the more popular commands have Presentation Manager versions. Avoid using these in command file processing.

Table 7.5. Disk and diskettes.

Command	*Description*
CACHE	Loads or monitors the disk cache for HPFS
CHKDSK or **PMCHKDSK**	Scans a disk and checks it for errors; the PM version displays a pie chart of space usage; the /F option fixes drive errors; HPFS has 4 levels of checking
DISKCOMP	Compares the contents of two diskettes
DISKCOPY	Copies the contents of one diskette to another diskette
FDISK or **FDISKPM**	Enables you to partition the hard disks on your system; FDISKPM is a Presentation Manager version; the FDISK /D option run from a floppy boot deletes the primary partition

continues

Table 7.5. continued

Command	*Description*
`FORMAT`	Prepares a disk to accept files; the `/FS` parameter specifies the file system
`LABEL`	Displays the volume serial number and creates or changes the volume identification label on a disk
`VERIFY`	Confirms that data written to a disk has been written correctly
`VMDISK`	Creates an image file of a DOS startup diskette
`VOL`	Displays the disk volume label and serial number

Table 7.6 lists the program management commands.

Table 7.6. Program management commands.

Command	*Description*
`CMD`	Starts an OS/2 session; `/C` runs a program and closes the session, `/K` keeps running
`COMMAND`	Starts a DOS session
`DETACH`	Starts a noninteractive program
`EXIT`	Ends a command-line session
`HELP`	Provides a help line as part of the command prompt, a help screen, and information related to warning and error messages
`START`	Starts another program in another session (either DOS or OS/2)

Table 7.7 has several utility programs that ensure better reliability, availability, and serviceability (RAS). These tools are provided to help in gathering information to isolate and correct system problems.

Table 7.7. Problem determination commands.

Utility	*Description*
AUTOFAIL	Displays system error information (ON¦OFF)
CREATEDD	Creates a dump diskette for use with the Stand-Alone Dump procedure
MAKEINI	Creates a new OS2.INI file containing default information
PATCH	Allows you to apply IBM-supplied patches to make repairs to software
PSTAT	Displays process /P, thread /S, shared memory /M, and dynamic-link library /L information
SYSLEVEL	Displays operating system service level
SYSLOG	Starts or stops adding system event information to the System Log file
TRACE	Sets or selects system trace
TRACEFMT	Displays formatted trace records in reverse time stamp order

Table 7.8 lists commands for customizing the system and command-line interface. Setting the PATH and PROMPT variables are very important and should be entered in CONFIG.SYS.

Table 7.8. System customization commands.

Command	*Description*
ANSI	Allows extended keyboard and display support (ON¦OFF)
BOOT	Switches operating systems (DOS¦OS2); /Q displays the current setting (it can be issued from an OS/2 or VDM session; the same command is also used to switch the hard disk to reboot OS/2 2.1 from MS/PC-DOS)
CHCP	Displays or changes the current system code page
CLS	Clears the display screen
DATE	Displays or sets the system date
DDINSTAL	Provides an automated way to install new device drivers after the operating system has been installed
DPATH	Specifies the search path for data files outside a current directory
KEYB	Specifies a special keyboard layout that replaces the current keyboard layout
KEYS	Retrieves previously issued commands for editing or reuse (ON¦OFF¦LIST)
MODE	Sets operation modes for printer, communications, console, and disk devices
PATH	Specifies the search path for programs and commands
PROMPT	Sets the system prompt

Command	Description
SET	Sets one string value in the environment equal to another string for later use in programs
SETBOOT	Switch operating systems and set parameters for the Boot Manager
SPOOL	Intercepts and separates data from different sources going to the printer so that printer output is not intermixed
TIME	Displays or changes the time known to the system and resets the time of your computer
VER	Displays the OS/2 version number

Programming with Command Files

A command file is an ASCII text file with a batch of OS/2 commands. The command processor reads this file and performs one line at a time. Repetitive tasks process quicker with fewer typing errors. Simple language statements are provided for conditional execution, parameter passing, and error handling. Command files have the extension .CMD and are similar to DOS batch files (.BAT). More advanced operations can build on these command files and include REXX language statements. These will be discussed briefly in the following sections and explained in detail in Chapter 15.

Several methods are used to create and edit command files. Simple files can be created with the `COPY` command and the console device:

```
COPY CON MYFILE.CMD
```

The cursor moves to the next line in column one. Type the command text, editing each line as you go. Pressing Enter moves the cursor to the next line, and there is no way to edit previous lines. Press F6 or enter Ctrl-Z to save the file. Ctrl-C aborts this process. Another useful option is available with the command history facility.

If KEYS is set to ON, type the desired commands and redirect the list to a file

```
KEYS LIST > MYFILE.CMD
```

This text has unwanted line numbers and extraneous commands that can be easily edited. Any text editor or word processor can handle this task. OS/2 includes two editors for this purpose, the system editor (E) and the enhanced editor (EPM). Of course, command files can be composed from scratch.

Comment lines start with the REM statement and can be as long as 123 characters. The comments will display as the file is processed unless ECHO is set to OFF. An @ sign in front of any command line will suppress display of that individual line. Any number of comment lines can be added. REM on a line by itself can separate comment sections and make the text more readable.

Command files can be run directly from the command prompt. They can be installed in the Workplace Shell and assigned object settings. They can appear in object pop-up menus by association with a file type. Command files can also call other command files.

Each file line is read from disk before processing. Performance will improve when these files are stored on a virtual disk.

STARTUP.CMD is a special command file that is automatically processed at system startup. This file must be in the root directory and is often used to initialize sessions or start network operations. New command sessions started

from a Workplace Shell object can also begin with a command file. This is useful for setting environment strings such as the prompt. The name of this file is entered at the Program page Optional Parameters box shown in Figure 7.18.

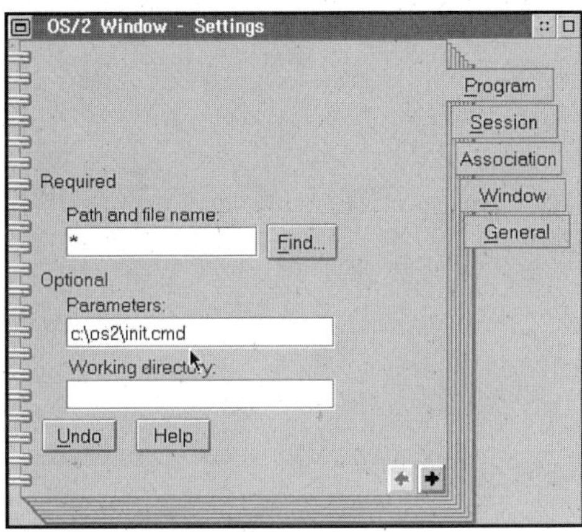

Figure 7.18. Adding a command file to the object settings.

The commands in Table 7.9 are specific to batch file processing and will not work at the command prompt. Combine these with the OS/2 commands listed in Tables 7.4 through 7.8 and other executables to achieve the desired result. (Note that the OS/2-specific batch commands are set in boldface type in the following table.)

Table 7.9. Batch file processing commands.

Command	*Description*
`CALL`	Nests a batch file within a batch file
`ECHO`	Allows or prevents the display of OS/2 commands when a batch file is running
`ENDLOCAL`	Restores the drive, directory, and variables that were in effect before a SETLOCAL command was issued

continues

Table 7.9. continued

Command	*Description*
EXTPROC	Defines an external batch-file processor. This statement must be on the first line. Calling CMD.EXE might set up an infinite loop!
FOR	Allows repetitive processing of commands within a batch file
GOTO	Transfers batch processing to a specified label
IF	Allows conditional processing of commands within a batch file
PAUSE	Suspends batch-file processing
REM	Displays remarks from within a batch file
SETLOCAL	Sets the drive, directory, and variables that are local to the current batch file
SHIFT	Allows more than 10 replaceable parameters to be processed from a batch file

The following examples demonstrate the use of batch commands. Processes repeat continuously in the `GOTO` loop in Listing 7.2. Pressing Ctrl-Break will stop this cycle.

Listing 7.2. Continuous loop command file.

```
REM Stress test the hard drive...
:TOP
DIR OS2 /W
CHKDSK
TREE /F
GOTO TOP
```

Multiple files are processed with the FOR command in Listing 7.3. Each is assigned to parameter number 1 and compiled. The output is directed to a common error file.

Listing 7.3. Processing multiple files with FOR.

```
REM Compile each of three files
FOR %%1 IN (MOD1 MOD2 MOD3) DO CL /C %%1.C >> MOD.OUT
```

Up to ten parameters can be read from the command line and assigned positional numbers. These numbers are replaced by the parameters in the command file. If more than ten are needed, use SHIFT to cycle through the others. Listing 7.4 processes any number of command files and uses CALL to execute the file.

The number of characters allowed on the command line will limit the number of parameters. This varies with different command processors.

Listing 7.4. Processing any number of command files.

```
REM Each parameter is a command file without .CMD.
@ECHO OFF
:TOP
IF "%1" == "" GOTO FINISH
CALL %1
SHIFT
GOTO TOP
:FINISH
ECHO Processing complete!
```

Environment strings can also be used as parameters by passing their names in percent symbols. Listing 7.5 checks the value of COMSPEC before proceeding.

Listing 7.5. Testing environment strings in a command file.

```
REM DO not proceed with an alternate command processor.
IF NOT "%COMSPEC%" == "C:\OS2\CMD.EXE" CALL PROCESS
```

Error checking is provided by the IF statement. Most commands and utilities return a status code. The ERRORLEVEL of the previous command can be tested. The existence of a file is checked with EXIST. Both techniques are demonstrated in Listing 7.6.

Listing 7.6. Command file error checking.

```
REM Make sure the file exists, copy it from the root.
@ECHO OFF
IF NOT EXIST C:\OS2\SYSTEM\CONFIG.DOS THEN GOTO PROBLEM
COPY C:\OS2\SYSTEM\CONFIG.DOS D:\CONFIG.BAK
IF NOT ERRORLEVEL 1 GOTO END
ECHO Copy failed, check the drive
GOTO END
:PROBLEM
ECHO Can't find the DOS config file!
:END
```

Command files can be extended further using the REXX procedure language, discussed in detail in Chapter 15. REXXTRY.CMD in the OS2 directory is the only REXX program that installs with OS/2. It allows testing of REXX syntax from the command line, as shown in Figure 7.19.

The text for REXXTRY.CMD demonstrates some very important capabilities that are lacking in command files. The first line of text must be a comment surrounded by /* and */. That is how the command processor knows to call REXX. The program accepts arguments from the command line, calls procedures and functions, controls the screen display, accepts input, and more. Any line which is not a REXX statement or comment is passed back to the command processor for proper handling. Use REXX statements to control the console and let OS/2 commands do the utility work.

```
OS/2 Window
 OS/2     Ctrl+Esc = Window List                              Type HELP = help
[c:\os2]rexxtry
  REXXTRY.CMD lets you interactively try REXX statements.
    Each string is executed when you hit Enter.
      Enter 'call tell' for a description of the features.
  Go on - try a few...              Enter 'exit' to end.
say Bill was here
BILL WAS HERE
  ............................................... REXXTRY.CMD on OS/2
say 125634 / 268
468.783582
  ............................................... REXXTRY.CMD on OS/2
say Bill || 234 * 15
BILL3510
  ............................................... REXXTRY.CMD on OS/2
ver

4OS2 1.0    OS/2 Version is 2.0
  rc = 0 ........................................ REXXTRY.CMD on OS/2
```

Figure 7.19. Testing REXX syntax with REXXTRY.

Some OS/2 command symbols such as * and : confuse REXX. Surround command parameters in quotation marks to make them literal strings. These are passed to the command processor intact.

Alternate Command Processors

CMD.EXE is a character-based OS/2 program. It is possible to replace it with another program of similar design. This might provide enhanced functionality, rigid security, or auditing features. There are several alternate command processors on the market. The most notable are the Hamilton C Shell by Hamilton Software Labs and 4OS2 by JP Software. The Hamilton C Shell provides UNIX-style commands and shell scripts. 4OS2 is modeled on the popular 4DOS utility and is an extension of standard OS/2 commands. The shareware version of 4OS2 is included on the companion disk and will be explained in detail in the following paragraphs.

The OS/2 command processor is defined by two entries in CONFIG.SYS. OS2_SHELL is the default processor used when a command session is started from a Workplace Shell object. It also processes command file objects and runs character applications. The second entry is COMSPEC, which defines the processor used when an application shells to the operating system. Creating a new session with START relies on COMSPEC. These two entries are listed in the environment table, but only COMSPEC can be changed as needed with the SET command.

Different programs can be used for OS2_SHELL and COMSPEC. CMD.EXE might be the default shell and 4OS2.EXE could be used for new START sessions.

4OS2 has an installation program that handles these adjustments. It can also be installed manually by editing the entries in CONFIG.SYS and restarting the system. For casual use, call it as a program from the command line or add it to the Workplace Shell as a new object. This method is preferred when strict CMD.EXE compatibility is required.

The rich 4OS2 feature set complements the standard OS/2 commands and is a valuable addition for novice and advanced users. Most of the features are identical in the DOS version called 4DOS. This processor can be installed for DOS sessions by setting the SHELL variable in CONFIG.SYS or by creating a Workplace object. The DOS equivalent of COMSPEC is entered in the DOS Settings. JP Software sells a combination package that includes both programs.

Ease of use and customization are strong points of 40S2. The command-line editing keys are improved and include neat tricks like the completion of a filespec with a single keystroke. The command history can be loaded and saved from a file. The Page Up key displays the scrolling command history shown in Figure 7.20.

Aliases are named macros that abbreviate commands. They can also be loaded from a file. Additional help is provided, especially with the /? command-line option. The OS/2 *Command Reference* and 4OS2 reference books are loaded when F1 is pressed or HELP is entered at the prompt. The environment

has several additional variables and can be global to all sessions using the SHRALIAS utility. Environment strings can be edited with ESET instead of the usual retyping required by CMD.EXE.

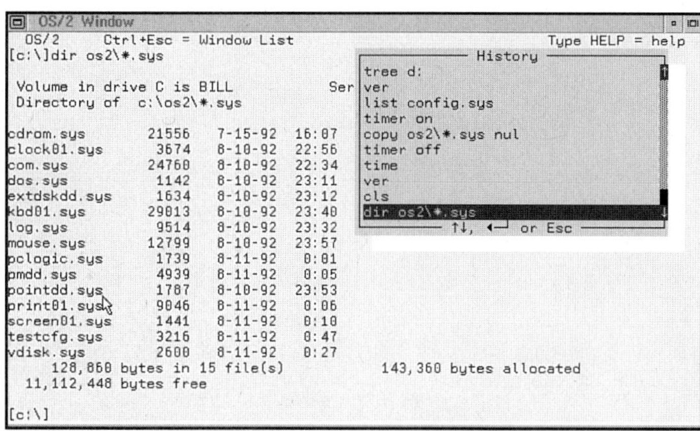

Figure 7.20. 4OS2 command history picklist.

Video customization includes line drawing, text placement, boxes, menus, and named color controls. The `COLOR` command sets the text color and uses names rather than numbers:

```
COLOR BRI WHITE ON BLUE
```

The command screen and major utilities can have separate color schemes. Many of these settings can be stored in the 4OS2.INI text file. One of the most popular features is the colorized directory listing. Color names can be assigned to directories and various file extensions. Any use of the `DIR` command displays a colorful barrage with .EXEs in one color, .DOCs in another, and .BAK files blinking wildly.

Additionally, 4OS2 added several new commands that should be part of OS/2 and DOS. `FREE` shows the amount of disk space available on a drive. `MEMORY` shows RAM usage in DOS and the largest block of memory in OS/2. `DESCRIBE` adds useful comments to filenames and stores them in a hidden text file. These are automatically displayed when the user does a `DIR`. Many other options are provided for `DIR` including `/2` and `/4` for two- and four-column lists, `/F` for full path names, `/L` for lowercase, and `/T` for attributes.

TIMER is a utility that clocks execution time. It is very useful for performance testing and works well in command files. `LIST` displays files in a scrolling window with a handy find option. `SELECT` is combined with other commands for picklist input. The statement that follows displays a full-screen multiple-selection list (*.SYS) and deletes the files marked in Figure 7.21:

```
SELECT DEL (*.SYS)
```

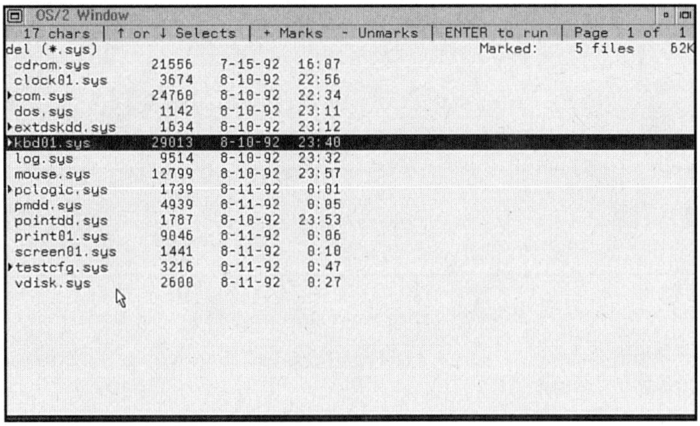

```
OS/2 Window
 17 chars | ↑ or ↓ Selects | + Marks  - Unmarks | ENTER to run | Page  1 of  1
del (*.sys)                                       Marked:     5 files     62K
 cdrom.sys        21556   7-15-92   16:07
 clock01.sys       3674   8-10-92   22:56
▸com.sys          24760   8-10-92   22:34
 dos.sys           1142   8-10-92   23:11
▸extdskdd.sys      1634   8-10-92   23:12
▸kbd01.sys        29013   8-10-92   23:40
 log.sys           9514   8-10-92   23:32
 mouse.sys        12799   8-10-92   23:57
▸pclogic.sys       1739   8-11-92    0:01
 pmdd.sys          4939   8-11-92    0:05
 pointdd.sys       1787   8-10-92   23:53
 print01.sys       9046   8-11-92    0:06
 screen01.sys      1441   8-11-92    0:10
▸testcfg.sys       3216   8-11-92    0:47
 vdisk.sys         2600   8-11-92    0:27
```

Figure 7.21. Selecting files for deletion in 4OS2.

Batch processing enhancements offer the advanced user unlimited control of command procedures. Internal variables provide the program with system information such as process number, screen position, and application type. Functions include mathematics, date and filename formatting, and string handling. Blocks of text can be displayed with the `TEXT` and `ENDTEXT` operators. These can be combined with screen controls and input commands to create powerful menu-driven utilities.

The batch files can be stored in the traditional .CMD text format or in a .BTM file. The latter process is much quicker because the file is kept in memory instead of individual lines being read off the disk. Two special command files are used by 4OS2 sessions. `4START` is processed whenever a new command-line session is started. `4EXIT` runs whenever a session is closed or exited. Of course, 4OS2 is also compatible with the REXX language. If you use the command line, give this program a try.

Author Bio

Bill Wolff is founder and president of Wolff Data Systems, a client/server database consulting firm in the Delaware Valley. His development and training focus primarily on OS/2 LANs and database servers. Wolff is Vice President of the Delaware Valley SQL Server Users Group.

8

Virtual DOS Machines

In This Chapter

One of the most exciting features of IBM's OS/2 2.1 is its ability to run multiple DOS sessions in a high-performance, protected environment. This chapter introduces the multiple virtual DOS machine component of OS/2 2.1 and examines its design, architecture, performance, and usage. This chapter also shows you how OS/2 2.1 can boot native DOS in separate sessions, how to get the most out of the multiple virtual DOS machine environment, how to maximize the performance of common DOS applications, and how to integrate multiple virtual DOS machines into the OS/2 2.1 environment.

General Virtual DOS Machine Parameters

A virtual DOS machine (VDM) creates an environment that many DOS programs may recognize as plain DOS. It services interrupts and provides disk and RAM resources and ports for printing and modem activity. In fact, the only way you can tell that DOS applications are not running in DOS is that any application's function that returns the version of the operating system (such as dBase IV's `OS()` operator) says "DOS 20.10."

Each virtual DOS machine functions independently of other DOS machines, OS/2 native applications, and WINOS2 applications. Each VDM can have up to 32M of Lotus Intel Microsoft (LIM) Version 4.0 memory, 512M of DOS Protect Mode Interface (DPMI) Version 0.9 memory, 16M of Lotus Intel Microsoft AST Extended (LIMA XMS) Version 2.1 memory, and anywhere from 630K to 740K of total conventional memory, which can be used in most of the same ways that a typical DOS environment could be used. DOS utilities can be loaded into upper memory blocks (UMBs), and network redirecters can make use of the high memory area (HMA).

Virtual DOS Machine Defaults

Out of the box, OS/2 2.1 provides a default of approximately 640K of conventional memory, 2M of LIM expanded memory, 4M of DPMI memory, and 2M of XMS memory for each VDM. DPMI memory is not actually activated or committed (and therefore doesn't impact system resources) unless an application such as Lotus 1-2-3 3.1+ accesses it. LIM and XMS memory,

however, do impact system resources immediately. Unless an application actually needs these types of memory, it's probably wise to reduce the DOS settings for that kind of memory to 0 (refer to the "DOS Settings" section later in this chapter).

Don't be afraid to experiment with the DOS session parameters (discussed in greater detail later). In a DOS system, changing one line in CONFIG.SYS or AUTOEXEC.BAT can lock a system, and in extreme cases of this type, the user has to hunt down a DOS boot disk, boot the system, and correct the error before any more work can be done. With OS/2 2.1's virtual DOS machines, rebooting a session is as simple as killing the session and starting again. When you also consider that OS/2 2.1 protects each DOS session, experimenting with different combinations of drivers, memory settings, and other parameters is no longer so dangerous or time consuming as it was under DOS.

Accessing DOS Settings

The total amount of available memory, as well as what types of memory are available, are controlled through the DOS settings notebook, available through the Session tab in the MVDM session's icon settings. (DOS settings in general are discussed in more detail later in the "DOS Settings" section.) To access the settings notebook, follow these steps:

1. Place the mouse pointer over the DOS Window icon (or any DOS session icon you want to alter).
2. Press mouse button 2 (MB2) once to bring up a context-sensitive menu.
3. Place the mouse pointer on the arrow beside the Open option and press mouse button 1 (MB1).
4. On the resulting menu, use MB1 to click on Settings.

5. The settings notebook is now on screen. OS/2 2.1 has implemented a notebook motif for its system navigation and maintenance. Use MB1 to click on the Session tab.
6. Use MB1 to click on the DOS Settings button.

The resulting screen shows all of the configurable DOS settings (see Figure 8.1).

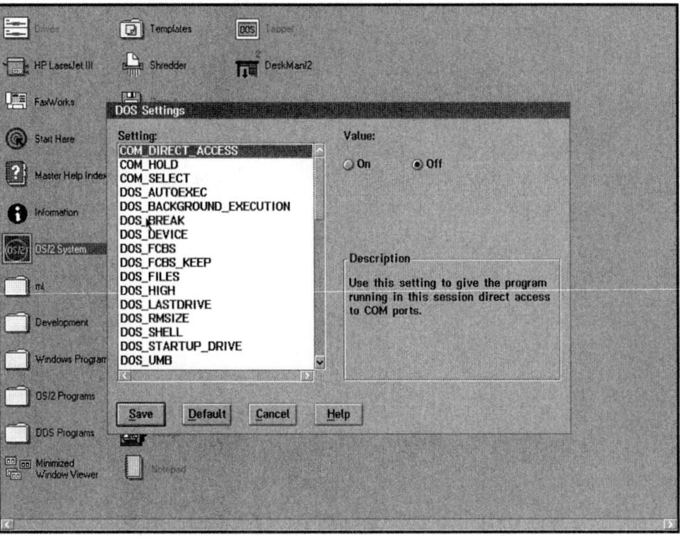

Figure 8.1. *The DOS settings.*

How much conventional RAM is available? The answer is found in another question: how much conventional RAM does an application need? A basic MVDM opens with approximately 608,096 free bytes. That's a respectable number, but for DOS customers accustomed to DOS memory managers, it may not be terribly exciting (note the following settings in Table 8.1).

The following settings build up from a default DOS session that includes `DOS_HIGH` Off and `DOS_UMB` Off, the defaults that ship with OS/2 2.1. Note that individual results may vary somewhat from machine to machine.

Table 8.1. MVDM Memory Settings and Effects.

Setting	*Effect*
611,986	Default
636,048	`DOS_HIGH` On
642,496	`DOS_UMB` On
740,544	`VIDEO_MODE_RESTRICTION` CGA

When the `VIDEO_MODE_RESTRICTION` is set to CGA, only CGA-level graphics work correctly because this setting tells the session that it is running on CGA hardware. Text output is not affected and appears at the normal resolution of the graphics adapter and monitor.

The amount of RAM is not greatly affected by any OS/2 2.1 device driver (even drivers that provide service to the MVDM sessions). Network drivers, for example, may insert a Virtual Device Driver stub into the MVDM, but its conventional memory impact is practically nil. This is one area where OS/2 2.1 is better than DOS. Realizing 730,576 bytes of free conventional memory with a 3270 host session and a LAN attachment on a DOS system is nearly impossible, but with OS/2 2.1's VDMs, it is not at all difficult.

OS/2 2.1 typically installs with two default MVDM icons: DOS Full Screen and DOS Window. Creating a new icon is a simple task. One way to do this is based on the assumption that the user installed OS/2 2.1 with the default DOS support that provides two DOS icons: one for a DOS Window, and one for a DOS Full Screen. To create another DOS session, use the following steps:

1. Position the mouse pointer on top of the icon (either the DOS Full Screen or the DOS Window) and press the selection button.
2. Click once with MB1 on the Copy option.
3. Type the icon's new name in the New Name field after positioning the mouse pointer over that field and pressing MB1.
4. Press Enter.

These actions create a new DOS icon. At this point, the user can go into that icon's DOS settings notebook and customize the session's memory, device drivers, and other configurable options.

Another way to create an icon is to use the Template folder with the following steps:

1. Position the mouse pointer over the Template folder and press MB1 rapidly twice.
2. Click once on the Program icon with MB1. Press and hold MB2 and drag the icon to the desktop or into any desired folder. Releasing MB2 drops the icon.
3. The settings notebook comes up automatically, and you can make changes to the path and filename, as well as the session title here. To simply create another DOS icon, type an asterisk in the Path and Filename field, select the Session tab, and click once with MB1 on either the DOS Full Screen or the DOS Window pushbutton. When you double click with MB1 on the system icon (the square in the upper-left corner of the window), the changes are saved.

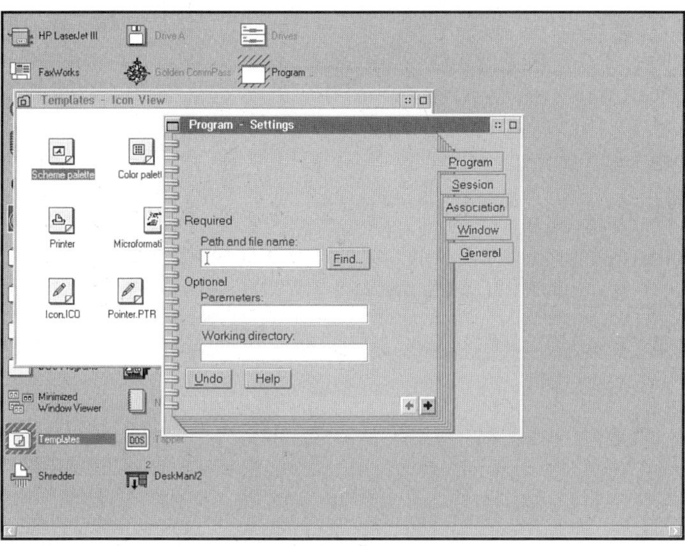

Figure 8.2. The Program Settings notebook.

TIP

It's a good idea to use the Template folder to create all new programs and other desktop objects. It is also a good idea to customize the individual template objects to closely meet your needs. It may be wise, for example, to go into the DOS settings of the program icon and disable EMS and DPMI memory to conserve system resources. Setting the XMS memory to 64 reduces the physical RAM requirements, too.

Material on the inner workings of the MVDM architecture is presented in more detail in *OS/2 Version 2.0 Volume 2: DOS and Windows Environment.* This redbook, produced by IBM's

International Technical Support Center, is an outstanding reference for anyone who has to support VDM usage in a corporate setting or anyone who simply wants to understand the VDM technology.

Specific DOS Versions

The 8086 emulation component of OS/2 Version 2.1 provides an environment so much like an 8086-based microcomputer that DOS or other 8086-based operating systems besides the OS/2 DOS emulation (DOSKRNL) can be used. (IBM, however, officially supports only IBM PC DOS 3.1, 3.2, 3.3, 4.0, 4.01, and 5.0.) The following examples cover setting up and using IBM PC DOS 5.0.

What's the rationale for this feature? The preceding discussions about the VDM DOS kernel noted that the kernel supported all documented and many undocumented DOS calls and interrupts. Some programs rely on undocumented features of DOS that may not be present or supported in a VDM environment. Streaming tape drives and some network drivers are good examples. By providing the ability to load not only VDM DOS emulation, but other native versions of DOS as well, IBM is providing tangible features to support its claim that it is interested in protecting the customer's investment in DOS software. There is no need to discard existing investments in DOS software. If the program doesn't run in a VDM, boot a native version of DOS while still running OS/2 2.1.

The specific DOS implementation is so complete that you can use it to establish a test LAN on your OS/2 desktop. Although this is discussed in more detail later, the point here is that there is no better platform than OS/2 2.1 for the DOS developer.

Booting a specific DOS session is similar to booting a VDM. All of the session initialization procedures up to and including the 8086 emulation mode are the same. Specific DOS sessions make use of Virtual Device Drivers. Interrupts and port accesses are accomplished in the same manner as they are handled under a MVDM. A specific DOS session can access high performance file system (HPFS) drives, which are normally invisible to DOS, through FSFILTER.SYS (described in more detail later), which enables a DOS 3.x session to access a fixed disk larger than 32M. DOS 3.x is limited to 32M partitions, but FSFILTER.SYS works with the OS/2 file system to provide those services, much as a network file server makes its larger drives available to DOS 3.x clients.

A major difference between a specific DOS session and a VDM is that a specific DOS session can bypass virtual device drivers and access physical devices in some circumstances. If a system is not running any OS/2 LAN software, for example, that system could still boot a specific DOS session with the appropriate DOS LAN drivers, which directly control the network adapter. This disallows any other session from using that network adapter, but at least the system can get network access without changing the user's existing software. To the network software, it appears as if it is running on a native DOS workstation.

Memory resources are controlled through an interesting combination of DOS settings accessed from the OS/2 2.1 desktop and the CONFIG.SYS and AUTOEXEC.BAT of the specific DOS session. In an MVDM, all setup and control is accomplished through the DOSKRNL, which is controlled by the desktop DOS settings—a combination of DOS and 8086 emulation settings. The DOSKRNL level is missing in a specific DOS session because it substitutes IBMBIO.COM, IBMDOS.COM, and COMMAND.COM from the specific version of DOS.

MS DOS 5.0 uses IO.SYS and MSDOS.SYS instead of IBMBIO.COM and IBMCOM.COM. Both sets of files accomplish the same purpose: they provide basic DOS services.

This division means that some DOS settings, like DOS_HIGH, have no tangible effect on the specific DOS session. Memory settings such as EMS_MEMORY_LIMIT also have no effect. Settings that control 8086 or hardware level activity, however, affect the specific DOS session. VIDEO_MODE_RESTRICTION is a good example. With VIDEO_MODE_RESTRICTION set to NONE, the session provides video resolution at the limit of the adapter. When it is set to CGA, however, much of the A0000-BFFFF area is freed and the session has more conventional memory free.

If memory-related activity cannot be controlled by the DOS settings, how are they controlled? OS/2 2.1 ships with two memory management programs, HIMEM.SYS and EMM386.SYS, that can and should be used in a specific DOS session. HIMEM.SYS provides XMS services, including the A20 wrap-around support, just as the native DOS HIMEM.SYS does. EMM386.SYS provides the expanded memory support for specific DOS sessions. These drivers should be used instead of the files that ship with the specific DOS version. The OS/2 2.1 files are written to interface with the 8086 emulation code, and the others are not.

Table 8.2 contains a summary of how the various DOS settings and CONFIG.SYS settings affect the available conventional RAM (these figures were gathered using an MS DOS 5.0 specific DOS session).

Table 8.2. Specific DOS session and conventional memory.

Setting	*Effect*
567232	Default
567232	DOS_HIGH On
567152	DOS_UMB On
567024	HIMEM.SYS Loaded
521408	HIMEM.SYS Loaded, DOS=HIGH,NOUMB
621408	HIMEM.SYS Loaded, DOS=HIGH,UMB
718688	VIDEO_MODE_RESTRICTION Set to CGA

Notice that the maximum available conventional RAM is greatest under a MVDM. Even with a specific DOS session, however, more than 700K of conventional RAM can be made available.

Two primary methods are used to prepare a specific DOS session: using a disk boot from drive A (or another disk drive) or creating an image of a boot disk and storing it on the fixed disk. The first method is easier, but much slower during operation. The second method takes a little extra time to set up, but is much faster and easier to maintain. The following section focuses on the second method.

To create a specific DOS session, start with the IBM PC DOS 5.0's installation disk (other versions of DOS will be similar).

1. Insert a bootable DOS system disk in drive A (it's important to include a simple text editor such as EDLIN on the disk).
2. Open an OS/2 command prompt.
3. Create a subdirectory to store all the boot image files. To create a directory called C:\VBOOT, type `MD VBOOT`, then type `CD VBOOT`. The OS/2 prompt should now be `[C:\VBOOT]`.
4. OS/2 2.1 ships with a utility called VMDISK to create the DOS boot images. Type `VMDISK A: MYDOS.IMG` (`MYDOS.IMG` is the name given to the file that holds your boot image). OS/2 2.1 then displays a message saying "x percent of the disk has been copied" (*x* is the percentage of the total boot disk that has been read). The message "The system files have been transferred" displays when the process is complete. Note that the original DOS boot disk is not changed.
5. Exit the OS/2 prompt by typing `EXIT`. Remove the disk from drive A.
6. Double click with MB1 on the Template folder to display the templates. Move the mouse pointer on top of the Program icon and press MB1 once. Press and hold MB2 and drag the icon onto the desktop (or into a folder). The Program settings notebook now automatically opens up.
7. Type an asterisk (*) in the path and filename field. Click once with MB1 on the Session tab.

If you have an application that requires special DOS environmental variables or terminate-and-stay resident (TSR) programs, OS/2 2.1 can simulate an addition to the system's AUTOEXEC.BAT. For example, a program like Arago dBXL requires the DOS environmental variable `ARAGOHOME` to function correctly. Instead of adding it to the system-wide AUTOEXEC.BAT, you could add it to a separate BAT file. This BAT file should be specified in the path and filename field. It executes just after the standard AUTOEXEC.BAT executes. Note that as soon as the last line of the BAT file is executed, the DOS session terminates.

8. Click once with MB1 on the DOS Window pushbutton. (If you prefer, you can click once on the DOS Full Screen pushbutton instead.)
9. Click once with MB1 on the DOS settings pushbutton. Click once on the `DOS_STARTUP_DRIVE` option under Setting. Click once with MB1 anywhere in the Value field. The `DOS_STARTUP_DRIVE` setting tells OS/2 2.1 to use the DOS boot image just created with VMDISK. Type the full path and filename. In this case, type `C:\VBOOT\MYDOS.IMG`.
10. Click once with MB1 on the Save pushbutton.
11. Double click rapidly with MB1 on the system icon (the box in the upper-left corner of the window) to close the Settings folder.
12. Double click with MB1 on the new icon and verify that it opens as expected. If you use the IBM PC DOS 5.0 installation disk, you have to break out of the installation program by pressing F3 and answering Yes to the confirmation prompt. Use EDLIN or another simple editor that you copied onto the disk prior to it being VMDISKed to change the CONFIG.SYS. Notice that DOS thinks it has booted from drive A. CONFIG.SYS and AUTOEXEC.BAT for the specific DOS session is on a phantom drive A:, a drive that has no connection to drive A hardware. The A: drive for this session is (physically) the MYDOS file created with VMDISK.

13. While editing the CONFIG.SYS file, add the line `DEVICE=C:\OS2\MDOS\FSFILTER.SYS` near the top of the file. This line enables the specific DOS session to interact with the OS/2 2.1 file system. If you want expanded and XMS memory support, add the lines `DEVICE=C:\OS2\MDOS\HIMEM.SYS` and `DEVICE=C:\OS2\MDOS\EMM386.SYS` to the CONFIG.SYS.

> TIP
>
> Users who are familiar with the horrors of configuring an EMS page frame on a DOS machine are in for a treat with OS/2 2.1. EMS LIM 3.x and 4.0 work best with a single page frame of 64K. In the case of LIM 4.0, the page frame can be carved into separate 16K chunks, but that sacrifices backward compatibility with some applications that need LIM 3.x. The 64K page frame typically goes between A0000 and FFFFF. If a system has more than a few adapters, those areas of memory can go quickly and leave the system with no room for a page frame.
>
> OS/2 2.1 controls the 8086 emulation layer and "below" (it virtualizes the resources at those levels to DOS; OS/2 2.1 presents a virtual image of a microcomputer's hardware resources). If a specific DOS session doesn't need direct access to hardware, you can tell OS/2 2.1, through the `MEM_INCLUDE_REGIONS`, to use even memory that's claimed by an adapter. Only OS/2 2.1 needs physical access to the device. Virtual device drivers working with physical device drivers provide the function of that adapter to the VDM or specific DOS session. You can then include the `FRAME=C0000` switch on the EMM386.SYS line to provide LIM 3.x and 4.0 support to the applications that need EMS memory.

14. Save the CONFIG.SYS and edit the AUTOEXEC.BAT to suit your application. If you just want a standard DOS environment, add the lines `PATH=A:` and `PROMPT $p$g`.

Now, close the DOS 5.0 session and reopen it to verify that it works. Note that typing `EXIT` and pressing Enter won't work with a specific DOS session.

You have to select the system icon, select Close, and then select Yes. The reason for this is simple: from DOS's perspective, there's nothing to exit to. The specific DOS kernel owns the session and thinks it is the only thing running. On a native DOS system, typing `EXIT` has no effect. The same rules apply here.

Step 12 mentioned that the specific DOS session thinks drive A is the MYDOS boot image created with VMDISK. There may be times when you need to access the physical disk drive. OS/2 2.1 offers a way to do this with a program called FSACCESS.

FSACCESS redirects calls from phantom drives to the physical drives. It can also cancel that redirection. The command `FSACCESS A:`, when issued from within a specific DOS session, causes future attempts to access drive A to go to the physical disk drive. In this way, the physical disk drive is available to copy files onto the fixed disk or install DOS applications from drive A.

Be cautious when using FSACCESS. Typically, in a specific DOS session, the `COMSPEC` and `SHELL` statements in the AUTOEXEC.BAT and CONFIG.SYS point to drive A. The `COMSPEC` statement from the preceding example is probably `A:\COMMAND.COM`. Using FSACCESS to access the physical A: drive, for example, could cause the "Invalid COMMAND.COM" message to come up and lock the session unless this situation is corrected because the phantom drive that DOS expects is now gone in favor of the physical disk drive.

The way around this is to create a C:\DOS subdirectory and copy the basic DOS system files from the phantom drive A into the subdirectory on the fixed disk. Then, change references to A:\COMMAND.COM in CONFIG.SYS and AUTOEXEC.BAT to point to C:\DOS. In this way, you are free to use FSACCESS without hanging your session.

A specific DOS session behaves in much the same way as a VDM—performance is roughly the same, navigation is roughly the same. The only difference is at the DOS kernel level.

MVDM Window Management

An advantage that OS/2 2.1 has over OS/2 Version 1.x is its capability to run DOS programs on the Workplace Shell desktop, along side OS/2 Version 1.x, OS/2 Version 2.x, and Microsoft Windows 3.x applications. These windowed VDMs or specific DOS sessions can be manipulated in much the same way that an OS/2 window can be manipulated.

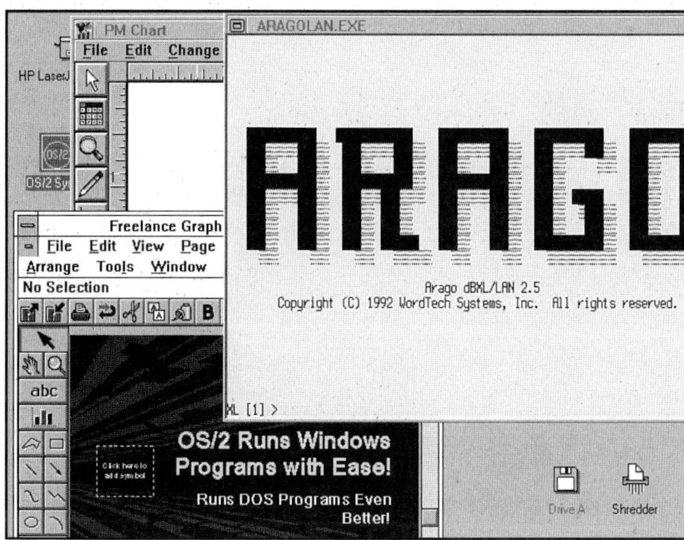

Figure 8.3. An example of DOS VDM, WINOS2, and OS/2 sessions on the OS/2 2.1 desktop.

Opening a session is easy. First, create an icon following the methods outlined in the previous sections or select an existing icon. Click twice with MB1 to open the session.

A DOS windowed session can be switched to a DOS full-screen session by pressing and holding the Alt key, then tapping the Home key. On PS/2-style keyboards, the Home key on the numeric keypad won't work—use the other Home key. The Alt-Home sequence toggles the DOS session from full screen to a window and back again.

Are you tired of having to manually expand windows every time you start an application? OS/2 2.1 has a solution: open the DOS window, position the mouse pointer over the Maximize button to the right of the Title bar, press and hold the Shift key, then press MB2—the window is now maximized.From that point forward, all windowed command prompts and applications open maximized.

Fonts can also be changed globally. As shipped, OS/2 2.1 defaults to a usable font that, when maximized, forces the window to take up two-thirds to three-fourths of the screen. If more of that information needs to appear in a smaller window, the user can change fonts using the following steps:

1. Click once on the System icon with MB1.
2. Click once on Font Size with MB1.
3. OS/2 2.1 displays a number of settings. Click once on "14 x 6" with MB1. Note that a given system's monitor/adapter combination may not show this setting.
4. Click once on Save with MB1.

The DOS windowed session now has a different font. Even the OS/2 windowed session has this font. Experiment with the various fonts to see which ones most closely meet your needs.

There are three ways to close an MVDM and one OS/2 2.1-supplied way to close a specific DOS session. In an MVDM, simply type `Exit` and press Enter to close the session. Of course, there are times when an erring DOS application may seriously conflict with its environment, and the session may crash. In that case, click once on the system icon with MB1 and select Close (or double click with MB1 on the system icon). Select Yes with MB1 to close the session. Either close method effectively yanks the rug out from under the DOS session—data files are not saved.

A third way to close a session is to press Ctrl-Esc to bring up the Task window list. Position the mouse on top of the session you want to end and press MB1 once. Press MB2 and click Close once with MB1 (the effect is the same as selecting Close from the system icon).

Specific DOS versions can be closed using the last two approaches. A quick way to do this is to be sure that the specific DOS version session has the desktop focus. Then press and release Alt, press C, and press Y. Alt, C, Y quickly closes the session.

DOS Settings

A few DOS settings that pertained specifically to RAM allocation appeared earlier in the chapter. This section evaluates selected DOS settings with an emphasis on maximizing overall system and session performance. Some of the more commonly-used DOS settings include real-world examples.

COM_DIRECT_ACCESS

Some DOS applications require direct access to COM port hardware. This parameter enables applications running in a VDM direct access to the port. It must be set before the session is started.

COM_HOLD

This setting locks the COM port that the DOS session uses to prevent interruption from other sessions. This setting is useful, but it is also dangerous (if a system has two COM ports and an LPT1 port, for example, and the STARTUP.CMD [the OS/2 2.1 AUTOEXEC.BAT file] contains the line SPOOL /D:LPT1 /O:COM2). If the DOS session locks the COM ports, it could potentially prevent any other sessions, DOS or OS/2, from printing, since the COM ports the session is using are locked, and one of those ports is being used for system-wide printing. (This setting affects both VDMs and specific DOS image sessions.)

COM_SELECT

Some DOS applications try to take control of all available COM ports regardless of what they actually use. Once this type of DOS program starts, other applications may not be able to access any COM ports. COM_SELECT prevents the DOS program from taking control of unnecessary resources. The field for this setting can be A11, COM1, COM2, COM3, or COM4. The field defines the COM ports the application can access. You must change this setting before you start the VDM.

DOS_AUTOEXEC

A Tip earlier in this chapter discusses setting up an AUTOEXEC.BAT supplement for certain applications that need SET commands or TSR programs loaded for that particular session. In that Tip, the default AUTOEXEC.BAT ran first, then the user-specified BAT file. OS/2 2.1 offers a way to replace the default AUTOEXEC.BAT file for specific VDMs.

The DOS_AUTOEXEC setting holds the path and filename of a substitute BAT file. The BAT file can contain any valid DOS BAT commands or structures. The user could set up a separate AUTOEXEC.BAT for every application. Leaving this setting blank forces the system to use the AUTOEXEC.BAT in the root directory of the OS/2 boot drive. This setting works for VDMs, but has no effect in specific DOS image sessions.

DOS_BACKGROUND_EXECUTION

The whole point of OS/2 2.1 is that it allows DOS applications to multitask safely along side OS/2 and MS Windows applications. However, there may be times when you want to disable that function for a specific session. WordPerfect can provide a good reason. It constantly polls the keyboard for input, and this inhales CPU cycles. If WordPerfect will not be printing in the background, and if a number of other applications will be running simultaneously, set DOS_BACKGROUND_EXECUTION to Off. This setting affects both VDMs and specific DOS image sessions.

DOS_DEVICE

Some DOS sessions may have a need to load device drivers that other DOS sessions do not need. Instead of placing these drivers in CONFIG.SYS, which would force the drivers to load into every VDM, OS/2 provides the `DOS_DEVICE` setting for the user to specify device drivers specific to a single VDM.

For example, if the user wanted to add the VDM version of ANSI.SYS to a specific session, the user could add the entry `C:\OS2\MDOS\ANSI.SYS`, assuming that OS/2 2.1 was installed on the C: drive. This line forces ANSI.SYS to load for that VDM only.

DOS device drivers can also be loaded in CONFIG.SYS. As noted earlier, DOS device drivers do not cause OS/2 2.1 any problems during the system boot. If OS/2 2.1 encounters a DOS device driver in CONFIG.SYS, OS/2 2.1 waits to load and invoke that device driver until any MVDM or specific DOS image is started. If a device driver is loaded in CONFIG.SYS, they affect all VDMs. This setting has no effect on specific DOS image sessions, but works for VDMs.

DOS_HIGH

This is the equivalent to the DOS 5.0 `DOS=HIGH` CONFIG.SYS parameter. XMS memory must be enabled (it is by default) for this to function correctly. There are few reasons to not set this to On, even though it is Off by default. In the original OS/2 2.1, `DOS=HIGH` prevents Windows 3.x applications from running.

The default for this setting can be set in the OS/2 CONFIG.SYS's `DOS=LOW,NOUMB`. The `LOW` parameter defines the `DOS_HIGH` default state. The default state does not override any icons or applications that are already defined. If the user has created one DOS application icon that set `DOS_HIGH` Off, the CONFIG.SYS setting has no affect on that application. If the user is going to create a new application using the Template's program icon, then the default conforms to the CONFIG.SYS setting. The exception is if the user has manually changed the Template folder's program icon's `DOS_HIGH` setting.

Setting DOS_HIGH to On tells OS/2 2.1 to load part of DOS in high DOS memory. This frees about 24,432 bytes of conventional RAM for DOS applications. This setting works for VDMs and has no effect on specific DOS image sessions.

DOS_STARTUP_DRIVE

This is the parameter that tells OS/2 2.1 to load a specific DOS image session. Though IBM doesn't explicitly support anything except IBM PC DOS 3.1, 3.2, 3.3, 4.0, and 5.0, it is possible to boot Digital Research DOS from this setting. It is even possible to boot a PS/2 reference disk (on a PS/2 only, of course) as long as you don't run diagnostics or change the system configuration. This parameter, of course, is used only for specific DOS version boots.

If the user specifies a drive letter here, OS/2 2.1 will not load the usual DOSKERNL and associated OS/2 DOS files. Instead, OS/2 looks to the specified disk drive and begins to load the operating system as if that session were a unique microcomputer. In other words, the user can think of that session as a PC being turned on and booting from disk.

DOS_UMB

This works with DOS_HIGH to make the most conventional memory available to an MVDM. This parameter opens up the upper-memory blocks between, basically, C0000 to DFFFF on PS/2-class machines. The DOS command LOADHIGH or CONFIG.SYS parameter DEVICEHIGH can then be used to load application or system code in the UMB region. The UMB region can be maximized with one or both of the following approaches.

First, use MEMORY_INCLUDE_REGIONS to block C0000 to DFFFF. Don't use this if a session needs direct hardware access to an adapter whose adapter RAM or ROM is in that region.

Second, don't use LIM Expanded Memory. This saves the page frame RAM, which is 64K. Of course, if an application needs expanded memory, this isn't an option. The default setting for DOS_UMB is set in the OS/2

CONFIG.SYS's DOS=LOW,NOUMB. The NOUMB aspect of that setting sets the default for DOS_UMB.

As with the DOS=LOW parameter, changing the CONFIG.SYS setting has no affect on existing applications. This setting works for VDMs and has no effect on specific DOS image sessions.

DOS_VERSION

DOS version is vital to some applications that need to think they are running on DOS 5.0 or less. Some applications, like dBase IV 1.1 and 1.5, check the DOS version when they load. If it's too low, or if they can't understand it (as is the case with DOS 20.10, which is what OS/2 2.1 returns), then that application may not function correctly. Some device drivers, like selected Microsoft CD-ROM drivers, fall into this category. DOS_VERSION tells the application that it is running under another version of DOS. The syntax to add a program is MYPROG.EXE,5,00,255. MYPROG.EXE can be any DOS program name, and it is not limited to EXE files. The number 5 represents the DOS major version. It could also be 3 or 4, or any other valid DOS major version. 00 is the DOS minor version, as in DOS 3.3. 255 tells DOS_VERSION to return the specific DOS version to the application no matter how many times it checks.

This setting works only in a VDM. Under specific DOS session boots, applications inquiring about the operating system's version receive the version of the specific DOS that was booted.

The OS/2 2.1 VER command can provide more information about the current session's version than is documented in the command reference. Typing VER /R displays the command processor's version, as the user might expect. It goes on to display the OS/2 kernel revision level. The VER /R command also displays whether or not DOS is loaded into HMA.

EMS_FRAME_LOCATION

You can use EMS_FRAME_LOCATION to disable EMS entirely, specify a certain range for the page frame, or allow the session to select the frame automatically. Setting it to None disables it.

LIM expanded memory requires a page frame. There are two basic types: continuous and discontinuous. Older applications that support LIM expanded memory, like Lotus 1-2-3 2.01, require a specific version: LIM 3.2. LIM 3.2 needs a page frame of 64K, in one continuous chunk (i.e., located at C0000 to CFFFF, or D0000 to DFFFF). Newer applications that support LIM 4.0 memory, like Lotus 1-2-3 2.4, still need 64K, but that 64K can be in four distinct and discontinuous 16K segments.

OS/2 2.1 does not give the user the ability to specify multiple 16K segments. Instead, it forces the user to specify a single 64K segment. This should not pose a problem, because OS/2 2.1 can virtualize any adapter RAM in the high memory area. See the section "Specific DOS Versions," in this chapter for a more detailed discussion of this point. This setting works for VDMs and specific DOS image sessions.

EMS_MEMORY_LIMIT

Before this setting will work, the EMS_PAGE_FRAME must be set correctly. The EMS_MEMORY_LIMIT setting controls how much expanded memory that OS/2 provides for a session. Each session can be configured independently from one another.

EMS memory consumes system resources quickly. Specifying 2M (the default) and opening five sessions commits 10M of EMS memory. On a system with 8M of memory available after loading OS/2 2.1, this causes the SWAPPER.DAT file to grow by at least 2M. SWAPPER.DAT is the file OS/2 2.1 uses to page RAM to disk when the demand for RAM resources exceeds the total amount of RAM installed in the system. If applications don't require EMS, don't waste resources and degrade performance by having an EMS_MEMORY_LIMIT other than 0. If an application needs 1M of EMS RAM, set EMS_MEMORY_LIMIT to 1024.

It is best to start by specifying a low amount (or none if the user's application doesn't need EMS memory). If the user has a Lotus 1-2-3 2.01 spreadsheet that needs 500K or so of expanded memory, then the user could start by specifying 1024 as the `EMS_MEMORY_LIMIT`. As the spreadsheet grows, the user can increase the `EMS_MEMORY_LIMIT` as necessary.

As discussed earlier in the chapter, EMS memory directly affects the amount of RAM available to the system. If performance degrades as more and more DOS applications use EMS, adding more RAM to the system should increase performance. The exception is on some older machines whose BIOS will not support more than 16M of physical RAM. On those machines, 16M is the maximum that can be added to the system. This setting affects VDMs and specific DOS versions.

IDLE_SECONDS

The OS/2 2.1 task scheduling component watches the MVDMs to make sure they're doing useful work. `IDLE_SECONDS` gives an MVDM application a grace period before the system reduces the resources to the MVDM. Ordinarily, `IDLE_SECONDS` is set to 0, and this tells OS/2 2.1 to reduce resources immediately if the MVDM appears to be waiting. However, some games may pause briefly before moving on, and some timing-dependent programs may be adversely affected if `IDLE_SECONDS` is set to 0. Setting this to 1 or 2 will gives an MVDM application 1 to 2 seconds to do something before their processor resource allocation is reduced. This parameter works for both VDMs and specific DOS versions.

IDLE_SENSITIVITY

The OS/2 2.1 task scheduling component monitors how much a given MVDM application polls for keyboard input. Such a polling action is generally, though not always, an indication that an application is idle and is just waiting for user input. `IDLE_SENSITIVITY` is a percentage that OS/2 2.1 applies to the rate the application is polling versus the maximum potential rate of polling for that session. If the setting is 75 percent, then OS/2 2.1 only reduces resources to that MVDM's application if that application polls at over 75 percent of the

maximum potential polling rate. In other words, if an application can potentially poll the keyboard 10 times a second and actually polls it 8 times, OS/2 assumes that the application is idle and reduces the amount of system resources allocated to that application.

Some programs, like Procomm Plus and other Async communications programs, may appear to be idle, when they are in reality receiving screen information from a remote host or are conducting a file transfer. If this setting is too low for those applications, the screen may appear to freeze, even when that application is in the foreground. The setting should be increased to 80 or 90 for some timing-dependent applications, and it should be set to 100 for many Async applications.

Of course, setting it too high degrades overall system performance. This setting can be changed while the session is running to facilitate easy experimentation. For most applications, this setting can be set low (around 10 to 20) to maximize the CPU resources to other applications. This setting works for VDMs and specific DOS version sessions.

INT_DURING_IO

In a native DOS system, and in a default VDM session, writing to a file prevents that session from receiving any interrupts. This is done to protect the integrity of the information in a DOS environment. After all, under DOS, only one thing should be running at a time, so why go to great lengths to protect disk I/O?

OS/2 2.1's `INT_DURING_IO` leverages off of the VDM's interaction with the OS/2 file system. Because OS/2 2.1 is handling the I/O at a level independent from the VDM, the user can set `INT_DURING_IO` to On, which allows the session to receive interrupts even while the I/O operating is incomplete. Multimedia applications benefit especially from this setting because they will be able to continue to service interrupts from a sound adapter or special video display even while they are reading or writing to the fixed disk from a VDM or WIN-OS2 session.

An application that produces sound for a Windows 3.1 application, for example, can work fine under OS/2 2.1. However, if there is a significant amount of disk I/O happening at this time, like loading a Windows application in the WINOS2 session, that I/O can place such a high demand on the processor that the sound producing application can produce garbled sound. Setting `INT_DURING_IO` On tells OS/2 to go ahead and service the sound-producing interrupt requests in a timely manner. I/O performance is degraded with `INT_DURING_IO` set On because OS/2 has to add the overhead of checking for interrupts often during the file I/O operation. This setting applies to both specific DOS image sessions and the VDMs.

KBD_BUFFER_EXTEND

What power user hasn't complained about DOS's small typeahead buffer? While there are many utilities available that increase the buffer, OS/2 2.1 provides the ability as part of the operating system. The power-user can type blithely on and not be subjected to the annoying beeps of DOS complaining that its keyboard buffer is full.

This setting works best with DOS and OS/2 command prompt windows or full-screen sessions. It also works well with specific DOS version sessions. Some DOS applications, however, will not benefit from the extended keyboard buffer. dBase IV, for example, has its own typeahead buffer. Its maximum setting, if set below the `KBD_BUFFER_EXTEND` buffer size, takes precedence. This setting affects both VDMs and specific DOS version sessions.

KBD_CTRL_BYPASS

OS/2 2.1 uses Ctrl-Esc and Alt-Esc to maneuver among windowed sessions and the Task List. Some DOS programs may depend on those keystrokes for their function. The IBM 3270 Entry Level Emulation Version 2.0 program, for example, now uses Ctrl-Esc to switch from DOS to the 3270 emulator session. Use `KBD_CTRL_BYPASS` to give DOS the ability to continue to use those keystrokes.

When the session with `KBD_CTRL_BYPASS` set On is in the foreground, the keystroke that is set to be bypassed performs no OS/2 function. Instead, it functions as the DOS application wants it to. In the case of the IBM 3270

Emulation program, pressing Ctrl-Esc toggles the DOS session to the host emulator screen and back. Alt-Esc still takes the user to the next application that is running on the Task List. The user cannot bypass both Ctrl-Esc and Alt-Esc. Otherwise, the user could become trapped in that session! This setting affects both VDMs and specific DOS version sessions.

MEM_EXCLUDE_REGIONS

There are times when you may not want OS/2 2.1 to allow a DOS session to interact with certain portions of RAM between A0000 and FFFFF. This setting pretends to be ROM in whatever region or regions you specify. It prevents the VDM from using the area as UMB memory or as an EMS page frame. Both VDMs and specific DOS versions are affected by this setting.

MEM_INCLUDE_REGIONS

Typically, VDMs and specific DOS image sessions don't need to directly access the system's hardware. Most devices are accessed via the virtual device drivers working with physical device drivers at the OS/2 2.1 level. That means systems with VGA adapters, for example, can make the C0000 to DFFFF range available for UMBs or an EMS page frame without affecting a VDM or specific DOS image session's access to OS/2-controlled software.

For example, the IBM Token Ring Adapter takes up UMB-area memory for its adapter ROM and RAM. That UMB-area could be from C0000 to CFFFF. In a DOS system, that memory would be completely unavailable if the user wanted LAN access because the adapter needs to communicate with the device drivers and the system unit, and to do that it needs to be present in the UMB memory area. However, under an MVDM or specific DOS image session, that memory can be specified in `MEM_INCLUDE_REGIONS` to provide UMB memory or an EMS LIM 4.0 page frame, and if the OS/2 2.1 LAN drivers are loaded, the VDM or specific DOS image session still enjoy all of the LAN connectivity available to OS/2. This parameter influences both VDMs and specific DOS versions.

MOUSE_EXCLUSIVE_ACCESS

Pertaining only to windowed DOS sessions, `MOUSE_EXCLUSIVE_ACCESS` controls whether or not the window uses the desktop mouse pointer or requires that the window completely control the mouse pointer. WordPerfect, for example, doesn't work correctly with the desktop pointer. Whenever WordPerfect senses mouse movement, it invokes its own pointer, and then the WordPerfect mouse pointer, a block, moves along with the desktop pointer. The WordPerfect pointer is slightly out of sync with the OS/2 pointer, and the results can be confusing.

Setting `MOUSE_EXCLUSIVE_ACCESS` On eliminates this situation. As soon as the mouse pointer is invoked in WordPerfect's windowed DOS session, the WordPerfect block mouse pointer takes over. The desktop pointer disappears. Pressing Ctrl-Esc or Alt-Esc restores the desktop pointer's function.

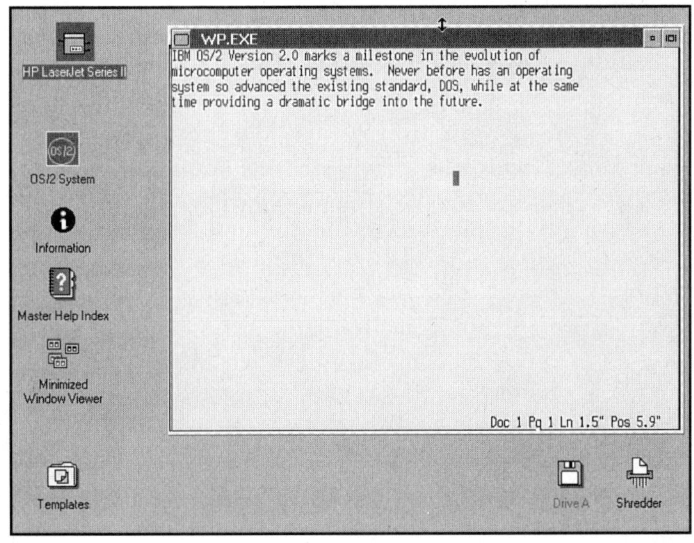

Figure 8.4. *WordPerfect's mouse point can conflict with the OS/2 2.1 desktop mouse pointer.*

At an OS/2 level, when `MOUSE_EXCLUSIVE_ACCESS` is set On, after the first mouse click within the application's windowed session, OS/2 2.1 no longer tries to update the mouse cursor position—the VDM now holds the mouse pointer captive. Pressing Alt-Tab, Alt-Esc, or Ctrl-Esc changes the OS/2 desktop's focus from the VDM to another session or to the desktop itself, and OS/2 then begins to update the mouse cursor position again. The setting controls both VDMs and specific DOS versions.

PRINT_TIMEOUT

Some DOS applications have a nasty tendency not to tell the operating system when they are done printing with an end-of-job code. Consequently, it may be difficult for the operating system to tell when to release a print job. In a single-tasking DOS environment, this isn't a problem because only one application at a time accesses the printer (unless the printer is itself shared among multiple computers, of course). Under a multitasking environment, though, the results could be frustrating as multiple jobs interrupt each other.

OS/2 2.1's print spooler functions much like a LAN Server's print queue. Instead of sending information to the printer as its received from an application, OS/2 collects the information into a file. OS/2 then watches the size of that file. If the spooler receives an end-of-job code, or if the spool file doesn't grow after a specified period of time, it releases the job.

`PRINT_TIMEOUT` controls that period of time. The default is 15 seconds. Some programs legitimately need that time. Database programs may need to do a lot of file I/O to prepare multiple parts of a report. Other programs may just not send an end-of-job code. Setting `PRINT_TIMEOUT` to a lower number releases the job more quickly. (This parameter affects VDMs and specific DOS versions.)

Some DOS applications may not release their print jobs, regardless of this setting, until the user exits the application. If this happens, the user should add the line `C:\OS2\MDOS\LPTDD.SYS` to the `DOS_DEVICE` selection discussed earlier.

VIDEO_FASTPASTE

Within windowed sessions, OS/2 2.1 allows the user to cut information from one session and paste it into another. This pasting is accomplished by stuffing the keyboard buffer from the OS/2 Clipboard. Setting this On allows for faster pasting.

Some applications may rebuffer keyboard input or may tamper with the keyboard buffer in other ways. If those applications don't work with this setting On, setting it Off may help. This setting affects both VDMs and specific DOS image sessions.

VIDEO_MODE_RESTRICTION

Video memory for VGA systems occupies roughly the A0000 to BFFFF area of upper memory (there's a gap of 32K in the regions, but it's of little consequence to this setting). That's around 96K of memory that is taken up in case you want to display VGA-quality graphics.

If an application doesn't use VGA graphics, setting the `VIDEO_MODE_RESTRICTION` to CGA frees up an extra 96K of memory for the DOS session. In many cases, total available conventional RAM can exceed 700K in a DOS session because of this, even with network and other drivers loaded!

The user should exercise caution with this setting. In some cases, applications can become less stable with the `VIDEO_MODE_RESTRICTION` set to CGA. The reason why is not clear, but if the user changes this setting to CGA and sees an immediate stability impact, the user should change this back to None. This setting works with VDMs and specific DOS versions.

This setting only frees up the RAM. Applications that query this RAM area to verify the existence of VGA Graphics work fine. Some applications that check hardware registers may try to use that memory for graphics production and thus corrupt application memory. In other words, the application could crash dramatically.

VIDEO_ONDEMAND_MEMORY

When OS/2 2.1 kicks off a VDM full screen, it allocates enough RAM for a virtual video buffer that can handle buffering the largest potential image for that session (i.e., a full-screen, full-resolution graphic). If the system is low on memory, setting this to On could help. The default is Off.

The drawback is that if the system is critically low on memory, and if the full-screen DOS session locks up because of insufficient virtual video buffer space, you could lose all of the unsaved data in that application. This setting impacts both the VDMs and specific DOS image sessions.

VIDEO_RETRACE_EMULATION

In ancient days, on CGA-level adapters, some applications would cause visual snow on the monitor by trying to write to the screen in between retrace intervals. Some programs began polling the retrace status port and would only update the screen at the appropriate interval. Technology progressed, and it is now safe on EGA and VGA screens to write anytime. A handful of programs, however, still poll the status port, and this negatively impacts performance.

The virtual DOS machines have an answer! `VIDEO_RETRACE_EMULATION` tells the polling application that it is safe to write to the screen, no matter when the application asks. On the balance, this provides better performance. There are a very small number of applications that write only during vertical retrace operations, and their performance may be negatively impacted if the `VIDEO_RETRACE_EMULATION` is On (the default). This setting affects both VDMs and specific DOS image sessions.

VIDEO_ROM_EMULATION

This function allows software to emulate video ROM, and thus provides higher performance than could be obtained by going through the hardware-level ROM for the video adapter. Under normal circumstances, this should be set On, which is the default that provides maximum performance. Some applications rely on undocumented INT 10h calls or rely on features provided by a particular brand of video adapter. If either of these is the case, `VIDEO_ROM_EMULATION` should be set Off. Performance, of course, will suffer. This setting impacts specific DOS and VDM sessions.

The higher performance that this function provides is most evident in a windowed session.

VIDEO_SWITCH_NOTIFICATION

With most CGA, mono, EGA, and VGA screens and adapters, this setting should remain Off. Its function is to notify the DOS session when the session has been changed from a full screen to a windowed screen. Some DOS applications, particularly Windows 2.x and 3.x applications, use this setting (and in their case, this should be set On). A few other DOS programs do as well.

It may also be valuable to some applications that use non-standard video modes that OS/2 doesn't support. This setting lets the application redraw its screen as appropriate.

For an IBM 8514 adapter (and compatible adapters as well), `VIDEO_SWITCH_NOTIFICATION` can increase redraw performance by telling the application when it can redraw to virtual space (i.e., the virtual device driver can know when to display data in a windowed session of a full-screen session, and when it can simply send the output to the virtual memory buffer and not the screen). This settings affects both the VDMs and specific DOS image sessions.

VIDEO_WINDOW_REFRESH

This setting controls the video refresh rate for the given session. The time is adjusted and shown in tenths of a second. Some graphics programs write often

to video memory. Adjusting the VIDEO_WINDOW_REFRESH rate higher (for example, to 5 tenths of a second) frees the processor from making frequent window/session screen refreshes. This setting also affects full-screen, scrolling (TTY) commands like DIR. This setting affects both VDMs and specific DOS image sessions.

XMS_MEMORY_LIMIT

This setting controls the maximum number of kilobytes that OS/2 2.1 gives to the DOS session. It can be set in 4K increments. By default, this is set to 4096, or 4M. In most cases, this is wasted because most DOS applications (and the DOS kernel itself) simply want the first 64K of XMS to use for DOS=HIGH. In fact, I recommend that unless you specifically need more XMS memory for a RAM disk or if a DOS application can use XMS memory, you should set this to 64. XMS_MEMORY_LIMIT is valid for VDMs and specific DOS image sessions.

Setting this to less than 64 disables DOS=HIGH and reduces the total amount of conventional RAM in a DOS session because DOS can no longer be loaded high.

Maximizing Common Applications

This section presents specific products that provide a variety of scenarios to OS/2 2.1's DOS compatibility. Although almost all current DOS applications run under OS/2 2.1, not all run well with the default settings. This section provides examples that can be applied in a typical business or personal microcomputer environment. In some cases, the section provides an application workaround for a situation, and in others, an OS/2-level workaround. OS/2 2.1 is so robust and flexible that it often offers not one, but several ways of achieving an end.

The following list of DOS applications is not intended to present a value judgment on the applications. Although I have selected WordPerfect 5.1 as the application to be presented, I am not suggesting that it is the best, or that other word processors are inferior.

Keep in mind that OS/2 2.1 provides unparalleled capabilities for the user to experiment with DOS settings. The user can change system-level settings, such as `XMA_MEMORY_LIMIT` settings, and see the result immediately by simply closing the VDM and reopening it. Users no longer have to be subjected to the torture of waiting for lengthy reboots to see if the latest attempt to squeeze one or two more kilobytes out of conventional RAM was successful. Verification is an Exit and a double click away.

Borland's Arago dBXL/Quicksilver 2.5

Arago dBXL 2.5 is an xBase interpreter product. Though Borland does not intend to market the product anymore, its technology will be incorporated into dBase IV, and the product has several characteristics that demonstrate many `DOS_SETTINGs`.

The Arago product line is typically well-behaved, but it has a few quirks that don't integrate well with the VDM default settings. The first manifests itself during the installation process. Arago's installation routine attempts to find the disk from which the system booted. OS/2 2.1 apparently returns an answer that Arago can't accept because it displays the phrase "Cannot locate a drive upon which DOS boots; No access to a boot drive. Cannot confirm values in AUTOEXEC.BAT and CONFIG.SYS." Perhaps the cause is that Arago can't find the DOS hidden system files. In any event, CONFIG.SYS and AUTOEXEC.BAT are not updated.

It's not a great matter to correct this. Table 8.3 shows the changes that need to be made.

DOS

Table 8.3. Arago-VDM Changes.

Change Where	*Change*
DOS_FILES	Increase to at lease 99
CONFIG.SYS	Increase BUFFERS to about 50
AUTOEXEC.BAT	Add `x:\ARAGO\BIN` to `PATH` statement (x = drive)
AUTOEXEC.BAT	Add `SET ARAGOHOME=x:\ARAGO\BIN` (x = drive)

These changes should enable both Arago products to run as largely as expected.

Arago's CUA-screen presentation fonts are a good example of another problem a program can get into with OS/2 2.1's VDMs and specific DOS image sessions.

Arago, and any program that manipulates screen fonts, can run into trouble when it is run in a windowed session. In Arago's case, the product has remapped several of the high-ASCII characters to provide more rounded edges for pushbuttons, half-circles to build circular radio buttons, and other similar CUA screen items. These display fine in a full-screen session. In a window, the results are unpredictable.

PC Tools 7.x takes a similar approach to its CUA-style menu and screen events.

OS/2 2.1 itself offers an alternative. Arago senses the type of video adapter it starts up under. Under a VGA-level monitor, it enables its font remapping. Under a CGA-level monitor, however, it doesn't. Changing the session's `VIDEO_MODE_RESTRICTION` to CGA disables the fonts as effectively as `SET ARAGOFONT=OFF`. It is a happy side effect of changing the restriction to CGA that Arago performs faster. The CGA setting allocates 96K more RAM from the video RAM area to conventional RAM, and the more conventional RAM that is available, the better Arago performs.

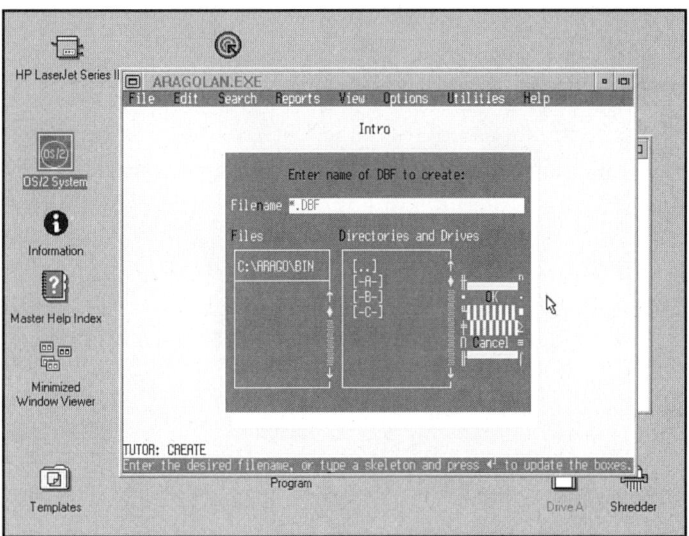

Figure 8.5. Arago dBXL 2.5's CUA font problem. Note the distorted edges on the OK and Cancel pushbuttons.

Arago QuickLink, its linker, works with expanded memory and upper memory blocks (UMBs) to achieve its greatest performance. On some systems, however, QuickLink locks up with an error message that says it has encountered a memory allocation error and cannot load COMMAND.COM. Correcting this error shows why its helpful to understand what settings control the VDM's memory environment.

A memory allocation error can happen in conventional RAM, UMB RAM, EMB RAM, XMS memory, expanded memory, or DPMI memory. Changing the corresponding DOS settings that control the different RAM areas isolates the problem. In this particular case, setting `DOS_UMB` to No corrected the problem. Apparently, on some systems, something in the environment causes QuickLink to malfunction when it tries to access UMBs.

The manuals that come with Arago mention in several places that Arago works best with large amounts of expanded memory. The DOS setting `EMS_MEMORY_LIMIT` specifies how much EMS memory is available. Deciding how high to set the `EMS_MEMORY_LIMIT` is a function of the complexity of the application to be run, but 2048, the default, is a good place to start.

dBase IV 1.5/Runtime 1.5

Borland's dBase line is the market leader for database products designed specifically for the microcomputer platform. dBase IV 1.5 is an interpretative environment, much like Arago dBXL. It includes screen designing tools, report building tools, and an application building tool, and these are accessed through the dBase IV Control Center. For advanced microcomputer database designers, it offers what is widely considered to be the standard xBase language for application development.

The dBase IV 1.5 Runtime allows the royalty-free distribution of dBase IV applications. It is not a compiler, but it achieves nearly the same purpose. In this section, the statements that apply to dBase IV 1.5 also apply to the Runtime, unless otherwise noted.

Simple dBase IV 1.5 scenarios run in a VDM without changes to the default settings. One problem manifests itself in more complex dBase IV activities because dBase IV 1.5 employs a unique method of allocating internal file handles for itself. When it fires up, it checks the version of DOS it is running on. If it encounters a version it is not familiar with, but is a version higher than the lowest version of DOS it supports, dBase IV allocates a default of 20 file handles. This is fine for routine control center activity, but no application of any complexity can run at all.

Knowing this characteristic of dBase IV made it easy to understand how to correct the problem. Changing the DOS_VERSION setting to tell dBase IV that it was running under DOS 5.0 corrected the internal dBase IV problem, and increasing the DOS_FILES to 60 solved the second.

The default FILES= for VDMs can be changed in CONFIG.SYS by increasing the FILES= statement.

The precise lines to add to DOS_VERSION are as follows:

```
DBASE.EXE,5,00,255
RUNTIME.EXE,5,00,255
```

With these changes made, dBase IV will not run as expected in a standalone mode.

Lotus 1-2-3 Version 3.1+

Lotus 1-2-3 Version 3.1+ is one of two current versions of Lotus Corporation's market leading character-based spreadsheet programs. It offers three-dimensional spreadsheet capabilities, as well as DPMI memory support to work with huge spreadsheets. It also has rudimentary graphics capabilities.

Like many DOS programs, 1-2-3 3.1+ checks what version of DOS it is running under to verify the version is supported by the product. Like many DOS programs, it doesn't know how to deal with DOS Version 20.10. Therefore, it is essential to change the `DOS_VERSION` setting for this application to work.

Experimentation is the key to discovering all of the EXE and COM files that require a notation in the `DOS_VERSION` slot. One of the first things to do if a program doesn't work it to add it to `DOS_VERSION` and retry the application.

Table 8.4 shows the Lotus 1-2-3 3.1+ EXE files that should be added to `DOS_VERSION`, along with an appropriate DOS version number.

Table 8.4. Lotus 1-2-3 3.1+ EXE DOS_VERSION settings.

123.EXE	4,00,255
123DOS.EXE	4,00,255
LOTUS.EXE	4,00,255
INSTALL.EXE	4,00,255
TRANS.EXE	4,00,255

If you plan to run just 123.EXE, only 123.EXE and 123DOS.EXE need to be set.

Trying to run 1-2-3 3.1+ now results in either poor performance or a failure. That's because 1-2-3 doesn't have its DPMI memory settings correctly

established yet. Lotus 1-2-3 3.1+ requires two things to correctly address DPMI memory: an adequate amount of addressable DPMI memory and a DOS environmental variable.

The first thing to do is set the `DPMI_MEMORY_LIMIT`. This number should be tailored by considering a number of variables, including how large the spreadsheets Lotus 1-2-3 3.1+ will be working with, how much physical RAM is in the system unit, and how much of that physical RAM is already committed or is likely to be committed to other applications or to the operating system when 1-2-3 3.1+ loads and begins its work.

Of course, the larger the spreadsheets are going to be, the higher the `DPMI_MEMORY_LIMIT` has to be set. If the system unit is in a RAM-constrained situation (i.e., it has 4M to 8M of RAM), setting `DPMI_MEMORY_LIMIT` too high can negatively impact overall system performance. If this can't be helped, if the spreadsheets need at least, say, 4M of RAM, OS/2 2.1 provides it by swapping other sessions' contents to disk while 1-2-3 3.1+ has the processor's attention. Overall performance suffers, but at least the system will still be operational. If, on the other hand, the system has 16M of RAM and only a few other programs will be running simultaneously, a `DPMI_MEMORY_LIMIT` setting of 4096 causes little or no performance degradation. The key here is to set what 1-2-3 3.1+ needs under normal circumstances. The user can always increase the limit for special cases. Try setting it to 2048 to start.

The next thing to do is set the 1-2-3 DOS environmental variable. A Tip earlier in this chapter discusses establishing a special supplement to the standard AUTOEXEC.BAT for an individual MVDM. To create one called 12331.BAT, see Listing 8.1.

Listing 8.1. 12331.BAT.

```
@ECHO OFF
SET 123MEMSIZE=2048
PATH=%PATH%;C:\123R31
123
```

Remember that this needs to be placed in the path and filename field in the DOS settings notebook.

This batch file does several things. First, `@ECHO OFF` turns `ECHO OFF`, which means the rest of the commands won't echo onto the screen. `@` means the `ECHO OFF` itself won't show either.

`SET 123MEMSIZE=2048` is required by 1-2-3 3.1+ to tell the program how much DPMI memory to expect and to use. This number must equal or be lower than the amount of DPMI memory specified above.

The `PATH` statement appends C:\123R31 to the existing `PATH` as stated in the AUTOEXEC.BAT. If you installed 1-2-3 3.1+ in a directory other than C:\123R31, you should specify it on this line. Appending C:\123R31 to the existing `PATH` enables 1-2-3 3.1+ to be run from any other directory, and it preserves the default `PATH` as stated in AUTOEXEC.BAT. You can eliminate the need for this line by substituting `CD\123R31`. If you have installed 1-2-3 3.1+ on a drive other than the default, include a line `X:` before `CD\123R31`, where `X:` is the drive you have used. The last line, `123`, starts the program.

There is one final thing that needs to be done. Lotus 1-2-3 3.1+ is basically a graphical application, even when not run in its WYSIWYG mode. That means it should be run as a full-screen application. Open the DOS settings notebook, select the Session tab, and select the DOS full-screen pushbutton.

Although this approach gives you access to the full set of functionality within 1-2-3 3.1+, starting 1-2-3 3.1+ via the `LOTUS` command may behave oddly when quitting out of 1-2-3. You will probably get the error message "Access cannot run the program you selected." There is no other abnormal behavior at this point, and our experience suggests this error can be ignored.

Since this approach starts the session without an asterisk in the path and filename field, the session will probably close when you quit 1-2-3 3.1+. This is the default behavior. You can change that by opening DOS Settings, selecting the Session tab, and deselecting the Close window in exit checkbox.

Procomm Plus 2.x

Procomm Plus is an asynchronous communications package. It began its days as a shareware application. It became highly popular because of its ease of use and support of many file transfer protocols. Datastorm, the manufacturer, has released the package into the commercial world, where it enjoys a loyal customer following and good market penetration.

Programs like Procomm Plus require intensive access to a serial port, where a modem is connected. The application must constantly monitor the asynchronous port for communications input and it must constantly manage output to the screen or to disk (for instance, from the keyboard or during a file transfer). This can present a performance problem for the rest of the system. If most of the system resources are dedicated to handling the asynchronous port, the rest of the system can slow down noticeably. On the other hand, too little resources devoted to the Procomm Plus session can cause screen scrolls or file transfers to fail.

This is what can happen when the `IDLE_SENSITIVITY` is set to its default, 75. If you attach to a remote asynchronous host like a BBS, the data stream coming into your system typically scrolls vertically on your screen. With an `IDLE_SENSITIVITY` set to 75, that scroll can sometimes stop. The OS/2 2.1 task scheduler doesn't interpret input from the asynchronous port to be session activity, at least in the same sense as keyboard or mouse input. The task scheduler considers the task to be idle if it is simply receiving asynchronous input, and the session receives less processor time. This is why the screen seems to freeze sometimes, and also why file transfers can fail. Both conditions are made much worse at higher baud rates like 9600.

The solution is to set `IDLE_SENSITIVITY` to 100. Although this has a negative performance impact for the rest of the system for asynchronous connections at or more than 9600, it does allow for reliable operation of Procomm Plus and packages like it.

Don't switch from a full-screen to a windowed session during a file transfer. You can hang the session and abort a download or upload.

You may be tempted to set COM_HOLD On for an asynchronous program. Although that makes sense to do, it is typically not necessary. The virtual device driver for the COM port handles conflicts in most cases.

WordPerfect 5.1

WordPerfect 5.1 is the undisputed market leader in the word processing arena. The application offers a tremendous breadth of function in an easy-to-use package. Its printer support is unparalleled, and the company has demonstrated a desire to support new printers as they become available. The company's free 1-800 support program has won the package many loyal customers.

WordPerfect also shares an annoying tendency with many other DOS programs: it polls the keyboard constantly. This continuous polling can degrade overall system performance. In fact, if you are not prepared for it, the results can be surprising. With the default settings, WordPerfect under OS/2 2.1 can reduce even an 80486 system to 80286-performance levels.

Fortunately, OS/2 2.1 again demonstrates its flexibility by providing a fix for this situation: IDLE_SENSITIVITY. As discussed in the "DOS Settings" section, IDLE_SENSITIVITY monitors the application's polling rate and compares it to the maximum possible polling rate estimated for that session. When the application exceeds the threshold set in IDLE_SENSITIVITY, OS/2 2.1 assumes the session is idle, and reduces the amount of processor time allocated to it.

The best IDLE_SENSITIVITY setting for WordPerfect appears to be around 20. This allows the application to function without apparent degradation, yet reduces the unnecessary stress on the processor by allowing the operating system to recognize more quickly when WordPerfect is just polling the keyboard.

With IDLE_SENSITIVITY set to 20, WordPerfect's printing performance can be reduced. It may be a good idea to temporarily set IDLE_SENSITIVITY to 50 or 60 during printing sessions. To do this, use the following instructions:

1. If the WordPerfect session is not already running in a windowed session, press Alt-Home to place it in one.

2. Click once on the System icon (the small box on the left of window's the title bar) with the selection mouse button (the left mouse button).
3. Click once with the left mouse button on the DOS Settings option.
4. Click once with left mouse button on the `IDLE_SENSITIVITY` option in the Settings list box, then use the mouse (or manually type in the value) to increase the value to 50 or 60.

Changing the setting here (instead of changing it from the session's icon) will not make the change permanent.

WordPerfect has exhibited one more odd behavior when run in a VDM. Sometimes, for no apparent reason, WordPerfect stops accepting keystrokes. Ordinarily, this would be a cause for panic. However, because OS/2 2.1 provides a mouse interface that WordPerfect can use, you can still save your work and get out of the session. If your WordPerfect session stops taking keyboard input, simply press the manipulation mouse button (the right mouse button) to bring up the WordPerfect menu, select Save, save your work, then press the right mouse button and select Exit. You have to have the WordPerfect menu enabled for this to be possible, and you have to have the mouse interface enabled. It is typically enabled by default. WordPerfect runs with approximately the same characteristics in a VDM or a specific DOS image session.

Integrating MVDMs Into the OS/2 Environment

OS/2 2.1 can run windowed VDMs side by side with OS/2 2.1 windowed applications and seamless Windows 3.x applications. To the user, all three types of applications appear to be equal because they all run at the same time. There may or may not be visual differences: a character-based OS/2 application cannot be distinguished from its equivalent DOS-based cousin without an intimate knowledge of the products. IBM has done this intentionally to support OS/2 2.1's role as the integrating platform. This integration goes beyond the cosmetic. IBM has provided tools to help OS/2, DOS, and Windows applications communicate and work together.

The degree of integration of the VDM extends to the `VER` command issued in any VDM session. `VER /R` in MS/PC-DOS returns the internal revision number. The same command entered into any VDM returns the internal revision of the OS/2 kernel.

Clipboard

The Clipboard is perhaps the most obvious manifestation of this concept. Basically, the Clipboard can be used to transfer information from one session to another. The method varies subtly for different types of sessions. In DOS windowed sessions and OS/2 windowed sessions, you mark text or graphics to be copied by clicking once with MB1 on the System icon and selecting Mark. The cursor then turns into a cropping tool. Place the tool on the upper-right corner of the rectangle that you want to copy, then press and hold MB1. Move the mouse until the area to copy is highlighted, then release MB1. The area is now marked and is ready to copy. To actually copy the data to the Clipboard, click on the System icon with MB1 and click once with MB1 on Copy. (Note that this method works for both text and graphic elements.)

Some OS/2 2.1 programs support copies or moves to the Clipboard through a menu option within the program. For those programs, the Mark option may not be available under the System icon. Use the OS/2 program's menu option to perform the copies or moves.

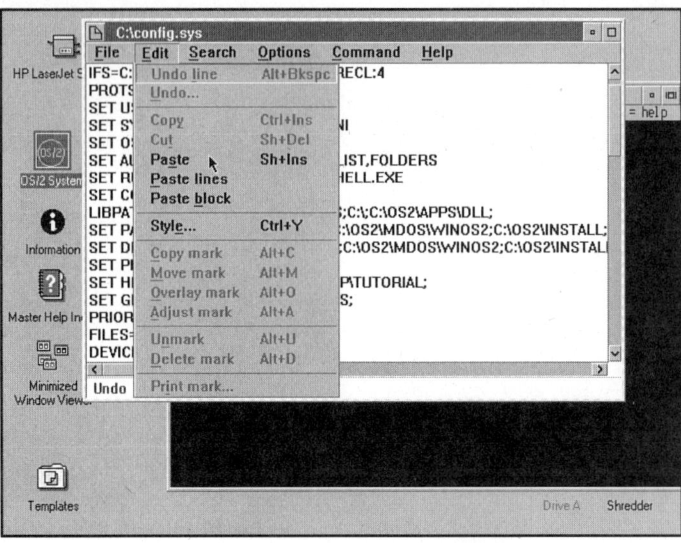

Figure 8.6. The OS/2 2.1 Enhanced Editor includes the Paste option under the Edit menu selection.

Getting data to the Clipboard from full-screen sessions is a little less flexible. For a DOS full-screen session, the method is to use an icon to start the program. While the program is running in full-screen mode, use Ctrl-Esc to get back to the Workplace Shell desktop. Click once with MB1 on the program's icon, then once with MB2. Position the mouse pointer on the Copy All option near the bottom (just above Paste and below windowed) and click once with MB1. The entire contents of the screen should be dumped to the Clipboard. However, for the sake of precision and flexibility, it makes more sense to press Alt-Home to convert the full-screen session temporarily to a windowed session and use the method described in the previous paragraph to copy or move the data.

For an OS/2 full-screen session, the only way to cut information is if the program running in that session supports copies to the Clipboard. If it does, the option is typically located off the Edit option of the application's main menu bar (similar to the editor in Figure 8.6). The Cut option under Edit should move data to the Clipboard.

OS/2 2.1 comes with a tool that lets you see just what got copied or moved to the Clipboard before the data is pasted into another application. In the OS/2 System icon (in the Productivity folder) is an application called Clipboard Viewer (assuming that the user installed the Productivity Aids). This application shows the contents of the Clipboard. This is useful to verify your copy before you paste the Clipboard contents into the target application.

The method to move information into an application, otherwise known as pasting, depends on what kind of session and application the target is. For a windowed DOS session, click once with MB1 on the System icon, then click once with MB1 on Paste. The contents of the Clipboard are transferred to the DOS session through the keyboard buffer (for text transfers), beginning at the cursor's current position. OS/2 2.1 is intelligent enough not to provide the Paste option for graphic Clipboard contents when the target is a text-based session.

If you experience difficulties when pasting into a DOS application, try changing the setting for `VIDEO_FASTPASTE`. Some applications may not correctly interpret the keyboard buffer input and may hang the session. Be aware that there may be limitations on how the DOS application interprets the paste operation. A word processor is perfect for accepting pastes. The end of a line is marked with a carriage return and a line feed for Clipboard text, and a carriage return advances the cursor to the next line in a word processor. The word processor simply thinks it is being used by an extraordinarily fast typist.

Spreadsheet applications may not fare as well. They may interpret a carriage return as a command to close a cell, but not advance the cursor. This could result in the entire contents of the Clipboard overlaying itself until only the last line remains. To transfer data to a spreadsheet, it may be best to transfer the Clipboard to a text editor, save the contents as a file, and use the spreadsheet's Import option to bring that text file in.

A real-world example of Clipboard usage is a corporate environment where information is accessed through a mainframe computer and a 3270 link. For this example, assume that the user is attached to an information service through OS/2 Extended Services 1.0's Communication Manager and that there is information on the mainframe the user wants to get into WordPerfect 5.1, but would prefer not to retype. Again, OS/2 2.1 provides the answer!

The user can bring the information up on the 3270 screen. For the Communication Manager, there's no need to use MB1 on the System icon to select Mark: Communications Manager interprets an LMB click and hold as the beginning of a block mark. The user then positions the mouse pointer to the upper-left corner of the text to be copied and presses and holds MB1. Using the mouse to expand the rectangle, the user highlights the block of text that needs copied and releases MB1. Clicking once with MB1 on the System icon reveals the Copy option, which the user clicks with MB1. The contents of the 3270 screen are now in the Clipboard.

The user should now bring up WordPerfect 5.1. With the cursor blinking where the user wants the 3270 screen's information to begin, the user clicks once with MB1 on the System icon, then once on Paste. The contents of the 3270 screen are now fed through the keyboard buffer into the WordPerfect document.

This process can be repeated as many times as necessary. Of course, if the source of the data is 30 or 40 screens, it may be more beneficial to find a way to get a host file with the information for download and import. However, if the choice is between cutting and pasting or retyping, the decision is obvious. If the user selects Paste and the operation does not behave as expected, pressing Esc halts the Paste operation.

Rudimentary MVDM-OS/2 Communications

Multiple virtual DOS machines are independent of one another and of any running OS/2 2.1 sessions. This is a good thing in general because that scheme maintains system integrity. There are times, however, when the user may want to access OS/2 2.1 functions from a VDM. What if the user wants to initiate a file transfer using Extended Services 1.0's Communications Manager to a mainframe host from within an application running in a VDM? What if a dBase IV program automatically backs up its databases using the BACKUP command, which is not available in a DOS session under 2.1? Can that application be moved without change to OS/2 2.1's VDMs? IBM has a solution: named pipes.

DOS

OS/2 2.1 sessions can serve as named pipe servers to VDM clients. Although this is an elegant and efficient method, named pipe knowledge is rare, even among highly technical microcomputer specialists. There is another way to accomplish many of the same things, however, building on existing batch command knowledge through a combination of BAT and CMD files.

For example, the first need just mentioned was a VDM initiating a file transfer to the host computer through the Communications Manager. In an OS/2 session, this is no problem. If the PATH is set correctly, simply invoking the SEND or RECEIVE commands to transfer the files accomplishes the function. However, Version 1.0 of Extended Services offers no SEND/RECEIVE commands that work in a VDM. The situation seems hopeless until the user remembers that she or he is running under OS/2 2.1, which must offer a workaround somewhere.

The solution is to create a queuing environment where the VDM makes a request of the OS/2 2.1 system. This can be done with a BAT file and a CMD file. BAT files are DOS batch files that contain lists of DOS commands. CMD files are DOS batch files that contain lists of DOS commands for OS/2 sessions. The BAT file can copy a file into a queue directory. The OS/2 CMD file can be running in that directory, and it can constantly check for the existence of the predetermined filename that will be copied by the BAT file. When the CMD file sees it, the CMD performs whatever actions necessary to initiate the upload.

A VDM application, a database program, for example, needs to send reports to the host. In the strict DOS environment of the old days, it would issue a SEND command similar to SEND C:\DATA\REPORT.TXT REPORT SCRIPT (ASCII CRLF. In a VDM, the replacement is a created file called SEND.BAT that has the following lines:

```
@ECHO OFF
COPY C:\DATA\REPORT.TXT C:\QUEUE\REPORT.TXT
```

An OS/2 2.1 windowed or full-screen session should already be running at this point. It should be executing a CMD file, called CHKQ.CMD, located in the C:\QUEUE directory. The contents of the CHKQ.CMD file are shown in Listing 8.2.

DOS

Listing 8.2. The contents of C:\QUEUE\CHKQ.CMD.

```
@ECHO OFF
IF EXIST REPORT.TXT GOTO UPGO
GOTO RERUN
:UPGO
SEND REPORT.TXT REPORT TXT (ASCII CRLF
ERASE REPORT.TXT
GOTO RERUN
:RERUN
CHKQ
```

This file runs constantly. As soon as it sees the REPORT.TXT copied into its directory, it branches to the :UPGO routine, where the report is uploaded to the host. CHKQ.CMD erases REPORT.TXT to be sure it doesn't try to upload the report file again, then passes control to the `:RERUN` routine, which runs the CMD file again.

Another example is a dBase IV program that has to run a BACKUP program to backup its *.DBF (database) files. dBase IV and other xBase languages (that is, languages based loosely on the dBase IV standard) allow programs to run DOS programs by prefacing the command with an exclamation point (!). To run a BACKUP program, then, the dBase IV command is `!BACKUP C:\DATA\*.DBF A: /S`. This works fine in a DOS system, but it doesn't work at all in a VDM.

The same queuing paradigm solves this problem, too. First, create a small file called BACKTRIG.TXT with a text editor (it needs only a single blank line). Then create a BACKUP.BAT file in the dBase IV program's directory that contains the following lines:

```
@ECHO OFF
COPY BACKTRIG.TXT C:\QUEUE
```

In the C:\QUEUE directory, create a continuously running CMD file called CHKQ2.CMD. It should contain the following lines:

```
@ECHO OFF
IF EXIST BACKTRIG.TXT GOTO BACKGO
GOTO RERUN
:BACKGO
BACKUP C:\DATA\*.DBF A: /S
ERASE BACKTRIG.TXT
```

```
GOTO RERUN
:RERUN
CHKQ2
```

This program continuously checks for the existence of BACKTRIG.TXT. When it sees that file in the C:\QUEUE directory, CHKQ2.CMD issues the BACKUP command and backs up the *.DBF files in C:\DATA. When it is done with that, CHKQ2.CMD erases the BACKTRIG.TXT file in C:\QUEUE and passes control to :RERUN, which runs the CMD file again.

This example could easily be expanded to cover multiple BACKUP options. BACKTR1.TXT could signal the OS/2 session to begin a BACKUP of C:\DATA*.NDX, the index files; BACKTR2.TXT could trigger a BACKUP of the *.DBO files (the tokenized dBase IV program files). In fact, CHKQ2.CMD and CHKQ.CMD could be combined into one VDM event handling CMD program. Any VDM could make a request of the OS/2 2.1 host system, and OS/2 2.1 could handle the requests. It almost turns OS/2 2.1 into a batch processing environment!

A continuously running (looping) batch file might affect system performance, especially on a minimal system with 4M to 6M of system memory.

LANs and VDMs

OS/2 2.1 Unleashed discusses LANs in more detail in Chapter 17, "Networking." However, the VDM environmental relationship to the OS/2 2.1 LAN connectivity world warrants some preliminary discussion.

OS/2 2.1 works well with both the OS/2 LAN Requester for connections to an IBM OS/2 LAN server domain controller and the Novell NetWare Requester for OS/2 2.1 for connectivity to a NetWare 3.x server. This section focuses on the OS/2 LAN Requester environment, but much of the material applies to the NetWare Requester for OS/2 2.1 as well.

After the user logs into an OS/2 LAN server domain controller through an OS/2 session, all network drive and printer assignments are available to the virtual DOS machines. If the user has a network drive I, for example, the VDM sees and is able to use that drive. This works fine for most nondatabase environments such as word processors and many spreadsheets. However, when the user needs to invoke NetBIOS services, the user needs to take additional steps.

NetBIOS is a protocol that provides DOS and OS/2 with file and record locking services across a LAN. These services ensure that during multiple, concurrent accesses of a database, the database users don't overwrite themselves when they make changes to a database record. If one system is updating record 10 and another tries to do the same thing, NetBIOS provides a record locking function that prevents the second user from getting to the record during the update process. Database programs such as dBase IV can also lock a record while the first machine is looking at it to ensure that when the first machine updates the record it doesn't overwrite changes made by another workstation. This dBase IV capability is based on NetBIOS services.

The problem here is that NetBIOS resources aren't automatically made available to the VDMs. The user has to take another step—run SETUPVDD to update CONFIG.SYS with the virtual device drivers (VDDs) for NetBIOS.

To run this program, open an OS/2 session and type `SETUPVDD`. `SETUPVDD` is in C:\IBMCOM (or the \IBMCOM directory on the drive where the user installed LAN Requester). It adds lines for two VDDs to CONFIG.SYS, and after the user reboots the next time, NetBIOS resources are available to the DOS session.

The Novell NetWare Requester for OS/2 2.1 has the capability to provide NetBIOS services to VDMs itself. There are a number of options to invoke this, but in general, if you are also running IBM's LAN Requester, it's safest to use the IBM VDDs. However, if you are only running Novell's Requester, then by all means use it to provide NetBIOS to the VDMs. The NetBIOS support option is available on the Configure screen.

There are two circumstances where simply adding NetBIOS support may not be enough. The first circumstance was mentioned earlier under the dBase IV considerations: some database programs don't detect NetBIOS by itself and need a network redirector loaded. NetBIOS is still necessary in this case because the network redirector software requires NetBIOS.

The second circumstance occurs when the DOS application developer needs to run a small LAN to test applications. Loading a network program like the IBM DOS LAN Requester 2.0 can simulate up to a four-station network, right on the OS/2 desktop!

The steps to load the network redirector are given, in general, below. Note that this is not an attempt to give you step-by-step instructions. These steps are intended to provide you with an operational overview.

1. At least double the NetBIOS commands, sessions, and names in the LAN Support and Protocol session.
2. Create a specific DOS version boot image using VMDISK, following the instructions given earlier in this chapter.
3. In the specific DOS session's AUTOEXEC.BAT, add the line to configure the NetBIOS parameters. An example of the command is `LTSVCFG C=14 S=14`.
4. Close the specific DOS session and reopen it.
5. Install the IBM DOS LAN Requester 2.0 (from the OS/2 LAN Server Entry 2.0 or Advanced 2.0—previous versions won't work). Note that the user has to run `FSACCESS=A:` to open the physical disk drive.

After the installation is complete, the user can issue a `NET START` to load the redirector. For dBase IV and other software looking for a redirector, this is all that is necessary. The specific DOS session also still has access to the drive assignments from the OS/2 LAN Requester's log in. For DOS network application development and testing, however, the user should log into the domain controller from the specific DOS session. The user can do this by issuing the `NET LOGON` command or using the full-screen interface.

> NOTE
> You cannot use the same machine name or log-in name for the DOS LAN Requester that you are using for the OS/2 LAN Requester. Each specific DOS session and its DOS LAN Requester session should be treated as if they are separate and unique microcomputers. Each one needs its own machine and log-in IDs.

Up to four DLR sessions can run inside specific DOS sessions at any given time, assuming that the system has sufficient network adapter resources to support the NetBIOS sessions, command, and names.

Once the user logs into a domain controller from a specific DOS session, the user no longer sees the log-in assignments from the OS/2 LAN Requester. The drive assignments for that specific DOS session depend on the log-in name and whatever network assignments the network administrator specified for it.

> A number of combinations of active network software is possible. OS/2 LAN Requester can be running concurrently with the NetWare Requester for OS/2 2.1 (if the latter is installed using the LANSUP option) at the same time one or more DOS LAN Requester sessions are running. In that case, you can be logged into an OS/2 LAN Server domain, a Novell NetWare 3.x server, and another (or the same) OS/2 LAN Server domain controller. The most difficult thing about OS/2 2.1, VDMs, and LANs is keeping track of what session is doing what.

Author Bio

Terrance Crow began working in the microcomputer support and consulting department of a major insurance company in July 1986. He worked on the roll-out and support team for IBM OS/2 Extended Edition 1.0, and he has worked on every version since then. Crow is now responsible for the deployment and support strategy for IBM OS/2 2.1.

9

WIN-OS/2—Windows in OS/2

In This Chapter

It is possible to run applications written for Microsoft Windows in OS/2 2.1. It is even possible to run Windows applications on the OS/2 desktop. All this is made possible because of an agreement between IBM and Microsoft that gives IBM access to the source code for Microsoft Windows. IBM used this capability to create a special version of Windows 3.1 (called WIN-OS/2) that runs under OS/2 2.1.

When Microsoft Windows runs under DOS on an 80386-based system, it is a DOS protected-mode interface (DPMI) server that allows client Windows programs to access up to three times the amount of RAM installed in the computer. One of the changes IBM made in developing WIN-OS/2 was to place the DPMI server capability directly into the operating system and remove it from the Windows code they converted to run as a part of OS/2 2.1. This means that each DOS application can address up to 512 megabytes of DPMI memory under OS/2 2.1, provided the computer has enough resources (RAM and hard disk space).

When you run Windows applications in OS/2 2.1, you can elect to run them in their own full-screen session. If you choose this method, the result looks as if you are running Microsoft Windows. You can also elect to run Windows applications in a WIN-OS/2 window on the OS/2 desktop. This last mode of operation is often called seamless windows or just seamless.

If you are a veteran Windows user, you'll be pleased to discover that most things you've gotten used to using—most of the tricks, the INI file settings, and the shortcuts—still work in WIN-OS/2. For those of you who haven't spent much time with Windows, I'll try to point out some things that make using WIN-OS/2 a bit easier.

Installation

If you didn't install Windows or DOS support when you installed OS/2, you can install it now. Find the OS/2 system icon on your desktop and open it. Then open the system setup icon and open the selective install icon (your desktop should look like the one shown in Figure 9.1).

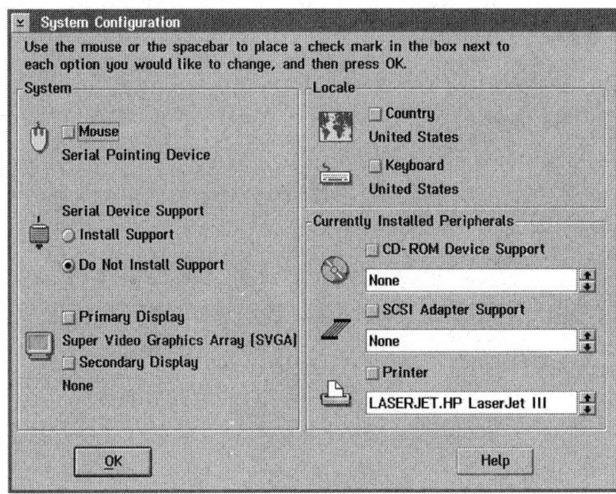

Figure 9.1. The first window in the selective install process.

If you don't have any changes, click the OK button to continue. On the next screen select the check box for OS/2 DOS and WIN-OS/2 Support (see Figures 9.2 and 9.3) and then select the associated More pushbutton.

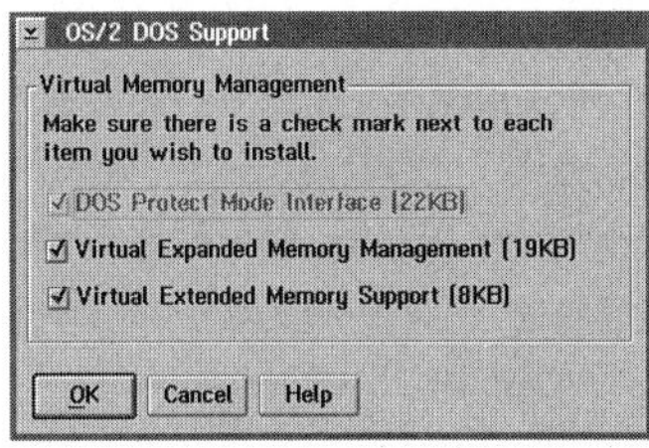

Figure 9.2. Installing DOS support.

TIP

Be sure you have enough disk space available. (The space required for each component is shown on each line). The dialog in the lower-right corner of the screen shows the amount of disk space

available and the amount of space required. If you plan to install WIN-OS/2 over a prior version, you may not need as much space.

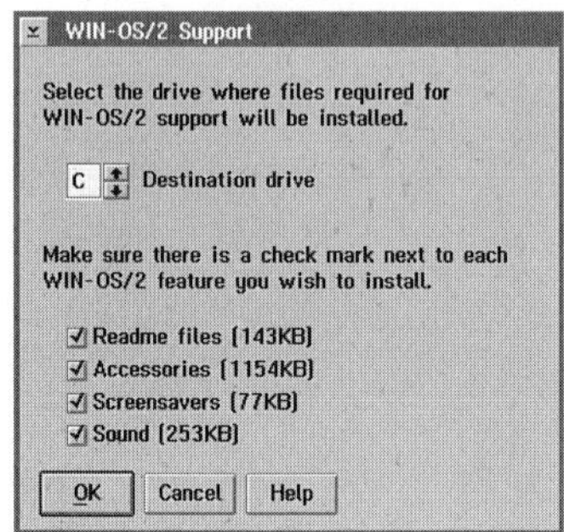

Figure 9.3. Installing WIN-OS/2 support.

When you have selected the features of DOS and WIN-OS/2 support that you would like to install, return to the previous screen. Click on the Install button and insert the disks when prompted.

Migration and Setup

When you install WIN-OS/2 consider letting the migration facility do some of the setup for you. The migration tool supplied with OS/2 does some things that can make using Windows applications in OS/2 a bit easier.

The migration facility scans the Windows WIN.INI file for the [Extensions] section. It uses the information it finds to set up the OS/2 object associations so that opening a data file opens the corresponding Windows application (exactly the same way it does in the Windows File Manager).

The migration phase of WIN-OS/2 installation creates Windows program objects on the OS/2 desktop. The migration utility uses a database that comes with OS/2 to determine the settings. If an application isn't there, you may have to edit the settings notebook pages for the application manually (to set or change the DPMI memory limit). The migration facility also scans existing Windows group (GRP) files and creates desktop folders with contents that correspond to the Windows groups.

You can change the operation of the migration facility if you change the contents of the migration database (DATABASE.TXT in the \OS2\INSTALL directory). You need to consult the DBTAGS.DAT file in the same directory for the proper values for each of the possible settings (see the migration section in Chapter 3, "System Configuration, Setup, and Tuning," for details).

OS/2 Setup

Whether you added WIN-OS/2 support or installed it when you initially installed OS/2, you should still make changes to the default setup conditions. You can change the global defaults for all WIN-OS/2 sessions as well as the specific settings for any given session. In addition, you can also affect the way WIN-OS/2 runs by making changes in the appropriate WIN-OS/2 initialization files (they are usually text-based INI files).

The installation process for WIN-OS/2 adds an icon to the System Setup folder. Double-click mouse button 1 to open the WIN-OS/2 Setup settings notebook (see Figure 9.4 for a picture of the icon and Figure 9.7 for the notebook page).

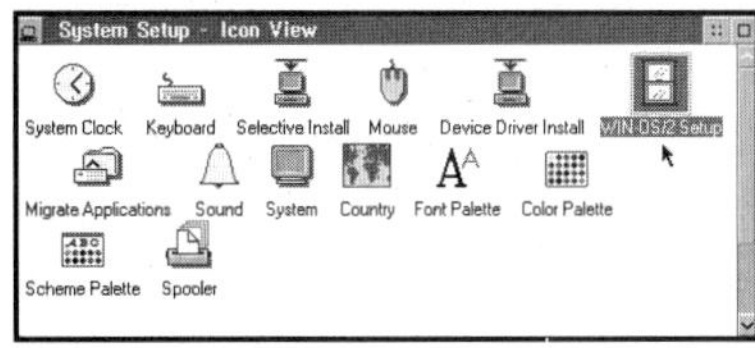

Figure 9.4. The WIN-OS/2 setup icon view in the OS/2 System folder.

Separate Versus Multiple Sessions

In Microsoft Windows, applications share a common address space. This means that a failure in one Windows application can bring down the whole system. The original designs for WIN-OS/2 before its first release called for each Windows application to run in its own separate virtual DOS machine (VDM) for extra protection. Although it worked, it had an impact on performance; a copy of WIN-OS/2 had to be loaded for each Windows application.

Now you have a choice. You can elect to have each Windows application run in a separate session or you can allow Windows applications to share a single session (one for seamless WIN-OS/2 operation and one for each full-screen execution of WIN-OS/2). I'll cover some of the ramifications of this capability a bit later in the chapter (see "Clipboard and Dynamic Data Exchange").

Earlier in this chapter I mentioned that one of the changes IBM originally made to Windows was to allow each Windows application to run in its own VDM. There are some interesting by-products of this decision that might not be obvious.

In real Microsoft Windows, a single buggy application can still do something to generate a protection fault that wipes out the entire system. In OS/2 2.1 this same application might wipe out the entire WIN-OS/2 session. If you are running multiple applications within the session, the results could be catastrophic.

Instead, you can elect to run each WIN-OS/2 application in a separate session. If the application crashes, the only thing affected is this one program. Separate sessions isolate each application and provide full protection. In addition, the separate session also allows the WIN-OS/2 applications to participate in full preemptive multitasking (versus the cooperative multitasking that is a normal part of Windows and WIN-OS/2 operation).

Second, some Windows applications do not allow more than one invocation to be active at any one time. By running the program in separate sessions you can get around this limitation. To setup separate sessions for all WIN-OS/2 windows, check the WIN-OS/2 window and check the Separate session button immediately under it (see Figure 9.5). You can also run applications in a separate session if you select WIN-OS/2 full screen.

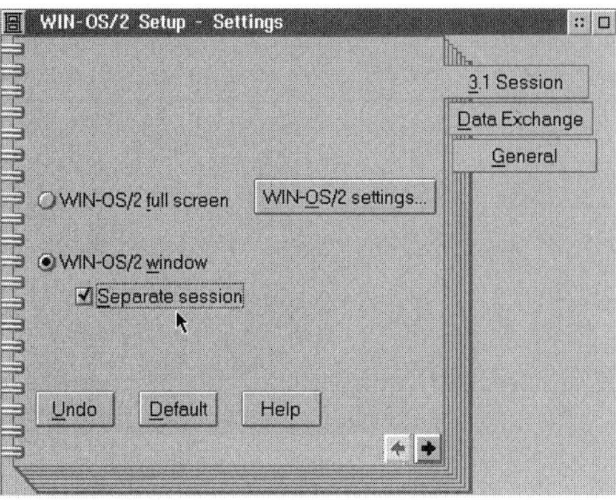

Figure 9.5. You can select separate sessions for all WIN-OS/2 windows.

If you make this selection, the price is increased load time for each application. You can elect to have specific applications run in a separate session by choosing the corresponding selection on the individual applications Sessions setting page.

WIN-OS/2 Settings

Push the WIN-OS/2 Settings pushbutton (see Figure 9.5) to view or change settings. You should see a dialog box that looks like the one shown in Figure 9.6.

The Settings area is a list box that contains the various parameters that can be changed. The settings in the list include most of the settings available for a DOS session. There are some parameters that only show in a WIN-OS/2 settings page. The Value changes for each selected parameter in the setting list box. Similarly, the Description also changes to provide parameter-specific help.

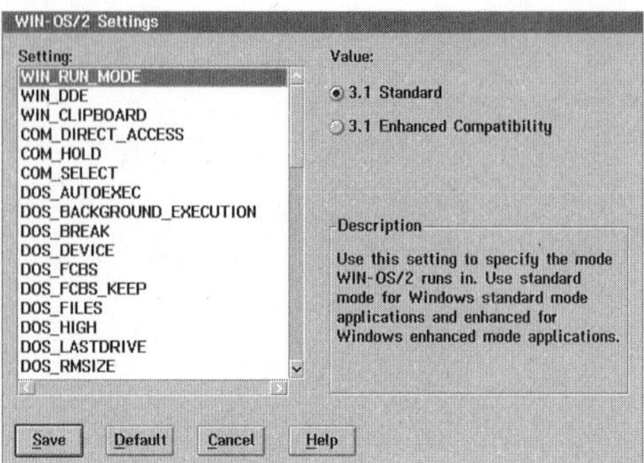

Figure 9.6. Changing settings for WIN-OS/2.

The following sections provide information about the most common changes for WIN-OS/2. There are other parameters you could change besides those in the following listings. Feel free to experiment. There isn't one single right set of settings that will produce the optimal results for everyone.

Other than WIN_XXXX settings, all of the values listed apply to any VDM (see Chapter 8, "Virtual DOS Machines").

WIN_RUNMODE

Proposed value: 3.1 STANDARD

Comment: This is the default value. If you have an application that requires enhanced mode, make the appropriate selection here.

If you try to launch your enhanced-mode application from a WIN-OS/2 standard-mode program manager it will not work. Be sure the mode of the Program Manager matches all of the applications you want to run in that session.

It is possible to have WIN-OS/2 applications run in separate sessions if their `WIN_RUNMODE` settings do not agree. For example, if you start the Calculator accessory with the `WIN_RUNMODE` setting equal 3.1 STANDARD and start the File Manager tool with the setting 3.1 ENHANCED, they will run in separate sessions. Thereafter, every standard mode application runs in the standard session and every enhanced mode application runs in its corresponding session.

WIN_DDE and WIN_CLIPBOARD

Proposed value for both: ON

Comment: These settings correspond to the global default DDE & Clipboard found on the WIN-OS/2 setup object that is discussed in the next section. When they are ON, the corresponding item (either DDE or CLIPBOARD) is shared between this WIN-OS/2 application and OS/2 sessions. To make them private, set the value OFF.

If you elect either a private DDE or Clipboard, the WIN-OS/2 application shares the Clipboard or DDE with any other WIN-OS/2 session. *Private* refers to the communications link with OS/2 applications (severed when the parameter is OFF).

DPMI_MEMORY_LIMIT

Proposed value: 64 (or more)

Comment: The default value provides up to 64 megabytes of storage to each WIN-OS/2 session. You can change this value for each WIN-OS/2 session.

Sme applications try to access all available memory during their initializations. Performance may improve if you reduce this value for these applications.

You can get additional memory for some Windows applications if you run the application full screen without the WIN-OS/2 program manager. In some cases this can make an additional 1M of memory available without changing this setting. Some applications need more memory. It doesn't hurt to set this value higher. It describes the upper limit of WIN-OS/2 memory, not the amount automatically used.

INT_DURING_IO

Proposed value: ON

Comment: The help for this setting suggests that it is useful for Windows multimedia applications. The help suggests the ON setting enables interrupts during disk I/O. What it really means is that OS/2 starts a second thread to handle the interrupts. This can sometimes improve the performance of all DOS sessions, not just Windows multimedia applications.

You might want to make this a default for all VDM sessions. I haven't found any case where it hurts performance.

KBD_CTRL_BYPASS

Proposed value: CTRL-ESC

Comment: If you want the CTRL-ESC sequence to bring up the WIN-OS/2 Task List in a full-screen WIN-OS/2 session, change this setting as indicated. If you leave the default value (NONE) CTRL-ESC takes you back to the OS/2 desktop.

If you do not enable the Windows Task list as suggested, use the WIN-OS/2 fast application-switch keyboard combination Alt-Tab to select the WIN-OS/2 application you want. If a special WIN-OS/2 keyboard combination doesn't appear to work, check the value of this setting.

OS/2 allows you to pick one bypass combination from the list. It would be nice if multiple selections were possible.

KBD_RATE_LOCK

Proposed value: ON

Comment: The WIN-OS/2 control panel provides the ability to change the keyboard response rate. If the initial rate set is different from your personal choice, you could be surprised to discover the keyboard behavior changes. If you turn this parameter ON it prevents any WIN-OS/2 session from changing the keyboard repeat rate.

MOUSE_EXCLUSIVE_ACCESS

Proposed value: OFF (normally)

Comment: This is the default value. If you run a seamless WIN-OS/2 application and you see two mouse pointers, change this setting to ON and click inside the WIN-OS/2 window; the second mouse pointer should disappear.

To gain mouse access to your desktop, you have to use a keyboard sequence (e.g., Ctrl-Esc) to enable the mouse for operation outside the "exclusive" window.

VIDEO_8514A_XGA_IOTRAP

Proposed value: OFF

This parameter is not present unless you have either an 8514a, XGA, or compatible video adapter.

Together with the notification parameter documented below, changing this setting may improve performance on supported hardware.

You should experiment with this parameter to discover the optimal setting for your hardware.

VIDEO_ONDEMAND_MEMORY

Proposed value: ON (normally)

Comment: If set OFF it may prevent a high-resolution, full-screen WIN-OS/2 session from failing due to insufficient memory to save the complete screen image.

The default value is usually better for performance. Don't change this setting unless you experience problems.

VIDEO_SWITCH_NOTIFICATION

Proposed value: ON

Comment: You may want to play with this setting to see if it helps improve performance. Some Windows display drivers don't require the video buffer to be saved and restored on their behalf by OS/2 2.1 (for example, the 85141A driver). If your adapter supports the capability, this can make switching between the OS/2 desktop and a full-screen WIN-OS/2 session a bit faster and smoother.

If your hardware supports the capability, setting this parameter ON may also allow full-screen WIN-OS/2 sessions to run in the background.

When you finish with your changes, click mouse button 1 on the Save pushbutton. The Cancel button will undo any changes you've made. Selecting either of these two buttons dismisses the settings page and returns you to the notebook. The Default button restores the system default for the selected (or highlighted) parameter.

If you want to change all of the parameter settings to the factory defaults, select the Default button shown in the screen that matches Figure 9.7. The Undo on this screen restores the previously saved values. You do not have to do anything to explicitly save the changes, just close the notebook.

All of the changes I've mentioned are also available for individual Windows applications. Click mouse button 2 on the object to bring up its context menu then select Open-Settings to get the notebook. If you change a specific application, it overrides the default settings.

Clipboard and Dynamic Data Exchange

The default conditions provide both public DDE and public Clipboard. This means that you can share information among the three types of applications supported by OS/2 (OS/2, DOS, and Windows). There may be times when

you do not want to let this happen. You can elect to make the Clipboard or DDE private to WIN-OS/2 sessions only.

Select the Date Exchange tab on the notebook (see Figure 9.7). There are two areas on the page. The top area allows you to determine if DDE should be shared between WIN-OS/2 and OS/2 sessions (Public) or non-shared (Private). Click the appropriate button. The same choices are available for the Clipboard.

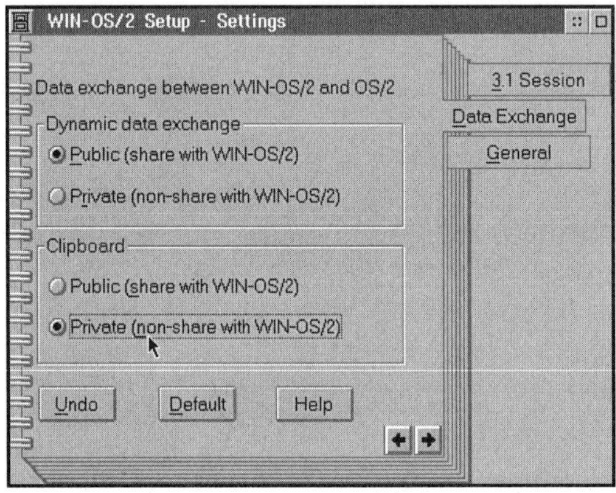

Figure 9.7. *Changing the settings for the WIN-OS/2 Clipboard and DDE.*

If you elect to make the Clipboard private, you will have separate clipboards: one for all OS/2 and character-based DOS sessions and another for WIN-OS/2 sessions.

Even if you elected separate sessions for your seamless applications, they can still share data using the WIN-OS/2 Clipboard and DDE.

TIP

For some Windows applications that deal with heavy real-time data exchange you may see an improvement in performance if you make the DDE private. If you make the Clipboard private, you will not be able to use the WIN-OS/2 Clipboard to share information with either an OS/2 application or a DOS window on the OS/2 desktop.

Windows Setup (the INI Files)

You can change all of the settings in the various initialization (INI) files for WIN-OS/2. Almost any book on Microsoft Windows that documents the settings can also be used for WIN-OS/2. IBM has added some additional settings to the WIN-OS/2 SYSTEM.INI file that are explained in following sections.

The settings that follow are all from the [BOOT] section of the WIN-OS/2 SYSTEM.INI file.

useos2shield

Value: 1

Comments: If set to 1, the parameter `os2shield` is used by WIN-OS/2 to determine the first application program to start in each new WIN-OS/2 session. If set to 0, the value of `os2shield` is ignored; no icon is displayed.

You may need to set `useos2shield` to 0 if you wish to run an application that requires that it is the very first program to run in a WIN-OS/2 session. The Norton Desktop is an example of such an application.

os2shield

Value: winsheld.exe

Comments: This statement determines what application program is responsible for managing all interaction between the WIN-OS/2 session and the other components of OS/2 2.1. The default program, winshield.exe, communicates with an equivalent program running in the OS/2 Workplace Shell. Both are responsible for exchanging data for the Clipboard and DDE, managing the contents of the WIN-OS/2 Task List, and, for seamless WIN-OS/2 Windows, the portions of the display screen available to the WIN-OS/2 applications.

MAVDMAPPS

Value: !printman

Comments: MAVDMAPPS stands for multiple application VDM applications. It is used whenever a full-screen WIN-OS/2 session runs multiple application programs. The applications named on this line are started in addition to the Program Manager and any applications that are in the WIN-OS/2 startup group. The default setting starts up the WIN-OS/2 Print Manager. The exclamation point means that the application is started as minimized; you can list multiple applications on the line (each separated by a comma).

SAVDMAPPS

Value: (unused)

Comments: SAVDMAPPS stands for single application VDM applications. It is used whenever a full-screen WIN-OS/2 session that will run only a single application is started. Like MAVDMAPPS, it determines what other programs to start in addition to the single application you select. This setting is unused in a default WIN-OS/2 installation.

WAVDMAPPS

Value: (unused)

Comments: `WAVDMAPPS` stands for Windowed application VDM applications. It is used whenever a seamless WIN-OS/2 Windowed session is started and, like `MAVDMAPPS`, determines what other programs to start in addition to the application you select. This setting is unused in a default WIN-OS/2 installation.

sdisplay.drv

Value: swinvga.drv

Comments: Setup during WIN-OS/2 installation, it is the normal seamless WIN-OS/2 display driver. If you install a new driver using Display Driver install utility, it changes this value appropriately. See Chapter 11, "The Video Subsystem," for more information.

display.drv

Value: t800.drv

Comments: This is a vendor-supplied Windows driver used for full-screen WIN-OS/2 sessions. In this case it is the 800x600x256 color driver for the Trident TVGA 8900LC2 adapter.

WIN-OS/2 does not provide a mechanism to change display drivers from within WIN-OS/2. It is possible to edit the INI files manually to make changes, or you may be able to use the display driver installation utility that OS/2 2.1 provides.

NOTE Almost all of the other Windows INI settings are documented in books about Microsoft Windows. In operation, WIN-OS/2 is very similar to Microsoft Windows. However, some of the Windows INI settings are not relevant to WIN-OS/2; for the most part, these extra settings are ignored.

Running Windows Applications

The release of OS/2 2.1 provides a WIN-OS/2 layer compatible with Windows 3.1. You can run almost every Windows application, including the shells for DOS applications (for example, 4SHELL, a Windows Shell for Korenthal Associates' 4PRINT). You can run them in a window on the OS/2 desktop or in their own full-screen session.

Seamless Windows

The seamless operation of WIN-OS/2 on the OS/2 desktop is a cooperative process between the WIN-OS/2 display driver and the OS/2 Presentation Manager display driver. A special OS/2 virtual driver device, VWIN.SYS (loaded in the CONFIG.SYS file at boot time), provides the mechanism for these two display drivers to communicate with each other. The WIN-OS/2 window display driver device is defined by the `SDISPLAY` setting in the [Boot] section of the WIN-OS/2, is SYSTEM.INI file.

If a WIN-OS/2 session doesn't run on the desktop, be sure the following line appears in the CONFIG.SYS file:

```
DEVICE=C:\OS2\MDOS\VWIN.SYS
```

The OS/2 PM display driver provides an opening or "hole" on the desktop to allow the Windows application to appear. The seamless WIN-OS/2 driver has to be written to operate within the hole. Specifically, the seamless WIN-OS/2 driver has to be aware that it can only display what fits into the hole versus what fits on the entire screen.

The preceding paragraph explains why you can't use a standard Windows video driver for seamless operation. It also explains why the seamless driver has to be supplied either by IBM or by the maker of your video adapter.

In addition to the display drivers, OS/2 2.1 has special components known as *Shields* that are used to communicate between the OS/2 Presentation Manager and the WIN-OS/2 window managers. There is a shield that executes in each WIN-OS/2 session as well as a shield that executes in the Presentation Manager desktop. Each of these communicate with each other (using the VWIN device driver), providing information on what application windows are visible in which areas of your display screen. The shields effectively control who has access to the "holes" on your desktop in which WIN-OS/2 applications appear. The shield component is also responsible for all Clipboard and DDE activity.

The migration utility may not find everything on your hard disk (you may install a Windows application after you install WIN-OS/2). Either way, the procedure to add a seamless application to your desktop is the same.

1. Open the template icon on the OS/2 Workplace Shell desktop.
2. Drag a copy of the program icon to where you want it.
3. Fill in the appropriate information on the first notebook page (see Figure 9.8).

On the second page of the notebook, (the Session page), select WIN-OS2 window. If you want your windows applications to each be in a separate session, check the appropriate box (see Figure 9.9).

Once you've added the WIN-OS/2 application to the desktop, you can use it as you would any other application regardless of type. After you've installed the applications you want on the desktop, you have a few choices. Figure 9.10 shows the WIN-OS/2 Program Manager on the OS/2 desktop.

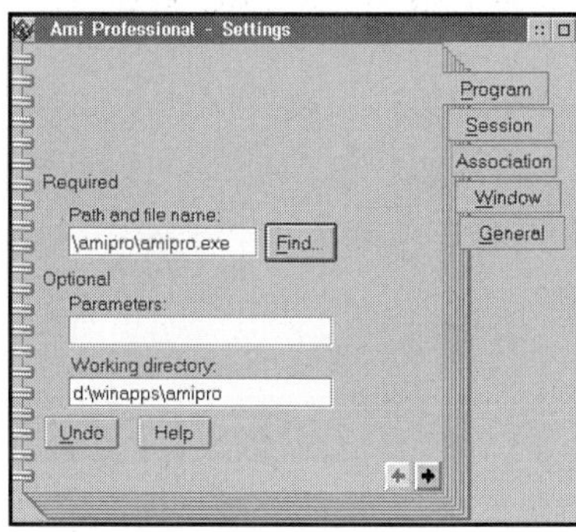

Figure 9.8. Setting up the program information.

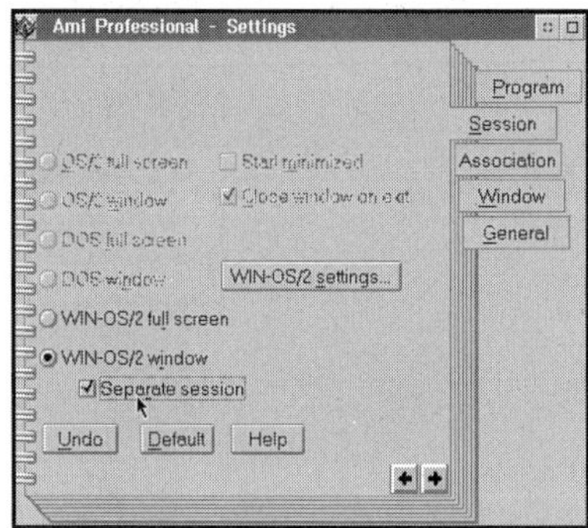

Figure 9.9. Mark as a separate section on the OS/2 desktop.

If you compare this to Figure 9.11, you'll see the content of the Program Manager in both figures is identical. The full-screen session has the WinShield application running (see the icon in the lower-left corner). As noted previously, you can use your vendor-supplied Windows driver for your full-screen session. It is important that you follow the instructions in the following Caution box, otherwise you may experience unexpected results when you switch between the OS/2 desktop and the full-screen WIN-OS/2 session.

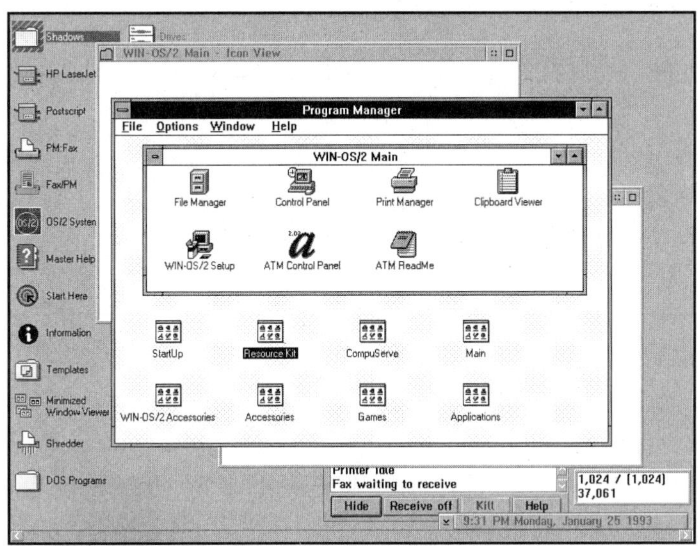

Figure 9.10. The WIN-OS/2 Program Manager on the OS/2 desktop.

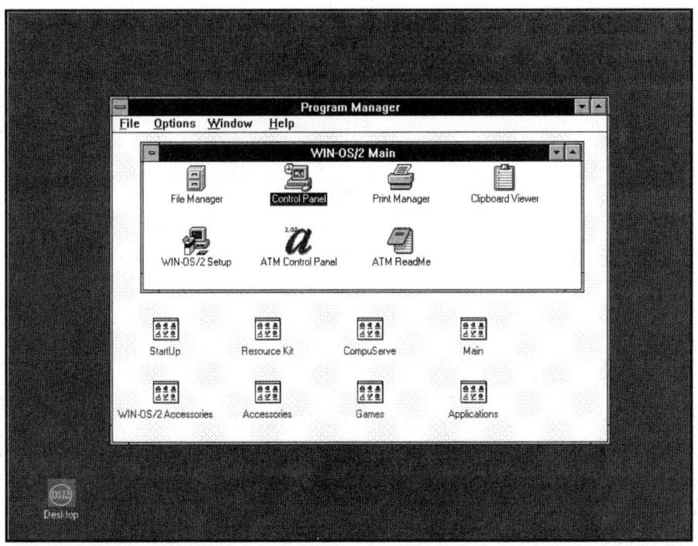

Figure 9.11. The full-screen WIN-OS/2 Program Manager.

If you have a super VGA adapter, you must run SVGA ON in a full-screen DOS session to create the proper PMI file for your adapter. This file contains adapter-specific instructions to tell OS/2 video drivers how to change video modes for the adapter. If you don't perform this step you may discover a new definition for screen garbage! See Chapter 11 for information on the SVGA command.

You can start a Windows application in a seamless window from the OS/2 command line by typing `WINDOWS_PROGRAM_NAME`. You may have to enter the full path, too.

Screen Blanker

WIN-OS/2 includes a screen blanker that you can use with the OS/2 desktop. To activate it, configure the screen saver from the WIN-OS/2 control panel desktop icon. Then follow the procedure in this chapter to install any Windows application for seamless operation on the OS/2 desktop. Whenever a WIN-OS/2 session is active on the desktop, the WIN-OS/2 screen saver is operational.

If you don't use the mouse that much on the OS/2 desktop, specify as long a delay time as possible. Sometimes a Windows screen saver misses keystrokes headed for OS/2 desktop and activates prematurely. (Mouse movement is caught by the screen saver.)

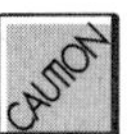

You can also specify a password for the WIN-OS/2 screen saver. Do not use both the OS/2 system lockup facility and the WIN-OS/2 facility (with a password) at the same time.

Screen Capture and Other Utilities

It is possible to use almost any WIN-OS/2 utility on the desktop, even screen capture utilities. Figure 9.12 is a picture of the OS/2 Workplace Shell desktop taken with a Windows screen capture utility. The only way you can tell the difference is the presence of the Collage:PM windows; if you used the PM version of the tool, they would not be visible. In fact, most of the Windows utilities I've tried work in OS/2, including the Windows For Workgroups File Manager, all of the games, and other utilities.

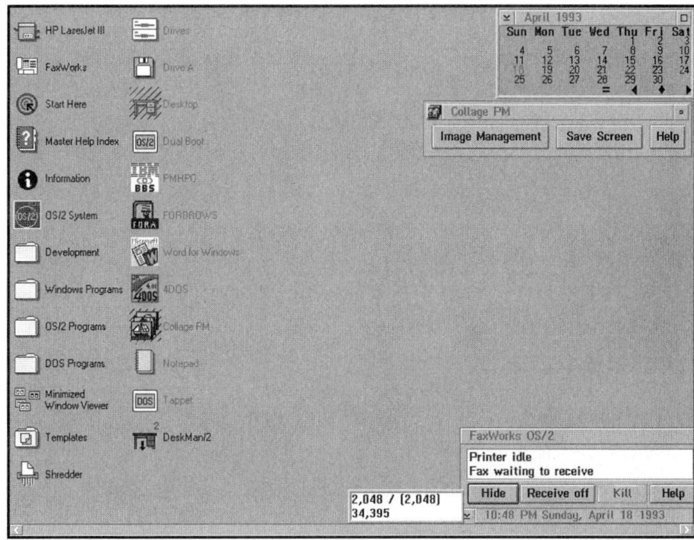

Figure 9.12. *An OS/2 desktop screen capture using a Windows application.*

Full-Screen Sessions

Windows applications run faster in a full-screen session than they do seamless on the OS/2 desktop. Depending upon what you're trying to do, the difference in speed may make a difference. In addition, some applications behave differently between full-screen and seamless sessions. In general both DDE and the Clipboard function properly in either environment.

I use a Windows high-resolution video driver for full-screen sessions to get higher resolution and 256 colors. It is a good idea to use the highest resolution that is comfortably possible for your display adapter and monitor combination. A graphical user interface chews up a lot of screen real-estate very quickly.

Running WIN-OS/2 in a VMDISK Session

It is possible to run WIN-OS/2 in a DOS image session created with the VMDISK.EXE utility. Follow the instructions to create the disk in Chapter 8 with the following modification: be sure the HIMEM.SYS and EMM386.SYS drivers specified in the VMDISK CONFIG.SYS file are the ones located in the \OS2\MDOS directory—not the ones that shipped with DOS. Change the following settings for the DOS image session:

- `DOS_STARTUP_DRIVE` should point to the image created by VMDISK.
- Set `DOS_FILES` to 40.
- Set the `DPMI_MEMORY_LIMIT` to at least 4.

Be sure you follow all of the steps in this section. If you omit one, WIN-OS/2 will not run.

Drivers

It is possible that you may need to load device drivers for WIN-OS/2 that are separate from the drivers supplied by IBM. The WIN-OS/2 control panel provides a way to install multimedia drivers, and the WIN-OS/2 setup allows you to install a network that will work with WIN-OS/2. If you want to install any other device driver, you have to edit the appropriate INI file manually; if an installation tool isn't supplied with the device, check with the manufacturer.

Printers

You can add printer drivers to WIN-OS/2 separately from OS/2. In fact, you may have to do this. If you install a printer driver using the OS/2 template for a new printer, this may only install the OS/2 driver. OS/2 2.1 will install a printer driver for WIN-OS/2 at the same time as you install an OS/2 printer driver only if there is an equivalent driver available on the OS/2 disks—in some cases there is no equivalent WIN-OS/2 driver. However, there may be a substitute driver that will work for you, or you may have your own printer driver, in this case you have to install the driver in an independent step.

The fastest way to install a WIN-OS/2 printer driver is to start a full-screen WIN-OS/2 session and open the WIN-OS/2 control panel and select the printers icon. Follow the instructions to add a new printer.

WIN-OS/2 does not use the Windows Print Manager if the WIN-OS/2 printer points to a parallel port with an associated OS/2 spooler queue. This results in improved printing performance in WIN-OS/2 versus Windows.

Video Adapter

If you want to change the display driver for full-screen WIN-OS/2 sessions, you may have to do it manually. IBM did not provide the capability to change drivers in the WIN-OS/2 setup tool, but there is a display driver installation tool provided with OS/2 2.1 (see Chapter 11). The best advice is to check with the vendor of your video adapter to see if they have specific instructions. If they don't, and you already have a video driver from a previous installation of Microsoft Windows, you can use that driver as is. Copy the driver to the WINOS2\SYSTEM directory and set the `DISPLAY` setting in the WIN-OS/2 SYSTEM.INI file to the full name of the file.

Fax

There are two different types of fax software that can run in WIN-OS/2. The first is a standard Windows application. This type of application lets you send (or receive) facsimiles only from within WIN-OS/2. If you also establish a seamless icon on your OS/2 desktop, this may extend the capabilities to provide limited support for OS/2 applications and DOS VDM windows.

The degree of support for DOS or OS/2 sessions depends on the features and capabilities of the Windows application.

A better alternative is to use an OS/2 2.1-based fax software package that also provides either a driver or mechanism to support WIN-OS/2. Once installed, you should be able to receive a fax in the OS/2 application and send a fax from any session.

Differences Between Microsoft Windows 3.1 and the WIN-OS/2 Environment

There are minor differences between WIN-OS/2 and Windows 3.1. Although I've talked about some of them, including multiple sessions and multiple clipboards, there is one important factor, the common denominator for most of the variances between the two products: Windows 3.1 relies on DOS.

Managing Memory

In the DOS/Windows combination, an application is limited to accessing 3 times the amount of installed system memory. In OS/2 2.1 each DOS or Windows application can access up to 512M of RAM.

In Windows 3.1 you only get virtual memory if you run in enhanced mode on a 386-based system. If Windows 3.1 executes in standard mode, it allows access to, at most, 16M of memory. In OS/2 2.1 the full 512M of DPMI memory is always available for applications.

Failures, Fractures, and Faults

In Windows an application can crash and potentially take out the entire system. In OS/2 the same application can still crash, but it is much less likely to lock up the entire system. The normal name given to this type of failure is called a general protection failure or GPF for short. The usual cause of the problem: the application tried to use memory it did not own.

Windows applications share a common address space. If this type of failure occurs it is more likely to cause a system-wide problem than the same failure in an OS/2 application. There are two modes of operating Windows applications under OS/2: seamless or full-screen. By definition, full-screen sessions are each unique—a failure in one normally doesn't impact another full-screen session. If you run Windows applications in separate full-screen sessions, they are each isolated from each other.

Seamless applications (as well as those applications started within a single full-screen session) are different. Applications started this way use the same memory model as Microsoft Windows running in DOS: Windows applications share the address space.

You could elect to run each seamless application in a separate session. However, if you do, remember that there are trade-offs. With a single seamless session, the first Windows application takes a while to load. Not only does OS/2 2.1 load the application, it also loads both the DOS and WIN-OS/2 support. Subsequent Windows applications will not take as long to load because WIN-OS/2 support is already present.

Separate sessions provide increased protection between applications at the expense of load time. Each separate seamless session needs its own copy of WIN-OS/2 support. This also means that more memory is required.

If you want separation of Windows applications, consider running them each as full-screen sessions. Although it will take the same minimum 4M of address space per process, the application will have more memory at its disposal. Switching between full-screen sessions, however, is not as convenient as switching between seamless applications.

Local Ctrl-Alt-Del

In Windows you can stop an application that is not responding by using the Ctrl-Alt-Del key sequence. This brings up a screen that gives you the option to either reboot the computer (hit the sequence again) or end a non-responding

application. In OS/2 you can hit Ctrl-Esc to get a screen for a non-responsive application (if the entire system appears to be frozen) or close the specific session.

Using Ctrl-Alt-Del on OS/2 2.1 causes your computer to restart immediately. You will not see any prompt!

Troubleshooting

Some of the techniques you might have adopted for troubleshooting in Microsoft Windows will work for WIN-OS/2. However, there are some differences. If you are upgrading to OS/2 2.1 from either OS/2 2.0 or Windows 3.0 there are some things to consider.

Applications Don't Work

If you have a problem attempting to run a Windows application in OS/2 2.1 the first thing to do is check the WIN-OS/2 application settings screens to make sure both the path and working directory are correct. If there is an error message, you can keep the window or full-screen session open by adding a `PAUSE` statement to the batch file specified by the `DOS_AUTOEXEC` parameter (see Chapter 8 for details).

The next area to check is the amount of memory assigned to the session. In any Windows 3.1-aware application (Word for Windows is an example) you can open the About box (found under the Help menu item). This tells you the amount of available memory for this session. You can increase this by changing the amount of DPMI memory assigned (`DPMI_MEMORY_LIMIT` on the WIN-OS/2 application settings notebook). Some applications won't give you an indication of a memory problem, but they will not load, either. Sometimes increasing the DPMI memory limit will do the trick.

The actual amount of available memory is the smaller of the DPMI_MEMORY_LIMIT and the actual amount of space available on the hard disk that you have selected for your swapper file. Increasing the DPMI_MEMORY_LIMIT above the amount of free space on your hard disk is not going to help. Memory is a real resource, it doesn't appear out of thin air!

Finally, some WIN-OS/2 applications may not properly install. Check the settings page for the application. The setting pushbutton should read "WIN-OS/2 settings" and either the WIN-OS/2 full-screen or the WIN-OS/2 seamless should be checked. If the pushbutton reads "DOS settings," select one of the WIN-OS/2 settings manually. This should change the pushbutton to read WIN-OS/2. If it doesn't, reinstall the application.

Applications That Used to Work, Don't

If you have applications that used to work with Windows 3.0 (or the corresponding version of WIN-OS/2) that don't work with OS/2 2.1, check the [compatibility] section in the WIN.INI file. It is possible you will have to contact technical support to get a corresponding "patch" for WIN-OS/2.

True Type Fonts Don't Work

If you upgraded to OS/2 2.1 from a prior version and True Type fonts don't work, you may have to get an updated printer driver for your system. The OS/2 install program installs known drivers for both OS/2 2.1 and WIN-OS/2. However, if you have a special driver for your printer, you may have to contact the manufacturer to get an update. Tell them you need a driver for Windows 3.1 (not Windows for Workgroups).

Fatal Exit Codes

If you see a fatal exit code 0x0401 when you try to start WIN-OS/2, this usually means that something in the SYSTEM.INI file is not set properly. The other possibility: check the path specified in the file specified by the `DOS_AUTOEXEC` setting parameter for this session. It is possible that something may either be incorrect or out of order that is causing the system to load incorrect drivers.

Summary

There is a lot of flexibility and capability inherent in using Windows applications in OS/2. Do not be afraid to experiment with some of the settings and parameters discussed in this chapter. Be sure you either write down the working settings or make a backup copy of any working INI files. If something doesn't work, don't be discouraged, try something else.

Author Bio

David Moskowitz, president of Productivity Solutions, was the original developer and instructor of the IBM OS/2 Conversion Workshops. Moskowitz developed a set of workshops presented by IBM to members of their Developer Assistance Program to help them migrate their applications to OS/2. He is a frequent speaker at conferences and symposiums including Miller Freeman's Software Development Conferences. He is the author of a book about DOS to OS/2 migration, Converting Applications to OS/2 *(1989, Brady Books). He has written many articles about OS/2 and object-oriented development for various publications including* OS/2 Monthly, VAR Herald, *and IBM's* OS/2 Developer.

10

File Systems and Drive Objects

In This Chapter

One of the chief responsibilities of an operating system is to allow rapid, reliable access to a user's data. This type of access comes in two forms: the physical aspect of disk input/output and performance, and the more abstract concept of organized, human-accessible mechanisms to manipulate data. In the OS/2 operating system, the term *file systems* is used to describe the portion of the operating system that allows physical access to data. OS/2 2.1 includes the second concept directly into the Workplace Shell desktop metaphor with drive objects. Obviously, these two ideas are closely related, and knowing more about one aids in the use of the other.

File Systems

The OS/2 2.1 file system provides access to directories and files. To introduce the OS/2 file systems, this section begins with the file allocation table (FAT) file system, which is built into the operating system, and discusses how OS/2 2.1 is able to support additional file systems. The high performance file system (HPFS) is also discussed—a capable, performance-oriented file system that is included with OS/2 2.1 and can be installed optionally.

The File Allocation Table

The FAT file system that is built into DOS (and OS/2 2.1) is a relatively robust file system designed for single-process disk access. Although FAT has been modified to support fixed disk drives and tolerate multiple processes accessing data concurrently, it has not been optimized. In addition, because many software vendors take advantage of knowing how the FAT file system is laid out, it is virtually impossible to add new features to the file system without breaking many pieces of existing software.

OS/2 2.1 pushes FAT even further. With the OS/2 2.1 operating system, IBM introduced enhanced caching, 32-bit code, and lazy writes to FAT file system access, making it considerably faster than previous FAT implementations. Because OS/2 2.1 controls access to the FAT file system, it is able to add

features such as extended attributes without limiting existing DOS applications access to data files. OS/2 2.1 maintains the FAT file system compatibility so that even native DOS can access the file system.

The FAT file system, however, still suffers from limitations such as the 8.3 file naming convention, excessive head movements to access files, and file fragmentation. The OS/2 operating system could clearly do better, and so the installable file system (IFS) concept was born.

The Installable File System

The installable file system (IFS) was introduced with OS/2 1.2. An IFS is a file system in which the mechanics of file system access are transparent to the applications using it. Applications perform file access through an application programming interface (API), which standardizes the way applications access the file system. In addition, as the name suggests, the file system is installed on top of the operating system, not built as a part of it. Applications written to an IFS interface are more portable than those written to a hard-coded file system like FAT.

Each drive is managed by only one file system, whether it is an IFS or FAT. Remember, though, that one physical drive can be partitioned into multiple partitions or logical drives so you can have multiple file systems running on the same physical drive.

What happens if, for some reason, the IFS driver is not loaded properly at startup and the system has a drive formatted for an IFS? In this case it turns out that the FAT file system tries to access the drive (assuming that if it were an IFS drive, the IFS would have taken control of it). In the case of an HPFS drive, FAT does not recognize the HPFS layout, so it cannot access the data on the drive. An error message displays when you try to access the data. If the drive in question is the boot drive, the boot fails.

The High Performance File System

The high performance file system (HPFS), also introduced with OS/2 1.2, was the first implementation of an OS/2 IFS. HPFS, however, is not a derivative of FAT; rather it is a new file system created specifically for OS/2's multitasking environment. HPFS was designed to provide multiple, concurrent access to data and to speed access to large volumes and large numbers of files and directories. HPFS was designed to avoid fragmentation, a problem that plagues FAT. HPFS allows users to specify filenames up to 254 characters in length (with case preserved). In contrast, FAT filenames must conform to the 8.3 naming convention (case is not preserved).

TIP

On an HPFS drive, case is preserved but not required. In other words, when you use a mixture of upper- and lowercase letters for a filename, OS/2 preserves the case. To access the file, however, you don't need to specify the same mixture of case that you originally used. For example, suppose you create a file called Senate_Voting_Records. The file is saved on the drive as Senate_Voting_Records, but you can access it on the command line by typing `Senate_Voting_Records`, `senate_voting_records`, `SENATE_VOTING_RECORDS`, or even `sENATe_VoTINg_RecoRDS`.

This may be a small victory for the user, but it's a nice one. Contrast the way DOS (FAT) or most UNIX implementations handle case. With DOS, all filenames are converted to uppercase letters. UNIX goes to the other extreme, where case is preserved and required. In other words, Senate_Voting_Records and Senate_Voting_RecordS are recognized as two different files, which can lead to confusion.

Where FAT is based on a simple, linear table to locate files and directories, HPFS is based on a "Balanced Tree" or "B-Tree" structure. Instead of a plodding lookup through an unsorted linear table, HPFS quickly traverses the B-Tree structure to find data. The only disadvantage to B-Tree is that it must be created when a file is created, thus slightly slowing write operations. Use of the lazy write capability (discussed shortly), however, hides this extra work.

HPFS also excels at locating free disk space for allocating new files or expanding additional ones. HPFS keeps free-space information in a compact bitmap structure actually located near the free space. HPFS also keeps its directory information near the center of the drive to further reduce head movement, and FAT keeps directory information near the home track, which results in excessive disk head moves.

FAT uses relatively large allocation units—clusters of 2 kilobytes or larger—resulting in an average of 1 kilobyte of wasted space per file. HPFS allocates disk space on sector boundaries, which is more efficient in terms of disk space. The average amount of wasted disk space with HPFS is only 256 bytes (1/2 of a 512-byte sector).

If FAT is built into OS/2 and HPFS is not, how does OS/2 boot off an HPFS drive and read the CONFIG.SYS file that FAT cannot recognize? The CONFIG.SYS has to be read for the IFS driver to be loaded. But the driver itself is probably on an HPFS drive also, not to mention the disk drivers. The operating system has enough knowledge of HPFS to find the CONFIG.SYS file and load the base drivers (those drivers that get loaded with the `BASEDEV=` statement instead of the `DEVICE=` statement) and the IFS. Once HPFS is running, the other boot files can be read.

Lazy Write

In OS/2 2.1, both HPFS and FAT optionally use a caching technique called lazy write. Lazy write means that data is written into a cache instead of directly to a disk. The program that performed the write does not know that the data has not physically been written to the disk yet. The file system writes the data to the disk as a background task according to a well-defined set of parameters.

Some people believe that lazy write is inherently more dangerous than conventional write-through techniques. There is perhaps some truth to this because there is always a possibility of power failure or other errors that, combined with the worst possible timing, could result in data loss. However, applications (on an individual file basis) have the option to write through the cache and ensure that critical data is written before the application proceeds.

My experience in three years of using HPFS with lazy write is that I have not lost data due to a lazy write-related problem. I can't say that I have never lost data, but when I do, it always seems to be operator error. If you are not comfortable with the idea of lazy write, however, you may want to consider disabling it (see the following section or refer to the OS/2 *Command Reference*).

HPFS Performance Versus FAT Performance

Is HPFS significantly faster than FAT? The answer, like many answers in computing, is that it depends on the situation. HPFS is clearly faster for large volumes and for dealing with many files. HPFS also takes advantage of an enlarged cache. However, on a small- to medium-size disk drive, or on a system with 8 or less megabytes of memory, the difference in performance between these two file systems is negligible. If you have a larger volume or more memory to give to the HPFS cache, HPFS is probably going to give you better performance.

Benchmarking the OS/2 file systems can provide clues as to which file system may perform better with your needs and system setup. I used Synetik Systems' benchmarking product, BenchTech for OS/2, to compare HPFS performance versus FAT performance. As automobile manufacturers are quick to point out, your mileage may vary— disk performance varies because of factors such as fragmentation, how full the drive is, and partitioning. These are synthetic benchmarks, running stand-alone, and operating on a single file. Keep in mind that HPFS is designed to maintain good performance in more complicated scenarios.

The results shown in Figure 10.1 are from a 486/33 ISA clone with a Maxtor 7120 IDE drive and 8 megabytes of memory (lazy write enabled). As you can see, FAT performance was virtually identical to HPFS in sequential

write operations. HPFS writes required more overhead than their FAT counterparts because HPFS must take the time to add to the B-Tree structure. Enlarging the cache sizes dramatically improves performance. Keep in mind, however, that enlarging the cache takes away memory from applications, and, if you have less than 10 megabytes of memory installed, increases swapping, which actually degrades overall performance. HPFS appears to benefit more than FAT from a larger cache, presumably because of the more sophisticated caching algorithm used by HPFS.

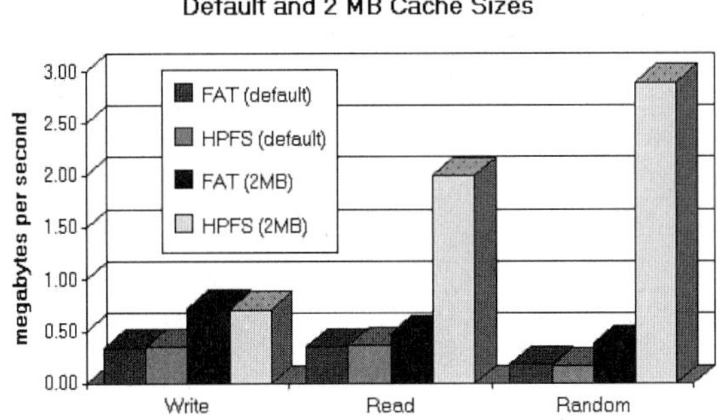

Figure 10.1. The relative HPFS and FAT benchmark results.

HPFS Versus FAT—Other Factors

Although performance is a major concern, there are other factors to consider when selecting which file system to use with OS/2 2.1.

Multiple File Systems

Remember that because you can create multiple partitions on a single-disk drive, you can elect to have both FAT and HPFS. This can be useful in an environment where native DOS support is needed and HPFS performance and features are also important.

Memory Usage

If you have any HPFS drives on your system, you must have the HPFS device driver loaded. This driver takes approximately 300 kilobytes of memory—memory that otherwise could be used for applications. If you have less than 8 megabytes, avoid installing HPFS.

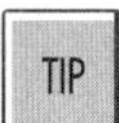

If HPFS support was installed on your system and you don't have any drives formatted with HPFS, you should comment out the IFS statement in your CONFIG.SYS.

```
IFS=D:\OS2\HPFS.IFS  /CACHE:384 /CRECL:4 /AUTOCHECK:DE
```

for example, becomes

```
REM IFS=D:\OS2\HPFS.IFS  /CACHE:384 /CRECL:4 /AUTOCHECK:DE
```

Put HPFS partitions at the end of your drive list if you boot real DOS.

DOS Support

Because FAT is the native file system for DOS, your FAT formatted drives are accessible to DOS, either in an OS/2 virtual DOS machine (VDM) or stand-alone DOS. HPFS is another story. HPFS data is laid out in an entirely different manner than data on a FAT drive. Native DOS simply cannot access files on an HPFS drive.

All is not lost, however, because DOS programs running in a VDM go through OS/2 to access data, so DOS or Windows applications can access files on your HPFS formatted drive. Files with long filenames, however, are not available to DOS applications.

CAUTION: There are certain DOS programs, especially those that use low-level system calls, that cannot be used on HPFS drives.

When making the choice about which file system to use, you need to estimate how reliant you are on DOS programs. If you are reliant on a DOS program that won't run under OS/2 2.1, you need to have at least one FAT formatted drive. If the DOS programs that you use run well under OS/2 2.1, you should be able to get by without FAT if you choose.

Long Filenames

HPFS supports long filenames; FAT does not. However, the Workplace Shell allows you to use long filenames on objects contained on a FAT formatted drive. If you look at them with the command line, the filenames comply with the 8.3 naming convention. What is happening here?

OS/2 supports extended attributes (EAs), which allow the operating system to attach additional information to a file (see the section later in this chapter concerning EAs). One of the things OS/2 can attach is a longer filename; the Workplace Shell refers to this name as the title of an object. If, for example, you use the Workplace Shell to create a file on a FAT drive called College Basketball Stats 1992/93.XLS, the real filename will be something like COLLEGE_.XLS. You can use the details view for a folder or the settings notebook for an object to compare titles versus real names.

There are pluses and minuses associated with this approach. DOS programs are able to read and write to the file because they see the short filename. The long filename usually disappears if you write to the file because DOS programs don't know anything about EAs. What's worse, OS/2 programs may not save your long filename. For example, the OS/2 System Editor retains the long filename, but Microsoft Excel for OS/2 does not.

"Long filename" means any filename that is acceptable to HPFS but not to DOS. For example, the filename Sept.15.92 is not especially long, but it is not a valid DOS filename because it has two periods in it.

Although you can get some long filename support out of FAT, if you really want to use long filenames, use HPFS. When it comes to file systems in OS/2, you have a choice. There are good reasons for going to HPFS, and there are good reasons to stay with FAT. You need to think about your particular requirements and decide which one is the best for you. Fortunately, it's not an all-or-nothing decision—you can choose to partition your drive and use both FAT and HPFS. If you have less than a 120-megabyte drive, or less than 8 megabytes of memory in your system, you should probably stay with FAT.

Shutdown

One of the minor penalties that a user must pay for the multitasking and disk caches under OS/2 is the shutdown process. Even under DOS, shutting your computer off at an inopportune moment can cause data loss. Shutting down under DOS usually means that you exit the program you're using and get back to the C: prompt before you turn the machine off. Because there aren't other processes running, you're assured that there aren't any open files.

Because there are usually several processes running simultaneously under OS/2 2.1, a more formal procedure is needed to ensure that no data is lost when your computer gets turned off. In addition, data may be being held in the OS/2 system cache that has not yet been physically written to disk because of lazy write.

Shutdown is designed to cleanly close all files and make your system ready to be turned off. It is important to get into the habit of shutting down your system. OS/2 is not alone in asking you to do this; Apple Macintosh and most UNIX systems are examples of other operating systems with shutdown procedures.

Depending on the application's design, when you shut down the application may give you an opportunity to save any unsaved data. Applications also have the opportunity to cancel the shut down. Usually if you have unsaved data, a message box that says something like "File not saved. Save it? Yes, No, or Cancel" appears on-screen. Selecting Cancel cancels the shutdown and the program does not close. Not all applications are designed this way, however, so it is obviously more prudent to save data before beginning shutdown.

Under OS/2 2.1, shutting down also saves the state of your desktop so that it can be restored when you reboot or restart your system. It takes diligent use of shutdown to make this feature work properly.

At some point you may find yourself in too much of a hurry to shut down your system. If so, don't just shut off your machine. Use the following trick to ensure that, at a minimum, the cache buffers are cleared and written to disk properly: press Ctrl+Alt+Delete, just like you are going to reboot. This action flushes the buffers. When the system beeps, shutdown your system.

What happens when you don't shutdown? Accidents happen, not to mention power outages. In order to protect the integrity of your system, OS/2 sets a bit indicating whether HPFS file systems went through an orderly shutdown when last reset. If not, it initiates the Check Disk (CHKDSK) program to make sure that the file system is okay before proceeding to boot OS/2. Because this procedure can take quite a while, it's worth shutting down just to avoid this delay when starting your system. The `AC` parameter on the `DISKCACHE` and/or `IFS=HPFS` statements in your CONFIG.SYS dictate whether or not the CHKDSK program is run at startup. OS/2 adds the autocheck for all HPFS drives. If you want the same for FAT drives, add the `AC` parameter to the `DISKCACHE` statement in your CONFIG.SYS.

Disk Support

All OS/2 disks are formatted using FAT—there is no HPFS support for disks. OS/2 disks are interchangeable with DOS disks. If you use the Workplace Shell to copy files to and from disks, the HPFS long filenames are preserved.

OS/2 can also be booted from disk. One simple method of booting an OS/2 command-line session is as follows:

1. Insert the OS/2 installation disk in the bootable disk drive.
2. Shut down and reboot the machine or, if it is off, turn it on.
3. When prompted, insert installation disk #1.
4. When the first OS/2 installation panel appears, press Esc.
5. The OS/2 command prompt should appear at this point.

You can reduce this to a one disk load by creating a customized OS/2 boot disk. To do this, you need to create a disk that has the OS/2 system files and device drivers for your type of system. Check CompuServe in the IBM OS/2 forums for examples, and refer to Chapter 2, "Multiple Configurations," for instructions.

Optimizing Your File Systems

Both FAT and HPFS have several tunable parameters that can be adjusted to optimize disk I/O performance in the OS/2 2.1 environment. Before I present them, however, I need to make the following points about objectives and expectations about performance tuning:

- Don't expect miracles. Although tuning may improve disk performance considerably, it is not a cure-all for other performance problems. For example, you can adjust all the disk parameters you want, but if your main performance problem is insufficient memory, you'll see little or no improvement in overall system performance.
- Be careful that you don't degrade overall system performance for the sake of improving disk performance. A common mistake is enlarging a cache when the system is short of memory. Enlarging a cache uses system memory that may be better used by your applications.
- Know your applications. If you have a specific application that you want to optimize, you need to understand as much as you can about how it accesses data. Does it perform sequential reads and writes or is the data accessed in a more random manner? Does it use the OS/2 system cache or specify write through?
- Know your system. If your system has a 16-megabyte caching disk controller, using the OS/2 cache may actually slow your system down. Understanding the components in your system will help your tuning effort.
- Don't stray far from the OS/2 defaults for your system. If you do change a parameter by a large factor, be aware of the system-wide impact of the change.

Disk Performance Parameters

The BUFFERS statement in CONFIG.SYS—the BUFFERS parameter applies to both FAT and HPFS file systems. These buffers are used in addition to cache memory as the place to put blocks of data that don't occupy complete 512-kilobyte sectors. Increasing the number of BUFFERS may help performance when reading smaller files.

The DISKCACHE statement in CONFIG.SYS—the n parameter in the DISKCACHE statement specifies the number of kilobytes used for the FAT file system cache. Increasing this value decreases the amount of real memory that is available to your system. If you have less than 8 megabytes of real memory, avoid increasing this number. IBM recommends that systems with 6 or less megabytes of memory use a value of 64 kilobytes, and those with more use a value of 256 kilobytes. The LW parameter specifies the use of FAT lazy write. Omit the LW parameter to disable FAT lazy write. The threshold parameter T can be modified for specific applications, but changing the value is not recommended for general OS/2 use.

The IFS (HPFS.IFS) statement in CONFIG.SYS—the IFS statement for the HPFS IFS driver contains parameters that specify the size and maximum record size for the HPFS cache. The CACHE parameter specifies the cache size in kilobytes, and it can be as high as 2,048 kilobytes (2 megabytes). As with the DISKCACHE size, enlarging the cache size reduces the amount of real memory available to the system.

The CACHE command—this command allows you to specify four parameters, all pertaining to HPFS lazy write. The LAZY parameter specifies whether lazy write is enabled or not. Specify /LAZY:OFF to disable HPFS lazy write. If you disable lazy write, the other parameters become meaningless. The second parameter, MAXAGE, specifies the maximum age that dirty pages are left in the cache. DISKIDLE specifies how long the disk should be idle before the writes take place. The BUFFERIDLE parameter specifies how much buffer idle time can elapse before the cache data must be written out.

Because the CACHE command can be executed from the command line (as well as in the CONFIG.SYS with a RUN= statement), it is the easiest to tune. Changes made to parameters in the CONFIG.SYS require a shutdown and reboot to take effect. The CACHE command allows you to change the lazy write parameters on the fly.

Making the Most of Long Filenames

The ability to specify filenames longer than the DOS 8-character plus 3-character extension standard is a major benefit of HPFS and, in a more limited sense, the FAT file system under OS/2 2.1. Although you may never use 254 characters for your filenames, you may find yourself routinely using 15 or more characters. Not only do you get more characters to work with, but you are also free of some of the other constraints of the DOS file system, such as being able to use spaces in the name or to specify more than one period.

I won't repeat the rules for filenames here, but I will offer some advice on how to take advantage of the longer filenames. The first thing you can use long filenames for is to make filenames more descriptive and easier to find. "Letter to Editor about Prairie Dogs" is certainly more descriptive than PR_DOG.LET. The second name would probably be quicker to type, however, given that it is less than half the length of the first. Because the first filename has spaces in it, it is necessary to enclose the name in quotes when using it on the command line. A better compromise might be something like Prairie_Dog_Letter, which is shorter and contains no spaces, but still conveys what the file contains.

If you write a large number of letters to the editor about prairie dogs, you may need to add a bit more to the name to help keep things organized. You may want to append a number or the date to the name. HPFS keeps track of the creation date and last modification date for you, so adding the date may be redundant for data contained on HPFS drives.

OS/2 reserves certain directory names and filenames for itself. However, OS/2 does not always tell you if a file that you are creating has a reserved filename. The following list presents some examples of reserved names (see the OS/2 online help for the complete list):

PRN or LPT1 through LPT3
COM1 through COM4
PIPE on HPFS Volume 3

Extensions

OS/2 2.1 uses one of two pieces of information to determine the object type of a given file. The first method is to use the file extension. The second method of deciding the object type is to use the file type (if it exists) that is kept in extended attributes (more on extended attributes later). The file extension or type is primarily used for associating the file with an application. Using the file type for associations becomes more prevalent as more applications are written to take advantage of it. Most OS/2 applications, as well as DOS and Windows programs running under OS/2, use the second method. What this means is that many of your data files need an extension, even if they are long filenames. For example, if the letter to the editor were a Microsoft Word for OS/2 document, the name would need to be something like Prairie_Dog_Letter.DOC. The DeScribe Word Processor, on the other hand, takes advantage of file types so you won't need to tack on an extension.

What is the extension? Under the 8.3 naming convention, the extension is the three characters to the right of the period. Under HPFS, the concept is the same, although it is slightly more

> difficult to explain. If the file has at least one period and three or fewer characters to the right of the last period, these three characters are the extension.

The Workplace Shell has a feature that makes the business of carrying around these extensions a bit easier. Because renaming or deleting a file extension, such as changing Prairie_Dog_Letter.DOC to Prairie_Dog_Letter.TMP would break the association with its application, the Workplace Shell by default asks you if you really want to change the extension. If you do, the Workplace Shell asks you if you want to carry over the association. This feature can get you over the hump of having to provide an extension, although it is a little extra work. OS/2 also lets you turn this feature off so applications that don't rely on extensions can be renamed without confirmation.

There is one area, however, where you shouldn't change file extensions: executable programs, command files, and batch files. These extensions determine how the programs are initially loaded for execution. Renaming WP.EXE to WP.CMD prevents OS/2 from running the program.

Workplace Shell Drive Objects

OS/2 2.1 provides a graphical mechanism for accessing and manipulating files and directories. Files are represented by objects, and directories are represented by folders. At the top of the hierarchy is a folder called Drives. Drives is unique in a number of respects. First, you can't delete the Drives folder, nor can you delete the drives that are in it. Drives won't let you move a drive object out of the Drives folder, but it will let you make a shadow of the drive. The Drives folder contains one drive object for each disk drive in your system. If you have a drive with multiple partitions, each partition or logical drive has its own drive object. By default, the Drives folder is located in the OS/2 System folder, although you may want to move it to the desktop for easier access.

Both OS/2 1.x and Microsoft Windows feature a program called File Manager, which lets you access files and directories graphically. In OS/2 2.1, the File Manager is replaced by a set of Workplace Shell objects, headed by the Drives folder.

Drive Objects

A drive object can be opened to access the folders and objects that it contains. Opening a view of a drive object lets you see the contents of that drive. File objects are represented by an icon with the name of the file below it. Most folders have an icon that looks like a file folder, but some have special icons. Opening the drive object produces a view of the files and folders it contains.

By default, the view shown when you double-click on a drive object is the tree view, a hierarchical view of your directories (represented in the Workplace Shell by folders). The tree view is useful because it allows you to open a folder that is several levels down in the hierarchy without opening the folders that contain it. Folders that have subfolders are shown with a plus sign next to them. To expand the tree and see the lower-level folders, click on the plus sign. The tree view also displays the amount of disk space available on that drive. The disadvantage of this view is that the nonfolder objects that the folder contains are not displayed.

The amount of available disk space that is shown on the tree view is not always current because another process may use or free disk space in the background. To get the most current value, select Refresh from the Drive's pop-up menu.

There are two other views of the drive object: the icon view and the details view. Most folders in the Workplace Shell have icon view as the default view. If you prefer the icon or details view over the tree view, you can change the

default. On the Menu page of the settings notebook for the folder you want to change (in this case a drive object), select Open, and then select Settings. In the ensuing window, there is an option to set the default action for the Open menu. Use it to select icon or details view as the default.

The tilde character (~) in a menu definition tells OS/2 to underline the next character and make that character the keyboard shortcut for the menu option.

Deleting Files

And I was working at my desk on other things, literally cleaning up files on lots of things, and when I would finish with a handful of documents, I'd walk up, walk past them [two investigators from the Attorney General's Office], out the door—you know where the shredder was—turn the corner, turn on the shredder, and drop them in.

-Lt. Colonel Oliver L. North,
Testifying before Congress about the Iran-Contra Affair

Apparently, none of the data shredded by Lt. Colonel North was recovered. However, many pieces of evidence in the investigation came from the National Security Council's IBM PROFS system—messages that staffers deleted. The system kept a copy of the messages in a central data base.

For more conventional users of computer systems, recovering deleted data is considered a necessity. Although OS/2 2.1 provides an "undelete" capability, you do have to make a minor change to your system configuration to enable it.

There are two ways to use the Workplace Shell to delete an object: dragging it to the shredder or selecting Delete from the object's pop-up menu. You can also delete files or directories from the command line using the DELETE and

RMDIR commands, but keep in mind that with the exception of DEL x, where x is a directory or a wildcard combination representing all of the files in a directory, the command-line versions do not ask you to confirm deletions.

By default, the Workplace Shell makes you confirm object deletions once (if the object is a folder, you must confirm your deletion twice). You can, however, instruct Workplace Shell not to confirm deletions. These settings are contained in the system object, located (initially) in the System Setup folder, which in turn is located in the OS/2 System folder.

Asking you to confirm what you are about to delete is good, but what about the cases where you are not quite sure what the object is? For example, deleting an object that refers to a program is quite a bit different from deleting the program itself, even though they usually have the same icon. In the same way, deleting a shadow of an object is harmless; deleting the object itself, however, is more consequential. Unfortunately, the Workplace Shell comes up somewhat short in this area. When it asks you to confirm the deletion of an object, it does not tell you what type of object it is. There are two things that you can look at to help with these situations. First, in the case of a program object versus a program file object, the former usually has a longer, more descriptive name, such as Microsoft Excel for OS/2, and the latter usually has a name like EXCEL.EXE. In the case of deleting a shadow versus the original, you might try changing the color of the shadow text to make it more distinctive than a regular object's text.

Mistakes occur, of course, and even with the best confirmation approach, you still may find yourself accidentally deleting this month's revenue figures. OS/2 provides support for a limited capability to undelete deleted files, yet this support is not enabled by default. To enable it, you need to edit your CONFIG.SYS file and remove REM from the line that is similar to the following line:

```
REM SET DELDIR=C:\DELETE,512;D:\DELETE,512;E:\DELETE,512;
```

Do this now so that when that unfortunate time comes your system will be ready. You have to shut down and reboot your system for this change to take effect. In the preceding example line, `512` means that up to 512 kilobytes of disk space are used for undelete. You can make this amount larger or smaller if needed. If you routinely use files larger than 512 kilobytes and have sufficient disk space, it's probably wise to make it larger.

Why did IBM choose to inhibit this feature? Apparently there was an argument among the engineers just before 2.0 was released concerning the way in which free disk space is reported. Should the amount of free disk space reflect the amount in use by deleted files? Although this is probably an important subject to debate, it really shouldn't have stopped them from enabling the undelete.

Enabling undelete may cause many operations to be performed more slowly because deleted files must be moved to the undelete directory.

To recover your files, use the `UNDELETE` command from an OS/2 command line. To use it, use CD to change directories to the directory where the lost file existed. When you enter `UNDELETE` with no parameters, you will be prompted as to which files are available and if you want to recover them. Alternatively, you can run `UNDELETE` with parameters to specify how you want the command to work. Refer to the OS/2 Command Reference to obtain the `UNDELETE` command syntax.

At some point, you may temporarily want to use the disk space that the undelete feature is using. You can free up this space by issuing the following undelete command in an OS/2 window. First, change drives to the one you want cleared and type the following line:

```
UNDELETE /f /s /a
```

The `/a` parameter is optional. Using it bypasses prompting for each deleted file.

Laying Out Your Data

A little planning can go a long way toward the goal of having an organized, accessible data layout in your system. OS/2 provides several mechanisms to facilitate almost any data layout that you might want to try. Support for multiple drives, partitions, and logical drives is a basic feature of OS/2, and Boot Manager and the dual boot mechanism enable you to have multiple, bootable operating systems on the same system. Although system setup is covered in Chapter 3, "Configuration and Setup," I want to touch on it here because of the relevance to laying out your programs and data.

A one-partition system is the simplest approach, and it may have the edge in performance compared to multiple partitions. Because data is always read from and written to the same drive, the cache may be more effective in a one-partition system. For a small drive, less than 120 megabytes, for example, one partition is probably the only effective approach. For larger drives, however, the benefits of a multiple-partition system may override the simplicity and slight performance edge of the one-partition system. Breaking a large drive into smaller partitions may help performance, especially for the FAT file system, because directory and file access paths are shortened. Multiple partitions may also provide more data security and operating system flexibility.

Security

To illustrate the potential for enhanced data security with a multiple-partition system, compare the data layouts shown in Figure 10.2. Configuration A has all programs and data on one partition: the C drive. Configuration B has DOS 5.0 installed on drive C, OS/2 2.0 on drive D, and OS/2 applications and data on drive E. If, for example, the file system on the drive containing OS/2 fails, the user with Configuration A may lose all data; with Configuration B, the user would only have to reinstall OS/2. In addition, backup becomes easier because the only drive that needs to be backed up consistently is drive E. (The other drives contain some configuration data, and the user needs to evaluate what, if anything, needs to be backed up from the C and D drives.)

Making Multiple Drives Work with Workplace Shell

You probably have noticed by now that the OS/2 desktop is really just another Workplace Shell folder. You can store program objects, folders, and even data objects on the desktop. Because the desktop is a directory on the drive that contains OS/2, placing data in a folder on the desktop is no different than keeping it in a folder in the drive object, except that it is contained in a directory called \DESKTOP.

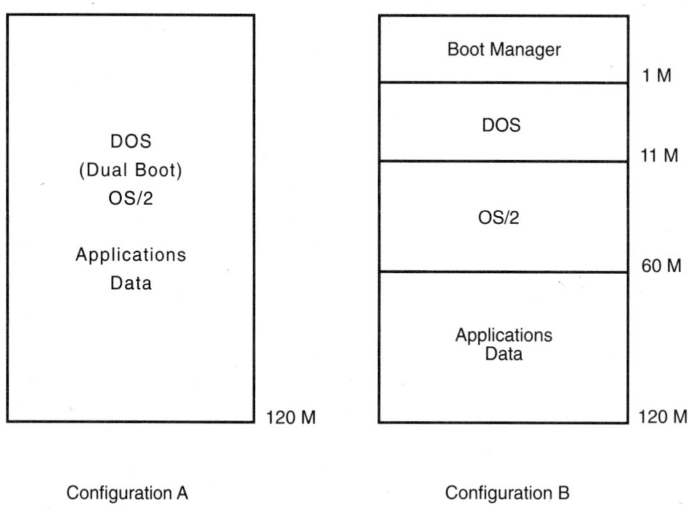

Figure 10.2. Two OS/2 disk configurations.

Because the desktop is just another folder on the drive where OS/2 is installed, storing data on a folder on the desktop means that it is stored on the OS/2 drive. Data stored on another drive must be accessed through the drive objects. If, however, you still want the accessibility of having folders on the desktop without storing data on the drive that contains the desktop, there is a simple answer: store the data where you want it and make a shadow of the data object or of the folder that contains it. Then place the shadow on the desktop.

Swap File and Spooler

Although you may only have 8 megabytes of physical memory on your machine, with OS/2 2.1 you can run an application that uses 10 or more megabytes. OS/2 2.1 uses the concept of *virtual memory* to allow applications to use practically as much memory as they need. The operating system uses some of your disk space to swap out sections of memory that aren't often used. The swapped-out memory is written to a file called the swap file. If your system is swapping a great deal, performance will suffer, but this can be remedied by adding more real memory to your system.

What happens, though, when your disk drive that contains the swap file runs out of space? In general, OS/2 is able to detect the shortage of virtual memory (swap space) and report to you, in no uncertain terms, that you'd better do something about it. If you choose to ignore this error message, programs and OS/2 itself may start to fail. There are two things that you can do when this situation occurs. First, you'll probably need to close at least one application. When OS/2 pops up the message that says your swap file partition is full, you are given a chance to close the application that was allocating memory when the shortage occurred. You may take this approach or close one yourself. It is generally less risky to close the one that OS/2 is asking you to close. After you do this, your system is probably safe for the moment. You can either close more applications or free up some disk space on the drive that contains the swap file.

The print spooler is another system function that can use large amounts of disk space. Print spooling is a handy feature of OS/2 2.1 that gives you considerable control over how and when multiple print jobs are sent to the printer. If you have spooling enabled, each time you print a file the print image is written to a file in the spooler directory. After it is printed, the print image is deleted.

If you run out of space on the drive that the print spooler writes to, a pop-up message appears. Normally, this isn't too much of a problem—you can cancel the print job and free up more space to start it again. There is a situation that can occur that is potentially more dangerous, however. If the print spooler and the swap file are both written to the same drive, and you run out of disk space, your system may or may not be able to recover. The problem is that there are three or more parties—the swapper, the print spooler, and your application—all in need of the same vanquished resource. One solution to this problem is to configure your system so that your spool file is on a different drive or partition than the swap file. To change the spool file location, use the spooler object located in the System Setup folder (located in the OS/2 System folder). To change the location of the swap file, edit the line in your CONFIG.SYS. (See Chapter 1 for information about swap file location, and Chapter 3 for information about CONFIG.SYS and the swap path.)

Dealing with Fragmentation

In the FAT file system, as files are erased or enlarged, fragmentation occurs. Fragmentation is the scattering of the sectors of disk files. Fragmentation hurts disk read/write performance because the disk heads have to move further and more often than they would for a file that is laid out in a contiguous fashion. The more files that are erased, written, expanded, and so on, the more fragmentation that occurs.

Although fragmentation does tend to degrade disk performance over time, it is too often blamed for performance problems. Major performance problem or not, a great deal of time has to be spent fixing this problem. Defragmenting DOS disks has evolved from a science into a religion. Most general-purpose utility packages for DOS contain defragmenters. Even though these tools are good for reporting how badly a disk is fragmented, they may be overkill as far as fixing the problem. The easiest way to fix fragmentation, provided you have a reliable backup system, is to do a complete file backup of the drive, format it, and then restore the contents. In this way, files are written back to the disk in a contiguous fashion.

The designers of HPFS seized the opportunity to reduce the problem of fragmentation by assigning consecutive sectors to files whenever possible. When a file is created, HPFS uses the specified file size to find a contiguous set of sectors and then uses that spot to place the file. When a file is extended, a contiguous set of sectors is searched for that meets the requested extension size, plus a predetermined amount for good measure. If the file grows again, it may not have to be re-extended because of the extra space allocated in the first extension. HPFS can also detect when two files are created simultaneously; it then tries to place them in different areas on the disk so the potential that they fragment each other is reduced.

As you might guess, HPFS is very successful at eliminating fragmentation if there is adequate space on the disk. If a large file is written to the drive and there are no contiguous sections available, the file is stored in noncontiguous sectors. As of this writing, file utilities for HPFS are scarce. However, the GammaTech utilities provide HPFS fragmentation reports and offer an HPFS defragmentation utility.

OS/2 Disk Utilities

OS/2 provides some utility programs for your file systems. CHKDSK.EXE and PMCHKDSK.EXE search for and optionally correct allocation problems on a drive. CHKDSK.EXE is a command-line utility. PMCHKDSK.EXE can be issued from the command line, but it is also available on the pop-up menus of drive objects. FDISK.EXE and FDISKPM.EXE are utilities that allow you to modify the partitions on a drive. They also allow you to change the parameters for Boot Manager.

Deleting a partition destroys any previous data contained in the partition. Use FDISK.EXE and FDISKPM.EXE with care.

File Attributes

File attributes are information that OS/2, and most operating systems, maintains about files and directories. The date and time that a file was last modified is an example of the type of information that the operating system might record. OS/2 2.1 provides for simple file attributes with an extension of this concept called, appropriately, extended attributes.

The FAT file system provides an associated set of attributes (in addition to the file's data) for each file and directory. Sometimes called simple attributes, these attributes record the size of the file and its allocated size, last modification date and time, and a set of four "flags" for the file or directory. The flags indicate whether a file is read-only, a hidden file, a system file, or a file that should be backed up (archived). HPFS also adds other simple attributes such as the creation date and time and last-accessed date and time.

Extended Attributes

OS/2 provides for attributes that go beyond the simple attributes listed above. An application can tack on virtually any kind of information to a file. An example of an extended attribute is a comment like the author's name. In DOS and early OS/2 word processors, the application, if it were to support saving the author's name, would have to save it as part of the data file itself or in a separate file. Using extended attributes, the comment can be maintained by an application or the File Pages of the settings notebook for the object.

HPFS provides direct support for extended attributes, but the FAT file system does not. In order to implement extended attributes under FAT, the OS/2 designers chose to save all extended attributes in a special file called "EA DATA. SF". Because the file is marked "hidden" and "system," you normally can't see it. Obviously, this approach sacrifices performance somewhat because of the second file.

Do not delete "EA DATA. SF". Deleting this file is the OS/2 equivalent of shooting yourself in the foot.

Special Extended Attribute—File Type

One extended attribute that is used by many applications and the Workplace Shell is the type attribute. Although most Workplace Shell objects have an associated type, in this discussion I'll stick to file objects. The type of an object is one method that OS/2 uses to determine what application is to be associated with the object (i.e., what application is opened when you double-click on the object). The OS/2 System Editor requires that when a file is saved, it must have a file type. Although this may be overkill, OS/2 is trying to introduce you to file types.

Usually, your application takes care of setting the file type, but you can also have a say in the matter. To view the file type, open the settings notebook for any file object. Usually the Types page in the notebook shows you what types are defined for the file. For example, a spreadsheet created with Microsoft Excel has a file type similar to "Microsoft Excel 3.0 Spreadsheet." If you remove the type, the association with the application is also removed.

If you add a new file type, a new association is formed. For example, suppose that you have created a "Plain Text" file using the OS/2 System Editor and you now want to switch to the DeScribe Word Processor. If DeScribe is installed on your system, you can create a DeScribe Document object. You could create such an object and then cut and paste the "Plain Text" data into the new object. This would solve the problem, but it would be somewhat messy. Now that you know about file types, you could use the Types page in the settings notebook to add the DeScribe Document type to the file. If you are going to exclusively use DeScribe on the object, you may want to delete the "Plain Text" type.

Attach a Comment or Key Phrase to Your File

OS/2 also enables you to attach comments or key phrases to your files. This feature may be useful in an environment where many people have access to data files, and you need to be able to record the author's name or other information about the file without modifying the file's contents. To add a comment or key phrase to a file, use File Page Number 3 of the settings notebook for the file.

Attaching an Icon in Extended Attributes

Another piece of information that can be attached to a file's extended attributes is an icon. As you might have guessed, when you edit a file's icon on the General page of the settings notebook for a file, you are either modifying the icon as it exists in the file's extended attributes or you are adding a new icon to its extended attributes. Actually, extended attributes also allow you to add bitmaps (raster-based images) or metafiles (vector-based images) to a file's extended attributes; the icon, however, is more interesting because it is visible.

Using the Edit option on the General page of the settings notebook for an object is only one way to add an icon to a file's extended attributes. Applications may also attach an icon to a file by writing the icon data directly to the file's extended attributes. You can do the same thing using a little bit of REXX programming. Listing 10.1 is a REXX command file called PutIcon.CMD. You can use it to attach an icon file to any other file. The simple version listed here could be adapted to modify any number of files. For example, if you have an icon that you would like to apply to all of your CMD files, modify PutIcon.CMD to call `SysPutEA` for each CMD file on your system.

Listing 10.1. REXX command file PutIcon.CMD

```
/* ********************************************************** */
/*                   >>>>> PutIcon.CMD <<<<<                  */
/*                    by Chris Parsons 9/29/92                */
/*                     for OS/2 2.1 Unleashed                 */
/*                                                            */
```

```
/* Description: A simple OS/2 REXX command file that             */
/* demonstrates the use of REXX and OS/2 Extended Attributes.   */
/*                                                               */
/* Usage: PutIcon.CMD (The program prompts for filenames).      */
/*                                                               */
/* Function: Takes an icon file created by the Icon Editor      */
/* and attaches it to a file in the files extended attributes. */
/*                                                               */
/* Note: This program doesn't do any error checking; that is    */
/* it doesn't check that the icon file actually contains an     */
/* icon or if an icon is already attached to the file.          */
/* ********************************************************** */
 call RxFuncAdd SysPutEA,RexxUtil,SysPutEA
 call RxFuncAdd SysFileTree,RexxUtil,SysFileTree

 say
 say "This CMD file will add an icon to a "
 say "file's extended attributes"
 say

    /* Get the filenames from the user */
 say "Enter Icon Filename..."
 pull Icon_File
 say "Enter Target_File Filename..."
 pull Target_File

    /* Get the size of the icon file */
 call SysFileTree Icon_File,'FileArray','F'
 Size = word(FileArray.1,3)

    /* Read in the icon data */
 Icon_Data = charin(Icon_File,1,Size)

    /* Set up the data for the call to SysPutEA          */
    /* Note: the F9FF is the value for EAT_ICON from the */
    /* Toolkit, which is the EA identifier for icons.    */
 EA_Data = 'F9FF'x ¦¦ d2c(Size) ¦¦ Icon_Data

    /* Call the REXX function SysPutEA to write the icon data */
 call SysPutEA Target_File,".ICON",EA_Data;

    /* Inform the user of the result code */
 say
 if result = 0 then say Icon_File' was attached to 'Target_File'
➥successfully.'
 else                say 'Error trying to add Icon to File.'

 exit
    /* end of PutIcon.CMD */
```

Reclaiming Disk Space from Extended Attributes

Although extended attributes are generally useful, at some point you may decide that the EAs for a file or set of files are simply wasting disk space. All is not lost, however, because you can reclaim some of the space if you proceed carefully. OS/2 provides a command-line-only utility called EAUTIL that allows you to separate a file's EAs into another file. If there are extended attributes attached to a file and you want them all removed, use EAUTIL and delete the EA file that it creates. If you need to be selective, you can edit the file and rejoin the EAs. For programmers who have access to the OS/2 Toolkit, one sample program allows you to interactively view and edit EAs. Hopefully, someone will capitalize on the idea and provide a more complete EA utility.

Avoid Losing EAs When Sending Files

What happens to extended attributes when you use a communications program to send an OS/2 file? As a general rule, they are lost unless you do something about it. Imagine writing a REXX command file that you want to share with others. You create a flashy icon and attach it to the file. If you hand it to someone on a disk, OS/2 takes care of the icon for you. If, however, you send the file with your favorite communications package, the EAs, and consequently the icon, will be lost.

One way to avoid this problem is to use EAUTIL to split the EAs into another file and then send both files. This is probably not the most elegant solution, however, because it burdens the receiving user to rejoin the EA file. A better solution is to pack the file or files using a file compression tool that supports extended attributes. One example of such a tool is the OS/2 `PACK` and `UNPACK` commands. Unfortunately, `PACK` only exists in the OS/2 Toolkit.

The LH2 utility on the companion disk to this book supports compression and restoration of EAs.

Alternatives to Drive Objects

After a little bit of orientation with the Workplace Shell, the drive objects ease of use and utility shine. Until the time that it becomes second nature, however, you might long for an alternative. This section describes some alternatives and some of the pros and cons of each approach. If you upgraded to OS/2 2.1 from OS/2 1.2 or 1.3, you may want to try the OS/2 File Manager from those versions. If you upgraded to OS/2 2.1 from Microsoft Windows, you may want to try the File Manager from Windows or Windows for Workgroups. There are also other alternatives, such as Norton's Commander for OS/2, the OS/2 or DOS command-line interfaces, the 4OS2 command-line utility, or Norton's Desktop for DOS or Windows.

OS/2 1.3 File Manager

To install the 1.3 File Manager, use the UNPACK.EXE program to copy the following file from the 1.3 installation disks to a directory on your OS/2 system and execute PMFILE.EXE:

```
PMFILE.DLL
PMFILE.EXE
PMFILEH.HLP
```

The best way to accomplish this is to create a program object for File Manager. File Manager runs just fine under OS/2 2.1, although it does not use the newer CUA 91 guidelines. You may find yourself trying to get a pop-up menu for the files with mouse button 2.

Like any OS/2 application that has DLLs or HLP files, the DLL files need to be in your `LIBPATH` (if your `LIBPATH` has the `;` to indicate the current directory, then the current directory is adequate) and the HLP file needs to be in your `HELP` path or the current directory.

Windows File Manager

The Windows 3.1 File Manager is included with WIN-OS/2 support and works fine under OS/2 2.1, even on HPFS drives. Like any DOS application, the Windows File Manager does not have access to the files with filenames that don't conform to the FAT 8.3 naming convention.

Command Line

Chapter 7, "Command Line Interface," deals with the OS/2 command line. The command-line interface has considerable power when working with file systems and the data they contain. For some users, the command line is the operating system, and a GUI only slows them down and gets in their way. Personally, the command line represents altogether too much typing for my feeble typing skills, but I do find myself using it on occasion.

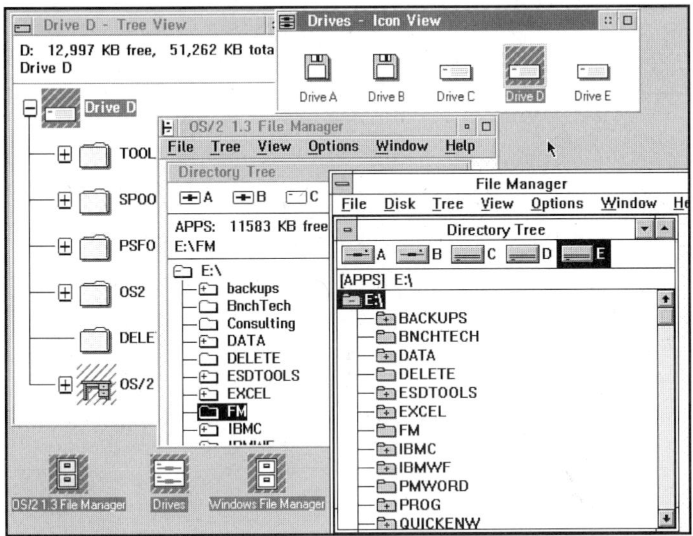

Figure 10.3. A Drives folder, the OS/2 1.3 File Manager, and the Windows File Manager running on the same desktop.

There are a few items about the GUI versus the command-line way of dealing with files that are worth mentioning:

- Copying HPFS files to FAT file systems, especially disks: using the Workplace Shell you can preserve long filenames, but the command-line interface doesn't allow for this. This is especially useful when transferring data from one HPFS drive to another via disk.

- Using the Workplace Shell, there are several levels of protection against making mistakes, such as deleting wanted files, renaming file extensions, and moving objects. In general, no such protection is afforded to the command-line equivalent of these operations. There are only a few command-line entries that require confirmation by the operating system (i.e., `DEL *.*`, `FORMAT C:`, and so on).

- It is often much easier to delete whole directories that may in turn contain more directories using the Workplace Shell. Using the command line, it takes two commands to delete a directory (`DEL dir_name` and `RMDIR dir_name`). If there are subdirectories, one has to delete these prior to deleting the higher-level directories. Using the Workplace Shell, just drop the directory icon on the shredder, even if there are many lower-level subdirectories.

Summary

OS/2 2.1 provides the most advanced file systems for desktop computers. A skilled user can take advantage of OS/2's HPFS and Workplace Shell access to file objects. HPFS provides excellent performance, portability, and expandability. Instead of being limited by the old FAT file system, users can now consider the personal computer a solid platform for disk-intensive applications. New users get many of the advantages of the system because of the easy-to-understand, easy-to-use data access metaphor. The FAT file system is fully supported, making the transition from DOS to OS/2 2.1 smooth. The command-line interface, the Windows File Manager, and the OS/2 File Manager can also make it easier for people coming to the OS/2 2.1 environment from Windows, OS/2 1.2 or 1.3, or UNIX.

Author Bio

Chris Parsons has a diverse range of experience in computer software ranging from assessment of the IBM RISC/6000 workstation to work on an MVS-based satellite tracking station located in the Australian Outback. He develops and markets 32-bit OS/2 performance measurement tools and other OS/2 applications. An avid OS/2 user since Version 1.1, he is an independent software consultant and developer. He holds a degree in physics from the University of Colorado at Boulder. Contact him via CompuServe at 70403,126.

The Video Subsystem

In This Chapter

Video support in OS/2 2.1 comprises four principal components:

- base video handlers
- video virtual device drivers
- Presentation Manager display drivers
- WIN-OS/2 display drivers

This chapter discusses these components of OS/2 2.1 that support a wide range of video adapters, display driver installation, and driver customization.

The Base Video Handler

Base video handlers (BVHs) manage the different modes that switch video adapters between displaying text or graphics at various resolutions. When you switch between a full-screen OS/2 session and an application using Presentation Manager (PM), the BVH remembers the current video mode for this full-screen session. The video adapter then switches into the mode required for the Presentation Manager.

Another function of the BVH is to provide support for text display in full-screen mode and, for OS/2 applications, in a Presentation Manager window.

Dynamic link libraries (DLLs) contain BVH support and are loaded during system initialization according to statements in the CONFIG.SYS file. System installation places these statements there depending on the available video adapters. The following example shows the statements used for a VGA video adapter:

```
SET VIDEO_DEVICES=VIO_VGA
SET VIO_VGA=DEVICE(BVHVGA)
```

The first line, `VIDEO_DEVICES`, specifies what video adapters are available on your computer. You can specify more than one, separated by a comma.

The value set here tells OS/2 2.1 what to look for in CONFIG.SYS when searching for the name of the BVH for each adapter.

For each value set for the `VIDEO_DEVICES` there is a statement assigning the names of the BVHs to be used. In this example, `DEVICE(BVHVGA)` specifies the handler used for a VGA adapter. This indicates that the filename of the DLL is BVHVGA.DLL.

Some video adapters combine VGA functions with more complex operating modes. The design of the OS/2 2.1 video system allows BVHs to be built on top of existing support. For example, the 8514/A, XGA, and SVGA video adapters include all the VGA functions in addition to their own extended graphics modes. The BVHs for these adapters do not include all the VGA support, but instead build on top of the BVHVGA.DLL. SVGA devices, for example, are configured in CONFIG.SYS as shown in the following example:

```
SET VIDEO_DEVICES=VIO_VGA
SET VIO_VGA=DEVICE(BVHVGA,BVHSVGA)
```

The OS/2 2.1 video system supports multiple video adapters. You can assign one adapter as the primary display and the other as the secondary display. If you configure your computer with two displays—one connected to a VGA and the other to an 8514/A adapter—the CONFIG.SYS file will include the following statements:

```
SET VIDEO_DEVICES=VIO_8514A,VIO_VGA
SET VIO_8514A=DEVICE(BVHVGA,BVH8514A)
SET VIO_VGA=DEVICE(BVHVGA)
```

The first adapter specified in the `VIDEO_DEVICES` statement is the primary display.

OS/2 2.1 provides BVHs for a number of video adapters. Table 11.1 lists the types of supported video adapters and the names of the base video handlers and virtual device drivers (VDDs) used for each one.

Table 11.1. Adapter families supported by OS/2 2.1 BVH and video VDD.

Adapter Family	*BVH Files*	*Video VDD Files*
Monochrome Adapter	BVHMPA.DLL	VMONO.SYS
CGA	BVHCGA.DLL	VCGA.SYS
EGA	BVHEGA.DLL	VEGA.SYS
VGA	BVHVGA.DLL	VVGA.SYS
SVGA	BVHVGA.DLL, BVHSVGA.DLL	VSVGA.SYS
8514/A	BVHVGA.DLL, BVH8514A.DLL	VVGA.SYS, V8514A.SYS
XGA	BVHVGA.DLL, BVHXGA.DLL	VVGA.SYS, VXGA.SYS

The Video Virtual Device Driver

The video virtual device driver performs functions for DOS applications that are similar to functions the BVH performs for OS/2 full-screen applications. Most DOS-based applications run in OS/2 2.1 without any problems. Some of these applications are text-based and others take advantage of VGA or SVGA graphics modes. OS/2 2.1 provides support for both types of application.

DOS applications normally operate by writing directly to the video adapter hardware. Because OS/2 enforces protection between different applications, they are not allowed to directly access hardware. Therefore, the video VDD is responsible for controlling access to this hardware by DOS applications. The large number of different operating modes available in modern video adapters makes this task complex.

When a DOS application executes as the foreground application in full-screen mode, the video VDD normally allows unrestricted access to the video adapter hardware. When a DOS application executes in the background or in a window on the Presentation Manager desktop, the application cannot access the video adapter hardware. Instead, the video VDD emulates the video adapter so that the application can continue to execute as if it had access to the hardware; this is known as *hardware virtualization*—hence the name given to this type of device driver.

The video VDD maintains a copy of the screen in memory. This copy remains invisible for DOS applications executing in the background until you switch them back to full-screen mode. For applications executing in a Presentation Manager window (foreground or background) the Presentation Manager device driver regularly updates the screen from the video VDD's copy.

Not all the possible video adapter modes are virtualized by the video VDDs. Whenever a DOS application in the background or in a window tries to use a graphics mode that is not virtualized, the video VDD suspends that application until you switch it into full-screen. Table 11.2 lists the BIOS video modes.

Table 11.2. VGA video adapter modes emulated by Video VDDs.

BIOS Mode	*Text/Graphics*	*Continue to Execute*
0	40 x 25 text	Yes
1	40 x 25 text	Yes
2	80 x 25 text	Yes
3	80 x 25 text	Yes
7	80 x 25 text	Yes
4	320 x 200 graphics	Yes
5	320 x 200 graphics	Yes
6	640 x 200 graphics	Yes

continues

Table 11.2. continued

BIOS Mode	*Text/Graphics*	*Continue to Execute*
D	320 x 200 graphics	On VGA + 8514/A hardware only
E	640 x 200 graphics	On VGA + 8514/A hardware only
F	640 x 350 graphics	On VGA + 8514/A hardware only
10	640 x 350 graphics	On VGA + 8514/A hardware only
11	640 x 480 graphics	On VGA + 8514/A hardware only
12	640 x 480 graphics	On VGA + 8514/A hardware only
13	320 x 200 graphics	On VGA + 8514/A hardware only

(This table shows that video VDDs only virtualize graphics modes supported by the CGA adapter. Other modes require a VGA adapter.)

Video VDDs can virtualize the VGA graphics modes only with the assistance of VGA video adapter hardware. If you have an XGA video adapter, the VGA modes are not available for use by the video VDD while the XGA is operating in its extended graphics modes.

The 8514/A does not have this restriction for its extended graphics modes because a VGA adapter is always present with an 8514/A.

Even if the DOS application suspends when you switch it into a Presentation Manager window, the current screen image appears in the window so you can use the Clipboard to copy the image.

Text-based DOS applications always continue to execute in the background unless you turn off the `DOS_BACKGROUND_EXECUTION` DOS setting.

Device drivers contain video VDD support and load during system initialization according to statements in the CONFIG.SYS file. System installation places these statements there depending on the available video adapters. The following example shows the statement used for a VGA video adapter:

```
DEVICE=D:\OS2\MDOS\VVGA.SYS
```

You can add additional statements for other video adapters installed in your computer or for adapters that have extended graphics modes. Use both VVGA.SYS and VXGA.SYS for the XGA video adapter, which supports both VGA and extended XGA modes.

SVGA video adapters contain a special VDD that you use instead of the VGA VDD to support a wide range of SVGA adapters. The following line shows the statement in CONFIG.SYS for all supported SVGA adapters.

```
DEVICE=D:\OS2\MDOS\VSVGA.SYS
```

The SVGA VDD normally operates in exactly the same way as the VGA VDD until you enable it for SVGA modes with the command `SVGA ON`. This command generates a special configuration file called SVGADATA.PMI (see the following section entitled "The SVGA Command and PMI Files"). The SVGA.SYS virtual device driver reads the contents of this file (if it is present) when OS/2 2.1 initializes and uses the information when setting SVGA extended graphics modes.

An ATI 8514/Ultra installs as an 8514/A adapter, although it supports SVGA modes in addition to VGA and 8514 modes. You should ensure that the video VDD specified in CONFIG.SYS is the VSVGA.SYS so you can use these additional modes.

Because the SVGA video VDD operates exactly as a VGA video VDD when there is no PMI file present, it is a good idea to use this VDD at all times if you have an SVGA adapter. (You may have to manually change your CONFIG.SYS file to match the example above.)

The SVGA Command and PMI Files

To enable the SVGA video VDD to support the extended graphics modes of your SVGA adapter, you must execute the SVGA command. `SVGA ON` activates the extended mode support; `SVGA OFF` disables it.

Always execute `SVGA ON` from a full-screen DOS command-line prompt. You cannot run it in a window because the video VDD intercepts the calls to set the SVGA modes. The command will appear to complete properly if it is run in a window, but the values will be incorrect. If you do not have an SVGA card, the command immediately exits with a warning message.

When you execute the `SVGA ON` command, you set the video adapter into each of the SVGA modes that OS/2 2.1 supports using the BIOS function calls. Information is read back from the video hardware registers for each mode

and saved in a file called SVGADATA.PMI in the \OS2 directory on the boot drive. Table 11.3 lists all the modes supported in OS/2 2.1.

When you install a Presentation Manager display driver, the DSPINSTL program executes the `SVGA ON` command automatically, which enables the SVGA modes for you.

Table 11.3. Extended SVGA modes supported by SVGA video VDD.

H x V Resolution	*Colors*
640 x 480	256
800 x 600	16
800 x 600	256
1024 x 768	16
1024 x 768	256
132 x 25	text only
132 x 43	text only
132 x 44	text only

The saved .PMI file contains the following information:

- the video chip set used on the SVGA adapter
- the modes (see Table 11.3) that can be supported by the video adapter
- the values in the video hardware registers for each mode

The SVGA video VDD uses the register values to save and restore the video mode when OS/2 2.1 switches between DOS full-screen and Presentation Manager applications.

The generated SVGADATA.PMI file is specific to each machine, video adapter, and display combination. You cannot copy this file and use it on another system. Always execute the `SVGA ON` command to generate the correct .PMI file.

If you experience problems using extended SVGA modes, even after you execute the `SVGA ON` command, it is possibly because the .PMI file is incorrect. Even if you execute the `SVGA ON` command in an OS/2 full-screen sesson, it is still possible for the `SVGA` command to incorrectly read the SVGA chip registers. If you suspect this is the problem, you can start real DOS (from disk, or using multiboot) and execute the command `SVGA ON DOS` that generates a file called SVGADATA.DOS. The parameter `DOS` tells the `SVGA` command that it is not executing in an OS/2 2.1 virtual DOS environment; it also tells the `SVGA` command to generate a file with an extension of .DOS. You can then compare this file with the .PMI file generated when you ran `SVGA ON` in OS/2 2.1 to learn if there are any differences that may be causing your problems. To use the data generated when running the `SVGA` command in real DOS, you must rename it to SVGADATA.PMI and restart OS/2 2.1.

The `SVGA OFF` command deletes the SVGADATA.PMI file created and thus disables support for the extended SVGA graphics modes.

Do not try to run video adapter test programs provided with your SVGA adapter on OS/2 2.1 unless the manufacturer explicitly verifies that it works. In some cases the video VDD in OS/2 2.1 affects the results of the test.

Switching Between Full-Screen and Presentation Manager Applications

When switching between full-screen DOS applications and Presentation Manager applications, the video VDD saves a copy of the entire screen buffer being used by the DOS application before returning control to the Presentation Manager display driver.

Depending on the video adapter mode being used, the video VDD may have to save a significant amount of information. On XGA and some SVGA adapters, up to one megabyte of data is copied from the video memory buffer to system memory. On most systems this saves to the hard disk in the SWAPPER.DAT file so other applications can use the memory.

> TIP
>
> Switching from DOS to Presentation Manager on some SVGA systems while the DOS application is still drawing may cause some corruption on the desktop. If this occurs, switch back to the DOS screen and wait until the drawing has completed before returning to the Presentation Manager desktop.

Once the Presentation Manager desktop restores, all applications that are visible start to redraw their windows.

These two processes can take a significant amount of time. OS/2 2.1 has video DOS settings that can improve the performance in some circumstances. Chapter 8, "Virtual DOS Machines," describes the DOS settings that affect operation of the video subsystem and with all the other DOS settings. The settings, which may contribute to improved screen switching performance, are:

```
VIDEO_8514A_XGA_IOTRAP
VIDEO_SWITCH_NOTIFICATION
VIDEO_MODE_RESTRICTION
```

Use the `VIDEO_8514A_XGA_IOTRAP` setting to tell OS/2 2.1 not to save the 1 megabyte of video memory buffer used by the 8514/A and XGA adapters. To notify DOS applications when they switch to or from full-screen, use the

VIDEO_SWITCH_NOTIFICATION setting so OS/2 2.1 does not have to save the video memory buffer. This setting works only if the DOS application supports the screen switching protocol. Use VIDEO_MODE_RESTRICTION to limit the availability of video adapter modes; this setting helps to reduce the size of the video memory buffer that OS/2 2.1 has to save.

Be careful with these DOS settings—they will not always work well for all applications and video adapters. If changing any one causes screen corruption when switching to or from the full-screen session, you need to reset it. Do not change any of these settings when a DOS application is executing. Most applications only check for screen switch notification protocol during their initialization.

Some full-screen WIN-OS/2 display drivers recognize the screen switching protocol. Setting the VIDEO_SWITCH_NOTIFICATION for these can save a significant amount of memory.

The Presentation Manager Display Driver

Presentation Manager display drivers translate graphics requests from the OS/2 graphics engine into text, lines, and color for screen display, or storage in memory bitmaps.

DOS applications and OS/2 full-screen applications that execute in a window on the Presentation Manager desktop also use the Presentation Manager display driver to display text or graphics instead of writing directly to the video adapter hardware.

For DOS applications, the video VDD holds a copy of the current screen. The window command-line code in OS/2 2.1 regularly copies this to the display. You can use the DOS setting `VIDEO_WINDOW_REFRESH` to change the update frequency (by default it is set to the maximum rate of 10 times per second). In the case of OS/2 full-screen applications, a special BVH (BVHWNDW.DLL) sends output directly to the Presentation Manager display driver.

The different ways that DOS and OS/2 full-screen applications are windowed onto the Presentation Manager desktop explains why it is possible to switch between full-screen and windowed sessions for DOS applications but not for OS/2 applications. OS/2 applications indirectly link with the BVHWNDW.DLL file when they start up and this cannot change while the application is executing.

On all versions of the OS/2 operating system, up to and including 2.0, the Presentation Manager display driver is always contained in a dynamic link library called DISPLAY.DLL. Installing or changing the driver requires only that you change this DLL. On OS/2 2.1, however, this is no longer the case (see "Installing Display Drivers" later in this chapter).

The WIN-OS/2 Device Driver

OS/2 2.1 includes support for Windows applications running either in their own full-screen session or on the same Presentation Manager desktop as the Workplace Shell and other PM applications. This second mode of operation is known as running in a WIN-OS/2 Window (sometimes also called Seamless WIN-OS/2).

OS/2 2.1 includes WIN-OS/2 support for all the video adapters that it recognizes. Some work on full-screen modes only, and others support WIN-OS/2 Window operation.

Full-Screen WIN-OS/2

In full-screen WIN-OS/2 you can use the same display driver that you use with Microsoft Windows. Many display drivers provided by manufacturers of Windows accelerator cards work successfully in full-screen mode, although you may have to manually install the display driver into the \WINOS2\SYSTEM directory on your hard disk and update the SYSTEM.INI file to change the display driver name. (See "Step 5: The WIN-OS/2 Display Driver" later in this chapter for guidance on manually installing WIN-OS/2 display drivers.)

OS/2 2.1 handles the video output from the WIN-OS/2 display driver just as if it were output from any other DOS-based application. The VDD for the video adapter has to be able to recognize the requested mode or allow unrestricted access to the video adapter. To successfully switch between the WIN-OS/2 full-screen session and any other program, the OS/2 video VDD must recognize the adapter and mode that is being used. If it does not, the screen may become corrupted.

If you have an SVGA video adapter, always be sure that the CONFIG.SYS file is set up with the SVGA BVH and video VDD.

If you get video corruption when switching, it is usually possible to recover by closing the WIN-OS/2 full-screen session and switching back to the Presentation Manager desktop from a full-screen DOS prompt.

WIN-OS/2 Window

To allow Windows applications to run in a WIN-OS/2 window on the same desktop, OS/2 2.1 requires a special display driver for both the Presentation Manager and WIN-OS/2. OS/2 2.1 includes support for the following drivers:

- VGA display driver
- SVGA display drivers included with OS/2 2.1
- 8514/A display driver
- XGA display driver

When operating in WIN-OS/2 Window mode, the application uses a special display driver that cooperates with the Presentation Manager display driver and window manager to control its access to the video memory buffer. When a WIN-OS/2 application needs to display information on-screen, the WIN-OS/2 display driver must first request access to the adapter from the Presentation Manager display driver. It then retains this access permission until the Presentation Manager display driver asks for it back again.

Every time a WIN-OS/2 application opens, closes, or repositions a top-level window it notifies the Presentation Manager window manager so it can keep track of what windows are visible on-screen. This extra overhead explains the slightly slower performance for applications when they execute in a WIN-OS/2 window. This slight performance penalty, however, is usually acceptable for the enhanced usability provided in this mode.

Changing Display Resolutions

Some video adapters are capable of operating in one of a number of different display resolutions and colors, depending upon the display monitor connected to it. For example, the IBM XGA adapter can operate in 640 x 480 mode or 1024 x 768 mode. For these types of adapters it is possible to switch the resolution used by the OS/2 Presentation Manager.

Software support for switching display resolution is provided either by changing the display device driver or by telling the driver to operate the adapter in a different mode with settings configured inside the OS2.INI file. For display drivers that support resolution switching through the OS2.INI file, a system setting page labeled Screen is present in the system configuration settings notebook in the System Setup folder.

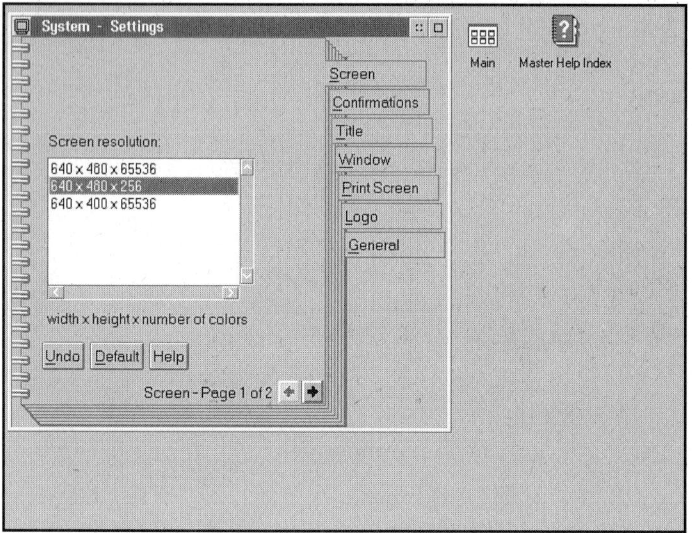

Figure 11.1. A screen page in the system settings notebook.

OS/2 2.1 includes display drivers that support multiple resolutions using both of these methods. The SVGA display drivers are resolution specific—each mode requires a new DLL. However, the XGA display driver supports any of the XGA video adapter's resolutions (select these in the system configuration settings notebook). In both cases it is necessary to shut down and restart OS/2 2.1, after selecting a new resolution, before it becomes active.

To change display resolution on systems with an XGA display driver, select the system icon from within the System Setup folder:

1. Double-click on the System Setup folder icon.
2. Double-click on the system icon.
3. Select the Screen page on the settings notebook tabs (this may be the first page displayed).
4. Select the resolution.
5. Close the settings notebook.
6. Shutdown OS/2 2.1 from the desktop popup menu and restart your computer.

The list of available resolutions displayed depends on whether the adapter is an XGA or the newer XGA-2 and the type of display monitor plugged into your computer.

If the screen settings page is not available, you must install a new display driver to change the screen resolution (see "Installing Display Drivers" later in this chapter).

After changing display resolutions, you may notice that the icon and folder window positions are different—you may have to rearrange your folders again.

You can avoid this annoyance if you use the flowed format of icon view on the Workplace Shell desktop (see Chapter 4, "The Workplace Shell").

Why Would I Want to Change Resolution?

Before OS/2 2.1, most Presentation Manager display drivers supported only one resolution and users had little or no control over it. On XGA or SVGA adapters with 512K of video memory, the 1024 x 768 modes support up to 16 colors; however, if you reduce the resolution to 640 x 480, up to 256 colors from a palette of 262,144 colors are available. For many applications the increased color selection is more important than higher resolution.

Multimedia-type applications are examples of applications that need more color than resolution. When these applications try to support live-motion video, the technology is not yet available to decompress and display live motion at 1024 x 768 resolution in anything larger than a small box on the screen. Reducing the overall display resolution improves the appearance of the motion video.

Screen resolution has a direct effect on the amount of information that you can view on the display. The three screen resolutions most commonly used in OS/2 2.1 are:

- 640 x 480
- 800 x 600
- 1024 x 768

Although not widely used, OS/2 2.1 does support both larger and smaller resolutions. The smallest screen resolution that most users find acceptable is 640 x 480—the standard VGA resolution. For most purposes this is adequate for OS/2 2.1.

A common SVGA resolution is 800 x 600, an ideal intermediate step between the lower and higher resolutions. On many SVGA video adapters, this is the highest resolution available that does not require extra memory for the display buffer while providing 50 percent more screen area for Presentation Manager and WIN-OS/2 applications.

The highest resolution available at an affordable price is 1024 x 768. First introduced on the 8514/A video adapter, it is now common on most SVGA adapters. More than 150 percent more screen area is available for applications (compared to the standard VGA modes), making it very easy to work with multiple applications. A cut-and-paste operation between applications is much easier when you can see a nearly complete view on-screen.

One drawback of 1024 x 768 resolution is the relatively high cost of compatible display monitors and, for adapters that do not have hardware assistance, slower performance. Also, sometimes text can appear very small and, therefore, more difficult to read. In this case, use the features of the Workplace Shell to change the fonts.

TIP

You can change the default font used in windowed command lines and the fonts used in many other areas of the Workplace Shell. You can use this feature to find fonts that are easy for you to read.

At all of these resolutions, a choice of 16, 256, 32,768, or even 65,536 colors may be available depending on the video adapter type and the size of the video memory buffer. In many cases, the number of available colors decreases as resolution increases. Your choice of resolution may have to be a compromise between these two features.

You may choose to operate your video adapter at the highest screen resolution that it supports. OS/2 2.1 uses color dithering to simulate colors if there are only 16 available when an application asks for one that is not in the default 16. If your video adapter is capable of producing 256 colors at its highest resolution, you can use this, although there may be a performance penalty (see "Display Performance" later in this chapter).

If you have a choice between many colors at a lower resolution or fewer colors at a higher resolution, it is usually better to choose the higher resolution. Few applications require the extra colors.

If you require accurate color representation for photo-realistic images, you should consider a video adapter capable of producing 32,768 or 65,536 colors.

Supported Resolutions for Presentation Manager

Presentation Manager supports a wide range of display resolutions and colors, although no single video adapter or device driver is able to support the complete range. Table 11.4 lists all the currently supported combinations of resolution and color and indicates whether the mode can use a color lookup table (CLT). (See "Colors and the Palette Manager" later in this chapter for a description of color lookup tables.)

Table 11.4. Graphics modes supported by the Presentation Manager.

H x V Resolution	*Colors*	*CLT*	*Comments*
640 x 200	2	No	CGA only
640 x 350	16	No	EGA only
640 x 480	16	No	VGA only
640 x 480	256	Yes	from 256 thousand or 16 million
640 x 480	65536	Direct	
800 x 600	16	No	
800 x 600	256	Yes	from 256 thousand or 16 million
800 x 600	65536	Direct	
1024 x 768	16	No	
1024 x 768	256	Yes	from 256 thousand or 16 million

The first two resolutions (640 x 200 and 640 x 350) are for CGA and EGA video adapters only. Such low resolution does not work well on the graphical user interface of the Workplace Shell, and I do not recommend anything less than 640 x 480 for OS/2 2.1. These are uncommon adapters to find on systems that are OS/2 2.1 capable, although some portable systems use double-scan CGA adapters.

Most SVGA adapters and display drivers support all the resolutions from 640 x 480 up to 1024 x 768. Some SVGA display drivers, however, support only the 256-color modes and others support only the 16-color modes.

The 8514/A driver supports the 1024 x 768 256-color mode only. The XGA adapter supports the 640 x 480 256-color mode and the 1024 x 768 16-color and 256-color modes.

The XGA-2 adapter supports all modes from 640 x 480 16-color upwards, although support of 800 x 600 is dependent on the display monitor attached. The 9515 and 9517 monitors from IBM do not support these modes (some non-IBM monitors, however, do support these modes). XGA-2 can also operate at resolutions of 1280 x 960 and 1280 x 1024, in interlaced modes, if you have a display monitor capable of such high resolutions. Currently, however, this is uncommon.

Display Mode Query and Set (DMQS)

During installation, and each time it initializes, OS/2 2.1 queries the type of display monitor. The system uses this information to determine how to operate and what video display modes can be used. Some displays, for example, are capable of 640 x 480 but not 1024 x 768 resolution.

Because of the limited number of identification bits available for all display manufacturers, many display monitors have the same identification although they are capable of different operating modes.

The XGA-2 adapter and OS/2 2.1 use a scheme called display mode query and set (DMQS) that provides far greater information to the operating system about the modes supported by the display monitor. When you install OS/2 2.1 on systems with an XGA video adapter, a directory called XGA$DMQS is created on the boot drive. This contains a number of configuration files for different display monitors.

Systems preloaded with OS/2 2.1 do not have this directory created by default. If your computer has XGA, OS/2 creates the directory automatically when you set up XGA support.

The OS/2 operating system selects which DMQS file to use based on the identification reported for the display monitor. In some cases the display monitor supports additional modes. To access these modes with the XGA-2 video adapter, you can override the DMQS file in use.

If you have an XGA-2 video adapter you can do this on OS/2 2.1 in the System settings notebook from the System Setup folder. The second page in the screen section enables you to select a video adapter and display monitor type. In Figure 11.2 note the "page 2 of 2" text on the first screen page; this indicates that you need to click the mouse button on the left arrow to access the preceding page in the same section.

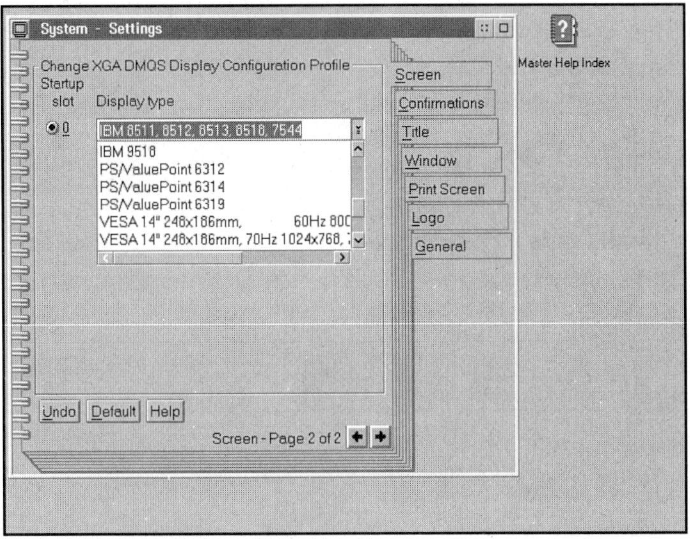

Figure 11.2. The DMQS page in the OS/2 System settings notebook.

If you have more than one XGA-2 video adapter installed in your computer, you can select the adapter you want Presentation Manager to use. For each of the adapters installed, you can tell OS/2 2.1 what type of display monitor is connected to it using the drop-down list box.

Choosing incorrect settings for your display monitor may result in an unusable display. If this happens, you must remove the XGASETUP.PRO file from the XGA$DMQS directory to undo the changes. It is possible to damage your display monitor if you use incorrect settings.

If you change your display monitor, you should delete the XGASETUP.PRO file before connecting the new display.

Using this system setting enables the XGA-2 adapter to operate your display monitor in the best available mode—possibly permitting a wider selection of screen resolutions or noninterlaced modes.

The Effect on WIN-OS/2

Changing display resolution for Presentation Manager and Workplace Shell affects the resolution used for WIN-OS/2. If you used the screen page in the System settings notebook, or any installation utility that also installed the WIN-OS/2 display driver, the resolution changes automatically apply to the WIN-OS/2 environment.

If you manually changed the Presentation Manager display driver, the full-screen WIN-OS/2 environment is unaffected and continues to operate as before. The WIN-OS/2 Window display driver is unlikely to continue working and you need to update this manually too (see "Manually Changing Display Drivers" later in this chapter).

Colors and the Palette Manager

The preceding sections discussed the different display resolutions supported by the Presentation Manager. Directly related to resolution are the range of colors available and the ways in which OS/2 2.1 manages color selection.

Presentation Manager display drivers support four principal color modes:

- 16 fixed colors
- 256 colors with palette management
- 256 colors without palette management

• 65,536 direct colors

These modes determine the number of colors (and the available range, or palette, of colors) that you can display simultaneously.

16 Fixed Colors

The simplest mode operation supports 16 fixed colors based on the three primary colors. Because of this limited number of colors, it is not possible for applications or users to change them. Display drivers use a technique known as *dithering* when you request colors that do not match one of the fixed 16.

Table 11.5. The 16 fixed colors in OS/2 2.1.

Black	Dark Gray
Blue	Dark Blue
Red	Dark Red
Pink	Dark Pink
Green	Dark Green
Cyan	Dark Cyan
Yellow	Brown
Light Gray	Intense White

Dithering is a process that combines two of the 16 fixed colors in a pattern that causes the human eye to believe that it is seeing a different color. Lines and text do not dither because it does not work well for these types of graphics. It does, however, work well for filled areas.

The number of colors that you can simulate depends on the number of solid colors used by the algorithm and the size of the dither pattern area. Display drivers implement the algorithm used, and the results can vary from one video adapter and display driver to another.

The VGA display driver uses an 8 x 8 pixel grid for the dither pattern area, and all of the 16 fixed colors participate in the algorithm. This results in a good range of simulated colors. You can see this best on gradient fills in graphics-based applications such as the PM Chart applet provided with OS/2 2.1.

The XGA display driver uses a 2 x 2 pixel grid for the dither pattern area. This results is a smaller range of simulated colors and slightly higher performance. This is not usually a problem for the XGA driver because most XGA systems operate in 256-color modes and don't require dithering.

256 Colors

Video adapters capable of displaying 256 colors simultaneously also have a hardware component known as a color lookup table (CLT) or palette. An 8-bit number represents each pixel on the screen and is an index into a table of 256 entries. Each entry contains an intensity level for Red, Green, and Blue. These primary colors combine to produce any one of a large number of unique colors.

The number of intensities that each of the primary colors can be set to determines the range of available colors that any one entry in the color lookup table can represent. Video adapters use either 6-bit or 8-bit intensity values giving 64 or 256 levels for each of the three primary colors. These are known as 18-bit or 24-bit color lookup tables and, therefore, support a total range of 262,144 or 16,777,216 colors.

As a gray scale requires all the primary colors to be set at the same level, the number of grays that an adapter can display is the minimum of the number of color indexes and the number of levels in the color lookup table for each primary color. If the adapter uses 18 bits in the color lookup table, you can display a maximum of 64 grays. This is usually not a problem because the human eye becomes unable to distinguish between two gray neighbors when the range is somewhere between 32 and 64 levels.

The 8514/A and XGA adapters use 18-bit colors. The newer XGA-2 and many SVGAs use a 24-bit color lookup table.

OS/2 Presentation Manager display drivers load the 256-color lookup table with a range of colors designed to give a broad range from light to dark across the color spectrum. In the center of the color table (from index 112 to 143) are 32 shades of gray. Color values, composed from 7 shades of red, 8 shades of green, and 4 shades of blue, make up the remaining 224 entries (7 x 8 x 4 = 224). The different number of shades used for each primary color accounts for the nonlinear response of the human eye. The eye is very sensitive to green and much less sensitive to blue.

256 Colors with the Palette Manager

Palette management is a technique that gives applications control over the precise levels of red, green, and blue that each entry in the color lookup table can take. It also allows applications to change entries in the table while they are in use to cause an effect known as *palette animation*. You can find an example of the special effects that this can produce in the PALETTE sample included with the IBM OS/2 2.1 Developers Toolkit.

The most important feature of palette management, however, is the ability to handle multiple applications all requesting specific colors at the same time. The display hardware is capable of displaying 256 colors simultaneously through its color lookup table. The palette manager assigns entries in the lookup table when an application tries to create a *logical* palette (a logical palette is essentially a table that maps from a color index, used by an application, to an entry in the video adapter's hardware color lookup table, or CLT). Once the application has this logical palette it can control the intensity levels for each of the primary colors in the palette.

When multiple applications cause the demand for colors to exceed the maximum 256 possible, the palette manager assigns priority to the foreground application (the one currently in use) to guarantee all its color requirements. Background applications get what is left of the color lookup table. Dithering is used after the table is completely full to simulate the requested colors.

It is possible for the palette manager to assign the same entry in the color lookup table to multiple applications if all the applications are asking for exactly the same color. However, as applications cannot create a palette larger than 256 entries, OS/2 2.1 guarantees the foreground application all the entries in the color lookup table it requests.

OS/2 2.1 can support applications that do not use the palette manager while other applications are executing and using the palette manager. The color lookup table used for these applications reduces in size, in a number of steps, as the palette manager's requirements increase. The first step reduces it to 128 entries (8 grays and 120 colors from 5 red, 6 green, and 4 blue). The second step reduces it to 64 entries (4 grays and 60 colors from 4 red, 5 green, and 3 blue). The final step uses the 16 fixed colors listed in Table 11.5.

Most 256-color display device drivers support palette management in OS/2 2.1, although the 8514/A driver released with OS/2 2.1 currently does not support it.

256 Colors without the Palette Manager

If a display device driver supports 256 colors but does not support the palette manager, OS/2 2.1 does allow an application to replace the entire color lookup table. However, OS/2 2.1 does not control this and it may affect the appearance of other applications on the screen. If at all possible, you should use a driver that supports the palette manager.

Direct Color

A number of video adapters are available that support a mode known as *direct color.* In this mode there is no color lookup table. Instead of an 8-bit index into a 256-entry table of colors, a 16-bit or 24-bit value represents each pixel on the screen. This value comprises three components, each representing red, green, and blue intensity levels.

The 24-bit direct color modes assign 8 bits per primary color for a total of 16,777,216 possible colors! The 24-bit-per-pixel video adapters are expensive because of the large size of the video memory buffer and the complex hardware required to send the data from memory to the display monitor at the high frequency required.

The 16-bit direct color modes assign 6 bits to green, 5 bits to red, and 5 bits to blue primary colors. Again, green has highest priority because the human eye is most sensitive to this color. The 16-bit direct color modes allow simultaneous display of 65,536 colors. The XGA-2 adapter supports this at both 640 x 480 and 800 x 600 resolution modes, as do many SVGA adapters.

Because of the large range of colors available in direct color mode, the display drivers do not require either palette management or dithering. You can display high-quality photo-realistic images.

OS/2 2.1 and the Workplace Shell do not require all the colors available in direct color modes, but if you have image applications or intend to work with digital representations of photographs, this mode is invaluable.

Black-and-White Liquid Crystal Displays (LCD)

Most people use OS/2 2.1 on color display systems. With the increasing importance of notebook and laptop computers, however, OS/2 2.1 includes a number of features to support this environment. Of particular concern for the OS/2 video subsystem are black-and-white liquid crystal displays (LCDs).

Black-and-white LCDs typically have poor contrast, poor brightness, and are slow to respond to movement. OS/2 includes two special features to improve your use of these displays:

- an alternative color scheme
- a larger mouse pointer and a text I-beam cursor

Color LCD displays based on Thin Film Transistor (TFT) technology do not have the poor contrast and slow responsiveness problems typically found with black-and-white LCDs.

Alternative Color Scheme

OS/2 2.1 includes a special color scheme specifically designed to provide good contrast and highlighting when used on black-and-white LCDs. The colors are also suitable for occasional use on color displays, for example, when giving a presentation at a customer location, so it is not necessary to frequently switch between schemes. To select the alternate color scheme:

1. Open the System Setup folder icon (double-click).
2. Open the Scheme Palette object icon. In this window there are two color schemes marked as monochrome. The first (on the left) is true black and white, the second (on the right) is the scheme designed for LCDs.
3. Press and hold mouse button 2 on the second monochrome scheme and drag it.
4. When the scheme icon is over the desktop background, press and hold the Alt key on the keyboard and release the mouse button.

Holding down the Alt key when completing the drag and drop operation makes the changes system-wide—it takes a few seconds to complete the save to the hard disk.

After applying this color scheme, you may want to readjust the contrast of the LCD display. Notice the foreground and background combination for selected and highlighted text. Instead of white on dark gray, it is black on light gray (adjust the contrast for clarity).

Bigger Cursors

Because of the poor contrast and slow response of LCD displays, many users find the mouse pointer difficult to locate on the screen, especially after movement. Increasing the size of the mouse pointer makes it much easier to locate. The VGA and SVGA display drivers included with OS/2 2.1 have larger pointers available for the following:

- the standard pointer (the upper-left pointing arrow)
- the text pointer (sometimes called the I-beam because of its shape)

These larger pointers are significantly larger and selected automatically when OS/2 2.1 initializes. The VGA display driver selects the large size pointers whenever it detects that the display type is black-and-white LCD. On some machines the display driver may obtain incorrect information and thus the pointer size may be inappropriate. In this case it is possible to change the pointer size by changing a setting in the OS2.INI file.

Using an INI file editor, the entry to change is as follows:

```
Application name: PM_IBMVGA
Key name: CURSOR_SIZE
```

and the values recognized are integers:

`'0'` = Automatic selection
`'1'` = Force large-size pointers
`'2'` = Force standard-size pointers

If you do not have access to an INI file editor, you can create a REXX command program. Listing 11.1 contains LARGE.CMD, which sets the pointer size to `large`.

Listing 11.1. The REXX command to set a large pointer size.

```
/* LARGE.CMD Set VGA pointers to large */
/* (c) Copyright IBM Corp. 1992, All rights reserved */
call RxFuncAdd 'SysIni', 'RexxUtil', 'SysIni'
call SysIni 'USER', 'PM_IBMVGA', 'CURSOR_SIZE', '1'
say Result
exit
```

The final parameter of the call to SysIni is the value to write. After you execute the REXX command, you must restart OS/2 2.1 for the change to take effect.

Large pointer sizes are only available with the VGA and SVGA display drivers included with OS/2 2.1. All other display drivers, including the 8514/A and XGA, contain standard size pointers.

Installing Display Drivers

When you install OS/2 2.1 on your computer, it attempts to automatically determine the available video adapter types. There may be more than one adapter in a system, and in this case one becomes the primary display and one other becomes the secondary display.

If there are multiple displays, the Presentation Manager uses the primary display, and full-screen OS/2 or DOS-based applications use the secondary display. An example of such a configuration is an IBM PS/2 Model 70 with an 8514/A video adapter card (in addition to the VGA video adapter built into the computer).

If the video adapter type sensed by OS/2 2.1 is different from what is actually available, or if you want to reassign the primary and secondary displays, you can change them. Do this either when initially installing OS/2 2.1 or anytime using Selective Install in the System Setup folder.

During the installation process, OS/2 2.1 treats the video adapter as a standard VGA in 640 x 480 resolution, regardless of the type of video adapter found. If the adapter is not capable of this, OS/2 2.1 uses the CGA 640 x 200 resolution mode (this is the case with some laptop or portable systems based on double-scan CGA technology).

On systems preloaded with the OS/2 operating system, the VGA display driver is the default. Many of these systems have XGA, XGA-2, Tseng, or other

SVGA video adapters capable of higher performance or resolution. Display drivers for these adapters can be found on the hard disks of preloaded systems, and you can use the configuration tools provided to select an appropriate display driver.

The most reliable way to change OS/2 2.1 display drivers is to use an installation tool provided with OS/2 2.1 or the supplier of the device driver. Manually replacing the display driver is possible (see "Manually Changing Display Drivers" later in this chapter).

With each new release of the OS/2 operating system, the complexity of the display subsystem increases. In OS/2 2.1, the act of changing a video adapter can affect each of the following components; this may require you to install new files or make changes to the configuration of the existing ones:

- the Presentation Manager display driver
- WIN-OS/2 display driver
- base video handler
- DOS video virtual device driver
- fonts
- display mode query and set (DMQS) files
- OS2.INI
- WIN.INI
- SYSTEM.INI

Although it is still possible to replace or modify a display configuration manually, the increased complexity of the video subsystem makes the process difficult. It is usually better to use one of the installation tools.

Using Installation Tools

The choice of which installation tool to use depends on whether OS/2 2.1 includes a display driver to support the adapter type installed in your computer. If it does include a display driver, the tool to use depends on whether OS/2 2.1 was already preloaded on your computer's hard disk or you installed it from disk.

If the adapter manufacturer supplied the OS/2 2.1 display driver, you should use the instructions provided with the driver. If OS/2 2.1 includes a display driver that supports your video adapter, you can use the OS/2 2.1 installation and configuration tools.

The following sections were written with the assumption that OS/2 2.1 includes the display driver you want to install. For display drivers obtained from another source, refer to the instructions that accompany them.

You can find out whether your copy of OS/2 2.1 includes a display driver for your video adapter by running the installation tool. If you run the installation tools, you can cancel it if the list of supported adapters does not include the one you have installed.

Systems Installed from Disk

If you installed OS/2 2.1 from disk, you should use the Selective Install utility in the System Setup folder to install a display driver that came with OS/2 2.1. This prompts a window to appear with a number of options (see Figure 11.3)—select the Primary Display option.

Selecting the OK pushbutton prompts a second window to appear. On OS/2 2.1 you can only select a video adapter that the operating system supplies a display driver for. If the list includes your video adapter type, then select it; if not, check the Other option and select the OK pushbutton. You will then be asked to insert Disk 6 into the disk drive.

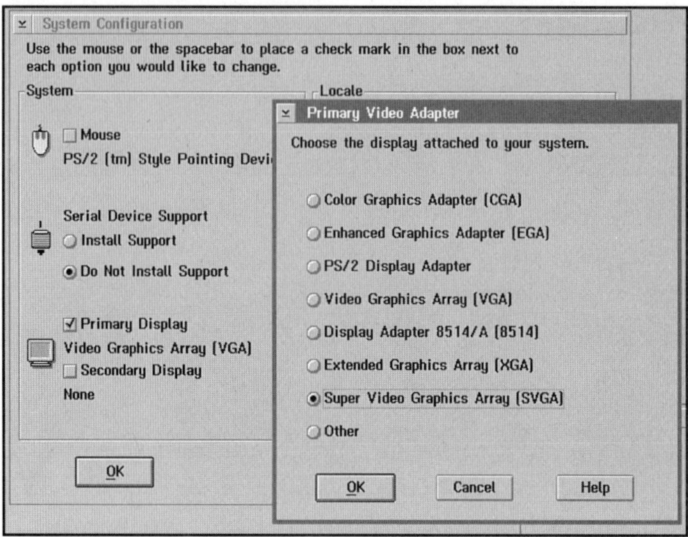

Figure 11.3. Changing the primary display from Selective Install.

Systems Preloaded with OS/2 2.1

If OS/2 2.1 was preloaded on your computer and you have not removed it and reinstalled from disk, you should use the Configure System utility provided in the Welcome folder. This is similar to the Selective Install utility, but it searches for the files on the hard disk instead of the disks.

The Configure System utility displays a window that matches the Selective Install utility. If you select to change the display driver, the DSPINSTL utility, described in the next section, executes.

The Display Driver Install Utility

OS/2 2.1 includes a display driver installation program. This program simplifies the process of installing a new display driver, regardless of whether it comes with OS/2 2.1 or the video adapter manufacturer provided it.

You can execute the DSPINSTL command from an OS/2 command line. A panel will appear from which you select either Primary or Secondary display driver.

The DSPINSTL program installs only display drivers; it does not ensure that you have the correct fonts installed. "Fonts and Display Drivers," later in this chapter, explains the close relationship between fonts and display drivers. You may have to manually change your fonts depending on those that are currently on your system. You should use the Selective Install and Configure System utilities if you are unsure if your fonts need changing or if you don't want to do it manually.

After selecting the Primary or Secondary display options, a list of all the supported video adapters appears. Figure 11.4 shows a typical list.

When you select the video adapter type that matches your system, the utility copies the required files from the disk (or directory) and makes all necessary updates to the OS2.INI, SYSTEM.INI, and WIN.INI files.

If you select Super VGA, the `SVGA ON` command executes so OS/2 2.1 can determine the type of SVGA adapter installed (see "The SVGA Command and PMI Files" earlier in this chapter).

When the installation is complete you must shutdown OS/2 2.1 and restart your computer.

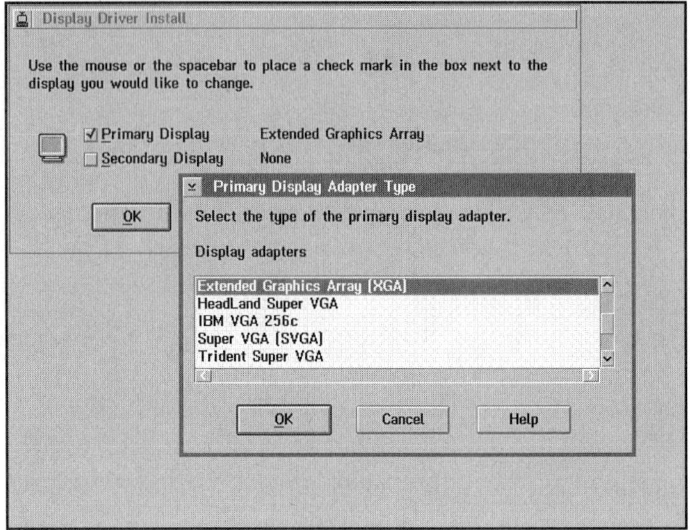

Figure 11.4. A list of video adapters from DSPINSTL.

Manually Changing Display Drivers

As mentioned earlier, the display subsystem in the OS/2 operating system is becoming more complex with each new release. Because of this I do not recommend manually replacing or modifying the display driver configuration. The process is discussed here, however, as it serves to highlight some of the features and configurations to be aware of in OS/2 2.1. It may also help you install display drivers for some video adapters that have incomplete installation tools (or none at all).

Version Differences

On all versions of the OS/2 operating system before release 2.00.1, the Presentation Manager display device driver is a single dynamic link library with the name DISPLAY.DLL (it could not be called anything else). Changing the display driver used by the Presentation Manager required changing this file.

With the introduction of the 32-bit graphics engine, the Presentation Manager display device driver can be, and is, named differently.

There is still a file called DISPLAY.DLL but this is *not* the Presentation Manager display driver. Its purpose is to support those printer drivers that use functions in this DLL. Its name cannot change because existing printer drivers would not continue working. Do not attempt to replace this DLL in OS/2 2.1.

Before attempting to change the display driver configuration manually, make a backup copy of your current configuration and data files. The files that you should back up are

```
CONFIG.SYS
OS2.INI
WIN.INI
SYSTEM.INI
```

Have an OS/2 2.1 boot disk available to aid recovery. If the display driver configuration becomes corrupted, OS/2 2.1 may be unable to boot from the hard disk or parts of the operating system may function incorrectly.

Replacing Files in Use

When manually installing display drivers, you may find that you are unable to overwrite a file with a new version because it is in use by OS/2 2.1. In this case you have two alternatives:

1. Boot from disk and copy the new file onto the disk.
2. Place the new files in a separate directory and change the CONFIG.SYS file to point to the new location.

Always remember to make a backup copy of any files you replace or change (including CONFIG.SYS).

If you choose the second step, the statement to edit in CONFIG.SYS is the `LIBPATH=` line. Be sure to place the name of the new directory at the front of the list so OS/2 2.1 loads your new DLLs before any other DLLs. For .SYS files, edit the line that contains the `DEVICE=` statement for the file being added so it points to the version in your new directory.

When you restart OS/2 2.1, it picks up your new files. You can now copy them on top of the old files that they are replacing and then restore the backup copy of CONFIG.SYS.

Step 1: Finding the Files

The first step in manually installing a new display driver is to find all the files that you will need. You need to locate the following:

- the display driver dynamic link libraries
- device drivers (.SYS files) for CONFIG.SYS
- base video handlers
- video virtual device drivers
- font files

If you are installing the drivers manually, you should already have the DLL and SYS files available. If you do not know where to locate them, you should be using an installation tool provided with OS/2 2.1 or the display driver.

On OS/2 2.1 all the display drivers are located on separate disks in packed files. The names of the packed files represent the target video adapter. The Presentation Manager display drivers for all non-SVGA chip sets are packed into the following files:

CGA
EGA

VGA
XGA
8514

The disks also include the WIN-OS/2 display drivers packed into separate files. The name is prefixed with the letters *WIN*:

WINCGA
WINEGA
WINVGA
WINXGA
WIN8514

The SVGA display drivers for Presentation Manager and WIN-OS/2 are individually packed on the disks. They have filenames with extensions of .DL_ (for Presentation Manager) and .DR_ (for WIN-OS/2). The underscore indicates that the files are packed.

The display driver disks also contain files with extensions of .DSP that the DSPINSTL utility in OS/2 2.1 uses to control what configuration changes and files are required for each video adapter when you install a new display driver.

You can use the `UNPACK` command with the `/SHOW` parameter to list the contents of the packed files. For more information on the `UNPACK` command, type `HELP UNPACK` at any OS/2 command-line prompt.

Some display drivers comprise multiple files. The 32-bit VGA display driver is made up of three DLLs:

```
IBMVGA32.DLL
IBMDEV32.DLL
DSPRES.DLL
```

The 32-bit XGA display driver uses the following files:

```
IBMXGA32.DLL
DSPRES.DLL
XGA.SYS
DMQS Files
```

OS/2 2.1 includes 32-bit SVGA drivers based on the VGA display driver, and they share two of the DLLs: IBMVGA32 and DSPRES. There could be a different version of the IBMDEV32 dynamic link library for each of the SVGA chip sets and resolutions that the OS/2 operating system supports. Later in this chapter, Table 11.13 lists all the chip sets that OS/2 2.1 supports.

OS/2 2.1 uses a single DLL for each of the supported chip sets, but it has a different DLL for each resolution. You will find these DLLs on the display driver disks:

```
SV480256.DLL
SV600256.DLL
SV768256.DLL
```

These DLLs support 640 x 480, 800 x 600 and 1024 x 768 resolutions respectively, all in their 256-color modes. When OS/2 2.1 installs one of these, it renames it to IBMDEV32.DLL so that the common DLL, IBMVGA32, can load it correctly. The SVGA display driver determines which chip set you are using from the SVGA device driver. To operate correctly you must execute the `SVGA ON` command at least once.

Step 2: Base Video Handler

When OS/2 2.1 installs, the BVHs and virtual device drivers install also. You should not have to search through all the disks looking for the files you need; they should be on your hard disk already. (See Table 11.1 for the names of all the BVH and VDD files and the video adapters that you use them for.)

Although the files may be on your hard disk, the CONFIG.SYS file may not load them. Be sure that you have the right statements (shown earlier in this chapter).

Step 3: Fonts

If you currently use an XGA, 8514/A, or any SVGA display driver, you should not change the font files already installed—they contain fonts for both 96 x 96 and 120 x 120 logical font resolution devices. (See "Fonts and Display Drivers" later in this chapter for an explanation of the logical font resolution and the ways in which fonts and display drivers interact.)

If you use any other driver and you are manually installing a display driver that offers a resolution of 1024 x 768 or higher, you need to replace the fonts with those designed for the higher resolution devices. If either of your HELV.FON or TIMES.FON files are less than 100K in size, you need to replace these fonts.

The necessary fonts are bundled together into files on disks or on the hard file of preloaded systems. The actual disk number depends on the OS/2 operating system version. The files to look for are:

```
COURIER.BMP
TIMES.BMP
HELV.BMP
```

There may be several files with these names on the OS/2 disks. You need to use the `UNPACK` command with the `/SHOW` parameter to find which files have the right fonts. The following example shows the output from the `UNPACK` command when executed against one of the COURIER.BMP files on the OS/2 installation disks.

```
[D:\]unpack courier.bmp /show
COURIER.BMP
->\OS2\DLL\COURIER.BGA
[D:\]
```

This shows that the packed file contains the correct font file (it has the extension of BGA). On preloaded systems, the file contains multiple font files with different extensions. You only need the one with the BGA extension. When you find the right packed files, use the `UNPACK` command with the `/N` parameter to extract the one file you need (note the following example).

```
[D:\]unpack courier.bmp /N:courier.bga
COURIER.BMP
- \OS2\DLL\COURIER.BGA
     0 file(s) copied.
     1 file(s) unpacked.
[D:\]
```

The `UNPACK` command unpacks the files into the target directory specified when the files were packed—in this case, the \OS2\DLL directory.

Once you have extracted the three files (HELV.BGA, COURIER.BGA, and TIMES.BGA) you need to rename them to HELV.FON, COURIER.FON, and TIMES.FON. Because these filenames are already in use, it is necessary to uninstall them using the Workplace Shell font palette before renaming the .BGA files to .FON and installing them. Unfortunately, you cannot do this while the fonts are in use. The simplest and quickest solution is to restart OS/2 2.1 from disk and overwrite the old .FON files.

If the .BGA files you unpacked are the same size as the .FON files of the same name already installed in the \OS2\DLL directory, there is no need to replace them.

Step 4: The Presentation Manager Display Driver

If the display driver has any .SYS device drivers, you must place a `DEVICE=` statement or `BASEDEV=` statement into CONFIG.SYS for each of them.

The 32-bit and 16-bit XGA display drivers use different .SYS device drivers and statements in your CONFIG.SYS file. The following code line shows the statement for the 32-bit XGA driver (included with OS/2 2.1):

```
BASEDEV=XGA.SYS
```

The following code line is the statement used by the 16-bit XGA driver:

```
DEVICE=XGARING0.SYS
```

You may see both of these statements in your CONFIG.SYS file. The 32-bit version of the XGA display driver does not use the XGARING0.SYS device driver. OS/2 2.1 still installs it, however, for compatibility with the Audio Video Connection (AVC) multimedia application. If you don't run AVC and you have the 32-bit graphics engine, you can remove this device driver from CONFIG.SYS.

To add your new Presentation Manager display driver to OS/2 2.1, you should copy the display driver DLL and any associated DLLs into the \OS2\DLL directory. You must now update two statements in the OS2.INI file so that the graphics engine knows what DLL to load.

Using an INI file editor, the entry to change is:

```
Application name: PM_DISPLAYDRIVERS
Key name: CURRENTDRIVER
```

The value set is a string representing the name of the display device driver (for example, IBMVGA32). There also needs to be another INI file entry with a key name of IBMVGA32:

```
Application name: PM_DISPLAYDRIVERS
Key name: <Value set for CURRENTDRIVER>
```

The value set for this is a string representing the name of the dynamic link library that is the display driver. If you do not specify any directory path or file extension, the file is assumed to be located in your `LIBPATH` with an extension of .DLL.

If you do not have access to an INI file editor, you can create a REXX command program. Listing 11.2 shows SETVGA.CMD, which sets the current display driver to IBMVGA32.

Listing 11.2. The REXX command to set the IBMVGA32 display driver.

```
/* SETVGA.CMD Set display driver */
/* (c) Copyright IBM Corp. 1992, All rights reserved */
call RxFuncAdd 'SysIni', 'RexxUtil', 'SysIni'
DriverName = 'IBMVGA32'
call SysIni 'USER', 'PM_DISPLAYDRIVERS', 'CURRENTDRIVER',
➥DriverName||x2c(0)
say Result
call SysIni 'USER', 'PM_DISPLAYDRIVERS', DriverName,
➥DriverName||x2c(0)
say Result
exit
```

The values for the display driver name written to the INI file terminate with a null character. The `x2c(0)` function ensures this.

There is also an entry in the INI file for `PM_DISPLAYDRIVERS, DEFAULTDRIVER`. The graphics engine uses this entry if it is unable to load the driver specified in the `CURRENTDRIVER` entry.

Step 5: The WIN-OS/2 Display Driver

OS/2 2.1 keeps the WIN-OS/2 display drivers in the \OS2\MDOS\WINOS2\SYSTEM directory on your hard file. There are usually two driver files (with .DRV extensions) for each display type: one for full-screen WIN-OS/2 operation and the other for a WIN-OS/2 Window. There may also be separate drivers for different resolutions. For example, Table 11.6 shows the files used by the XGA and SVGA WIN-OS/2 display drivers on OS/2 2.1

Table 11.6. XGA and SVGA WIN-OS/2 display drivers on OS/2 2.1.

File Name	*Chip Set*	*Display Driver Purpose*
SXGA.DRV	XGA	WIN-OS/2 Window (all resolutions)
XGA.DRV	XGA	Full-screen WIN-OS/2 (all resolutions)
WSPDSSF.DRV	SVGA	WIN-OS/2 Window small fonts
WSPDSF.DRV	SVGA	Full-screen WIN-OS/2 small fonts
WSPDSBF.DRV	SVGA	WIN-OS/2 Window large fonts (1024 x 768)
WSPDBF.DRV	SVGA	Full-screen WIN-OS/2 large fonts (1024 x 768)

The SVGA drivers with small fonts support 640 x 480 and 800 x 600 resolutions. The large font drivers support a 1024 x 768 resolution.

WIN-OS/2 determines which display driver to use based on entries in the SYSTEM.INI file. This is a plain text file that you can edit with any text editor; it is located in the \OS2\MDOS\WINOS2 directory. The entries that specify the driver names are:

Application name	`[boot]`
Full-screen WIN-OS/2 display driver	`display.drv =`
WIN-OS/2 Window display driver	`sdisplay.drv =`

When changing WIN-OS/2 display drivers it may also be necessary to change the fonts used by WIN-OS/2. There are three entries in SYSTEM.INI that you may need to change. Table 11.7 lists the key names and the names of the font files you may use for 640 x 480 (and 800 x 600) and 1024 x 768 resolutions.

Table 11.7. The WIN-OS/2 display driver fonts in SYSTEM.INI.

Application Name	*Key Name*	*640 x 480 Files*	*1024 x 768 Files*
[boot]	fonts.fon	VGASYS.FON	XGASYS.FON
[boot]	fixedfon.fon	VGAFIX.FON	XGAFIX.FON
[boot]	oemfonts.fon	VGAOEM.FON	XGAOEM.FON

If you are installing a WIN-OS/2 display driver that did not come with OS/2 2.1, the driver may come with its own font files. In this case you should use the ones supplied with the driver.

For fonts that are not part of the display driver, it may be necessary to select ones with different logical font resolutions (see "Fonts and Display Drivers" later in this chapter for more information). For WIN-OS/2 the WIN.INI file includes the list of fonts to load. Table 11.8 lists the key names and the names of the font files used for 640 x 480 and 1024 x 768 resolutions.

Table 11.8. The WIN-OS/2 System fonts in WIN.INI.

Application Name	*Key Name*	*640 x 480 Files*	*1024 x 768 Files*
[fonts]	Symbol	SYMBOLE.FON	SYMBOLG.FON
[fonts]	Courier	COURE.FON	COURG.FON
[fonts]	Tms Rmn	TMSRE.FON	TMSRG.FON
[fonts]	Helv	HELVE.FON	HELVG.FON

You may have to edit these fields in WIN.INI to select different fonts for different screen resolutions.

Fonts and Display Drivers

There is a close relationship between the Presentation Manager display driver and the fonts used on OS/2 2.1. There are two basic types of fonts used in OS/2 2.1: bitmap fonts and outline fonts.

An artist designs bitmap fonts for use on a specific device (a printer or a display) at a specific size. It is important, therefore, that you use them on the specific device. If you use them on an incorrect device, the resulting font could look incorrect in size, aspect ratio, or quality.

OS/2 2.1 tries to match bitmap fonts to the correct device by using a measure called the logical font resolution. This is a value in dots per inch that is used for calculating the size of a font. Font size is normally measured in *points* (there are 72 points in an inch). This is a measure used by the printing and publishing industry to measure the size of a font on paper. When displaying fonts on a screen you need to calculate the size of a font in pixels. The relationship between points and pixels is

```
Size in pixels = (logical font resolution) x (point size)
                 ----------------------------------------
                                   72
```

OS/2 2.1 uses a font on a specific display only if the logical font resolution exactly matches the resolution specified in the font. Table 11.9 lists the logical font resolutions used by OS/2 2.1.

Table 11.9. Logical font resolutions in OS/2 2.1.

Adapter Type	*Screen Size*	*Logical Font Resolution*
CGA	640 x 200	96 x 48
EGA	640 x 350	96 x 72
VGA, SVGA, XGA	640 x 480	96 x 96
SVGA, XGA	800 x 600	96 x 96
SVGA, XGA, 8514	1024 x 768	120 x 120

The logical font resolution is not exactly the same as the actual resolution of the displayed screen. It is usually larger by approximately 20 percent to account for the greater viewing distance for display monitors when compared to paper.

OS/2 2.1 detects the display type during installation and only installs the fonts designed for the logical font resolution required. This can save more than 1 megabyte of hard disk space. Because of this you may notice that some applications which do not attempt to match the font resolution with the display appear to offer fewer font sizes on OS/2 2.1 than on OS/2 1.3.

You can use outline fonts on any device, and OS/2 2.1 scales them to match the logical font resolution of the target device at the size requested. OS/2 2.1 and WIN-OS/2 use the Adobe Type Manager technology for outline fonts; Microsoft Windows 3.1 uses a similar technology called TrueType. You can either display these on-screen or print them on paper.

Fonts Provided by the Display Driver

Display drivers are responsible for providing at least two types of bitmap fonts for use in the various modes that the display driver supports:

- System Proportional font
- Windowed command-line fonts

System Proportional

The System Proportional font is the default font used for all text in Presentation Manager application windows, menus, and dialog boxes. Display drivers are responsible for providing this default font for a number of reasons:

1. It must always be available.
2. Performance must be fast because it is frequently used.
3. It may have to change in size or design for different display sizes and resolutions.

The font is usually a proportional-spaced, sans-serif typeface with a logical size of 10 points. The actual size of the font in pixels, however, depends on the display resolution.

There are three sizes of the System Proportional font currently being used in all the major display drivers (see Table 11.10).

Table 11.10. System Proportional font sizes.

Point Size	*Display Resolution*	*Height in Pixels*	*Ave Character Width in Pixels*	*Physical Screen Size*
10 pt	640 x 480	16	6	All
10 pt	800 x 600	16	6	All
10 pt	1024 x 768	20	8	> 16 inches
12 pt	1024 x 768	22*	10	< 16 inches

*Some display drivers use a font that is 23 pixels high.

Sometimes you may see application dialog boxes with text only partially visible. This situation usually occurs because the application developer designed the dialog on one display type and did not test thoroughly on different displays and adapters.

Notice that two different sizes of fonts are available for display resolution 1024 x 768. The larger font is for smaller display monitors because the 10-point font is too small on monitors less than 16 inches to meet the requirements of German DIN standards. The display driver automatically selects which font to use based on the display monitor type connected to the video adapter. Currently, the display drivers that automatically switch fonts are the 8514/A adapter and the XGA adapter.

The display driver switches to the larger font when the display monitor attached is an IBM 8515 (14 inches) and uses the smaller font for larger display monitors.

It is possible to change this behavior so that OS/2 2.1 uses the same font for all display monitor types. You may want to do this if you find the default selection too small or too large. You can make this change by modifying a setting in the OS2.INI file.

Using an INI editor, the entry to change is:

Application name:	PM_SystemFonts
Key name:	DefaultFont

The value to set is the point size for the font and the typeface name, separated by a period. For example, "10.System Proportional" would request the smaller of the two fonts provided in the XGA and 8514/A display drivers.

Changing the default font may affect the size of application dialog windows. If you select a smaller font, you may see some text clipped at the right with some applications.

If you do not have access to an INI file editor, you can create a REXX command program. Listing 11.3 shows SETFONT.CMD, which sets the default font to 10 point system proportional.

Listing 11.3. REXX Command to set the default font.

```
/* SETFONT.CMD Set default system font */
/* (c) Copyright IBM Corp. 1992, All rights reserved */
call RxFuncAdd 'SysIni', 'RexxUtil', 'SysIni'
FontName = '10.System Proportional'
call SysIni 'USER','PM_SystemFonts','DefaultFont',FontName¦¦x2c(0)
say Result
exit
```

The final parameter of the call is the value to write, specifying the size and name of the font to use. Once you execute the REXX command, you must restart OS/2 2.1 for the change to take effect.

An added benefit of specifying the exact font you want, using this technique, is that OS/2 2.1 loads all the fonts from the display

driver, including the fixed-spaced, windowed, command-line fonts. These can then be used in any Presentation Manager application. This is particularly useful in text editors, like the OS/2 Enhanced Editor or System Editor provided in the Productivity Folder.

You can also change the fonts used for window titles, menus, and icons from the font palette object in the Workplace Shell system settings.

Windowed Command Lines

The display driver also includes the fonts used in windowed command lines (both OS/2 and DOS). These are all fixed-space fonts designed for compatibility with the fonts used in full-screen, command-line sessions.

In addition to windowed command lines using these fonts, any Presentation Manager application that uses the Advanced Video (AVIO) function calls will also use these fonts. For this reason, these fonts are frequently known as AVIO fonts. Some of the applications that use them are

- OS/2 Extended Services terminal emulators
- The PM Terminal emulator applet in OS/2 2.1

Display drivers can include a number of different sizes for these fonts, and AVIO applications or the windowed command lines can select any one of them. The number of different sizes available depends on the display driver.

It is not possible to change the number of fonts or their sizes without rewriting the display driver—this can usually only be done by the supplier of the driver.

Table 11.11 shows all the AVIO font sizes that OS/2 2.1 uses. Not all of these are available on all display drivers.

Table 11.11. Windowed command-line (AVIO) font sizes.

Width x Height	*VGA, SVGA 640 x 480*	*SVGA 800 x 600*	*SVGA, XGA, 8514/A 1024 x 768*
5 x 12	*	*	
5 x 16	*	*	
6 x 10	*	*	*
6 x 14	*	*	*
7 x 15			*
7 x 25			*
8 x 8	*	*	*
8 x 10	*	*	*
8 x 12	*	*	*
8 x 14	*	*	*
8 x 16	*	*	*
8 x 18	*	*	*
10 x 18		*	*
12 x 16			*
12 x 20			*
12 x 22			*
12 x 30			*

Table 11.11 shows that the VGA display driver provides 10 different sizes and both the XGA and 8514/A drivers provide a choice of 15 sizes. On previous versions of the OS/2 operating system the number of fonts available was often much fewer than this; some display drivers often do not include as wide a range of sizes.

No display driver offers a selection of more than 15 AVIO fonts because some applications have limits that allow only a maximum of 15 AVIO fonts!

The performance of text display in a windowed command line can vary widely and is a function of the font size and video adapter being used. Larger fonts are slower because of the greater number of pixels that each character contains. However, small fonts can be slow if they are of odd width or height—many video adapters and drivers are most efficient when handling bitmaps of even width and height.

The VGA video adapter hardware and driver are most efficient when working with fonts 8 pixels wide. There is a significant improvement in performance over the 5-pixel-wide or 6-pixel-wide fonts.

In OS/2 2.0 each display driver includes both the System Proportional and the AVIO fonts inside the driver's DLL. With the release of OS/2 2.1, the VGA, SVGA, and XGA drivers now load these fonts from a separate library known as DSPRES.DLL. This DLL contains only the fonts used by the display driver.

Application developers can use the GpiLoadFonts API call on the display device driver DLL to obtain access to all the AVIO fonts from the Presentation Manager GPI.

International Standards and How They Affect Fonts

Two important international standards exist that cover the use of computer display monitors and fonts.

- German DIN 66234
- International Standards Organization (ISO) 9241 Part 3

Both these standards address fonts and displays and how they affect health and safety for workers. The ISO standard is becoming increasingly important as it becomes a European standard; many countries in the European Community require new computer systems installed in offices to meet the standard starting in 1993.

For fonts, the standard requires that characters meet certain minimum sizes and contrast ratios between the foreground and background colors. Some of the requirements are:

- character descenders must not touch ascenders or national language accents on the following line
- underlines must not touch ascenders or national language accents on the following line
- the contrast between foreground and background elements both within a character and between characters must be 3 to 1
- every character must be uniquely recognizable, even when underlined
- horizontal and vertical strokes should be the same width

These are just some examples of the requirements. For OS/2 2.1, all the bitmap fonts were redesigned to meet the ISO standard where possible. The affected fonts are the windowed command-line fonts, System Proportional as well as the bitmap Courier, Tms Rmn, and Helv fonts.

Tms Rmn and Helv are similar to the Times and Helvetica typeface designs.

> The redesign of System Proportional makes some characters wider than they were before. Because of this, some application dialog boxes may have text characters clipped at their right extremes.

The redesigned fonts for Courier, Helv, and Tms Rmn do not replace the old ones; OS/2 2.1 includes them in addition to the old ones and adds the letters 'ISO' to their face name. Also, the WIN-OS/2 fonts were not redesigned or tested for compliance with the standards.

The redesigned fonts have been tested for compliance to ISO 9241 Part 3 on the IBM display monitors 9515, 9517, and 9518. It is possible that display monitors from other manufacturers also meet the standards, but no testing has been performed to confirm this.

It is not possible for all font sizes to meet the standards. If you select one of the redesigned fonts (Helv, Tms Rmn, Courier, or AVIO) and it does not pass the standards, you will see a message in the font selection dialog ("Font may not be ISO-compliant").

Table 11.12 lists all the fonts in OS/2 2.1 tested for compliance with the ISO standard and the results on the 9515, 9517, and 9518 displays. This table assumes black text displayed on a white background for all fonts except the AVIO command line, for which is assumed white text on a black background.

Table 11.12. Fonts tested for ISO 9241 Part 3 compliance.

	9518 at	*9515 at*	*9517 at*	
Font face name	*Size*	*640 x 480*	*1024 x 768*	*1024 x 768*
System Proportional	10 pt	Y	N/A	Y
System Proportional	12 pt	N/A	Y	N/A
System Monospace	10 pt	Y	Y	Y
Helv ISO	8 pt	1		

continues

Table 11.12. continued

	9518 at	*9515 at*	*9517 at*	
Font face name	*Size*	*640 x 480*	*1024 x 768*	*1024 x 768*
Helv ISO	9 pt	Y	Y	Y
	10 pt	Y	Y	Y
	12 pt	Y	Y	Y
	14 pt	Y	Y	Y
	18 pt	Y	Y	Y
	24 pt	Y	Y	Y
Tms Rmn ISO	8 pt	1		
	9 pt	Y	N/A	N/A
	10 pt	Y	2	
	12 pt	Y	Y	Y
	14 pt	Y	Y	Y
	18 pt	Y	Y	Y
	24 pt	Y	Y	Y
Courier ISO	8 pt	1		
	9 pt	Y	N/A	N/A
	10 pt	Y	2	
	12 pt	Y	Y	Y
System VIO	5 x 12	3		
	5 x 16			
	6 x 10			
	6 x 14			
	7 x 15			

Font face name	*9518 at Size*	*9515 at 640 x 480*	*9517 at 1024 x 768*	*1024 x 768*
System VIO	7 x 25			
	8 x 8			
	8 x 10			
	8 x 12			
	8 x 14	Y	4	
	8 x 16	Y		
	8 x 18	Y		
	10 x 18	Y		
	12 x 16	Y		
	12 x 20	Y		Y
	12 x 22	Y	Y	Y
	12 x 30	Y	Y	Y

[1]All 8-point fonts fail because they do not meet the minimum size requirements.

[2]10-point Tms Rmn and Courier fail on both 1024 x 768 displays because they do not meet the inner contrast ratio requirements.

[3]All AVIO fonts smaller than 14-pixels high or 8-pixels wide fail because they do not meet the minimum size requirements.

[4]All 8-pixel-wide AVIO fonts fail on both 1024 x 768 displays because they do not meet the inner contrast ratio requirements.

(The 9518 is a 14-inch display capable of 640 x 480 resolution; the 9515 is a 14-inch display capable of 1024 x 768 resolution; and the 9517 is a 17-inch display capable of 1024 x 768 resolution.)

Where to Get Display Drivers

OS/2 2.1 includes a number of Presentation Manager and WIN-OS/2 display drivers for a selection of video adapters. The SVGA display drivers try to support as wide a range of SVGA adapters as possible. In some cases this may mean that the display driver does not use hardware accelerators available on some display cards. Many suppliers of these cards choose to enhance their support of OS/2 2.1 by providing display drivers specifically designed for optimum performance with their video adapter cards.

On systems preloaded with OS/2 2.1, the VGA display driver is the default. If you have a system with XGA or SVGA, go to the Welcome folder to install a more appropriate display driver.

Up-to-date information on supported video adapters can be found on a number of bulletin board systems (BBS):

- CompuServe
- IBM National Support Center BBS
- OS/2 BBS

Video adapter and personal computer manufacturers often maintain their own bulletin board systems and these contain up-to-date information on OS/2 display driver support for their systems. In many cases you can download display drivers for OS/2 2.1.

If you have a non-IBM video adapter, always check with the supplier so that you have the best display driver for OS/2 2.1 currently available.

How to Select the Best Video Adapter for OS/2 2.1

A wide range of video adapters is available for personal computers. In most cases you already have a video adapter suitable for use by OS/2 2.1. If you are considering replacing it, it is important to ensure that it is compatible with OS/2 2.1.

Compatibility Considerations—VGA

The VGA video adapter architecture is the dominant video technology in the industry. First introduced in 1987 on the PS/2 range of personal computers, it has evolved into an accepted industry standard.

Nearly all video adapters available today either complement or are compatible with the VGA. For this reason, supporting the VGA architecture has been (and is likely to remain) of primary importance in the OS/2 operating system.

The display architecture replaced by VGA, the CGA, and EGA, is now generally considered obsolete. OS/2 2.1, however, does support both of these adapters for the few machines still in use that do not have VGA video adapters but are otherwise capable of running OS/2 2.1. (8514/A, the XGA, and various SVGA chip sets extend the VGA architecture.)

While it is possible to use CGA and EGA on machines equipped with a VGA, I don't recommend it. Generally, the Workplace Shell does not work well on screen resolutions less than 640 x 480, and enhancements to CGA and EGA support are unlikely.

The 8514/A

IBM introduced the 8514/A at the same time as the VGA to complement the VGA adapter. It provides 1024 x 768 resolution in either 16 colors or 256 colors. Software support for the 8514/A got off to a slow start because the hardware interface specification was not published. This reason alone probably contributes to the wide number of SVGA designs rather than designs compatible with the 8514/A.

Despite the lack of information on the hardware interface, the introduction of the ATI 8514/Ultra and device drivers for Microsoft Windows and the OS/2 operating system make the 8514/A architecture a common choice for many users.

Regarding a choice of video adapter for use with OS/2 2.1, you should be aware of the following concerns:

1. IBM has withdrawn the 8514/A video adapter card. The ATI 8514/Ultra is still available, although it is being replaced with newer designs.
2. The hardware architecture is not well suited to 32-bit operating systems.

This last point is the most critical for future compatibility. The 8514/A does not allow any operating system or application direct access to the video memory buffer. All access is through I/O ports (this is significantly slower than addressing memory directly). Additionally, I/O operations are privileged in OS/2 2.1, and a process known as a *ring transition* must take place to switch the processor from user mode (with hardware protection) to kernel mode (when hardware access is permitted). This makes the 8514/A slower than designs that allow direct memory access.

XGA

IBM introduced the XGA video adapter in 1990, and it was a significant improvement over the 8514/A and many other SVGA designs. Designed to be used by 32-bit operating systems, it provides memory-mapped access to almost all hardware registers and the video memory buffer. Infrequent operations, like initialization, still use I/O registers, but because these operations are rare, this is not a problem for XGA performance.

Display drivers for Microsoft Windows and the OS/2 operating system have been available since the introduction of the XGA adapter, and there have been significant improvements made since then. In OS/2 2.1, the XGA display driver is implemented in 32-bit code and provides support for WIN-OS/2 Window mode. This makes the XGA (now the XGA-2) one of the best video adapters currently supported by OS/2 2.1.

The XGA was expensive when first introduced and only operated in interlaced modes, which made it unattractive to many users. An updated adapter, the XGA-2, is now available in both Microchannel and ISA bus versions and offers improved performance in more noninterlaced modes at a competitive price.

SVGA

There are several SVGA video adapters available from a number of manufacturers. Many of these share the same basic chip sets. There is no single SVGA architecture, although all of them support the original VGA video modes. The extended graphics modes usually follow a similar architecture to the original VGA using I/O ports to control the adapter and direct access to the video memory buffer for drawing operations. Performance can vary depending on how much hardware assistance features are available, the implementation of the video adapter card, and the device driver software.

OS/2 2.1 provides good support and compatibility for many of the SVGA video adapters currently available. It is hard to predict how well future SVGA designs will work with OS/2 2.1. However, as noted earlier in this chapter, the design of the SVGA support in OS/2 2.1 is as generic as possible between adapter types so that support for future video adapters should be fairly easy to provide.

The SVGA chip sets currently supported by OS/2 2.1 are listed in Table 11.13. These are the SVGA chips that the `SVGA ON` command recognizes to provide DOS full-screen support. In many cases these SVGA chips are available from several suppliers who include them on their own adapter cards.

Table 11.13. SVGA Chip sets supported by OS/2 2.1.

Manufacturer	*Chip Set*	*DOS Full-Screen*	*PM Driver*	*WIN-OS/2 Driver*
ATI	18800	Y		
	28800 (Wonder XL)	Y	Y	Y
Cirrus Logic	CL-D5422	Y	Y	Y
	CL-D5424	Y	Y	Y
	CL-D5426 (as a 5424)	Y	Y	Y
Headland	HT205	Y		
	HT208	Y		
	HT209	Y	Y	Y
IBM	VGA 256c	Y	Y	Y
Trident	8800	Y		
	8900b	Y	Y	Y
	8900c	Y	Y	Y
Tseng	ET3000	Y		
	ET4000	Y	Y	Y
Western Digital	PVGA1A	Y		
	WD9000 (PVGA1B)	Y		
	WD90C11 (PVGA1C)	Y	Y	Y
	WD90C30 (PVGA1D)	Y	Y	Y
	WD90C31	Y	Y	Y

Where OS/2 2.1 provides DOS full-screen support for an SVGA adapter, you can run any DOS application that uses an SVGA extended graphics mode. The OS/2 2.1 video virtual device driver correctly recognizes the mode, and you can switch between the DOS application and any Presentation Manager or other windowed applications.

OS/2 2.1 includes Presentation Manager and WIN-OS/2 display drivers for a subset of these SVGA chips, as marked. Because of the difference between adapter cards, it is not possible to declare that all cards with a given SVGA chip will work with the display drivers included. The video adapter cards known to work with OS/2 2.1 are listed in Table 11.14. It is very likely that cards from other manufacturers based on similar SVGA chip set designs also work with these Presentation Manager and WIN-OS/2 display drivers.

Table 11.14. SVGA adapter cards known to work with OS/2 2.1 display drivers.

Manufacturer	*Adapter Card*
ATI Technologies, Inc.	8514/Ultra
ATI Technologies, Inc.	VGA Wonder XL
Boca Research, Inc.	SuperVga
Diamond Computer Systems, Inc.	SpeedStar SuperVGA
Everex System, Inc.	Viewport NI
Headland Technology, Inc.	Video Seven
Orchid Technology, Inc.	ProDesigner II/MC
Sigma Designs, Inc.	SigmaVGA Legend II
STB Systems, Inc.	PowerGraph VGA
STB Systems, Inc.	Ergo-VGA/MC
Trident Microsytems, Inc.	TVGA 8900C
VGA Graphic Card	JAX-8212
Western Digital Corporation	Paradise VGA
Wyse Technology, Inc.	Amdek SmartVision/SVGA

Up-to-date information on which cards have been explicitly tested is available on the bulletin board systems listed in "Where To Get Display Drivers." As other manufacturers' SVGA chip sets become widely used, you can expect OS/2 2.1 device drivers to become available. Always ask the manufacturer for the latest information on OS/2 2.1 support, or keep an eye on the bulletin board systems.

Resolution, Performance, and Flicker

When choosing a video adapter and display monitor for use with OS/2 2.1, there are three features to consider:

- screen resolution
- performance
- flicker

Screen Resolution

The discussion in "Why Would I Want to Change Resolution?" earlier in this chapter will help give you an idea of what type of video adapter is appropriate for you.

I recommend a minimum screen resolution of 640 x 480, and this is likely to be all that most people will require. If you plan to make heavy use of Presentation Manager or WIN-OS/2 applications, it's a good idea to use an adapter that is capable of at least 800 x 600 resolution or higher.

Display Performance

You will see an improvement in the overall system responsiveness of OS/2 2.1 if you have a fast video adapter. Although the video adapter has no effect on areas such as the file system, printing, memory management, or mathematics, it directly affects the most important part of OS/2 2.1: the user interface.

The difference in performance among video adapters is great. Even on the same adapter, performance can vary depending on the mode of operation. Because performance varies so much between video adapters, I did not include specific measurements here. Instead, I included some guidelines to help you choose between adapters and operating modes.

Video adapters with hardware to assist with basic drawing operations usually perform faster than adapters without hardware assistance. Common operations, which many adapters provide hardware assistance for, are line drawing, area fill, and bit-blt (bitmap move or copy operations). An example of such an adapter is the XGA-2.

Higher resolution modes require the display driver to work with more information in the video memory buffer. This usually causes higher resolution modes to operate slower than the lower resolution modes, although hardware assistance in the video adapter can make the difference in performance small.

Many adapters offer hardware assistance only in their higher resolution extended graphics modes. This could make these modes perform faster than the lower resolution modes!

If the number of available colors changes from 16 to 256, the amount of memory used for the video buffer doubles. It doubles again if you go to 65,536 colors. This doubles the amount of data that the display driver needs to work with and can significantly decrease performance. Again, the availability of hardware assistance can help maintain the performance level.

Screen Flicker

You may see screen flicker if the video adapter has to redraw the image onto the display monitor at a rate slow enough for the human eye to notice. It can be particularly noticeable when you see a display screen from the corner of your eye or perhaps from the other side of a room.

Flicker often occurs when a video adapter has to scan down the screen twice to redraw the entire image. Each pass down the screen draws every second horizontal line of the image, alternating between even and odd lines. This type of operation is known as interlaced and used to be a common feature of video adapters at their 1024 x 768 resolutions.

Interlaced operation, however, can cause severe flicker on display monitors, especially for some patterns and horizontal lines. For this reason, noninterlaced video adapters and monitors produce a far more stable and pleasant image. As the cost of electronics decreases, the availability of noninterlaced displays increases.

Another factor influencing the increased use of noninterlaced displays is concern for the health and safety of users of computer displays. It is generally accepted that noninterlaced displays are less tiring to work with over extended periods of time. The International Standards Organization specifies reduced flicker, among other display characteristics, in the ISO 9241 Part 3 standard that is being adopted by the European Community.

When buying a new display monitor, always look for one capable of noninterlaced operation, and check to be sure that your video adapter supports noninterlaced modes. Ask what internationally recognized standards the display monitor meets. A high-quality display monitor will significantly improve your comfort when working at your computer.

The standards do not specify exactly how fast a video adapter should update the entire display to reduce the flicker to a level that is not noticeable to the human eye. The video adapter and display monitor industry has standardized on frequencies between 70 Hz and 75 Hz, depending on the display mode. By contrast, interlaced displays refresh at between 80 Hz and 90 Hz, but only draw half the image each time, effectively updating the entire image 40 to 45 times per second.

Flicker generally occurs only on cathode ray tube (CRT) display monitors. LCD displays, especially TFT technology, do not flicker.

Author Bio

David A. Kerr is an Advisory Programmer with the OS/2 development team in Boca Raton, Florida. He joined IBM in 1985 at the Hursley Laboratories, England, where he worked on the design and implementation of the GDDM-OS/2 Link product. In 1989 he joined the Presentation Manager team in the technical planning office and moved into the OS/2 planning department in Boca Raton the following year. His broad knowledge of all aspects of the internals of OS/2 has earned him the recognition as an expert on the Presentation Manager and a position as a key member in the OS/2 design team. He frequently speaks at conferences and seminars for OS/2 customers and developers in Europe, Australia, the Far East, and America. David holds a BSc in Computer Science and Electronics from the University of Edinburgh, Scotland.

12

Printing

In This Chapter

This chapter describes the OS/2 print subsystem and the Workplace Shell print objects, their uses, and how the WIN-OS2 print subsystem is related to them. The Workplace Shell extensions for LAN printing complete the description of the user interfaces to the OS/2 print subsystem. I will also describe some example configurations that you can use for your own requirements.

An important aspect of printing is application printing. I will describe the printing interface for several OS/2 applications, including those shipped with OS/2 2.1. The last part of the chapter contains a section for troubleshooting problems with the OS/2 print subsystem.

Print Workplace Objects

The print subsystem consists of a user interface (the Workplace Shell), a spooler, and printer drivers. This section describes the user interface. It consists of six objects in the Workplace Shell:

- The printer object that represents a spooler queue of print jobs.
- The job object that represents a print job.
- The port object that represents a port (for example, LPT1).
- The printer driver object that represents a printer driver.
- A queue driver object that represents a queue driver.
- A spooler object that represents the spooler.

Printer Object

The printer object is the main controlling object of the print subsystem. It allows you to access all the other objects except the spooler object, which is in the OS/2 Setup folder. Each printer object represents a single spooler queue of print jobs and all the associated configurations to make it print.

Printer objects are similar to all other objects in the Workplace Shell in that you can create, delete, copy, move, shadow, or open them. In addition, there are some unique features such as selecting one to be the default, changing the status to be held or released, and deleting all the print jobs.

There is also a subclass of the printer object: the network printer object, which is available if you have a network environment.

Creating a Printer Object

There are four ways you can create a printer object:

1. Creating a printer object during system installation:

   When installing the operating system, OS/2 2.1 asks you whether you want to install a printer. Then OS/2 2.1 displays a dialog with a list of supported printers and a list of possible port names. The installation program installs the appropriate printer driver for OS/2 2.1 and, if it exists, the one for WIN-OS2. During the next system restart, OS/2 2.1 creates the appropriate printer object and automatically derives the name of the printer object from the name of the printer driver.

2. Creating a printer object from a template:

   The Templates folder contains a template named printer. Dragging this template to another folder or the desktop results in a dialog. The dialog presents a list of printer drivers. You can select a printer driver and port to use with the new printer object. There is an additional pushbutton called Install new printer driver that takes you to the printer driver installation dialog.

   The Create a Printer dialog is shown in Figure 12.1. You give the name of the printer object in the Create a Printer dialog. The printer object name has blanks and illegal characters removed (for example, \) and is truncated to eight characters. The spooler then uses this name to create a spool subdirectory name and queue name. In case of duplicate names, OS/2 2.1 overwrites the name with increasing numbers (for example, IBM40291, IBM40292, and so on). Older PM applications use this name rather than the longer printer object name, which is actually the queue description. You can see this queue name in the View setting page of a printer object in the field named Physical name.

TIP

Make the first eight characters of your printer object name unique and meaningful so that you can readily distinguish the Physical name displayed by older OS/2 applications.

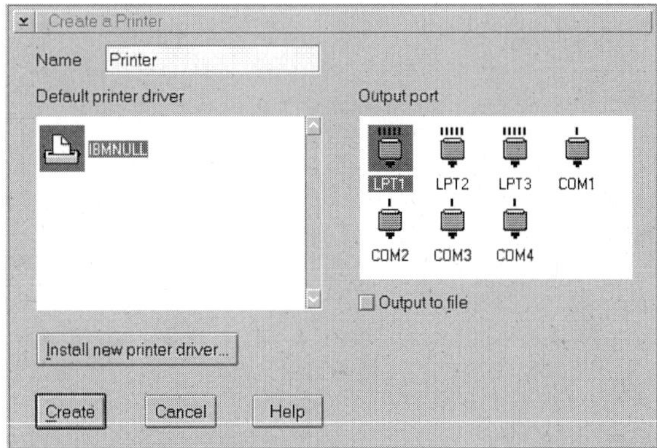

Figure 12.1. The Create a Printer dialog.

3. Creating a printer object from an existing printer object:

   Selecting Create another on a printer object context menu is the same as using a printer object template; OS/2 2.1 displays the dialog shown in Figure 12.1.

4. Creating a printer object from a printer driver:

   Open a folder containing a printer driver. For example, the folder could be A:\ or C:\OS2\DLL\PSCRIPT. If you double-click on the printer driver icon, OS/2 2.1 displays a window listing the different printer models (or types) supported by the printer driver (see Figure 12.2).

   Drag the one that corresponds to your printer to another folder (for example, the Desktop folder). This action installs the printer driver and creates a printer object. OS/2 2.1 automatically chooses the next available port name. OS/2 2.1 derives the printer object name from the printer driver.

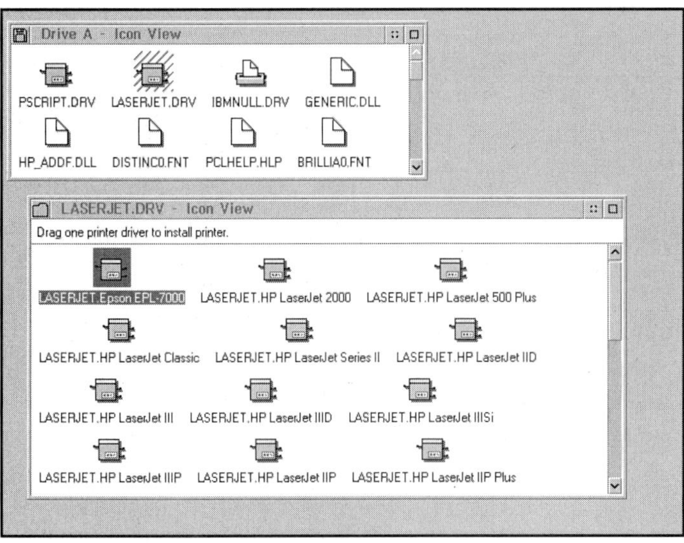

***Figure 12.2.** Creating a printer object from a printer driver.*

In the last three cases, OS/2 2.1 checks to see whether it can create an equivalent WIN-OS2 configuration. OS/2 2.1 checks a file named DRVMAP.INF to see whether an equivalent Windows printer driver is available. If it is, OS/2 2.1 asks you whether you want to install an equivalent WIN-OS2 printer configuration. If you need to install a WIN-OS2 printer driver, the system displays an installation dialog. The installation process updates the WIN.INI file appropriately when this is completed successfully. The DRVMAP.INF file is in the \OS2\MDOS\WINOS2 directory.

> TIP
>
> In larger system environments, you may want to manually edit the DRVMAP.INF file so that you can install a Windows printer driver not shipped with OS/2 2.1.

In OS/2 2.1 you can enter any path; you are not limited to installing from Disk A.

Deleting a Printer Object

To delete a printer object, you can use the normal operation of choosing Delete from the context menu or dragging it to the shredder.

If the printer object is currently printing a job, OS/2 2.1 completes the job before it deletes any other jobs and deletes the printer object.

Copying a Printer Object

You can copy a printer object. OS/2 2.1 copies all the settings of the printer object, including the name and the status (held or released), to the new object.

The most common use of copy is to create two printer objects with the same settings but with different default job properties—for example, IBM4029 Landscape and IBM4029 Portrait or LaserJet Foils and LaserJet Paper.

Moving a Printer Object

You can move a printer object just like any other Workplace object. I recommend leaving printer objects on the desktop for easy access. Some users, particularly those on a network, may wish to have a folder to hold all printer objects.

Shadowing a Printer Object

I recommend shadowing printer objects to work area folders as required; for example, you may want to use only certain printer objects with certain types of printing activity from applications within a work area folder.

Open Printer Object—Icon View

Icon view is the default open operation, although you can change this default in the printer object settings. Double-clicking on a printer object shows a window of icons, each of which represents a print job. Each job can have one of the following five states: spooling, waiting in queue, held in queue, printing, or error. OS/2 2.1 uses a different icon for each job state.

Open Printer Object—Details View

Details view shows print jobs in a details layout. The job state is shown descriptively. The details view fields are very similar to the OS/2 1.3 Print Manager. You can obtain a context menu for a job object by clicking with mouse button 2 on the job name.

A printer object shows only one open view at a time. For example, if you open an icon view and then open a details view, OS/2 2.1 closes the icon view. This is not the same as other objects in the Workplace Shell.

Open Printer Object—Settings

A printer object has seven setting pages. The last two pages, named Window and General, are the same as those for any other Workplace object. Five pages are of interest:

- View
- Printer driver

- Output
- Queue options
- Print options

NOTE

You need to close the printer object settings notebook for all the changes to take effect. This is different from other objects in the Workplace Shell.

The View page (see Figure 12.3) contains the printer object Physical name. This is the name of the queue and also the spool subdirectory. Older PM applications may display this name. It is a read-only field for reference purposes only. The other field is named Default View and contains radio buttons to choose the default open view for a printer object. This is a unique feature of the printer object. OS/2 2.1 reserves the rest of the blank space in the dialog for options that apply only to a network printer object.

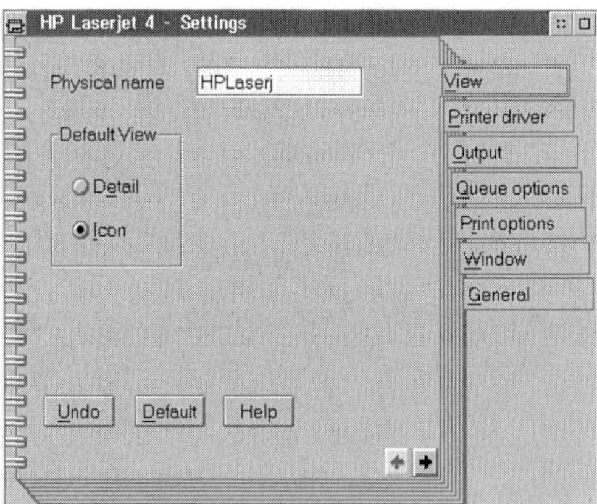

Figure 12.3. *Printer object View settings page.*

The Printer driver page (see Figure 12.4) shows the list of installed printer drivers in the upper window. You can select one or more of these printer drivers for the printer object. You can select more than one printer driver if you use sharing.

The lower window lists all the printer drivers selected from the upper window. You can select only one printer driver in the lower window, which becomes the default printer driver for this printer object.

The icons represent printer driver objects; you can display a context menu for each object. You cannot move the objects from the window, however, or drop any objects into these windows.

Use the Job properties pushbutton to display the Job properties dialog of the default printer driver. Job properties are the options to use with a print job. The print subsystem stores the results as defaults for the printer object. Any print jobs submitted without job properties (mostly from non-PM applications) have these defaults applied to them. If you have not set any defaults, OS/2 2.1 queries the printer driver for its "device defaults" and uses these for a print job.

When you use sharing, OS/2 2.1 can select two or more printer drivers in the upper window. If you deselect one, close and reopen the settings, the driver may still be selected. This is because OS/2 2.1 prevents you from defining an illegal configuration; the printer driver is used by other printer objects that are sharing the same port.

The Output page (see Figure 12.5) shows a list of installed ports. You can select zero, one, or more of these ports for the printer object. You can select no port by clicking on any blank space inside the Output port window. If you select no port, the printer object "holds" print jobs in the printer object until you select a port.

The icons represent port objects. You can display a context menu for each object. You cannot move the objects from the window or drop any objects into this window.

Use the Output to file checkbox to direct application print output to a file. If you select this checkbox, and you are printing from a PM application, OS/2

2.1 displays a dialog to prompt for the name of the output file. This filename can be any valid filename including a Universal Naming Convention (UNC) name (for example, \\SERVER\DISK\OUTPUT.TMP), a pipe (for example, \PIPE\APP1), or a port name (for example, LPT1).

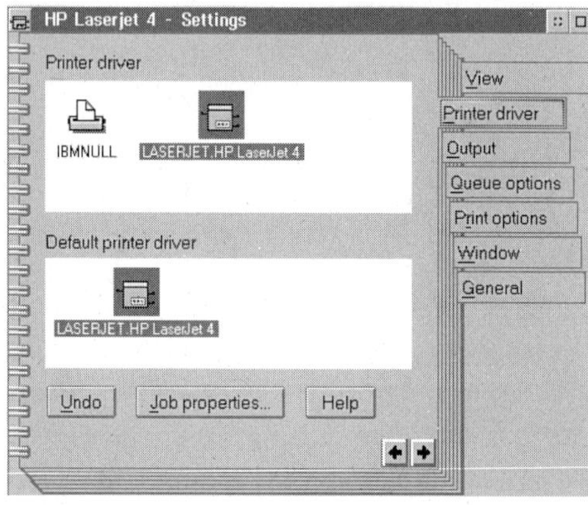

Figure 12.4. The printer object Printer driver settings page.

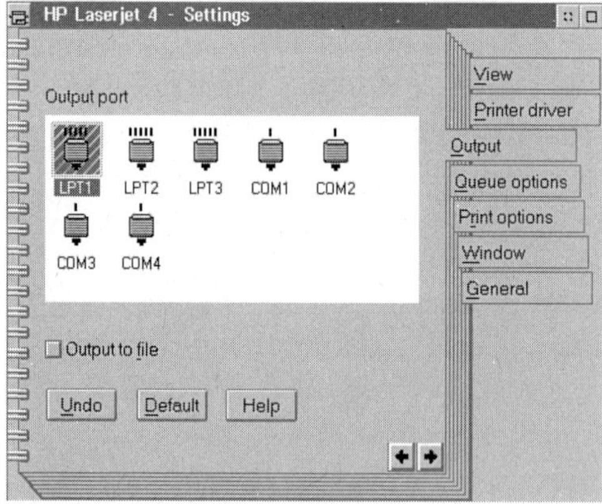

Figure 12.5. The printer object Output settings page.

The Queue options page (see Figure 12.6) shows the list of installed queue drivers. You can select one of these queue drivers for the printer object.

The icons represent queue driver objects. You can display a context menu for each object. You cannot move the objects from the window or drop any objects into this window.

The Job dialog before print option is used only for drag-and-drop printing. If you select this option, OS/2 2.1 displays a Job properties dialog for each drag-and-drop print action on this printer object. This feature allows you to vary the options (Job properties) used with each drag-and-drop print operation.

Use the Printer-specific format option to indicate that OS/2 2.1 will process all your jobs for this printer object into the printer commands before placing them onto the spooler queue. This option causes OS/2 2.1 to create much larger jobs on the disk or send them across the network, but it does shorten the time it takes to receive the first page of output when used in conjunction with the Print while spooling option.

Use the Print while spooling option to indicate that OS/2 2.1 should try to send job data to the printer while the application is still spooling the job data. This is useful for a multipage document because the time taken to receive the first page from the printer is reduced. The Print while spooling option is effective only for non-PM applications or if you select the Printer-specific format option.

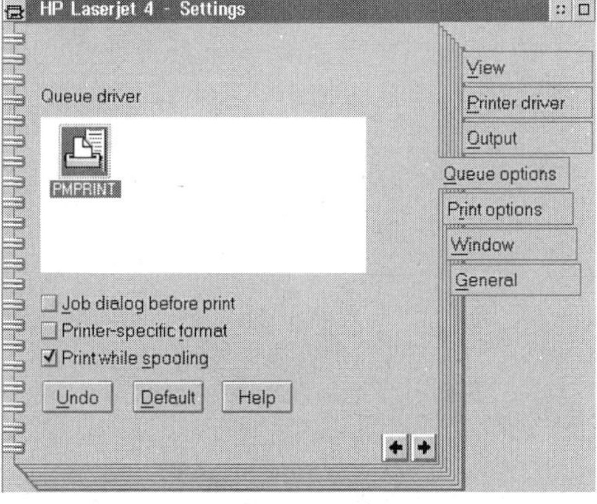

Figure 12.6. The printer object Queue options settings page.

The Print options page (see Figure 12.7) contains the name of the separator file. Use separator files to define a header page for the print job—the page that OS/2 2.1 prints before the actual job. Normally, you will probably use the separator page in a network environment so that users can identify their own jobs. Two sample separator files named SAMPLE.SEP and PSCRIPT.SEP are distributed with OS/2 2.1, and you can find them in the \OS2 directory. You can also use separator files to send printer-specific commands to a printer that take effect before the actual print job, providing you specify the IBMNULL printer driver.

The Start Time and Stop Time options define when the printer object is available to actually print jobs. You can typically use these options in a network environment to define, for example, an overnight queue for large print jobs. You can also use this option to start printing jobs at a specific time.

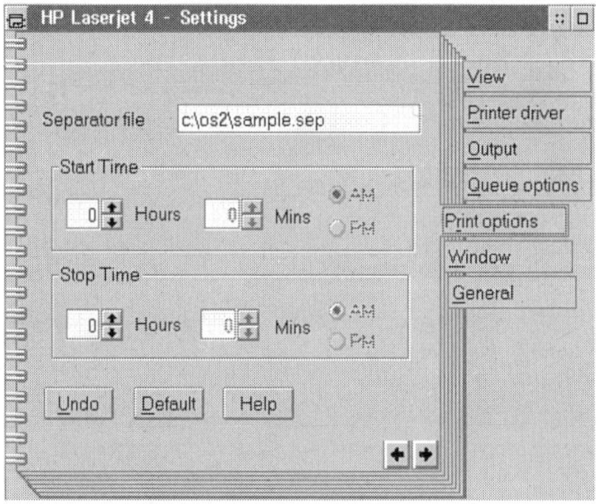

Figure 12.7. The printer object Print options settings page.

Set Default Printer Object

Use the Set default option (see Figure 12.8) on the printer object context menu to select the default printer object. OS/2 2.1 uses the default printer object if you are using an application that does not allow you to choose the printer object for the print job (for example, non-PM applications or some PM applications such as Print Screen, Help, and PICVIEW).

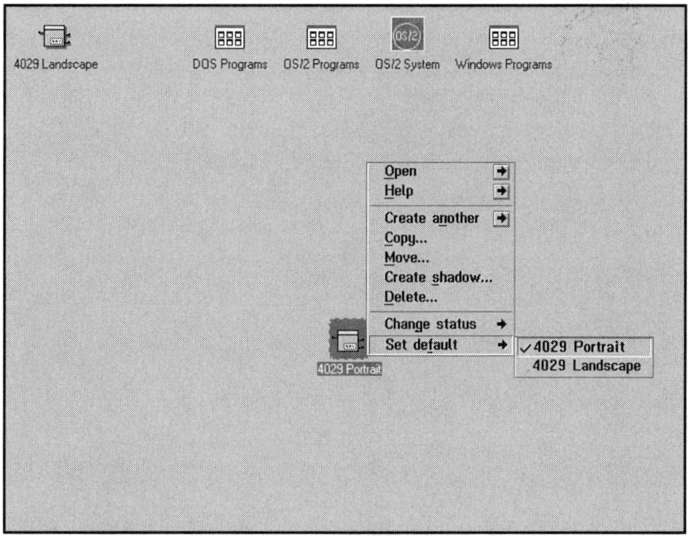

Figure 12.8. Setting the default printer object.

Changing Printer Object Status (Hold or Release)

Use the Change status option on the printer object context menu to either hold or release the printer object. Holding the printer object means that OS/2 2.1 does not print any jobs until you change the printer object status to released. If you have the printer object window open, you will see the status line change appropriately when you change the printer status.

Deleting All Jobs from a Printer Object

Use the Delete all jobs option on the printer object context menu to delete all jobs queued in the printer object. This menu option appears only if there is one or more jobs in the queue.

Do not confuse this with the delete option, which will cause OS/2 2.1 to delete the printer object itself, as well as all the jobs.

Job Object

The job object represents a print job queued in a printer object. There are five job states: spooling, waiting in queue, held, printing, and job error. For the printer object icon view there is a different icon for each state (see Figure 12.9).

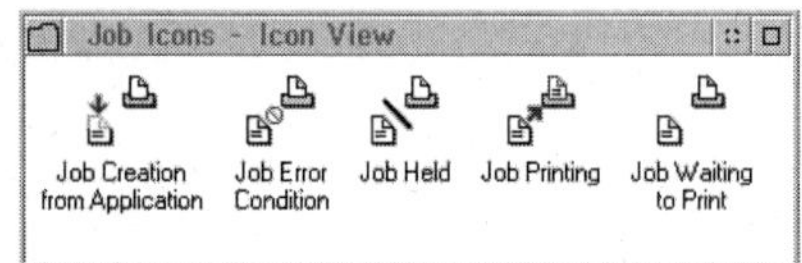

Figure 12.9. Job object state icons.

Creating a Job Object

Job objects are print jobs, and you create them by printing from applications. These applications are contained in one of the following groups:

- Printing from the command line using the `COPY` or `PRINT` commands.
- DOS applications such as Lotus 1-2-3 2.2.
- WIN-OS2 applications (such as Freelance Graphics).
- OS/2 full-screen applications such as WordPerfect 5.0 for OS/2.
- OS/2 PM applications such as Describe.
- Workplace Shell drag-and-drop printing.

Print jobs created by the first four groups are all in the printer-specific command language. Print jobs created by the last two groups can be either in the printer-specific language or in a device-independent format—a PM metafile; it depends upon the application and the Printer-specific format setting for the printer object.

Many PM applications, when they list the printer objects in OS/2 2.1, do not use the printer object name but rather the Physical name. Be sure to check the Physical name in the printer object settings. Note also that some PM applications such as PM Chart applet and Lotus 1-2-3/G use an internal name which is an alias for the port. This can lead to some further confusion because you get only one name for each port rather than one name for each printer object. This internal name is usually the same as the first printer object Physical name created for that port.

Deleting a Job Object

To delete a job object, choose Delete from its context menu. You cannot drag a job object to the shredder. If you try to delete a job in the middle of printing, OS/2 2.1 aborts the printing at a suitable point, such as the end of a page, and then deletes the job.

Moving/Shadowing a Job Object

Job objects cannot be moved or shadowed. They exist only within a printer object.

Copying a Job Object

To copy a job object, choose Copy from its context menu. You cannot copy the job by dragging it to another printer object for the same reason that you cannot move a job.

Open a Job Object—Job Content

You can view the actual content of a print job by selecting Open and Job content from the job object context menu or by double-clicking on the job object (see Figure 12.10).

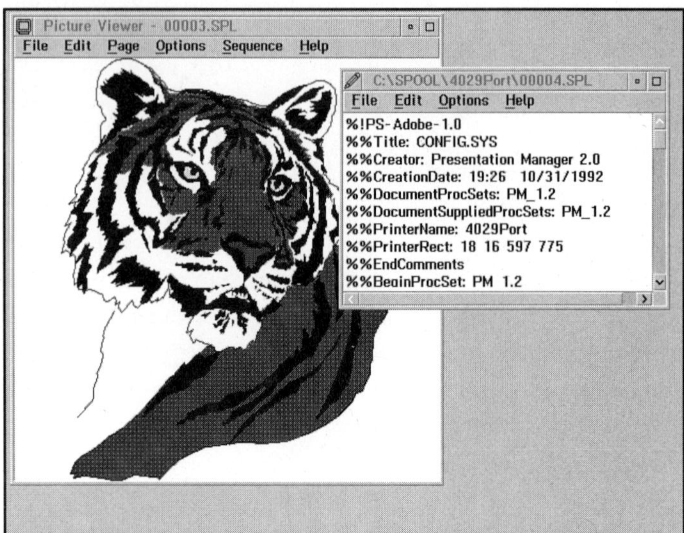

Figure 12.10. Print job content.

For print jobs in printer-specific format, OS/2 2.1 uses the OS/2 editor as a browser. Note that the editor cannot cope with hex command strings that may be present in some printer-specific format print jobs. For print jobs in the PM device-independent format (a PM metafile), OS/2 2.1 uses the PICVIEW applet to view the spool file.

Open a Job Object—Settings

A job object has as many as three settings pages:

- printing options
- submission data
- queue options

NOTE: You need to close the job object settings notebook to make any changes take effect.

The Printing options page (see Figure 12.11) contains fields giving the Job identifier and the Job position in the queue. As you change the job priority, OS/2 2.1 alters the Job position.

The Copies field is the number of collated copies. For each copy, OS/2 2.1 re-sends the complete print job. For improved performance, you can select the uncollated copies option that is available with the LaserJet and Postscript printer drivers in the Job properties dialog. You then have to collate the document yourself.

You can change the Priority field to increase or decrease the relative priority of print jobs in the queue. This option is most useful in a network environment when the administrator needs to rush a high-priority job through. You need to ask an administrator to increase your job priority.

The Form name is the name of the form (such as Letter, Legal, A4) that OS/2 2.1 should use to print the job. It is supplied by PM applications. The Job status field gives the state of the print job or shows an error message if the print job is in an error state.

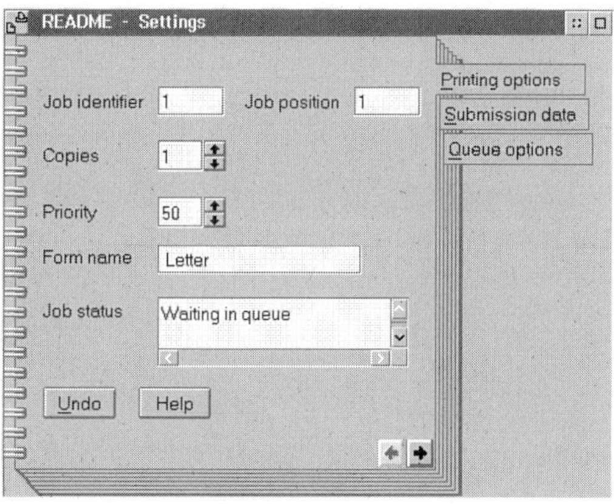

Figure 12.11. *The job object Printing options settings page.*

The Submission data page (see Figure 12.12) contains data about the print job itself (for example, the date and time of submission, the file size, and a comment string).

There is also a window with the printer driver object that OS/2 2.1 uses to print the job. You can double-click on this printer driver object to get the job properties that OS/2 2.1 uses when printing this job (for example, you can change the number of uncollated copies).

Changing the printer driver object Job properties has no effect once the job starts to print.

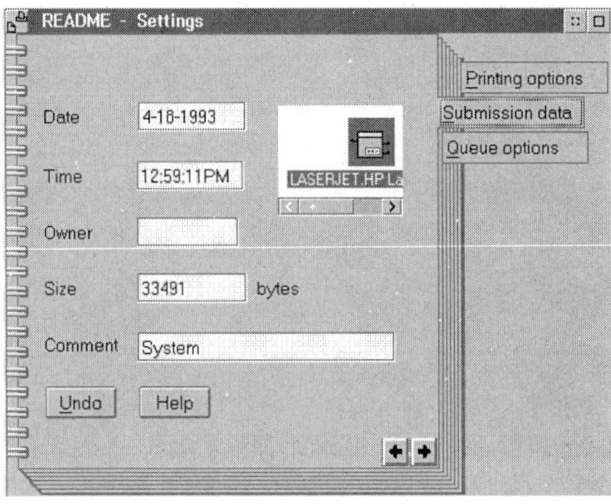

Figure 12.12. The job object Submission data settings page.

The Queue options page (see Figure 12.13) is present for only those print jobs that are in device-independent format. Device-independent format can be readily converted to the printer-specific commands for any type of printer, providing that a printer driver is available. The queue options are used to apply some transforms such as color mapping or scaling to the data before it is printed. PM applications can define queue options when they create the print job or they can let OS/2 2.1 use defaults, some of which can be modified in this settings page.

The Type of Output and Color Mapping fields determine the color of the output. You can change the Code page so that OS/2 2.1 prints the job with a code page other than the system code page.

OS/2 2.1 specifies and maps the code page in a network environment, so you do not need to worry about a requestor and server using the same code page.

The window shows the queue driver that OS/2 2.1 will use when the job is printed. It is the queue driver that uses the queue options to determine how to print the job.

The Queue driver options field shows some application-supplied transforms that tell the queue driver how to position and scale the output on the page. The user has the option to override these transforms if supplied by a PM application. Otherwise, both of these fields are blank and grayed.

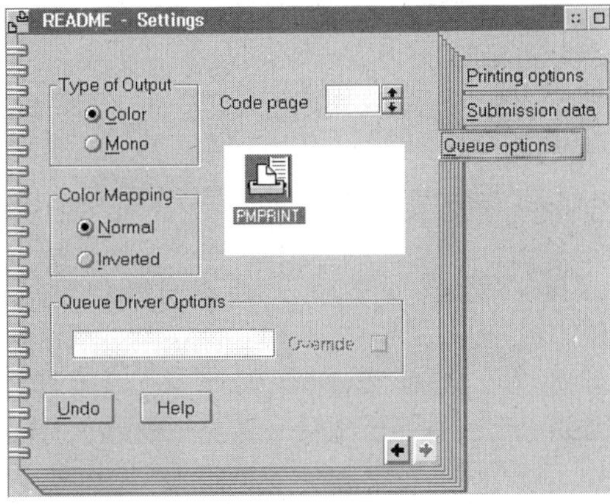

Figure 12.13. The job object Queue options settings page.

Changing Job Object Status (Hold or Release)

Use the Change status option on the job object context menu to either hold or release the job object. Holding the job object means that OS/2 2.1 does not send the job to the printer until you change the status to released.

Start Printing a Job Object Again

Use the Start again option on the job object context menu to restart a print job that is currently printing. You should use this option if there is some error during the currently printing job and you want to start printing it again.

Printing a Job Object Next

Use the Print next option on the job object context menu to change the order in which OS/2 2.1 prints jobs. The job object moves to the front of the queue, but its priority is not changed. This position setting takes precedence over the job object's priority setting.

Port Object

A port object represents a physical port attached to your system. The ports are divided into three groups:

- Predefined physical ports such as LPT1 to LPT3 and COM1 to COM4.
- Logical ports used for networking or emulation switching such as LPT1 to LPT9.
- Installable ports such as LPT10 to LPT32.

OS/2 2.1 uses a port driver to display the port configuration dialog. OS/2 2.1 pre-installs port drivers for LPT1 to LPT3 and COM1 to COM4. It is expected that manufacturers of adapter cards that support additional ports will supply a device driver and a port driver.

Installing a Port Object

To install a port object, choose Install from the context menu. You can install a port object provided that a port driver exists for that port. For example, you can delete LPT3 and then reinstall it by installing from the directory \OS2\DLL on the boot drive.

You can install ports directly into the OS2SYS.INI file (for example, LPT4 to LPT9 for networking). In this case no configuration dialog is available. An example of a REXX program to add LPT4 to LPT9 is shown in Listing 12.1.

Listing 12.1. Adding LPT4 to LPT9 ports to OS2SYS.INI file.

```
/* add LPT4 to LPT9 into OS2SYS.INI */
call RxFuncAdd 'SysIni', 'RexxUtil', 'SysIni'
do i=4 to 9
     call SysIni 'SYSTEM','PM_SPOOLER_PORT','LPT'||i, ';'||'00'x
end
exit
```

Using a REXX program similar to the one in Listing 12.1, you also can add a port name, which is a filename, and then select the file in the Output settings page of a printer object.

Deleting a Port Object

To delete a port object, choose Delete from its context menu. You cannot drag the port object to the shredder. If the port object you are deleting is being used by any other printer object, OS/2 2.1 displays a dialog (see Figure 12.14) that shows the printer objects that are using that port object. If you still want to delete the port object, you must open the settings for each printer object, change the port object, and close the settings. When there are no more printer objects using the port object, OS/2 2.1 deletes it.

It is not possible to delete LPT1 and COM1 port objects because these ports always exist and at least one port object is required so that new ones can be installed.

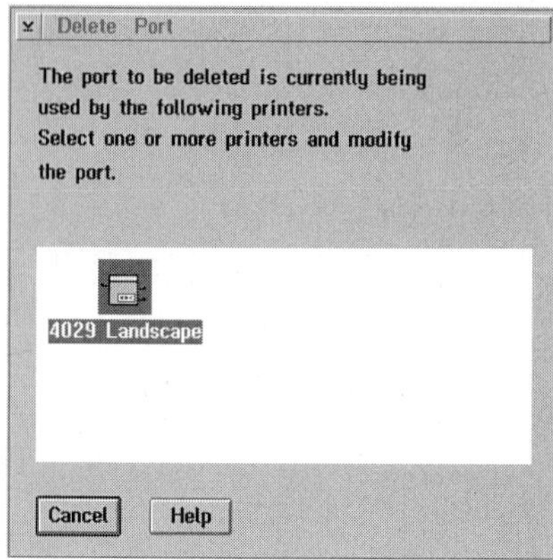

Figure 12.14. Port object in use dialog.

Open Port Object—Settings

A port object does not have a settings notebook as expected. Instead, each port object has a configuration dialog that is displayed, providing there is a port driver connected with that port.

The parallel ports LPT1 to LPT3 display the dialog shown in Figure 12.15 with the OS/2-supplied port driver (PARALLEL.PDR). The Timeout option is used to specify the time that OS/2 2.1 should wait before informing the user that the printer is not communicating with the system. The default of 45 seconds is recommended for laser printers, but this can be reduced to 15 seconds for a dot matrix printer or increased to 120 seconds for Postscript or other intelligent printers that can take some time to process and print a single page.

The Port sharing check box allows multiple DOS applications to simultaneously access the parallel port. This is useful for DOS applications that use an attached security device (such as a dongle) or other devices such as a network adapter or SCSI drive to LPT1, LPT2, or LPT3.

Printing from several DOS applications can cause the output from one application to be intermixed with the output from another.

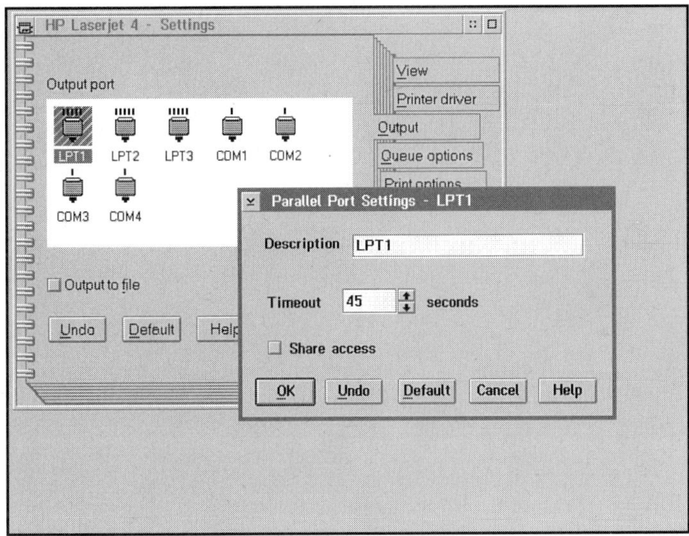

Figure 12.15. Parallel port object configuration dialog.

The serial ports COM1 to COM4 display the dialog shown in Figure 12.16 with the OS/2-supplied port driver (SERIAL.PDR). The Timeout option is used to specify the amount of time that OS/2 2.1 should wait before informing the user that the printer is not communicating with the system.

The Baud rate, Word length, Parity, and Stop bits are the normal communication parameters; the most common values of 9600, 8, N, and 1 are used as defaults, respectively. In some circumstances, the plotter or printer may use other values—check the device manual and any DIP switches on the device. Most serially attached plotters or printers use hardware handshaking, but you should verify this with your plotter or printer user manual.

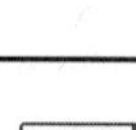

The serial port configuration in the WIN-OS2 control panel must match that used in the port object.

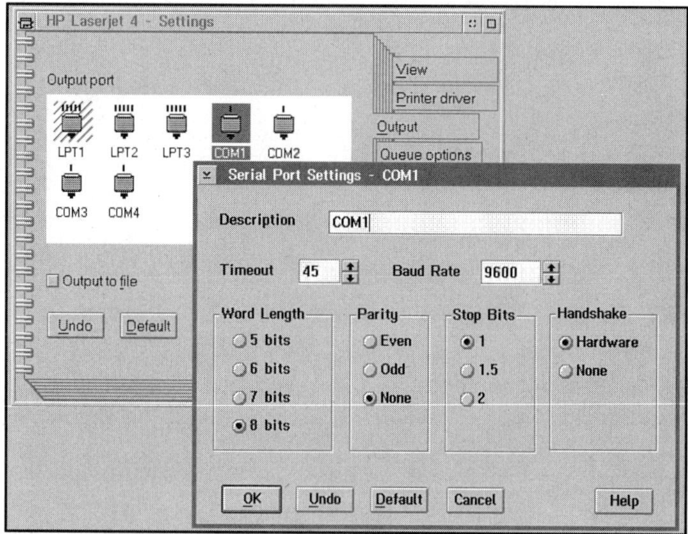

Figure 12.16. Serial port object configuration dialog.

Device adapters for other ports such as LPT10 to LPT32 must provide their own device driver and port driver to replace those provided with OS/2 2.1.

OS/2 2.1 does not support SCSI attached printers.

Copying/Moving/Shadowing a Port Object

Port objects cannot be moved, copied, or shadowed. They exist only within a printer object.

Redirection of a Port Object

The Redirection option on the port object context menu is used to redirect one port to another. The option is available only when you define two or more printer objects and at least one is configured to use LPT1, LPT2, or LPT3. You can redirect LPT1 through LPT3 to any other port, but you cannot redirect COM1 through COM4. Redirection is the Workplace Shell interface to the SPOOL command available at an OS/2 command prompt.

If you use a PM application to print to a printer object, the data will not get redirected; redirection applies only to non-PM application printing.

Printer Driver Object

A printer driver object represents the driver required for a particular model or emulation mode of a printer. For example, the printer driver object for a LaserJet III with Postscript cartridge is named PSCRIPT.LaserJet III v52_2. A single driver module such as PSCRIPT.DRV can support many Postscript printer models. A single printer such as the HP LaserJet III can be driven with several driver modules (LASERJET and PSCRIPT).

Installing a Printer Driver Object

A printer driver object is installed using the Printer driver install dialog shown in Figure 12.17.

If you want to install one of the printer drivers shipped with OS/2 2.1, scroll down the list until you find the right one and select Install. You will be prompted either to install the correct disk or CD-ROM, or to enter the correct directory for the printer driver. This works with all the different cases, such as installing from disk, CD-ROM, or across a network. It also works with preinstalled systems.

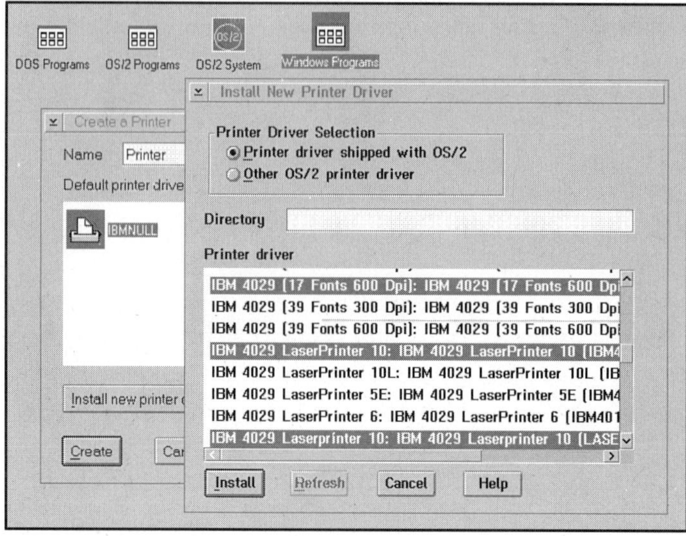

Figure 12.17. The Printer driver install dialog.

If you want to install a printer driver from a different source (for example, if you received a disk from a printer manufacturer), select the pushbutton labeled Other printer driver and select Refresh. Select the required printer driver object(s) from the list and select Install.

The OS/2 operating system always installs the IBMNULL printer driver so that at least one printer driver is installed.

Deleting a Printer Driver Object

To delete a printer driver object, select Delete from the context menu. You cannot drag the printer driver object to the shredder. If the printer driver object you are deleting is used by a printer object, a dialog is displayed (see Figure 12.18) that shows the printer objects that are using that printer driver object. If you still want to delete the printer driver object, you should open settings on each printer object, change the printer driver object, and close the settings.

You cannot delete a printer driver if there are outstanding print jobs that need the printer driver to print.

When there are no more printer objects using the printer driver object, you are asked whether you want to delete the files associated with the printer driver. If you press the OK pushbutton, OS/2 2.1 tries to delete the files. It is not possible to delete the driver files if they have been loaded by the system. (See "Replacing Printer Drivers" later in this chapter.)

It is not possible to delete the last printer driver object. You need at least one printer driver object so that new printer driver objects can be installed.

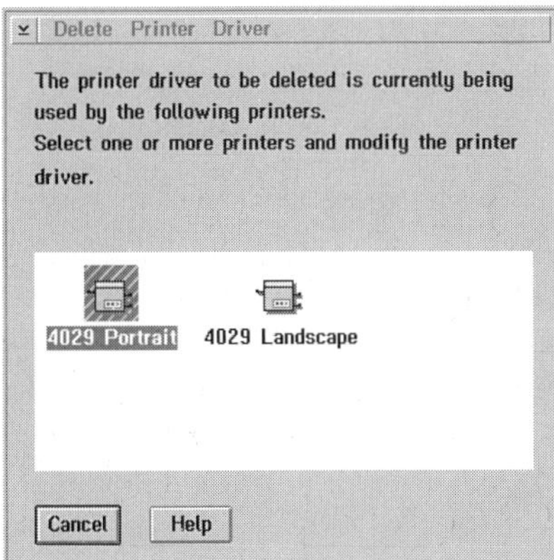

Figure 12.18. The printer driver object in use dialog.

Open Printer Driver Object—Settings

A printer driver object does not have a settings notebook as you might expect. Instead, each different printer driver object has a configuration dialog provided by the printer driver module. This configuration dialog is the driver Printer

Properties dialog. An example Printer Properties dialog is shown in Figure 12.19.

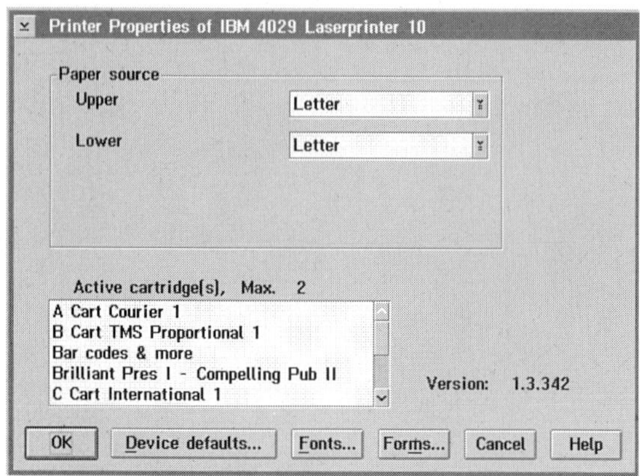

Figure 12.19. The printer properties dialog for the LASERJET driver.

Printer Properties and Job Properties

Each printer driver object has a Printer Properties dialog. Printer properties are configuration parameters about the printer hardware setup, such as which form is loaded into which paper trays or which font cartridges are installed.

A printer driver object also has a Job properties dialog, which is either accessed through a PM application or by selecting the Job properties pushbutton on the Printer driver settings page of a printer object. Job properties are options that are used on a per-job basis, such as orientation, resolution, or form.

All Printer Properties dialogs have combined printer hardware configuration parameters and other fields that look like Job properties. For some drivers these parameters are accessed through a pushbutton named Device defaults. The Device defaults dialog looks very similar to the Job properties dialog. These device defaults are used by OS/2 2.1 when printing a job that does not have any Job properties associated with it.

When the Printer setup menu item is selected for some older applications, these applications display a Printer Properties dialog instead of a Job Properties dialog. These applications are incorrect because any changes on this dialog also affect the printer object printer properties. These older applications also tend to list the printer name—an alias for the port rather than the printer object Physical name.

Copying/Moving/Shadowing a Printer Driver Object

Printer driver objects cannot be moved, copied, or shadowed. They exist only within a printer object.

Queue Driver Object

A queue driver object represents a queue driver. The queue driver is called upon by the spooler to pass print jobs on to the printer driver. There are two queue drivers shipped with OS/2 2.1: PMPRINT and PMPLOT. PMPRINT is the default queue driver and is used most frequently.

You should use PMPLOT queue driver when sending print jobs to a plotter to reverse clip the data. Reverse clipping is a process that clips overlapping areas so that the correct output is produced. Overlapping areas on a plotter can cause problems such as the wrong final color, running inks, and even torn paper that is overloaded with ink.

Installing a Queue Driver Object

A queue driver object can be installed using the Install context menu option on a queue driver object. The queue driver installation dialog is similar to the port object installation dialog.

Deleting a Queue Driver Object

To delete a queue driver object, select Delete from its context menu. You cannot drag the queue driver object to the shredder. If the queue driver object you are deleting is being used by the printer object, a dialog is displayed that shows the printer objects that are using that queue driver object. If you still want to delete the queue driver object, you should open settings on each printer object, change the queue driver object, and close the settings. When there are no more printer objects using the queue driver object, it is deleted.

It is not possible to delete the last queue driver object. You need at least one queue driver object so that new queue driver objects can be installed. This is why OS/2 2.1 always installs the PMPRINT queue driver.

Open Queue Driver Object—Settings

The two system queue drivers, PMPRINT and PMPLOT, have no settings, so the open settings context menu option is not available. Queue drivers from other sources may have a settings dialog.

Copying/Moving/Shadowing a Queue Driver Object

Queue driver objects cannot be moved, copied, or shadowed. They exist only within a printer object.

Spooler Object

The spooler object initially resides in the System Setup folder under the OS/2 System folder. The spooler object allows control over the spooler, which is responsible for queuing and dequeueing all print jobs (job objects).

The spooler object can only be moved, shadowed, or opened. In addition, it has some unique features such as disabling and enabling the spooler.

Open Spooler Object—Settings

The spooler object has two settings pages: Spool path and Print priority.

The Spool path page contains one field with the name of the spool path. This is where all print jobs are stored—in subdirectories under this path. If you are running out of space on your install disk, you can move this spool path to another disk that has more space. You can change the spool path only when there are no print jobs in any of the printer objects.

The Print priority page (Figure 12.20) contains a slider that allows you to alter the priority of printing jobs in OS/2 2.1; the higher the value, the higher the priority given to the print subsystem. For general system use, the default value should not be changed. For print servers, the value can be increased to 150 or more, although the rest of OS/2 2.1 (for example, the user interface) will seem very sluggish.

Disabling the Spooler

The spooler can be disabled using the Disable spooler option on the context menu. There are few reasons ever to disable the OS/2 spooler. One reason would be that you are using only WIN-OS2 applications, and you want to see all print jobs in the WIN-OS2 Print Manager rather than a printer object.

The disabling of the spooler does not take effect until you restart your system.

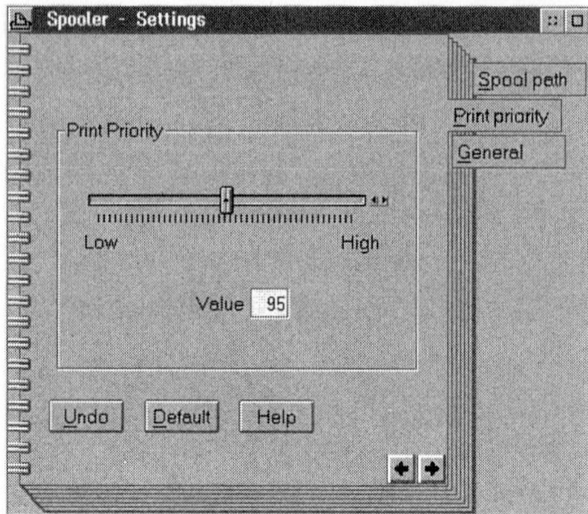

Figure 12.20. Spooler object Print priority settings page.

When the spooler is disabled, print jobs from different sources can appear on the same sheet of paper because OS/2 2.1 has no way of keeping the print jobs separate without the spooler.

Enabling the Spooler

The spooler can be enabled (if previously disabled) using the Enable spooler option on its context menu. This option takes effect immediately.

Differences Between OS/2 2.1 and OS/2 1.3 Print Subsystems

If you are familiar with the OS/2 1.3 Print Manager and Control Panel, this section will help you understand where they went in OS/2 2.1.

The 1.3 Print Manager displayed the jobs for all print queues in one list. For 2.1, the jobs for each queue are displayed in a printer object open view. A printer object details view closely matches the 1.3 Print Manager job list.

The set-up of queues and printers is now all done in printer object settings pages. The end-user concept of queues and printers no longer exists. It is replaced with printer objects that are related one-to-one with 1.3 print queues. For example, two queues connected to one printer can be set up in 2.1 as two printer objects with the same port selected in the Output settings page, and a queue connected to two printers can be set up in 2.1 as a single printer object with multiple ports selected in the Output settings page.

The 2.1 printer object, unlike the 1.3 Print Manager, does not allow any illegal configurations. Also, the 2.1 printer object ensures that any printer objects connected to the same port but with different printer drivers do not allow the user to deselect printer drivers that are actually used by other printer objects. This is why sometimes when you deselect a printer driver, close the settings notebook, and then reopen the notebook, the printer driver is selected again.

The 1.3 Control Panel installation of printer drivers, queue drivers, and port configurations has been moved to port, printer driver, and queue driver objects within a printer object settings notebook.

WIN-OS2 Print Subsystem

The WIN-OS2 print support is provided through the WIN-OS2 Control Panel and WIN-OS2 Print Manager. If you run WIN-OS2 applications frequently in a window, you may want to create Control Panel and Print Manager icons and shadow them onto your desktop.

WIN-OS2 Control Panel

The WIN-OS2 Control Panel allows you to configure your WIN-OS2 printers and ports. When you create a printer object, OS/2 2.1 checks to see whether it can create an equivalent WIN-OS2 configuration and asks you whether you want to do this. In other cases you may have to create a WIN-OS2 printer yourself.

If you create a WIN-OS2 printer, you should create an equivalent printer object. If there is no OS/2 equivalent printer driver, IBMNULL can be used. You can use this printer object to manage all print jobs in one central place.

I recommend that you select ports with names like LPT1.OS2. Ports with the .OS2 extension have better spooling performance. If these ports do not exist, you can manually edit WIN.INI and insert them into the ports section.

If you are using COM1 to COM4 serial ports, you must ensure that the port configuration in WIN-OS2 matches the OS/2 port configuration.

WIN-OS2 Print Manager

To get the advantages of multithreading and multiple printer objects, leave the OS/2 spooler enabled, even if you print only from WIN-OS2. If you do this, print jobs for a parallel port do not show up in the WIN-OS2 Print Manager, but in the equivalent printer object instead.

Leave the WIN-OS2 Print Manager enabled so that you will be able to see print jobs destined for COM1 to COM4. It does no harm because print jobs destined for LPT1 to LPT3 will not be spooled twice; OS/2 2.1 captures the data before it arrives at the WIN-OS2 Print Manager and creates a print job in the printer object.

Network Printing

This section describes how to print on the network. It also describes the Workplace Shell features that make it easier for you to perform network printing and network print management.

This section also concentrates on the relationship of the network-independent shell and print subsystem. The other details of the network-independent shell are given in Chapter 5, "Workplace Shell Objects." This section describes the network printer object and how it relates to the printer object described earlier in this chapter. It also describes the differences between the printer object and network printer object. Throughout this section on network printing, a printer object is referred to as a *local* printer object to differentiate it from a *network* printer object.

Network Printer Object

You can find network printer objects in the Network Object folder. First you need to open the network object, then the network group object, and finally the server object. There is also a network printer object template in the Templates folder.

Network printer objects represent print queues on a remote network server. Many of the same actions for a local printer object are also available for a network printer object. There are some restrictions, but there are also some additional functions.

Creating a Network Printer Object

You cannot ordinarily create network printer objects. The network printer objects that OS/2 2.1 displays in a server folder object are objects that refer to the actual print queues on the server. It is possible for a LAN administrator, using either the Workplace Shell or the network requester-specific interfaces, to create print queues on a server. Once created, OS/2 2.1 shows these new network printer objects in the Network folder.

Deleting a Network Printer Object

You can delete a network printer object in the usual way. You should note, however, that because these objects are references, you have deleted only the reference, not the real object. Hence, you will see these network printer objects reappear in the Server folder.

If you delete a network printer object, you also uninitialize it.

Copying, Moving, and Shadowing a Network Printer Object

You can copy, move, or shadow a network printer object in the usual way. I recommend that you shadow network printer objects onto your desktop for future use. Whenever you copy, move, or shadow a network printer object, some extra initialization is performed.

Open Network Printer Object—Icon View

Icon view is the default open view. The network printer object uses an icon to represent each job object in the queue. In the icon view you can see both print jobs that belong to you and print jobs that belong to others. OS/2 2.1 shows other people's jobs as grayed icons; you cannot act on these icons (see Figure 12.21). Using the Network Job View setting, you can choose to show all the print jobs in the queue or just the print jobs that belong to you.

If you have administrator privilege, you have access to all the print jobs in the queue; OS/2 2.1 does not gray any job object icons.

Open Network Printer Object—Details View

Details view is similar to icon view in that OS/2 2.1 shows grayed detail lines for those print jobs to which you do not have access.

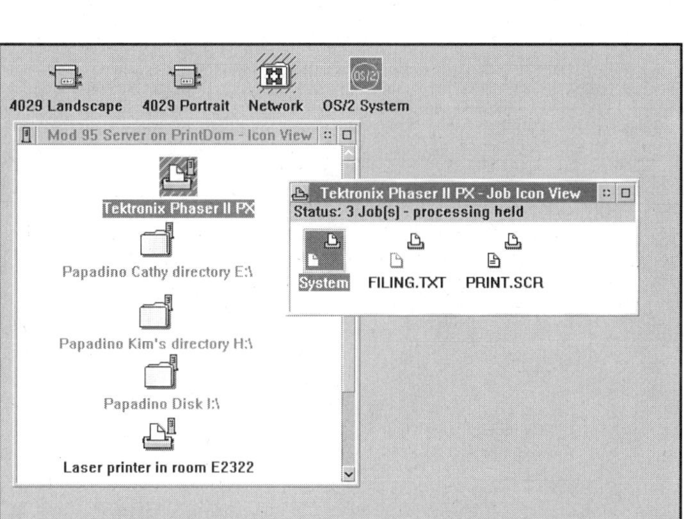

Figure 12.21. Icon view for network printer object.

Open Network Printer Object—Settings

A network printer object can have as many as seven settings pages. The Window page is the same as that for any other Workplace object. The last page is a new page named Network status. The General page is not available for a network printer object. The other five pages are similar to the five for local printer object. The differences are described as follows.

The View page for a network printer object (see Figure 12.22) has two extra fields. Use the Network Job View pushbutton group to select whether a network printer object open view shows all the jobs in the print queue, or just the jobs that belong to you.

TIP If you show all the jobs, you can see the ordering of your jobs among the rest of the jobs in the queue. If you show just your

own jobs, you can view a shorter list of jobs and know that you can manipulate all the jobs in this open view.

You can use the Refresh interval field to determine how often OS/2 2.1 refreshes an open view of the network printer object. I recommend keeping the refresh interval at least 30 seconds or longer because the network printer object does a network query at the end of each interval that affects the performance of your machine.

For network printer objects with large queues (more than 100 jobs), you should set the interval even higher, to 300 seconds, for example.

You can use the Refresh context menu item on a network printer object to refresh the open view at any time.

A network printer object still queries the network even if you minimize or hide the open view of a network printer object. To avoid this network traffic, close the open view instead of minimizing it.

A Refresh interval set to zero turns off automatic refreshing of the network printer object open view. You can use Refresh from the context menu to refresh the open view.

The Printer driver page is the same format as for a local printer object. The Printer driver window is read-only for network printer objects on an IBM LAN Server. It reflects the printer drivers installed on the server. If you are an administrator, the Printer driver window is read-write. You cannot install or delete printer drivers unless you go to the server itself.

For network printer objects on a Novell NetWare server, the Printer driver window reflects the printer drivers installed on your local machine because NetWare does not recognize the concept of printer drivers.

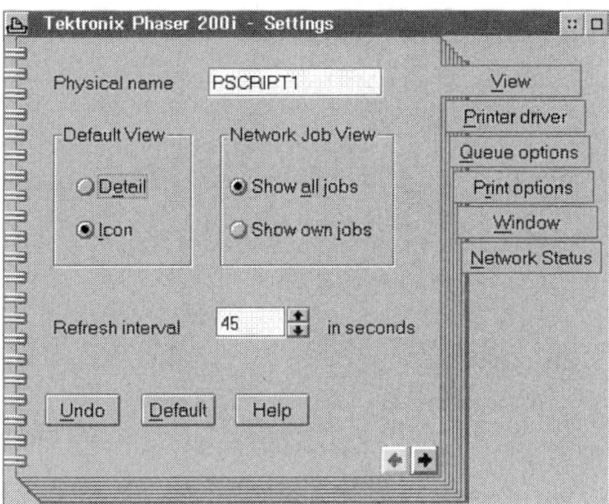

Figure 12.22. *Network printer object View settings page.*

The Default printer driver window is also read-only for network printer objects on an IBM LAN Server. If you have LAN Server administrator authority, you can select a different printer driver as the default.

If you are using Novell NetWare, the Default printer driver window is read/write. If you alter the default printer driver, it may no longer match the printer connected to the server and you will get the wrong results. Of course, you may alter it to match the printer that you know is connected to the server.

If you are a Novell NetWare administrator, I recommend that you set the printer driver for the network printer object. Then when a user initializes this network printer object, OS/2 2.1 will prompt for the correct printer driver.

If you are an administrator, do not change the Default printer driver unless you are willing to have all your users update their configurations, too. A better idea is to create a new network printer object and phase out the old one over time.

A printer driver object settings (printer properties) dialog is available if you are an administrator and if the network printer object exists on a server that uses IBM LAN Server 2.0 or later.

The network printer object Job properties pushbutton and subsequent printer driver Job properties dialog is always available. OS/2 2.1 stores the default job properties for the network printer on your local machine. It is even possible to copy a network printer object, change the default job properties, and have more than one network printer object pointing to a print queue on a server. This is particularly useful if you want variations on a standard network printer object provided by the administrator.

If you are an administrator, OS/2 2.1 stores any changes you make to the network printer object job properties on the server.

The Output page is shown only if you are an administrator and the network printer object is on a server running IBM LAN Server. The Output port window displays the port objects that are available on the server. You cannot install or delete a port object unless you go to the server itself. You can, however, change the ports that are used by the network printer object.

The port objects in this window may use a different icon than what you expect. This is the default port icon when the port object does not provide one.

The Queue options page has a queue driver window that displays the queue driver objects available on the server. You cannot install or delete a queue driver object unless you go to the server itself. If you have administrator privilege you can, however, change the queue driver object that is used by the network printer object.

The Job dialog before print option is available for network printer objects.

OS/2 2.1 checks and grays the Printer-specific format option for network printer objects on a Novell NetWare server. This denotes that NetWare print server queues accept print data only in a format ready for printing; they cannot accept the PM device-independent format because the servers run native DOS.

You can check the Printer-specific format option for a server running IBM LAN Server. This results in much more network traffic, however, because the print job is much larger than it would be using the PM device-independent format.

The Print while spooling option is unavailable for a network printer object; it is removed from the dialog. This is because OS/2 2.1 cannot allow printing while spooling to a network printer object; one user with a long print job or a bad application could block the whole print queue from everyone else.

The Print options page is read-only unless you are an administrator. The reason that OS/2 2.1 still shows the Print options page is so that you can see the start and stop times for the network printer object. If you have administrator privilege, you can alter all the fields on this dialog.

You must enter a filename in the Separator file field that refers to a valid path and filename from the server's point of view—not from your point of view.

The Network Status page (see Figure 12.23) shows read-only information about the network printer object.

The Resource field is also the physical name of the network queue and the name with which the administrator is probably familiar.

The resource name of the network printer object should be unique across the network or set of printers that the user may use. This is because OS/2 2.1 uses the resource name on the user's workstation, and some applications may present these physical names, rather than the printer object descriptions, in a list.

The network Description is the name of the network printer object. The administrator may not have defined a description for the print queue on the

server. In this case OS/2 2.1 derives a name from the Network, Server, and Resource fields such as LS\LANSRV2\LAN4019.

The administrator should always provide a description of the network printer object. The first seven or eight characters of this name should match the resource name. The rest of the description can provide more detail, such as the room or department where the printer is kept.

The Assigned port field shows whether there is a port assigned to this network printer object. An assigned port is necessary only for non-PM application printing.

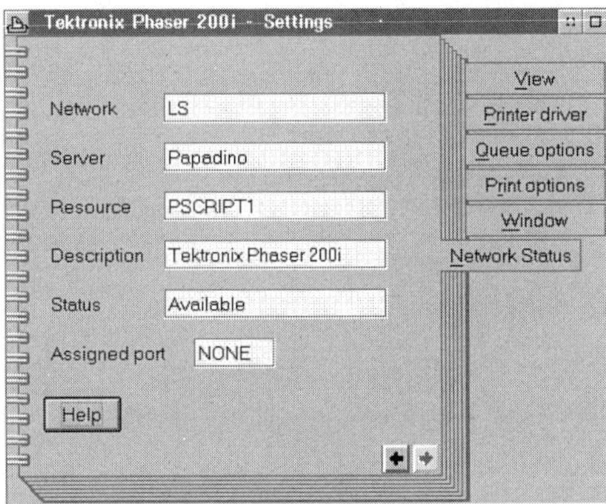

Figure 12.23. Network printer object Network Status page.

Set Default (Network) Printer Object

OS/2 2.1 defines the list of printer objects for the Set default list. The list contains all local printer objects and all network printer objects that you have initialized. This means that you can select a network printer object as your default printer.

The Set default list does *not* contain all the network printer objects available on the network because this list would be too large; it lists only those you have initialized.

Changing Network Printer Status (Hold or Release)

OS/2 2.1 adds the Change status option to a network printer object context menu only if you have administrator privilege.

Deleting All Jobs from a Network Printer Object

OS/2 2.1 adds the Delete all jobs option to a network printer object context menu only if you have administrator privilege and there are print jobs in the queue.

Refreshing a Network Printer Object

You can refresh the contents of a network printer object open view at any time by selecting Refresh from the context menu.

If you select Refresh, OS/2 2.1 resets the Refresh interval timer. This prevents OS/2 2.1 from performing an unwanted refresh immediately after you selected the Refresh action.

Login/Logout from a Network Printer Object

If you log in to a network, you can choose to log out at any time by selecting Logout from the network printer object context menu. Logout is also available on other network objects. You can log in to a network using the Login context menu item.

The names for the Login and Logout menu items are meant to be generic; other users may be more familiar with logon and logoff.

The network printer object shows either Login or Logout on the context menu, depending upon which is applicable at the time.

The network printer object determines the level of network authorization required and displays all the appropriate Login dialogs. For example, a network printer object resource on a server running IBM LAN Server may require a Log-in at the network level and at the server level. OS/2 2.1, therefore, displays two Login dialogs.

Assign/Unassign Port for a Network Printer Object

You can assign a port such as LPT1 or LPT7 for the network printer object by selecting Assign port from the context menu. OS/2 2.1 displays a further dialog consisting of a list of ports LPT1 to LPT3. OS/2 2.1 does not show any ports already assigned to other network printer objects. The port assignment is equivalent to doing an IBM LAN Server `NET USE` command or a Novell NetWare `MAP` command. You can find the current port assignment for a network printer object on the Network Status settings page. You can use this port assignment for any applications that print using a port name such as LPT1 or LPT7.

You may wish to install LPT4 to LPT9 using the REXX program in Listing 12.1 (shown previously) so that more ports are available for the Assign port.

You can remove the port assignment using the Unassign port option on the network printer object context menu.

Accessing Another Network Printer Object

You can access a network printer object on other domains or in other networks in three different ways:

1. Add the IBM LAN Server domain names to the `OTHDOMAIN` statement in your IBMLAN.INI file.
2. Select Access another on the context menu of any network printer object.
3. Use the Network printer template that can be found in the Templates folder.

If you use the first method, the servers and network printer objects will be accessible via the Network folder as usual. The other two methods both present the same Access another network printer dialog (see Figure 12.24). You can select the network and enter the name of the server and network printer object that you want to access. The dialog also provides drop-down list boxes that show accessible network printer objects.

After you enter valid names and select OK, OS/2 2.1 initializes the network printer object. If the initialization is successful, OS/2 2.1 adds the network printer object to the desktop.

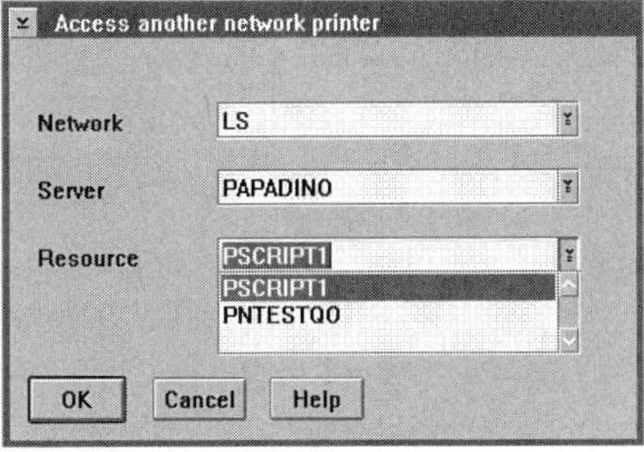

Figure 12.24. Access another network printer dialog.

Remote Administration on a Network Printer Object

If you have administrator privilege, you can perform some extra remote administration functions for network printer objects on an IBM LAN Server server.

Three extra functions are available from the Remote admin context menu item:

Create You can create new network printer objects on the server using the Create menu item. OS/2 2.1 displays the local printer object Create another dialog and prompts you for the printer driver and port objects to use with this network printer object. You cannot install new printer drivers or port objects from this dialog. You will need to share this printer object before other users can access it from their Network folders.

Delete You can delete a network printer object from the server using the Delete menu item. OS/2 2.1 will automatically unshare the network printer object.

Copy You can copy an existing network printer object on the server using the Copy menu item. The new network printer object is created on the same server. You will need to share this network printer object before other users can access it from their Network folders.

Initialization of a Network Printer Object

This section on initialization of a network printer object is key to your understanding of network printer objects. OS/2 2.1 automatically initializes the network printer object when you perform one of the following functions on the network printer object:

1. Copy, move, or shadow it outside the network folder.
2. Access another network printer object.
3. Drag/drop a file into the network printer object.
4. Change the printer driver settings or job properties.

In the first three cases, OS/2 2.1 initializes the network printer object because it assumes that you want to use this object in the future. In the last two cases, OS/2 2.1 initializes the printer object in order to perform the function required by the user.

TIP

The best method to initialize a network printer object is to move it outside the network folder to the desktop. This is because you can then readily remove it from the Set default and application list by deleting it. In the other cases you may not be able to do this because the object may no longer exist on the network and therefore cannot be deleted.

To initialize a network printer object, you must install a printer driver model that matches the default printer driver model used by the network printer object on the server. OS/2 2.1 prompts you for the printer driver name (see Figure 12.25) and if you want to continue, OS/2 2.1 displays the Printer driver install dialog (see Figure 12.17). If you cancel the printer driver install, then OS/2 2.1 cancels the network printer object initialization. The operation that started the initialization, such as a drag/drop of a file, is cancelled.

If the printer driver is already installed in your system, you do not have to install it. OS/2 2.1 recognizes that you have the correct printer driver installed and initializes the network printer object.

You must install the exact printer driver that OS/2 2.1 asks for in the dialog, otherwise OS/2 2.1 may prompt you again.

For network printer objects on Novell NetWare servers, OS/2 2.1 may not prompt you because it cannot determine the printer driver used by the network printer object (remember that NetWare may not use printer drivers on the server). In this case, OS/2 2.1 selects the default printer driver object used by the default local printer object.

The initialization of a network printer object causes OS/2 2.1 to create a hidden local printer object. OS/2 2.1 derives the configuration of this local hidden printer object from the network printer object. When you change settings such as Job dialog before print or Job properties, OS/2 2.1 stores this with the hidden local printer object. You can change other settings such as the

port object only if you have administrator access, because this causes OS/2 2.1 to change the setting on the server for the network printer object.

The hidden local printer object is *not* connected to ports; OS/2 2.1 handles the redirection of the print data to the network printer object. Because OS/2 2.1 does not limit you to using port names, you can print using a PM application to any number of network printer objects. OS/2 1.3 had a limitation of nine (LPT1 to LPT9) network printers. The limit for non-PM applications is still nine network printers at any one time because they need to print on one of the LPT1 to LPT9 port names.

Once you initialize a network printer object, OS/2 2.1 lists it in the Set default printer object list. The network printer objects also appear in PM application print destination lists. The hidden local printer object is shown in the Set default printer object list and in PM applications.

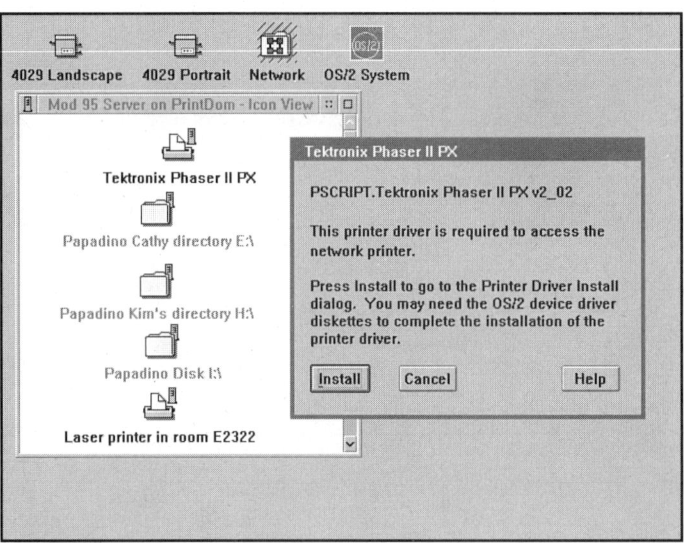

Figure 12.25. *Initialization of a network printer object.*

> TIP
>
> If you delete a network printer object, it is uninitialized. When you refresh the Server folder, the network printer object reappears. You may find this useful if the printer driver on the server has changed and you need to reinstall a new printer driver to match the server.

Job Objects in a Network Printer Object

As mentioned earlier, when you open a network printer object, you see jobs that belong to you and jobs that belong to other users. The only available context menu item for jobs that do not belong to you is Help.

For those jobs that belong to you, the following subset of functions is not available, compared to jobs in a local printer object:

- You cannot copy the job unless the server is running IBM LAN Server 2.0 or later.
- You cannot start the job again unless you have administrator privilege.
- You cannot print the job next unless you have administrator privilege.
- You cannot increase the priority of your job, but only decrease it, unless you have administrator privilege.
- You cannot open settings on the job printer driver object unless the server is IBM LAN Server.

Distributing Printer Drivers for Network Users

As an administrator for a network, you can configure the network so that your users can always pick up printer drivers from a standard place on the network. This is particularly useful when they want to initialize a network printer object.

From a maintenance point of view, you can control the level of printer driver available to users.

The best method for copying the printer drivers to the network is to create a separate subdirectory for each printer driver disk. Then when OS/2 2.1 prompts for the disk, your users can insert a standard UNC (Universal Naming Convention) path name such as \\SERVER\DISK\PRTDRV\DISK1.

It is even easier if your users installed OS/2 2.1 using LAN installation. OS/2 2.1 and later versions prompt for a standard directory derived from the LAN installation path, such as \\SERVER\OS2INST\DISK1.

Printing to a Network Printer

There are several ways you can print to a network printer, depending upon the type of application. For PM applications such as Describe and Workplace Shell drag/drop, you should initialize the network printer object first.

For non-PM applications including WIN-OS2, you must assign a port, such as LPT2, to a network printer object using either the Assign port context menu item or using a command unique to the LAN requester, such as `NET USE` or `MAP`. Then the application prints to the port and OS/2 2.1 redirects the data to the network printer object. You can also print to a network printer from the command line:

```
PRINT CONFIG.SYS /D:LPT2
COPY CONFIG.SYS LPT4
COPY CONFIG.SYS \\SERVER\4029LAND
```

Print Subsystem Configurations

There are a few different print subsystem configurations that you will find useful:

- print to a file
- sharing

- single printer objects with multiple ports
- multiple printer objects with multiple ports
- separator files
- DOS and WIN-OS/2 considerations

Print to File

There are many reasons for printing to a file. The most common is to provide a printer-specific print file that you can print on another system. This could be because the system with the printer connected does not have your application or you do not have the printer. For example, you print draft Postscript on your local printer and then generate a final version print file for printing on an imagesetter (typesetter).

The type of this print file is set to PRINTER_SPECIFIC. When you drop this file on a printer object, OS.2 2.1 does not bother prompting you for the file type: plain text or printer-specific.

To print to file, select Print to file on the Output settings notebook page. Note that the Output port window is now inactive. When the PM application prints, OS/2 2.1 displays a dialog for you to enter the filename. This filename could be any valid filename including a UNC name (for example, \\SERVER\DISK\OUTPUT.TMP), a pipe (for example, \PIPE\APP1), or a port name (for example, LPT1).

OS/2 2.1 does not provide a printer driver that just outputs text with no printer commands.

For non-PM applications, the application is responsible for generating the printer-specific print data—the OS/2 printer driver cannot do this.

Port with Multiple Printer Objects (Sharing)

Printer sharing is the ability to have multiple printer objects all using the same port and therefore the same printer. For example, you could configure two printer objects with different settings and drag/drop to each, depending on which settings you wanted. The sharing avoids the need to keep reconfiguring the print subsystem. There are three scenarios in which sharing is useful.

Multiple Forms

You may wish to print on two types of paper—say, legal and letter sizes— even though your printer supports only one input tray. In this case you create two printer objects named Letter LaserJet and Legal LaserJet (see Figure 12.26). Then in the job properties dialog for the printer driver, you select Letter for one printer object and Legal for the other. In the printer properties dialog for your printer object, you select the form that is in the printer (for example, letter). Any jobs directed to the letter printer object will print and OS/2 2.1 holds any directed to the legal printer object with a forms mismatch status. You may also want to hold the legal printer object. When you change the paper in the printer to legal and change the printer properties to match, jobs in the legal printer object will print and OS/2 2.1 holds those in the letter printer object with a forms mismatch status.

> **NOTE** A printer object holds print jobs with a forms mismatch status only if the application submitted a form name with the print job (using the `FORM=` parameter). This form name is in the Form name field of a job object Printing options setting page. For print jobs that do not have a form name, the printer driver displays a forms mismatch error message.

The second case to consider is when the printer has two input trays and is, therefore, capable of printing both letter and legal sizes. In the printer properties dialog you should set up the forms so that they match the printer; for example, legal in the top tray and letter in the bottom tray. Then use the job properties dialog of each printer driver object to select the appropriate form for each job.

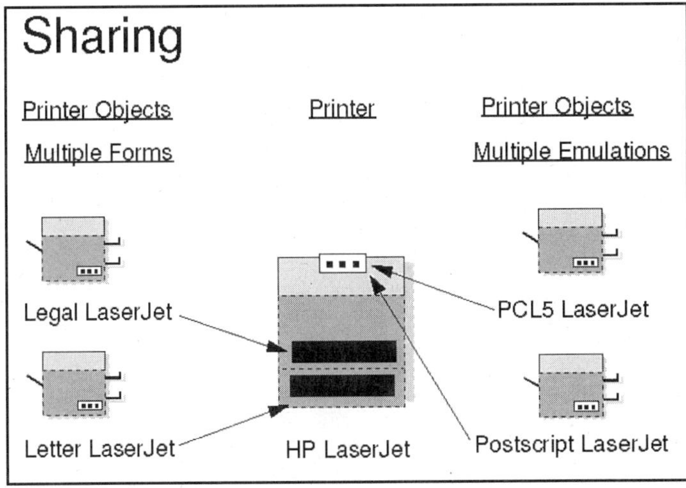

Figure 12.26. Printer object sharing.

You can set up a separator file with the appropriate printer commands so that the separator page is pulled from a different input tray. This allows for colored separator sheets.

The scenario of forms sharing is particularly useful for network environments.

Multiple Emulations

Some printers support two or more different emulation modes. For example, the IBM 4029 Laserprinter supports (with appropriate options) IBM PPDS, HP PCL4, HP PCL5, Postscript, and HP GL. For these printers you may want to drive the printer in different emulation modes, depending upon which application or type of output you require.

For those printers that have software emulation mode switching (such as HP LaserJet IIIsi or IBM 4029 Laserprinter), you can set up two printer objects with the appropriate printer drivers (such as LASERJET and PSCRIPT) and name them, for example, PCL5 LaserJet and Postscript LaserJet (see Figure 12.26). The printer drivers send the appropriate printer command to switch the printer emulation mode before sending the actual print data.

IBM provides a software emulation switching program named AES with the IBM 4019 and 4029 Laserprinters. This program was produced before OS/2 printer drivers incorporated emulation switching. However, the AES program can still be used for non-PM application printing because it allows you to print to multiple ports and route all the data to just one port. For example, you can send LaserJet output to LPT1 and Postscript output to LPT2 and ask AES to send all data to LPT1.

Other printers require you to manually switch the emulation mode; you should set up two printer objects with the appropriate printer drivers (for example, LASERJET and PSCRIPT). You then need to hold the printer object that uses the emulation mode to which the printer is not switched.

A few printers provide intelligent emulation switching in the printer itself. This method is reliable for most print jobs, but the software can occasionally get it wrong.

Using the IBMNULL Printer Driver

This case is an extension of multiple emulation modes. You can configure printer objects using the same port with different printer drivers that do not relate to the actual printer you are using. The most common example is to use IBMNULL in conjunction with another printer driver.

Select the printer object with the IBMNULL driver as the default printer object. OS/2 2.1 can now correctly print jobs originating from non-PM applications without a printer reset. All printer drivers, except IBMNULL, reset the printer so that it is in a known state. This printer reset may interfere with command sequences from the non-PM application.

Printer Object with Multiple Ports (Pooling)

Printer pooling is the ability to have a single printer object connected to multiple output ports. You can achieve pooling by simply selecting more than one port in the Output settings page of the printer object.

Printer pooling is most useful in a network environment in which there are several identically configured printers connected to a server. Pooling allows the print subsystem to spread the load of printing from one printer object onto more than one physical printer (see Figure 12.27).

"Identical" means that the printers have the same or similar configuration. For example, you could have an IBM 4029 Laserprinter and an IBM 4019 Laserprinter both using the IBM4019 driver with the 4019 Laserprinter model name.

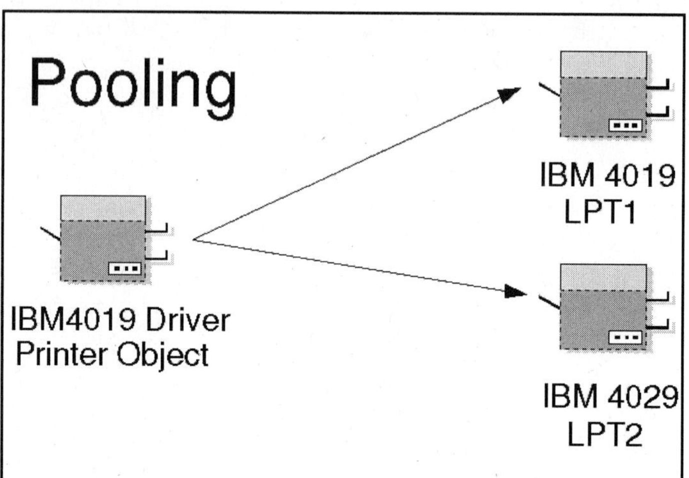

Figure 12.27. Pooling three printers that use the same printer driver.

Multiple Printer Objects with Multiple Ports

You can use sharing and pooling in combination to provide a variety of configurations. For example, you can connect two printers to a network server: one with two paper trays and the other with one paper tray. The printer with two paper trays also has a Postscript mode. You could create three printer objects: one pooled for the two printers using letter paper, one for legal paper in the first printer, and one for Postscript with letter and legal paper.

Separator Files

You can use separator files for several purposes. The normal use is in a network environment to print a separator page between two print jobs. The separator page may contain data about the time and date of job submission, the job identifier, the printer object name, and the owner of the print job.

The second use of a separator file is to configure a printer a certain way before OS/2 2.1 sends the data to the printer. You will need to use the IBMNULL printer driver because it does not reset the printer at the beginning of each job. Two sample separator files named SAMPLE.SEP and PSCRIPT.SEP are distributed with OS/2 2.1, and you can find them in the \OS2 directory.

DOS Considerations

There are three ways that a DOS application can print:

1. Using a call into DOS via the INT 21 interface.

   The OS/2 DOS emulation traps the request and sends it through the file system to the spooler.

2. Using a call into BIOS via the INT 17 interface.

   OS/2 2.1 captures the data from the DOS application using a virtual device driver (VLPT.SYS) in the VDM. Note that DOS applications that use the INT 17 interface cannot close the port, so OS/2 2.1 does not know when the print job is complete. OS/2 2.1 has two mechanisms to bypass this problem: the user can press the keyboard sequence Ctrl-Alt-Print Screen or use the system timeout. The default timeout is 15 seconds, but you can alter this with the DOS setting named `PRINT_TIMEOUT`.

3. Writing directly to the port hardware.

   OS/2 2.1 cannot capture this print data but prevents the OS/2 spooler from printing a job to the port at the same time that a DOS application is printing to the port.

In some cases a terminate-and-stay-resident (TSR) program needs to capture all INT 17 interrupts. For applications like this, you must load the DOS device driver LPTDD.SYS on system startup or on a DOS session startup. Printing from the VDM, however, will be slower. The configuration line you need for CONFIG.SYS or the `DOS_DEVICE` DOS setting is the following:

```
DEVICE=C:\OS2\MDOS\LPTDD.SYS
```

Another use for LPTDD.SYS is for applications that use INT 21 but do not close the port. LPTDD.SYS converts the INT 21 interupts to INT 17 interrupts. Then the keyboard sequence Ctrl-Alt-Print Screen or the timeout closes the print job.

Some DOS applications require the use of a parallel port attached security device (such as a dongle) before they print. This can be a problem because the application opens the port to read the security device but then OS/2 2.1 does not allow the spooler to open the same port for printing. This is not a problem with DOS, but OS/2 2.1 tries to prevent output from two applications from getting intermixed on the printer by spooling the data. If you have an application that needs a security device, you should use the Port sharing check box in the LPT configuration dialog.

You can use redirection to print to a serially attached printer (for example, COM1) from an older DOS program that can only print to LPT1. You need to create two printer objects, one connected to COM1 and the other connected to LPT1. In the Output settings page of the first printer object, select Redirection from the LPT1 port and select COM1. Now OS/2 2.1 redirects all output destined for LPT1 to the printer object connected to COM1.

The data created by PM applications is not redirected. In the previous example, any PM application print jobs for the printer object connected to LPT1 are not redirected to COM1.

For some DOS applications, you do not want the OS/2 printer driver to reset the printer. Instead, you want OS/2 2.1 to pass the data from the application to the printer unchanged. In this case I recommend that you create a printer object with the IBMNULL printer driver and select this as your default printer object. See "System-Wide Sharing" later in this chapter.

WIN-OS2 Considerations

You must ensure that the WIN-OS2 printer driver matches the OS/2 printer driver. If no match is available, you should use the OS/2 IBMNULL printer driver. Also, if you are using serial ports, the WIN-OS2 configuration in the Control Panel must match the OS/2 configuration in the printer object.

Print jobs printed to a serial port are not queued in a printer object but are queued in the WIN-OS2 Print Manager, if it is enabled. One alternative to this problem is to print to LPT1 in WIN-OS2 and redirect LPT1 to COM1. The print data from WIN-OS2 is queued in the printer object connected to COM1.

Printing from OS/2 Applications

This section describes considerations for printing from various OS/2 applications.

Workplace Shell Drag and Drop

The Workplace shell drag-and-drop interface is the most powerful part of the shell. This section describes dragging and dropping on a printer object only. See Chapter 4, "The Workplace Shell," for more information on drag and drop.

Selecting Print from the context menu of an object has the same effect, but it allows you to choose the printer object from a drop-down list.

When you drop a data file on a printer object, you may be presented with a dialog (see Figure 12.28) in which you have to choose the format of the data.

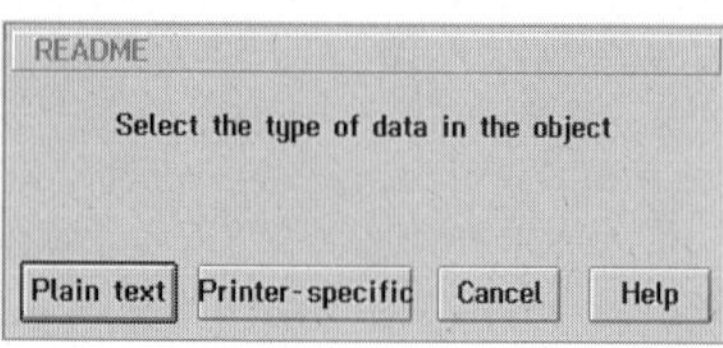

Figure 12.28. Data file selection dialog.

Select Printer-specific if the data file contains data in a format that the printer can understand (for example, PCL4 for an HP LaserJet printer or Postscript for a postscript-capable printer). Select Plain text if the data is in a normal ASCII format. OS/2 2.1 prints plain text by converting the data into a device-independent format that can be printed on any printer, even a postscript printer.

If you select the data type of the file to be Printer-specific or Plain text by using the Type settings page of a data object, the selection dialog is not displayed. Also, if the data file has been previously created by a print-to-file operation, OS/2 2.1 marks the data file as printer-specific.

If you want to vary the options each time you print with the Workplace Shell, you can set the option named Job dialog before print on the printer object Queue options settings page. OS/2 2.1 now displays the printer driver Job properties dialog for each file that you print.

Print Screen Key

If you press the Print Screen key while a DOS or OS/2 full-screen window is displayed, then OS/2 2.1 spools the data to the printer object connected to LPT1.

If you press the Print Screen key while the OS/2 desktop is displayed, OS/2 2.1 captures the screen and queues a print job to the default printer object. The print job data depends upon what is under the mouse pointer. If the mouse pointer is over a window that is in focus, then just that window is printed. The window could be a context menu or a minimized window on the desktop. If the mouse pointer is over the desktop background, the whole PM

session is printed. See Figure 12.29 for an example of the entire PM session print screen.

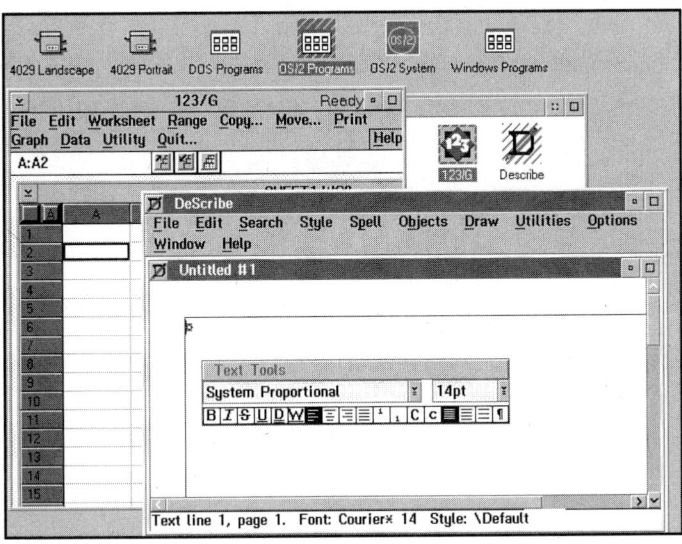

Figure 12.29. Print Screen of entire PM session.

A system menu, list box, or scroll bar, for example, is also a window. But print screen always chooses to print the parent window; that is, the outermost window.

OS/2 2.1 tries to fill as much of the paper as possible, so the size of the print screen on the printer page varies. Also, for monochrome printers, the printer driver has to map colors to either black or white. For example, printer drivers typically map yellow to white and hence it “disappears.” This may be okay if yellow is a background color with black text, but it may be incorrect if it is yellow text on a white background; OS/2 2.1 cannot tell.

TIP

Use a color printer for the best quality results from a print screen. Another alternative is to change the system color scheme to monochrome, do the print screen, and then change it back to the old color scheme.

You can disable or enable the Workplace Shell print screen function using the system object in the OS/2 System Setup folder. You may want to disable the print screen function if you have an application that also uses the Print Screen key.

OS/2 2.1 reserves the key sequence Shift-Print Screen for PM applications. If the PM application recognizes this key sequence, then it prints the area within its main window.

OS/2 Online Help and View Program

When you select the print function in the Help system, it queues a print job to the default printer object. Online Help prints text in WYSIWYG (what-you-see-is-what-you-get) format. This is why it may take longer than you may expect.

The online Help does not print graphics or bitmap data.

PICVIEW Applet

When you select the print function from the PICVIEW applet, it queues the print job to the default printer object. You can choose the number of copies you want on the print dialog.

The most common use of the PICVIEW applet is when you have selected Job content on a job object context menu. The print function is not available when you are viewing the job content of a print job.

PMCHART Applet

The PMCHART applet is a converted Windows program that executes under native OS/2 Presentation Manager; OS/2 2.1 maps Windows API calls to native OS/2 calls.

As PMCHART is derived from a Windows application, it understands only the concept of one printer per port. It does not understand print queues. Hence, if your configuration has sharing (a port with multiple printer objects), OS/2 2.1 queues the print job in the "first" printer object.

Describe

Describe is a word processor application. The Printer Setup dialog for Describe shows a list of printer object physical names (see Figure 12.30). You can ignore the name before the brackets; it is the alias for the port. Use the Change setup pushbutton to change the job properties for the print job.

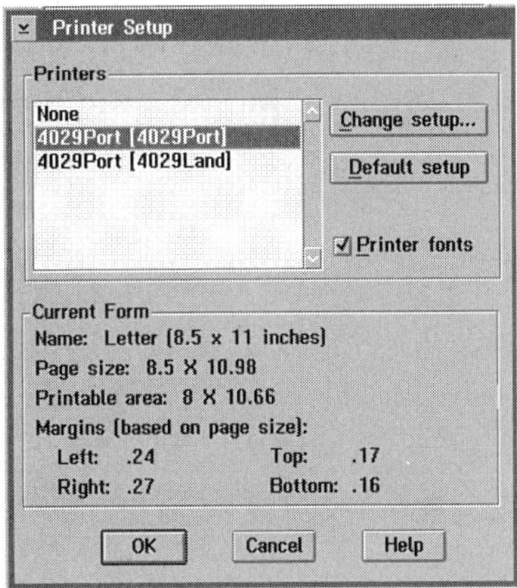

Figure 12.30. A list of printers in Describe.

Lotus 1-2-3/G (Version 1.1)

Lotus 1-2-3/G is the OS/2 version of the Lotus spreadsheet application. In Version 1.1 and later, the File Print Destination dialog for Lotus 1-2-3/G shows a list of printer object physical names (see Figure 12.31). Use the Setup push button to change the job properties for the print job.

Earlier versions of Lotus 1-2-3/G used the port alias names instead of the printer object names. I recommend that you upgrade to Version 1.1 or later.

Troubleshooting

This section presents a list of common problems with possible solutions.

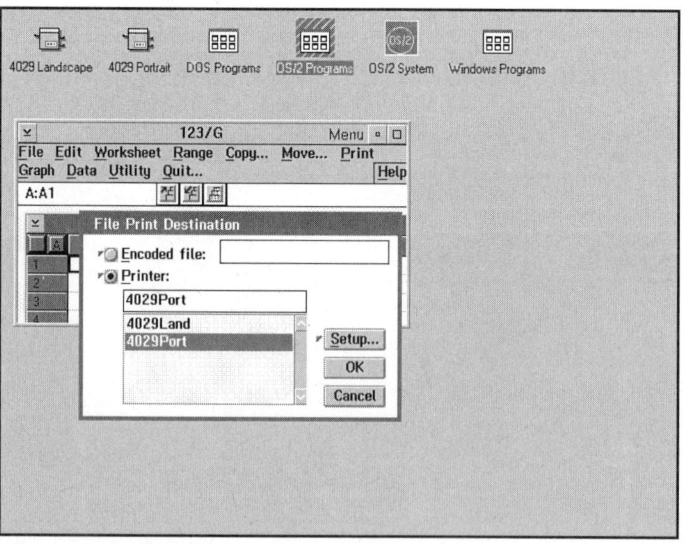

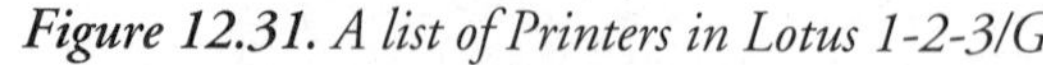

Figure 12.31. A list of Printers in Lotus 1-2-3/G.

Cannot Print Under OS/2 2.1

If you receive either of the following two messages:

- LPT1 not responding
- Printer off-line.....Retry Abort Ignore

then you need to check the following:

- The printer is connected to your system and is online
- You are using the correct printer driver and the correct OS/2 configuration

If there is still a problem, the most likely cause is that you have an interrupt problem. If the printer prints only one character or briefly flashes the busy signals and prints nothing, you have an interrupt problem. You can also verify an interrupt problem by running an interrupt test program under native DOS, such as PRNINTST, which is available on Compuserve in the OS2SUPPORT forum library 17 in PRNTST.ZIP.

OS/2 2.1 uses interrupts for printing so that it can effectively multitask. The interrupt wakes up OS/2 2.1 to the fact that the printer is ready to receive more data. Without interrupts, OS/2 2.1 would need to keep checking the signal wires waiting for the change that indicates that the printer is ready to receive more data, which slows end-user responsiveness during printing.

There are three causes for an interrupt problem, and you should check each in the order given as follows:

1. There is an interrupt conflict.

   For printing to LPT1, OS/2 2.1 requires IRQ7 (interrupt request level 7), and for printing to LPT2, it usually needs IRQ5. You should check other adapter cards in your system to ensure that they do not use the interrupt required by OS/2 2.1. One example of a card that causes problems is the Soundblaster audio card, which comes preconfigured to use IRQ7.

Table 12.1 lists the standard port addresses and interrupt request levels for different configurations of LPT1, LPT2, and LPT3.

Table 12.1. Standard port address and IRQ settings for OS/2 2.1.

Port	*ISA*	*EISA**	*MICROCHANNEL*
LPT1	3BC/IRQ7	3BC/IRQ5 or IRQ7	3BC/IRQ7
LPT2	278/IRQ5	378/IRQ5 or IRQ7	378/IRQ7
or			
LPT1	378/IRQ7	378/IRQ5 or IRQ7	378/IRQ7
LPT2	278/IRQ5	278/IRQ5 or IRQ7	278/IRQ7
or			
LPT1	3BC/IRQ7	3BC/IRQ5 or IRQ7	3BC/IRQ7
LPT2	378/IRQ7	378/IRQ5 or IRQ7	378/IRQ7
LPT3	278/IRQ5	278/IRQ5 or IRQ7	278/IRQ7

*Using IRQ5 or IRQ7 depends upon the EISA parallel card hardware.

2. There is a problem with your printer cable.

   Some cables do not meet the IBM PC specifications for parallel port cables because the manufacturer tried to reduce costs. All the interface lines should be wired and the cable should be double-shielded. DOS prints with this cable because DOS does not use all the interface signals in the cable. You should purchase a new cable that meets the specifications or that you know works with OS/2 2.1. The part number for an IBM cable is 1525612.

3. There is a problem with your interface card.

   To reduce costs, some manufacturers did not follow the IBM PC specifications for parallel interface. For example, the hardware fails to generate interrupts properly. You should replace the interface card with another one that works with OS/2 2.1.

Printing Starts When DOS Application Ends

If you can print successfully from some DOS or OS/2 applications but not from a particular DOS application, then the application is probably not closing the port. You can verify this by opening the printer object and finding a job object showing the job spooling icon—the green arrow is pointing towards the document.

After loading the LPTDD.SYS driver, you can use the key sequence Ctrl-Alt-Print Screen to signal the end of the print job.

DOS Application Holds Up Other Printing

If you start a DOS application and perhaps print some data and then find you cannot print from any other application until the DOS application ends, the DOS application is accessing the parallel port hardware directly. OS/2 2.1 prevents more than one application (including the printer object) from accessing the parallel port simultaneously in order to prevent overlapping of output data.

The solution to this problem is to end the DOS application after printing. You can also select the Port sharing check box in the parallel port configuration dialog.

Cannot Print from DOS with a Security Device on LPT1

You should select the Port sharing check box in the LPT port object configuration dialog (see Figure 12.14).

DOS Application Creates Many Print Jobs

Some DOS applications open and close a printer port for every buffer to be printed. This does not present a problem under DOS, but it causes OS/2 2.1 to create many print jobs: one for each open-and-close of the printer port. One solution to this problem is to disable the OS/2 spooler.

Disabling the OS/2 spooler may cause print output from several applications to be intermixed on the printer.

Forms Mismatch Message

This message occurs in the printer object when the form in the printer does not match the form required by the print job. You should insert the correct paper in the printer and update the printer properties by double-clicking on the correct printer driver in the printer object Printer driver settings page. The print job will then print.

You can also modify the form for the print job itself by double-clicking on the printer driver in the Submission data settings page of the print job and changing the form. This works only if the job has not yet started to print. You should use this option with caution because the application has formatted the data to fit one size of paper and you have now changed the paper size, so some print data may be missing.

Because some PM applications do not submit the correct job parameters, you may not be able to print any other jobs until you have corrected the forms mismatch for the current job. Other well-behaved PM applications will submit print jobs so that if a forms mismatch occurs, the printer object can continue to print jobs with the correct form. This latter case is particularly useful in a network environment because OS/2 2.1 reduces the number of times an administrator needs to change the form in a printer.

Job Stays in Printer Object Without Printing

A released job remains in a printer object without printing for two reasons:

- There is a forms mismatch error.
- The driver does not match. In this case, either resubmit the job or change the printer object configuration to use the correct driver. This problem only occurs if you change the printer object configuration while you are submitting jobs to it, or still have jobs held in the printer object which you later release for printing.

Performance Tips

Here are some tips to help you get the best performance from the print subsystem:

- For OS/2 PM applications, try to use device fonts whenever possible.
- For the OS/2 Postscript driver, set the number of fonts that can be downloaded to suit the available memory in your printer.
- For the OS/2 LASERJET and IBM4019 printer drivers you should select the Fast System Fonts check box (this is the default). If you have overlapping text and graphics you may get printing errors. In this case, you can get better results by disabling this option.
- If you are printing a draft document, try selecting a lower resolution in the printer driver job properties dialog (for example, 150 dpi rather than 300 dpi).
- For better application response time and less disk usage, ensure that you do *not* select Printer-specific format in the printer object settings page.
- If printing from a WIN-OS2 application is slow but acceptable elsewhere, you should try increasing the DPMI memory to 4 or even 6 Mbytes.
- If you own a PS/2 system that supports direct memory access (DMA) parallel ports (PS/2 models released in the last couple of years), then you should configure the parallel port adapter arbitration level to SHARED7 (enabled) to get DMA printing.
- You can increase the OS/2 spooler priority in the spooler object Print Priority settings page, but OS/2 2.1 will be less responsive.

Replacing Printer Drivers

You may want to replace the printer driver on your system for a variety of reasons. For example, if you have a new version from a bulletin board or you believe the existing driver is malfunctioning in some way.

The best method to replace a printer driver in your system is to use an OS/2 service pack. If you cannot do this, then the first step is to determine the state of the printer driver. A printer driver is active if OS/2 2.1 loads it to print or display the printer or job properties dialog.

If a printer driver is active, you cannot replace it. Therefore, ensure that no print jobs are using the printer driver, complete any printing, hold any printer objects, shutdown, and restart OS/2 2.1 so that the printer driver is inactive. Change the settings of all your printer objects to ensure that no printer objects are using the printer driver. Then delete the printer driver.

Install the new printer driver using the Install printer driver dialog and change the settings of all your printer objects to use the new printer driver object. You will also need to reconfigure the printer driver by opening the printer driver settings (printer properties dialog) in one printer object and selecting job properties for all the printer objects.

Printing Text on a Postscript Printer

If you simply copy a text file to a Postscript printer, the printer tries to interpret the text as a Postscript file. Here are several solutions:

- Drag and drop the data file onto the printer object. OS/2 2.1 creates a device-independent format print job that can be printed on the Postscript printer.
- Use a stand-alone application to convert the text into Postscript. Listing 12.2 gives a REXX program to print plain text on a Postscript printer. Many enhancements could be made, such as allowing 2-up (two logical pages on one sheet) or adding a parameter to vary the number of lines per page.

Listing 12.2. REXX Program to print text on Postscript printer.

```
/* PRINTPS.CMD - Print an ASCII file on a Postscript printer */
/* Written by Michael Perks (10/31/92) */
/* (C) Copyright IBM Corp. 1992 */
output = 'LPT1'
numlines = 80  /* lines per page */
pagelength = 792  /* points or 11 inches */
topmargin =  36   /* points or 0.5 inch  */
bottommargin = 36 /* points or 0.5 inch  */
leftmargin = 54   /* points or 0.75 inch */
linesize = (pagelength - topmargin - bottommargin) / numlines
parse arg filename
call stream filename, C, 'query exists'
if result = "" then
do
     say 'PRINTPS.CMD: Error, cannot find' filename
     exit
end
/* PS file header */
call lineout output, '% PRINTPS.CMD PostScript OUTPUT'
call lineout output, '/cour /Courier findfont 'linesize' scalefont
➥def'
call lineout output, 'cour setfont gsave'
/* read each line, quote characters and then output */
linecount = 0
pagethrow = 0
do until lines(filename)=0
     line = linein(filename)
     if pagethrow then do
          call lineout output, 'showpage grestore gsave'
     pagethrow = 0
     end
     line = quotechar(line, '\', '\')
     line = quotechar(line, '(', '\')
     line = quotechar(line, ')', '\')
     ycoord = pagelength - topmargin - linecount*linesize
     call lineout output, leftmargin ycoord 'moveto ('line') show'
     linecount = linecount + 1
     if linecount = numlines then do
          pagethrow = 1
          linecount = 0
     end
end
if pagethrow ¦ linecount<>0 then call lineout output, 'showpage
➥grestore'
call lineout output /* close output */
exit
```

continues

Listing 12.2. continued

```
/* quotechar - returns string with character "quoted" by another
character */
/* the quote character is also known as the escape character */
quotechar:
     parse arg newline, char, quote
     index = pos(char,newline,1)
     do while index<>0
          newline = insert(quote,newline,index-1)
          index = pos(char,newline,index+2)
     end
return newline
```

- You can install a device monitor that looks for textual data and converts it to Postscript. An example of this program is TEXTORPS, which is available from Compuserve.
- Start a word processor application and format the text file appropriately. You could choose to improve the text a little (such as putting headings in bold) before printing.

References

User References

- OS/2 On-line Help in Master Index and Printer object.
- *OS/2 Version 2.0 Volume 5: Print Subsystem* (Redbook) from IBM; order number GG24-3775.
- Schroeder, Frank J., "DOS Application Printing: Understanding the Differences under OS/2," *IBM OS/2 Developer* (Summer 1992), p.58-66.
- Schroeder, Frank J., "Configuring Parallel Ports for OS/2," *IBM Personal Systems Technical Solutions* (October 1992), p. 66-70.

Application Developer References

- "Chapter 18: Print Job Submission and Manipulation," *The OS/2 Programming Guide Volume III: Graphic Programming Interface.*
- *OS/2 2.1 Toolkit* PRTSAMP sample print program.
- Perks, Michael, "Application Printing using OS/2 2.1," *IBM OS/2 Developer* (Summer 1992), p.42-51.

Author Bio

Mike Perks (IBM Corporation) is an advisory programmer in OS/2 Technical Planning. He is responsible for OS/2 Presentation Manager planning. He was the designer for the OS/2 2.0 print subsystem and the OS/2 network-independent shell. He joined IBM in 1984 and has worked on many aspects of OS/2 since 1986. He received a B.S. from Loughborough University of Technology in the United Kingdom.

13

Productivity Applets

In This Chapter

Built into OS/2 2.1 are lots of programs that can get you started in OS/2 computing. You won't even have to go out and purchase any more software! (Just kidding!) These small programs are called the productivity applets. Although OS/2 1.x included some programs, such as System Editor and File Manager, most of those programs were designed to perform system utilities. In OS/2 2.1, the list of applications is extensive. Some are system utilities such as System Editor and the Enhanced Editor. There also are many other programs that perform a variety of functions for everyday use.

Productivity applets can be used right out of the box to draw charts, schedule lists of activities, set up alarms, create small telephone directories, calculate spreadsheets, and other tasks. There are 24 different programs. These programs are found inside the Productivity folder in the OS/2 System folder. The OS/2 System folder is one of the folders created during the initial installation and is found on your Workplace Shell desktop.

The Productivity folder is accessed by double-clicking mouse button 1 on the OS/2 system icon. For more information about using your mouse on the desktop, see Chapter 4, "The Workplace Shell." Inside the OS/2 System folder are many other folders, such as Drives, Startup, System Setup, Command Prompts, Games, and Productivity.

You may not see all of the applets described in this chapter if you did not do a full install of the operating system. One of the install options is to do a selective install that allows you not to install some applets.

The Origin of Applets

Most of these applets originated from IBM's own internal-use-only software. The Daily Planner and the other 14 programs associated with it were once part of a program called PM Diary that was created by Jeff Kerr from IBM UK. These were available to IBM employees only, and were later found on many electronic BBSs around the country.

In addition to the IBM internal-use software, several major software companies were contracted by IBM to create some of the other applets. One example is PM Chart, a draw mini-program developed by Micrografx. Another example is PM Terminal, developed by Softronics as a scaled-down version of their own Softerm Modular program. These applets can be found in the Productivity folder, shown in Figure 13.1.

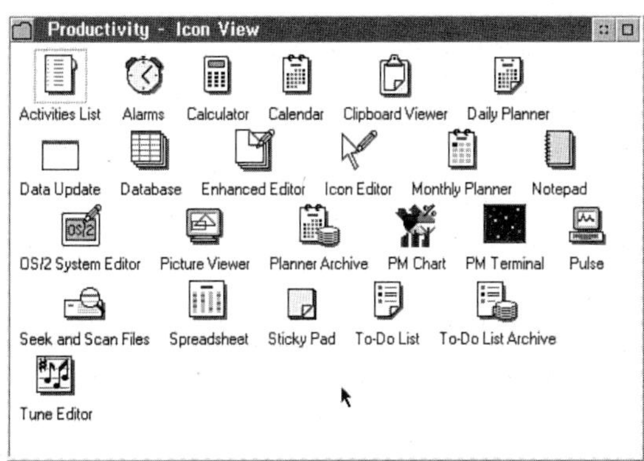

Figure 13.1. The Productivity folder with all the applets.

In this chapter, I try to describe most of the applets in as much detail as possible. Some of the applets such as the Notepad are quite simple, but others such as PM Terminal, a communication program, are more complicated applications, and to cover them in detail would be the subject for an entire book. To begin, I talk about my favorite applet: Daily Planner. With such a simple program, you can manage your schedules more efficiently. This applet is the driving force behind other programs.

Of Time and Planning—PM Diary

One of the most practical and useful applets in the Productivity folder is actually a collection of many programs that work together. The origin of these programs related to time planning, is from the IBM internal-use-only software. The original name of these programs was PM Diary. The number of programs that were part of PM Diary has grown from 8 to 14 and the list may grow even larger with subsequent releases.

Some of these programs share information; that is, when something is entered into one of them, the others reflect that change. Six programs share information: Alarms, Calendar, Daily Planner, Monthly Planner, Activities List, and Tune Editor. The best way to illustrate this is with an example from Daily Planner.

Daily Planner

To type the entry, place the mouse pointer on the first line and begin typing at the beginning of the first line. All the lines are divided into columns. Each column represents a field. The fields are Start, End, Alarms, and so on. Under the heading of Start you can type the hour and minutes of your appointment. The format has to be in hh:mm or, for example, 6:30PM. You can enter a blank space in front of the 6 or put a leading zero in front of the first digit. Simply fill in the entry completely and the cursor skips over to the next field. You can also use the Tab key or your mouse to move to another field. The completed entry is shown in Figure 13.2.

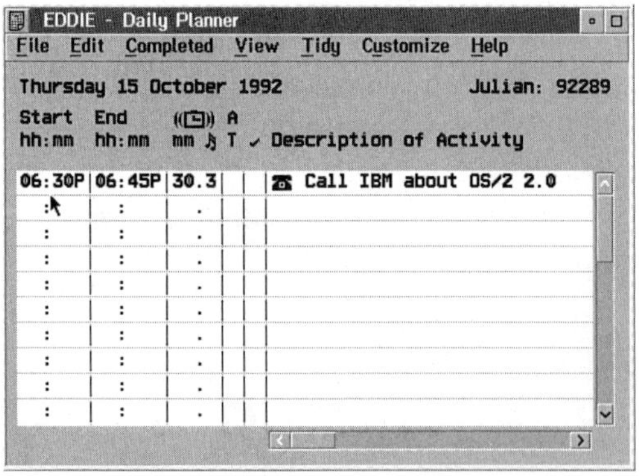

Figure 13.2. *The Daily Planner with a completed entry.*

Once you have completed the Start and End times, the next thing to enter under the mm field is the number of minutes before your appointment that

you would like the alarm to sound. You can enter a number from 00 to 59, or leave it blank. Leaving the field blank is interpreted as a zero.

You are required to enter only the Start time. The next field is where you choose the alarm tune to play from the Tune Editor. You can type the number of the tune to play or choose the tune from a list. To get the list of available alarm tunes, click on the Edit menu and choose the Select alarm tune. A pop-up dialog box follows that allows you to select a number for the alarm tune. If you leave this field blank it is the same as selecting the default tune, which is zero.

You can also add a graphic symbol to your entry and place it in the Description of Activity. This allows you to view the statistics on your planner archive files. To add a graphic symbol to your entry, select Edit to bring up a dialog box where you can click your mouse pointer (that graphic appears with your entry). In Figure 13.2, I chose the telephone graphic icon to remind me that this entry has to do with a telephone. By placing the graphic symbol at the beginning of the Description of Activity column, the program allows you to view the statistics related to the PMDIARY file. To view statistics on PMDIARY, select to bring up the pop-up dialog box with all the statistics of your file.

Using the following two steps, you can set up the alarms in the Daily Planner and they will automatically be updated into Alarms. Set the master planner file in Alarms by selecting Customize/Set master planner file from the pull-down menu.

1. Make an entry into Daily Planner and save the file.
2. Open Alarm and set the Master Planner File to the name used in Step 1.

> TIP
>
> You can set the Daily Planner to automatically start up when you first turn on your machine. Open the settings notebook in your Daily Planner. In the Program tab's parameters field type the name, of your planner file. You need to type only the first part of the name without the extension. Then make a shadow of Daily Planner and place it in the Startup folder. When your system

starts up, it opens the Daily Planner with your personal file and the alarms associated with your file. The alarms in this case will be minimized.

Activities List

The Activities List program in the Productivity folder is a read-only type of program. In other words, you can't edit any of the entries directly. To edit the entries in the Activities Planner, you have to start the Daily Planner or simply double-click with mouse button 1 on the item in the Activities List. All the entries in Activities List are from Daily Planner. This includes entries that have been deleted from the Daily Planner and moved to the Planner Archive. This program can be used to search for entries made to the Daily Planner and to print out a list of activities.

By typing the filename in the settings notebook, you can begin to use these programs in an integrated fashion. Once you start Daily Planner, the alarms will also be started and minimized. If you close Daily Planner, the alarms remain open and all the entries made in Daily Planner with an alarm continue to work.

Another way to automatically start Daily Planner with your filename is to create a filename association between Daily Planner and a data-file object. Do this by opening the settings notebook and selecting the Association tab. Under New name type `*.$D$`, the default file extension for PM Diary. Then create a shadow of your Daily Planner data file to add to the Startup folder. On initial start-up, your Daily Planner program will start and automatically load your data file.

For more information about how to add filename association to your data objects, see the Master Help Index icon on your desktop and search for "association."

Additionally, you can create a new type association instead of the filename association, but this requires an entry into the OS2.INI file using REXX to add this to your Workplace Shell. There is a program by Mike Felix called ADDEA.ZIP, found on the companion disk, that will assist you in adding new file types to your Workplace Shell.

Modifying your OS2.INI file using REXX requires extreme care. Be sure to back up your OS2.INI and OS2SYS.INI files before attempting this procedure. To back up your OS2.INI and OS2SYS.INI files, you need to place an additional statement in your CONFIG.SYS file and execute a reboot or IPL. For more information on backing up your .INI files, see the configuring sections in this book to back up your .INI files.

Listing 13.1 is the REXX code example for adding new file types to your OS2.INI file.

Listing 13.1. A REXX code example for adding new file types.

```
/* */
call RxFuncAdd "SysLoadFuncs", "RexxUtil", "SysLoadFuncs"
call SysLoadFuncs
call SysCreateObject "WPProgram", "Title", "<WP_DESKTOP>",
➥"EXENAME=EPM.EXE;ASS
➥OCTYPE=Type 1, Type 2, Type 3,,"
```

By typing your filename in the settings notebook, you can start all your PM Diary applets when you double-click on their respective icons to have them work together. Even if you choose not to type a filename in the settings notebook, they still integrate the information. The advantage of having your filename set in the settings notebook is that when you start each program, you'll be able to view information without having to use the File/Open pull-down menu to select a file to open.

Calendar

The Calendar program is another applet that is integrated in PM Diary. When you start Calendar, you have to use the File/Open pull-down menu to select the file to use. Again, the other alternative is to use the settings notebook to specify the file to use as the default. By using the same technique used earlier, you can put the name of your Planner file to use in the Program tab parameters field.

If you start the Calendar program and then choose a particular day by double-clicking mouse button 1, you start Daily Planner and it displays the day you selected. Calendar shows different colors for the days displayed. There is a color designating the current day of the month, one for every day that has an entry in Daily Planner, and also a color for the holidays, days you are out of the office, and weekends. You can change the default colors from the Customize/ Colors pull-down menu. This program is great for setting up appointments for many days at a time. You can also view the statistics for any month and it will show you the number of times that a particular type of appointment occurred. You must use a graphic symbol at the start of a complete or incomplete Daily Planner description entry.

Monthly Planner

The last two integrated applets in PM Diary are Monthly Planner and Tune Editor. Both of these use the information from Daily Planner. You can use Monthly Planner to provide you with an at-a-glance view of your monthly appointments. The Monthly Planner shows you each of the activities from Daily Planner and Alarms. The entire month is displayed in Figure 13.4.

When you double-click mouse button 1 on a particular day, the Daily Planner for that day pops up. I recommend setting the settings notebook to your PM Diary file.

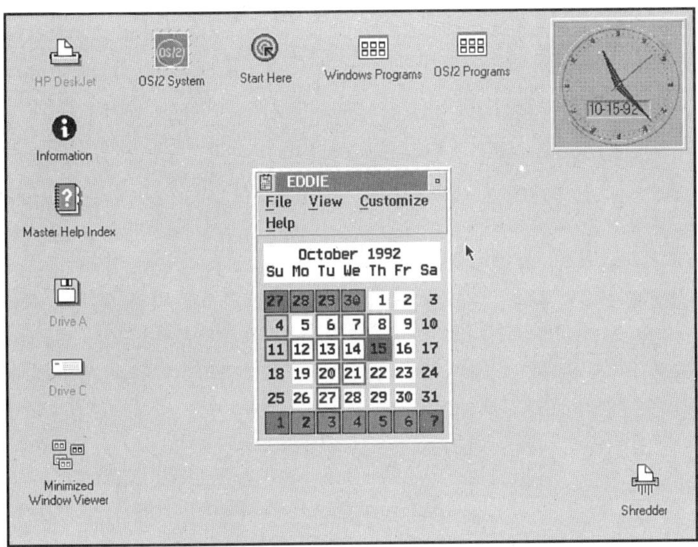

Figure 13.3. The Calendar program.

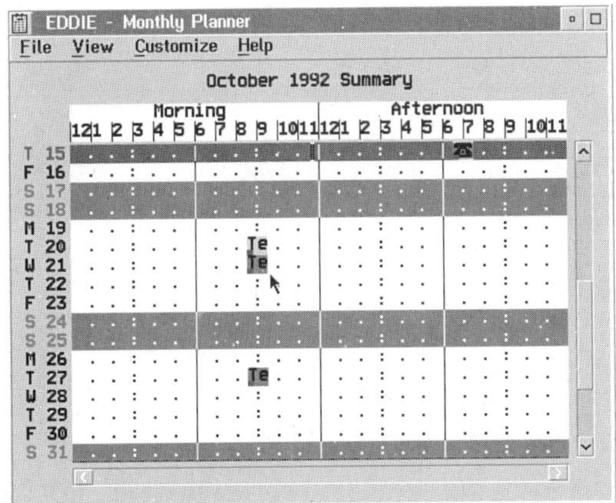

Figure 13.4. The Monthly Planner file.

Tune Editor

The Tune Editor provides the alarm tunes for PM Diary. This is the applet you use to edit and change the tunes that the Alarms program plays. If you feel like composing music, you certainly can do it with the Tune Editor, although I wouldn't recomend it! This applet uses the internal speaker in your computer to play tunes. These are used with the Alarms program. The tunes you can play are simple, but if you feel musically inclined, you can make them as "symphonic" as you want. Each file you create can have up to 36 individual tunes.

To create a new file, select File/New. When you first open Tune Editor, you have an untitled file. Figure 13.5 shows the Tune Editor with a Default tune in the tune title box. This tune is always your first tune unless you create a new one. To open existing files, use File/Open to open a dialog box showing your Tune Editor files in the \OS2\APPS subdirectory. These files have a $$A file extension. Double-click mouse button 1 on the highlighted file to load it into Tune Editor.

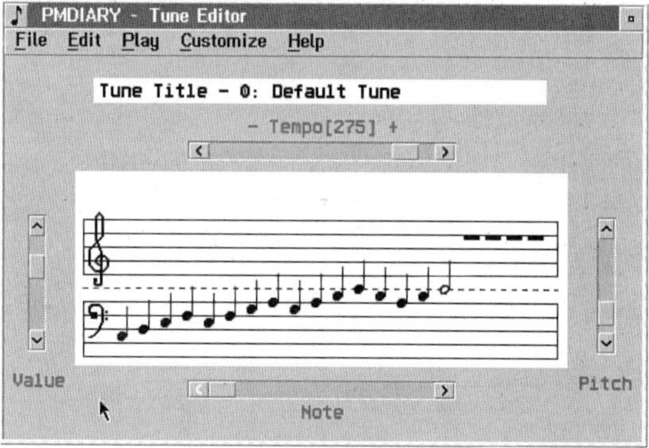

Figure 13.5. The Tune Editor started with an untitled file.

If you know how to write music, you can begin by using the slider arms on both sides and below the window to create tunes. To select a note, move the slider arm at the bottom, or move your mouse pointer and single-click mouse button 1 over the note. Select a Value for the note by moving the slider arm on the left. To select a Pitch, move the slider arm on the right, or click mouse button 1 to the new location. Finally, select a Tempo by moving the slider arm at the top of the window. There are 20 possible notes for each tune. The active note appears as a different color than the rest of the notes.

There are other possible notes you can place in the tune by selecting the Edit pull-down menu. This menu provides many choices not available when using the slider arms on the window. As you complete one tune, you can add more to your file by using the File/Open tune from the pull-down menu. Then select File/Save as to save your work the first time. When you save your file, choose a name and leave out the extension or use the $$A extension. The program automatically inserts the $$A extension. This way, the next time you want to use the file, it appears in the list box. After you create an entire file of tunes, make changes and save it using File/Save.

If you create a new file with your own custom tunes and you want to use that file in the Alarms program, rename the PMDIARY.$$A file to PMDIARY.TMP or some other name (your file will be changed to the PMDIARY.$$A filename). This is the default filename that works with Alarms.

Once you create a tune, you can begin to play it by selecting Play/Play current tune or Play all tunes from the menu. By experimenting with different notes, even a novice musician can be creative! As always, you can obtain more information from the online help by selecting Help from the pull-down menu.

Archiving

Both Daily Planner and To-Do List have programs associated with them called Planner Archive and To-Do List Archive. These programs provide a means to store your completed entries. You must mark your entries as completed and then choose to archive the entries. From the pull-down menu of Daily Planner, choose Completed/Mark line as completed, or select one of the other choices in this menu. After you mark your selection, archive that entry. Both these programs create files to store the archived entries. Planner Archive creates a filename with an extension of $DA; the To-Do List Archive creates an extension with $TA. I will have more to say about the To-Do List program later in this chapter.

Integrating the Five PM Diary Applets

One way to demonstrate the interrelationship of these 5 PM Diary applets is to open the program settings notebook on the following programs: Calendar, Daily Planner, Monthly Planner, Tune Editor, and Activities List. In the parameters, type the name of the file that you intend to use in Daily Planner. Now that you have typed the same filenames into all the programs that use PM Diary, open Daily Planner by double-clicking on the icon. Next, open the Activities List the same way. Now type an entry into Daily Planner and watch the Activities List as you select the File/Save from the pull-down menu. Did you notice that an entry was added to the Activities List? This entry is added only if you save the Daily Planner file. The same is true for the other applets mentioned previously. Once you execute the File/Save, all four programs will be updated at once.

Database

Database is another applet in the series. This program is intended as a simple way to store information, such as telephone numbers and addresses. Once you have created this database with phone numbers and addresses, you also can use this program to dial phone numbers.

To start a new database, select File/New from the pull-down menu. You need to type headings for your fields. A field is like a category in the database. An example of a field is Name—the name of a person. Another example is Address. The Edit menu has most of the functions you'll be using to create your new database. To begin, select with your mouse pointer over Edit/Edit line headings on the pull-down menu. Your cursor will appear in a newly created section, to the left of the rows of lines. This is the place where you can enter the headings of each field you plan to use.

You can type up to 8 characters for the name of each field. The contents of fields can be a maximum of 30 characters in length. After typing each field, you can move to the next one by pressing Enter. When you have completed typing the contents of each field, select File/Save before adding any more new records. To begin entering more new records, select Edit/Add a new record. Each record consists of 8 lines (or fields) and 30 characters in each line. You can have up to 5,000 records in each database; however, if you do have that many records in your database, you might consider getting a database program that can handle things like multiple indexing of records and creating customized queries and reports.

This database program is capable of sorting on 8 fields individually. To sort on a given field, choose the View command on the pull-down menu and select the field you want to use for sorting (see Figure 13.6). Place your mouse pointer on the Search Key box. Simply type a letter that you want to use for your sort. When you are finished typing the letter, you can see your records being sorted in the box below.

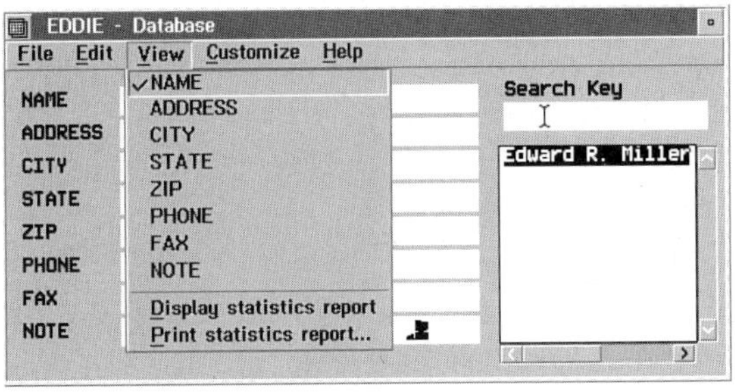

***Figure 13.6.** The sorting capability of Database.*

Once you have entered all your records into your database, save all your work with the File/Save pull-down menu. When you first save your database, you are able to access only the File/Save As menu. The reason for this is to allow you to pick a name for your database file. Once you are working with an existing file, you are able to use the File/Save menu.

TIP

To access your database quickly, open your settings notebook and look for the Program tab. In the parameters section, type the name of the database filename that you commonly use. You need to type only the filename (without the extension). Close the settings notebook. Every time you double-click on the Database icon, your database file is started automatically. If you are thinking about importing a database into this OS/2 applet, you need to have it in a format that includes a header on each file with a 183-character control record containing the line headings, the sort sequence, and the saved print list. You also need to have the fields separated by a split-bar character (ASCII 124).

Alarms

This applet has many different uses. Some of them are quite subtle, such as starting other applications. Others are just the usual ones of reminding you to make phone calls, send faxes, and attend meetings. Although there are more sophisticated programs for time management or personal information management, it's helpful to have a simple program to remind you of day-to-day tasks. This little program performs wonderfully when it comes to reminding you of important events. You can even start a program such as Golden CommPass, a CompuServe communications program, and check your messages on CompuServe or any other time-critical program.

Before you begin using Alarms, attach this program to the PM Diary file you have been using. In the previous section you learned that PM Diary consists of many different programs working together. To use Alarms together with other PM Diary programs, you must customize it. To do that, attach the Set master planner file to the same file you are using in Daily Planner. Figure 13.7 shows how to select Customize/Set master planner file. Once you start Daily Planner, all the alarms you set there will be updated in Alarms.

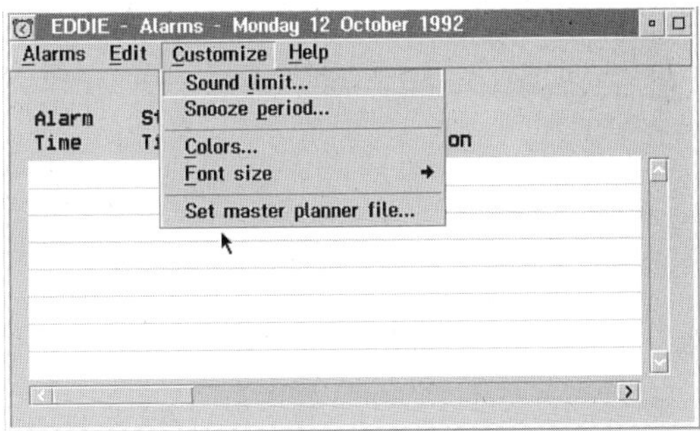

Figure 13.7. Customizing Alarms to work with Daily Planner.

You can set the Alarms from Daily Planner, Alarms, or Snooze. The last one, Snooze, is not an actual program but rather a selection once an alarm has gone off. Normally all alarms are set in the Daily Planner. You can also set up an alarm through the Alarms program. If you set up an alarm through the Alarms program, you will not make an entry into the Daily Planner. Figure 13.8 shows the Set Alarm pop-up dialog box, where you can set up the alarm and also have comments executed as commands. This example shows a comment to start a communications program at 8:55 p.m. This comment will be executed as `C:\GCPCOM\COMMPASS.EXE` at the preset time in the Alarms program, which starts the Golden CommPass program.

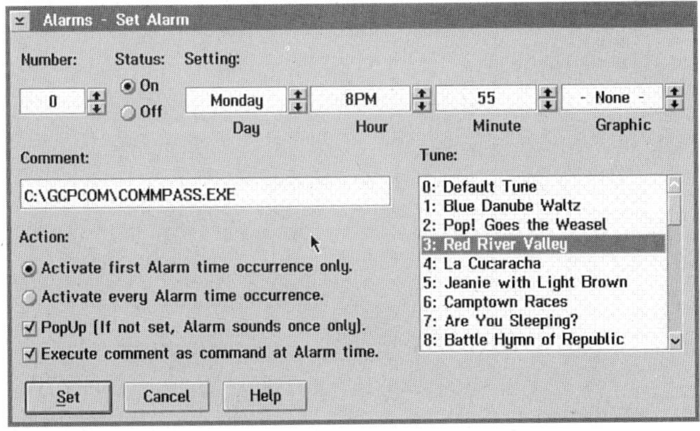

Figure 13.8. The Alarms dialog box to start an alarm or a program.

From the Customize pull-down menu you can preset several options. Some of them are Sound limit, Snooze period, Colors, Fonts, and Set master planner file. Using Sound limit, you can set the number of times an alarm should play the tune in the Tune Editor. For instance, how many times should you listen to "La Cucaracha" when 8:55 p.m. arrives? Surely even the most staunch Mexican folk song lover can have his or her fill of this song.

The Snooze period is set to default to 5 minutes, but you can change this to a different value. When the alarm sounds, you can choose the PopUp option in the Set Alarm dialog box (see Figure 13.8) and you'll be given the opportunity to select the "snooze" button. If you select "snooze" at that time, the alarm stops and is reset to go off 5 minutes later, just like a typical alarm clock.

Double-clicking with mouse button 1 on an entry in Alarms that was entered in the Daily Planner takes you back to Daily Planner, where you can edit the alarm information. If you select an entry with mouse button 1 in Alarms and then double-click mouse button 1 on it, the Daily Planner applet opens and displays that entry.

TIP

You can also set an alarm through your System Clock: open the system clock object settings notebook and select the Alarm tab. In this tab, you can set the date and time of the alarm and select a message box for the alarm. This gives you an alarm without any other notification. If you want a specific message to appear, you should probably use the Alarms program.

PM Chart for Business Presentations

Of all the applets in the Productivity folder, PM Chart and PM Terminal are the most powerful. To say that PM Chart is a complete application would be an understatement. This is a powerful implementation of the Windows versions of the Micrografx Designer program. What you may not see in this version are the extensive clip art, manipulation tools, file import/export, and visual effects available in the other versions. But make no mistake, you can do almost as much with this program as you can with the full versions! This is a very powerful program, and in many ways it has a better interface and runs faster than its counterpart in Windows. This is a preview of things to come from Micrografx in the OS/2 arena.

The best way to learn how to use this program is by example. In this example, I'll show you how to use most of the features of PM Chart, including drawing, clip art, using spreadsheets for graphs and charts, and text. You'll see how to use PM Chart for business presentations, but it will be up to you to experiment and learn all the features available. This section is meant as a brief introduction to PM Chart, not a full tutorial.

Some of the drawing tools require some practice, so don't be disappointed if your drawings don't come out well the first few times. Any professional graphic designer could tell you how difficult it is the first few times.

Using the Toolbar

Before I get started on the sample business presentation, I would like to highlight the many features of PM Chart by explaining how most buttons on the toolbar perform. The toolbar in PM Chart is located on the left side of the ruler. In Figure 13.9, the mouse points to the default select arrow tool. This tool is used to make selections from the pull-down menu and on the main screen. Use this tool for selecting and deselecting the objects you create. The toolbar includes the following tools:

- select
- worksheet
- view pages

- draw
- charts
- text objects
- color/style

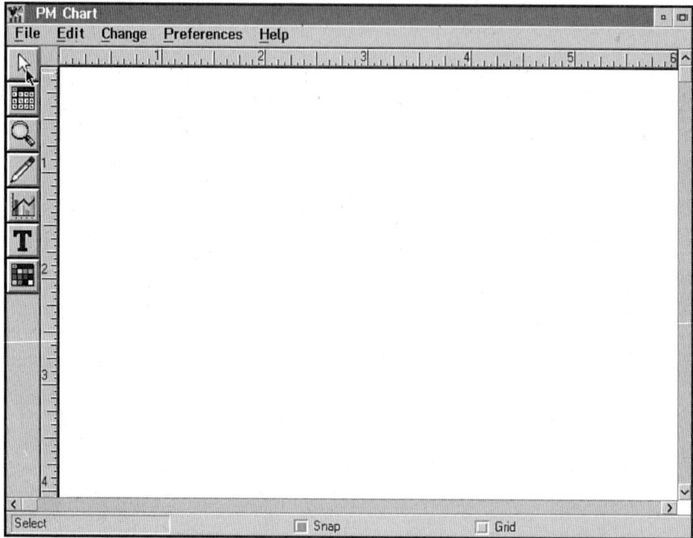

Figure 13.9. The toolbar in PM Chart.

TIP

To select an object on the screen without changing the tool on the toolbar, move the mouse pointer to that object and quickly click on it. When you do this, the object is surrounded by the selection symbol. To remove the selection symbol from that object, click the pointer outside the selection area.

The toolbar consists of icon buttons that represent functions to be performed by the program. In PM Chart you will find a new way of putting more tools into a small screen. The toolbar buttons contain subbuttons, thereby

minimizing the real estate used on the screen (see Figure 13.10). As programs become rich with features, they become more and more complex in the way they represent their features. Such an uncluttered screen in a program is certainly a welcome change.

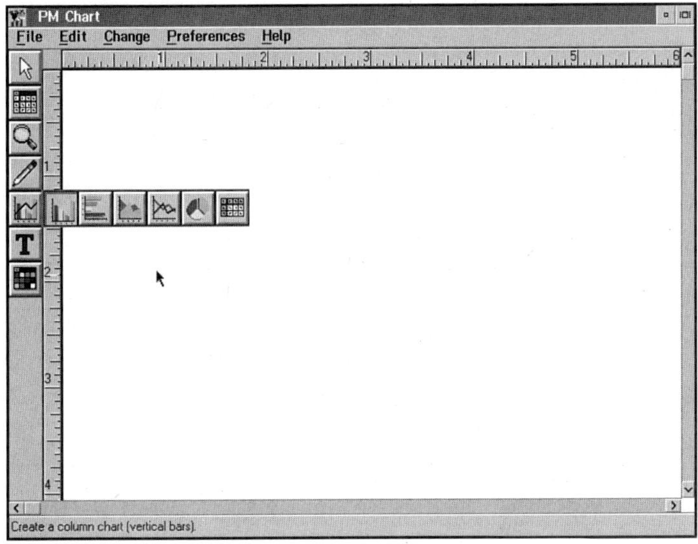

Figure 13.10. Subbuttons and the status line.

The toolbar consists of many different tools. It may not be obvious what each button on this toolbar represents. For this reason, there is a status line for each button in the lower-left corner of your program window. Figure 13.10 shows the description as "Create a column chart (vertical bars)." When you select a button under the main toolbar, you also get a description of what it performs (it appears only during the time you are depressing mouse button 1). Needless to say, this description appears only briefly. If you blink—you miss it!

The two toolbar buttons that are often misunderstood are View Pages and the draw tools. For that reason I have included a list of each button description for the View Pages button in Table 13.1 and the Draw button in Table 13.2. For more information on what each individual one performs, see the online help for this program.

Table 13.1. Descriptions of subbuttons in the View Pages tool.

Button	*Description*
1	View PM Chart work area at actual size
2	View the entire page
3	View all pages
4	View all pages containing symbols
5	Zoom in on selected area
6	Return to previous view
7	Redraw the PM Chart work area

Table 13.2. Descriptions of subbuttons in the Draw tool.

Button	*Description*
1	Rectangle or square
2	Rectangle with round corners
3	Ellipse or circle
4	Single line or multipoint line
5	Freehand object
6	Elliptical arc

Opening Existing Files

Begin by retrieving one of the sample files included in the program to show some of the basic uses of the program, and then follow this with a simple example of your own. The first step is to select the File/Open pull-down menu to select the file

GREEN.GRF. All PM Chart files are saved as *.GRF or *.DRW files. These are Micrografx Charisma graphic files and Micrografx draw files. Several other file extensions can also be imported, including *.XLS, *.WKS, and so on. The import of any of your spreadsheets created under Lotus 1-2-3, Quattro Pro, and Excel, can be used to create your business presentations.

First, change the default setting for printing from portrait to landscape. To do this, select Preferences/Pages to bring up a pop-up dialog box. Here you can choose not only the type of paper you want, but you can also change the orientation from portrait to landscape. The purpose of changing to landscape is twofold: to show the place to change the paper settings, and to allow you to do the next example with more screen area. Choose the toolbar button to view the entire page. Just place your pointer on the view pages icon and the other icon buttons appear. Choose the subbutton that has the page icon. The screen area is now 11 inches across the top by about 7 inches on the bottom.

Now that you have selected GREEN.GRF, your screen should look like the one shown in Figure 13.11. This is a file that shows the relationship between the awareness of the environment and time. By the looks of this graph, environmental awareness is on the increase, something we all hope is happening.

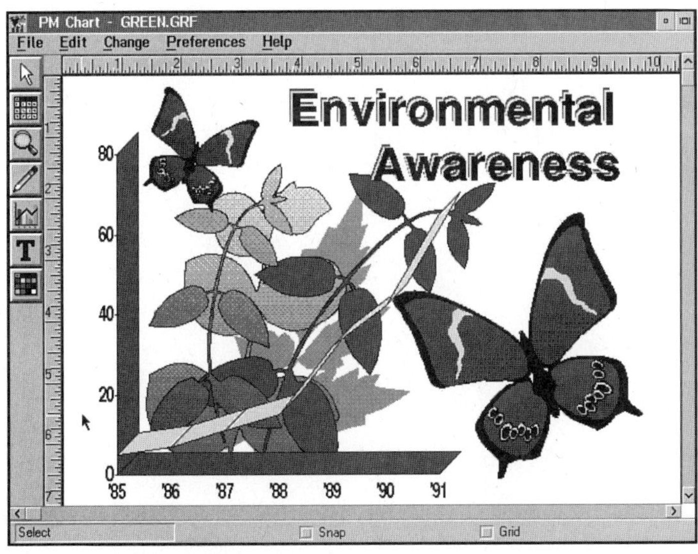

Figure 13.11. The file GREEN.GRF loaded into PM Chart.

Selecting and Manipulating Objects

Each presentation is composed of a worksheet data file, a graph, and several graphic objects and/or text objects. In PM Chart, all of the components of each file are individual objects—graphic objects, text objects, or chart objects. As objects, you can manipulate them by changing their size, shape, and color.

You can make an object active by placing the select pointer on an object and clicking mouse button 1 on it. Do that now, selecting the large butterfly on the lower-right side of the screen. The large butterfly should be surrounded by small square "handles." Place your pointer over the object and, while holding down mouse button 1, drag the pointer to the left part of your screen. After you release the pointer, the screen begins to redraw itself. The butterfly appears behind the other graphic objects. Why does this happen? It happens because the butterfly was previously set to Change/Move to/Back, using the pull-down menus, and you just moved it to the left, behind the graph. You can place an object either in front or in back of another object, creating the illusion of three-dimensional space. Congratulations! You have just mastered moving an object! By creating and moving objects around, you can place them where you want them for your presentation.

A pointer is the same as the cursor in a word processing program: it shows you where you are working. Also, there are various "pointer shapes" that appear, depending on what toolbar you have selected. The default is the select pointer. You get it by clicking on the top button of the toolbar (the one shaped like an arrow). An object must be selected before you can manipulate it with the Change pull-down menu. Be sure to select the object by placing the pointer on it and single-clicking mouse button 1. To verify that you have selected an object, check to see that the object is surrounded by little square handles.

Dragging an object and changing its size, as well as placing it in back or in front of another object, is most of what is done to create business presentations.

In the menu bar there are three choices that involve object manipulation. The first is the familiar Edit menu that involves the usual cut-and-paste choices, as well as the capabilities to Block Select and Select all. When you draw a graphic picture, sometimes you may want to connect objects together—for example, a series of lines in a drawing—and this is where these two Select choices are useful. More information on these menu choices is available in the online help.

The other menu selection is Change, with which you can move objects into background or foreground, flip, combine, disconnect, or duplicate them. To really learn how to use these tools, you need a demonstration. I will show you some of the uses of these menu choices. First, look at the example on the screen in Figure 13.11. This file is a completed presentation that was prepared by utilizing some of the menu items already discussed.

For example, the Flip menu choice allows you to make an object "flip" upside down. Try this by selecting the large butterfly on the right side of your screen, and then use the Change/Flip/Vertical menu. After your screen redraws, the butterfly appears to have been rotated around a horizontal axis; that is, the top of the object is moved vertically to the bottom, and vice versa.

You can manipulate any object this way, even if the object is composed of text. To be sure that I'm telling the truth, select the "Awareness" title at the top and try to flip it. You can try this a second time and restore the object to its original position. There are a lot of different ways to manipulate an object. You can resize it, that is, reshape its points. Try resizing an object now as an example. First, select the small butterfly on the top left part of your screen of the GREEN.GRF file. You should have the square handles around that object. Next, move your pointer to the lower-right corner and drag that corner diagonally to the right. When you release mouse button 1, the screen will begin to redraw and the butterfly will have increased in size, as shown in Figure 13.12.

Any object, whether in graphics or text, can be resized. This is one of the many ways you can create visual effects in your presentations. If you have clip art of an airplane and it's not large enough for your purpose, simply open the clip art, load it to PM Chart, and resize it to the desired size.

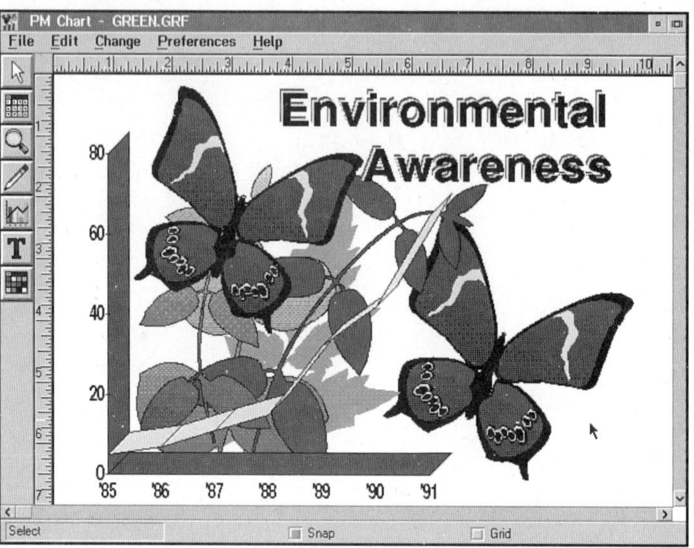

Figure 13.12. Resizing an object.

Using Clip Art

Most business presentations use graphics extensively. The graphics can be in the form of drawings or clip art. Drawing requires practice and some real expertise to obtain professional-quality graphics. The easiest way to obtain this quality without being an expert is to use clip art, which is a collection of predrawn graphics created by professional artists and sold free of copyrights. You can purchase them separately from various vendors.

Micrografx sells a separate package that includes hundreds of pieces of clip art that work with PM Chart or one of their other products. There are also other vendors who specialize in selling clip art. For more information about clip art, select the Help/

Product Information on the pull-down menu, and when you see the pop-up dialog box, place your pointer over the icon on the far right side and click it with mouse button 1. This gives you information about where to find out more about clip art.

The images in clip art are loaded by means of the File/Clipart menu. By clicking the Open button in the dialog box with mouse button 1, the Clip Art - Load and Select dialog box appears (see Figure 13.13) and thumbnail-size pictures are displayed on the right side of the dialog box. This enables you to preview the clip art without loading it into your file.

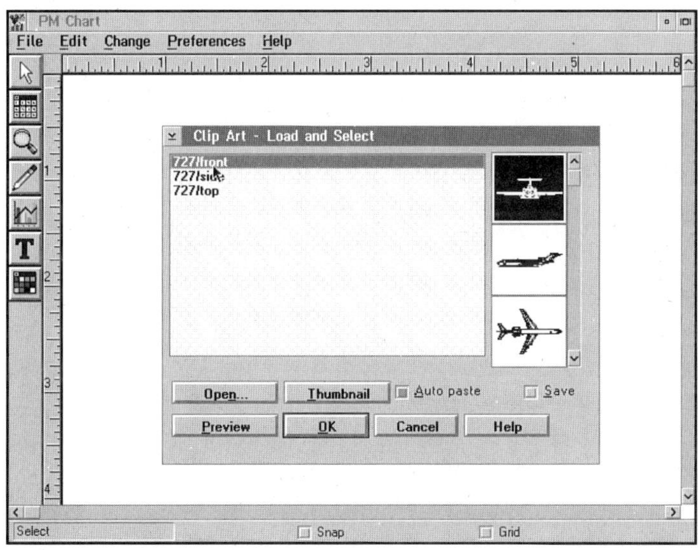

Figure 13.13. The Clip Art - Load and Select dialog box.

You can now select a piece of clip art from your file and load it into PM Chart or select all the choices for display.

Professional-quality drawings require talent and lots of experience. You can take full advantage of somebody else's talents by purchasing clip art and creating some quality work with them. Once you have the clip art loaded into your file, you can combine it with worksheet data and create charts and/or graphs. Now that you have all the elements present in your file, you can complete the business presentation.

Using Worksheet Data and Importing Other Formats

Most of the information you will have to communicate in a business presentation involves data that can be represented in a worksheet, or spreadsheet. These worksheets can be entered into PM Chart or imported. I will show you how to enter data into the built-in worksheet. If the data is simple and not too long, entering it to PM Chart is quite easy.

To enter the data, click mouse button 1 on the worksheet icon on the toolbar, or single-click mouse button 2 to pop up the worksheet on-screen. The worksheet that appears is small in comparison to a spreadsheet program. This worksheet is 100 rows by 100 columns. You can enlarge the worksheet area that appears on the screen by dragging one of the edges. The columns are labeled from A to CV, and the rows from 1 to 100. Each cell can accommodate up to 80 characters, with some of the characters hidden. The charts or graphs that are plotted use only the first 17 characters.

Moving around the worksheet is rather cumbersome. This worksheet does not support the navigation shortcut keys that you may be accustomed to using. In other words, you won't be able to use Home or other shortcut keys. To move to the right, use the Tab key; to the left, use Shift-Tab. The Up and Down arrow keys are used to move one row at a time. You can also use your mouse pointer to move around the worksheet quickly. This is probably the best way of navigating in this case.

For labels, the worksheet uses category labels from the first row or column of data. Value labels are automatically generated when you create a chart or graph. The range or scale determines the value labels on the chart.

You will not be able to enter formulas into the worksheet. All formulas entered are interpreted as labels. The purpose of this worksheet is not to be a substitute for a spreadsheet program, but rather a quick way to create graphs or charts. There is a way to do math on this worksheet, but it involves adding, substracting, mutiplying, and dividing values by a constant. To do that, use your mouse pointer to select the area of the worksheet that you want to use and select Data/Math on the pull-down menu. This pops up a dialog box that enables you to choose the type of math you want to perform. For more information, see the online Help.

If you have been trying the examples in this section, make sure that if you alter the sample files included, you don't save the changes when you close the files. Select Cancel from the dialog box (the changes will not be saved).

To illustrate the use of the worksheet, try an example. First select File/New so that you can start with a fresh new PM Chart file. Move your mouse pointer to the worksheet toolbar icon and click on it. You can also click mouse button 2. Both methods bring up an empty worksheet. Next, select File/Open Data to open a dialog box. From this dialog box you can choose any of the sample *.DAT files or use the file list to navigate to where you keep your favorite spreadsheet file. If you want to find your spreadsheet file, be sure that you select the file type from the dialog box. For this example, select the GREEN.DAT file. Your screen should look something like the one shown in Figure 13.14, which represents data for the Environmental Awareness screen.

The worksheet viewing area can be enlarged by dragging the edge of the window to the desired size. There is no Maximize or Minimize button on the worksheet.

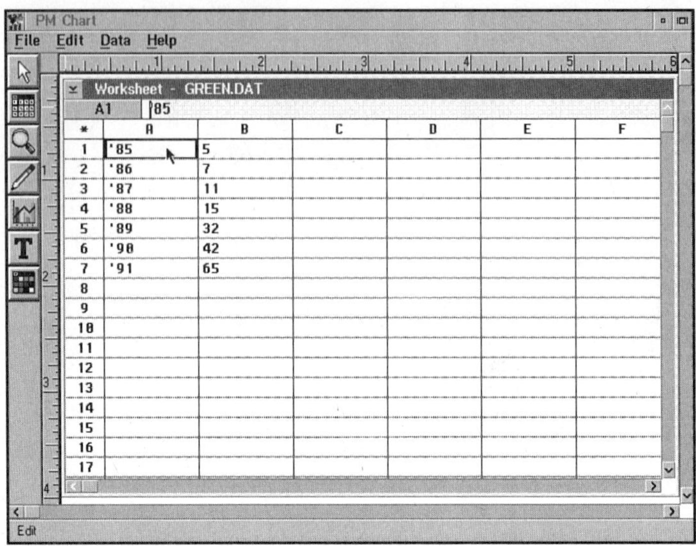

Figure 13.14. The worksheet containing the GREEN.DAT file.

Now that you have your worksheet GREEN.DAT file loaded, create a simple chart with this data. The first thing you need to do is to make sure that the data you want to use for the chart is selected in the worksheet. Do this by clicking the mouse pointer and dragging it over the part of the worksheet you want to use. To makes things easy, PM Chart has a way to select the entire worksheet. At the top of the A column and above the 1st row, you'll see the * symbol. Single-click your mouse pointer, using mouse button 1, over this symbol to select the entire region of the worksheet. The worksheet should appear now with all the rows and columns highlighted. Close the worksheet by double-clicking mouse button 1 on the system icon in the top-left corner. Closing the worksheet will not discard your data. Your PM Chart screen now appears blank.

The next step is to single-click mouse button 1 on the charts tool. This tool expands and shows several choices of different charts or graphs from which to choose. Icons on each button of the toolbar show you which type they represent. Select the icon button to the left of the pie-chart icon. This is the choice for the line chart graph. Your screen now pops up a dialog box for the line chart graph and shows the following: 3D, Legend, Table, Auto paste, and Save. The buttons on the bottom allow you to choose Overlay, Replace, New, and so on. Select 3D and New for a basic graph. Later you can add color, legend, text, and clip art to make it a more professional presentation. For more information about using this type of graph or any other, refer to the online Help information.

Regarding importing other spreadsheets into the PM Chart worksheet, you have a choice of the available import formats listed in the File/Open dialog box. When you import these spreadsheets, you lose the formulas contained in them. The formulas are interpreted as labels. For Presentation Graphics, it makes sense to import values anyway. If you have a large spreadsheet that has formulas and values, try to copy the values to another spreadsheet and then import them into PM Chart.

I hope that you are beginning to see the process of building a business presentation more clearly. With the clip art and the worksheet data loaded in PM Chart, you are left now with the task of combining these two and adding color and text to complete the presentation. There are an infinite number of ways to combine electronic artwork, graphs, and text to create snappy business presentations. You have to experiment a bit to find the ideal combination for your work. To learn more about this subject, consult your library for information on presentation graphics, desktop publishing, and electronic art.

TIP

If you are a member of CompuServe, you can take advantage of the wealth of information in many of the forums. One in particular is DTPFORUM (the desktop publishing forum). To get there type `go dtpforum` at the CompuServe prompt. In this forum, you will find many messages from other users relating to DTP and electronic publishing. In the libraries there are plenty of demo programs, fonts, and clip art samples.

Text and Labeling

There are also ways to add pizzaz to your presentation with labeling and text. PM Chart has some built-in text tools that allow you to make some forms of typography. With the right labels or signs, you can make your presentations easier to understand and you can focus on a particular subject. Keep in mind that anything created by the text tool can be manipulated as though it were a graphic object; in fact, text *is* a form of graphic object.

The text tool looks similar to that found in many word processors. Using buttons, scroll bars, and text entry boxes, you can specify the type size, fonts, and type weights (normal, bold, italic, and bold italic). For business presentations, you can use a fancy font, utilizing all the ATM type 1 fonts that are part of the OS/2 2.1 base system. With PM Chart, you can use a simple ATM font and manipulate it to give it a more appealing look. To get a taste of this text tool, try an example. In this exercise, you will use the dialog box to specify the type size and font, and then you will manipulate it a bit to see some of the things you can do with PM Chart.

Before you begin, start with a blank screen in the program. Select File/New, and when you are asked to save the changes to PM Chart, click on No in the dialog box. Next, select the text tool by single-clicking with mouse button 1 on the icon button that has the letter *T*. The toolbar expands and you have a choice of three buttons: create a text object, select font style or size, or select text alignment. Use mouse button 1 to click on the select font style and size icon.

If you select the Helevetica Outline font and increase the font size to 30 points, you could also add bold or any other type style here as well. For now, however, pick a simple choice. Select the create a text object tool from the text toolbar. Place your mouse pointer inside your blank screen, note, the pointer changes to a "text tool" pointer. Single-click the mouse pointer to the right of the "1" marked by the ruler. Notice the large cursor appearing on your screen. This is where you will begin to type text. Type `I love PM Chart!!!`.

After you finish typing, click on the select tool icon at the top of the toolbar and place the pointer over your text. Single-click on your text object. The text object has the familiar square handles, indicating that you have selected this object. Now that the text object is selected, you can manipulate this object just like a graphic object. You can try to stretch the object and see whether you can increase its size. Do this by placing your pointer over any of the square handles until the pointer changes into a "stretch" pointer. Drag it one direction and notice that when you release the mouse pointer, the screen redraws with a larger text object (see Figure 13.15). As an exercise, see how many ways you can manipulate these text objects.

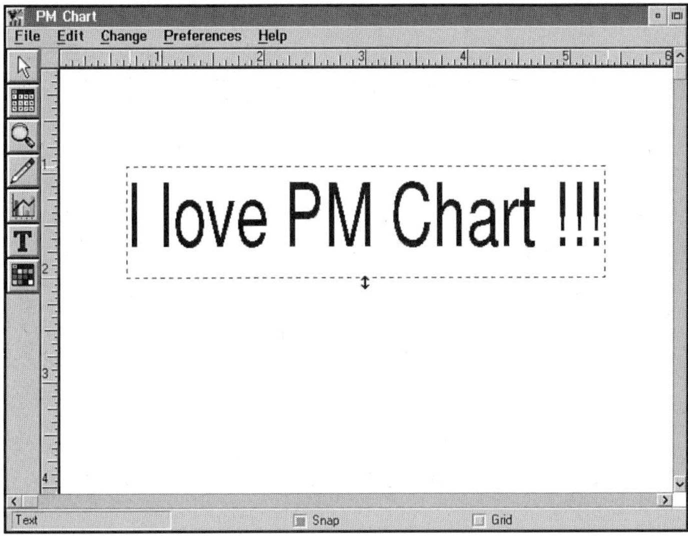

Figure 13.15. Manipulating a text object.

If you have additional ATM fonts installed, you have more fonts to pick from in the dialog box than those shown in Figure 13.15. Your installed printer should also appear in this box, under "printer." In the previous example, the printer is HP Deskjet.

Using Draw, Color, and Style

The last two areas to cover on PM Chart are drawing tools and combining everything with color and style. As I mentioned earlier in this section, drawing graphic art requires a great deal of practice and expertise. The same holds true for using color and style. These two tools are the most exciting and the most difficult. I can point out only some simple examples for these two powerful tools. It's up to you to experiment and exploit these tools.

Creating graphic art in the simplest form involves putting together lines and curves. The PM Chart drawing tools were described earlier in this section. The drawing tools consist of several rectangles and ellipses tools and some curve and straight-line tools. Draw using your mouse and mouse button 1. Drawing with the mouse is a challenge because it's not as precise as your hand and a pencil or pen. It takes some practice!

Begin with a simple drawing involving the use of two of the draw tools: the rectangle tool and the free-hand tool. When you are finished, your completed "wireframe" drawing should look like the one shown in Figure 13.16.

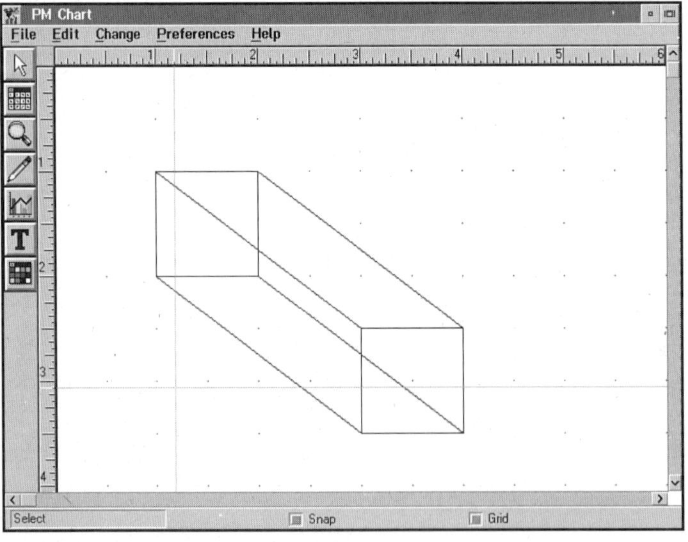

Figure 13.16. The completed wireframe drawing.

A *wireframe* is a term used in computer-aided design (CAD) to define the outline of the drawing, before color or any other solid hatching is used.

Before you begin the drawing, change some of the settings in the program. This makes it easier to draw precisely. First, be sure that the Snap and Grid boxes are on in the lower part of the screen. By setting Snap to On, you are really saying Snap to rulers. This means that drawing and moving is controlled by the rulers. You can get an idea of what this does by selecting Preferences/ Crosshairs from the pull-down menu. Now place your mouse pointer on the screen and move it around with mouse button 1 depressed. The first thing you will notice is that it tends to move in a jerky manner. It appears to be going from one ruler guide to another.

You can turn the Snap to Off by clicking mouse button 1 on the button below. By repeating the same exercise, the mouse pointer this time moves more smoothly. Having Snap on allows you to create geometric shapes more precisely. The Grid is useful when you need to check the measurements of your drawing. It allows you to align your drawing with the rulers when you combine it with the crosshairs.

Now that you have everything set, select the rectangle drawing tool from the toolbar. From the previous exercise, you should also have the Snap, Grid, and Crosshairs turned on. Place your pointer so that it lines up under the top 1" and the left 1" markers. There should be a grid mark at this intersection. Now drag the pointer from this point to the right until you are aligned with the top 2" marker, then continue to drag downward until you reach the 2" marker on the right ruler. Release the pointer and you should have a 1" square drawing.

Repeat this process again starting at the 3" top marker and the 4" right marker. Proceed again to the right and downward, until you have drawn another 1" square.

To complete your drawing, simply select the line drawing tool from the toolbar and, starting at the top square, draw a line joining the two squares.

Repeat this process until you have created four lines, each one joining a corner of one square to a corner of the other square.

Drawing lines and polygons in PM Chart is similar to a painting type of program. When you draw a straight line, double-click mouse button 1 so that the line is not continued from the two points you picked. Otherwise, your line will continue to be drawn beyond the two points.

This drawing can be improved tremendously with a few more squares and lines. If you added two more squares and some lines, this drawing might actually resemble a kite! You can try adding these on your own—the process is quite simple.

To delete an object after drawing it on the screen, double-click your pointer on the object until you see the familiar square handles, and then use the Delete key or use the Edit/Clear menu command.

You have just created a simple drawing consisting of squares and lines to form a kite. If you want to add more features, you can manipulate this drawing by changing its position with rotation, or you could resize it to make it smaller or larger. There are many ways to improve the drawing. One quick way to improve it is to add color, the next topic.

When you draw a picture or create a graphic object, you are combining many separate lines and curves together. To apply color, PM Chart needs to group or connect objects together. Once these objects are grouped or connected, you can manipulate them in many different ways. You can rotate, stretch, resize, flip, fill with color, or apply a gradient of color. Text objects need not be grouped to have color applied to them. The Change command on the pull-down menu has many different choices. I will not explain each one of

these commands, but only the ones that apply to this example. To obtain more information about each of these commands, see the online Help file.

Apply some color to the last example to demonstrate basic coloring techniques. You still should have the kite you created previously. If you don't, try to recreate it. To select a color, display the Color dialog box. You can do this by clicking the bottom icon button on the toolbar. After you click this button, the dialog box appears on the screen, as seen in Figure 13.17.

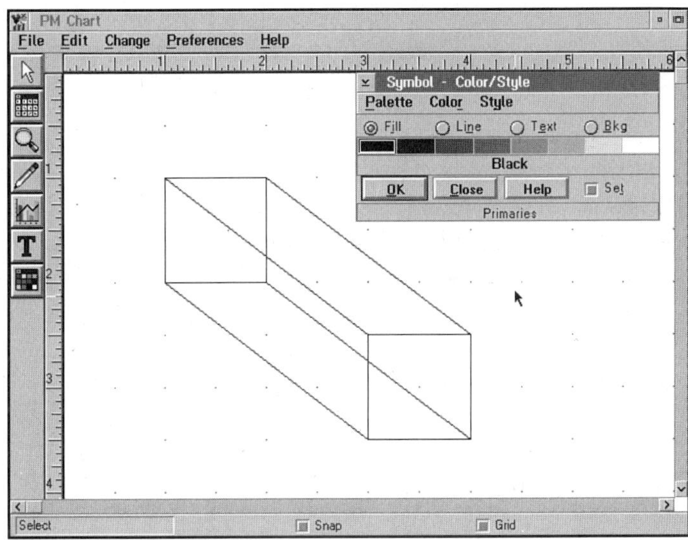

Figure 13.17. The Color dialog box.

Now that you have this dialog box on the screen, I can explain a few things about its use. There are three basic menus on the pull-down menu: Palette, Color, and Style. With Palette you can pick different color choices. The program default colors are the primary colors. By choosing a different set of colors, you have more variety to choose from. For now, use the default colors. Most of the other choices on the pull-down menu are self-explanatory and require some experimentation to understand their use.

A symbol in PM Chart is the same as a graphic object.

You have a choice in this dialog box to use Fill, Line, Text, or Bkg for your color choices. Select Fill to color a symbol completely, depending on the style. Select Line to change colors, width, or the style of a line. Text changes the color of what you type. Bkg changes the color of the symbol's background. With this you can change the background color independently of the foreground.

NOTE The Color dialog box remains on the screen if you click on the Set box. If the dialog box is closed with the Close button, just click on its toolbar icon button to pop it up again.

Fill the square areas with red in your kite example. You might remember from earlier discussions that every symbol needs to be selected before you can apply any changes. Select the square object by choosing the select tool from the toolbar and then single-clicking with mouse button 1 on the square until the square's handles appear.

Now that you have the square selected, you can move the pointer to the Color dialog box and select Fill and the red color. You select colors by clicking directly on the palette. Next, click on the OK button. This fills the rest of the objects with colors. If you would like an object to appear behind or in front of another, simply select the object. Then, from the pull-down menu choose Change/Move to/Front or Back. The coloring of all your symbols can be accomplished this way.

The Color command in the Color dialog box allows you to fill the colors with solids, choose a gradient of color, change chart colors, and change the screen color. In the last example, you colored one of the squares red. This time, color the other square in red, but instead of a solid color, use a gradient. To do this, select the symbol first. Then select Color/Gradient and Style and pick the last one of the choices of the gradients. Now click on the red color and select the Start button and the OK button. You also need to choose the End color.

Pick the white color and click OK. Your screen should look like the one shown in Figure 13.18.

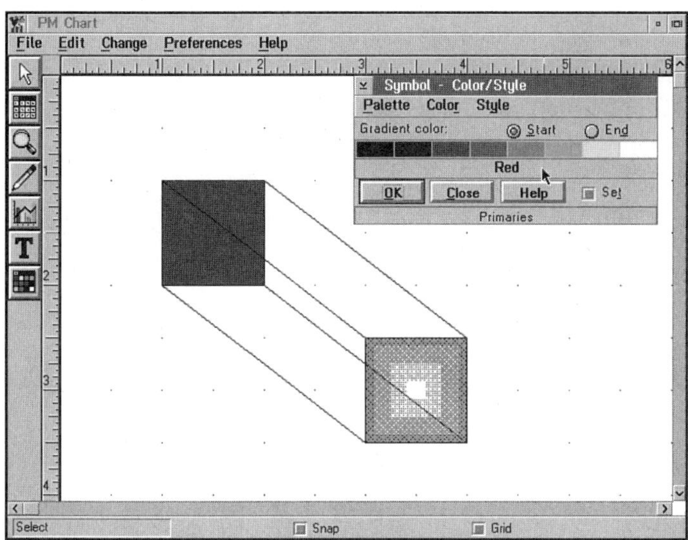

Figure 13.18. Using color gradients on your symbols.

There are many different ways to use the Change command to affect the way your symbols will appear on the screen. Try experimenting with this command to see how many different ways you can manipulate your symbols.

I hope you have been able to see how powerful PM Chart is, and the many ways you can use it to create not only business presentations, but graphic artwork to use in your everyday business documents. You can combine a chart created in PM Chart with a word processor file, or draw an organizational chart for your office. This program has a variety of uses. One of the few drawbacks is the export capability. If you don't have a word processor that allows you to import a *.DRW or *.GRF file, you may have to use a different program to translate these files into a format that's acceptable to use.

One way to export your file in a format other than *.DRW or *.GRF is to install a Generic PostScript Printer printer driver on your OS/2 desktop. Select that printer as your default printer. When you select that printer, select the Options button and choose to print to an Encapsulated PostScript file (EPS). You have to give this a filename. When you print, you will have your PM Chart saved to an EPS format that you can use with your word processors. One caveat on this: EPS files can grow to very large sizes. Be prepared to expend several megabytes of disk space when using this method.

PM Terminal

For many, this program will seem like one of the games included in the Games folder, instead of the Productivity folder where it resides. Traversing through what seems like an endless choice of menus may seem like an adventure game! With all the emphasis on object-oriented applications, PM Terminal may seem out of place. This program offers a unique interface, however, that eliminates some of the confusing elements of the newer PM applications. There are no button bars or floating icons in this program, so all your selections are done in a straightforward fashion, using your mouse and highlighting your choice from a list of entries. By double-clicking with mouse button 1, the Session Phonebook of your choice is started.

PM Terminal is a scaled-down version of the Softerm Modular communications program sold by Softronics of Colorado Springs, Colorado. Their Modular version offers a plethora of features. Some of the features missing from this version are as follows: robust scripting, session scrollback, ZMODEM and IND$FILE transfer protocols (plus many more), and extensive LAN/Gateway connectivity. The Modular version has nearly four times as many terminal emulations as PM Terminal. The additional features are too numerous to mention. Softerm Modular is truly an impressive terminal program! Even

without all the features of the Modular version, PM Terminal is still a complete Asynchronous Terminal Emulation program.

You will be able to start using this program immediately to call your favorite BBSs, CompuServe, the IBM Information Network, or other online services. This program supports many different terminal emulations, as well as character and binary transfer of files. With it, you can do binary file transfers to speeds of 19,200 bps, using the 10 protocols found in the list that follows. Also, it has a keystroke recording for creating macros. This enables you to automate some of your keystrokes into macros. After you create a keyboard macro, use the keyboard remap facility to assign it to a particular key.

File Transfer Protocols
Character
KERMIT
KERMIT Server
SOFTRANS
XMODEM
XMODEM -1K
YMODEM
YMODEM -1K
YMODEM -G
YMODEM -G 1K

Modes of Operation

When you start PM Terminal, the first thing you see is the Softerm Session Manager. In this Session Manager is a directory type listing of your Session Phonebook. The Session Phonebook is where you add your individual entries into your directory of all the places you wish to call. This program allows you to customize each of your entries in your Session Phonebook, to allow for different terminal emulators, transfer protocols, communication ports, and so on. To understand the operation of PM Terminal, I'll take you through an example of how to set up a new profile and use it to perform a call.

When you create a new entry in your Session Phonebook you are essentially creating an entry into the configuration database. This database is a file called CUSTOM.MDB, and its backup CUSTOM.BAK file. Your program automatically updates these files after you have exited the program. PM Terminal has only one configuration database.

There are several modes of operation for this program. When you first start the program and you are making changes to a profile, you are in the User Interface Mode. As soon as you begin your call, you will be in the Terminal Emulation Mode. Finally, if you decide to download or upload a file, you will be in the File Transfer Mode. It is useful to remember that the interface changes every time you are in a different mode. This may seem confusing at first, but knowing what to expect will help you troubleshoot any problems you may have in a session.

Configuring PM Terminal

Start with an example of how to add an electronic bulletin board entry into our Session Phonebook, and how to set up a profile for this entry. In this example, I added the entry for OS/2 Connection BBS, which is an electronic BBS found in the San Diego area. To begin, start the PM Terminal program. Your screen should look like the one shown in Figure 13.19. This figure shows the completed entry for OS/2 Connection BBS.

The next step is to click on Session/Add to take you to the Add Session dialog box, where you type the following in the Comment section: `San Diego's OS/2 Bulletin Board` (see Figure 13.20).

The comment appears to the right of the Phonebook entry. Notice that below your comment the choice of profiles appears: terminal emulation, connection path, system environment, and file transfer.

These profiles define the different configurations for the new entry. The default profiles are shown in Figure 13.20. If you want to accept the default profiles, you can enter the new name of the host computer and the phone number and proceed with your communication session. More than likely, however, you will have to modify one of the profiles slightly. Before you proceed with the example, I would like to explain what each of these profiles does.

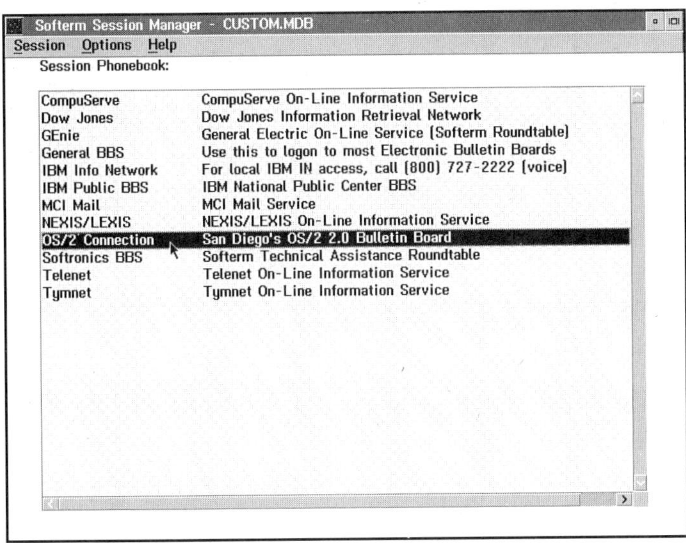

Figure 13.19. Session Manager for PM Terminal with the new entry.

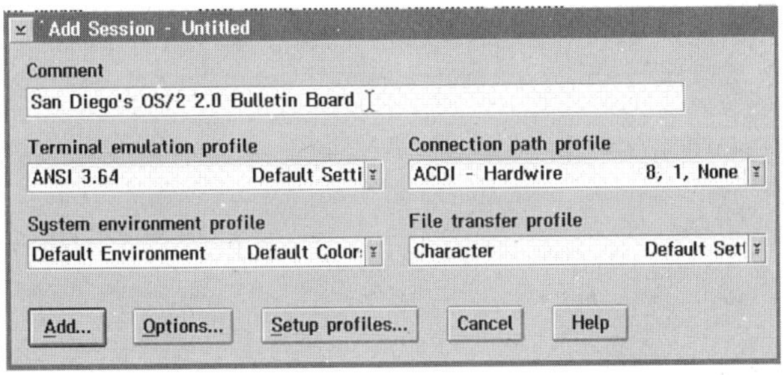

Figure 13.20. The Add Session dialog box.

The terminal emulation profile provides the interface to allow the host computer to "think" it's communicating with the correct terminal. This emulation interprets the host-initiated command and control sequences and also transmits the appropriate controls back to the host.

The connection path profile defines the communication interface that is to be used by the connection. It takes the information from the modem profile, such as the method of connection (modem or hardwire) and the communication port, for example, COM1.

The system environment profile maintains all system-wide parameters for your session. This includes the default printer, Nationality profile (if you are interested in displaying characters outside the U.S.), disk drive and directory path, terminal emulation screen area (colors), and your default Video Code Page used by your terminal emulation to display characters.

The file transfer profile allows you to specify the file transfer profile for your session. The protocol-specific parameters can be saved with your file transfer profile.

The telephone network profile defines the prefix and suffix to be used when accessing a particular telephone network, such as PBX, and forms part of the admittance data.

Additionally, PM Terminal has profiles that deal with your print path and keyboard. These are set up from within some of the major profiles already mentioned.

As you continue with the example, you will see how to find and set up these profiles. Proceeding with the example, the Add Session dialog box shown in Figure 13.20 has a button for setup profiles. Clicking on this button takes you to the Setup Profiles dialog box, which shows the five main profiles as seen in Figure 13.21. The individual profiles are then accessed by clicking on the buttons in the Profile's box. For this example, click on the Terminal button, which takes you to the Terminal Emulation Profile Module for the CUSTOM.MDB database. This dialog box gives you a choice of the type of terminal emulation that you wish to use. The list that follows shows the many different terminal emulations available with PM Terminal.

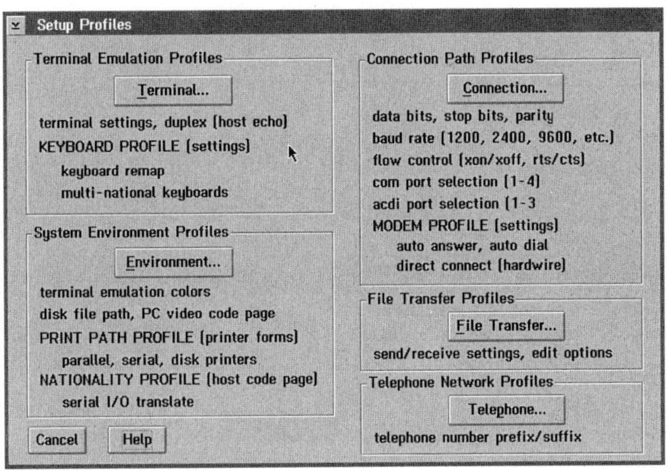

Figure 13.21. The Setup Profiles dialog box.

Terminal Emulations Available in PM Terminal
A NSI 3.64
DEC VT100
DEC VT52
GEnie terminal
IBM ANSI
IBM INVT100
IBM 3101 - 10
IBM 3101 - 20
TTY

TIP

If you wish to change the default settings for your particular terminal emulation, select Add from the terminal emulation profile and then create a "clone" of the default emulation, but with the custom changes you want, by using the Save As button from the dialog box. This renames that custom emulation. In this manner, you always preserve your initial default settings. If you make a mistake or are troubleshooting a problem, you can go back and start with settings that you know will work. If you decide to add another terminal emulation, you always have a known starting point.

For this example, choose the IBM ANSI terminal emulation. Click your pointer to highlight that choice. If that choice is not visible, use the scroll bar on the right of the box to find it. Now click on Close to accept your choice with its default settings. In the example, you don't have any fancy changes to make to the default settings. At this point, you need to make sure that your connection path profile is what you want. The program is shipped with default settings for COM1 with 8 data bits, 1 stop bit, no parity, Hayes 1200-baud auto-dial modem, and a VT100 customized emulator with AT 84-key keyboard. You may have a set up as COM2 port, or 2400-baud, so these settings will have to be changed.

The connection path profile button takes you to the Connection Path Profile Module, where there should be a list box showing the default settings. There are two basic types of connections listed in this dialog box: standard COM (serial port) and IBM's ACDI. Either of these can be a hardwire connection or some type of modem. The OS/2 Connection BBS in the example requires you to use COM modem and 8, 1, None for settings. Remember that the default baud rate is 1200, so you must change that if you want faster throughput. As with the terminal emulation, it's better to create a new connection path profile than to alter the default settings. To start, click on Add, which produces Add Connection Path. A communication interface list box appears, where you choose Standard COM. (The other choice would be ACDI if you have one.) Click on the OK button and the Connection Path Settings dialog box appears as shown in Figure 13.22.

If a Connection Path requires a modem profile, but none is provided, it will default to a Standard COM hardwire. This means that you will not get the Admittance Data dialog box.

No initialization string will be provided to your modem, and you will have to manually initiate the connection inside the Session Window with Hayes AT commands.

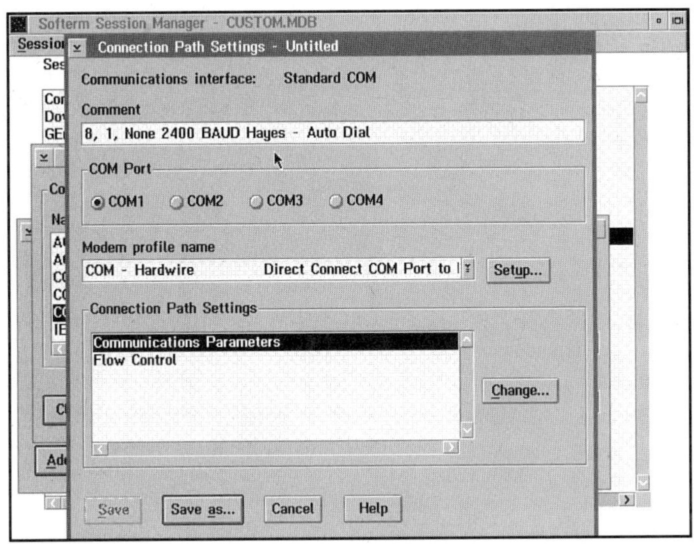

Figure 13.22. The Connection Path Settings dialog box.

You need to access COM2, so click on that radio button. Select the Communication Parameters below and double-click on it. This brings up Communications Parameters so that you can select the 2400 Baud, 8, 1, None settings from the list box. Click on the OK button and double-click on Flow Control to set the desired setting. The last step is to select a modem profile. The list box in the middle is where you can select a Hayes 2400 Baud, Auto Dial modem.

You need to make sure that the modem initialization string is what you need before you select it. First, click on Add to set up a clone of this profile. You will be guided through several dialog boxes, the first one being the Add Modem (standard COM), then the Connection Path (Auto Dial), then the modem type (Hayes Smartmodem 2400). Now you should be able to customize your modem settings. If you select Device Initialization String by double-clicking on it, you can modify the default string.

When you are finished with all these steps, click on Save As and give your Connection Path a unique name that will remind you of the changes you made to the default profile. Click the Close button to bring back the Add Session dialog box. Choose a File transfer profile from the list box (Xmodem 1K), and click the OK button.

The final step is to fill in the Admittance Data dialog box. Enter the phone number (see Figure 13.23) and decide whether you want this dialog box to be present every time you use this entry. By leaving out the check mark on the Display this dialog box, you go directly to the Session Window after you initiate a session. You could also place a check mark on "Bypass the autodial information message" to forego the Auto Dial dialog at connect time. The final step in the configuration processs is to Save as to the name of your online service or BBS, in this case, OS/2 Connection.

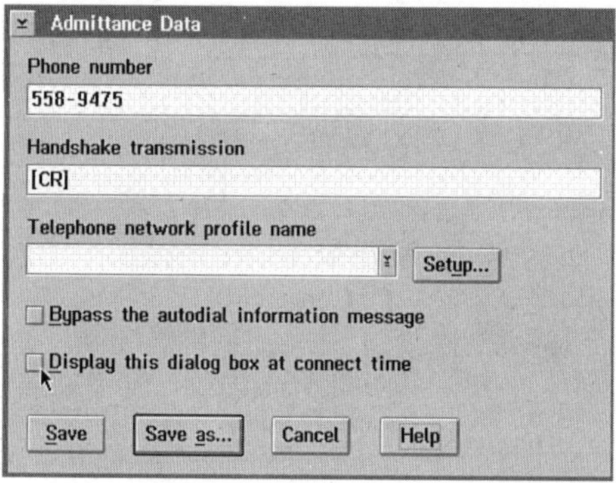

Figure 13.23. The Admittance Data dialog box.

Now that you have configured your entry into the Phonebook directory, you can start a session by double-clicking that entry, or select the Session/Start from the menu. The program displays the Admittance Data dialog box (if you checked that box) or simply goes directly to the Session Window.

From the Session Window, you can select "on-the-fly" changes to the following: Terminal emulation, Connection path, Keyboard, System environment, and Print path. The changes you make in this window will be used only for the duration of your session. When you exit, you have the option to save the changes you make. Also, from the Session Window you can perform file transfers by selecting File/Send file or Receive file.

The overview of PM Terminal has included setting up an entry into the Phonebook Directory and the steps to take to configure this new entry. This overview was designed to give you only an introduction to the program. There are many other areas that were not covered. I hope that this gives you enough information to encourage you to experiment and learn more about this program. For further information on this program or topics, search the online help.

The Icon Editor

The Icon Editor program was included in the productivity applets to create, edit, and save icons. Many of the applications that you use could have an icon that you would like to replace, or no icon at all. This is where Icon Editor comes in handy. It can also create bitmaps and pointers. The program can be started in two ways: from the Productivity folder icon and from the settings notebook. If you use the settings notebook, you have to start the Icon Editor just as if you clicked the icon in the Productivity folder. If you save your icons and use the ICO extension, give the icon the same name as your program so the icon will be used automatically. You must save the .ICO file in the same directory as your program for this feature to work.

When you start the program, it looks just like a painting program. Most of what you need for creating icons is available from the pull-down menus. Before you begin to create your icon, however, it may be useful to review some of the available options.

If you select Options/Preferences on the menu, you can see most of the main settings of the program (see Figure 13.24). The Safe prompt allows the program to warn you that you need to save your work before exiting. Safe state on exit stores the following conditions: all user preferences, the predefined device list, current pen size, screen and inverse colors, the hot spot setting, and display options such as X background or Draw straight. Suppress Warnings prevents the program from displaying warning messages about memory, palette operation, availablility of help, and file size. Use Display status area when you want to show status on your primary window. Reset options and modes is used to restore the program settings to their original state. As always, a check mark appears next to the option you have selected.

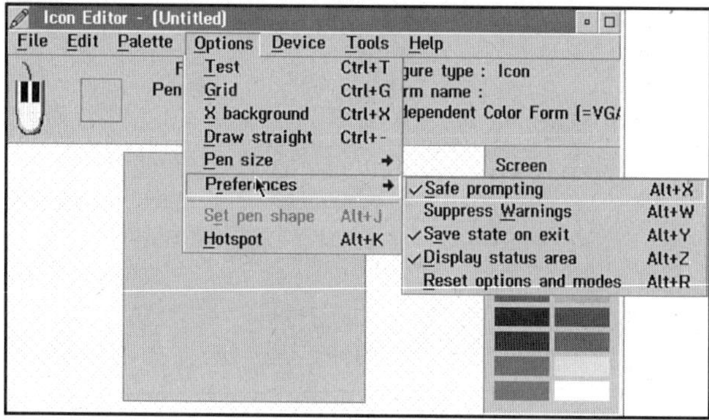

Figure 13.24. The Options menu and submenus.

The area below the menu bar is known as the status area. Here you find four different sections. The mouse on the left side of the dialog box below the menu bar shows the colors assigned to the two mouse buttons. You can change the assigned colors by clicking with your mouse button over the color palette area, selecting the color for that button. If you click mouse button 1 over a certain color, the color is assigned to that button. The same thing holds true for mouse button 2. Next is the icon and pointer display area. This is where you can view how the icon will appear on the screen. Figure statistics are next, showing the form size, pen location, pen size, and hot spot. Figure characteristics show the figure type, form name, and status line.

Icon Editor allows you to change the colors of your palette by creating a customized palette. From the colors you see on the palette, you can delete and add new ones. To change colors in the palette, select Palette/Edit color to bring up the Edit color dialog box. You can use slider arms to choose a color, then return to the main program with that selection.

You can create a bitmap file in any application and copy it to the Clipboard. From the Clipboard you can paste it into your Icon Editor program.

Using this tip, I found it easier to create icons in the PM Chart applet and copy them to the Clipboard. In the following example I created an icon using PM Chart for a DOS program. As you might recall from earlier in this chapter, PM Chart has a lot of precise drawing tools. With these tools, you can create circles, squares, and curves, and you can color them with the tools in PM Chart and move them to the Clipboard. Figure 13.25 shows a bitmap pasted from the Clipboard into the Icon Editor. This now allows you to create some professional-quality icons you never thought possible!

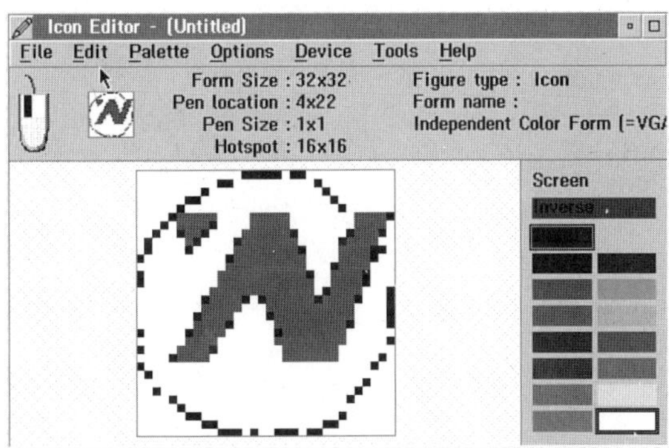

Figure 13.25. A bitmap pasted into Icon Editor from the Clipboard.

Don't forget to experiment with the program! This overview of Icon Editor will get you started, and if you have any specific questions about a feature of this program, select Help from the menu.

The Enhanced PM Editor

The Enhanced Editor (EPM) is one of the most misunderstood programs in the Productivity folder. Some people think of it as yet another editor in the long list of ones they have used in the past. Others are glad to see a replacement for the old edlin editor from early DOS versions and the OS/2 System Editor from early OS/2 versions.

EPM is a pure text editor. It creates and modifies files in ASCII form. This editor, combined with some extra support files released recently in CompuServe, can be one of the most powerful and useful programs included in your OS/2 2.1 package.

Originally, EPM was developed by several IBM employees as an internal-use-only program. The program was so popular among IBM employees that they decided to release it inside the OS/2 2.1 package. This program has been described by IBM as a "simple application built on top of a toolkit." You'll find that EPM is capable of simple text editing, or it can be used as a programmer's editor. You can configure the editor by way of the Options menu, use macros, or use the REXX language that's included with OS/2 2.1.

EPM is found in the Productivity folder. To start the program, open that folder and double-click mouse button 1 on the Enhanced Editor icon. The editor starts with an untitled file opened. This is because you haven't named your file. You may notice that the editor has a top-of-file marker and a bottom-of-file marker (see Figure 13.26). At a glance, EPM looks just like the System Editor. You really have to explore the pull-down menus to notice the differences. For example, select the Edit menu to see quite a few more available editing commands. You could use EPM as a word processor. It has some of the same features that most word processors have. You can format characters, words, paragraphs, make changes, and cut and paste. Remember that this editor is only for pure ASCII files! It will not translate embedded codes put in by other word processors.

Editors used for text editing come in two flavors: a line editor or a stream editor. The EPM editor is a line editor and the System Editor is a stream editor.

A line editor is one that uses a file as a sequence of lines that are separated by an end-of-line character. A stream editor uses the file as a long stream of characters. The most commonly used word processors are stream editors.

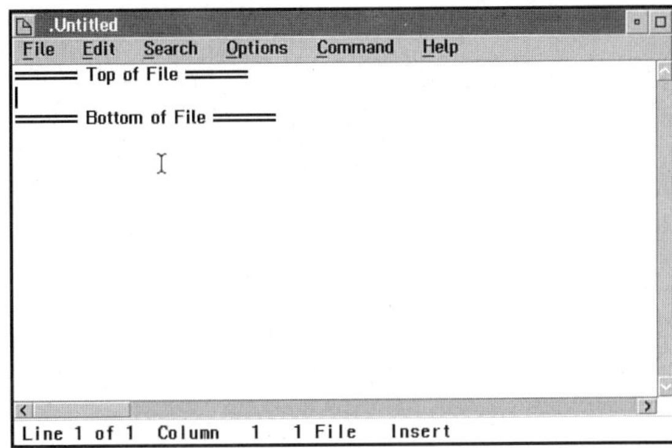

Figure 13.26. An untitled file in EPM.

Because most users are accustomed to working with stream editors, EPM can be configured in stream mode. To configure EPM as a stream editor, start the editor, and from the pull-down menu, select Options/Preferences/Stream editing. Then make sure to select Options/Save options to save this setting for future use.

For more information about the differences between line editors and stream editors, see the online help.

Basic Editing Techniques

As with most word processors, you can use your mouse pointer to move around the editor. If you want the cursor to move to a different position, position your mouse pointer over the new position and single-click mouse button 1. You can do this a few times to verify that you understand how to move your cursor. The

pointer, as in all OS/2 programs, is used for positioning your cursor, marking blocks of text, and selecting menus.

You will notice that when your pointer appears on the editing area, it changes to an editing pointer called an I-beam. When you move outside the editing area, it changes back to a normal mouse pointer. Sometimes while in the editing area, you might lose track of your editing pointer. Some background colors make the pointer "blend" on the screen. To find your pointer, in this case, move your mouse outside the editing area and look for your regular pointer.

Some commands can be selected by using keystrokes. If you are used to keystrokes, you may want to learn a few basic ones to use in this editor. There is a keystroke equivalent for most mouse actions. You can find out what these are by using the online help. Table 13.3 below shows some of the basic function key assignments.

Table 13.3. Function key assignments.

Function Key	*Assignment*
F1	Help
F2	Save and continue
F3	Quit without save
F4	Save and quit
F5	Open dialog
F6	Show draw options
F7	Change filename
F8	Edit new file
F9	Undo current line
F10	Activate menu
F11	Previous file
F12	Next file

You can change the definitions of any keystrokes by using macros. If you are more familiar with another kind of editor, BRIEF, for example, or the Emacs editor, you can change EPM to have the look and feel of your favorite editor.

Review the pull-down menu commands and the Options settings notebook. First select the File menu. Table 13.4 describes each command in this menu.

Table 13.4. The File menu commands.

Menu Item	*Description*
New	Open a new file to replace the current one
Open .Untitled	Open a new file with .Untitled used as the name
Open	Open an existing file
Import text file	Retrieve a file and insert it into the current one
Rename	Used to change the name of your current file
Save	Store your current file to disk
Save as	Store the current file under a particular name
Save and close	Store the current file and then quit
Quit	Close the current file and quit if it's the last one
Print file	Print the current file

The Edit menu can be expanded with more advanced features. Only the basic features are shown in Table 13.5. Notice that some of the commands are greyed-out. These are available only after you have modified your file and marked a block of text.

Table 13.5. Basic commands of the Edit menu.

Menu Item	*Description*
Undo line	Reverse any changes in the current line
Undo	Reverse changes from a session through a slider bar
Copy	Copy text into the Clipboard
Cut	Copy text to the Clipboard and delete it
Paste	Insert text into the cursor position from Clipboard
Paste lines	Insert text into the cursor position, adding lines
Paste block	Insert a rectangular block of text to cursor position
Style	Change the font or color of marked text
Copy mark	Copy marked text into cursor position
Move mark	Move marked text into cursor position
Overlay mark	Overwrite text with a copy of marked text
Adjust mark	Overwrite text at cursor position and leave blanks at source
Unmark	Remove any mark on the current window
Delete mark	Remove mark and delete text in it, leaving spaces
Print mark	Print a copy of the marked text

The Search menu pops up as a dialog box. This dialog box is where you can specify the characters you want to find, or in the case of Grep, you can search for special pattern-matching characters within the search string. This option uses a pattern-matching string expression to find your characters. For examples of this, see the online help file under Grep.

Table 13.6. Search menu commands.

Menu Item	*Description*
Search	Display the search pop-up dialog box for file search
Find next	Find the next occurrence of the initial search
Change next	Repeat the previous change command
Bookmarks	Create, list, and find bookmarks in your current file

By now you should already know how to start the program. After starting your program, type the following text (with the spelling errors):

```
   The Privacy Act of 1974 provides that each Federal Agency inform
individuals, whom it asks to information supply, of the authrity for
the solcitation of the information and whether disclosure of such
information is mandatory or voluntary;..
```

As you can see, the paragraph contains numerous typos and words that are not spelled correctly. Figure 13.27 shows an EPM file with typed text, except that the text extends beyond the screen. This is because the margin has a default setting of 254 for the right margin. You can change the margin by selecting Options/Preferences/Settings to pop up the familiar dialog box on your screen that looks like one of your program settings notebooks.

Click with your mouse on the Margins tab and you discover why you couldn't see all the text on your screen. Here you can change the left and right margin, and also a paragraph margin. This paragraph margin allows you to place the first line in a new paragraph to a different margin. The number for the paragraph margin has to fall between the left and right margin. Now change the right margin to 80. Click on one of the buttons below to have the change take effect.

For the purpose of this example, enter the number 80 on the right margin and click on Apply. If you decide later to make your change permanent, you can choose the Set button instead. You should have a pop-up dialog box that asks you whether you want to reflow the document to the new margins. Select the Yes button with your mouse pointer and click. The text should now be reformatted to the new margins. Now correct the typo in the phrase *of the authrity.* Place your pointer where the *o* should be placed in *authority* and type `o`. The letter should be inserted and the line will reflow to accomodate the extra character.

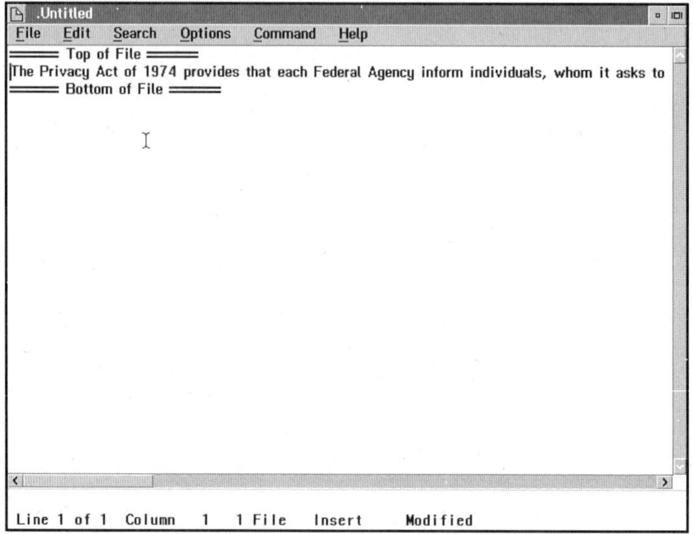

Figure 13.27. A text file in EPM.

Try the Search command by selecting Search/Search. Type `solcitation` in the Search box. Your screen should look like the one shown in Figure 13.28. In the Replace box, type `solicitation` and click the Find button. Notice that the word has been found and there is a large circle around the word in the editing window. Now you have several choices: click on Change, then find; Change; or Change, cancel. Click on Change and then find, and you will notice that the typo was replaced by "solicitation." Also, the circle around the found word is gone. The Search dialog box remains on-screen until you select the Cancel button.

In this example, move the word *information* behind the word *supply* so that the sentence ends with *supply information.* This requires using Edit/Cut, followed by Edit/Paste. First, mark the block with your pointer. To do this, position your mouse pointer and click on the beginning of the word *information*, then drag the highlighted block to the end of the word. Select Edit/Cut and notice that the word is deleted. Actually, it was deleted, but it was also copied to the Clipboard. You can then place the pointer to the new position for your word and select Edit/Paste. Voila! The word is back!

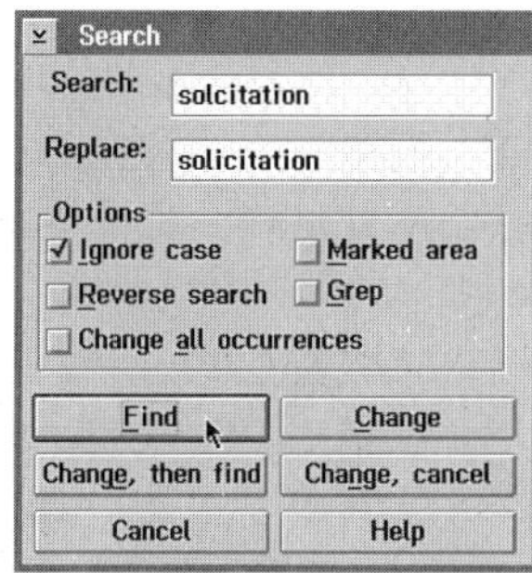

Figure 13.28. Searching in EPM.

I have demonstrated some simple editing techniques. The marking of the block is performed with the mouse pointer. The keyboard equivalent of marking a word is Shift and the right arrow key to mark the text to the right of the cursor. If you don't have a mouse, using OS/2 2.1 can be quite tedious! Occasionally, using keystrokes is faster than using a mouse, except that you do have to remember what the keystrokes are. You could use EPM as a word processor, but its real power lies in using its advanced features as a programmer's editor. (Other editing operations found in the Edit menu are covered in the online help.)

Power Features

With all new programs, it is tempting for users to experiment and try new things. With this program you can edit files, just like with a word processor. You should be careful, however, when you decide to create macros or REXX programs using this editor.

As with all changes to your original default settings, be sure that you have backed up your files before you begin to change anything on the editor or the OS/2 desktop. If you disregard this warning, you might change your editor or your system setup and not be able to restore your program back to its original state!

As an example, assume that you have logged on to CompuServe and retrieved the support files mentioned in the following list. You are probably wondering what to do with all this! Well, for starters, you can change the Enhanced Editor configuration and customize the way the editor works. The EPM editor is programmable in several ways.

Some EPM Support files in CompuServe OS2SUP Library 17.

EPMBK.ZIP	User's Guide and Tech. Reg in INF format
EPMMAC.ZIP	Macros used to build standard files
EPMHLP.ZIP	New help files
EPMSMP.ZIP	Sample macros
EBOOKE.ZIP	Add-on for Bookmaster support
LAMPDQ.ZIP	Lets you enter commands in EPM to send to VM host
EPMREX.ZIP	Sample REXX macros

If you want to get started using macros with EPM, but don't need all the support files, download the first four files. The other files are needed only if you want to do REXX programming or need VM host support.

The simplest way to customize EPM is to choose Options/Preferences. In this fashion, you can change the way that marking a block behaves by choosing the Options/Preferences/Advanced marking. Basically, this changes your mode of marking text from the simple CUA style to an Advanced mode that utilizes

both mouse buttons. Another change could be to reconfigure the Enter key. There are about six ways to do just that.

The next level of configuration is to write macros. By writing macros, you can take complete advantage of all the EPM's features. With macros, you can make the editor behave like another one with which you are more familiar. For example, if you are more familiar with the EMACS editor, you could reconfigure EPM to behave like the EMACS editor. Writing macros requires that you install the new support files and move your EPM editor to a new subdirectory. The default installation has EPM residing in the \OS2\APPS subdirectory.

There is also a way to control EPM via the DDE. This is how the Workframe/2 IBM compiler product works with EPM.

Some other features in EPM involve using the Command dialog box. By knowing some simple commands, you can perform search and replace operations more effectively, run OS/2 commands from inside EPM, change margins dynamically, change the default colors, and more.

One of the most powerful ways to use EPM without writing macros is to use editing commands. The Enhanced Editor has a variety of general-purpose editing commands. Several of them are already available through the menu bar. You can use commands through the Command/Command dialog. This brings up a dialog box so you can type commands and execute them from within EPM. EPM has an extensive list of available commands. You can also execute any OS/2 command from within EPM. Note the following example of an EPM editing command:

```
MARGINS 1 75 5
```

In the previous example, you set the right margin to column 75, the left margin to column 1, and the paragraph indent to column 5. This command allows you to set your margins by typing into the Command dialog box instead of having to change the settings notebook. The advantage of this approach is that you can make changes to your editor dynamically and much faster. Also, there are more options available to you through commands than using the menu. Later in this section I will talk about how to use macros. Both commands and macros can be used together to configure your editor.

At this point, it may be useful to try a few more examples of commands to give you a taste of the power of EPM. If you want to look for all the README files on your hard drive, you could use your Seek and Scan Files (PMSEEK) utility applet, although then you would have to load the file into EPM the old-fashioned way. Even if you selected EPM as your default editor under PMSEEK, you still couldn't edit multiple files.

Type the following line in your Command dialog window. You can use either the mouse or the keyboard (Ctrl-I) to bring up the dialog box. When the dialog box pops up, type the following command in the box:

```
LIST README
```

The result of the `LIST` command should appear between the file markers inside the editor window. What you have is a list of all the files matching your specification. From this point, you can select the file to edit by selecting the file with your mouse pointer and then using Alt-1 (Alt and number 1) with the keyboard. This loads the README file into the EPM window.

Had you selected some options by having the Options/Preferences - Ring enabled, you could then recall your original directory of the README files and select another file from that directory. As you can see, you could edit files much quicker this way than by using the Open menu bar.

TIP

Using the Command dialog box as I just described, you can create a SHELL for OS/2 commands inside EPM. If you need to run them, you can select that EPM window and type the command. This is useful for recording to file the intermediate results of OS/2 commands, without having to use the OS/2 I/O redirection commands. To use this example, type `SHELL` in the Command dialog box. A new EPM window called .command_shell 1 appears, and inside EPM is an OS/2 command prompt. You can type `DIR` to get a directory listing of your current directory. If the

command results in a long listing, you can use the scroll bars in EPM to view the rest. I use this technique when I want to view what's inside a zipped file. If you use the OS/2 full-screen session, the results will sometimes scroll off the top of the screen. With this technique, you can use the scroll bars to view what went past the top of the screen. If you want to get rid of your SHELL file, close that EPM file.

There are many more editing commands that you will find useful. For a complete listing and explanation of these commands, read the online help file.

One last power feature to mention about EPM is the direct manipulation of the file icon object. First, the file icon is located to the left of the title bar. Some of the things you can do with this icon are as follows:

- print the current file
- copy a file to another edit window
- create another edit window for your file
- copy the file to a desktop folder

To manipulate the file icon, you need to use mouse button 2 to click on the icon. You can, for example, hold the button and move the pointer to Print Manager to print the file loaded into EPM. You can also drag the icon to another EPM window to copy the file. If you drag the icon to a folder, it creates an icon for that file. This is one of the new implementations of CUA '91, and you'll probably see more programs implement this standard in the future.

Macros

Macros are text files containing source code in E language. They can also include EPM commands embedded in the source code. First you create them with an editor and save them under the .E extension. Then compile them with the ETPM compiler to create .EX, which are executable macros. These .EX executable macros are interpreted at runtime. You can control EPM's mode of operation with the macros. Also, you can add new commands or change the existing commands. There is a standard EPM.EX file that's included in the base package and contains the standard default values in EPM.

For macro creation, you need to become familiar with the E language. Then modify the source code of some existing macros and recompile them with the ETPM compiler. You can control macros on two different levels: one level is to create a MYCNF.E file and set flags to control the EPM editor; the second level is to actually write your own macros.

Included in the support package are files that were copied over to the \EDIT\EMACROS subdirectory. These files are the constants written in E source code for the standard configuration of EPM. Some of the files, for example, are STDCNF.E and COLOR.E, which control the colors displayed on the screen as well as margin settings, tab settings, cursor size, terminal emulation to be used during host sessions, and so on. Changing the constants in the default STDCNF.E file (or any of the distributed E files) is not recommended. You can override the STDCNF.E file settings by using an MYCNF.E file. The advantages of controlling EPM through the MYCNF.E file are as follows:

- Upgrading the toolkit to a newer version is simple by copying over the old files. You won't have to merge modified STDCNF.E code with the new one.
- Macro writers can include your MYCNF.E file and also use the constants you defined, even if their own code isn't included in the base set of E code.

Before you proceed with the next example, be sure that you have a backup of the files you'll be examining. If you accidently modify these standard files, your EPM editor may become erratic.

To better understand the sequence of events in macro creation, examine the EPM.E source code file. This file is the standard file that compiles into EPM.EX and is executed at runtime. Start your EPM editor, select File/Open, and click the File list button. Next, double-click on the \EDIT subdirectory under the file list box and double-click on the \EMACROS subdirectory. Scroll the bar in the file box until you find the EPM.E file. When you find it, select it with your pointer and click on the Open button. The EPM.E file will appear in a new EPM window. Be sure that you don't inadvertently modify this file! Notice the source code in this file in Listing 13.2.

Listing 13.2. Source code of the EPM.E file.

```
========== Top of File ========
include 'e.e' -- This is the main file for all versions of E.
==========Bottom of File ======
```

The only line in the source code is an `include` statement pointing to the E.E file. To continue your quest for knowledge, select File/Quit to close this file. Now select File/Open and follow the last steps you did to find the E.E file in the EMACROS subdirectory. Load that file into EPM (see Figure 13.29) and note the source code.

Now you can see how the different .E files are linked together in EPM. The EPM.E file has one `include` statement pointing to the E.E file. The E.E file has all the rest of the `include` statements, defining all the configurable aspects of EPM. Notice also that there are statements in this file with command language. These are the next level of configuration for the Enhanced Editor. For more information on the correct syntax of the E language and the command language, see the *EPM Users Guide* included in the EPMBK.ZIP file (EPMUSER.INF and EPMTECH.INF).

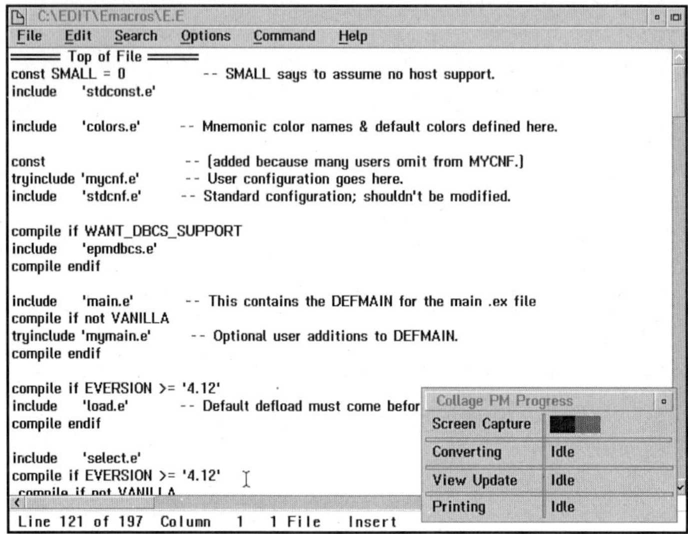

Figure 13.29. The E.E file in our EPM window.

The macros must be compiled from the .E file into an .EX file using the ETPM compiler included in the support package. Once compiled, the EPM will be configured with your new changes. If you compile a macro to create an EPM command, you can execute that command from the Command/Command dialog menu, as mentioned previously.

Macro language is described in detail in one of the files included in EPMBK.ZIP. This file contains the *EPM Users Guide* and the *EPM Technical Reference Guide,* both viewable with the VIEW.EXE command.

I have discussed the macro language and how it is used to make configuration changes to the Enhanced Editor. I hope you have been able to see the

power of macros and what steps to take to create and compile them. Many of the functions of EPM, however, are programmable by using the Options menu command.

Understanding the Options Menu

The Options menu offers an extensive number of choices. These are available through the individual submenus under each of the commands. In this section I discuss only the Preferences and the Frame controls submenus. The others are left as an exercise for the interested reader. The Options/Preferences/Settings menu brings up the settings notebook.

Each tab in your notebook has different options that you can change. Table 13.7 shows the available options in the notebook and their meanings.

Table 13.7. The settings notebook options.

Option	*Description*
Tabs	Enter a number for a fixed-tab interval
Margins	Set the left, right, and paragraph margins
Colors	Change the different colors in EPM
Paths	Set up the Autosave and Temporary paths for your files
Autosave	Number of modifications before your file is autosaved
Fonts	Change the default EPM font and attribute
Keys	Allows you to change some of the keystroke definitions

In addition to the Preferences/Settings, there are options you can set from the menu bar that modify EPM in several ways. Table 13.8 shows the commands and what they do.

Table 13.8. The Options/Preferences menu bar.

Option	*Description*
Settings	You can choose the settings notebook
Advanced marking	Switches between basic marking mode to advanced
Stream editing	Switches between stream-mode and line-mode editing
Ring enabled	Allows mulitple files to exist in the edit ring
Stack commands	Enables or disables stack-related commands in edit

The Advanced marking command allows you to change how EPM responds to marking blocks. If you have not selected this option, the mouse behaves like the normal CUA block-pointing device. That is, you can select an object (word) by clicking mouse button 1. If you want to extend the mark to the whole word, double-click mouse button 1. To continue the block to include the paragraph, hold mouse button 1 and drag the pointer until the highlight is over the whole paragraph.

Once you select Advanced marking, you have four ways to mark a block:

- block mark
- line mark
- word mark
- character mark

For a block mark, you can follow these basic steps:

1. Place the mouse pointer over the position where you want to start the mark.
2. Hold mouse button 1.
3. Drag the mouse pointer until you form a rectangular box around your object.
4. Release mouse button 1.

For a line mark, do the following:

1. Place the mouse pointer on the line where you want to start the mark.
2. Hold mouse button 2.
3. Drag the pointer to the end of the last line you wish to mark.
4. Release mouse button 2.

For a word mark, do the following:

Double-click mouse button 2 over the word you wish to mark.

For the character mark, do the following:

1. Place the mouse pointer over the character you want to mark.
2. Hold down the Ctrl key and mouse button 2.
3. Drag the mouse pointer to the new location.

You can also use your keyboard to do the marking. For more information, check the online help file.

Once you get used to the advanced marking method, you'll probably have trouble going back to the old basic way. If you thought that was enough, there are still more features in EPM that are enabled by Ring enabled and the Stack commands menu.

The Ring enabled settings allow you to set up multiple files to exist in a ring list. This means that you'll be able to load a file in the ring list and switch between files by clicking on the circular button on the top-right side of the menu bar. If you enable this feature, you also add another selection in the Options menu called List ring. This is extremely helpful for edits on multiple files.

Stack commands are enabled with a click on the menu bar and appear as additional commands in the Edit menu. If you look at your Edit menu after enabling the Stack commands, you'll notice all the extra ones available. For those of you not familiar with the functions of a stack, this is what a programming register in the CPU is called; it allows you to put things into it—like a Clipboard—and retrieve them for later use.

The next part of the Options menu I want to discuss is the Frame controls menu. Here is the place where you can configure EPM to show you messages, scroll bars, status line, rotate buttons (for ring list), and change the information displayed. All the settings you make in this menu and the Preferences menu will not be saved unless you click your mouse pointer over the Options/Save options button.

If you make changes to your EPM editor and later want to restore the defaults, one quick way is to find the EPM.INI file, usually found in the \OS2 subdirectory, and delete it. Your program will create a new EPM.INI file the next time you start the editor. Remember that by doing so, you lose any configuration settings you may have preset.

Under the Help menu bar is the Quick reference selection. This takes you to a pop-up help screen that you can edit, and to your own help information. Also on this help screen is a summary of all the editing keystrokes available in EPM.

Printing and Formatting

The last part of the Enhanced Editor to discuss is how to print with this program and what features are available for formatting text. If you select File/Print file from the menu bar, it brings up a Print dialog box like the one shown in Figure 13.30.

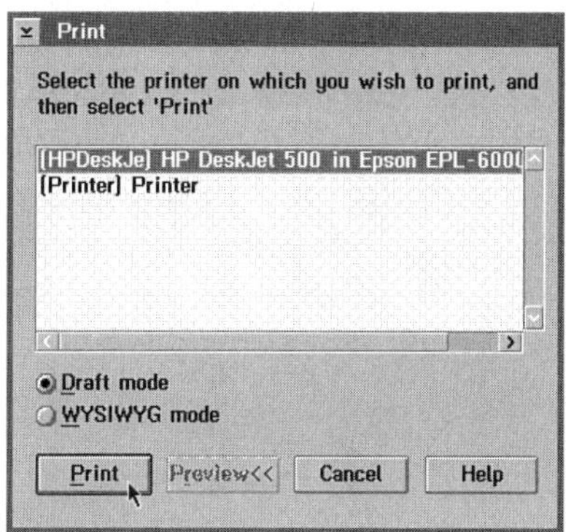

Figure 13.30. *The Print file dialog box.*

From this dialog box you must choose the printer (if you have more than one) and whether you want to print in draft mode or in WYSIWYG (what-you-see-is-what-you-get) mode. The differences are listed as follows:

WYSIWYG	What you see is what you get. The printed text looks exactly as it does on the screen, including font and sizes. Also, when you select WYSIWYG, the Preview mode is enabled. This lets you preview several pages if you have them.
Draft mode	Text is printed from the default printer font. It ignores the fonts you selected and the sizes.

If you are using WYSIWYG mode, the light foreground colors do not appear on a noncolor printer. Also, background colors are ignored in this mode.

Formatting files involves using the Edit menu. In this menu you will see the Style command. First, mark the block, select the Edit/Style command, and pick a particular font, size, color, or attribute you want to apply.

The Style menu pops up a dialog box (see Figure 13.31) where you can apply the formatting you want, create style combinations, and register it with your program. Then you can reuse it from this dialog box without having to recreate it. If you register your style, you'll be able to save it under a Style name and recall it from the list box.

Figure 13.31. The Style dialog box.

Formatting capabilities are limited in EPM, but you must realize that this program was not intended to be a word processor. If you need to create documents with many different types of styles, a word processor might be better suited for your work. Also, in this release of Enhanced Editor, there is no spell checking capability. The spell checker is sold separately as an add-on product by IBM.

Other OS/2 Applets

In this section I'll cover a few more applets. You will find that the applets not mentioned in this chapter are fairly straightforward and don't require much explanation. Don't forget to check the online help menu for more information.

Seek and Scan Files—OS/2 2.1's Most Useful Applet!

This applet, sometimes referred to as PMSEEK, is so useful in your everyday activities that you may want to make a shadow of this on your desktop. With this applet you can find those pesky files that seem to be lost in that 20 gigabyte drive on your notebook computer. You can also search for text found inside files and then start your editor. This program is in the Productivity folder. Start this applet by double-clicking on the icon.

After you start the program, you'll notice the different choices available (see Figure 13.32). In this program you can search for the filename, including using the wildcard specification `*.*`, although I don't recommend searching without having something more than a wildcard. It's helpful to do searches with some part of the filename. You can also choose a text to search and specify the drives and the editor you want to use to edit.

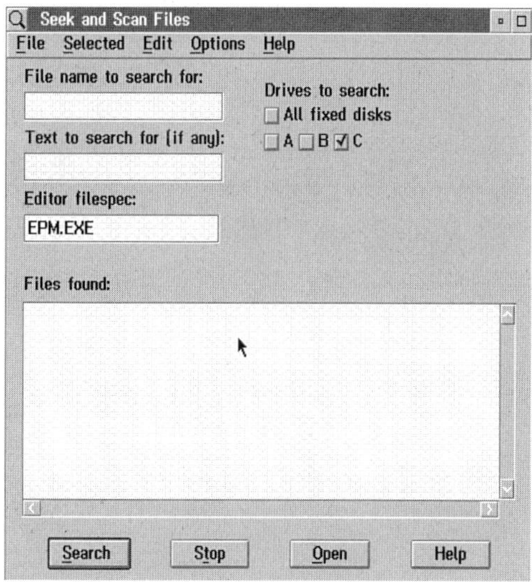

Figure 13.32. PMSEEK's dialog box.

Once you begin the search with the button, the files found window lists all the files matching the specification you chose. From here you can start your editor by selecting the file with your mouse pointer and then clicking the Open button. Another way to start the EPM editor (if that's your editor of choice) is to use the drag-and-drop technique. The EPM editor would have to be started, or the icon visible, for you to use this technique. Then you simply select the file from the Files found window and click mouse button 2. While depressing mouse button 2, drag it into the EPM icon and drop it inside. This starts EPM with the file you selected. Also, remember from the discussion on the EPM editor that you can follow the procedure as described and drop the file into the titlebar of EPM. Both methods start an EPM window with our file opened inside.

After you have completed your search, you can also start the programs you've found, or you can use the Selected/Command to run `COPY`, `ERASE`, `RENAME` or any other OS/2 commnands. The Selected/Process command is the one to use to start the selected program.

The PMSEEK program should become a daily part of your OS/2 computing life. With the ability to find your files with a wildcard, filename, or text search, PMSEEK makes your job of finding files a lot easier. If you have found the file you need, you can stop PMSEEK and begin editing, or perform any OS/2 commands on the selected file. This last part is great for finding duplicate files and deleting them (see Figure 13.33).

> TIP
>
> You can also start PMSEEK from the OS/2 command line. Just type `PMSEEK` with the search specifications and the program starts, bringing up the Seek and Scan Files dialog box with the filename box already listing a choice. The only disadvantage of doing this is that you won't be able specify a search to multiple drives or text search until after the dialog box pops up and the search is complete.

You won't be able to use Options/Set defaults to save the settings on your session. This is a known bug in OS/2 2.1 and probably will be corrected with the next release. In the meantime, you'll have to set your Options every time you start this program.

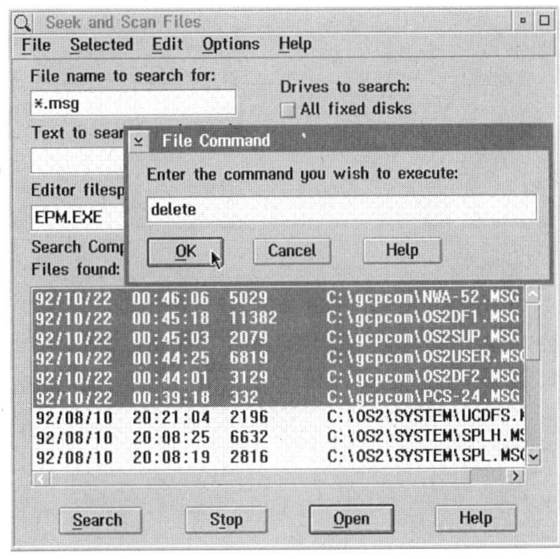

Figure 13.33. Using PMSEEK to find and delete unwanted files.

Pulse—Monitor CPU Performance

This applet shows a graphical presentation (see Figure 13.34) of the CPU's activity. By having Pulse started, you can monitor how much CPU time a particular program is using. Like all the other applets, Pulse is found inside the Productivity folder. The scale of the graph displays a window where 0 percent is represented by the bottom of the window, and 100 percent is at the top. Before you start Pulse, you can set up some startup options (see Table 13.9) in your settings notebook under Parameters.

Table 13.9. Startup options for Pulse.

Option	*Description*
NOICON	Show a minature graph of pulse when the program is minimized, instead of an icon
NOMENU	Don't show a menu bar
SMOOTH	Show a smooth line graph
FILL	Show a filled graph

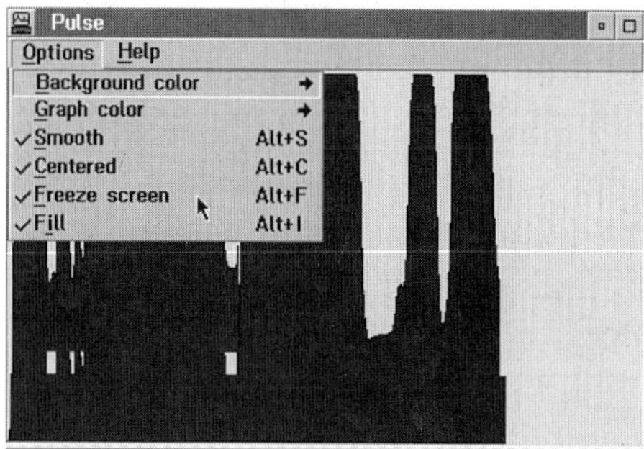

Figure 13.34. Pulse showing the Options menu bar.

One of the many uses I have found for Pulse is to monitor how much the CPU is being used when running DOS programs in VDM environment. In the DOS settings notebook, you can fine-tune the program using the Session tab (see Figure 13.34), adjust the `IDLE_SENSITIVITY`, and affect the polling time before the system reduces the polling program's portion of CPU time.

There is one caveat to using Pulse for this purpose. Pulse could give erroneous information in the case of a program that constantly polls the keyboard (Word Perfect 5.1). It may be idle, but Pulse thinks the CPU has a lot of activity; therefore, it shows the graph at 100 percent all the time.

Clipboard Viewer—Exchange Data Between OS/2 and WINOS/2

To view the contents of the Clipboard, you can select the Clipboard Viewer icon found in the Productivity folder and double-click on it with mouse button 1. Once started (see Figure 13.35), you can use the menu bar to Display/ Render in various formats.

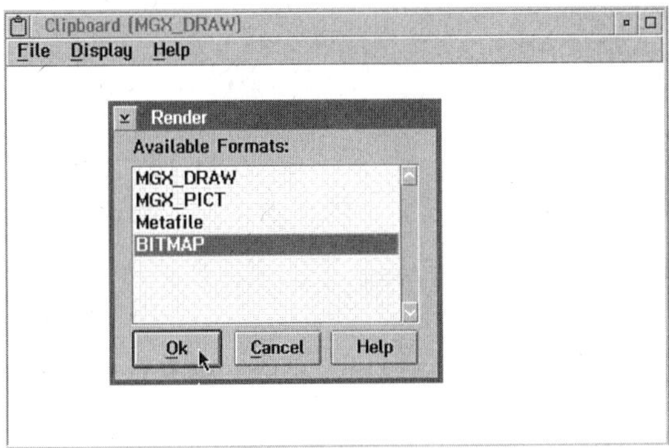

Figure 13.35. Clipboard Viewer with the Render formats.

Under the OS/2 System folder there is an icon for WIN-OS/2 Setup. If you double-click on this icon, you'll be able to open the settings notebook. In this notebook is a tab for Data Exchange. Here is the place to turn things on or off with respect to the DDE and the Clipboard to private or public. See Chapter 9, "WIN-OS/2—Windows in OS/2," for more information on the differences between public and private clipboards.

Picture Viewer

This program will display metafiles (.MET), picture interchange (.PIF), and spool files (.SPL). Picture Viewer is located in the Productivity folder and can be started by double-clicking the icon with mouse button 1. Once started, you can select File/Open to bring up the Picture Viewer dialog box. In this box you can select from the file list the one you wish to view. The lower part of the box contains the button to pick for the type of file you want. By clicking on that type, you can discriminate when selecting from the file list. In other words, if you click on *.MET, the metafiles will be the only ones listed (see Figure 13.36) in the files window.

Once you find a file, you can open the file or simply select it with your mouse, then double-click on it. This loads that file into the Picture Viewer window, where you can view, cut-and-paste to the Clipboard, and print it. You can also zoom on the picture by moving the pointer to the area you want to zoom and double-clicking mouse button 1. The picture can be zoomed five times. Once you enlarge the picture you can use the scroll bars to view it. To zoom out of the picture, hold the Shift key and double-click mouse button 1 again.

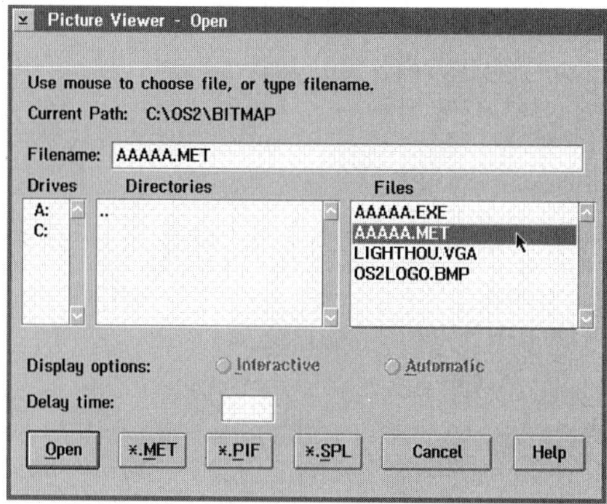

Figure 13.36. Picture Viewer File/Open dialog box.

There is some practical use for viewing pictures, but the most useful feature of Picture Viewer is the ability to display .SPL files. These are the files created when you send something to the printer. The files will have names such as

000001.SPL, and by opening your Print Manager, you can double-click on the print object and the .SPL file will be loaded into the Picture Viewer (if it's a metafile) or the System Editor. The best way to clear up this confusion is to illustrate this with an example. First, select your printer object and double-click on the icon. When the printer object opens, select the system menu (see Figure 13.37). This is the menu that appears at the top-left corner of the window when you click once on the Print Manager icon. Now select Change status/ Hold on the menu bar. This prevents the file from being printed before you have a chance to view it. Next, open the Information folder and the Command Reference book icon.

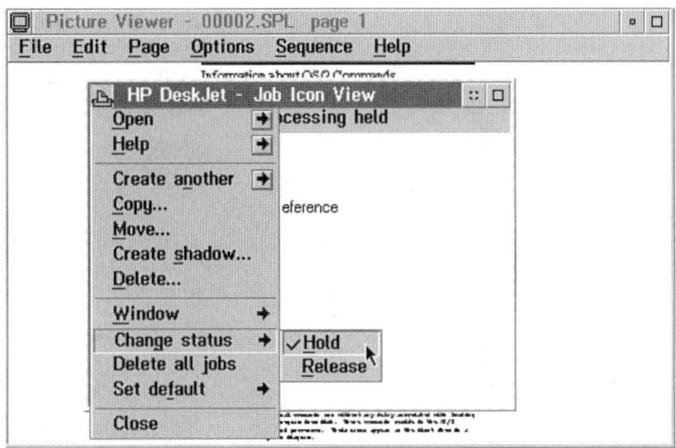

Figure 13.37. Making your printer object hold all jobs.

When the OS/2 Command Reference file is opened, select the Introduction for topic and double-click on it. You should have the Introduction information appearing on your screen. Now, click on the Print button at the bottom of the window. When the Print dialog box appears, select the This section button and then the Print button. Wait for the Print dialog box to disappear, then close the OS/2 Command Reference file. Now open your printer object and you'll notice the print object appear. It should not be printing, because you selected to Hold all jobs in the queue. Next, double-click on the print object and your

Picture Viewer will be started with your 000001.SPL file loaded. The information will appear in WYSIWYG format, so it's an excellent time to check the format of the page. From here you can zoom to double size the area that you want, cut and paste, or view the next page if you have multiple pages.

This little applet can let you preview your print jobs, even if they don't originate from a word processor or any program that already has a printing preview mode. Although it may not replace the preview mode of the Enahanced Editor, or other OS/2 programs, it does provide that capability in a limited fashion. In the exercise you just performed, don't forget to reset your printer object so that the future print jobs won't be held in the queue.

When you send files to the spooler as in the preceding example, the files will be named beginning with 00001.SPL, the next will be 000002.SPL, and so on.

Sticky Pad

This program is the electronic equivalent of the yellow Post-It notes. You can use it to make reminder notes that you can "stick" on the screen. Use Sticky Pad to write up to ten notes on your screen and include picture graphics (from the same one as the PMDIARY program) and itemized activities. After you create these notes you can stick them in any of the four corners of your computer screen.

To start the program, double-click on the Sticky Pad icon in the Productivity folder. The first window with Sticky-0 on the title bar (see Figure 13.38) will appear on the screen. You can begin typing your note. The program will date-stamp your note; however, this can be reset by way of the Edit/Reset timestamp. From this pull-down menu you can also select many other choices, such as Edit/Graphics. Also, the program can be customized to save the position of the pad on the screen, colors, font size, and icon position.

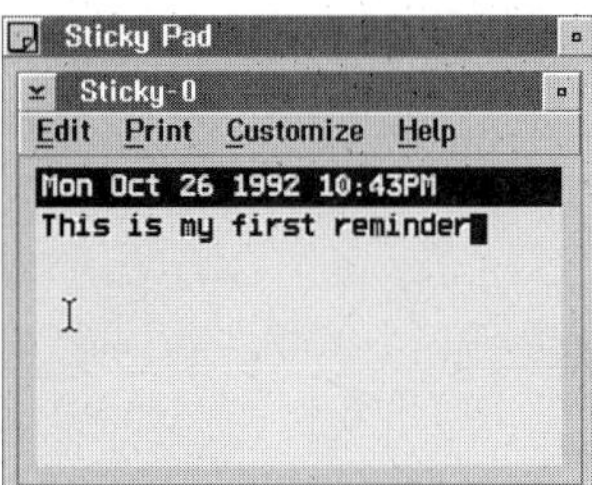

Figure 13.38. Sticky Pad started with first note.

To place the Sticky-0 note somewhere on the screen, select the title bar and drag it somewhere away from the applet. As soon as you drag the first note, the Sticky-1 note will appear. You can choose to leave the notes open or minimize them. When you minimize them, they will appear as small yellow squares with their corresponding number. The position of the minimized note depends on the Customize/Icon position you selected. If you attach the note to a folder, the note will disappear when you close or minimize the folder. After you open that folder again, the note will once again surface. To open the minimized notes, double-click on the small squared icon.

If you close the Sticky Pad program, *all* notes will disappear with it. They won't reappear until you start Sticky Pad again. This is a current bug in the OS/2 2.1 code.

Summary

By now you should have a better understanding of the power of OS/2 programs. The applets presented in this chapter can get you started toward being more productive with your computer. Some are just programs created to introduce you to their more powerful commercial versions. The others provide limited capability due to their features. I think you'll find use for some of them, if not all of them. Certainly the Enhanced Editor, PM Terminal, and PM Chart could easily surpass some DOS and Windows programs in their performance. The best part about these Productivity Applets is the price—they're free!

Author Bio

While in the United States Air Force, Edward Miller became active as an independent computer consultant. As a consultant, he worked with small businesses and professionals, designing and developing DBMSs using dBASE II and later RBASE. In March of 1984, he was hired by Northwest Airlines as an airline pilot. He currently flies as a First Officer on a DC10 based out of Boston, flying mostly Europe and Hawaii. In addition to his flying duties, he works with the Airline Pilot Association (ALPA) as their technical consultant on the Information Services Committee. He helped in the development and testing of a mainframe access system-using CIS as a gateway to access the IBM and Unisys mainframes by crewmembers. In this capacity, he set up a CompuServe forum for Northwest Airlines to support mainframe access.

14

Learning to Program—Tools, Tips, and Techniques

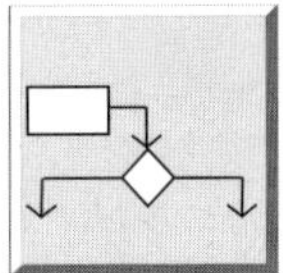

In This Chapter

OS/2 2.1 can be such an enjoyable environment to use, it's easy to forget that its primary (and rather mundane) purpose is to control the execution of computer programs. Similarly, in the course of executing these programs, it is easy to dismiss your favorite application and regard it simply as a consummate companion or ever-present business tool. Easy to dismiss, that is, unless you are a programmer. The simple and obvious truth of the matter is that every program you use, from spreadsheets to word processors to communications programs, needs to be written. The typical OS/2 programmer does not take this simple fact for granted, and you don't have to either. You don't need to be a professional programmer to learn how to program OS/2. All it takes is a little bit of hard work and perseverance.

This chapter is intended to provide new OS/2 programmers with an understanding of the issues that must be tackled before successfully developing OS/2 programs. I'll begin by introducing a few of the programming issues that make developing applications for OS/2 unique, and then I'll delve into the programming languages and tools you might use to create your own masterpieces. Because it is currently the most widely used collection of development tools available for OS/2 programming, I'll conclude with a discussion of IBM's WorkSet/2 product.

Basic OS/2 Programming Concepts

For application developers, OS/2's expanded capabilities do not come without a price. Moving to the OS/2 platform from DOS or Windows means tackling a new set of programming challenges and problems. At the same time, the multitasking and memory protection afforded by OS/2 gives the programmer a stable and dependable development environment. OS/2 quickly catches and shuts down programming errors that typically cause simple operating systems to freeze up or become corrupt. Although OS/2 forcibly stops errant programs, the rest of the operating system continues to function normally. For this reason alone, writing programs under OS/2 is much easier and considerably less frustrating than writing similar programs under other less-protected operating systems.

The topic of OS/2 programming is a large and complex one. Because OS/2 offers the user so much flexibility with regard to graphical interfaces, process control, device support, and system services, the programmer faces a daunting array of development tasks. Even a simple program that does little more than displaying a window with an innocuous "Hello World" message may span several pages of code. This additional complexity is understandably intimidating for many programmers.

Don't panic. The key to successfully mastering OS/2 programming involves patience and a slow, deliberate approach. You're likely to succeed if you don't try to learn everything at once. Although a comprehensive treatment of programming issues is beyond the scope of this chapter, several concepts are crucial to writing effective and efficient OS/2 applications. Specifically, the intelligent use of multithreading and dynamic link libraries (DLLs) can go a long way toward making your programs run faster, occupy less space, and operate in a way that a typical user might expect. Remember, a program that simply works is not necessarily a good OS/2 program.

Working with Messages

As you probably know, the Workplace Shell is the graphical interface you are presented with when you start OS/2. The Workplace Shell, in turn, runs on top of a subsystem called the Presentation Manager (PM). Programs that run in the PM environment and use the graphical presentation services it provides are called PM programs. Strictly speaking, it is possible to write OS/2 programs that are not PM programs, but this is the exception. The reason for this is simple: OS/2 was designed as a graphical environment, and a program needs to use the services that PM provides if it wants to take advantage of this fact. Still, there are many programs that do not use PM and operate in text mode. Device drivers, command-line utilities, data entry applications, and terminal emulators are a few of the program types that do not require—and are sometimes restricted by—a PM interface.

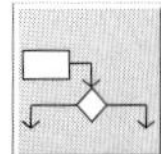

The Presentation Manager is based on an event-oriented messaging system. PM programs spend much of their time waiting for the user to initiate actions. As the user interacts with the PM interface, OS/2 generates event messages. For example, when a user clicks the button, a "Button Clicked" message is generated. When the user strikes a key on the keyboard, a "Key Pressed" message is generated. Some events may generate a flurry of messages, depending on the action's complexity. Programs may also send customized messages to themselves or other applications.

Programs using the traditional programming model execute blocks of code and pause for user input when necessary. PM programs, on the other hand, react to a stream of messages. This unique programming approach takes a little getting used to, especially if you have a lot of experience using the older procedural methods. The message-based model is a difficult hurdle facing the novice PM programmer, but once conquered, the rest of the learning experience is considerably easier.

Multitasking and Multithreading

One of OS/2's great strengths is its capability to run more than one program at a time. This feature, called multitasking, enables the machine's user to work simultaneously on several tasks at once. This capability's benefit becomes clear the first time you try to format a floppy disk while working in a spreadsheet or the first time you do a communications download while typing a memo with your word processor. Instead of waiting for a program to finish a lengthy task, multitasking effectively enables you to break away and do something else until the program is finished.

OS/2 uses a powerful multitasking variant called preemptive multitasking. Under the preemptive model, programs share the processor in a manner mandated by the operating system. Each program executes for a discrete period of time: a *time slice*. When the program's time slice ends, the operating system forcibly suspends the application and allows other programs to execute. This model ensures that no single program can monopolize the system's most precious resource: the microprocessor. Microsoft Windows, by comparison, uses cooperative multitasking. This model relies on the good behavior of individual programs to guarantee equal access to the processor. Because applications need to voluntarily yield the processor to other programs, a single, greedy program can dominate the entire operating system.

Multitasking alone, however, has several inherent limitations. For example, take the case of a user who is working on a document and wants to print a rough draft. Ideally, the user wants to tell the word processor to print the job in the background while she or he continues to edit the document in the foreground. With traditional multitasking operating systems, the individual can switch out and start another application; however, they still constrain the word processor to a single strand of execution and force the program to send the entire job to the printer before returning control to the user. Although there are ways around this problem, none are elegant, and all are resource-hungry.

Multithreading allows multiple parts of the same program to execute simultaneously. In the previous example, an OS/2 word processor could use a separate thread to process the print job and return control to the user almost immediately. The background thread would continue spooling the print job to the printer without locking up the program's user interface.

From a technical perspective, OS/2 distinguishes between processes and threads. A process contains its own main thread, virtual memory address space, file handles, and other crucial system resources. OS/2 considers these resources private and ensures that they are not accessible by other processes that may be running on the system. A process may create other threads that execute in parallel to the process' main thread. These threads can be created much more quickly than separate processes and can communicate with each other through shared memory.

I cannot overemphasize the importance of using efficient multithreading programming techniques. Too often, OS/2 programmers concentrate on sophisticated processing algorithms or impressive user interfaces without paying enough attention to the intelligent use of OS/2's multithreading facilities. Some programmers try to compensate for this by replacing the mouse pointer with the dreaded "ticking clock" icon and waiting for the lengthy processing to conclude. Although this helps to notify you to wait for a task to finish, it doesn't take advantage of the operating system services that make OS/2 so powerful. More importantly, it doesn't make the program as responsive or effective as it should be.

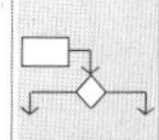

Dynamic Link Libraries

Dynamic link libraries are collections of code, data, and resources that are separated into external files. They are occasionally a source of confusion, not because they are particularly hard to understand, but because it is sometimes difficult to decide when and where they should be used. The simple truth is that all but the most trivial OS/2 programs can effectively use DLLs.

When you run a program that uses DLLs, the operating system figures out which DLLs the program needs and loads them into memory. Once a DLL is loaded, the program can call functions in the DLL as if they resided in the executable file. Data and PM resources embedded within the DLL can also be accessed and manipulated seamlessly. A DLL that is loaded into memory can share its code and data resources with any process running on the machine. This is tremendously useful when you want to share a piece of code between several separate programs.

Consider, for example, a large accounting system that includes several programs. Most programs have a significant amount of code in common—both the accounts receivable module and the accounts payable module might need to retrieve information from the master ledger database. By placing the routines that interact with ledger files into a single DLL, you can ensure that only one copy of the code is simultaneously in memory. This procedure also ensures that only one copy of the code needs to be shipped with the system. This saves storage space and requires less memory—two of the sacred cows for programming in any environment. Figure 14.1 illustrates how such an accounting system might use DLLs to minimize duplicated code and wasted memory.

Dynamic link libraries are excellent mechanisms for extending OS/2's system services or for providing your own new operating system services. If a developer wants to provide electronic mail services to OS/2 programs, code can be placed in a DLL and installed in a directory on the `LIBPATH`. In this way, any application that knows which functions are in the DLL can access and use the E-mail services.

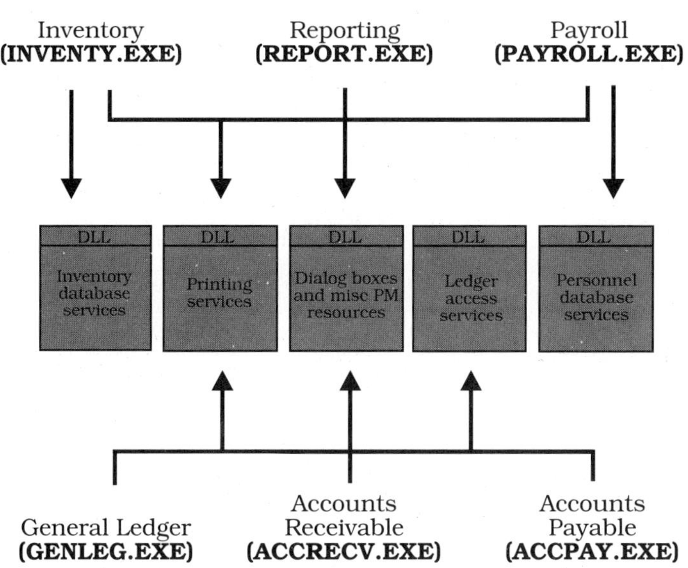

Figure 14.1. A hypothetical accounting system DLL usage.

> NOTE
>
> When choosing names for your DLLs, try to think up something that is intuitive and specific. If you choose a generic name, chances are high that someone else might use the same name when building a DLL. You can imagine the resulting chaos if both DLLs were installed on the same system. (Don't laugh, this is not an uncommon occurrence.) You could name an accounting DLL containing common code something like ACCCMMN.DLL or CMMNACC.DLL, not COMMON.DLL. An even better solution is to incorporate your company's name or initials into the DLL name.

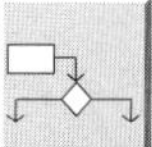

Language Choices

A variety of language compilers and interpreters are available that support the creation of native 32-bit OS/2 applications. IBM has compilers that support programs written in C, C++, Macro Assembler, COBOL, and FORTRAN. Programming languages that are offered or supported by third-party vendors include Ada, Basic, C, C++, COBOL, FORTRAN, Modula-2, Pascal, Prolog, Smalltalk, and many others. Clearly the number of development options available to the OS/2 programmer is growing at a rapid pace.

Since the early days of OS/2, C has been its primary programming language. C has traditionally been the mainstream language that has received the strongest support from IBM and third-party developers. The vast majority of existing OS/2 applications are written in C, and most companies regard C as the language of choice for OS/2 development. I think you will find that it is the language with the largest variety of supporting programming tools and utilities.

Object-Oriented Programming

Lately, a lot of talk has surrounded object-oriented programming (OOP), and no discussion of OS/2 programming is complete without some mention of it. Most contemporary computer languages encourage the use of a programming style called structured programming. Programmers who employ this model can write complex programs quite easily, so it comes as no surprise that these languages have prospered. However, a common complaint about structured languages is that as a program grows in size it becomes considerably more difficult to understand and support. By the time a C or Pascal program nears 75,000 lines of code it has typically turned into a maintenance nightmare. It is rare to find a programmer that can completely understand all the nuances of a program that large.

Object-oriented languages (including C++) are designed to help alleviate the burden of maintaining large programs. In doing so, these languages have also bridged a conceptual gap that has always existed between the way a program is written and the way people interact with the world. Perhaps the following example most clearly demonstrates this. In the real world, a person doesn't need to understand the details of how the internal combustion engine operates just to drive a car.

In the course of our day-to-day lives, we constantly deal with objects. Objects are items that possess distinct characteristics and traits. Basketball objects are round, book objects have pages, and ice cube objects are cold. There are a whole range of actions that you can perform on or with these objects. You can bounce a basketball and read a book. Sometimes these actions can modify the attributes of the object. If you heat an ice cube it is no longer ice, it is water. OOP uses these sorts of object/action relationships as the foundation for a programming technology.

Programmers create their own objects by first defining object classes. These classes provide a description of an object's traits (class variables) and possible actions (class methods). Individual objects that belong to a particular class are called instances. When you want to perform an action on or with the object, you send an object instance a message telling it to execute one of its methods.

As an example, take the programmer who has been asked to design an automobile class. Such a class might contain data that describes the car's various attributes. There may be one variable that details the car's color, another that identifies how many doors the car has, and yet another that represents the direction the car is facing. Because objects describe both data and potential actions, the car class might contain a method that controls the engine's acceleration. Another method might turn the car left or right. The developer could then create an instance of this class, and by sending a message to it, execute the "TurnLeft" method. This method, in turn, would change the value of the variable that stores the direction the car is facing.

Perceiving a programming task as simply defining the interactions between preexisting objects can help to dramatically reduce program complexity. But OOP can also reduce the program's physical number of source code lines. The key lies in using an object-oriented programming mechanism called inheritance. An object class that is said to be inherited from another object class is called a derived object class; the original object class is called the base object class. Instances of the derived class get all of the same variables and methods as instances of the base class. Only the variables and methods that make the inherited class unique need to be added to the new class definition. As an

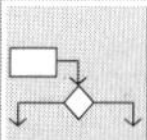

example, you could create a derived car class called `SportsCar`. Instances of this class would still have the `Color`, `NumDoors`, and `FacingDirection` variables. These instances would also have the same turning and acceleration methods. These variables and methods would be automatically available to the `SportsCar` class, even though they are not directly defined in that class' definition. Then you could augment your derived class by giving it additional variables and methods to represent insurance penalties and better performance characteristics.

Sophisticated programs construct large hierarchies of object classes, each inheriting the attributes and methods of its base class. This cuts down dramatically on the amount of code duplicated in the system and allows buy fixes and performance improvements to cascade down the inheritance chain without physically changing every object class definition.

Although C remains the dominant language in OS/2 development, it's getting a lot of competition from object-oriented languages such as C++ and Smalltalk. Object-oriented languages are especially well suited for writing graphical programs, and PM programs in particular. This is because, in many ways, the PM programming interface model is already object-oriented. User interface controls in PM have an inherent knowledge of their internal state, and programs manipulate these internal states by sending messages to them. For instance, an entry-field control "knows" what its current contents are, and you can either set or query this value by sending specific messages to it.

Picking the Tools

Developers use programming environments in much the same way that a secretary might use a word processor or an accountant might use a spreadsheet. Without an effective set of tools at your disposal, OS/2 programming rapidly becomes a difficult and unpleasant opponent. Many products fall under the nebulous category of "development tools," so before you start concentrating on specific products, it's probably beneficial to review the classes of tools that you might want to use.

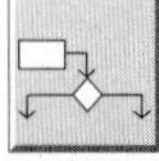

One phrase that you will encounter often is *integrated development environment*, or IDE. IDEs provide a single access point for all the development tools that you might need. Instead of interacting with an editor, compiler, and project control system as separate components, an IDE couples them together so that they work in harmony. For example, a common feature implemented in many IDEs relates to the processing of compiler error messages. Most compilers display a line number when they encounter a programming error that prevents them from continuing. Many IDEs enable the user to select the error message text, and by performing some action, start the programmer's editor and place the cursor on the offending line. This is a dramatic improvement over the separate tool approach. Using separate tools, this operation usually requires the programmer to pipe the compiler's output into a file, examine the file to find the line number, and then use the cursor keys or editor "jump" command to move manually to the line. As you might imagine, IDEs are especially useful for inexperienced programmers who have not yet mastered the arcane art of command-line compilers and make files.

Language Compilers and Interpreters

When programmers talk about tools, they are actually talking about several classes of products. Perhaps the most obvious of these is the language compiler. Depending on the product you purchase, this could be a command-line compiler, a compiler functioning inside an integrated development environment, or a compiler that is built into an integrated environment. Borland's C++, for example, can function as a command-line compiler. The IBM C Set/2 compiler, when used inside the WorkFrame/2 environment, runs in a PM window that is part of an integrated product. Finally, the incremental compiler supplied with Digitalk's Smalltalk/V is built into the development environment.

Most vendors ship their command-line compilers with a make program. The make program enables you to describe your program's structure so that the compiler only recompiles those modules that have changed or are dependent on the modules that have changed. Although this may not seem like such a big deal for smaller programs, for a large project with many source files, this becomes a very valuable and desirable capability. If your compiler is of the command-line variety, ensure that you acquire a make program that will work with it.

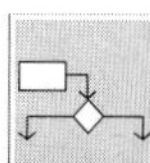

Developer's Toolkits

Some compilers might require you to invest in a developer's toolkit if you want to take advantage of all of OS/2's programming interfaces. The C Set/2 and Symantec's C++ compilers require the IBM Developer's Toolkit to write PM programs because it supplies the crucial header files needed to use functions in the standard OS/2 DLLs. The IBM toolkit also offers online documentation; utilities for creating icons, bitmaps, and dialog boxes; and other programming conveniences that help to make your life easier. Other vendors may decide to license the header files directly from IBM and provide their own utilities. This approach, which is the one taken by Borland, makes purchasing a separate toolkit unnecessary.

If you need to develop Workplace Shell objects, be sure your compiler provides som bindings. If it doesn't, you may have to also acquire the IBM Developer's Toolkit.

Debuggers

An important item in any developer's toolbox, professional or otherwise, is an effective debugger. A debugger enables you to easily move through your program—a line at a time if necessary—to investigate the values of program variables, registers, and memory segments. A good debugger helps you specify certain lines at which to stop execution (breakpoints). A good debugger also helps you to select a particular variable or memory address and stop execution when its value is changed (watchpoints). Almost every compiler vendor supplies a debugger with their compiler (or sells a debugger compatible with their compiler as a separate product).

Class Libraries

The concept of a class library is intimately coupled with object-oriented programming. Class libraries are collections of objects that programmers can

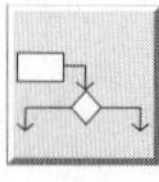

incorporate into their own programs. Because objects are complete unto themselves, a programmer need only know how to use the object—the rest is up to the object library. Some vendors have taken the idea of a class library and extended it to the idea of an applications framework. Technically speaking, applications frameworks are simply large class libraries, but they are usually constructed so they completely shape and direct the way you develop your program. Applications frameworks, because they try to be so comprehensive, usually contain a large collection of user-interface objects. Many also incorporate a variety of general-purpose classes.

Examples of application frameworks on the DOS and Windows side of the fence include Borland's TurboVision, the Object Windows Libraries (OWL), and the Microsoft Foundation Classes (MFC). Borland says that a version of OWL for OS/2 is in the works; because it will be based on a set of class libraries developed for Windows NT, OS/2 developers will probably have to wait a while before these frameworks become widely available. However, more specialized class libraries are available from a variety of other third-party sources. In addition, most C++ compilers ship with general-purpose class libraries of some sort. The Smalltalk language is notable because its standard implementation calls for a large set of ready-to-use object classes.

CASE Tools

If you need to get a program or prototype together as quickly as possible, you might be interested in one of the CASE tools available for OS/2 PM. CASE, which stands for computer aided software engineering, can quickly generate parts of your program's user-interface or execution logic. Tools like Gpf 2.0 from Gpf Systems or Case:PM VIP from Caseworks Inc. enable you to construct dialog boxes and windowed interfaces using a variety of easy-to-use editors and code builders. When your design is completed, the CASE tool generates the C code necessary to carry out your interface. The generated code is usually extensively commented and can be very useful as a learning aid that shows various programming techniques and operations. However, because the code is usually limited to the user interface, you need to modify it in strategic areas and add the customized functionally that your application requires. The CASE tools generally suggest where you should add your own processing logic and help you incorporate it into the final executable file.

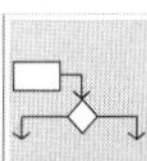

Most CASE tools do not come with a compiler or debugger and may also require that you purchase a developer's toolkit. Although this isn't a major failing, don't forget to factor these expenses into your purchasing decision.

IBM's Offerings

During OS/2's development, IBM realized that a key to getting developers to write quality 32-bit applications was to provide them with a robust and sophisticated suite of tools. Their answer was the C Set/2 compiler and debugger, the Developer's Toolkit, and the WorkFrame/2 (bundled together, IBM calls these tools the WorkSet/2). Because IBM's tools are so important and are in such widespread use, I will provide a more detailed look at these tools in later sections.

The C Set/2 compiler is a native 32-bit C and C++ compiler that can build full-screen text-mode, windowed text-mode, and PM programs (with the optional Developer's Toolkit). The compiler supports all the standard OS/2 system facilities such as multithreading, DLLs, and double-byte character sets. As of 2.1, the compiler also supports the creation of virtual device drivers (VDDs) and programs written in C++ (including advanced features like templates and exception handling). Hardware and software manufacturers typically use VDDs to allow integrated operation of their products in the OS/2 environment. The compiler supports IBM's Systems Application Architecture (SAA) and the American National Standards Institute (ANSI) C language specification.

A 32-bit PM debugger accompanies the C Set/2 compiler. With this debugger, you can view your source in its native format, assembly language, or a combination of the two. It has extensive support for breakpoints and watchpoints, in addition to an interesting variable monitor display with which you can display structures in detail or collapse them into a single entity. You can easily trace and examine linked lists and other dynamic data structures that depend on pointer links. Absent, however, is the capability to cast an arbitrary piece of memory into a given structure.

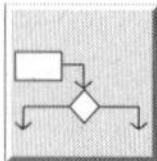

> TIP
>
> Like many PM-based debuggers, effective use of the C Set/2 debugger often requires opening many separate windows for variable inspectors, source views, register displays, and so on. Therefore, I highly recommend using the debugger with a high-resolution display adapter (800x600) and a large monitor (15 inches diagonal or greater). At normal VGA resolutions, you can easily run out of screen real estate.

One of the most innovative components of IBM's tool offering is the WorkFrame/2. In its simplest form, it is an integrated development environment. Perhaps the most interesting facet of the WorkFrame's approach is that it is inherently tool-independent. Unlike Borland's IDE, which forces you to use the environment's built-in editor, the WorkFrame enables you to use your own text editor. You can usually easily integrate any external tool into the WorkFrame environment. You can add most third-party utilities and development tools to the WorkFrame environment simply by filling in a dialog box.

Borland's Offerings

Borland's popular and elegant development products have long been favorites of professional and amateur programmers. Borland was the first company to release a comprehensive and affordable C++ compiler for DOS and Windows platforms. IBM realized early on that versions of Borland's C++ products would help dramatically boost developers' interest in OS/2. Borland's C++ comprises several separate components. Although a host of accompanying utilities are included, the main tools are the IDE, the command-line compiler, and the debugger. Figure 14.2 shows the IDE and the debugger in action.

Although integrated programming environments have been around for years, Borland set the standard when it introduced its DOS-based C++ product in 1990. Since then, the company has continued to refine the IDE's interface, and OS/2 programmers now have the opportunity to use a faithful port of the DOS favorite.

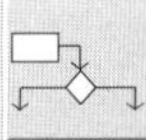

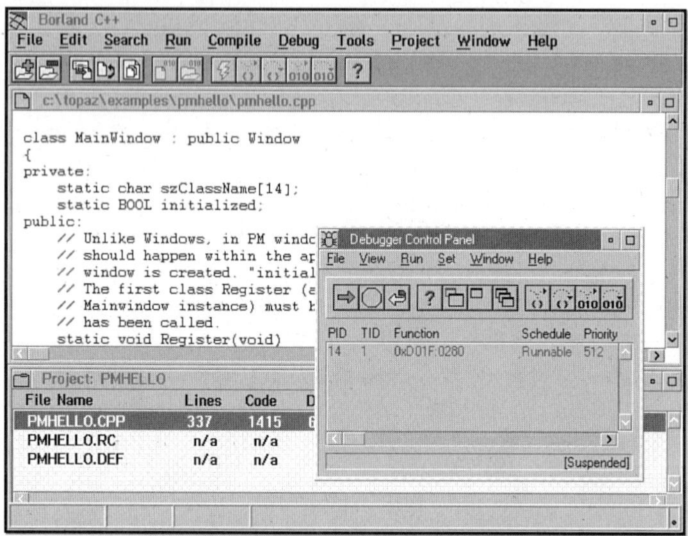

Figure 14.2. Borland's C++ for OS/2.

The OS/2 version takes advantage of the operating system's capability to efficiently multitask (editing source files while seamlessly compiling in the background). Borland's grouping of programs into projects allows the built-in compiler to generate internal dependency lists with ease. The compiler only recompiles those modules that need it, saving you time that might be wasted if the system recompiled all your source code every time you made a change to a module. The IDE's editor also offers syntax highlighting. With this interesting feature, you can display various parts of your program in different colors, depending on the function. You might specify that reserved words, for example, should appear in black and variable names should appear in green. This feature is definitely an acquired taste and takes a little time to get used to.

The IDE has its own built-in compiler, but Borland also supplies the same compiler in a command-line version, complete with accompanying make program. One of the IDE's biggest deficiencies is that to fully take advantage of it you need to use the editor supplied with the environment. Although this editor is more than adequate for most programmers, it may not have the same features or keyboard mappings of your favorite text editor. Although you can change the keyboard mappings (with some difficulty), you'll have a hard

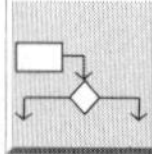

time simulating features that are not built-in to the IDE's editor. With the command-line version of the compiler, you are not tied into using the IDE and its editor. If you opt to use the command-line version, you lose the IDE's project management capabilities, syntax highlighting, integrated debugger, and "fill-in-the-blanks" compiler support. Instead, you are free to use any editor you want. Because OS/2 supports virtually any DOS, Windows, or native OS/2 program, I'm sure that many programmers waive the sexy IDE in favor of their favorite editor. I should also note that Borland supports integration of their command-line compiler with IBM's generic WorkFrame/2 (discussed later in this chapter). If you are a fan of IDEs but are determined to use your own editor, the WorkFrame may be just the right compromise.

One of the most successful DOS/Windows debuggers is Borland's Turbo Debugger. Although the Borland development team built the Turbo Debugger for OS/2 from scratch, it retains many strengths and features that have made its DOS-based siblings so endearing to programmers. However, this debugger is OS/2 all the way through—it supports the dynamic tracking of multithreaded programs and is particularly effective in debugging PM programs. Borland used mouse button 2 in a project before IBM made it an integral part of the Workplace Shell, and the button's continued use in the Turbo Debugger gives it the look and feel of a native Workplace Shell application. Because this debugger resembles IBM's C Set/2 debugger in many ways, the same advice about using a high-resolution display definitely applies to the Borland counterpart.

Other Vendors

It is a credit to OS/2's growing popularity that I can't even come close to listing all the fine programming products and development aids available from independent software vendors. A recent copy of *IBM's OS/2 Application Solutions* catalog contained more than 1,400 OS/2 program titles (more than 250 of them are development-oriented applications). I will, however, point out some prominent names that are shipping or working on new OS/2 releases.

Watcom, Symantec, and MicroWay have announced intentions to bring C or C++ compilers to market. Digitalk is the Smalltalk powerhouse under OS/2 2.1 with their Smalltalk/V PM product. Micro Focus, a longtime supporter of

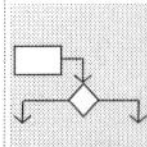

OS/2, is working on an OS/2 2.1 COBOL product. Clarion is keeping busy as it readies C, C++, Modula-2, and Pascal compilers. Most of these vendors already have supporters from previous versions of products targeted for OS/2 or DOS, so support for these offerings should be very positive.

CASE tool vendors are heating up the market in a big way. Caseworks Inc. has updated Case:PM to take advantage of the operating system's new capabilities. This new version is called Case:PM VIP and supports all the new OS/2 controls, as well as those constructs required to comply with IBM's ambitious CUA '91 user-interface guideline specification. Gpf Systems has released a 32-bit version of their impressive and well-received Gpf applications development tool. Enfin Software Corp, Guild Products, and Intelligent Environments are making other CASE tools available. The Stirling Group is releasing several useful tools, including a comprehensive resource editor called ResourceShield that enables programmers to edit icons, bitmaps, dialog boxes, and other PM objects.

Shareware and Freeware

Although many products are available from third-party commercial software vendors, people are often amazed to find affordable software as freeware and shareware. Freeware is just that: free. You can copy a program marked as freeware, give it away, and indiscriminately use it at will. Shareware typically involves a small fee, but these prices are often considerably cheaper than their commercial equivalents.

Some freeware or shareware authors allow others to use their programs only under specific conditions. For example, an author may say that a program and its source code are absolutely free, but only if you do not alter them and pass them on to other individuals. Be sure you understand a program's restrictions before using it.

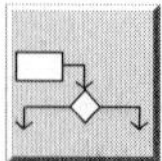

The primary sources of freeware and shareware are electronic bulletin boards and large online services like BIX, Prodigy, and CompuServe. CompuServe's OS2DEV forum contains an assortment of programming-related files available for downloading. One gem that can be found online is INIMAINT, a program that helps you browse and modify your INI files. Your OS2.INI and OS2SYS.INI files contain most of the information about the Workplace Shell desktop, and with this program you can get at almost all of it. SHOWDLLS is a program that displays a list of the DLLs used by an EXE or DLL. This program is invaluable for tracking down the hordes of problems that can arise when multiple versions of the same DLL are accidentally or inappropriately installed on the same machine. You can find a large assortment of sample OS/2 source code online. One effective way to learn how to program OS/2 is to pick through the source code of a proven program.

In a bit of irony, one of the first C++ compilers available for OS/2 is absolutely free. You can locate the GNU C/C++ compiler from the Free Software Foundation on Internet and electronic bulletin boards across the country. Although this package does not include many frills apart from the compiler, it hardly matters considering the price you'll pay (you even need to obtain the make program separately, although the Free Software Foundation's version is also free). The GNU compiler is a mature product, and renowned companies like NeXT and Quarterdeck have adopted it as their C compiler standard.

If you have experience on UNIX systems, you will be happy to hear that many UNIX development tools have been ported to OS/2. Many of these programs are available for free or for a nominal price. Various programmers have ported the Free Software Foundation versions of Awk and Make. The GNU Make program is unique in that it supports different compilings on separate threads. Other UNIX utilities found on various bulletin boards and CompuServe include YACC and GREP. Aficionados of the remarkably complete EMACs editor will not be disappointed; the full-blown EMACs are available under OS/2, as well as a scaled-down version called MicroEMACs.

IBM has begun a unique program that distributes useful and interesting programs and programming aids that employees have developed on their own time. Many of these programs are extremely useful, although not all of them are related to programming. My favorite, PMTREE, enables the programmer to manipulate PM windows and modify their internal attributes. You can send event messages and user-defined messages to almost any window. BOOT20 can be a lifesaver of a program if you need to boot from a floppy disk drive to perform maintenance work. With this, you can create an OS/2 boot disk with varying levels of Workplace Shell support. This program is especially useful if OS/2 was already installed on your computer without accompanying installation disks. These programs—and others that IBM has approved for release through their OS/2 Employee Written Software program (OS2EWS)—are available on IBM's OS/2 bulletin board system and CompuServe.

The programs mentioned here are only a few examples of the kind of quality software that you can find online. Spending a brief amount of time tracking down a useful utility can often save hours of frustrating work later.

Installing the WorkSet/2

As I noted earlier, IBM's WorkSet/2 product is a bundling of the C Set/2 compiler, the Developer's Toolkit, and the WorkFrame/2 integrated development environment. Although IBM delivers these components together, they are each individual tools that you need to install separately.

If you plan to use the WorkFrame/2 with the C Set/2 compiler, you must install the WorkFrame first. The C Set/2 installation program copies certain configuration files and DLLs into WorkFrame directories. If you do not install the WorkFrame, these directories will not exist, and the compiler installation program will assume that you don't want to use the C Set/2 in accord with the WorkFrame.

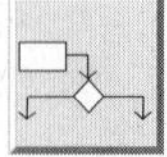

Installing the WorkFrame/2

The WorkFrame installation process begins by placing the disk labeled IBM WorkFrame/2, Diskette 1 into the A: drive and running the INSTALL program. The initial install options for this component are straightforward; set the target drive and path appropriately. If you choose to not have your CONFIG.SYS file modified, you must manually add the WorkFrame DLL directory to your `LIBPATH` statement. The basic installation takes up a little more than 1.5 megabytes of hard disk space, so be sure you plan accordingly.

You can easily install the WorkFrame from a LAN drive by using the `XCOPY` command to copy the installation disk to a directory on the shared disk. Users with access to this directory can then move into this directory and run the INSTALL program from there.

If you are interested in speeding up the installation process, here's a little trick that works for the WorkFrame/2, C Set/2 compiler, or Borland C++ compiler installations (unfortunately, you cannot use this procedure to install the Developer's Toolkit): create a directory on you local hard disk called \INSTALL and `XCOPY` the contents of the installs disks into it. Then move into this directory and run the appropriate installation program. When asked for the location of files, or when the program prompts you to insert the next disk, simply modify the default entries and make sure that they reference your new \INSTALL directory. You should not try to install all three of the above mentioned products at once. Copy one product's disks onto the hard disk, install it, erase the contents of the directory, and then move on to the next product. Because your hard disk is substantially faster than your floppy disk drive, the decompression procedures that all three of these products employ will run much faster.

You can also install the WorkFrame onto a network drive and share it with multiple users. To do this, install the WorkFrame into a directory on the shared LAN drive. Each user who wants access to the WorkFrame needs to run the

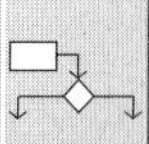

Adduser utility (shown in Figure 14.3) to establish the necessary environment. Although the Adduser program does not copy the WorkFrame executable files and DLLs to the user's workstation, it creates an IBMWF.INI into which it places the users' profile. If told to do so, the utility also copies language profiles, projects, and bitmaps. The WorkFrame uses the language profiles whenever it performs any useful actions (for example, compile, link, and build Help files). Therefore, the user should copy these profiles despite the Adduser utility's insistence that this operation is optional. Select the other two options as you deem appropriate.

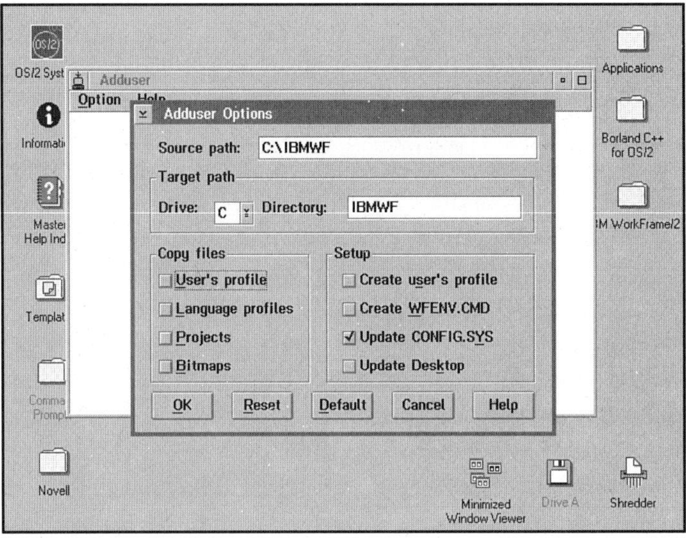

Figure 14.3. The Adduser installation utility.

Installing the C Set/2 Compiler

Begin the installation by placing the disk labeled IBM C Set/2, Diskette 1 into the A: drive and executing the INSTALL program. Remember that a complete installation consumes almost 10 megabytes of disk space.

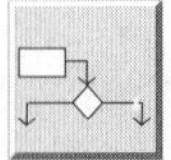

In the main installation dialog box, shown in Figure 14.4, you can specify which components you want to copy onto your hard disk. (The screen display depicted in Figure 14.4 shows a pre-release version of the IBM C Set/2, Version 2.0 installation program. Your screen may appear slightly different.) Most of the options are obvious—the check boxes for the compiler, debugger, profiler, C++ code browser, WorkFrame support, and sample programs select those items for installation. Except for the online portion that you can read with OS/2's VIEW utility, the documentation requires IBM's BookManager Read/2 product for viewing. IBM does not include the BookManager program with the compiler product, so unless you already have it on your machine, you can save more than 1.5 megabytes of disk space by opting not to install these electronic documents.

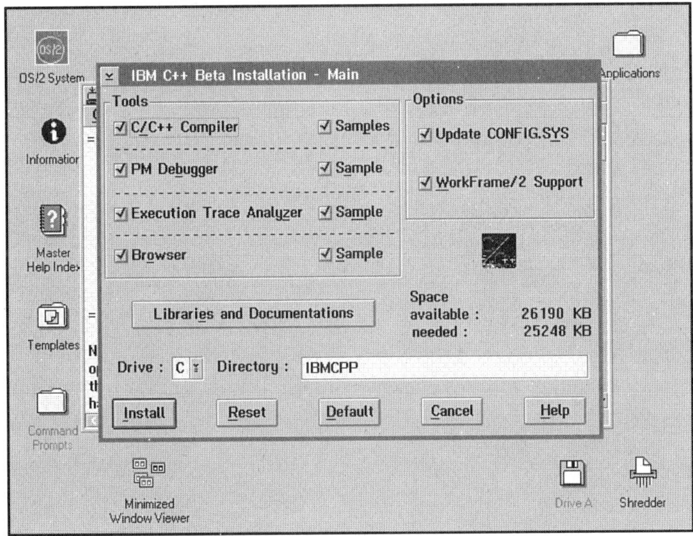

Figure 14.4. C Set/2 compiler installation options.

If you have trouble finding an explanation of the C Set/2 installation process in the documentation, don't despair. The procedure is described on a small reference card that is simply marked C Set/2 Installation.

Installing the IBM Developer's Toolkit for OS/2 2.1

The Developer's Toolkit is the largest of the three components, spanning nine 3.5-inch disks. Although you can write OS/2 programs without the Developer's Toolkit, you won't be able to write programs that interact and take advantage of the PM. You also won't be able to build and run all the sample WorkFrame projects that are shipped with the C Set/2 product. For these reasons, I strongly recommend that you install this component. The Toolkit occupies about 24 megabytes of disk space when fully installed.

Begin the installation by placing the disk labeled IBM OS/2 Developer's Toolkit, Diskette 1 into the A: drive and running the INSTALL program found on that disk. Unlike the previous two components, the Toolkit's installation program does not display an initial dialog box. As you can see in Figure 14.5, the program gives you the option of installing three separate items, all of which are useful and recommended, although only the third one (Development Tools) is absolutely required to develop PM programs. To begin the installation, choose the Install selection from the Options menu.

If you want to install the Toolkit on a drive other than the C: drive, choose the Set drives selection from the Options menu and make the appropriate changes in the presented dialog box. If you don't do this, the installation program will assume that you want the selected items to be copied to the C: drive.

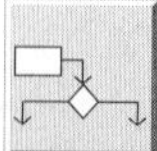

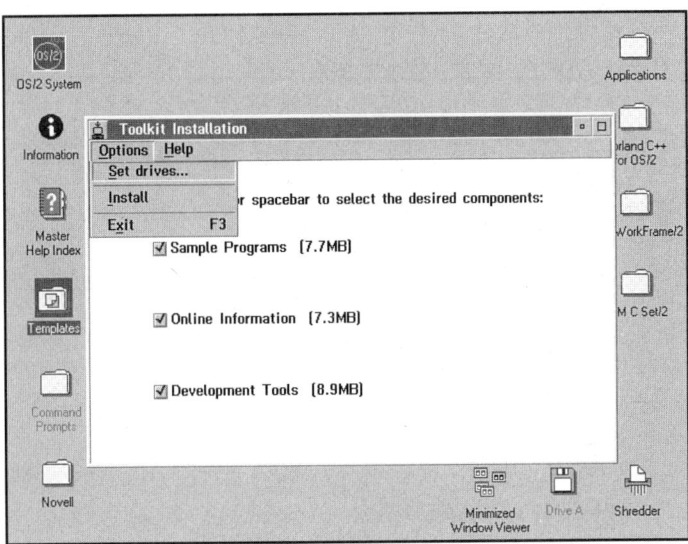

Figure 14.5. IBM Developer's Toolkit for OS/2 2.1 installation options.

At this point you should have all three of the WorkSet/2 components installed on your hard disk. You now need to reboot your computer for the changes made to your CONFIG.SYS to take effect. If you elected not to allow the installation programs to modify your CONFIG.SYS, be sure that you add the appropriate entries to your `LIBPATH` before using any of the components. Congratulations—you are finally ready to compile and run your first OS/2 program!

Starting and Testing the WorkFrame/2

The installation process has conveniently created two command files so you can set various environmental variables that the compiler, WorkFrame, and Toolkit need. You can find the first file, CSETENV.CMD, in the C Set/2 BIN directory (if you installed using the defaults, this is C:\IBMC\BIN). This command

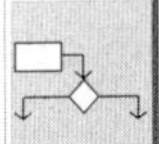

file prepares the environment but does not execute any program. You can find the second command file, IBMWF.CMD, in the WorkFrame BIN directory (if you installed using the defaults, this is C:\IBMWF\BIN). Because this command file runs the WorkFrame, you need to run the CSETENV.CMD file before this one. Of course, by combining the two command files, you can set up and run the entire environment at once. You may find it easier to launch the WorkFrame directly from the Workplace Shell objects that the installation programs created. If you allowed the installation programs to directly modify your CONFIG.SYS, this method should work fine.

If you are using the Developer's Toolkit and you did not allow the installation programs to modify your CONFIG.SYS, you may want to add the following entries to your CSETENV.CMD file. Be sure that the C:\TOOLKT20\C\OS2H directory is appended to the `INCLUDE` environmental variable and that the `LIB` environmental variable includes the C:\TOOLKT20\OS2LIB directory. Of course, if you installed the Toolkit on a drive other than the C: drive, you need to make changes accordingly.

> **TIP**
>
> If you need to program with multiple compilers, you might want to create a command file that sets up the appropriate environment for each product. You can then create a new Workplace Shell object for each command file. Place an asterisk in the path and filename field of the object's Program tab. This indicates to OS/2 that you want to start a new command prompt window. Now place the arguments `/K X.CMD` in the Parameters field, where `X` is your new command file's name. This tells OS/2 to execute the indicated command file immediately after creating the new prompt window. Now, every time you open this object, a new command-line appears that is specifically configured for one of your programming systems. Using this mechanism, I have four distinct development environments on my machine, each using a different compiler and set of tools.

To test your newly installed products, I recommend building one of the sample projects included with the C Set/2 compiler. Start the WorkFrame using the previously described command files or launch it from its desktop icon. You should see the central work environment screen illustrated in Figure 14.6. The WorkFrame segregates programs into separate projects (which I will discuss in detail a little later), and the C Set/2 compiler ships with four sample projects. The PMLINES program demonstrates multithreading and PM graphical programming techniques. You can select this project by double-clicking the project entry in the Project Control window. The window that appears is called the Project window, and it contains a list of all the relevant files that belong to this project. You can create the PMLINES program by selecting the Make option from the Actions menu or by simply typing `Ctrl-M`. After the Make window has appeared and the executable file has been built, you can run the program by selecting the Run option from the Actions menu or by typing `Ctrl-R`.

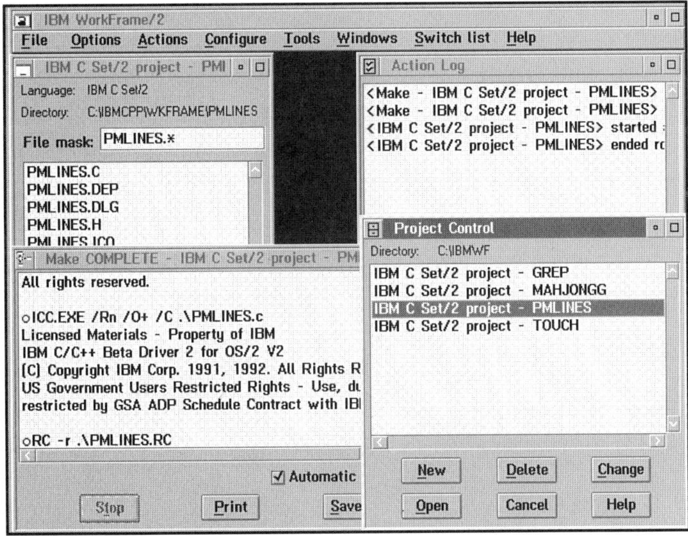

Figure 14.6. The IBM WorkFrame/2.

Using the WorkFrame/2

You can't deny that writing OS/2 applications can become a complex process, and WorkFrame does a good job of organizing the programming procedures that you will use. The WorkFrame accomplishes this is by giving you a great deal of flexibility in how you switch from one window to another and from one running program to another.

The Window Lists

One mechanism that the WorkFrame uses to help organize the development process is to divide on-screen windows into two categories: sessions and dialogs. A session window belongs to a program that is not an integral part of the WorkFrame. Examples of session windows include editors, command windows, and tools that you have indicated should run in the foreground. Conversely, a dialog window belongs to the WorkFrame program or a tool configured to run in background mode. Examples of dialog windows include the main Project Control dialog window, the Action Log window, and the individual Project windows. Dialog windows generally remain on top of the main WorkFrame/2 window; session windows may be hidden from view by placing them beneath the WorkFrame.

The key to switching rapidly between session windows and dialog windows is the Window menu that appears on the main WorkFrame menu bar. This menu contains two submenus that list the currently active session and dialog windows. You can move into any window listed on either of these menus by selecting the appropriate entry. Using the Window menu, you should quickly become accustomed to zipping from one view to the next.

The Switch List and the Window Shade

Although the WorkFrame allows a high level of integration with external tools and utilities, occasions will arise when you need to interact directly with OS/2 or use a program that you cannot incorporate into the WorkFrame. In these

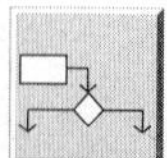

cases, you can use the switch list to jump to processes that are already running. You can also use the window shade to gain easy access to Workplace Shell objects.

The switch list, found under the Switch List menu, provides a limited display of those programs that are currently running. To switch to another program, simply select the desired program name from the switch list. However, because the switch list does not necessarily display all currently running programs, you may need to modify it. You can accomplish this by selecting the Switch List panel of the Configure menu. The WorkFrame presents you with a dialog box with a list of the currently running processes from which you can select programs.

This feature can be very useful, but I urge you to limit the number of entries that you add to the list. Although it is technically possible to add many active programs to the Switch List, this feature follows the law of diminishing returns. Once you have added seven or eight items, you will probably find yourself spending a significant amount of time searching for the desired program within the menu list. As a rule, the Switch List should be long enough to fit those processes that you use most often, but not long enough to hinder your ability to quickly switch from one program to another.

The window shade is just another way of looking at the central WorkFrame work window. A bit of experimentation reveals that you can resize this window just like any other Workplace Shell window. The user can raise or lower the window shade by "grabbing" the window's lower edge and dragging it up or down to its desired height. By furling and unfurling the window shade in this manner, you can reveal or hide the desktop and its associated views. Clicking desktop objects brings them to the top of the window stack and makes them easily accessible. The window shade provides a convenient way to conceal or expose parts of the desktop that are of interest to the developer. Although I don't find myself resizing the shade very often, I always keep it at a level that grants me at least partial access to the desktop.

Adding Tools to the Working Environment

The WorkFrame also provides an easy way to launch tools and utilities. The Tools menu provides access to features like make file generation and library services, but the programmer can also customize it. Tools placed on this menu also have a convenient hot key automatically assigned to them so you can quickly start a tool with a single keystroke. To add a tool entry to this menu, or to remove a tool that is already on it, select the Tools option from the Configure menu. You'll see a list of the tools already installed. From this dialog box, you can easily delete or modify tools that are already installed or add new programs. Clicking the New button brings up a dialog box like the one depicted in Figure 14.7.

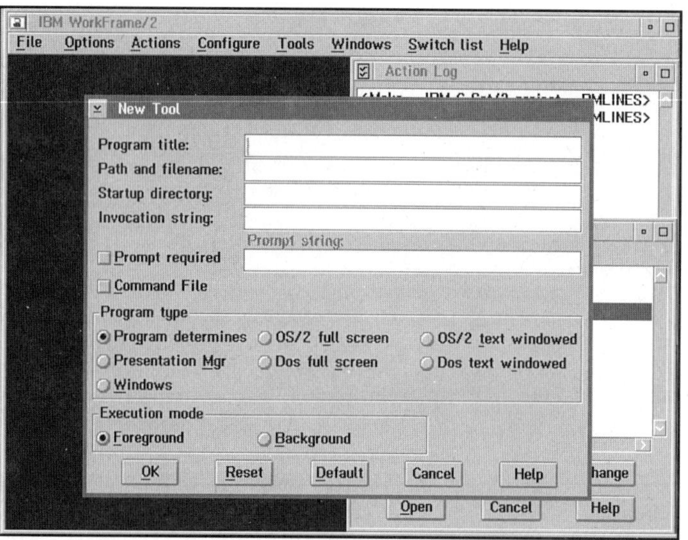

Figure 14.7. Adding tools to the WorkFrame/2 environment.

Filling in the New Tool dialog box is a straightforward process, although a couple of important things are probably worth mentioning. You can specify parameters to be passed through to the tool program by placing them in the Invocation string field. If you are starting a command file instead of an executable file, be sure to check the Command File box, or the spawning of the utility process will probably fail. The Background/Foreground radio button group dictates the specific screen behavior of the tool. Tools executing in the background are effectively invisible, and the user can't direct interactions with them; instead, the WorkFrame captures their output and presents it to the user in a Monitor window. On the other hand, tools executing in the foreground are created in their own window or full-screen session, and the programmer interacts with these programs in the appropriate manner. Remember that tools running in the foreground are added to the Sessions list in the Windows menu and that they can be optionally added to the Switch List.

Building a Project

WorkFrame organizes your development work into a collection of projects. A project is a collection of files contained in the same directory and a set of WorkFrame specific settings that describe the prominent characteristics associated with these files. These settings, which you can easily set using various WorkFrame dialog boxes, include features such as language profiles, compiler options, and linker settings.

Base and Composite Projects

The WorkFrame recognizes two different types of projects: base projects and composite projects. A base project has a single target that is either an executable file (.EXE) or a supporting dynamic link library (.DLL). To accommodate larger programming systems that may contain many executable files and DLLs, the WorkFrame supports composite projects. A composite project is a collection of base projects bound together into a single conceptual unit. Selecting the Make command from a base project builds that project's single target, whereas selecting Make from a composite project causes each of the included base projects to be built one at a time.

The WorkFrame displays projects in the central Project Control dialog box. (If this dialog box is not visible, you can open it using the Project Control item in the File menu). This dialog box contains options for creating new projects

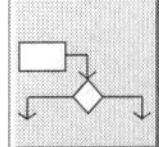

and deleting or modifying preexisting projects. You open project entries by clicking the Open button or by double-clicking directly the project entry. Each open base project has its own Project window that displays a list of the files that reside within the project directory. Each open composite project has a Project window that lists the base projects that belong to it. You can double-click these base project names to open their respective base Project windows.

You can limit the files displayed in the base Project windows by modifying the File Mask entry field. This field accepts one or more wild card expressions that determine which files get included in the main file list box. For example, if you only want to see your C source files and header files, you might enter a file mask entry of `*.C *.H`.

The Actions menu is one of the most frequently used WorkFrame menus. All the commands that you need to build, run, and debug your application appear in this menu, with accelerator keys defined for faster access. For example, to compile the source files currently selected in the base Project window, type `Ctrl-C`; to run your application in the C Set/2 debugger, type `Ctrl-D`. With regular use these keystrokes will become second nature to you.

The WorkFrame uses drag-and-drop extensively throughout its user interface. Source files can be dragged from project window to project window, providing an easy way to copy source code between projects. Files can also be dragged from project windows into the deletion window in much the same way that you can drag Workplace Shell objects into the shredder. Experiment! You might be surprised by some of the things that the WorkFrame lets you do.

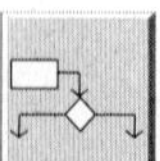

Setting C Set/2 Compiler Settings

Every compiler that supports the WorkFrame ships with a DLL that enables the user to seamlessly set command-line compiler switches through dialog boxes. The C Set/2 compiler is no exception. One of the first things you need to do when creating a new project is to ensure that the compiler settings are appropriate for the program you are trying to build.

When you first create a project, the WorkFrame prompts you with a dialog box containing buttons that relate to each of the program build phases (for example, make, compile, link, debug, and run). You can also get this dialog box by clicking the Change button in the Project Control window. Each of the displayed buttons causes the C Set/2 DLLs to display dialog boxes that relate to each of these phases. For example, clicking the Compile options button brings up a transitional dialog box that enables you to control many different aspects of the compilation phase. Clicking the Object code control options button displays the dialog box, shown in Figure 14.8, that enables you to set most of the important options relating to target type (EXE or DLL), multithreading, the target processor, and so on. Although you can modify and set many dialog boxes, anyone with command-line compiler experience will admit that this approach is much easier to understand and use. If you don't have any command-line experience, consider yourself lucky. This is definitely one of the quickest and least painful ways to break into OS/2 programming.

The compiler, linker, make, debug, and run settings are also individually accessible under the Options menu.

When you are satisfied that you've correctly adjusted your project settings, you need to generate the make file and dependency file that the WorkFrame uses to build your application. Do this by selecting the Make File Creation option from the Tools menu. With the Make File Creation dialog box, shown in Figure 14.9, you can select the files you want to include in the build process.

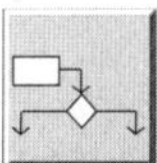

You also use this dialog box to indicate which actions you want to be incorporated into the build process. Therefore, you might select all the C files from the file list box on the right and the Compile and Link options from the Actions list box on the left. This ensures that the correct entries for compiling your source files into object modules are added to the make file and that the make file correctly links your object modules. If you are building a complex PM program, you might take advantage of the Resource compile, Message file, and IPF compile actions. Clicking the OK button creates the make file and enables the WorkFrame to build your target correctly.

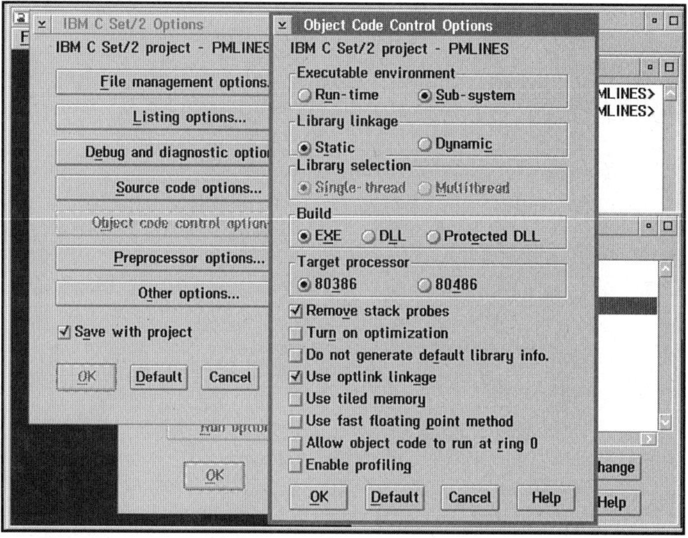

Figure 14.8. A C Set/2 compiler options dialog box.

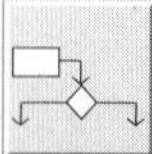

> **TIP**
>
> Buttons that enable you to modify your project's compile and link options are conveniently located in the center of this dialog box. If you realize that you've made a mistake when setting the compiler options or if you simply decide that you want to change a particular setting, you can access the appropriate setting by clicking one of these buttons.

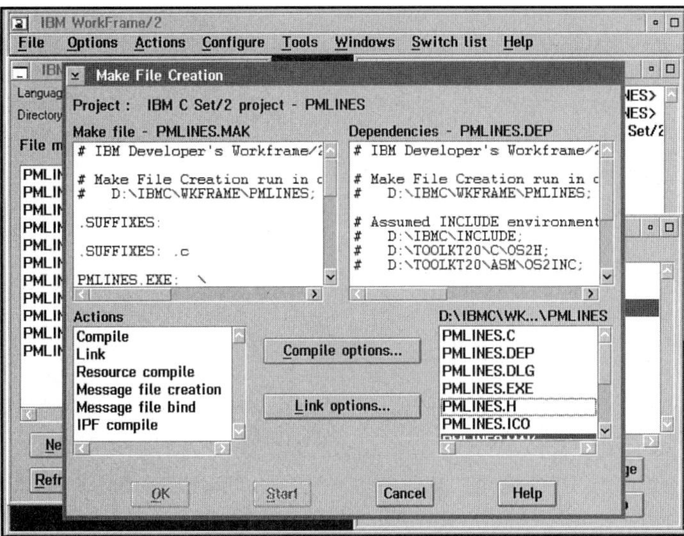

Figure 14.9. The Make File Creation dialog box.

Editing Source Files

Like programming tools, the WorkFrame treats program editors as external entities that can be set up and integrated directly into the development environment. You can find your editor configuration in the Editor selection under the Configure menu. The configuration dialog box prompts you for the path and filename of your editor's executable file and for any parameters that you want to be passed to the program in the form of command-line arguments. If you do not choose to provide your own editor, the WorkFrame defaults to the EPM editor that is installed with the base operating system.

TIP: If you normally start your editor through a command file, set the Current Editor field to CMD.EXE and place `/K X.CMD` in the Editor invocation string field (where `X` is the name of your command file).

The simplest way to edit a file is to double-click its entry in the Project window. This action starts your editor and makes it the active window. If your editor can accept filenames on its command-line, you may want to specify the substitution variables `%a %z` on the invocation string field of the editor's configuration dialog box. This allows the editor to automatically load the files selected in the Project window. Some editors even support close integration with the Make monitor window. If your editor can receive messages from the WorkFrame (consult your editor's documentation or call the editor's technical support line) you can double-click C Set error messages that appear in the Make window, and your editor will move the cursor to the appropriate line number. Although not many editors currently support this level of integration, hopefully this will change as WorkFrame use becomes more prevalent.

TIP: If your editor cannot accept multiple filenames on its command-line, use the substitution variable `%f` instead of `%a %z`. The `%f` variable specifies that only the first filename should be passed through to the editor, whereas the `%a %z` variables pass every selected filename. Passing too many filenames may cause your editor to generate errors or refuse to load.

Using the Online Documentation

The Developer's Toolkit comes with a great deal of online documentation in .INF file format. These files are read using the VIEW program that accompanies OS/2. If you let the installation programs modify your CONFIG.SYS,

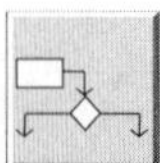

your environment has been set up to allow easy access to online documents. You should be able to acquire general OS/2 programming information by typing `VIEW PROGREF20` and PM programming information by typing `VIEW PMREF`.

If you did not directly modify your CONFIG.SYS at the time of installation, you may need to make a few modifications to your development environment in order to gain access to the online documentation. Be sure that the `BOOKSHELF` environmental variable is set (either from the command prompt, in your CONFIG.SYS, or in your CSETENV.CMD command file) so that the C:\TOOLKT20\BOOK directory is appended to it. If you installed the Developer's Toolkit somewhere other than the C: drive, be sure that you use the appropriate drive letter. To make access to the documentation even easier, I suggest you add the following entries to your CSETENV.CMD file:

```
SET PROGREF20=GUIREF20.INF
SET PMREF20=PMFUN.INF+PMGPI.INF+PMHOK.INF+PMMSG.INF+PMREL.INF+
➥PMWIN.INF+PMWKP.INF
```

When you first run VIEW to study the online documentation, it presents you with a Contents window that lists the major topics covered by the loaded INF files. The contents menu is hierarchical in nature, so you can expand the topics with subheadings by clicking the plus (+) sign that sits in the window's left margin (see Figure 14.10). Any heading or subheading can be double-clicked on; this displays the selected section in another window. You can efficiently browse the INF file using the buttons that run along the bottom of the main window, and you can search it using VIEW's built-in searching capabilities.

The general OS/2 programming information files cover those aspects of the operating system that are called Control Program functions. These functions are not directly related or linked to the PM, but they instead provide basic operating system services. Examples of such OS/2 constructs include dynamic linking, the file system, memory management, message management (not to be confused with PM messages), semaphores, named pipes, and so on.

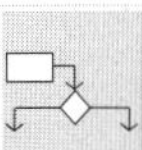

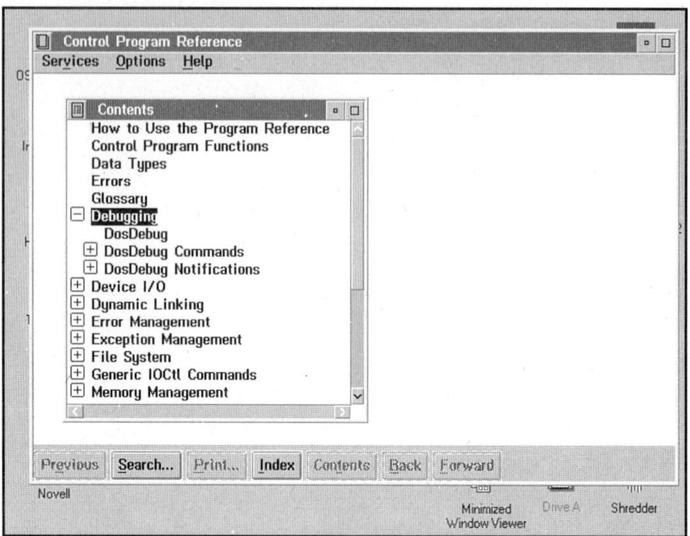

Figure 14.10. The VIEW program with Control Program Reference loaded.

The PM programming information files, on the other hand, relate to material exclusively related to PM, the Workplace Shell, and the System Object Model (SOM), which is the object-oriented programming foundation upon which the Workplace Shell sits. Because these systems can be quite complex, these INF files are considerably larger and a little more difficult to navigate.

The Developer's Toolkit includes a useful documentation browser called KWIKINF. This utility allows you to press a hot key sequence that displays a list of online file topics installed on your system. This facility works from within PM and text-mode sessions and is the most convenient way to get at .INF files quickly. Use it as a form of instant online help—if you've ever gotten tired of typing `VIEW PROGREF20`, or even just `help`, this program will quickly become a favorite.

KWIKINF uses special index files to help it find and search the online .INF files. These index files have an .NDX extension. In order for the utility to operate correctly, it is important that you define an environmental variable called HELPNDX that includes the name of your central KWIKINF index file. The program uses the BOOKSHELF environment variable when looking for this .NDX file, so be sure your index file can be found in one of the BOOKSHELF directories.

TIP

The KWIKINF program suffers from the annoying limitation of only being able to use a single index file. If you have two (or more) index files that you want to include in your topics list, you need to combine them into a single master index file. Do this using the COPY command. For example, assume that you want to combine the DDE4.NDX file (which you can find in the \IBMC\HELP directory) with the EPMKWHLP.NDX file (which you can find in the \TOOLKT20\BOOK directory). The following command concatenates the two files and places them into a single index file called MASTER.NDX.

```
COPY EPMKWHLP.NDX + DDE4.NDX MASTER.NDX
```

Be sure that your HELPNDX environment variable is set to this master index file and that the index file is located in one of the bookshelf directories.

Good Luck!

Although learning to program OS/2 can be intimidating at first, don't worry. Probably the most problematic aspect of the process relates to the fact that there is so much to learn. OS/2 is a large system with many exciting and interesting nooks and crannies. Don't feel like you need to explore them all at once. Keep at it. I guarantee you success.

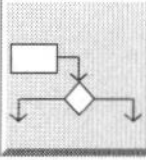

Author Bio

Chris Corry is a lead OS/2 2.1 developer for a programming team at American Management Systems in Arlington, Virginia. The team is responsible for developing a distributed IBM Client/Server imaging system that operates on LANs and host mainframes. His professional interests range from object-oriented programming to user-interface design. Corry holds a bachelor's degree form the University of Pennsylvania.

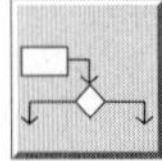

REXX Programming

In This Chapter

This chapter describes REXX programming on OS/2 2.1. You can get more information about any of the topics in this chapter online on OS/2 2.1 by clicking on the information icon, the blue circle containing the lowercase *i*, and selecting the book icon called REXX Information.

The REXX language support is a selectable option when you install OS/2 2.1. If you deselected the REXX support, you cannot use the REXX command and macro language on your computer. Because many applications can take advantage of REXX, it is usually a good idea to include REXX when you install OS/2 2.1—this is the default, so unless you specifically de-selected it, you do not have to do anything.

REXX Versus Batch

Batch in its simplest form is a program containing a series of commands that performs some useful task. By putting those commands that you enter repeatedly into a batch file, you automate that specific task by simply executing the name of your batch file at a command-line session. This improves efficiency by reducing the manual input of repeated tasks to a single call to a batch file program.

If you are using the OS/2 batch facility to automate your tasks in an OS/2 environment, you can extend the functionality of your programs using REXX. REXX is an easy-to-use, structured, interpreted programming language that offers many powerful features for the experienced programmer. For detailed REXX information, see the online REXX Information reference or the *OS/2.1 Technical Library Procedures Language/2 REXX Reference* manual.

Differences

You can use a REXX program anywhere you use OS/2 batch files, but the differences between REXX programs and batch files and what you can do with each of these are quite significant. Note the following areas in which REXX and batch differ:

- program structure
- program control
- variables
- functions
- external commands
- parsing/string manipulation
- mathematical operations
- error conditions/debugging
- application programming interfaces

Program Structure

REXX programs are structured programs, and batch files tend not to be structured. Each processes a list of commands, but REXX programs can be broken down into smaller functional pieces to perform a bigger task. These pieces form subroutines of the primary task or function of your program. Subroutines are called from within your REXX programs using the `REXX CALL` instruction. With structured programs in REXX, your programs are easier to read and understand.

You can modularize your tasks in batch programming by calling other batch files to do certain subtasks. This uses the OS/2 `CALL` command, and because the system needs to first locate your batch file before running it, this hinders your program's performance.

To distinguish a REXX program from a batch file, a REXX comment `/* */` must start in the first column of the first line of your program. This enables CMD.EXE to recognize the REXX program and invoke the REXX interpreter. In a batch file, there does not need to be a comment on the first line of the program, although comments (`REM` statements) make the program more readable. A batch file contains a list of commands as they appear if typed at a command-line session.

Program Control

There are just a few simple control instructions available to you in your batch files to control program flow. You can use the FOR instruction to process certain commands repeatedly, the IF instruction for conditional command processing, and the GOTO instruction for redirecting program flow.

REXX, on the other hand, enables better control of your programs with many control instructions that are available and easy to use:

- The DO instruction performs repetitive command processing. When issued with WHILE, UNTIL, or FOREVER, the DO instruction becomes much more flexible and can execute commands according to specified conditions. The DO instruction also enables you to use counters and expressions to control the number of iterations of your loop. REXX is not limited to executing just one command, repeatedly.
- The IF instruction controls the conditions by which certain commands are processed. The IF instruction accepts all types of valid expressions in evaluating conditional statements. This instruction controls whether a list of commands following the THEN clause or alternative commands following the ELSE clause should be processed. REXX is adept at controlling which sequence of commands need to be executed under certain conditions in a more structured manner.
- The SIGNAL and CALL instructions change the flow of control of your program. The SIGNAL instruction allows you to jump to another part of your program to process a sequence of commands, and it is most useful for transferring control to a common routine to handle certain error conditions. The CALL instruction transfers control to a subroutine in a structured manner and can also be used to set up special command processing for error conditions. With these instructions, REXX offers a much clearer flow of program control in your programs.

Variables

In batch programming, you can access environment variables to use their values and perhaps change them. The statement PATH %path%;C:\TOOLS, for example,

uses the current path environment variable to change its value by adding a C:\TOOLS path.

You can also use SETLOCAL and ENDLOCAL to establish new local environment settings within your program so as not to alter the currently active environment. In REXX, you can use all kinds of variables to store information within your program and as parameters to other programs. This extends far beyond the use of environment variables. REXX also provides the functions SETLOCAL and ENDLOCAL, which, like their respective commands in batch, save and restore current environment values. The VALUE function in REXX is used to access environment variables and optionally change their value.

Program variables can have meaningful names and can be easily assigned values by using REXX instructions such as ARG, PARSE, and PULL. REXX also provides compound and stem variables that enable you to store variables conveniently in arrays or lists and process them as collections.

Functions

In batch programming, there are no additional functions available beyond the capabilities of OS/2 system commands. With REXX, however, there are numerous built-in functions and handy REXX utilities available that can enhance your programs even further.

You can use built-in functions to manipulate characters or strings using SUBSTR, STRIP, or LENGTH; perform input/output operations using STREAM, LINEIN, LINEOUT, or QUEUED; convert or format data using X2D, C2X, or FORMAT; or obtain useful information using VALUE, SOURCELINE, TIME, or DATE.

The RexxUtil functions allow you to (among other things) search files and directories using SysFileTree, SysFileSearch, or SysSearchPath; work with extended information in files using SysGetEA, SysPutEA, or SysIni; or work with objects and classes using SysCreateObject, or SysQueryClassList.

In addition, REXX enables you to create your own functions and invoke them either internally to your REXX program or externally. REXX allows you to take advantage of these various function capabilities when you write your programs.

Rexx

External Commands

As you create more and more functional programs, the need to call these programs and other application programs as external commands increases as you set out to perform larger tasks. In your batch files, you can invoke OS/2 commands or make calls to other batch files using the OS/2 `CALL` command. This works as long as these commands are known within your current environment.

In REXX, your programs can invoke OS/2 commands and call other REXX programs using the `REXX CALL` instruction, but more importantly, REXX gives you the capability to invoke external commands to OS/2 applications. Applications can use REXX as a macro language by registering their environment to REXX and creating commands written in REXX to run in the application environment.

An external call simply becomes a command string passed to the current command environment. The `ADDRESS` instruction allows you to change your command environment and issue commands to your application. You can then establish a new default environment in which to make calls to your application within a simple REXX program.

In addition to the REXX built-in functions and the available RexxUtil functions, you can further enhance your programs by using external commands with other applications.

Parsing/String Manipulation

In batch programming, parameters `%1` through `%9` are available as arguments to your batch programs. Batch handles character strings as they appear with no special manipulation functions.

With REXX, you can parse up to 20 parameters in your function or subroutine. The `PARSE` instruction can parse these arguments, in addition to variables, or lines of input data. There are numerous parsing options that give you added flexibility to handle data in your programs.

REXX provides you with capabilities to manipulate character strings. Your programs can read and parse characters, numbers, and mixed input. With many

REXX built-in string functions, you can greatly enhance the way you use character strings in your programs.

Mathematical Operations

Mathematical operations are well-supported in REXX. In batch programming, you do not have integrated mathematical capabilities. REXX, however, provides easy-to-use and flexible operations. Even though numbers in REXX are represented as character strings, REXX allows you to perform mathematical operations and return string values. There are a number of REXX instructions and built-in functions that enable you to work with numeric data. `NUMERIC DIGITS`, for example, allows you to control the significant digits used in your calculations. `DATATYPE` function ensures the numeric type of your data.

Error Conditions/Debugging

When creating and running a large number of programs to automate your tasks, the capability to easily handle error conditions and debug your programs becomes important. In batch programming, you can set `ECHO ON` to display each command to the screen as it is being executed and determine which, if any, command is in error. You receive a system error message if an error occurs while running your batch file.

With REXX, there is a built-in `TRACE` instruction that allows you to step through your REXX program and see how each statement is interpreted in order to determine which, if any, statement is in error. If an error occurs in your REXX program, a meaningful REXX error description appears. Use the `PMREXX` command from OS/2 2.1 to interact with your REXX program and display its output in a Presentation Manager window.

REXX also provides special instructions to enable you to catch error conditions and handle them within your program. The `SIGNAL` instruction can be used to jump to an error-handling routine—`SIGNAL ON ERROR`, for example. The `CALL` instruction can also be used to transfer control to some condition-handling routine, but it resumes command processing after the routine completes.

Rexx

REXX enables you to break down your program's error handling into concise, common routines, and it offers easy-to-use debugging techniques.

When to Use REXX Programs

When to use batch files and when to write REXX programs depends on the way you intend to use your programs on OS/2 2.1. REXX programs are most useful if you need to do the following:

- build large structured programs to modularize your tasks
- specify varying conditions for repeating or distinguishing which commands are executed
- store and change data in variables or lists of variables
- run existing functions to manipulate data or perform input/output operations
- work with large lists of files or directories
- easily obtain and access system information within your programs
- write programs to address other OS/2 applications
- parse input data into usable forms
- handle various error conditions or interactively debug your programs
- use system application programming interfaces

For simply executing a series of commands from a single OS/2 environment to automate a certain task, batch files or a simple REXX program works nicely.

Why REXX is Faster—the Role of Extended Attributes in REXX

REXX programs use extended attributes to hold information about itself (which REXX uses when executing a program). This causes REXX programs to run faster because REXX only takes the time to store information about its

source file once, although the information in the extended attributes is accessed every time the REXX program is executed.

When REXX programs are executed on OS/2, they are first scanned into various tokens, and a tokenized image of the program is created. Then the program is run using this tokenized image. The tokenized image is saved in the extended attribute of each REXX program or source file where it is easily accessible. When you rerun your REXX programs, REXX simply executes the existing tokenized image instead of retokenizing the file.

There is a limit of 64K of information capable of being stored in an extended attribute, so for very large program files, REXX may not be able to store the tokenized image. Therefore, smaller functional REXX programs reward you with the best performance.

An Introduction to REXX Basics

REXX is a powerful structured language that is easy to learn and useful for both beginners and computer professionals. This section introduces REXX on OS/2 2.1 and describes REXX's features and concepts, instructions, built-in functions, and it also shows you how to send commands.

REXX is a very readable language because its syntax is similar to natural language. Many of its instructions use common English words, and computations use the familiar operators +, -, and so on. REXX has few rules about how to enter lines of code. You do not need to type any program line numbers. Except for the initial comment, program lines can start in any column. You can put any number of blanks between words or skip entire lines, and REXX assumes ending punctuation (the semicolon) at every line-end, so you don't have to type it. Case is not significant (*IF*, *If*, and *if* all have the same meaning). In this chapter, however, keywords are capitalized as examples.

REXX serves several roles on OS/2 2.1. When you use REXX as a procedural language, a REXX program serves as a script for the OS/2 program to follow. This enables you to reduce long, complicated, or repetitious tasks into a single command or program. You can run a REXX program anywhere that you can use an OS/2 command or batch file.

Rexx

You can also use REXX as a macro language. If you use an application program that you control with subcommands (for example, a word processor), a REXX program can issue a series of subcommands to the application.

REXX is also a good prototyping language because you can code programs fast, and REXX makes it easy to interface with system utilities for displaying input and output. REXX is suitable for many applications because you can use it for applications that otherwise require several languages.

You can run a REXX program from Presentation Manager in any of the following ways:

- the OS/2 windowed command line (enter the name of the .cmd file)
- the full-screen command line (enter the name of the .cmd file)
- the drives object (click on the program filename)
- the desktop (see Chapter 5, "Workplace Shell Objects," for information on creating a REXX program object)

Features and Concepts

A comment in REXX begins with `/*` and ends with `*/`. On the OS/2 operating system, the first line of your program must be a comment. This differentiates a REXX program from an OS/2 batch facility program. The comment must begin in the first column.

```
/* This is an example of a comment in REXX. */
```

Comments can be on the code line and can span more than one line:

```
dimes=dollars * 10  /* multiply dollars by 10 */
dimes=              /* multiply dollars by 10 */   dollars * 10
/* It's easy to use
block comments in REXX. */
```

An assignment takes the following form:

```
variable=expression
```

This stores the value of whatever is to the right of the equal sign into the variable named to the left of the equal sign. For example, a=1 assigns the value 1 to the variable a.

REXX treats all data as character strings. You do not need to define variables as strings or numbers, and you do not need to include certain characters in variable names to identify the data type.

A variable name can contain up to 250 characters. It must, however, start with a letter from A-Z, a-z, or a question mark (?), exclamation mark (!), or underscore (_). The rest of the name can include any of these characters as well as 0-9 and the period (.). For example, the following variable names are all valid:

```
day
Greetings!
word_1
```

The following variable names, however, are not valid:

```
.dot
1st_word
```

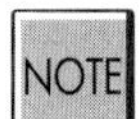

A symbol that begins with a number is a constant.

Again, case is not significant. The following variable names, for example, are essentially the same variable:

```
day
DAY
Day
```

A variable can have any value, up to the limit of storage. In REXX, a variable always has a value. If you use a variable name without giving that variable a value, its value is its own name in uppercase. For example, the variable name would have the value NAME.

A literal in REXX is called a literal string. Put quotation marks around a literal string:

```
"Hooray for REXX!"
```

In REXX, you can use single or double quotation marks. To include single or double quotation marks within the string, use the other form of quotation marks around the whole string:

```
string="Don't hurry"
```

Or you can use two of one form of quotation marks you want in the string:

```
string='Don''t hurry'
```

A literal string can be any length, to the limit of storage.

The line-end character for ending punctuation on an instruction is the semicolon. REXX automatically assumes a semicolon at every line end. To put more than one instruction on a single line, include semicolons to separate the instructions:

```
a=1; c=2
```

The continuation character is the comma. Use this for an instruction that is too long to fit on one line:

```
IF language='REstructured eXtended eXecutor' THEN SAY,
'REXX'
```

You cannot, however, continue a literal string from one line to the next.

```
IF language='REstructured extended,    /* This causes an error. */
eXecutor' THEN SAY "REXX"
```

Commas also separate multiple arguments in calls to built-in functions and multiple templates in parsing instructions.

Compound symbols make array handling easy. A compound symbol starts with a stem: a variable name followed by a period. After the stem is one or more symbols called a tail. A tail is somewhat like an array index. A tail doesn't have to be a number. The following compound symbols are all valid:

```
a.1
a.b
tree.1.10
tree.maple.red
```

You can assign the same value to all elements of an array without using a loop. To do this, simply use the stem in the assignment. For example, `number.=0` assigns the value `0` to all possible array elements starting with a stem of `number.` You can assign specific array elements any values (for example, `number.one=1` and `number.100=100`). If you use an array element that you have not separately assigned a value, its value is the value from the assignment using the stem: `number.new` has the value `0`.

Arithmetic operators in REXX include the familiar + (add), - (subtract), * (multiply), / (divide), and ** (exponentiation) symbols. To return only the integer part of the result of a division, use % (integer divide). To return the remainder of a division, use // (remainder). Additionally, - (prefix -) treats a term as if it were subtracted from 0; + (prefix +) treats a term as if it were added to 0.

Logical and comparison operations return 1 for true and 0 for false. Logical operators are shown in Table 15.1.

Table 15.1. Logical Operators

Operator	*Comparison Operation*
\	not
&	and
¦	inclusive or
&&	exclusive or

Comparison operators are the familiar = (equal), < (less than), and > (greater than) symbols, and they can be used with the logical not. (For example, ^= and \= both mean not equal.)

REXX offers two forms of comparisons: regular and strict. In regular comparisons, leading and trailing blanks are insignificant. For example, REXX treats '`the big top`' as equal to '` the big top`'.

Rexx

> **NOTE** If you are comparing two terms that are both numbers, REXX does a numeric comparison.

In strict comparisons the strings being compared must be identical to be considered equal. The strict comparison operators are == (strictly equal), >> (strictly greater than), and << (strictly less than). You can use these with the logical not (for example, ^==, \==, ^<<, \<<, and so on).

REXX has three concatenation operators. The blank concatenation operator concatenates with a blank between terms. The ¦¦ operator concatenates without an intervening blank. The abuttal operator concatenates without a blank; abuttal involves juxtaposing two terms (which must be of different types, such as a variable and a literal string).

```
a='good'
c='will'
d=a c       /* Uses blank operator. d='good will'    */
d=a¦¦c      /* Uses ¦¦ operator.    d='goodwill'     */
e='$'
money=e"2"  /* Uses abuttal.        money='$2'       */
money=e 2   /* Uses blank operator. money="$ 2".     */
            /* Note: money=e2 assigns "E2" to money. */
```

REXX Instructions

A keyword instruction is a REXX instruction. Case is not significant in keyword instructions. The following keywords all mean the same thing:

```
EXIT
exit
Exit
```

The following listing contains a few of the most indispensable instructions (to exit a REXX program, use the `EXIT` instruction):

```
/* All this REXX program does is exit. */
EXIT
SAY displays output to the user.
SAY "Goodbye"          /* Displays "Goodbye" */
SAY goodbye            /* Displays "GOODBYE" because the variable  */
                       /* goodbye has not yet been given a value.  */
```

```
goodbye='au revoir'
SAY goodbye          /* Displays 'au revoir' */
```

PULL gets the input the user types at the terminal. (PULL uppercases whatever the user inputs. PULL is also a parsing instruction.)

```
SAY "Enter a number from 1 to 13."
PULL number
SAY "Is" number "your lucky number?"
```

IF and SELECT allow conditional processing:

```
switch=0
IF switch=0 THEN SAY 'Off'
ELSE SAY 'On'
```

If you put ELSE on the same line as IF, you need a semicolon before ELSE:

```
IF switch=1 THEN SAY 'On'; ELSE SAY 'Off'
```

You can use SELECT instead of IF-THEN-ELSE coding. Each SELECT must conclude with END.

```
SELECT
WHEN landscape='white' THEN season='Winter'
WHEN landscape='green' THEN season='Spring'
WHEN landscape='red' THEN season='Autumn'
OTHERWISE season='summer'
END
```

OTHERWISE is usually optional, although it is a good coding practice to include it.

OTHERWISE is required in one case: if you have a SELECT where all the WHEN tests evaluate to true, omitting OTHERWISE causes an error.

You can nest IF and SELECT instructions. You can also specify a list of instructions after THEN using the DO instruction.

You can use DO to create loops and LEAVE to exit a loop. A list of instructions can follow DO; REXX requires an END statement after the list. DO has many forms: DO number, DO WHILE..., DO UNTIL..., and so on. (You can nest DO instructions.) The following examples all have the same effect:

```
DO 3
   SAY "Mercy!"
END
```

```
i=3
DO i
   SAY "Mercy!"
END
```

```
i=1
DO UNTIL i=4
   SAY "Mercy!"
   i=i+1
END
```

```
i=1
DO WHILE i<4
   SAY "Mercy!"
   i=i+1
END
```

```
DO i=1 TO 3
   SAY "Mercy"
   i=i+1
END
```

```
DO i=4 TO 1 BY -1
   SAY "Mercy"
END
```

An unusual variant is DO FOREVER. The REXX LEAVE instruction exits a DO FOREVER loop (and other DO loops). DO FOREVER can be very useful for processing files containing an unknown number of lines:

```
DO FOREVER
   SAY "Try to guess my name."
   PULL name
   IF name='RUMPLESTILSKIN' THEN DO
                                     SAY "That's right!!!!!"
                                     LEAVE
                                  END
END
```

NOP is a dummy instruction often used with IF.

```
IF filename="" THEN NOP
else ...
```

You can use CALL to transfer control to a subroutine. The subroutine must start with a label—a name composed of the same characters allowed in variable names and followed by a colon:

```
subroutine:
```

A label marks the start of an internal subroutine. Include a RETURN statement in the subroutine to transfer control back to the main program.

```
IF language='REXX' THEN CALL cheer
EXIT
cheer:
SAY "Hooray for REXX"
RETURN
```

Be sure you include an EXIT in your main routine, or you will "drop through" to the subroutine and execute the code in the subroutine.

You can also use the CALL instruction to call another program from your REXX program. Be careful not to confuse the REXX CALL instruction with the OS/2 instruction. To use the OS/2 instruction, put quotation marks around everything you do not want REXX to evaluate.

In REXX, all variables are global unless you make only selective variables known to a subroutine. You can do this by using PROCEDURE EXPOSE after the label:

```
var_a=1; var_b=2; var_c=3; counter=0
CALL sub
EXIT
sub: PROCEDURE EXPOSE var_a var_c
...
RETURN
```

In the preceding example, the subroutine knows the values of var_a and var_c but does not know the value of var_b or counter. With PROCEDURE EXPOSE you can use the same variable names in a subroutine that you use in a main routine without affecting the variables in the main routine. When you RETURN from the subroutine, the new versions of the variables are deleted.

By default, REXX's precision for arithmetic is nine digits, but REXX has flexible precision. You can alter the precision with the DIGITS variant of the NUMERIC instruction. (The only limit is storage.)

```
SAY 22/7            /* By default, displays: 3.14285714 */
NUMERIC DIGITS 20
SAY 22/7            /* Displays:  3.1428571428571428571 */
```

Other variants of `NUMERIC` control the number of decimal digits used in comparisons (`FUZZ`) and the format for exponential notation (`FORM`).

REXX provides built-in parsing. Parsing assigns parts of a source string into variables. It does this on the basis of a template, a model you specify in the `ARG`, `PARSE`, or `PULL` parsing instruction. You can parse the source string into words by using a template consisting only of variable names:

```
PARSE VALUE 'Samuel Taylor Coleridge' WITH firstname middlename
➥lastname
```

The preceding example assigns `Samuel` to `firstname`, `Taylor` to `middlename`, and `Coleridge` to `lastname`. The template is `firstname middlename lastname`.

The `ARG` and `PULL` parsing instructions uppercase the source string before parsing it. The `PARSE` instruction does not do this. If you want uppercase translation, you can include the `UPPER` keyword on the `PARSE` instruction (`PARSE UPPER...`). If you do not want uppercase translation, you can use `PARSE ARG` instead of `ARG` and `PARSE PULL` instead of `PULL`.

The `PARSE` instruction has many variants. The `PARSE VALUE` variant can parse literal strings or variables. `PARSE VAR` is only for variables.

`PARSE VALUE` requires the keyword `WITH`; none of the other variants use this. If you include `WITH` on a `PARSE VAR` instruction, it is treated as part of the template, not as a keyword. The following example assigns `"one"` to `WITH`, `"two"` to `word1`, and the null string to `word2`.

```
PARSE VAR "one two" WITH word1 word2
```

If there are more variables in the template than words in the source string, the extra variables receive nulls. If there are more words in the source string

than variables in the template, the last variable receives the extra words. Parsing removes leading and trailing blanks. But if the last variable is receiving multiple words, or if there is only one variable, parsing removes only one blank between words; parsing retains any additional blanks.

```
author='Samuel Taylor Coleridge'
PARSE VAR author firstname middlename lastname   /* same results */
```

A string may contain more data than you need to save in variables. You can use the period (.) placeholder instead of one or more variables in the template:

```
string='red yellow blue green'
PARSE VAR string . . azure .     /* Assigns only azure='blue' */
```

> **NOTE** Put at least one space between adjacent periods to avoid an error.

You can also include string or positional patterns in a template. Parsing splits the source string based on matching these patterns. If a template contains patterns, the source string is first split in accordance with these patterns; parsing into words follows this:

```
data='The Woman in White      Wilkie Collins'
PARSE VAR data 1 title 25 author
SAY author "wrote" title
data='The Woman in White      Collins, Wilkie'
PARSE VAR data title 25 lastname ", " firstname
SAY firstname lastname "wrote" title
```

Parsing with positional patterns splits the source string at the column number the pattern specifies. In the first example (the top portion of the preceding code listing), the positional pattern `25` splits the source string so that `title` receives data from columns 1 through 24 and `author` receives column 25 to the end of the string. The positional pattern `25` is an absolute positional pattern (`=25` works the same way). You can also use relative positional patterns, such as `+25` or `-25`.

Parsing with string patterns can skip over characters matching the specified string pattern. In the second example, parsing splits the source string at column 25 and at the string pattern `", "`. The variable `title` again receives the data from columns 1 through 24. The variable `lastname` receives from column 25 to

the start of the matching pattern `", "`; `firstname` receives characters from the one after the character matching `", "` to the end of the string.

A pattern can be in a variable. For a variable string pattern, simply place parentheses around the variable name in the parsing template:

```
data='The Woman in White      Collins, Wilkie'
varlit=", "
PARSE VAR data title 25 lastname (varlit) firstname
SAY firstname lastname 'wrote' title
/* Displays: Wilkie Collins wrote The Woman in White */
```

For a positional pattern, place parentheses around the variable and place a plus, minus, or equal sign before the left parentheses:

```
numpat=25
PARSE VAR data title =(numpat) lastname (varlit) firstname
SAY firstname lastname 'wrote' title
/* says Wilkie Collins wrote The Woman in White */
```

Parsing with a string pattern skips over the characters that match the string pattern except when the template contains a string pattern followed by a variable name and then a relative positional pattern.

The `ARG` parsing instruction passes arguments to a program or subroutine. Call a program by entering the name of the .cmd file followed by the arguments you want to pass, or call a subroutine with the `CALL` instruction followed by the arguments you want to pass. Use `ARG` as the first instruction in the program or subroutine. The next example shows you how to pass arguments when you call a program:

```
/* ADDTWO.CMD -- Call this program by entering ADDTWO and 2 numbers */
ARG num1 num2
IF num1="" THEN num1=0
IF num2="" THEN num2=0
SAY "The total is" num1+num2"."
```

Entering “addtwo 3 4” displays `'The total is 7.'` The next example shows passing arguments to a subroutine.

```
SAY 'Enter any 2 numbers.'
PULL num1 num2
IF num1='' THEN num1=0; IF num2='' THEN num2=0;
CALL subroutine num1 num2
EXIT
subroutine:
ARG num1 num2
```

Rexx

```
SAY "The total is" num1+num2
RETURN
```

The names of the variables on the ARG instruction in the subroutine need not be the same names in your main routine. For example, the first instruction in the subroutine could have been ARG n1 n2. (In this case, you need to use these variables in the addition operation as well.)

You can parse more than one string at a time by including more than one template on the PARSE ARG and ARG instructions. Separate the templates with commas.

Debugging REXX Programs

REXX has built-in tracing capabilities, plus an interactive debugging facility. The TRACE instruction helps you to debug programs by displaying information about your program while it is running. You can specify a certain number of lines to trace (for example, TRACE 10), or you can specify one of the tracing options. For example, TRACE ALL traces everything before execution; TRACE COMMANDS traces only commands to the underlying system before processing; TRACE RESULTS traces the final result of evaluating an expression; TRACE INTERMEDIATES shows all intermediate results; and TRACE OFF shuts off all tracing. You need to specify only the first letter of each option.

Each line in the trace includes a line number (line numbers are truncated after 99999) and a three-character prefix indicating the type of data. Note the following code example:

```
TRACE A
SAY "Enter 2 numbers"
PULL num.1 num.2
IF num.1+num.2 > 10 THEN SAY "Greater than 10"
ELSE SAY "Less than 10"
```

If the user enters the numbers 7 and 5 after PULL, the following code displays:

```
     2 *-* SAY "Enter 2 numbers"
Enter 2 numbers
     4 *-* PULL num.1 num.2
7 5
     5 *-* IF num.1+num.2 > 10
```

```
        *-* THEN
        *-* SAY "Greater than 10"
Greater than 10
```

Using `TRACE I` displays:

```
      2 *-* SAY "Enter 2 numbers"
Enter 2 numbers
      4 *-* PULL num.1 num.2
7 5
      5 *-* IF num.1+num.2 > 10
        >V> 7
        >V> 5
        >O> 12
        >L> 10
        >O> 0
        *-* THEN
        *-* SAY "Greater than 10"
Greater than 10
```

The `*-*` prefix indicates each program statement. (For a single line containing two instructions, such as `a=1; c=2`, `TRACE` displays two lines starting with `*-*`.) The `>V>` prefix indicates a variable, `>O>`, a completed operation, and `>L>`, a literal. Other important prefixes are `>>>` to indicate a result and `+++` to indicate a message.

Interactive debug pauses for your input after tracing each statement. To use interactive debug, code a `TRACE` instruction with a question mark (?) immediately before the option (for example, `TRACE ?A`). In interactive debug, you can do the following:

- press Enter to go to the next statement
- enter = to execute the same statement again
- enter `TRACE` followed by a number (this executes whatever number of statements you request without pausing for any further input from you)
- enter `TRACE` followed by a negative number to turn off all tracing for that number of statements
- dynamically enter statements

If your program contains the following code:

```
TRACE ?A
temp=90
```

```
IF temp>80 THEN SAY "Whew! It's hot!"
ELSE IF temp<40 THEN SAY "Brrr! I'm cold!"
ELSE SAY 'Nice day!'
```

if you simply press Enter at each pause, TRACE displays:

```
     3 *-* temp=90
     4 *-* IF temp>80
       *-* THEN
       *-* SAY "Whew! It's hot!"
Whew! It's hot!
```

But if you enter temp=30 during the pause after line 3, the following code is produced:

```
     3 *-* temp=90
temp=30
     4 *-* IF temp>80
     5 *-* ELSE
       *-* IF temp<40
       *-* THEN
       *-* SAY "Brrr! I'm cold!"
Brrr! I'm cold!
```

For programs with SAY and PULL statements to request and retrieve input, in interactive debug enter input after the PULL statement is displayed, rather than after the SAY statement is displayed.

Built-In Functions

REXX has 66 standard built-in functions. (REXX has additional built-in functions that are only for the OS/2 operating system.) A built-in function consists of the function name, a left parenthesis that is adjacent to the name, arguments, and an ending parenthesis—for example, RANDOM(1,10).

The function name is RANDOM. There can be no spaces between the name of the function and the left parenthesis. The arguments to the RANDOM function in this example are 1 and 10. Even if there are no arguments, you still need to include the parentheses. Separate multiple arguments with commas.

A built-in function always returns some data. You can assign this data into a variable by putting the function on the right side of an assignment: `rnumber=RANDOM(1,10)`, for example. Or you can display the result with a `SAY` instruction: `SAY RANDOM(1,10)`.

Twenty-five of the built-in functions are for string manipulation. `LENGTH`, for example, returns the length of a specified string, and `WORDS` returns the number of blank-delimited words in a string. `POS` returns the position of one string in another (or 0 if not found). `STRIP` removes leading or trailing blanks (or other specified characters). `SUBSTRING` extracts a substring from a string, starting at a specified position (and up to an optional length). `VERIFY` confirms that a string contains only characters in another string (by returning 0). For example, `VERIFY(char,'0123456789')` returns 0 if `char` is a number.

An `ARG` example shown earlier in this chapter, passed two numbers to a program that added them. You can use the `WORDS` built-in function to make the program more general.

```
/* ADDALL*/
ARG input
IF input="" THEN EXIT
words=words(input)
DO i=1 TO words
   PARSE VAR input word.i input
END
total=0
DO i=1 TO words
   total=total+word.i
END
SAY total
```

You can nest calls to built-in functions:

```
string='tempest in a teapot'
lastword=WORD(string,WORDS(string))    /* assigns: lastword='teapot' */
```

`WORDS` returns the number of (blank-delimited) words in the string, which is 4. Then `WORD` returns the fourth word in the string, which is `'teapot'`.

Note the following other main groups of built-in functions:

- mathematical built-in functions, such as `ABS` (which returns absolute value), `DIGITS`, `FORM`, and `FUZZ` (which return `NUMERIC` settings), `MAX` and `MIN` (which return the largest and smallest number in a list), and `SIGN` (which indicates the sign of a number)

- input and output functions
- conversion functions, which convert to or from character, decimal, hexadecimal, and binary

Using OS/2 Commands in REXX Programs

You can use OS/2 commands in REXX programs. Here's a trivial example of how it is done:

```
/* Trivial command example */
'DIR *.CMD'
```

The command is enclosed in quotation marks. This is not always required on commands, but it is usually a good idea. If this example were written without the quotes (`DIR *.CMD`), it would be treated by REXX as a multiplication of `DIR` and `.CMD`—hardly the desired result.

At times, however, you may want to write nontrivial commands that substitute a variable and so on. You can use the power of REXX expressions (variables, operators, and functions) in your commands:

```
'DIR C:\' || name || '.EXE'
'DIR' Substr(name,3,8)
'DIR' Driveletter':\'Directory'\'name
```

As an example of how you can replace long non-REXX .CMD files with REXX, the following example is the HELP.CMD file shipped with OS/2 2.1:

```
@echo off
rem SCCSID = @(#)help.cmd 6.4 91/08/05
rem *
rem * Process HELP requests:  verify specification of "ON" or "OFF"
rem *
if "%1" == ""    goto msg
if "%1" == "on"  goto yes
if "%1" == "off" goto no
if "%1" == "ON"  goto yes
if "%1" == "OFF" goto no
if "%1" == "On"  goto yes
if "%1" == "oN"  goto yes
if "%1" == "OFf" goto no
if "%1" == "OfF" goto no
if "%1" == "Off" goto no
if "%1" == "oFF" goto no
```

Rexx

```
if "%1" == "oFf" goto no
if "%1" == "ofF" goto no
helpmsg %1 %2
goto exit
:msg
helpmsg
goto exit
:yes
prompt $i[$p]
goto exit
:no
cls
prompt
:exit
```

The following listing is the equivalent listing in REXX:

```
/* HELP.CMD - REXX program to get help for a system message. */
ARG action .
SELECT
  WHEN action=''    THEN 'helpmsg'
  WHEN action='ON'  THEN 'prompt $i[$p]'
  WHEN action='OFF' THEN DO
                           'cls'
                           'prompt'
                         END
  OTHERWISE 'helpmsg' action
END
EXIT
```

REXX provides some functions that do the jobs of some of the more common commands. These functions run faster than the commands. Most of the functions are described in "The REXX Utility Library in OS/2 2.1" later in this chapter.

Table 15.2. Equivalent REXX or RexxUtil functions.

Command	*Equivalent REXX or RexxUtil functions*
CHDIR	Directory
CLS	SysCLS

Command	*Equivalent REXX or RexxUtil functions*
DIR	SysFileTree
ENDLOCAL	Endlocal
ERASE	SysFileDelete
FIND	SysFileSearch
MKDIR	SysMkDir
RMDIR	SysRmDir
SETLOCAL	SetLocal
VER	SysOS2Ver

If you are used to writing DOS .BAT and OS/2 non-REXX .CMD files, the following features can be used in REXX instead of the program control features of .BAT language:

Table 15.3. REXX instructions or functions.

.BAT Instructions	*REXX Instructions or Functions*
CALL	Call
IF EXISTS	If Stream(name,'C', 'Query Exists') <>'' Then
IF ERRORLEVEL n	If RC = n Then
SHIFT	Arg(number)
	Arg
	Parse Arg

continues

Table 15.3. continued

.BAT Instructions	*REXX Instructions or Functions*
`FOR`	`Do`
`PAUSE`	`Pull`
	Say instruction combined with SysGetKey function

Using REXXTRY

REXXTRY.CMD is a REXX program that comes with OS/2 2.1. It is a good tool to help you learn REXX by experimentation, and it enables you to do quick REXX operations without having to edit, save, and run a stand-alone program.

REXXTRY uses a REXX instruction called `INTERPRET`, which evaluates an expression and runs the result as a REXX instruction. For example, if you write the following:

```
name = 'Suzy'
instruction = 'Say'
Interpret instruction 'Hello' name
```

the message `"Hello Suzy"` is displayed. `INTERPRET` is a rather specialized instruction, however, and few programs need it.

If you have just one instruction, such calculating the average of a few numbers, you can have REXXTRY show you that result by giving it the proper `SAY` instruction:

```
[C:\]REXXTRY Say (88+92+97+79) /4
```

and the answer, 89, is displayed.

If you have several instructions you want to try, run REXXTRY with no arguments, and REXXTRY will go into a loop where it reads a line from the keyboard and `INTERPRET`s it, repeating the sequence for as long as you want. If

you want to experiment with a few REXX functions, your session with REXXTRY may look like the following:

```
[C:\]rexxtry
REXXTRY.CMD lets you interactively try REXX statements.
    Each string is executed when you hit Enter.
    Enter 'call tell' for a description of the features.
Go on - try a few...            Enter 'exit' to end.
a = Overlay('NEW', 'old string', 3)
........................................... REXXTRY.CMD on OS/2
Say a
olNEWtring
........................................... REXXTRY.CMD on OS/2
Say Length(a)
10
........................................... REXXTRY.CMD on OS/2
Say Reverse(a)
gnirtWENlo
........................................... REXXTRY.CMD on OS/2
Say Random() Random() Random() Random()
601 969 859 200
........................................... REXXTRY.CMD on OS/2
Say Time(Normal) Time(Civil) Time(Long) Time(Hours) Time(Minutes)
16:02:28 4:02pm 16:02:28.590000 16 962
........................................... REXXTRY.CMD on OS/2
Say Date(USA) Date(European) Date(Standard) Date(Month) Date(Weekday)
10/25/92 25/10/92 19921025 October Sunday
........................................... REXXTRY.CMD on OS/2
```

There are a few things to notice in this example. First, you can assign expression results to strings, just as you would in a program. Second, you need to use the `SAY` instruction to display a result. Also, REXXTRY writes out a line of periods after each interaction and identifies itself.

By the way, the filename REXXTRY.CMD and system name OS/2 are not written that way in the program. REXXTRY picks up its filename and system name when it starts up. This same version of REXXTRY works with other computer systems besides OS/2 2.1, as long as they support REXX.

You can issue OS/2 commands with REXXTRY. The following examples show that as usual, OS/2 2.1"echoes" the command being issued. If an error is detected by OS/2 2.1, you will see the error message. Also, REXXTRY displays the error level set by OS/2 commands, writing it at the beginning of the dividing line. This shows as `RC =` because error level values are automatically stored in the REXX variable `RC`.

```
'COPY C:\CONFIG.SYS F:'
[C:\]COPY C:\CONFIG.SYS F:
SYS0015: The system cannot find the drive specified.
rc = 1 ....................................... REXXTRY.CMD on OS/2
'COPY C:\CONFIG.SYS C:\CONFIG.CPY'
[C:\]COPY C:\CONFIG.SYS C:\CONFIG.CPY
      1 file(s) copied.
rc = 0 ....................................... REXXTRY.CMD on OS/2
```

What if you make an error in a line you enter? REXXTRY is written to handle this and to tell you what the error is. The following segment shows a few examples of this situation. In the first case, a closing parenthesis was left off a function call (line 1). In the second case (line 4), a command was written which included REXX special characters (a colon, which is used for labels, and a backslash, which is the logical `not` operator). Commands such as this should be enclosed in quotation marks, as in the preceding `COPY` command examples.

```
Say Substr("OS/2 Unleashed", 8, 5
 Oooops ! ... try again.     Unmatched "(" in expression
 rc = 36 ....................................... REXXTRY.CMD on OS/2
COPY C:\CONFIG.SYS F:
 Oooops ! ... try again.     Invalid expression
 rc = 35 ....................................... REXXTRY.CMD on OS/2
```

All the examples shown so far show just one REXX instruction per line. REXX does allow multiple instructions per line when you separate the instructions by a semicolon. This goes for REXXTRY, too. The most common case of this occurs when REXXTRY is writing a loop. `DO` and `END` must be entered in one input line:

```
Do i = 1 to 3; Say 'Hello, this is greeting number' i; End
Hello, this is greeting number 1
Hello, this is greeting number 2
Hello, this is greeting number 3
.............................................. REXXTRY.CMD on OS/2
```

How do you get out of REXXTRY? Because REXXTRY runs your input lines as REXX instructions, if you enter the instruction `EXIT`, REXXTRY ends.

More Advanced REXX

As you have learned, REXX is very useful for automating simple tasks and makes a powerful alternative for OS/2 batch command files. REXX, however, provides far more capability than a simple automation type task, as you will learn in the remainder of this chapter.

REXX Boilerplates

When writing programs, you may often find that you use certain bits of code in most of your programs. In fact, you may want to designate a standard starting point for each of your programs. These blocks of code are called boilerplates.

Minimal Boilerplates

One of the strengths of REXX, compared to some other widely used languages, is that REXX programs can be written with no required blocks of code, like variable declarations, before you get to the meat of your program. The minimal REXX program consists of nothing but a minimal comment:

```
/**/
```

The comment isn't required by REXX. It is required by the OS/2 operating system's command handler to distinguish REXX CMD files from batch language CMD files.

Although not required, there are several blocks of code you should use in larger REXX programs. These blocks make it easier for you to find and debug certain common programming errors. Some events that happen in a REXX program have an effect called "raising a condition." You can identify a routine in your code that you want to run when one of these conditions is raised. Your routine can take special actions to give details on an error or perhaps ask the user of the program what to do next.

One condition you have probably already encountered is called the SYTNAX condition. This happens when an unrecoverable error is encountered in a program, such as an incorrectly written instruction or an attempt to divide by zero. The normal REXX handling of this condition is to write out an error message and the line number the error is on, trace the failing line of code, and end the program. This often tells you enough to fix the program, but sometimes it does not. When it is not enough, sometimes you can figure out the problem if you look at the contents of some variables in your program. A SYTNAX routine lets you do that.

Before showing you an example, there are a few features of REXX I should tell you about. Whenever REXX calls a subroutine, function, or condition-handling routine, the variable SIGL is set to the line number of the line that was executing when the call was made. This can be used to help debug problems. REXX has a built-in function called SOURCELINE that returns the line of your program when you pass it a line number. When a SYTNAX condition is raised, REXX sets the variable RC to the REXX error number (there are about fifty REXX errors). Because an error number is not very meaningful, REXX has a built-in function called ERRORTEXT, which gives the text of the error message for any error number. REXX has an instruction called NOP, which does nothing. This is used in places where you need an instruction but don't need any action performed. The following segment is an example of a program with an obvious bug and a SYTNAX routine:

```
/* A program with a bug and a syntax routine                        */
/* The next line of code tells REXX to call the routine SYNTAX */
/* if a SYNTAX condition is raised.                                 */
Signal on Syntax
Say 'This program will now attempt to divide by zero'
a = 1/0
Say 'This SAY instruction will never run'
Exit
SYNTAX:
  Say 'A SYNTAX condition was raised on line' sigl'!'
  Say '  The error number is' rc', which means' Errortext(rc)
  Say '  The line of code is' Sourceline(sigl)
```

```
  Say '  Now entering interactive trace so you can examine variables'
  Trace ?r      /* This turns on tracing                          */
  Nop           /* This is traced, and the first debug pause      */
                /* happens AFTER it is traced.                    */

Exit
```

When you run this program, the result is as follows:

```
This program will now attempt to divide by zero
A SYNTAX condition was raised on line 6!
 The error number is 42, which means Arithmetic overflow/underflow
 The line of code is a = 1/0
 Now entering interactive trace so you can examine variables
  15 *-*   Nop;
  +++   Interactive trace. "Trace Off" to end debug, ENTER to Continue
```

You can debug this program by entering `SAY` instructions to display the contents of variables and so on. One thing you cannot do is have the program go back to where it was and continue executing from there. Once a program performs a jump because of a `SIGNAL`, there is no going back.

Another type of error that can occur is an endless loop. This happens when faulty logic controlling a `DO` loop leaves no means for the loop to end. If you have a REXX program that is taking too long and you want to force it to end, you can interrupt it to do so. There are two ways of causing this interruption. In an OS/2 command prompt session, press Ctrl-Break. In a PMREXX session, select the Action pull-down menu and select Halt. Either of these actions raises a condition called the `HALT` condition. As with the `SYNTAX` condition, this causes the REXX program to end with an error message and a trace of the line the program was on. Again, a `HALT` condition handler can be used to provide special handling of the condition. The following segment is an example of a program with an almost endless loop:

```
/* Program with a VERY long loop                            */
Signal on Halt
Say 'Starting a very long loop.  Interrupt the program now!'
Say '  (Use control-break or the "Action" pull-down)'

Do ii = 1 to 999999999
  Nop
End

Exit
Halt:
Say 'Halt Condition raised on line' sigl'!'
```

```
Say '  That line is' Sourceline(sigl)
Say '  You can now debug if you want to.'
Trace ?R
Nop

Exit
```

When you run this program, you should get the following result:

```
Starting a very long loop.  Interrupt the program now!
  (Use control-break or the "Action" pull-down)
Halt Condition raised on line 7!
 That line is Do ii = 1 to 999999999
 You can now debug if you want to.
  17 *-*   Nop;
  +++   Interactive trace. "Trace Off" to end debug, ENTER to Continue.
```

A third type of condition is the NOVALUE condition. As mentioned earlier, when you refer to a REXX variable that has not been set, the variable's name is used as its value. Besides supplying the default variable value, this raises the NOVALUE condition. Unlike SYNTAX and HALT, the default handling of NOVALUE does not stop the program. At times, having REXX provide a default value can make it hard to find bugs when you misspell the name of a variable in your program or use a variable incorrectly. When you accidently refer to a variable before it is set, the program continues on with an improper value. You can detect this when it happens with the NOVALUE condition. As with SYNTAX and HALT, use a SIGNAL ON instruction and set up a routine to handle the condition when it occurs. There's a built-in function that is quite useful, called CONDITION, which has several possible arguments, including 'Description', which cause it to return the description of the current condition. For NOVALUE conditions, it returns the name of the REXX variable that was used without having an assigned value. The following segment is an example of NOVALUE usage:

```
/* Program which raises the NOVALUE condition */
Signal On Novalue

Say 'This program is about to raise the NOVALUE condition'
a = b              /* Variable B is used without being set */
Exit
Novalue:
Say 'Novalue Condition raised on line' sigl'!'
Say '  The variable which caused it is' Condition('Description')
Say '  That line is' Sourceline(sigl)
```

```
Say '  You can now debug if you want to.'
Trace ?R
Nop

Exit
```

The output of this program is as follows:

```
This program is about to raise the NOVALUE condition
Novalue Condition raised on line 5!
 The variable which caused it is B
 That line is a = b       /* Variable B is used without being set */
 You can now debug if you want to.
  13 *-*   Nop;
  +++   Interactive trace. "Trace Off" to end debug, ENTER to Continue.
```

Of course, you can handle all three conditions in the same program, and you do not have to go into trace mode when you trap the condition. You can write a message to a log (perhaps on a LAN server) or type a message to the screen saying `"This program has encountered a problem. Call Suzy on phone 5098 and tell her to come take a look!"`

The following segment is an example of a boilerplate that sets up to handle all three conditions. There is one new feature used here: the instruction `SIGNAL`, which is used to activate condition handling, can also be used to force an immediate jump to a label. This allows you to share the code that all three condition-handling routines have in common, and makes it easier for you to make a change to the handling of all conditions.

```
/* Standard REXX boilerplate                                */
/* Program Purpose:                                         */
/* Author:                                                  */
/* Date Written:                                            */

Signal on Syntax
Signal on Halt
Signal on Novalue

/* Main program goes here                                   */

Exit

Syntax:
 Say 'A SYNTAX condition was raised on line' sigl'!'
 Say '  The error number is' rc', which means "'Errortext(rc)'"'
 problem_line = sigl
 Signal Abnormal_End
```

```
Halt:
 Say 'A Halt condition was raised on line' sigl'!'
 problem_line = sigl
 Signal Abnormal_End

Novalue:
 Say 'Novalue Condition raised on line' sigl'!'
 Say '  The variable which caused it is' Condition('Description')
 problem_line = sigl
 Signal Abnormal_End

Abnormal_End:
 Say '  That line is "'Sourceline(problem_line)'"'
 Say '  You can now debug if you want to.'
 Trace ?R
 Nop

Exit
```

Using REXX Queues

REXX uses several instructions to work with data structures called queues. Queues contain one or more lines of data. You can use queues as temporary holding areas for data and for passing data between different REXX programs. You can also collect output from commands through REXX queues.

REXX uses the instructions PUSH and QUEUE to add lines to a queue, the instructions PARSE PULL and PULL to remove lines, and the built-in function QUEUED to find out the number of lines the queue contains. Using these instructions you can work with a queue in your program and pass data between two programs where one calls the other. The following two programs exchange data using a queue:

```
/* QueueMain:  This program received data from the program it     */
/* calls, QueueSub.  (These programs are in different OS/2 files) */

Call QueueSub
OutputLines = Queued()
Say 'Program QueueSub returned' OutputLines 'lines of output.'
Say 'The lines are:'
Do OutputLines
 Parse Pull OneLine
 Say '  "'OneLine'"'
 End
Exit
```

```
/* QueueSub: This program puts several lines of data into a queue. */
Push 'Line one'
Push 'Line two'
Push 'Line three'
Push 'This is the last line'
Exit
```

The output from running QueueMain is:

```
Program QueueSub returned 4 lines of output.
The lines are:
  "This is the last line"
  "Line three"
  "Line two"
  "Line one"
```

OS/2 2.1 has several commands called filters, which process the output lines from other OS/2 commands (SORT and MORE are examples and RXQUEUE is another, which gives you a way to get the output of OS/2 commands into your program). Write the command followed by the vertical bar (¦) and the word *RXQUEUE*, being sure to put quotation marks around them. The following segment is a simple program that uses this approach to find all the environment variables in a session, as displayed by the SET command:

```
/* Display and count all the environment variables */

'SET ¦ RXQUEUE'
Do ii = 1 to Queued()
  Parse Pull OneLine
  Say 'Variable number' ii 'is' OneLine
  End
Say 'The total number of variables is' ii-1
```

The RXQUEUE filter has two options: /LIFO and /FIFO that determine which order the lines are placed into the queue. /LIFO means "last in, first out" and is similar to using the PUSH instruction. /FIFO means "first in, first out" and is similar to using the QUEUE instruction.

The following example shows this difference. The VOL command (which displays the disk volume label and serial number) is issued three times: once by itself, which writes the output lines directly to the screen, once with RXQUEUE /LIFO, and once with RXQUEUE /FIFO. (The default for RXQUEUE is /FIFO.)

```
/* LIFOFIFO:  A program to demonstrate RXQUEUE with /LIFO and /FIFO */

Say '*** Here is the command VOL C: D: without using RXQUEUE'
'VOL C: D:'n
```

```
Say '*************************************************************'
Say '*** Now RXQUEUE /LIFO will get the output lines'
'VOL C: D: ¦ RXQUEUE /LIFO'
Say '*** The VOL command produced' Queued() 'lines of output.'
Say '*** The lines are:'
Do ii = 1 to Queued()
  Parse Pull OneLine
  Say '---line number' ii 'is "'OneLine'"'
  End

Say '*************************************************************'
Say '*** Now here it is with /FIFO'
'VOL C: D: ¦ RXQUEUE /FIFO'
Say '*** The VOL command produced' Queued() 'lines of output.'
Say '*** The lines are:'
Do ii = 1 to Queued()
  Parse Pull OneLine
  Say '---line number' ii 'is "'OneLine'"'
  End
```

The following segment is the output of this program:

```
*** Here is the command VOL C: D: without using RXQUEUE

[C:\]VOL C: D:

 The volume label in drive C is OS2.
 The Volume Serial Number is A492:3C14

 The volume label in drive D is IDE_D920506.
 The Volume Serial Number is A499:C014
*************************************************************
*** Now RXQUEUE /LIFO will get the output lines

[C:\]VOL C: D:   ¦ RXQUEUE /LIFO
*** The VOL command produced 6 lines of output.
*** The lines are:
---line number 1 is " The Volume Serial Number is A499:C014"
---line number 2 is " The volume label in drive D is IDE_D920506."
---line number 3 is ""
---line number 4 is " The Volume Serial Number is A492:3C14"
---line number 5 is " The volume label in drive C is OS2."
---line number 6 is ""
*************************************************************
*** Now here it is with /FIFO

[C:\]VOL C: D:   ¦ RXQUEUE /FIFO
*** The VOL command produced 6 lines of output.
*** The lines are:
```

```
---line number 1 is ""
---line number 2 is " The volume label in drive C is OS2."
---line number 3 is " The Volume Serial Number is A492:3C14"
---line number 4 is ""
---line number 5 is " The volume label in drive D is IDE_D920506."
---line number 6 is " The Volume Serial Number is A499:C014"
```

These examples all use a single queue. Normally, only one queue exists for each REXX program, and it is shared with any program it calls. There is actually one queue for each OS/2 command prompt session you create, and one for each PMREXX session you run. This default queue is named SESSION.

There are times when you will find uses for having more than one queue in use at a time. To do this, use a built-in function called `RXQUEUE`. This is different from the `RXQUEUE` filter command previously discussed. This function creates and deletes queues by name, and it also selects a queue as the active one. There are several options available for the `RXQUEUE` function:

```
Call RXQUEUE 'CREATE', name
```

(This option creates a new queue with the given name. This also returns the queue name that was created.)

```
Call RXQUEUE 'CREATE'
```

(This option creates a new queue with a name chosen by REXX. This returns the name REXX chose.)

```
Call RXQUEUE 'DELETE', name
```

(This option deletes the queue with the given name and deletes any lines of data that may have been in the queue.)

```
Call RXQUEUE 'SET', name
```

(This option makes the given queue active, which means that `PUSH`, `PULL`, `QUEUE`, and `QUEUED()` all use that queue until another `RXQUEUE SET` call is made. This also returns the name of the queue that had been the previous active queue.)

```
Call RXQUEUE 'QUERY'
```

(This option returns the name of the queue that was most recently set.)

TIP

The RXQUEUE function does not have an option to tell you if a certain queue name is already in use. If you try to create a queue when that queue name is already in use, RXQUEUE creates a new queue anyway, but the name of the new queue is chosen by REXX. If you want to find out if a given queue already exists, use the following code:

```
/* Query the existence of a queue called MYNAME
by trying to create it */
NewName = RxQueue('CREATE', 'MYNAME')
If NewName = 'MYNAME' Then
   Say 'MYNAME did not exist before, but it does now.'
Else Do
   Say 'MYNAME already existed'
   Call RxQueue 'DELETE', NewName
   End
```

When you delete a queue that you have made active, you must remember to issue a new RXQUEUE SET call to make a different queue (one that still exists) active. If you forget, any future PUSH, PULL, or QUEUE instruction will fail.

The RXQUEUE function's SET option does not affect the operation of the RXQUEUE filter. To get the filter to use a queue other than the default, put the queue name on the command:

```
'VOL ¦ RXQUEUE /LIFO MYNAME'
```

Reading and Writing OS/2 Files with REXX

REXX provides several built-in functions that enable you to read and write files. The functions LINEIN, LINEOUT, and LINES operate on files one line at a time:

LINEIN: reads one line
LINEOUT: writes one line
LINES: tells if any more lines are left to read

The following segment is a simple program that copies a file:

```
/* COPY1.CMD:  Simple REXX program to copy a file use line         */
/* input and output functions                                      */
/* Input: Two file names: input-file output-file                   */

Arg InputFile OutputFile

Do While Lines(InputFile) > 0      /* Loop while some lines remain */
  DataLine = Linein(InputFile)     /* Read one line                */
  Call Lineout OutputFile, Dataline   /* Write the line just read  */
End
```

REXX doesn't require you to write function calls to open or close files; REXX does that automatically. REXX also provides functions that process files character-by-character instead of line-by-line. These functions are:

CHARIN: reads one or more characters
CHAROUT: writes one or more characters
CHARS: tells how many characters are left to read

The following segment is another program used to copy a file using the character input and output functions:

```
/* COPY2.CMD:  Simple REXX program to copy a file using character  */
/* input and output functions                                      */
/* Input: Two file names: input-file output-file                   */

Arg InputFile OutputFile

Do While Chars(InputFile) > 0         /* Loop while some characters */
                                      /* remain                     */
  DataChar = Charin(InputFile)        /* Read one character         */
  Call Charout OutputFile, DataChar   /* Write the character        */
End
```

Rexx

Although the LINES function just returns 1 if more lines (or partial lines) are left to be read, CHARS returns the actual number of characters left to be read. (Both functions return 0 when there is nothing to be read.) This allows you to write a third version of the copy program without using a loop at all:

```
/* COPY3.CMD:  Simple REXX program to copy a file using character  */
/* input and output functions, without using a loop.               */
/* Input: Two file names: input-file output-file                   */

Arg InputFile OutputFile

FileData = Charin(InputFile, 1, Chars(InputFile))
Call Charout OutputFile, FileData
```

These functions allow a variable number of arguments (all arguments are optional). For reference, the following sections contain complete statements of the arguments for the functions.

Linein

- `File name`: If omitted, the default is `STDIN:`, which is the name given to the program's main input stream. This is the keyboard, unless the program is running with redirection in use.
- `Line number`: The only valid argument is 1, which means to read from the first line of the file. If omitted, `LINEIN` reads from where the last read or write operation left off. If the file has not been read or written, `LINEIN` reads from the beginning of the file.
- `Number of lines to read`: 0 and 1 are the only valid options (the default is 1).
- `Return value of Linein`: The data read.

Lineout

- `File name`: If omitted the default is `STDOUT:`, which is the name given to the program's main output stream. This is the display, unless the program is running with redirection in use.

- `Data to be written`: If omitted, the file will be closed.
- `Line number to write at`: The only valid value is 1. If omitted, `LINEOUT` writes where the last read or write operation left off. If the file has not been read or written before, `LINEOUT` defaults to writing after the last line of the file.
- `Return value of Linein`: The number of lines not written; a successful write produces a return value of 0.

Lines

- `File name`: If omitted, the default is `STDIN:`.
- `Return value of Lines`: 1 if there is more data to read, 0 if not.

Charin

- `File name`: If omitted, the default is `STDIN:`.
- `Character position`: This may be any positive whole number within the size of the file. As with `LINEIN`, the default is to read from the current position, or from the start if the file has not been used before.
- `Number of characters to read`: The default is 1.
- `Return value of Charin`: The data read.

Charout

- `File name`: If omitted, the default is `STDOUT:`.
- `Data to be written`: If omitted, the file will be closed.
- `Character position to write at`: This may be any positive whole number within the size of the file. Again, the default is the current position or the end of the file if the file has not been used before.
- `Return value of Linein`: The number of characters not written; a successful write produces a return value of 0.

Chars

- `File name`: If omitted, the default is `STDIN:`
- `Return value of Chars`: The number of characters remaining to be read.

As with all REXX built-in functions, the input and output functions can be called as subroutines or as functions. Typically, people call the input functions (`LINEIN` and `CHARIN`) and query functions (`LINES` and `CHARS`) as functions, and the output functions (`LINEOUT` and `CHAROUT`) as subroutines.

This section only talks about doing input and output to files. The REXX I/O functions also can operate on OS/2 devices such as COM ports. However, for most devices, the `LINES` and `CHARS` functions always return 1 because data may arrive at any time, even though data may not be present at the moment the functions are called.

All the REXX I/O functions take an argument described here as `file name`. Strictly speaking, it should be stream name because it can be any type of I/O stream, not just a file.

Using the *STREAM* Function

Another function in REXX that works with the input and output functions is called `STREAM`, which enables you to do some specialized operations on files. `STREAM` contains the following three arguments:

1. `File name`
2. One of the following three words (which may be abbreviated to one letter):

   `Command`: A command is to be performed on the file.

   `State`: One of the four following words describing the state is returned:

   > **ERROR:** Some error has occurred when processing the file.
   >
   > **NOTREADY:** No further read or write operations may be done to the file in its present state. This usually indicates that a read operation has attempted to read beyond the end of the file. In this event, the file may be used again if the position is reset.
   >
   > **READY:** The file is ready for use.
   >
   > **UNKNOWN:** The condition of the file is not known. It has been closed, or it was never opened.

   `Description`: A description of the condition of the file is returned. The return value is one of the four state return values followed by a colon. If the state is `NOTREADY` or `ERROR`, additional information follows the colon. If the file is in an end-of-file condition, the return value is "NOTREADY:EOF". Other error conditions are indicated by a number after the colon.
3. `Stream command`: This is only allowed when argument 2 is `Command`. The `STREAM` function supports several groups of commands:

   OPEN: You usually do not have to open a file. One time when you would want to, however, is if you want to have two programs reading the same file at the same time. You can open the file as read-only, which makes it possible for two or more programs to read the file at once. Note the following open options:

   > **"OPEN READ":** open the file read-only.
   >
   > **"OPEN WRITE":** open the file for read and write.
   >
   > **"OPEN":** same as "OPEN WRITE".

CLOSE: REXX closes all files that have been used when a program ends, so you normally don't have to close a file explicitly. A case in which you might want to close a file is when you write out a file and want to use an OS/2 command such as `COPY` or `RENAME` on it. Commands are locked out until the file is closed. There is just one member in the CLOSE group:

> **"CLOSE":** close the file.

SEEK: REXX keeps a pointer to the current read/write position in the file. These seek commands let you move that pointer without doing a read or write. The number used in seek commands is a character location or count.

> **"SEEK number"**: place the pointer at this character number, counting from the start of the file.
>
> **"SEEK =number":** same as "SEEK number".
>
> **"SEEK +number":** move the pointer forward number characters.
>
> **"SEEK -number":** move the pointer backward number characters.
>
> **"SEEK <number"**: place the pointer number characters from the end of the file.

QUERY: There are several items you can find out about a file with queries.

> **"QUERY EXISTS"**: find out if a file exists. If it does, `STREAM(filename, 'Command', 'QUERY EXISTS')` returns the fully qualified filename, such as C:\DATA\APRIL.DAT. The function returns the null string if the file does not exist.
>
> **"QUERY SIZE"**: find out the size (in bytes) of the file.
>
> **"QUERY DATETIME"**: find out the date and time when the file was last updated. The returned information is in the form `MM-DD-YY HH:MM:SS`.

The stream command `QUERY EXISTS` only applies to files, not directories. To find out if a directory exists, use the `DIRECTORY` built-in function. Attempt to set the directory you are interested in as the current directory. If that succeeds, the directory exists (and you should set the directory back to what it was). If the operation fails, the directory does not exist.

The numbers returned by `STREAM(file name, Description)` are the same numbers other programming languages on the OS/2 operating system use for I/O error codes. Table 15.4 lists some of the common values.

Table 15.4. *STREAM* error codes.

Error code	*Explanation*
2	The file was not found.
3	The path was not found.
4	The maximum number of files that can be open at one time has been reached. A file must be closed before another can be opened.
5	Access was denied by the system. This usually means another program is using the file. When files are in use they are usually locked to ensure that programs get consistent results.

continues

Table 15.4. continued

Error code	*Explanation*
19	An attempt was made to write to a write-protected drive or disk.
99	The device is in use.
108	The drive is locked.
112	The disk is full.

The following program demonstrates some of the uses of the `STREAM` function and its commands:

```
/* Program to demonstrate some uses of the stream function. */

Say 'Opening the file "alphabet"'
Call Stream 'alphabet', 'Command', 'Open write'
Say 'The file description is now',
   '"'Stream('alphabet','Description')'"'
Call Charout 'alphabet', Xrange('a', 'z') ¦¦ Xrange('A','Z')
Say 'Now the file has been written to.  Now we will close and query it.'
Call Stream 'alphabet','Command','Close'
Say 'The file description is now',
   '"'Stream('alphabet','Description')'"'
Say 'The full file name is',
   '"'Stream('alphabet','Command', 'Query Exists')'"'
Say 'The file size is',
   Stream('alphabet','Command', 'Query Size')
Say 'The file was written at',
   Stream('alphabet','Command', 'Query Datetime')

Call Stream 'alphabet', 'Command', 'Open Read'
Call Stream 'alphabet', 'Command', 'Seek 5'
Say 'Using the stream command SEEK 5 gets us the character',
     charin(alphabet)
Call Stream 'alphabet', 'Command', 'Seek <5'
Say 'Using the stream command SEEK <5 gets us the character',
     charin(alphabet)
Call Stream 'alphabet', 'Command', 'Seek -1'
Say 'Using the stream command SEEK -1 gets us the character',
     charin(alphabet)
Say 'Notice that SEEK -1 gave us the same character as before.'
```

```
Say 'That is because reading that character' ,

     advanced our position by 1.'
```

Note the following output of the preceding program:

```
Opening the file "alphabet"
The file description is now "READY:"
Now the file has been written to.  Now we will close and query it.
The file description is now "UNKNOWN:"
The full file name is "D:\rexx\unleash\alphabet"
The file size is 52
The file was written at 11-08-92  19:18:14
Using the stream command SEEK 5 gets us the character e
Using the stream command SEEK <5 gets us the character V
Using the stream command SEEK -1 gets us the character V
Notice that SEEK -1 gave us the same character as before.
That is because reading that character advanced our position by 1.
```

Using the *NOTREADY* Condition

Earlier in this chapter, you were shown how the `SIGNAL` instruction can trap certain unusual conditions. Another condition that can be raised in a REXX program is the `NOTREADY` condition. This condition arises when a read operation hits the end of a file or some error occurs during input or output. The following program is another version of the program that copies a file. This version uses the `NOTREADY` condition to end the loop.

```
/* Simple REXX program to copy a file.                    */
/* SIGNAL ON NOTREADY is used to end the loop.            */
/* Input: Two file names: input-file output-file          */

Arg InputFile OutputFile

Signal on Notready
Do Forever
   DataLine = Linein(InputFile)
   Call Lineout OutputFile, Dataline
End
Exit
Notready:
Say 'All done copying the file'
Say 'The Input file description is now',
   Stream(InputFile, 'Description')
Say 'The Output file description is now',
   Stream(OutputFile, 'Description')
```

Note the following output of this program:

```
All done copying the file
The Input file description is now NOTREADY:EOF
The Output file description is now READY:
```

There are some advanced features of condition handling you may need some day. Besides using `SIGNAL ON NOTREADY`, you can use `CALL ON NOTREADY`. This works like `SIGNAL ON NOTREADY`, except that your condition handling routine can use the `RETURN` instruction to go back to the instruction after the one that raised the condition. `CALL ON` may also be used with the `HALT` condition, but not with the `SYNTAX` or `NOVALUE` conditions.

If you have a large program, you may want to have different condition handling routines for the same condition, although at different times. You can do this by putting a routine name into your `SIGNAL ON` or `CALL ON` instruction:

```
SIGNAL ON NOTREADY NAME InputError
```

Then have a routine that starts with the label `InputError:`. Later, you can use

```
SIGNAL ON NOTREADY NAME File2Error
```

to make a different routine handle `NOTREADY` conditions.

Using REXX Extensions

A number of OS/2 applications take advantage of REXX. They provide special commands or functions that REXX programs can use. This provides you with a way to customize the application to your taste, or make it more powerful. You may have used an application such as a word processor or spreadsheet that has its own macro language. REXX can be used as a macro language for many different applications, but only for applications that have support for REXX.

Besides applications that use or support REXX, there are products and packages that are written solely to extend REXX. I'll start by introducing two alternative means of having REXX programs work with applications: commands and external function calls. You've already seen that REXX programs can issue OS/2 commands; there are applications to which REXX programs can send commands just as easily. Also, applications can provide new functions for REXX programs to call, which extend the REXX language with application-related features.

Before I get into examples, however, a few words about preparing to use the commands and functions may be useful. In some cases, the extra features are only available when a REXX program is run directly from inside the application that provides the features. In this case, the REXX programs are called macros of the application. Usually, applications that run REXX programs this way provide commands, although sometimes they provide external functions, or both.

In other cases, the REXX programs are started independently of the application they work with and run in a separate session. With arrangements like this, you usually have to have the application started before the REXX programs use it, although you may have a REXX program start the application. Even if the application is already running, you may have to issue a special command to prepare the application to be used from REXX. Some of these applications provide commands for REXX programs, and others provide external functions.

This discussion of REXX working with applications talks about using REXX with one application at a time. One time when REXX really shines, though, is when a REXX program works with several applications at once. Consider a REXX program called as a macro from a spreadsheet, which takes several data rows from the spreadsheet, accesses a database server to get some additional data, merges the data together, and calls a communications application to send the results to a different computer system.

The *ADDRESS* Instruction

One REXX instruction not previously discussed is the `ADDRESS` instruction, which tells REXX what application to send commands to. Normally, REXX sends all commands (to REXX, any line of a program that is not recognized as a REXX instruction is considered to be a command) to an application for execution. The OS/2 operating system itself is the default "application" for commands found in REXX programs. There are two ways of using the `ADDRESS` instruction. The first way is the form, `ADDRESS environment`, where `environment` is a name defined by the application to identify itself as an application that is prepared to accept commands from REXX programs. This means that all commands issued after that point (until another `ADDRESS` instruction) go to the environment named here.

The name used for OS/2 commands is `CMD`. When you run a program in an OS/2 command-line session, it is run as if `ADDRESS CMD` has been issued. In fact, if you put the instruction `ADDRESS CMD` in a program you run from an OS/2 session, it produces the same results.

When you run a program in a PMREXX session, the PMREXX application sets an environment name of `PMREXX`. This allows PMREXX to provide special handling of OS/2 commands to run in a PM window, but it accepts most of the same commands as `ADDRESS CMD`.

The second form of the ADDRESS instruction is `ADDRESS environment command-string`. This sends one command to the named environment, but doesn't affect the destination of any other commands issued afterward. An example of this form is

```
ADDRESS CMD "COPY C:\CONFIG.SYS C:\BACKUP\CONFIG.1"
```

which, in a REXX program running in an OS/2 window session, would have the same result as simply typing

```
"COPY C:\CONFIG.SYS C:\BACKUP\CONFIG.1"
```

Built-In Functions Versus Libraries

Built-in functions are REXX functions that are always available to you to use in a REXX program. These functions do not have a consistent programming interface because they are designed to perform unique tasks with unique results. Built-in functions are base functions in REXX that cannot be extended in any way.

Libraries are used to make external functions available in your application programs using a consistent programming interface. In order to use these functions, they must be registered with REXX. Libraries extend the functions available to your application.

Using REXX Libraries

You can use REXX libraries to do the following:

- load functions available in the RexxUtil library
- register and create your own external functions

To make the RexxUtil functions available to your application programs, you need to use the following instructions:

```
/* Load the REXXUTIL functions.*/
call rxfuncadd 'SysLoadFuncs','RexxUtil','SysLoadFuncs'
call sysloadfuncs
```

Complete descriptions of RexxUtil functions can be found in the online REXX information reference and the *OS/2 2.1 Technical Library Procedures Language/2 REXX Reference* manual.

To use external functions that you created, you need to register your functions to the REXX language processor. In your application program, use the `RexxRegisterFunctionDll` function as follows to make your external library function available:

```
RexxRegisterFunctionDll(function name, library name,
                        entry point of function)
```

Within a REXX program, the `RxFuncAdd` function registers your external library functions. Your applications can take advantage of the capability of using extensive library functions with REXX.

The REXX Utility Library in OS/2 2.1

RexxUtil is a dynamic link library (DLL) package of the OS/2 operating system REXX functions available with OS/2 2.1. The following list briefly describes the RexxUtil functions. Complete descriptions of these RexxUtil functions can be found in the online REXX Information reference and the *OS/2 2.1 Technical Library Procedures Language/2 REXX Reference* manual.

Function	*Description*
`RXMESSAGEBOX`	Displays a Presentation Manager message box. This requires that you run your REXX program within the PMREXX utility provided with OS/2 2.1.
`SYSCLS`	Clears the screen quickly.
`SYSCREATEOBJECT`	Creates a new instance of a Workplace Shell object class.
`SYSCURPOS`	Queries cursor position and moves the cursor to a specified row, column.
`SYSCURSTATE`	Hides or displays the cursor.
`SYSDEREGISTEROBJECTCLASS`	Deregisters a Workplace Shell object class definition from the system.
`SYSDESTROYOBJECT`	Destroys a Workplace Shell object.
`SYSDRIVEINFO`	Returns drive information.
`SYSDRIVEMAP`	Returns string of drive letters of all accessible drives.

Function	*Description*
SYSDROPFUNCS	Drops all RexxUtil functions.
SYSFILEDELETE	Deletes a specified file.
SYSFILESEARCH	Finds all lines of a file containing the target string.
SYSFILETREE	Finds files and directories that match a certain specification.
SYSGETEA	Reads a file extended attribute.
SYSGETKEY	Reads the next key from the keyboard buffer.
SYSGETMESSAGE	Retrieves a message from an OS/2 operating system message file.
SYSINI	Stores and retrieves all types of profile data.
SYSMKDIR	Creates a file directory.
SYSOS2VER	Returns the OS/2 operating system version information.
SYSPUTEA	Write a named extended attribute to a file.
SYSQUERYCLASSLIST	Retrieves the complete list of registered Workplace Shell object classes.
SYSREGISTEROBJECTCLASS	Registers a new Workplace Shell object class definition.
SYSRMDIR	Deletes a file directory.
SYSSEARCHPATH	Searches a file path for a specified file.
SYSSETICON	Associates an icon with a file.
SYSSETOBJECTDATA	Updates a Workplace Shell object definition.

continues

Function	*Description*
`SYSSLEEP`	Pauses a REXX program for a specified time interval.
`SYSTEMPFILENAME`	Returns a unique file or directory name using a specified template
`SYSTEXTSCREENREAD`	Reads characters from a specified screen location.
`SYSTEXTSCREENSIZE`	Returns the screen size.
`SYSWAITNAMEDPIPE`	Performs a timed wait on a named pipe.

Once loaded with `SysLoadFuncs`, these RexxUtil functions can be used in your REXX programs from all OS/2 operating system sessions. Now you can extend the functions of your existing REXX programs by adding all these handy OS/2 tasks. Some of the more common ways in which these functions are used might be for the following:

- searching files and directories from within your REXX program to obtain needed information quickly
- saving information outside your REXX program to be retrieved and used whenever you need it
- obtaining system drive information to be used by your REXX programs
- controlling screen input and output when running your REXX program in an OS/2 window
- creating Workplace Shell objects and class definitions in your REXX programs

The following sections are intended to provide you with a slightly more detailed description and samples of the common usage of these functions.

Searching Files and Directories

RexxUtil functions `SysFileTree` and `SysFileSearch` enable you to search files and directories for specific information and use the results of your search in your application programs.

SysFileTree

```
rc = SysFileTree(filespec, stem, {options},
                 {target attribute mask}, {new attribute mask})
```

Note the following `options`:

F: file search
D: directory search
B: both file and directory search
S: subdirectory search
T: return date and time (YY/MM/DD/HH/MM)
O: return only file specifications

`target attribute mask` in the form `'ADHRS'` indicates the Archive, Directory, Hidden, Read-only, and System settings that are set (+), cleared (-), or contain any state (*).

`new attribute mask` in the form `'ADHRS'` indicates the Archive, Directory, Hidden, Read-only, and System settings that can be set (+), cleared (-), or not changed (*).

You can use the `SysFileTree` function to retrieve specific lists of files and directories in a REXX stem variable with information that can then be used in your application programs.

SysFileSearch

```
rc = SysFileSearch(target string, filespec, stem, {options})
```

Note the following `options`:

C: case-sensitive search
N: return line numbers with output

You can use the SysFileSearch function to retrieve a list of all lines of a file containing a specified target string in a REXX stem variable that can then be used in your application programs:

```
/* Search a list of files for a specified string and return     */
/* the file name and each line containing the specified string. */
parse arg filespec '"'string'"'
                                /* get list of files for search  */
call SysFileTree filespec , 'files' , 'FO'
do i = 1 to files.0             /* search each file              */
  call SysFileSearch string , files.i , 'line' , 'N'
  if line.0 > 0 then do         /* at least 1 occurrence         */
    say files.i                 /* display file name             */
    say 'Matches= ' line.0      /* number of matches             */
    do j = 1 to line.0
      say '    Line ' line.j    /* display line with line number */
    end
    say ''
  end
end /* do */
exit
```

Saving Information

RexxUtil functions SysIni, SysPutEA, and SysGetEA enable you to save useful information in profiles and extended attributes for accessibility to your applications programs.

SysIni

```
result = SysIni({inifile}, application name, keyword, value, stem)
```

The inifile can contain:

profile file specification
USER
SYSTEM
BOTH

You can use the `SysIni` function to modify many application settings that use INI profile files, such as the USER and SYSTEM profiles OS2.INI and OS2SYS.INI. You can use the `DELETE:` keyword to delete application information. This function also enables you to retrieve application information in a REXX stem variable using the `ALL:` keyword.

```
/* Store project file compilation options in profile              */
parse arg options               /* get the options                */
                                /* find the profile               */
profile = SysSearchPath('DPATH', 'PROFILE.INI')
if profile = '' then            /* find it?                       */
  profile = 'PROFILE.INI'       /* place in current directory     */
                                /* set the compile options        */
call SysIni profile, 'Compiler', 'Options', options
```

SysPutEA

```
result = SysPutEa(file, EAname, new value)
```

You can use the `SysPutEA` function to store application information in a file's extended attributes.

SysGetEA

```
result = SysGetEa(file, EAname, variable name)
```

You can use the `SysGetEA` function to retrieve application information stored in a file's extended attributes. `SysGetEA` places this information into a REXX variable that can be used in your application program:

```
/* Display extended attributes for a list of CMD files, or        */
/* set an  extended attribute, if none already exists.            */
rc = SysFileTree('c:\prog\*.cmd', 'cmdfiles', 'FO' )
if rc <> 0 then say 'No files found'
value = 'OS/2 Command file'
do i = 1 to cmdfiles.0
   if (SysGetEA(cmdfiles.i, '.TYPE', 'EAinfo') = 0) then
     say 'File: 'cmdfiles.i 'has TYPE 'EAinfo
   else
      call SysPutEA cmdfiles.i, '.TYPE', value
end /* do */
exit
```

Obtaining Drive Information

RexxUtil functions SysDriveInfo and SysDriveMap allow you to retrieve specific information regarding your system drives and drives having a certain status. This data is easily accessible to your application programs.

SysDriveInfo

```
drive info = SysDriveInfo(drive)
```

drive info contains the following information:

drive letter
free space on the drive
total size of the drive
drive label

You can use the SysDriveInfo function to retrieve system drive information in a form that can be easily accessed by your application program.

SysDriveMap

```
drive map = SysDriveMap({starting drive}, {options})
```

drive map information contains a list of drive letters. Its options include the following:

USED: drives in use
FREE: drives which are not in use
LOCAL: local drives
REMOTE: remote drives
DETACHED: detached resources

You can use the SysDriveMap function to retrieve a list of accessible drives that can be used in your program.

Controlling Screen Input and Output

RexxUtil functions `SysCurPos` and `SysGetKey` enable you to change the location of input fields on your screen and read screen input from within your application programs.

SysCurPos

```
position = SysCurPos(row, column)
```

You can use the `SysCurPos` function to change the location of the cursor on the screen being used by your application.

SysGetKey

```
key = SysGetKey({options})
```

Note the following `options`:

ECHO: echoes the key typed on the screen
NOECHO: does not echo the key

You can use the `SysGetKey` function to read input keys from the keyboard and access screen input from your application programs.

```
/* Reads a password from a specific field location on the       */
/* screen                                                       */
passwd = ''
call SysCls
call SysCurPos 12, 0
say 'Enter password for logon ===>'
do while (ch = SysGetKey('NOECHO') <> ETK)
  passwd = passwd¦¦ch
end /* do */
exit
```

REXX and the Workplace Shell

The RexxUtil library, described in the previous sections, includes a number of functions that allow you to control the Workplace Shell. From a REXX command program you can create objects, modify existing ones, and even execute DOS programs with specific DOS settings. This section describes these functions.

You will also find it useful to refer to Chapter 5 whenever you are using the RexxUtil functions to create or modify Workplace Shell objects.

Creating Workplace Shell Objects

The REXX `SysCreateObject` function can create new Workplace Shell objects or update the settings of existing objects. The syntax of `SysCreateObject` is as follows:

```
result = SysCreateObject(classname, title, location,
                   setupstring, replace)
```

where `classname` is a class currently registered with the Workplace Shell. This may be a class provided by OS/2 2.1 or a user-defined class that has been registered with `SysRegisterObjectClass` or by another application program that created its own object classes. Chapter 5 includes a list of many of the default object classes. The following Workplace Shell object classes are particularly useful:

`WPFolder`: a Workplace Shell folder object.

`WPProgram`: a Workplace Shell program object. A `WPProgram` object is a reference to a program, not an actual program file. `WPProgram` objects allow a single program file (.EXE or .CMD file) to be referenced and opened with different settings, parameters, or current directory.

`WPShadow`: a shadow of an existing Workplace Shell object. A shadow object allows an object to appear in multiple Workplace Shell folders.

The following small REXX program can display the list of currently available Workplace Shell classes:

```
/*   QCLASS.CMD - Display list of available object classes       */
call rxfuncadd 'SysLoadFuncs', 'REXXUTIL', 'SysLoadFuncs'
call sysloadfuncs                  /* register REXXUTIL functions*/
call SysQueryClassList "list."     /* get current class list     */
do i = 1 to list.0                 /* loop through returned list */
say 'Class' i 'is' list.i          /* display next class         */
end
```

In the syntax of `SysCreateObject`, `title` is the title you wish to give the object. The title is the long name for the object that is displayed under the object icon. You can use the line end character (`"0a"x`) to separate the title into multiple lines. For example, the title `"Lotus 1-2-3"||"0a"x||"Spreadsheets"` displays as follows:

```
Lotus 1-2-3
Spreadsheets
```

In the syntax of `SysCreateObject`, `location` is the folder where the object is created. There are three ways to specify the object location:

1. **Descriptive path**: The descriptive path is the fully qualified set of folder names in the Desktop folder hierarchy. For example, the location (on a FAT file system) C:\DESKTOP\OS!2_SYS\SYSTEM_2 creates an object in the System Configuration folder.

2. **File system name**: An object can be created in any directory of a disk drive by using a fully qualified path name. For example, a location of `"D:\LOTUS"` can be used to create an object in the "D:\LOTUS" drives folder. Every folder in the Workplace Shell desktop is a directory, so the fully qualified directory name can be used in place of the descriptive name. C:\DESKTOP\OS!2_SYS is the file system location of the system folder.

3. **Object identifier**: When an object is created, it can be given an identifier that is independent of the object location. Object identifiers have the syntax `<name>`. The object ID allows an object to be used without needing to know the object's physical location.

The initial system configuration gives object IDs to all of the standard Workplace Shell objects (for example, `<WP_DESKTOP>` for the Desktop folder and `<WP_OS2SYS>` for the OS/2 System folder). Chapter 5 includes a complete list of all the default object identifiers.

Object IDs can be given to objects created with `SysCreateObject`. The Workplace Shell stores the object IDs in the OS2.INI file. The following REXX program displays the current list of defined object IDs stored in the profile:

```
/* OBJECTID.CMD - Display object ids known to Workplace Shell */
call rxfuncadd 'SysLoadFuncs', 'REXXUTIL', 'SysLoadFuncs'
call sysloadfuncs               /* register REXXUTIL functions*/
call SysIni 'USER', 'PM_Workplace:Location', 'All:', 'ids.'
  do i=1 to ids.0
    Say ids.i
  end
```

In the syntax of `SysCreateObject`, `setupstring` is a string of options used to create or alter the object. The string is a set of `option=value` strings separated by semicolons. Each Workplace Shell class has a different set of options that the class can process. These options control the behavior and appearance of a Workplace Shell object. Setup strings can also be used with the REXX `SysSetObjectData` function.

In the syntax of `SysCreateObject`, `replace` is a single value that indicates what OS/2 2.1 should do if the object that you are trying to create already exists. You can set this parameter to one of three values:

- **"FAIL"** causes the function to fail with a bad return code if an object with the same ID already exists.
- **"REPLACE"** causes OS/2 2.1 to delete the existing object and replace it with a new object based on the parameters you provide in `SysCreateObject`.
- **"UPDATE"** causes OS/2 2.1 to replace the settings for the existing object with the new information you provide. This is effectively the same as using `SysSetObjectData`, but it is useful if you are not sure whether the object actually exists or not.

Common Setup Options

The options for the standard Workplace Shell object classes are documented in the OS/2 Technical Library. Because the Technical Library is not part of the general user documentation, however, it is worth repeating the information in this chapter.

Some of the setup string options are supported by all Workplace Shell classes. These options control the behaviors shared by all Workplace Shell objects, such as the icon position and appearance.

- "OBJECTID=<NAME>;" assigns an object identifier to a newly created object or identify a specific object for update. The object identifier is required for references to existing abstract objects such as programs or shadows.
- "OPEN=ACTION;" immediately opens the object using the specified OPEN action. The string "OPEN=DEFAULT;" opens the object using the default open action. This has the same effect as double-clicking on the object icon with the mouse. "OPEN=SETTINGS;" opens the object settings dialog, which is useful for objects that require information to be manually entered when created. The "OPEN=" option can also specify other open actions on the object pop-up menu:

```
/* DETAILS.CMD - Open details view of any directory */
call rxfuncadd 'SysLoadFuncs', 'REXXUTIL', 'SysLoadFuncs'
call sysloadfuncs            /* register REXXUTIL functions*/
parse arg directory          /* get the directory id       */
call SysSetObjectData directory, 'OPEN=DETAILS;'
```

- "MINWIN=" specifies how a window minimizes when the minimize button is selected. There are three possible minimize actions:

  HIDE: views of the object are hidden when minimized. The object can only be selected again from the Task List or with the original icon.

  VIEWER: the object icon appears in the Minimized Window Viewer when the object is minimized.

  DESKTOP: the icon of the minimized object appears on the Desktop folder. The default action depends on the default selected from the System Setup menu.

- "VIEWBUTTON=" specifies the appearance of the window minimize button. VIEWBUTTON can have the following settings:

  MINIMIZE: the window has a standard minimize button.

  HIDE: the window has a hide button rather than a minimize button.

- "CCVIEW=" specifies the action taken when the user opens an object. "CCVIEW=YES" creates a new view of the object each time it is selected. "CCVIEW=NO" resurfaces open views of the object rather than opening new views. If there are no open views, then the object is opened.

- "ICONFILE=FILENAME;" changes the icon associated with an object. The file must be an icon file created by the OS/2 icon editor. The icon can be changed for any type of object, including files in the drives directory. For example, the following program changes the icon of all files that match a wildcard specification:

```
/* SETICON.CMD - Change the icon used for a set of file objects */
call rxfuncadd 'SysLoadFuncs', 'REXXUTIL', 'SysLoadFuncs'
call sysloadfuncs                /* register REXXUTIL functions*/
parse arg filespec iconfile .    /* get the spec and file      */
                                 /* get the list of files      */
call SysFileTree filespec, 'files.', 'fr'
do i=1 to files.0                /* do for each file           */
                                 /* set the icon               */
  call SysSetObjectData files.0, 'ICONFILE='iconfile';'
end
```

- "ICONRESOURCE=ID,MODULE;" changes the icon displayed for an object using an icon resource contained in an OS/2 dynamic link library.

- "ICONPOS=X,Y;" sets the objects initial icon position within its folder. The X and Y coordinates are given as a percentage of the folder *x* and *y* size. For example, the string "ICONPOS=50,50;" places the icon in the center of a folder.

- "TEMPLATE=YES¦NO;" sets the object template property. If YES is specified, the object is a template object used to create additional instances of this type of object.

- HELP OPTIONS: assigns help information to an object. The "HELPLIBRARY=filename;" option associates a file containing object help

information with the object. The related option "HELPPANEL=id;" identifies the default help panel with the HELPLIBRARY.

- RESTRICTION OPTIONS: restricts the actions allowed on an object. These restrictions can be turned on, but cannot be turned off again without re-creating the entire object definition.

  NODELETE: the object cannot be deleted by the shredder.

  NOCOPY: the object cannot be copied.

  NOMOVE: the object cannot be moved to another folder; all attempts to move the object create a shadow object.

  NODRAG: the object cannot be dragged with the mouse.

  NOLINK: shadows of this object cannot be created.

  NOSHADOW: same as NOLINK.

  NORENAME: the object cannot be renamed.

  NOPRINT: the object cannot be dropped on the printer.

  NOTVISIBLE: the object icon is not displayed in its folder.

Creating Folders

The Workplace Shell has a special class, WPFolder, that is used for all of the Workplace Shell folders. All folders added to the desktop are created as directory entries under the C:\DESKTOP directory. In addition, all other drive directory entries appear as folders in the Drives desktop object.

Because folders are also directories, SysSetObjectData can address folders using the directory name or the assigned object ID. For example, you can use either <WP_OS2SYS> or C:\DESKTOP\OS!2_SYS to address the OS/2 System folder on a FAT file system. However, because the System folder can be moved off of the desktop into another folder, it is safer to use the object ID form. The object ID works regardless of the physical location of the folder.

Folder Views

All folder objects have three views, the icon view, the tree view, and the details view. You can open all three views and you can even have multiple versions of each if the "Open New Window" option has been selected. All of these names may be specified as an `OPEN=` action in a `SysCreateObject` or `SysSetObjectData` setup string.

The setup string can also tailor the appearance of the folder views using the `ICONVIEW`, `TREEVIEW`, and `DETAILS` view keywords. These keywords take a series of comma-delimited keywords that set the view appearance. For example, `"ICONVIEW=NONFLOWED,MINI;"` displays the folder icon view with smaller icons without flowing the items together. Note the following allowed view options:

> `FLOWED`: the folder items are flowed together in a "best fit" fashion depending on the icon title.
>
> `NONFLOWED`: the folder items are displayed in grid style, with equal space occupied by each icon.
>
> `NONGRID`: the folder items are displayed vertically, positioned against the left side of the folder window.
>
> `NORMAL`: normal-size icons are used for the folder items.
>
> `MINI`: folder icons are displayed in miniature form.
>
> `INVISIBLE`: folder icons are not displayed; only the object names appear in the folder.
>
> `LINES`: the tree view is displayed with lines connecting the tree structure.
>
> `NOLINES`: the tree view is displayed without connecting lines.

A folder can be made into a Work Area folder using the setup string option `"WORKAREA=YES;"`. The work area option is one that cannot be reversed using a setup string, as `"WORKAREA=NO;"` is not accepted.

You can specify the background that is used in a created folder with `"BACKGROUND=file;"`. The specified file must be in the C:\OS2\BITMAP directory. The following small REXX program, when started out of STARTUP.CMD, wakes up periodically and changes the desktop background to a different random bitmap file:

```
/* BITMAP.CMD - Randomly change the desktop background */
call RxFuncAdd "SysLoadFuncs", "REXXUTIL", "SysLoadFuncs"
call SysLoadFuncs
                                   /* get the bitmap list         */
call SysFileTree "C:\OS2\BITMAP\*.*", "bitmaps.", "O"
do forever                         /* keep doing this             */
  call SysSleep 600                /* sleep for 10 minutes        */
  index = random(1,bitmaps.0)      /* get bitmap index            */
                                   /* update the bitmap setting   */
  call SysSetObjectData "<WP_DESKTOP>", bitmaps.index
end
```

Creating Program References

Program objects are created using the `WPProgram` Workplace Shell class. Program objects are the same as objects created with the Program template from the Templates folder. As with the Program template, you need to specify the program name (EXENAME), the program parameters (PARAMETERS), and the program working directory (STARTUPDIR):

```
Call SysCreateObject "WPProgram", "Life Insurance", "<WP_DESKTOP>",,
"EXENAME=C:\VISION\VISION.EXE;PARAMETERS=C:\VISION\SAMPLE\LIFE.OVD;"||,
"STARTUPDIR=C:\VISION;"
```

The preceding segment creates a program reference for one of the Borland ObjectVision sample programs on the desktop. When the icon is selected, the Workplace Shell starts the program C:\VISION\VISION.EXE using the specified parameters and startup directory.

When you create a new program object, the Workplace Shell examines the program to determine the program type (OS/2, DOS, or Windows). When the object is opened, it is run in the appropriate session type. The object setup string can also force the program to a specific execution mode with the `PROGTYPE` keyword. Note the following available program types:

`FULLSCREEN`: the program is run in a full-screen (nonwindowed) OS/2 session.

`PM`: the program is run in a Presentation Manager session.

`WINDOWABLEVIO`: the program is run in a windowed OS/2 session.

`VDM`: the program is run in a full-screen virtual DOS machine.

`WINDOWEDVDM`: the program is run in a windowed virtual DOS machine.

`WIN`: the program is run in a full-screen WIN-OS/2 session; if a WIN-OS/2 session is already active, this program is added to the active session.

`SEPARATEWIN`: the program is run in a full-screen WIN-OS/2 session. This option always forces a new session to be opened.

`WINDOWEDWIN`: the program is run as WIN-OS/2 Window session on the Presentation Manager desktop; this option is not available with some video setups.

If you wish to create a command prompt session that doesn't run a specific program, use EXENAME=*; for the program name and specify the prompt type using `PROGTYPE`. For example, the setup string `EXENAME=*;PROGTYPE=WINDOWEDVDM;` creates a command prompt for a windowed virtual DOS machine.

For windowed sessions, you can also control how the program appears when first started. `MAXIMIZED=YES;` causes the program to first appear as a maximized window. `MINIMIZED=YES;` causes the program to start up minimized. A minimized window appears only as an icon in the position specified by the `MINWIN` keyword.

You can specify whether the session should be closed when the program terminates. `AUTOCLOSE=NO;` returns to a command prompt in an OS/2 full-screen, OS/2 windowed, DOS full-screen, or DOS windowed session when the program ends. `AUTOCLOSE=YES;` closes the session when the program ends.

Program Associations

When you create a program object, you can associate the program with data files. An association makes a program object an open action for the associated file objects. Associations can be created using a filename filter (`ASSOCFILTER` keyword) or by file type information (`ASSOCTYPE` keyword). The file filter association can name a specific file or multiple files using wildcard characters. For example, the following program associates all files with the extension .C to the Enhanced Editor available with OS/2 2.1:

```
/* Add .C association to the Enhanced Editor */
call RxFuncAdd "SysLoadFuncs", "REXXUTIL", "SysLoadFuncs"
call SysLoadFuncs
call SysSetObjectData "<WP_EPM>", "ASSOCFILTER=*.C;"
```

The ASSOCTYPE keyword associates program objects with named file types. OS/2 2.1 has a set of default file types with names such as OS/2 Command File and Plain Text. The list of associated types can be viewed with the Association page of a program object settings dialog or with following short REXX program:

```
/* LISTTYPE.CMD - Display current file types */
call RxFuncAdd "SysLoadFuncs", "REXXUTIL", "SysLoadFuncs"
call SysLoadFuncs                   /* register the package        */
                                    /* get the current type list   */
call SysIni 'USER', 'PMWP_ASSOC_TYPE', 'All:', 'types.'
do i=1 to types.0                   /* Display the list            */
  say types.i                       /* display a type              */
end
```

Additional file types can be created by writing an entry to the user .INI file. ADDTYPE.CMD below adds a new associated type to the system:

```
/* ADDTYPE.CMD - Add a new file type */
call RxFuncAdd "SysLoadFuncs", "REXXUTIL", "SysLoadFuncs"
parse arg type                      /* get the new type            */
type = strip(type)                  /* strip blanks for safety     */
                                    /* add the new type            */
call SysIni 'USER', 'PMWP_ASSOC_TYPE', type
```

Once a type is in the associated type list, the ASSOCTYPE keyword can add an association to a program object:

```
/* NEWASSOC.CMD - Display current file types */
call RxFuncAdd "SysLoadFuncs", "REXXUTIL", "SysLoadFuncs"
call SysLoadFuncs                   /* register the functions      */
parse arg id type                   /* get object id and type      */
type = strip(type)                  /* strip blanks for safety     */
                                    /* create the new association */
call SysSetObjectData id, 'ASSOCTYPE='type';'
```

The new file type can be assigned to a file by setting the .TYPE extended attribute for the target file. The .TYPE extended attribute must be set using a mixture of binary fields and the text type name. The first 6 bytes of the .TYPE extended attribute must be the extended attribute code for a multiple value attribute and the value count. For the .TYPE attribute, the count is always 1. The first six bytes must always be the value `'DFFF00000100'x`. `'DFFF'x` is the

Rexx

multiple value code; `'00000100'x` is the count of one. Following the first code is the type value. The type is an ASCII string, which has a special extended attribute form. An ASCII extended attribute field is identified by the code `'FDFF'x`, followed by the string length (two bytes, in byte-reversed order), followed by the type string. Note the following REXX code to construct a type extended attribute:

```
typevalue = 'DFFF00000100FDFF'x¦¦d2c(length(type))¦¦'00'x¦¦type
```

The `d2c()` built-in function encodes the string length in binary form, building up the correct type value. This encoded type value can be assigned to a file using the `SysPutEA` RexxUtil function. The following REXX program can assign a type to a specified list of files:

```
/* SETTYPE.CMD - Change the type for a set of file objects      */
call rxfuncadd 'SysLoadFuncs', 'REXXUTIL', 'SysLoadFuncs'
call SysLoadFuncs                  /* register REXXUTIL functions*/
parse arg filespec type            /* get the filespec and type  */
type = strip(type)                 /* strip blanks for safety    */
                                   /* get the list of files      */
call SysFileTree filespec, 'files.', 'fr'
                                   /* create the EA value        */
typevalue = 'DFFF00000100FDFF'x¦¦d2c(length(type))¦¦'00'x¦¦type
do i=1 to files.0                  /* do for each file           */
                                   /* set the file type          */
  call SysPutEa files.i, '.TYPE', typevalue
end
```

After a file type has been assigned, all the programs associated with the new type are part of the open actions for the object. For example, to create an association for `ObjectVision` application files, use the following steps:

1. Create a new type with ADDTYPE.CMD:

   ```
   addtype ObjectVision Application File
   ```

2. Create an ObjectVision program object with an object ID that can be referenced by NEWASSOC.CMD:

```
/* CREATEOV.CMD - Create an ObjectVision program object */
Call SysCreateObject "WPProgram", "ObjectVision", "<WP_DESKTOP>",
"EXENAME=C:\VISION\VISION.EXE;STARTUPDIR=C:\VISION;OBJECTID=<VISION>;"
```

CREATEOV.CMD builds an ObjectVision program object on the OS/2 desktop. Because this program is only used once, you may find it more convenient to invoke REXXTRY and just type in the `SysCreateObject` call on the REXXTRY command line. REXXTRY avoids the need to create a command file that is only used one time.

3. Add the association with NEWASSOC.CMD:

```
newassoc <VISION> ObjectVision Application File
```

4. Set the file type of the ObjectVision applications with SETTYPE.CMD:

```
settype c:\vision\sample\*.ovd ObjectVision Application File
```

Once these steps have been followed, opening one of the ObjectVision .OVD files automatically brings up ObjectVision to run the application. Because `ObjectVision` applications all use a .OVD extension, the association can also be set using a file filter association:

```
/* Add a file association filter to an application */
call RxFuncAdd "SysLoadFuncs", "REXXUTIL", "SysLoadFuncs"
call SysLoadFuncs                  /* register the functions     */
parse arg id filter                /* get object id and filter   */
                                   /* create the new association */
call SysSetObjectData id, "ASSOCFILTER="filter";"
```

DOS Program Settings

For DOS or Windows program types, you can also set the specific DOS characteristics with the `SysCreateObject` setup string. DOS characteristics are specified with a `"SET name=value;"` syntax, where `name` is a DOS setting that appears in the settings list box for a DOS program. The DOS settings include `DOS_SHELL`, `DPMI_MEMORY_LIMIT`, `IDLE_SECONDS`, and `VIDEO_FAST_PASTE`.

The DOS setting values are specified in the same way they are given in the DOS settings list box. Settings that have radio button selections to turn an option On or Off, use a 1 or a 0 to indicate each state respectively. For example, you would use `SET DOS_BACKGROUND_EXECUTION=1;` to allow a DOS program to run in the background. Settings such as `DOS_FILES` that take numeric values from an entry field or a slider dialog use a numeric value in the setup string. `SET DOS_FILES=50;` allows a DOS session to open up to 50 files concurrently.

`DOS_STARTUP_DRIVE` and other settings require a value entered in an entry field. Used in a setup string, the value can be given just at it appears in the

dialog entry field. For example, SET DOS_STARTUP_DRIVE=C:\DRDOS.VM; boots an image of Digital Research DOS when the program is started. The DOS_VERSION and DOS_DEVICE dialogs allow multiple values to be entered. Multiple values can be given in a setup string by separating the values by a line end character ('0a' hex). REXX interprets a line end character in a literal string as the end of the program line, the line end must be specified as a hex literal and concatenated into the setup string:

```
linend = '0a'x                          /* get a line end character   */
                                        /* create the version list    */
versions = "IBMCACHE.COM,3,4,255"||linend||"IBMCACHE.SYS,3,4,255;"
                                        /* create a dos window prompt */
call SysCreateObject "WPProgram", "Dos Window", "<WP_DESKTOP>",,
  "EXENAME=*;PROGTYPE=WINDOWEDVDM;SET DOS_VERSION="versions
```

The DPMI_DOS_API, EMS_FRAME_LOCATION, KBD_CTRL_BYPASS, and VIDEO_MODE_RESTRICTION settings use a list box selection mechanism to change the value settings. The values displayed in the list box can be used directly in a setup string to set the values. For example, SET KBD_CTRL_BYPASS=CTRL_ESC; allows a DOS program to use the Ctrl-Esc key sequence in this DOS session.

Special care needs to be taken with the VIDEO_MODE_RESTRICTION settings. The items in this list box contain trailing blanks that must also be included in the setup string. You can see the trailing blanks by selecting an item from the list box. The selected value appears in a darkened box with some trailing blanks included. These blanks must also appear in your setup string:

```
                                      /* create a dos window prompt */
call SysCreateObject "WPProgram", "Dos Window", "<WP_DESKTOP>",,
  "EXENAME=*;PROGTYPE=VDM;SET VIDEO_MODE_RESTRICTION=NONE     ;"
```

SysCreateObject can invoke DOS or Windows programs with specific session settings. This is particularly useful for programs that exist on a local area network and are not available until a LOGON or NET USE operation is done. To call the program, create a new program object and include OPEN=DEFAULT; in the setup string. The object will be created with the proper settings, then invoked. Because this is a temporary object, use <WP_NOWHERE> for the object location. <WP_NOWHERE> is a hidden folder used by the Workplace Shell for temporary objects. Objects created in the <WP_NOWHERE> folder do not show up as icons in the directory.

```
/* START123.CMD - Start Lotus 123 after accessing LAN resource */
call RxFuncAdd "SysLoadFuncs", "REXXUTIL", "SysLoadFuncs"
call SysLoadFuncs                       /* register the functions     */
'net use n: lotus'                      /* access the Lotus directory */
                                        /* call Lotus 123             */
call SysCreateObject 'WPProgram', 'Lotus 123', '<WP_NOWHERE>',,
'EXENAME=N:\123\123.EXE;PROGTYPE=WINDOWEDVDM;STARTUPDIR=N:\;OPEN=DEFAULT;'
```

`SysCreateObject` opens and runs a program asynchronously, without waiting for the program to complete. If you need to wait for the application to finish so resources can be released, the file system can be used to signal the completion of the application. Begin by creating a small .BAT file that calls the actual application:

```
REM RUN123.BAT - Run Lotus 123
@echo off
@123
REM Signal application completion
@echo >c:\123.sem
```

Change the calling REXX program to call the .BAT file rather than the application file. After `SysCreateObject` is called, the REXX program can wake up periodically and check for the creation of the semaphore file:

```
/* START123.CMD - Start Lotus 123 after accessing LAN resource */
call RxFuncAdd "SysLoadFuncs", "REXXUTIL", "SysLoadFuncs"
call SysLoadFuncs                       /* register the functions     */
'net use n: lotus'                      /* access the Lotus directory */
call SysFileDelete 'C:\123.sem'         /* delete the semaphore file  */
                                        /* call Lotus 123             */
call SysCreateObject 'WPProgram', 'Lotus 123', '<WP_NOWHERE>',,
   'EXENAME=N:\123\RUN123.EXE;PROGTYPE=WINDOWEDVDM;STARTUPDIR=N:\;'||,
   'OPEN=DEFAULT'
do forever                              /* wait until sem file created*/
  call SysSleep 1                       /* sleep 1 second             */
                                        /* file there yet?            */
  if stream('C:\123.sem','Command', 'Query Exists') <> ''
    then leave                          /* yes, terminate the loop    */
end
'net use n: /delete'                    /* release the lan resource   */
```

Creating Object Shadows

Another useful Workplace Shell object class is `WPShadow`. The `WPShadow` class is shadow objects that contain references to real objects located elsewhere.

Shadow objects can be created by dragging an object while holding down both the Ctrl and Shift keys. A shadow of another object can also be created using `SysCreateObject`. The object is created just like other objects, although the object class is `WPShadow` and the object setup string is a reference to the shadowed object. For example, to add a shadow of the Enhanced Editor from the Productivity folder to the desktop, use the following call:

```
call SysCreateObject 'WPShadow', 'Enhanced Editor', '<WP_DESKTOP>',,
    'SHADOWID=<WP_EPM>;'
```

Shadow objects are useful when you wish to access program objects from different folders, but only want to maintain one set of program settings. Shadow objects are also useful when placed in the Startup folder. The Startup folder contains objects that are started automatically when the system is restarted. To have the Enhanced Editor automatically started when the system is booted, add a shadow object to the `<WP_STARTUP>` folder.

```
call SysCreateObject 'WPShadow', 'Enhanced Editor', '<WP_DESKTOP>',,
    'SHADOWID=<WP_EPM>;'
```

Destroying Objects

You can delete an existing Workplace Shell object if you know its unique identifier, or full path and filename on your hard disk. You delete an object with `SysDestroyObject` and provide the object identifier or filename as the only parameter. This example deletes the program reference object for the Enhanced Editor:

```
call SysDestroyObject '<WP_EPM>'
```

The only way to reference abstract object types, like program references and shadows, is with the object's unique identifier. For objects that are files on your hard disk, you can use either an object identifier or the full path and filename. It is usually not a good idea to rely on the directory path or filename to uniquely identify an object because the path may vary between systems, depending on whether the FAT or HPFS file system is being used. This is especially true if you wish to execute any of your REXX programs on someone else's machine.

Registering Object Classes

The two functions `SysRegisterObjectClass` and `SysDeregisterObjectClass` are useful if you want to use a REXX program as a installation utility for any Workplace Shell object classes that you may be developing. You cannot create object classes themselves in REXX. On OS/2 2.1, Workplace Shell object classes must be within a dynamic link library (DLL) that the Workplace Shell loads. The `SysRegisterObjectClass` function lets you register this DLL, and each of the classes it contains, with the Workplace Shell. The syntax of the two functions are:

```
result = SysRegisterObjectClass(classname, modulename)
```

```
result = SysDeregisterObjectClass(classname)
```

In this syntax, `classname` is the name of the object class that you wish to register, or deregister, with the Workplace Shell. This class must be held within another DLL, which you specify with the `modulename` parameter. This DLL must be in the `LIBPATH` specified in your CONFIG.SYS file so that the Workplace Shell can successfully load it.

Both of these functions return a `result` of 1 (True) if they are successful and 0 (False) if they fail, for example:

```
IF SysRegisterObjectClass('MyNewClass','MYCLASS') THEN
   SAY 'Loaded my new class successfully'
```

You can query the list of all registered object classes using the example in the section "Creating Workplace Shell Objects" in this chapter. You will see all the registered object classes, including any you register with `SysRegisterObjectClass`, with their class name and the name of the DLL that contains them.

REXX and the OS/2 Communications Manager

The IBM product Extended Services includes a component called Communications Manager, or CM. CM provides several types of communication services,

including one called the Systems Application Architecture Common Programming Interface for Communications, or CPI-C, which supports program-to-program communication between different computers (even if they are different types, such as a PC and a mainframe). CPI-C defines many verbs for use in programs to tell the communications system what to do:

`CMINIT:`	initialize communications
`CMALLOC:`	make a connection
`CMSEND:`	send a block of data

CPI-C is one example where you must first have the application (Communications Manager) running before using CPI-C verbs. CPI-C provides a new command environment for REXX called CPICOMM. You must also prepare it for accepting commands from REXX by issuing a command called `CPICREXX` (which is issued to the CMD environment, not the CPICOMM environment). You only have to issue the command `CPICREXX` once, rather than every time you run a program that will use CPICOMM. You can tell whether the `CPICREXX` command has been issued by checking the return code from the command `RXSUBCOM QUERY CPICOMM` (a return code of zero means that `CPICREXX` has been run).

The following programs use CPI-C to transfer a file between systems. DEMOMAIN.CMD reads the program and sends it, and DEMOTP receives it and displays it. DEMOMAIN includes comments about how to configure Communications Manager in order to run both programs on one machine (sending the file to yourself):

```
/* DEMOMAIN.CMD: CPICOMM send program.
** This program will read a specified file, and send its contents
** via SAA CPI for Communications (CPICOMM) to another program.
** For the purposes of this demonstration, we assume will send the
** program to another program running on our own machine.
** Input arguments:
**   file name to send (optional.  You'll be prompted if it is not
     ➥provided)
** This requires the following set-up:
** 1) Install the Communication. Manager component of OS/2 Extended
      ➥Services,
**    including the optional programming interfaces.  During install and
**    configuration, ensure you select APPC support.
** 2) Select auto-start of the attach manager if you want the second
**    program to start up automatically.
```

```
** 3) Configure two Transaction programs as follows:
**    TPNAME: DEMOTPWIN
**    OS/2 program: C:\OS2\CMD.EXE
**    Parameter:    /K whatever\DEMOTP.CMD
**     (where "whatever" is the drive and directory you put the file in)
**    Presentation type: VIO-window
**    Operation type: Non-queued, Attach Manager started
**        (use this if you are autostarting the Attach Manager)
** 4) Configure Side Information as follows:
**    Symbolic Destination Name: DEMOWIN
**    Partner LU full name: your network.your node
**    Partner TP:   DEMOTPWIN
**    Security type: use what is appropriate for your system
**    Mode name: #INTER
*/
crlf = '0D0A'x          /* define carriage-return/line-feed */
/* get file name and ensure it exists */
Arg fn
Do While Stream(fn, 'C', 'Query Exists') = ''
   Say 'Sorry, that file does not exist.  Enter new name.'
   Parse Pull fn
end /* Do */
sym_dest_name = 'DEMOWIN'
/* To use CPICOMM, we must register the subcommand handler */
Address CMD '@RXSUBCOM QUERY CPICOMM'
if rc <> 0 then Address CMD '@CPICREXX'
Address CPICOMM
/* Initialize conversation  */
'CMINIT conv_id sym_dest_name cm_rc'
If cm_rc <> 0 Then
   Say 'CM_RC for CMINIT was' CM_RC
'CMALLC conv_id cm_rc'
If cm_rc <> 0 Then
   Say 'CM_RC for CMALLC was' CM_RC
/* Now we send our data.  We put cr/lf at the end of each line */
/* so that the receiving program can just dump the data to the */
/* screen, and it will appear with nice formatting.            */
/* send a header containing the file name */
first_buffer = crlf||crlf|| 'Contents of file "'fn'":' ||crlf||crlf
buffer_len = length(first_buffer)
'CMSEND conv_id first_buffer buffer_len rts_received cm_rc'
If cm_rc <> 0 Then
   Say 'CM_RC for first CMSEND was' CM_RC
/* Now send the file, line by line.  */
Do while lines(fn) > 0 & cm_rc = 0
   buffer = linein(fn)crlf
   buffer_len = length(buffer)
   'CMSEND conv_id buffer buffer_len rts_received cm_rc'
```

Rexx

```
    if cm_rc <> 0 then
       Say 'CM_RC for CMSEND was' CM_RC
end /* do */
/* Break the conversation and we are done */
'CMDEAL conv_id cm_rc'
If cm_rc <> 0 Then
   Say 'CM_RC for CMDEAL was' CM_RC
Exit
```

```
/* DEMOTP.CMD
** This program is part of a demonstration of SAA CPI for communications
** (CPICOMM).  It will receive buffers sent to it and display them
** on the screen.
*/
Address CPICOMM
'CMACCP Conversation_id CM_RC'
if CM_RC <> 0 Then Do
  Say 'error number' CM_RC 'on allocation'
  Exit CM_RC
  End
max_length = 32767        /* max size buffer to receive at once */
buffcnt = 1
Do Until \ (CM_RC = 0)
   'CMRCV Conversation_id buffer max_length data_received received_length',
      'status_received request_to_send_received CM_RC'
   Call charout , buffer
   buffer.buffcnt = buffer
   buffcnt = buffcnt + 1
   end /* do */
if cm_rc <> 18 then
   Say 'Terminating with an error, final receive RC =' CM_RC
Exit
```

One final note about CPICOMM: Communications Manager provides a file that defines the CPICOMM error codes and messages in the syntax of a REXX program. That file is called CMREXX.CPY. You can include it in a program as a subroutine and use the variables it defines.

The *HLLAPI* Function

Another service provided by Communications Manager is the High Level Language Application Programming Interface (HLLAPI). This lets programs read from, write to, and control host system emulator sessions, such as mainframe 3270 sessions. HLLAPI provides an external function, rather than a

command environment. It also needs a setup step before that function can be called. Rather than a command (like CPICPREXX for CPICOMM), HLLAPI requires a special call be made to the REXX built-in function RXFUNCADD. REXX prepares the connect to Communications Manager when the RXFUNCADD call is made. The following program is an example program that gets the time from a mainframe system. This example assumes that the user is logged onto a mainframe system known as virtual machine (VM), and that the terminal session A is to be used.

```
/* Program to show use of HLLAPI by getting the time from a
   ➥host system. */
terminal='A'
/* First get the HLLAPI connection made.  We make a query call
   ➥to find  */
/* out if the connection has already been set up, and make it if
   ➥we need */
/* to.                                                             */
If RxFuncQuery('hllapi') Then
  call RxFuncAdd 'HLLAPI','SAAHLAPI','HLLAPISRV'
/* The first step is to "connect" to the terminal session we want.  */
Call hllapi 'Connect',terminal
/* HLLAPI is a little tricky to use.  To ensure we are in sync with */
/* the mainframe, we perform a WAIT operation.                      */
Call hllapi 'Wait'
/* Now clear the terminal screen by sending the code
   ➥which represents    */
/* the clear key, and wait.                                         */
Call hllapi 'Sendkey', '@C'
Call hllapi 'Wait'
/* Now send the mainframe command which will cause the mainframe to */
/* display the time on the screen.                                  */
Call hllapi 'Sendkey', 'CP Query Time @E'
/* Wait for that to go through, and then perform an operation
   ➥called     */
/* "Search presentation space" to find the command output.          */
Call hllapi 'Wait'
search = hllapi('Search_ps','TIME IS ',1)
/* if that returned 0, the command did not work.                    */
If search=0 Then Say 'Sorry, the VM command did not work.'
Else Do
  /* Now we read the actual time, using the location returned
   ➥in the    */
  /* variable "search".                                             */
  hosttime = hllapi('Copy_ps_to_str', search + Length('TIME IS '), 8)
```

```
  Say 'The time on the mainframe is' hosttime
  End
/* We took over the VM system connection while we did this.  Now
   ➥we give */
/* it back with these two last calls.                              */
Call hllapi 'disconnect'
Call hllapi 'reset_system'
```

REXX and the Enhanced Editor

The Enhanced Editor of OS/2 2.1 (also known as the EPM editor) can be programmed using REXX as a macro language. The simplest way to invoke REXX is to write a normal .CMD file and type the .CMD filename on the EPM command line (accessed via the Command menu item or by pressing Ctrl-I). The REXX program runs, but it is little more than an OS/2 command file and is unable to take advantage of any of the EPM features. To make your program a true EPM macro, change the file extension to .ERX ("EPM REXX"). The EPM REXX macro can be invoked by typing `"RX name"` on the EPM command line.

Your EPM REXX macro now runs as an extension of the EPM editor. Any commands in your program will be processed by the editor rather than the OS/2 CMD.EXE command shell. This allows you to issue any of the editor commands from a REXX program that can be entered on the EPM command line. The Quick Reference section of the EPM online help has a short summary of the EPM commands.

As a first program, write a profile to change some initial settings in the editor. For now, the profile will only turn off language syntax expansion and change the current file directory to a current working directory. To create the profile, edit a file named PROFILE.ERX. The profile must reside within the current program PATH; C:\OS2\APPS is the same directory as the EPM editor, a handy place for the macro. Place the following two lines in the PROFILE.ERX file:

```
'expand off'
'cd c:\'
```

These are two of the commands listed in the EPM reference. The `EXPAND` command turns off the syntax expansion; the `CD` command changes the EPM current directory. The EPM commands are REXX expressions just as OS/2 commands in a .CMD file are, and must follow the same construction and quoting rules. Note that this REXX program does not begin with a REXX comment. The REXX comment required for .CMD files is used by CMD.EXE to distinguish REXX batch files from the older .CMD language files. Because EPM only uses REXX programs, the starting comment is not needed.

Before you can use PROFILE.ERX, you must tell the EPM editor that you wish to use a profile. Bring up the EPM command dialog (using the Command menu item or Ctrl-I) and enter the command `PROFILE ON`. This command enables EPM profile processing, but only for additional file windows opened in this session. To make the Profile option permanent, select Save Options from the Options menu item. Close the editor window, then reopen the editor; your new REXX program will execute, changing the editor settings as instructed. You should see a message on the EPM message line that the new current directory is now C:\.

The Enhanced Editor also has some special commands for use from REXX macros. The `EXTRACT` command is one of these special commands. `EXTRACT` "extracts" the value of some EPM variables and returns them to your REXX program. For example, the EPM variable `getline` is the contents of the current cursor line. The command `'extract /getline'` sets two REXX variables: `getline.0` and `getline.1`. The variable `getline.0` will be set to the count of `getline` values returned by the `EXTRACT` command, and `getline.1` will be the file line contents. The complete list of extractable values is given in the EPM Quick Reference. The following program uses the EPM `EXTRACT` command:

```
/* WORDCOUN.ERX:  an EPM macro to count the words in a file         */
'extract /last'                       /* extract the file size      */
WordTotal = 0                         /* No words so far            */
do ii = 1 to last.1                   /* loop for all lines         */
  ii                                  /* position at line 'ii'      */
  'extract /getline'                  /* extract the next line      */
                                      /* add in count of words      */
  WordTotal = WordTotal + Words(getline.1)
end
                                      /* display count in messagebox*/
'messagebox The number of words is' WordTotal
```

WORDCOUN.ERX extracts the EPM field `last`, which is the file size and then extracts `getline` for each line of the file. When it has counted all of the words, it displays the count in the EPM Message Box using another special EPM command, `MESSAGEBOX`.

REXX macros can also be added as EPM menu items. The following lines, when added to PROFILE.ERX, add WORDCOUN.ERX as a menu item:

```
'BuildSubMenu default 1990 CustomActions 0 0'
'BuildMenuItem default 1990 1991 WordCount 0 0 rx wordcoun'
'ShowMenu default'
```

The `BuildSubMenu` and `BuildMenuItem` commands build a named menu definition set that is enabled with the `ShowMenu` command. `BuildSubMenu` creates a menu item on the EPM action bar named CustomActions, associated with menu ID 1990. The last two arguments are the menu attributes and the help menu ID. A value of 0 is used to get the default attributes and help information. More information on these arguments can be found in the EPM Technical Reference. The `BuildMenuItem` command creates a submenu item named WordCount that appears on the pull-down menu named CustomActions. The menu item is assigned a menu ID of 1991 and is associated with the CustomActions ID 1990. When the menu item is selected, it processes the EPM command `rx wordcoun`. The menus created by `BuildMenuItem` and `BuildSubMenu` do not appear on the action bar until the named menu (`default`) is activated by the `ShowMenu` command.

WORDCOUN.ERX does an excellent job of counting the words in the file, but it isn't a very friendly EPM macro because it leaves the file sitting on the last line of the file. A better WORDCOUN macro would leave the cursor at the same starting location. The following segment is an improved version of WORDCOUN.ERX:

```
/* WORDCOUN.ERX:  an EPM macro to count the words in a file          */
'extract /last'                       /* extract the file size      */
'extract /line/col/cursorx/cursory'   /* extract positioning info   */
WordTotal = 0                         /* No words so far            */
do ii = 1 to last.1                   /* loop for all lines         */
  ii                                  /* position at line 'ii'      */
  'extract /getline'                  /* extract the next line      */
                                      /* add in count of words      */
  WordTotal = WordTotal + Words(getline.1)
end
```

Rexx

```
                                    /* reposition the cursor      */
call EtkSetFileField 'cursorx', cursorx.1
call EtkSetFileField 'cursory', cursory.1
call EtkSetFileField 'line', line.1
call EtkSetFileField 'col', col.1
                                    /* display count in messagebox*/
'sayerror The number of words is' WordTotal
```

The improved WORDCOUN.ERX extracts the cursor file position and the cursor window position. The `line`, `col`, `cursorx`, and `cursory` EPM variables are extracted with a single extract command, with each variable name separated by a `'/'`. After the words have been counted, WORDCOUN.ERX restores the cursor position and displays the word count with the `SAYERROR` command. The `SAYERROR` command displays the count on the EPM message line rather than bringing up the EPM message box.

The cursor position is not restored with an EPM command, but with a REXX function named `EtkSetFileField`, which is a function provided by the Enhanced Editor to change the EPM file settings. Many of the fields that you can retrieve with the `EXTRACT` command can be changed with `EtkSetFileField`. The EPM Quick Reference lists the EPM variables supported by `EtkSetFileField`.

`EtkSetFileField` is just one of the editor functions EPM provides. The functions `EtkDeleteText`, `EtkInsertText`, and `EtkReplaceText` allow REXX macros to change the file text by deleting, inserting, or replacing file lines. Create a simple macro that uses `EtkInsertText`. Create a file named BLOCK.ERX containing the following REXX lines:

```
/* BLOCKC.ERX insert a block comment delimiter into a REXX file     */
'extract /line'                     /* extract current position     */
call etkinserttext "/*"             /* insert starting delimiter    */
call etkinserttext " *"             /* middle line                  */
call etkinserttext " */"            /* and closing delimiter        */
                                    /* move up to inserted lines    */
call EtkSetFileField 'line', line.1 + 1
call EtkSetFileField 'col', 4       /* position at column 4         */
```

After you have saved the file, bring up the EPM command dialog again and enter the command `RX BLOCKC`. Three lines of text will be added to your program at the current cursor position, and the cursor will be positioned to enter the block comment text.

The block comment macro is as awkward to use as a command feature or as a menu item, but it would be an excellent feature to add to a keystroke sequence. The EPM allows commands to be bound to keystroke accelerators. The following lines, when added to PROFILE.ERX, allow you to invoke the BLOCKC function with the Ctrl-c key sequence:

```
AF_CHAR        =   1                    /* character key sequence      */
AF_VIRTUALKEY  =   2                    /* virtual key sequence        */
AF_SCANCODE    =   4                    /* specific keyboard scan code*/
AF_SHIFT       =   8                    /* shift key pressed           */
AF_CONTROL     =  16                    /* control key pressed         */
AF_ALT         =  32                    /* alt key pressed             */
VK_F1        = 32                       /* virtual function keys       */
VK_F2        = 33
VK_F3        = 34
VK_F4        = 35
VK_F5        = 36
VK_F6        = 37
VK_F7        = 38
VK_F8        = 39
VK_F9        = 40
VK_F10       = 41
VK_F11       = 42
VK_F12       = 43
'buildaccel blockc' (AF_CHAR + AF_CONTROL)  67 9000 'rx blockc'
'buildaccel blockc' (AF_CHAR + AF_CONTROL)  99 9001 'rx blockc'
'buildaccel blockc' (AF_VIRTUALKEY + AF_ALT)  VK_F1 9002 'rx blockc'
'activateaccel blockc'
```

The first lines create some constants that are used by the BUILDACCEL command. The BUILDACCEL command builds a named accelerator table that can be activated with the ACTIVATEACCEL command. The second parameter of BUILDACCEL defines the type of key accelerator. AF_CHAR + AF_CONTROL creates an accelerator for a Ctrl+char sequence. This accelerator table creates entries for Ctrl+c and Ctrl+C. If either of these sequences is used, the EPM command rx blockc is executed.

Accelerators can also be defined for virtual keys, which don't have an associated ASCII value. The AF_VIRTUALKEY value defines a virtual key accelerator. The following command creates an accelerator key for the sequence Alt+F1. The entire accelerator set is enabled by the ACTIVATEACCEL command.

```
'buildaccel blockc' (AF_VIRTUALKEY + AF_ALT)  VK_F1 9002 'rx blockc'
```

You can find further examples of using REXX as a macro language for the OS/2 2.1 Enhanced Editor on CompuServe in the IBM files section of the OS2USER forum. One example illustrates how powerful REXX can be as a macro language by allowing you to play the game of tic-tac-toe against the Enhanced Editor!

Using the VREXX Package

VREXX (which stands for Visual REXX) is a REXX extension package released by IBM through the Employee Written Software program. It provides a limited means for REXX programs to put PM windows. The package name on bulletin boards is VREXX2.

The IBM Employee Written Software program allows IBMers who write small OS/2 packages outside the scope of their regular job to release them. These packages are distributed on bulletin boards and are free to any user of OS/2. IBM releases the packages for free because IBM did not pay to have them developed—the only packages eligible for release as EWS are packages that were done on the employees' own time. To go along with the free price tag: the packages are unsupported; IBM makes no commitment to fix any problems you may have with them. As the saying goes, if it breaks, you get to keep both pieces. But VREXX and the other EWS packages work pretty reliably.

The VREXX package comes with some sample programs and a softcopy book describing the functions provided. It gives you the ability to display:

- **Dialogs**, including:

  Multiline message boxes
  Single- and multiple-entry boxes
  Scrollable list boxes

Radio button choices
Check box choices
Color selection
Font selection
File selection

- **Windows**, with a selection of the following:

 Size
 Position
 Text
 Color

- **Simple graphics**:

 lines
 circles and ellipses
 line and bar graphs

The following program is a sample program using a VREXX list box dialog:

```
/* Program to demonstrate VREXX package's list box */
If RxFuncQuery('Vinit') Then
   Call RxFuncAdd 'VInit', 'VREXX', 'VINIT'
Call VInit
If result = 'ERROR' Then Signal CLEANUP
Signal on Failure name CLEANUP
Signal on Halt name CLEANUP
Signal on Syntax name CLEANUP
list.1  = 'Ham and cheese'
list.2  = 'Turkey Club'
list.3  = 'Tuna Melt'
list.4  = 'Double Cheeseburger'
list.5  = 'Shaved Roast Beef'
list.0 = 5                      /* set the number of items      */
list.vstring = list.4           /* set the default selection    */
/* First set the position of the dialog box */
Call VDialogPos 50, 50
/* Now display the list, specifying the title, the variable     */
/* containing the choices, the width and height of the list box, */
/* and a code for the pushbuttons to display (just a YES button */
/* in this case).                                               */
Call VListBox 'Choose your sandwich', 'LIST', 35, 8, 1
/* Calling VExit at the end is important!                       */
CLEANUP:
   call VExit
Exit
```

Author Bios

Rick McGuire is a senior programmer in the IBM REXX Development organization. He joined IBM in 1981 and began working as a developer on REXX for the mainframe operating system, VM/SP Release 3. Since 1988, he has been concentrating on the development of REXX for all IBM systems, with a particular emphasis on OS/2. McGuire has a bachelor's degree in Computer and Information Sciences from the Ohio State University.

Stephen G. Price is an Advisory Programmer in the IBM SAA REXX Development department. He joined IBM in 1982, working on the System Test team for the first product to include REXX, the mainframe operating system VM/SP Release 3. He moved to SAA REXX Development in 1988 and has concentrated on the testing and development of OS/2 REXX since then. He has also worked on REXX for OS/400 and IBM's mainframe systems. Price has a bachelor's degree in Computer and Communication Sciences from the University of Michigan, and a masters's degree in Computer and Information Sciences from Syracuse University.

Jeff Gray is a senior associate programmer in the IBM REXX development group with responsibility for REXX service. He joined the REXX group in 1991 after working in VM/SP for four years. Gray has a B.S. in Computer Science from the Rochester Institute of Technology.

Ann Burkes received a B.A. in journalism and communications and English from Point Park College, Pittsburgh, in 1973. She received an M.A. in English in 1977 and an M.S. in Information Science in 1987 from the University of Pittsburgh. She worked at the University of Pittsburgh as a writer and editor from 1975 through 1986 and became an information developer at IBM Endicott in 1987 with responsibility for the SAA REXX manuals.

16

Troubleshooting

In This Chapter

Ideally, OS/2 2.1 does not crash, so the user never needs to recover from any operating system catastrophes. In reality, however, operating systems crash—even OS/2 2.1. This chapter presents information and procedures that help prevent problems—prevention, of course, being the most economical method of dealing with problems. Even the most cautious user encounters crashes or system failures. For these cases, this chapter discusses various methods of recovery and error-cause identification. Some errors are simple to correct, others require a great deal of effort, and still others require an effort similar to tracking down problems under an IBM mainframe operating system like MVS or VM. The latter may sound ominous, but IBM provides tools that ship with the OS/2 2.1 product that can turn the technical user into a master of OS/2 problem determination and recovery.

There are a variety of ways to approach OS/2 problem solving. This book has already presented several. In some cases, those approaches differ from the perspective of this chapter. The bottom line, however, is that the OS/2 operating system's robustness allows for many problem-solving methods.

IBM has created a document called "OS/2 Tips and Techniques" (IBM document number 53G1930). This document is available on CompuServe and a variety of other BBSs. It contains a wealth of information not only about problem recovery, but about general use of the OS/2 operating system.

The following sections focus on recovering from installation failures, preparing to recover from post-installation failures, recovering and isolating post-installation problems, and working with the OS/2 2.1 error-logging facilities.

IBM maintains two forums or two areas for file exchange and electronic discussion. On CompuServe, the forums OS2SUP and OS2USER can serve as a technical support link to IBM and other experienced OS/2 users. Posting a question in either of these

> forums usually sparks a response within a day or two. OS/2 users with a CompuServe ID may want to monitor these forums on a regular basis to pick up tips and techniques.

Installation Failure Recovery

This section presents methods to prevent and recover from errors that can happen during and just after the installation process. The user should only use the information in this section for those circumstances. A later section, "Post-Installation Failure Recovery," contains information about recovering from failures that occur after the system has been installed and operational for a period of time.

Preparing for Installation

OS/2 2.1 typically does an excellent job of installing on a newly formatted fixed disk. Generally, it does a good job installing itself over an existing DOS system. Most of the time, it does a good job installing over an existing OS/2 1.x system. Often, however, it doesn't do as well during an installation over an OS/2 1.x system with the IBM Extended Edition installed. This section discusses ways to avoid problems at all levels.

Step one is to backup the OS/2 2.1 installation disks. If any of the installation disks are bad, it is best to discover this before getting halfway through the installation process.

Step two is to backup the entire target fixed disk. Normally, OS/2 2.1 won't trash the entire fixed disk. But, as the saying goes, it is much better to be safe than sorry (for users who backup their fixed disks on a regular basis, this step should be nothing out of the ordinary).

Before installation, it is important to verify that the target fixed disk is in good shape. The disk must have absolutely no lost clusters, cross-linked files, or bad allocation units.

The best way to ensure this is to install OS/2 2.1 on a newly partitioned, newly formatted fixed disk. This is not an option if the user wants to install OS/2 over an existing operational system. If the user is going to install OS/2 over an existing operating system, there are a number of steps the user should take to ensure that the installation is a success.

For DOS systems, first verify that the following line is in CONFIG.SYS:

```
SHELL=C:\DOS\COMMAND.COM /P /E:1024
```

The examples in this chapter assume that drive C is the default operating system drive. This is the case for DOS and OS/2 1.x systems, but OS/2 2.1 can boot from nonprimary partitions such as a logical E: drive. For the sake of brevity, however, this section presents C as the operating system drive.

The OS/2 2.1 installation program scans CONFIG.SYS for this line so it knows where COMMAND.COM "lives." Without this line, the system is not able to dual boot. Also, be sure to verify that AUTOEXEC.BAT contains the following line:

```
SET COMSPEC=C:\DOS\COMMAND.COM
```

This line tells DOS, when the system is dual booted from OS/2 to DOS, where to find the command processor when DOS must reload the transient portion after running another command. Without these two lines, dual boot will not function.

The following steps show you what to do to prepare a DOS-based system for an OS/2 2.1 installation:

1. Boot the target system with a DOS system disk. Be sure this disk contains the files CHKDSK.COM, SYS.COM, and ATTRIB.EXE.

2. Without changing to the fixed disk C:, type `CHKDSK C: /F` and press Enter.

3. This is the important step! If anything shows up as abnormal, if CHKDSK reports any lost clusters or any files that are cross-linked, correct the problem before proceeding. In the case of lost clusters, allow CHKDSK to remove them. When prompted to convert the lost clusters to file, respond No. If CHKDSK finds cross-linked files, delete the offending files (CHKDSK will provide a list). Repeat Step 2 until CHKDSK reports no errors.

4. On the boot disk, create a directory called SYSBACK by going to the A: drive, typing `MD SYSBACK`, and pressing Enter. Then type `CD\SYSBACK` and press Enter. Copy C:\CONFIG.SYS and C:\AUTOEXEC.BAT into A:\SYSBACK using the following commands:

```
COPY C:\AUTOEXEC.BAT A:\SYSBACK
COPY C:\CONFIG.SYS A:\SYSBACK
```

The steps for preparing an OS/2 1.x system for upgrade are similar. The following steps include information about IBM's Extended Edition components of OS/2 1.x. If the user's system is not using these components, the user can skip these steps.

1. If the system is OS/2 1.3: no program should have the `Start When System is Started` property set. OS/2 2.1 often does not correctly translate these, and the resulting translated INI files can hang the system during the OS/2 2.1 boot process. To disable the `Start When System is Started` property, click on the program icon once. Then click on File, then Properties, then Options. If the Start When System is Started check box is selected (with an *x* or checkmark beside it), deselect it by clicking on the check box. Repeat this process for any and all options that autostart this way.

A common offender for the `Start When System is Started` property is the OS/2 1.3 Extended Edition Communications Manager. OS/2 2.1 correctly translates STARTUP.CMD entries from OS/2 1.x applications.

2. Insert the OS/2 1.x installation disk in drive A. Go to Desktop Manager by pressing Ctrl-Esc and clicking on Group Main from the Task List. Select the Desktop menu option, then select Shutdown.

Under OS/2 2.1, never reboot or turn the system off without performing a shutdown! This step should not be considered optional no matter how many times the user appears to get away without performing the shutdown. Sooner or later, not shutting down will damage the Workplace Shell.

3. After the system has successfully shutdown, press Ctrl-Alt-Del to reboot the system.
4. Wait for the OS/2 Welcome screen to display. Press Esc. OS/2 should display the A: prompt.
5. Type `DIR CHKDSK.*`. Odds are that CHKDSK.COM is not on the installation disk. If it is, go to Step 6. If it is not, replace the installation disk with OS/2 1.x Disk 1 in drive A:.
6. Type `CHKDSK C: /F`. Do not do anything to the C: drive before this step (including any DOS commands such as `DIR`). Any disk access could lock the disk and prevent CHKDSK from working correctly. If this happens, go back to Step 2.
7. If CHKDSK reports anything unusual, correct the error. If it reports lost clusters, allow CHKDSK to repair them without writing them to file. If it reports cross-linked files, delete the offending files (CHKDSK displays a list of the offending files). Insert the installation disk in A: and press Ctrl-Alt-Del. Go back to Step 4 and repeat. Step 7 is critical. Installing OS/2 2.1 on a disk that is already failing can have enormous negative ramifications for the stability of the entire system.

At this point, the user is almost ready to proceed with the installation. Notice that there are no recovery plans to return the system to OS/2 1.x if the OS/2 2.1 installation fails. This situation exists because OS/2 2.1 overwrites

the 1.x files during installation. The chances of being able to achieve a successful retreat to the 1.x system are practically nil. The best bet if the installation fails completely (i.e., if the user did not backup the 2.1 installation disk and the installation disk fails) is to restore the system from the backup done prior to 2.1 installation.

The last thing to do before installing the OS/2 2.1 upgrade to an existing DOS or OS/2 1.x system is to verify that the target system is ready for Version 2.1. Table 16.1 lists the general characteristics of a system for OS/2 2.1 installation:

Table 16.1. OS/2 2.1 system requirements.

System Point	*Requirement*
Processor:	80386SX 16Mhz Minimum, 80386DX 25Mhz Recommended
RAM:	4M Minimum, 8M Recommended
Free Disk Space (Upgrade from DOS):	35M free
Free Disk Space (Upgrade from OS/2 1.x):	25M free
Free Disk Space (Upgrade from OS/2 2.0):	10M free
Free Disk Space (Cleanly Formatted):	45M free
Disk Drive A:	1.44M 3.5-inch or 1.2M 5.25-inch

These numbers are based on my experience and may not exactly match those recommended by IBM.

A mouse is not strictly required for OS/2 2.1 because most functions have equivalent keystrokes, but the user's productivity will suffer greatly without a mouse. (IBM considers the mouse a requirement.) If the system passes all of the above tests and criteria, it should be ready for OS/2 2.1.

CONFIG.SYS Changes

During the installation process, OS/2 2.1 installs a specialized CONFIG.SYS. In addition to the usual settings in this file, a number of environment variables are initialized that keep track of how many disks are needed for the installation and which one is the current disk. Listing 16.1 shows an extract from an interim CONFIG.SYS used during OS/2 2.1 installation.

Listing 16.1. Example extracted from OS/2 2.1 Installation CONFIG.SYS.

```
SET DISKTYPE=1
SET FIRSTDISK=7
SET NUMDISKS=12
SET TARGETPATH=C:
```

If the OS/2 2.1 installation program fails in some way while it is reading a disk, it may be possible to temporarily stop the operation, use the installation backup disks, and continue the installation from a point just before the failure. The following paragraph discusses this procedure. Note that these steps should be used before restoring the system to the previous operating system (these steps could save a great deal of time).

The important lines to notice in the preceding CONFIG.SYS listing are `SET FIRSTDISK=7` and `SET NUMDISKS=12`. If the installation crashes during the installation process, follow the proceding steps to attempt to continue the installation:

1. Determine which disk the installation failed on: simply look at the last disk or boot with the installation disk, insert Disk 1 when prompted,

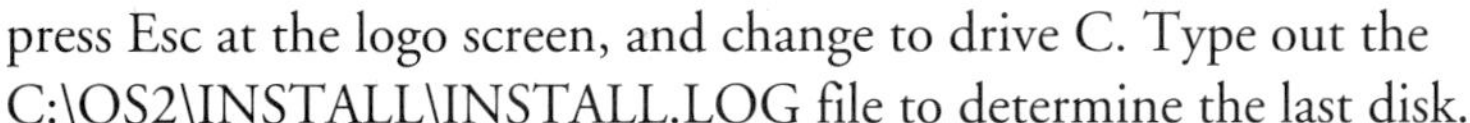

press Esc at the logo screen, and change to drive C. Type out the C:\OS2\INSTALL\INSTALL.LOG file to determine the last disk.

2. Subtract the number of the failing disk from the total number of installation disks (not including the first disk marked Install, or any of the device driver disks), then add 1.

This number is dependent on the exact version of OS/2 that you are installing.

3. If the user hasn't already booted with the installation disk, do so now. When prompted, insert Disk 1 and press Esc at the OS/2 logo screen.
4. Use a text editor to change the CONFIG.SYS. Set `SET FIRSTDISK` to the number of the disk that failed during installation. Set `SET NUMDISKS` to the number that is the result of the subtraction performed in Step 2.
5. Remove the disks from drive A and press Ctrl-Alt-Del. Click on the OK pushbutton and follow the prompts. The OS/2 installation program should pick up on the disk that failed.

If this process fails, try restoring the previous operating system (if DOS). Otherwise, restore the system from the backup.

Selective Install

After OS/2 2.1's installation program processes all of the disks, and after it prompts the user to remove the disk from the installation drive and press Enter to reboot, OS/2 2.1 goes through what many have no doubt affectionately called the "Monster Boot from Hell" (MBFH). The MBFH is so named because OS/2 can take from three to eight minutes to display the Workplace Shell after the screen clears. This delay is caused because OS/2 2.1 creates all of the extended attributes for the various Workplace Shell objects.

Do *not* interrupt the MBFH. It is important that OS/2 be allowed to continue this without interruption. Let the system run until the Workplace Shell displays. At that point, you should shutdown the system using the following steps:

1. Position the mouse pointer over the background and press mouse button 1 (MB1).
2. Press mouse button 2 (MB2) to bring up the menu.
3. Click once on Shutdown. Click on the Yes option to confirm.
4. When the message informing you that shutdown is complete appears, reboot the system with Ctrl-Alt-Del. The Workplace Shell should come up quickly now. At this point, the user can go through the tutorial, and I recommend that even highly skilled OS/2 users at least take a look at it.

These steps are desirable to ensure that all of the extended attributes are written to disk and that OS/2 2.1 is in an entirely stable condition when the user begins to work. The shutdown step may not be strictly necessary, but experience shows that not taking this step can result in a corrupted Workplace Shell desktop.

If the lengthy initial boot is interrupted, various undesirable events can occur—some folders or icons may be lost and, in some cases, entire classes of applications (like the Productivity programs, for example) may disappear. Fortunately, OS/2 2.1 provides a method to correct this situation without reinstallation.

If anything is missing from the OS/2 desktop, reboot the system and press and hold Alt-F1 from the time the OS/2 logo displays until the system displays a message that the .INI files were copied from the backup.

In extreme circumstances, the OS/2 installation process may corrupt the fixed disk or render some OS/2 folders and applications unusable. In this case, the following steps may prevent the user from having to reinstall the system:

1. Insert the Installation disk for OS/2 2.1 in drive A. Press Ctrl-Alt-Del to reboot. If the system does not respond, turn the system off.
2. When the installation disk prompts, replace it with Disk 1.
3. At the OS/2 logo screen, press Esc.

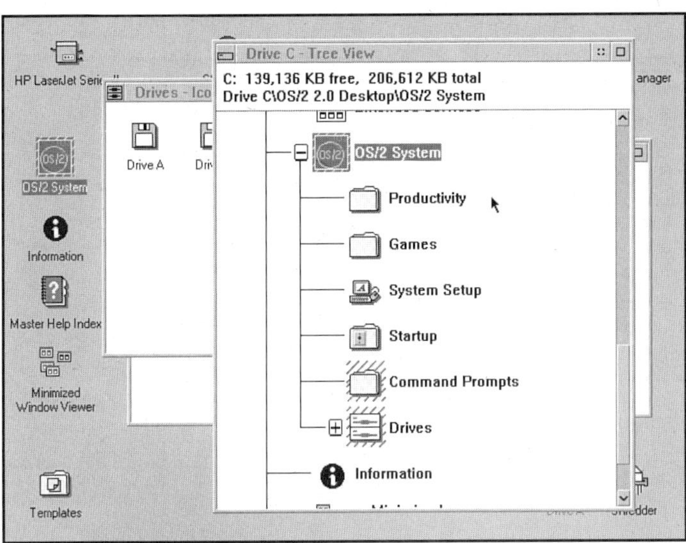

Figure 16.1. Locating the Productivity folder from the Drives icon.

4. Remove Disk 1 and insert Disk 2. Do not access drive C! Even a `DIR C:` command will lock the drive and prevent the next step from working.
5. Type `CHKDSK C: /F` and press Enter. If there are any lost clusters, allow CHKDSK to correct them. If there are cross-linked files, delete them from drive C and go back to Step 1 and begin again. When `CHKDSK C: /F` runs with no errors, proceed to Step 6.
6. Remove the disk from drive A. Reboot the system and press and hold Alt-F1 until the system displays a message saying that the INI files were copied from the backup, then release the keys. Ignore any beeping that the system issues prior to this point.
7. If the system displays the Workplace shell, the odds are favorable that the user can restore the system. Find the OS/2 System folder and double-click on it. Find the System Setup icon and double-click on it. Locate the Selective Install icon and double-click on it. This program will let the user reinstall any or all of the operating system components.

If the OS/2 System folder, or any of the icons beneath it, are missing, the user can invoke the Selective Installation program by getting to an OS/2 command prompt and typing the command `INSTALL`. Selective Installation should restore normal function to most of the OS/2 2.1 components.

The point of the preceding steps is to avoid reinstalling OS/2 2.1 unless it is absolutely necessary. The information in the preceding section should help prevent repeating the installation process.

Catastrophic Installation Failure

If the OS/2 2.1 installation fails catastrophically, the user can restore the DOS system to its original function. (Conditions are rare where such an event could happen.) However, if the user has the only copy of OS/2 2.1 for miles, if an installation disk is bad, and the user forgot to backup the installation disks before beginning the installation, these preparations prevent the user from experiencing excessive down time. Follow these steps if such a catastrophic installation failure occurs:

1. Remove any OS/2 installation disks from A:. Boot with the DOS boot disk (the one that has the A:\SYSBACK subdirectory).
2. Type `SYS C:` and press Enter. If the operation fails, type `ATTRIB -h C:\*.*` and press Enter. Then type `DEL C:\OS2BOOT` and press Enter and type `DEL C:\OS2LDR` and press Enter.
3. When the SYS operation completes successfully, the user should copy the DOS CONFIG.SYS and AUTOEXEC.BAT back to the fixed disk using the following DOS commands:

   ```
   COPY A:\SYSBACK\AUTOEXEC.BAT C:\
   COPY A:\SYSBACK\CONFIG.SYS C:\
   ```

4. Remove the boot disk from drive A and perform a warm boot (press Ctrl-Alt-Del). The system should now be restored to normal operation under DOS. The following list shows which directories should be deleted and removed from the fixed disk.

Not all of the directories may be present, depending on the point where the installation failed.

OS/2 Directories to Remove from the DOS Fixed Disk

C:\OS2 (and all directories beneath)
C:\DESKTOP (and all directories beneath)
C:\SPOOL
C:\PSFONTS
C:\NOWHERE

Some applications, such as Harvard Graphics for Windows, may use C:\PSFONTS. If the user has such a package installed on the fixed disk, do *not* delete that directory.

Problem Prevention and Recovery Preparation

The previous sections may have given you the impression that surviving the OS/2 2.1 installation process is a major feat. This is not the case at all. In the majority of cases, OS/2 2.1 installation works very well. When the user takes the precautions discussed in the previous section and prepares the machine correctly, the success percentage climbs even higher.

However, no operating system or any human creation can work all the time. All the testing in the world cannot find every defect or duplicate every combination of events and circumstances in the field. Sooner or later, a problem will impact most systems. This section discusses the preparation for such an eventuality so a potential disaster can be turned into a minor inconvenience.

Critical Files Backup

The key to the success of any preventative strategy is that once a strategy is implemented, the prevention should be painless and simple. Otherwise, the user will stop performing the task or tasks, and if a failure does occur, the user will not be ready. The following methodology is almost transparent once established.

OS/2 2.1 has several critical files. OS2.INI is located in C:\OS2. This is perhaps the most important file in the system. It includes information about programs, program icons, program locations (i.e., which folder a program is in), disk objects, folder positions, and various other Workplace Shell objects. It also holds printer driver information. If this file is damaged, the Workplace Shell is more or less inoperative.

OS2SYS.INI, located in C:\OS2, holds information about printer queues, communication port settings, and Presentation Manager window parameters. This file is also essential to OS/2 operation.

Of course, the CONFIG.SYS and STARTUP.CMD files are important and should be backed up, too. This can ordinarily be accomplished by the `BACKUP` command, but the OS2.INI and OS2SYS.INI files are locked during routine system operation, which means they are inaccessible and cannot be backed up. Although this appears to be very inconvenient, OS/2 would not be OS/2 if it did not offer an alternative. In this case, adding commands to the CONFIG.SYS, before the Workplace Shell fires up and locks the INI files, is the answer. The strategy is to back them up not once, but many times. After all, if CONFIG.SYS backs up the INI file to a single target file every time and then the system crashes, if the system has not stored multiple backups, the next time the system boots the good copy of the INI file will be corrupted. Using a combination of CONFIG.SYS and STARTUP.CMD solves this problem. Create a directory to store the backups and follow these steps:

1. Open an OS/2 command prompt.
2. Change directories to \OS2.
3. Type `MD RECOVERY` to create the backup directory.

Add the lines listed in Listing 16.2 to CONFIG.SYS after the `SET DPATH` statement:

Listing 16.2. Additions to CONFIG.SYS.

```
RUN=C:\OS2\XCOPY.EXE C:\OS2\OS2*.INI C:\OS2\RECOVER
RUN=C:\OS2\XCOPY.EXE C:\STARTUP.CMD C:\OS2\RECOVER
```

The first line in Listing 16.2 runs the OS/2 `XCOPY` command to copy both the OS2.INI and OS2SYS.INI files to C:\OS2\RECOVER. The second line copies STARTUP.CMD.

The next step prepares the user to build on some built-in OS/2 recovery methods. OS/2 2.1 has the capability to restore OS2.INI, OS2SYS.INI, and CONFIG.SYS from the C:\OS2\INSTALL subdirectory to the C:\OS2 subdirectory in the event of an INI file corruption. OS/2 2.1 builds these replacement files at installation time. If you cannot boot or you wish to reset the Workplace Shell to a basic level, simply press and hold the Alt and F1 keys after the OS/2 logo appears. You will soon see a message which indicates that the OS/2 files and the CONFIG.SYS have been replaced. Unfortunately, any changes the user has made to CONFIG.SYS or the Workplace Shell desktop will be destroyed.

Instead of taking the defaults, the following method enables the user to automatically recover with a backup of the user's INI files and CONFIG.SYS. This lessens the impact of an INI file crash and preserves any device driver and other options installed in CONFIG.SYS since the original installation.

1. Open an OS/2 command prompt.
2. Change to the C:\OS2\INSTALL subdirectory.
3. Type `COPY OS2.INI OS2INI.BAS`, `COPY OS2SYS.INI OS2SYS.BAS`, and `COPY CONFIG.SYS CONFIG.BAS`.

This now gives the user two crash restoration methods: the OS/2 2.1 Alt-F1 keystrokes or the CMD file (see the following listing). The difference between

these two methods is that Alt-F1 replaces the INIs and the CONFIG.SYS. The following CMD replaces INIs, CONFIG.SYS, and STARTUP.CMD.

Listing 16.3 shows the contents of STARTUP.CMD, which keeps the INI and related file backups fresh. This command file actually manages multiple copies of the backups.

Listing 16.3. STARTUP.CMD file contents.

```
@ECHO OFF
CD\OS2\RECOVER
IF EXIST OS2INI.003 GOTO STEP2
COPY OS2.INI OS2INI.001
COPY OS2.INI OS2INI.002
COPY OS2.INI OS2INI.003
GOTO STEP2
:STEP2
IF EXIST OS2SYS.003 GOTO STEP3
COPY OS2SYS.INI OS2SYS.001
COPY OS2SYS.INI OS2SYS.002
COPY OS2SYS.INI OS2SYS.003
GOTO STEP3
:STEP3
IF EXIST CONFIG.003 GOTO STEP4
COPY C:\CONFIG.SYS
COPY CONFIG.SYS CONFIG.001
COPY CONFIG.SYS CONFIG.002
COPY CONFIG.SYS CONFIG.003
GOTO STEP4
:STEP4
COPY OS2INI.002 OS2INI.003
COPY OS2INI.001 OS2INI.002
COPY OS2.INI OS2INI.001
COPY OS2SYS.002 OS2SYS.003
COPY OS2SYS.001 OS2SYS.002
COPY OS2SYS.INI OS2SYS.001
COPY C:\CONFIG.SYS
COPY CONFIG.002 CONFIG.003
COPY CONFIG.001 CONFIG.002
COPY CONFIG.SYS CONFIG.001
COPY CONFIG.003 \OS2\INSTALL\CONFIG.SYS
COPY OS2INI.003 \OS2\INSTALL\OS2.INI
COPY OS2SYS.003 \OS2\INSTALL\OS2SYS.INI
CD\
EXIT
```

> If the user wants to insert personalized entries into STARTUP.CMD, the user should place them just after `CD\` and before the `EXIT` statement.

This CMD file's functions are divided into three basic areas. The first `IF` statement checks to see if STARTUP.CMD has been run before by checking to see if the third copy of OS2.INI is present. If it is not, the CMD creates them based on the first copy of OS2.INI that the `RUN=XCOPY` statement in CONFIG.SYS placed in C:\OS2\RECOVER.

The program then checks to see if multiple generation OS2SYS.INIs have been copied before. If not, it uses the OS2SYS.INI copied by CONFIG.SYS and creates them.

The `STEP3` section performs a similar task for CONFIG.SYS. `STEP4` creates the multigeneration backups. The third backup is overwritten by the `002` copy, which is overwritten by the `001` copy, which is overwritten by the original. This means there are always three copies of both INI files (i.e., three boots' worth). The last step copies the third generation's files into C:\OS2\INSTALL.

The final step is to create a CMD file to handle crash recovery. Create a file called INI_REST.CMD in C:\OS2\RECOVER with the commands shown in Listing 16.4.

Listing 16.4. The contents of INI_REST.CMD.

```
@ECHO OFF
C:
CD\OS2\RECOVER
IF "%1"=="" GOTO NOONE
IF "%2"=="" GOTO NOTWO
COPY OS2INI.%1 C:\OS2\OS2.INI
COPY OS2SYS.%2 C:\OS2\OS2SYS.INI
COPY CONFIG.%1 C:\CONFIG.SYS
COPY STARTUP.CMD C:\STARTUP.CMD
GOTO DONE
:NOONE
ECHO YOU MUST SPECIFY WHICH VERSION OF OS2.INI TO RESTORE!
```

continues

Listing 16.4. continued

```
GOTO DONE
:NOTWO
ECHO YOU MUST SPECIFY WHICH VERSION OF OS2SYS.INI TO RESTORE!
GOTO DONE
:DONE
```

The syntax for INI_REST.CMD is `INI_REST 00x 00y`, where `x` is the version (`001`, `002`, or `003`) of the OS2.INI and CONFIG.SYS to restore, and `y` is the version (`001`, `002`, or `003`) of OS2SYS.INI to restore.

INI_REST.CMD cannot run while the Workplace Shell is up and operational. It must be run after booting from disk. The following "Boot Disks" section describes the creation of a boot disk. After booting from that disk, or using the installation disk and Disk 1 method of booting described previously, the user should follow these steps to run INI_REST.CMD:

1. Go to drive C and change to the \OS2\RECOVER subdirectory.
2. To restore the next-to-last versions of OS2.INI and OS2SYS.INI, type `INI_REST 002 002`. The program should restore the next-to-last INI files and restore CONFIG.SYS and STARTUP.CMD.

To verify system function after a failure, remove the boot disk from drive A and press Ctrl-Alt-Del. The alternative is not to boot with disk, but to reboot from the locked Workplace Shell, press and hold Alt-F1 just after the OS/2 logo screen, and wait for the message that says that OS/2 has copied the INI files. Most of the time, one of these approaches corrects the problem. Specifically, they correct problems associated with the INI file corruption. It does not, however, correct problems with extended attributes. However, a program called WPSBKUP, a shareware package, will correct those problems.

The Workplace Shell Backup Utility

Extended attributes are one of the key components of the Workplace Shell and its object-oriented paradigm. They are also one of the leading causes of

Workplace Shell problems. Extended attributes work with OS2.INI to define a Workplace Shell object's location, contents, settings, and so on. First, however, some words of caution about extended attributes.

- Some systems have dual boot capability. On these systems, when they are booted to DOS, the user should stay completely away from the OS/2 directories and the root directory.
- Most modern file compression/disk defragmentation programs should work harmlessly. However, programs that move files from one directory to another can be harmful. Avoid doing directory or file maintenance while booted to DOS.

These cautions do not apply to either a VDM or a specific DOS session under OS/2 2.1. In both cases, the OS/2 file system takes care of extended attributes maintenance.

Losing extended attributes is not always a disaster. Many times simply booting with an OS/2 boot disk and running CHKDSK C: /F corrects the problem, especially if the extended attributes dealt with data files. When the extended attributes for Workplace Shell objects become damaged, however, the Workplace Shell function can be impaired.

Under other circumstances, damaging extended attributes can impair or even destroy the Workplace Shell. If the INI files and extended attributes are damaged, the boot process may hang (typically just after the screen displays the Workplace Shell background).

The Workplace Shell Backup Utility (WPSBKUP) is designed to help the user recover under these circumstances. A 32-bit OS/2 application, it opens its own process (separate from the Workplace Shell) and copies all of the appropriate extended attributes and INI file contents into a directory that the user specifies. The entire process can take up to ten minutes, depending on the user's system and the complexity of Workplace Shell customization.

In my experience, when users lose their Workplace Shell from causes ranging from corrupted INI files to misallocated extended attributes, WPSBKUP restores the Workplace Shell every time. The target for the backup does not take up very much space—in many cases, less than 1M.

> **TIP** Use the OS/2 `XCOPY` command to copy the contents of the backup directory onto a floppy disk for safe keeping (i.e., `XCOPY C:\WPSBACK\*.* A: /S /E`). If the fixed disk is damaged and OS/2 2.1 must be reinstalled, the user can use `XCOPY` to copy the data from the floppy back onto the fixed disk and run the WPSBKUP restore procedure to rebuild the Workplace Shell desktop.

This package is very easy to use and operate. It comes with a READ.ME file and two EXE files: WPSBKUP.EXE (the actual backup and restore product) and WIPEWPS.EXE, which cleans out the destination (target) directory for the backups. WPSBKUP.EXE should be copied into C:\OS2, and WIPEWPS.EXE typically works best in C:\OS2\INSTALL. After the files are copied onto the user's fixed disk, follow these steps to add the program to the OS/2 desktop:

1. Open a command prompt. Create a directory called WPSBACK by typing `MD WPSBACK`. Close the command prompt by tying `EXIT` and pressing Enter.
2. Double-click on the Templates folder.
3. Place the curser over the Program icon and press and hold MB2. Drag the icon to the desired location on the desktop and release MB2. The Program Settings panel should display at this point.
4. Type `C:\OS2\WPSBKUP.EXE` in the path and filename field.
5. In the parameters field type `C:\WPSBACK`, which tells WPSBKUP where to store the backup information.
6. Click with MB1 on the General tab, and enter `WPSBKUP` for the title.
7. Double-click with MB1 on the System icon.

The program should now be operational. Double-click on its icon to verify its function.

WPSBKUP is a shareware package available on CompuServe.

The product as downloaded from CompuServe allows 15 backups before expiring. The registered package, of course, has unlimited executions. I encourage the user to register the package and support shareware.

Boot Disks

Most of the recovery methods discussed so far require the user to boot the system using disks. As shipped, the OS/2 2.1 disks can be used by booting with the installation disk, swapping it with Disk 1 when prompted, and pressing Esc at the next OS/2 logo screen. At this point, the OS/2 2.1 command prompt, [A:\], is displayed. The user can access CHKDSK by swapping Disk 1 with Disk 2.

This procedure works fine for the user who only needs to boot OS/2 2.1 from disk occasionally. If the user is part of a support network for a corporation, however, the extra time expended booting with two disks is time wasted. (See Chapter 1, "Installation," for information on creating a single boot disk.)

CHKDSK C: /F

The preceding sections mentioned CHKDSK /F as a method of recovery. It should also be used as a prevention tool. CHKDSK corrects errors in file allocation sizes, lost clusters, and extended attributes. These errors have a tendency to start out as minor errors that tend to deteriorate. Running CHKDSK /F after booting with a disk once a week can correct minor problems before they become major problems:

1. Boot with either the boot disk described in the previous section or the OS/2 2.1 installation disk. If you use the installation disk, switch the disk with Disk 1 when prompted. When the logo displays, press Esc and switch Disk 1 with Disk 2.

2. Type `CHKDSK C: /F` and press Enter. Do *not* do anything to access drive C first. Any fixed disk activity can lock the disk and force the CHKDSK C: /F to fail.

If there are any fixed disk errors, allow CHKDSK to correct them. When the process is complete, remove the disk from drive A and reboot the system.

Post-Installation Failure Recovery

Despite all attempts to keep a system running smoothly, some crashes eventually hit. This section divides the problems into several general areas. Each area includes information about what CONFIG.SYS files may be involved, what those files do, some common problems, and methods of recovery.

System Configuration (CMOS)

CONFIG.SYS settings involved: none

Other files involved: INSTALL.EXE

OS/2 2.1 and a given system unit's CMOS memory can sometimes conflict with each other. CMOS memory holds a number of things, including system configuration information and the system's date and time. For Industry Standard Architecture (ISA) systems, the system configuration information consists primarily of disk drive type, fixed disk type, amount of physical memory installed, and the video adapter type. For Extended Industry Standard Architecture (EISA) or Micro Channel Architecture, CMOS also holds information about the system's adapters (including, in many cases, interrupt levels and ROM/RAM address ranges), keyboard speed, and passwords, among other things.

The most common problem is that the disk drives are not correctly identified. In a system with a 3.5-inch, 1.44M drive A, for example, the system may work fine under DOS or DOS and Windows. However, if CMOS thinks the drive is a 5.25-inch, 1.2M disk, OS/2 2.1 will not be able to read past the 1.2M mark. So if OS/2 2.1 appears to be failing consistently at the same place during installation, if that same place is on the same disk, verify that the system's CMOS correctly identifies the disk drive types.

System RAM

CONFIG.SYS settings involved: various (none directly)

Other files involved: various (none directly)

OS/2 2.1 can fail with TRAP error messages. The most common non-application TRAP is 0002. It typically indicates a RAM hardware problem. TRAP 000D is usually a code-level problem.

TRAP 0002s almost always indicate that a problem exists with the physical memory. The most common causes are either single inline memory modules (SIMMs) that are not the same speed, memory that is not installed correctly, or failing memory components.

RAM comes in a variety of speeds from the somewhat slow (by today's standards) 85ns (nanoseconds) to the faster 70ns. Mixing 70ns and 85ns memory works fine under the less RAM-stressful environments of DOS and DOS with Windows, but industrial-strength operating systems like OS/2 2.1 push the memory much harder. If the user receives a TRAP 0002, the first thing to check is the speed of the RAM.

The second thing to do is to verify that all RAM, whether SIMMs or chips, are firmly seated. Rock SIMMs slightly in their slots, press the chips down firmly into their sockets, and retry the operation. If the TRAP 0002s persist, the unit probably has a defective memory adapter, memory chip, SIMM, or SIMM socket. If the user is adept at microcomputer hardware manipulation, the user should strip the system down to 4M and retry the operation. If the failure persists, the error is probably in the first 4M, which should be swapped

out with other memory from the system, returned for warranty replacement, or replaced. If the TRAP 0002 does not reoccur with the system running in 4M, the user should begin to add memory back into the system, in the smallest practical amount at a time, until the error reoccurs.

TRAP 000Ds are much more difficult to track down beause they are predominantly caused by application code. A TRAP 000D is the operating system's way of letting the user know that the application that failed tried to grab RAM that didn't belong to it. A new version of the failing application may solve the problem. If the user is coding an application in C, verify that return codes are the proper size, that the appropriate dynamic link libraries (DLLs) are loaded and called, and be sure that the stack is being manipulated correctly.

It is important to record the TRAP 000D (or TRAP 0002) error screen when contacting IBM or a corporate help desk. The information is several lines long, and the TRAP error screen may be in a Presentation Manager window (for less critical errors) or on a text-based screen, which generally indicates that the error will have more of a negative impact on the overall system. The PM-based windowed error message includes a pushbutton option to display the TRAP information, like Code Segment, CSLIM, and other register-level information. The text-based screen displays this information by default.

Press the Print Screen key to print a copy of the error message when OS/2 2.1 displays it in a PM window.

Applications can sometimes fail with the message "Internal Processing Fault Detected At" followed by a location. The user can work with the system unit's dealer to try to track down the offending RAM SIMM or chip.

HPFS-Related

There are two different kinds of file systems that the user can install for OS/2: the high performance file system (HPFS) or the file allocation table (FAT). HPFS offers resistance to disk fragmentation, high performance, long filenames (more than 250 characters long), and embedded extended attributes.

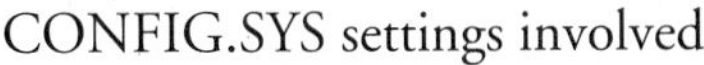

CONFIG.SYS settings involved:

```
IFS=C:\OS2\HPFS.IFS /C:64
BASEDEV=IBM2ADSK.ADD (or IBM2SCSI.ADD)
BASEDEV=OS2DASD.DMD
```

Other files involved: C:\OS2\DLL\UHPFS.DLL

The HPFS under OS/2 2.1 has approached the FAT structure in terms of reliability. However, because it cannot be accessed from a DOS boot disk and because it has its own, sometimes unexpected, way of dealing with the disk drive, it requires special handling.

One of the most startling and unnerving errors occurs when the system crashes and the user doesn't have a chance to perform a shutdown or reboot with Ctrl-Alt-Del.

Again, *never* turn off the system without performing an OS/2 2.1 shutdown!

After such an abnormal crash, booting with a disk and trying to access the C: drive, even with something simple like `DIR C:`, can result in the chilling error "Incorrect Internal Identifier"—the drive appears to be corrupted! Fortunately, this is a normal error message that appears if an HPFS drive is shutdown abnormally. To recover, simply run CHKDSK C: /F.

Include the `/AUTOCHECK:C` statement on the CONFIG.SYS statement to have OS/2 2.1 automatically check the hard disk for corruption every time OS/2 2.1 boots.

An HPFS drive attempts to perform routine maintenance, like running CHKDSK, whenever it has been booted abnormally or when it detects something amiss at boot time. An occasional CHKDSK message during the boot process (like a percentage of the disk that has been checked) is nothing to be concerned about.

By default, OS/2's ability to provide undelete support is REMed out of CONFIG.SYS. This is not a major problem under a FAT system because DOS utilities such as PC Tools can be used. However, only a handful of companies (GammaTech, for example) makes HPFS tools, so it is vital that the user unremark the CONFIG.SYS line `SET DELDIR=C:\DELETE,512;`. With that line unremarked, the user is able to recover deleted files on an HPFS partition using the OS/2 `UNDELETE` command.

A note on filenames: HPFS allows filenames more than 250 characters in length, and those names can include embedded spaces. A good example is the WP ROOT. SF file. To access these files or directories under an HPFS drive, include quotes. Note the following example of a `COPY` command.

```
COPY "C:\WP ROOT. SF" C:\OS2\RECOVER
```

Files whose names exceed the 8-character filename and the 3-character extension names are not visible to virtual DOS machines or specific DOS versions accessing the drive.

On systems with more than 8M of RAM, enlarging the size of the HPFS disk cache dramatically helps performance. Try changing the CONFIG.SYS line to read `IFS=C:\OS2\HPFS.IFS /C:128`.

FAT-Related

CONFIG.SYS settings involved:

```
DISKCACHE=384,LW
BASEDEV=IBM2ADSK.ADD (or IBM2SCSI.ADD)
BASEDEV=OS2DASD.DMD
```

Other files involved: "C:\EA DATA. SF" (note the spaces)

The FAT scheme of fixed disk management is venerable and stable. Except when it becomes fragmented, programs run fast under the OS/2 2.1 FAT environment.

Fragmentation, however, eventually degrades the performance of any FAT partition. Defragmenting is an answer, but this cannot be done while OS/2 2.1

is running because it will not allow any direct access to the fixed disk (that kind of access is what most defragmenters need). The answer would appear to be to boot to DOS.

Native DOS, however, is not familiar with extended attributes. OS/2 2.1 uses two reserved bytes in the directory entry (14h and 15h, near the date and time stamp) of a file to point to its entry in the "EA DATA. SF" file where the actual extended attributes are stored. Some defragmenter programs move the `DIR` entry as a single unit and do not manipulate the information inside. The bottom line is that if the user's defragmenter is well-behaved, the defragmentation operation should work without difficulty.

When using a VDM or a specific DOS session under OS/2, there is little chance that the "EA DATA. SF" file will become damaged. In the case of VDMs, they directly use the OS/2 file system, which takes care of the EAs. In the case of the specific DOS versions, they use the device driver FSFILTER.SYS, which interacts with the OS/2 file system. Only when booting to native DOS does the danger present itself.

Because the extended attributes for a given file are physically stored in "EA DATA. SF," there is the potential that an abnormal shutdown or reboot could damage the links between the files and their EAs. The severity of the damage depends on what kind of file owned the EAs. If the file is simply a data file, the damage will be minimal, though potentially inconvenient, because some program associations may be lost. These can be rebuilt or discarded after running CHKDSK C: /F from an OS/2 boot disk.

Do *not* run a DOS CHKDSK against an OS/2 partition. CHKDSK can misinterpret disk damage and increase the damage. Always boot with an OS/2 boot disk and use the OS/2 CHKDSK.

If the files with lost extended attributes are part of the Workplace Shell, the damage can range from lost icons to an inoperable desktop. The answer here is to either use Alt-F1 to restore the INI files and CONFIG.SYS, boot with an OS/2 boot disk, and run the INI_REST.CMD program, or boot with an OS/2 boot disk, run CHKDSK C: /F, and run the WPSBKUP program to restore the desktop.

Keyboard

CONFIG.SYS settings involved: `DEVINFO=KBD,US,C:\OS2\KEYBOARD.DCP`

Other files involved:

C:\OS2\SYSTEM\BDKBDM.EXE (bi-directional keyboard support)
C:\OS2\DLL\BKSCALLS.DLL (basic keyboard dynamic link library)
C:\OS2\DLL\FKA.DLL (function key dynamic link library)
C:\OS2\KBD01.SYS (keyboard support for non-Micro Channel systems)
C:\OS2\KBD02.SYS (keyboard support for Micro Channel systems)
C:\OS2\DLL\KBDCALLS.DLL (DLL for keyboard calls)
C:\OS2\MDOS\WINOS2\SYSTEM\KBDUS.DLL (US WINOS2 keyboard support)
C:\OS2\MDOS\VKBD.SYS (DOS virtual keyboard driver)
C:\OS2\MDOS\WINOS2\SYSTEM\KEYBOARD.DRV (WINOS2 keyboard driver)

Despite the large number of support files highlighted in the preceding listing, I have found few problems with the keyboard support under OS/2 2.1. The most difficulty comes from DOS programs that attempt to directly manipulate the keyboard buffer. For these situations, cut-and-pastes may not work correctly. You should attempt to set the `VIDEO_FASTPASTE` option to Off and retry the operation. If that doesn't work, try setting `KBD_BUFFER_EXTEND` to Off. Finally, set `KBD_RATE_LOCK` to On and retry. If none of these attempts work, check to see if the DOS program has keyboard settings of its own. WordPerfect has just such a settings menu, accessed through Shift-F1; select E for Environment, then C for Cursor Speed. Other applications may have similar keyboard buffer extender settings.

Of course, you should also check the obvious: verify that the keyboard is firmly plugged into the back of the system unit and check to be sure that the keyboard plus between the cable and the keyboard (for those systems that have such a setup) is firmly attached.

Mouse

CONFIG.SYS settings involved:

```
DEVICE=C:\OS2\MDOS\VMOUSE.SYS
DEVICE=C:\OS2\POINTDD.SYS
DEVICE=C:\OS2\MOUSE.SYS
```

Other files involved:

C:\OS2\DLL\MOUCALLS.DLL (mouse calls the dynamic link library)
C:\OS2\MDOS\WINOS2\MOUSE.DRV (mouse driver for WINOS2 session)

The most common difficulty with the mouse is more perceptual than an actual problem. In programs like WordPerfect, which don't use the standard mouse interface but choose instead to implement their own, trying to use the mouse while the program is running in a Windowed session produces two mouse pointers: the desktop pointer and one particular to the application. For these applications, open the DOS Settings and change `MOUSE_EXCLUSIVE_ACCESS` to Yes.

Changing `MOUSE_EXCLUSIVE_ACCESS`, however, also appears to cause a problem. With the mouse pointer more or less captured by WordPerfect or a similar program running in a Windowed session, how does the user regain control of the desktop mouse pointer? Press Ctrl-Esc to regain control.

If the mouse works fine until the user uses the dual boot feature to go from OS/2 to DOS and back to OS/2, there is a chance that the mouse will attempt to emulate another brand of mouse. The user should check the mouse documentation to see if the mode can indeed be changed. If it can, try selecting the mode for Microsoft Mouse emulation.

The desktop mouse pointer has been known from time to time to lock itself to the right margin of the screen. If it does this, stop trying to use the mouse or the keyboard and wait 15 seconds. Then try to use the mouse again. The mouse's position is relayed by three coordinates to the operating system, and sometimes static or other forces prevent one of the coordinates from arriving. When this happens, the mouse locks itself against the side of the screen. The mouse driver is designed to be smart enough to reset the mouse's position after 10 to 15 seconds of inactivity.

If waiting doesn't correct the situation, the only way to resync the mouse is to reboot the system. Just pressing Ctrl-Alt-Del won't do it. It is important to perform an orderly shutdown, but that is not easy without a mouse. Use the following steps to initiate a mouseless shutdown:

1. If a folder is open and in the foreground, press the space bar to deselect the currently selected icon and press Alt-Tab until no folders are in the foreground (i.e., the desktop itself has focus).
2. Press the space bar to deselect any desktop icon that was selected.
3. Press Shift-F10 to bring up the menu. Use the cursor keys to highlight Shutdown and press Enter.

Workplace Shell

CONFIG.SYS settings involved:

```
PROTSHELL=C:\OS2\PMSHELL.EXE
SET USER_INI=C:\OS2\OS2.INI
SET SYSTEM_INI=C:\OS2\OS2SYS.INI
SET AUTOSTART=PROGRAMS,TASKLIST,FOLDERS
SET RUNWORKPLACE=C:\OS2\PMSHELL.EXE
```

Other files involved:

C:\OS2\DLL\PMWP.DLL (Workplace Shell dynamic link library)
C:\OS2\DLL\PMWPMRI.DLL (Workplace Shell dynamic link library)
C:\OS2\DLL\WPCONFIG.DLL (Workplace Shell configuration DLL)

C:\OS2\DLL\WPCONMRI.DLL (Workplace Shell configuration DLL)
C:\OS2\HELP\GLOSS\WPGLOSS.HLP (Workplace Shell glossary help file)
C:\OS2\HELP\WPHELP.HLP (Workplace Shell help file)
C:\OS2\HELP\WPINDEX.HLP (Workplace Shell help index file)
C:\OS2\HELP\WPMSG.HLP (Workplace Shell message help file)
C:\OS2\DLL\WPPRINT.DLL (Workplace Shell printing DLL)
C:\OS2\DLL\WPPRTMRI.DLL (Workplace Shell printable translation support DLL)
C:\OS2\DLL\WPPWNDRV.DLL (Workplace Shell dynamic link library)
C:\DESKTOP (home directory for Workplace Shell)

The OS/2 2.1 Workplace shell is a complex combination of INI files and extended attributes. In general, if the user follows the rules discussed in the preceding sections, the Workplace Shell should function without difficulty. Even with the best preparations, however, some combination of application and circumstance may cause the Workplace Shell to fail. An application in an OS/2, DOS, or WINOS2 session, for example, could crash and take the system down with it. Because OS/2 by default tries to restore the desktop to the same pre-crash state, OS/2 may bring up the failing application and crash the system again (a seemingly endless loop).

Fortunately, there are two ways around this problem. The first is a keystroke combination. After pressing Ctrl-Alt-Del (or turning the computer off and on), wait for the mouse pointer to appear. Then press and hold Ctrl-Shift-F1 until the icons appear. If the system appears to freeze, briefly release the keys, then press and hold them again. Ctrl-Shift-F1 tells the Workplace Shell not to attempt to restart any applications.

The other alternative is preventative. If the user wants the Workplace Shell not to open any applications or folders when the system starts, the user can add the following line near the top of CONFIG.SYS:

```
SET RESTARTOBJECTS=STARTUPFOLDERSONLY
```

This line tells the Workplace Shell to only start those applications that are listed in the Startup folder. The user can replace the `STARTUPFOLDERSONLY` with `NO`, which causes the Workplace Shell to start up nothing. However, this defeats the purpose of the Startup folder.

If after booting the system the screen clears and the mouse pointer displays as the time clock, but the Workplace Shell never comes up and the system appears to freeze, there is a high probability that the INI files, the extended attributes, or both have been corrupted. Fortunately, the user who followed the advice in the preceding sections will be prepared. Follow these steps to recover:

1. If the user has created a boot disk, insert that disk in drive A, reboot the system, and wait for the [A:\] prompt to display. If the user is working with the OS/2 2.1 distribution disks, insert the installation disk in drive A and reboot. Wait for the prompt, then replace the installation disk with Disk 1 and press Enter.

2. If the user has a 1.44M, 3.5-inch boot disk, type `CHKDSK C: /F` and press Enter. If the user has a smaller boot disk or is using the OS/2 distribution disks, insert OS/2 2.1 Disk 2 in A, type `CHKDSK C: /F`, and press Enter. Allow CHKDSK to correct any problems. There is no need to write any corrections to file.

3. Change to drive C. If the user does not have WPSBKUP installed, change directories to C:\OS2\RECOVER by typing `CD \OS2\RECOVER` and pressing Enter. Type `INI_REST 002 002` and press Enter. When the process is complete, remove the disk from drive A and press Ctrl-Alt-Del. The system should come up as expected, unless the extended attributes were severely damaged. If they were, the Workplace Shell should still come up, although it may not resemble what the user expects. The user will probably have to rebuild the desktop if EAs were damaged.

4. If the user has installed and run WPSBKUP, the user should follow the restoration instructions that came with the package. If the package is unavailable, change back to A: and type `x:\PATH\WPSREST`, where `x:` is the fixed disk holding the Workplace Shell backup files and `PATH` is the

directory in which the backup is stored. When the process is finished, reboot the system.

If this procedure does not work, there is still hope. IBM creates a set of INI files in C:\OS2\INSTALL during the installation process, along with a basic CONFIG.SYS that was replaced with third generation backups of the user's INIs and CONFIG.SYS. During the boot process, the user should press Alt-F1 before the first OS/2 logo appears and hold the two keys for at least 20 seconds. A brief message saying that the original C:\OS2 INI files have been renamed and that the INI files from C:\OS2\INSTALL were copied will display. At that point, the user can release Alt-F1.

Worst case scenario: the user does not have INI_REST or WPSBKUP installed and the Alt-F1 procedure did not work. Is there anything to try short of reinstallation?

This is OS/2, so of course there is an alternative method. In C:\OS2 are a series of *.RC files. Each is either a basic OS2.INI file or a basic OS2SYS.INI file. Table 16.2 shows their names and the INI files they support:

Table 16.2. RC and INI files pairs.

.RC File	*.INI File*	*Description*
INI.RC	OS2.INI	Default OS2.INI File
INISYS.RC	OS2SYS.INI	Default OS2INI.SYS
WIN_30.RC	OS2.INI	Makes the OS/2 2.1 desktop look like Windows 3.0
OS2_13.RC	OS2.INI	Makes the OS/2 2.1 desktop look like OS/2 1.3

To access and work with these files, boot with the OS/2 distribution disks or with an OS/2 boot disk, go to drive C and change to C:\OS2.

A program called MAKEINI controls the re-creation of the INI files based on the RC file. It is best (when recovering from a crash) to re-create both OS2.INI and OS2SYS.INI:

1. Type `REN OS2.INI OS2DEAD.INI` and press Enter.
2. Type `REN OS2SYS.INI OS2SYSDE.AD` and press Enter.
3. Type `MAKEINI OS2.INI INI.RC` and press Enter. If the user would like to experiment (the desktop has been utterly destroyed anyway), the user could substitute `WIN_30.RC` for `INI.RC` to duplicate the look of Windows 3.0's desktop, or `OS2_13.RC` for `INI.RC` to duplicate the OS/2 1.3 desktop.
4. Type `MAKEINI OS2SYS.INI INISYS.RC` and press Enter.
5. It is important to clean up the directory structure so the new INIs don't conflict with the old structure. Change to the desktop directory and delete all the subdirectories. On a FAT-based system, type `CD \DESKTOP` and press Enter.
6. Delete all subfolders (subdirectories) in this directory.
7. Type `CD\` to change into the root directory.
8. There is a hidden file called WP ROOT. SF in the root directory. This holds information about the Workplace Shell configuration, and it, too, must be deleted. On a FAT-based system, type `ATTRIB -r -h -s WP*.*` and press Enter, then type `DEL WP*.*` and press Enter. On an HPFS-based system, type `ATTRIB -r -h -s "WP ROOT. SF"` and press Enter, then type `DEL "WP ROOT. SF"` and press Enter.
9. Reboot the system.

If you have just experienced a system crash and you're skipping directly to the preceding steps, be sure to run CHKDSK C: /F before accessing the C: drive.

The new INI files should now be in effect. As soon as the desktop is up and stable, perform an OS/2 shutdown and reboot. (See Chapter 6, "Configuring

the Workplace Shell," for more information about diagnosing Workplace Shell problems.)

Video

CONFIG.SYS settings involved:

Values shown are for a VGA-based system. Other systems are similar.

```
DEVICE=C:\OS2\MDOS\VVGA.SYS (for VGA systems)
SET VIDEO_DEVICES=VIO_VGA
SET VIO_VGA=DEVICE(BVHVGA)
DEVINFO=SCR,VGA,C:\OS2\VIOTBL.DCP
```

Other files involved:

C:\OS2\DLL\BVHSVGA.DLL (base video handler DLL)
C:\OS2\DLL\BVHVGA.DLL (base video handler DLL)
C:\OS2\MDOS\WINOS2\SYSTEM\COURE.FON (WINOS2 VGA Courier font)
C:\OS2\MDOS\WINOS2\SYSTEM\HELVE.FON (Helvetica font for WINOS2 VGA)
C:\OS2\SVGA.EXE (enables DOS SVGA support)
C:\OS2\MDOS\WINOS2\SYSTEM\SWINVGA.DRV (WINOS2 VGA driver)
C:\OS2\MDOS\WINOS2\SYSTEM\SYMBOLE.FON (WINOS2 Symbol font for VGA)
C:\OS2\MDOS\WINOS2\SYSTEM\TMSRE.FON (WINOS2 Times Roman font for VGA)
C:\OS2\DLL\VGA.DLL (VGA dynamic link library)
C:\OS2\MDOS\WINOS2\SYSTEM\VGA.DRV (WINOS2 VGA device driver)
C:\OS2\MDOS\WINOS2\SYSTEM\VGAxxx.FON (various WINOS2 fonts for VGA)
C:\OS2\MDOS\VSVGA.SYS (virtual device driver for VDM SVGA)

OS/2 2.1 was designed to support as many display adapters as possible. Most problems associated with video display can be traced to poor interaction between the OS/2 device drivers and the specific implementation of VGA, SVGA, or 8514 video standards on the adapters. The display adapters must be able to support switching between various, potentially different video environments. A DOS windowed session may display standard text, another may display a graphic, an OS/2 session displays a graphic application, and a WINOS2 session may also run on the desktop. Each one of these sessions has its own unique video requirements, and the video device driver must be able to handle them all simultaneously.

Of all the adapter modes that OS/2 supports, SVGA appears to cause the most problems. If SVGA resolution does not appear to be working correctly, verify the following:

1. Open a full-screen DOS session, type `SVGA ON`, and press Enter. Verify that the file SVGADATA.PMI has been created in C:\OS2.
2. Verify that the CONFIG.SYS line `DEVICE=C:\OS2\MDOS\VVGA.SYS` has been changed to `DEVICE=C:\OS2\MDOS\VSVGA.SYS`. If it has not, edit CONFIG.SYS to reflect this change.
3. Perform an orderly system shutdown and reboot. SVGA support should now be enabled for VDM sessions.

For SVGA resolution to work for OS/2 and WINOS2 sessions, the adapter's manufacturer needs to provide an SVGA driver for OS/2 and WINOS2.

Some SVGA adapters require a DOS program to initialize them to the correct video mode. These adapters typically display OS/2 session text incorrectly. Follow these steps to automate this process so the user doesn't have to open a DOS session and type the commands each time the system is restarted:

1. Create a DOS BAT file called SETVID.BAT. Include the commands necessary to set the display adapter's mode correctly. The last line of the BAT file should be `EXIT`.

2. Add the line `START /FS /DOS SETVID.BAT` to the STARTUP.CMD file.

From this point forward, each time the user reboots the system, the SETVID.BAT will run and correctly set the adapter's video mode.

If switching from an SVGA windowed DOS session running a graphics program to an OS/2 session results in a corrupted desktop display, immediately switch back to the windowed SVGA VDM and allow it to continue its drawing operation. When that operation is complete, the user should be able to return to the OS/2 desktop without corruption.

If the user encounters a SYS3176 (a program in this session encountered a problem and cannot continue), try following these steps:

1. Select the program's icon and press MB2 to bring up the menu.
2. Click once on the Open arrow.
3. Click once on Settings.
4. Click on the Session tab, then click on the DOS Settings pushbutton.
5. Press the letter *H* to quickly find the first DOS setting beginning with *H*, then click once with MB1 on the `HW_ROM_TO_RAM` setting. Click on the On radio button.
6. Click on the Save pushbutton, then double-click on the System icon in the upper-left portion of the panel.
7. Retry the operation.

On XGA systems, the user may encounter a situation that appears to be a problem, but is in reality merely an inconvenience. The default WINOS2 background may be uncomfortably bright and pulsating when run in full-screen mode. If this is the case, open the WINOS2 Control Panel, double-click on desktop, and select various combinations of patterns and wallpaper until the background is less painful.

Sometimes, switching from a WINOS2 full-screen session to the OS/2 desktop and back can cause distortion on the WINOS2 screen. If this is the case, follow these steps:

1. Select the program's icon, then press MB2 to bring up the menu.
2. Click once on the Open arrow.
3. Click once on Settings.
4. Click on the Session tab, then click on the DOS Settings pushbutton.
5. Press the letter *V* to quickly find the first DOS setting that begins with *V*. Click once on `VIDEO_SWITCH_NOTIFICATION`, then click once on the On radio button.
6. Click once on the Save option, then double-click on the System icon. Restart the WINOS2 session and retry the operation.

Printer

CONFIG.SYS settings involved:

```
PRINTMONBUFSIZE=134,134,134
BASEDEV=PRINT02.SYS
```

Other files involved:

C:\OS2\SYSTEM\BDPRTM.EXE (support for bi-directional printing)
C:\OS2\MDOS\WINOS2\SYSTEM\DRVMAP.INF (maps WINOS2 printers to OS/2 Presentation Manager printer drivers)
C:\OS2\DLL\PMPRINT.QPR (Presentation Manager print queue processor)
C:\OS2\PMSETUP.EXE (setup information used for printer driver installations)
C:\OS2\DLL\PMSPL.DLL (PM Spooler's DLL)
C:\OS2\PRINT.COM (sends output to a specified printer port)
C:\OS2\PRINT01.SYS (general printer driver for non-Micro Channel systems)
C:\OS2\MDOS\WINOS2\PRINTMAN.EXE (WINOS2 print manager)
C:\OS2\MDOS\WINOS2\PRINTMAN.HLP (WINOS2 print manager help)
C:\OS2\PSCRIPT.SEP (sample PostScript separator page)

C:\OS2\SAMPLE.SEP (sample separator page for non-PostScript printers)
C:\OS2\SPOOL.EXE (redirects printer output from LPTx to COMx for full-screen sessions)
C:\OS2\DLL\WPPRINT.DLL (Workplace Shell printer DLL)
C:\OS2\DLL\WPPRTMRI.DLL (Workplace Shell printable translation support DLL)

Printing to a Local Printer

OS/2 print services can be thought of on two levels: Workplace Shell and Presentation Manager application printing, and full-screen session printing. This division underscores the different ways the print subsystem handles requests.

In the case of the Workplace Shell and Presentation Manager application printing, the print subsystem routes everything through the Presentation Manager print driver, which varies from printer to printer. The printer drivers are located off the C:\OS2\DLL subdirectory under an abbreviation of the printer's name. For the HP LaserJet, for example, the driver is located beneath C:\OS2\DLL\HP. In fact, the actual *.DRV file is located in C:\OS2\DLL\HP\PCL\LASERJET. The C:\OS2\DBL\HP\PCL subdirectory contains font definition files for the HP Printer Control Language (PCL).

Presentation Manager printing is controlled through the printer's icon. If a PM application like Lotus 1-2-3 for OS/2 is not printing correctly, verify that the settings are correct by following these steps:

The proceeding steps presuppose that the user has already verified that the printer is turned on, the cables are secured correctly to the printer and system unit, the printer has paper and ink/toner, the printer is in a ready state, and that the correct printer device driver is installed.

1. Double-click on the printer icon.
2. Place the mouse pointer anywhere on the resulting panel (for example, the HP LaserJet Series II - Job Icon View) and press MB2.
3. Click once on the Open arrow.
4. Click once on the Settings option. The HP Laserjet Series II - Settings panel should now be displayed. The printer name will differ depending on what driver is installed.
5. Click once on the Printer driver tab. Verify that the correct driver is highlighted as the default printer driver. If it is not, double-click on the correct driver. On the ensuing Printer Properties screen, click on the OK pushbutton. If the correct printer driver is not displayed in the Printer driver box, select an existing driver, then, click once with MB2. Click on the Install menu option and select a printer from the resulting list. Follow the on-screen instructions and insert the correct disk(s) when prompted.
6. Click on the Output tab. Verify that the correct printer port is selected. If it is not, click twice on the appropriate port (LPT1, COM1, and so on). For an LPT port, click on the OK pushbutton on the Parallel Port Settings panel. For a COM port, be sure that the Baud Rate, Word Length, Parity, Stop Bits, and Handshake are set correctly. Table 16.3 illustrates a typical scenario:

Table 16.3. Typical COM port settings.

Time Out	45
Baud Rate	9600
Word Length	8 bits
Parity	None
Stop Bits	1
Handshake	Hardware

Many printers can handle speeds in excess of 9600 baud. If the user's printer can print faster than 9600 baud, set the Baud Rate to the printer's maximum and follow the instructions in the printer manual to match the Baud Rate. The faster the Baud Rate, the faster the print job will be completed, especially for graphics.

7. When the settings are completed, click on the OK pushbutton. Verify that the printer is expecting the correct type of input (i.e., parallel for LPT port output and serial for COM port output).
8. Click on the Queue options tab. Verify that the Print While Spooling option is selected.
9. Double-click on the System icon to close the panel.

If the print job still does not print correctly, follow these steps:

1. Double-click on the printer icon.
2. Place the mouse pointer anywhere on the resulting Job Icon View panel and press MB2.
3. Click once on Set default and verify that the correct printer has a check mark beside it. If it does not, click once on the correct printer.
4. If the menu is not now displayed, press MB2. Click once on Change status and verify that the check mark is beside Release. If it is not, click once on Release.
5. Double-click on the System icon to close the Job Icon View.

If there is still no output, verify in the application that cannot print that it is using the correct printer. If it is not, select the correct printer and try again.

If the printer still does not produce output, verify that the parallel port is using the correct interrupt (typically interrupt 7 for LPT1 and interrupt 5 for LPT2). If the user is working with COM2 or COM3, try changing the cable to COM1 and reconfiguring the Printer icon using the preceding steps.

Still no output? If the user is printing to a parallel printer whose cable is more than six feet long, the signal strength may be insufficient for the extended length. Try a six-foot or shorter parallel cable. If the parallel cable does not have all of its pins wired, as in the case with some less expensive cables, this could be causing the trouble. DOS does not use all of the pins—OS/2 2.1 does.

If replacing the cable doesn't correct the problem, there is a chance that the I/O adapter does not generate interrupts to process print jobs. Like an incorrectly wired cable, such an adapter would work fine under DOS. OS/2, however, uses interrupts to process print jobs, and the user may have to replace the I/O adapter.

The OS/2 print subsystem processes output from full-screen sessions a little differently. The print subsystem provides full spooling support, but it does not format the output because it only formats Presentation Manager or Workplace Shell application output. That means that the PM/WPS-level device redirection settings typically don't apply, either.

Specifically, if the user is printing to a COM port, a PM/WPS application automatically sends its output to the correct COM port based on the selection under the Output tab. A full-screen session will not heed that setting. The following two lines must be in STARTUP.CMD for LPT to COM redirection to work correctly for full-screen sessions (`x` should be replaced with the number of the LPT port to be redirected—1 or 2—and `y` should be replaced with the number of the destination COM port—1, 2, 3, or 4).

```
SPOOL /D:LPTx /O:COMy
MODE COMy:96,N,8,1
```

After you add these lines, shutdown the system and retry the operation. If the printer does not produce output, verify that the serial cable is correctly pinned according to the manufacturer's specifications (most printer manufacturers include pin specs for cables in the back of their manuals). If it does not, purchase a correct cable and retry the operation. If there is still no printer output, refer the preceding paragraphs that discuss interrupts and interrupt-capable I/O adapters.

If virtual DOS machines seem to take too long to print, the user should try going into the DOS Settings and reducing the value for `PRINT_TIMEOUT`.

Network Printing

Under either the OS/2 LAN Server or Novell NetWare, the user can have a network printer defined to replace a local printer port. For example, the network printer \\ACCT01\LASER01 can replace the local LPT1 port for printing to an OS/2 LAN Server's shared printer.

For Novell NetWare workstations, the user does not need to be concerned with a network printer icon. Novell's method of redirection appears to the operating system and applications to simply be the local printer. No reformatting is typically done at the server. Therefore, most of the information contained in the "Network Printing" section applies only to OS/2 LAN Server installations. The user just has to be sure that the OS/2 printer driver matches the redirected printer.

If the server is an OS/2 machine, the printer drivers on the server and on the workstation should match—if the server's printer is an HP LaserJet Series II, the workstation should have the HP LaserJet Series II printer driver installed (OS/2 includes the name of the printer driver as part of the print data stream to the server, and the server interprets this and tries to match drivers). If it has the correct driver, the print job is passed to the printer. If the server does not have the print driver, the server holds the job forever. If print jobs are holding in the server's queue, this could be the cause of the problem. Once a job is in the queue with an incorrect printer driver specified, it must be deleted from the server's queue or another print driver should be installed for the server.

Another somewhat perplexing condition occurs when the printer icon is on the workstation. If the user has not defined a network printer icon, and if the user is using the default printer icon, the user will not be able to see jobs spooling on the server. This may appear to be an error because the printer icon is supposed to be able to display information about queuing print jobs. However, this is working as designed. To correctly see server-level print queue activity, the user must use a network printer object, which appears in the Network folder, or the user can create a network printer icon from the Template folder.

1. Double-click on the Templates folder and wait for all of the icons to display.
2. Click once on the Network printer icon, then press and hold MB2. Drag the icon to the desktop and release MB2.

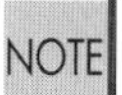

If the Network printer icon doesn't appear, verify that the Network icon is on the desktop. Some users place it in another folder to keep the desktop clean. If it is in another folder, bring it back to the desktop, close the Templates folder, and reopen it. Note that these steps only apply to OS/2 LAN Server LAN connections. If the Network printer icon still doesn't appear, open the existing desktop printer icon and set its output port to something other than LPT1. Perform a shutdown, open the Template folder, and try again.

3. Enter the correct information in the requested fields. If the user does not know the correct server parameters, the user should check with the OS/2 LAN server administrator responsible for maintaining the network.
4. Double-click on the local printer icon.
5. Position the mouse pointer anywhere on the Job Icon View panel and press MB2.
6. Click on Set Default and verify that the network printer definition is the default printer. If it is not, click on it.

The user should now be able to see network print jobs correctly displaying.

If a DOS session does not print to the network device, regardless of the DOS settings' `PRINT_TIMEOUT` value, the user should add the LPTDD.SYS device driver to the `DOS_DEVICE` setting for that DOS machine. The correct value to enter is `C:\OS2\MDOS\LPTDD.SYS` (this degrades that DOS machine's printer performance somewhat).

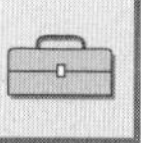

CD-ROM Drives

CONFIG.SYS settings involved:

`BASEDEV=IBM2SCSI.ADD` (for SCSI-based CD-ROM drives supported by OS/2)
`DEVICE=C:\OS2\MDOS\VCDROM.SYS`

Other files involved:

C:\OS2\CDFS.IFS (CD-ROM installable file system)
C:\OS2\CDROM.SYS (CD-ROM device driver)
C:\OS2\SYSTEM\DEV002.MSG (message file for CD-ROM file system)
C:\OS2\DLL\UCDFS.DLL (CD-ROM utilities DLL)
C:\OS2\SYSTEM\UCDFS.MSG (message file for CD-ROM utilities)

The current release of OS/2 has what IBM terms as "manufacturer-specific dependencies" in its CD-ROM support. The translation is that IBM has not tested its SCSI and non-SCSI CD-ROM support for all vendors. If the user has a supported internal or external SCSI-based CD-ROM drive, the OS/2 2.1 drivers provide access to all system sessions, including OS/2, DOS, and WINOS2.

This is not to say, however, that other manufacturers' drives will absolutely not work. The difficulty is that most of these drives use block device drivers, which work under native DOS but do not work under OS/2 2.1's VDMs. If the unsupported device has its own adapter, such support can be loaded in a specific DOS session by following these steps:

This section assumes that the CD-ROM device drivers were written for DOS.

1. Create a native DOS boot disk. This can most easily be done by locating a DOS installation disk for, say, IBM PC DOS 5.0. Perform a `DISKCOPY` to create a copy of the original, and put the original aside. Insert the copy in drive A.

Full instructions for creating a specific DOS version boot disk can be found in Chapter 7, "Command-Line Interface."

2. Copy the C:\OS2\MDOS\FSFILTER.SYS file onto the new boot disk. Copy the CD-ROM driver(s) and program(s) per the manufacturer's instructions onto the new boot disk. Create the CONFIG.SYS as shown in Listing 16.5.

Listing 16.5. Contents of CD-ROM Support CONFIG.SYS.

```
DEVICE=A:\FSFILTER.SYS
DEVICE=A:\CDROM.SYS (This will vary per manufacturer)
FILES=60
BUFFERS=30
SHELL=A:\COMMAND.COM /P /E:2048
```

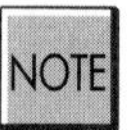

It is vital that FSFILTER.SYS be placed at the top of the CONFIG.SYS, especially in systems using HPFS. FSFILTER.SYS assigns the correct driver letters to the drives physically installed in the system, and DOS cannot see HPFS drives without the assistance of FSFILTER.SYS. When the CD-ROM driver loads, it will most likely assign a drive letter to the CD-ROM drive. If that drive conflicts with an HPFS drive, and if the CD-ROM drive is loaded before FSFILTER.SYS, unpredictable errors may occur.

3. Create an AUTOEXEC.BAT with the commands shown in Listing 16.6.

Listing 16.6. Contents of CD-ROM support AUTOEXEC.BAT.

```
@ECHO OFF
CLS
PROMPT $p$g
PATH=A:\
```

```
COMSPEC=A:\COMMAND.COM
CDROM.EXE (This will vary per manufacturer)
```

At this point, the CD-ROM device should be available. If it is not, if the CD-ROM software returns an "Incorrect DOS Version" error message, the user should go into the DOS Settings and add `CDROM.EXE,4,00,255` to the DOS version option. (The CDROM.EXE varies from manufacturer to manufacturer.)

If the drive is available but the mouse does not work correctly, the user may have to obtain a different version of the mouse driver. Check with the CD-ROM software manufacturer for information on supported versions.

If the user installs CD-ROM support for drives that OS/2 2.1 directly supports using selective install, the user should not attempt to install anything else at the same time. Install only the CD-ROM support, shutdown, and reboot.

OS/2 Error-Logging Facilities

Because of the complexity inherent in an operating system like OS/2 2.1, some problems can be difficult to diagnose or trace. For example, if the user has dBase IV running against data on an OS/2 LAN Server, and if the user has a problem, is dBASE the culprit? What if WordPerfect is also running and the OS/2 Communications Manager is providing host access? Which program is causing the problem?

OS/2 demonstrates once again that it deserves the title of world-class operating system by providing a variety of diagnostic tools built into the package. Some are easily accessible by the typical power user, and some require a little more work to decipher. But in all cases, the information is valuable when tracking down a problem.

These tools are unusual for the DOS and DOS-Windows world, but they are nothing new to mid-range systems and mainframe systems. IBM draws on its strength as a vendor of larger systems to bring their problem management facilities down to OS/2 2.1.

Although the following sections provide more detailed information, just after a system failure the user should issue the command `PSTAT > C:\RESULT.TXT` and copy the file onto a floppy disk (assuming the system is still operational—if not, reboot and perform the listed tasks).

PSTAT

PSTAT is a program that displays all of the operating system processes, threads, system-semaphores, and dynamic link libraries that are currently loaded and active in the system. This tool can reveal some tremendously useful information, but it can be somewhat difficult to read.

Figure 16.2 shows the result (first screen) of typing `PSTAT` and pressing Enter in an OS/2 windowed session. Figure 16.3 shows the second screen.

The headings are across the top of the screen: Process ID, then the Parent Process ID, Session ID, Process Name, Thread ID, Priority, Block ID, and State. The most important fields for routine trouble shooting are Process ID, Session ID, and Process Name.

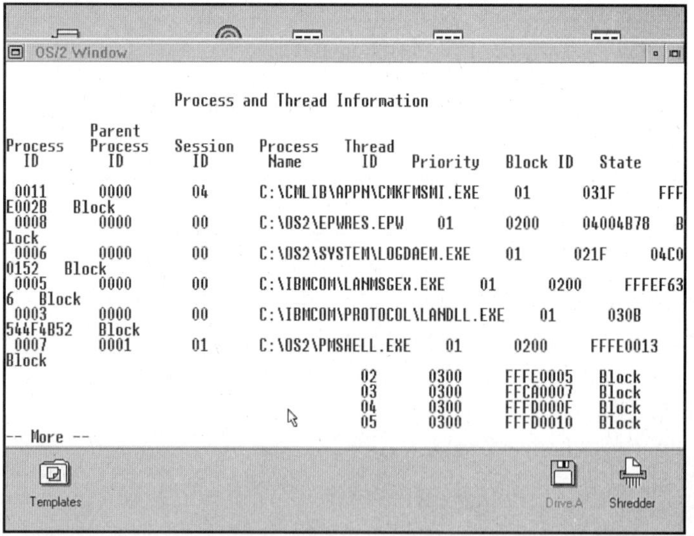

Figure 16.2. The first screen of PSTAT command results.

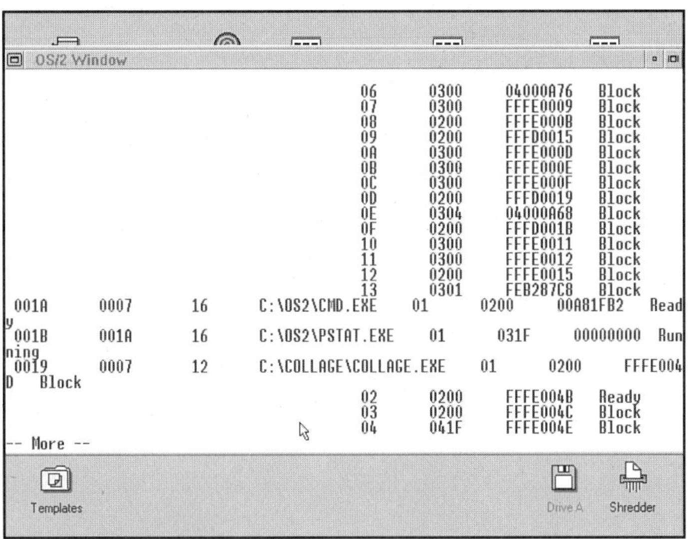

Figure 16.3. The second screen of PSTAT command results.

In the example, the C:\OS2\CMD.EXE program is Process identified as 001E on the second page. CMD.EXE is the OS/2 2.1 command processor. The first screen reveals a number of things about CMD.EXE. First, its Parent Process is 0007. Checking the Process ID column, starting on the first screen, you can see that Process ID 0007 is the PMSHELL.EXE program, or the desktop shell.

The State field, Block, means that CMD.EXE is waiting for a system event. Frozen means that a Process has ordered that Thread to stop execution until the Process issues a Thaw. Ready means the Thread is running normally.

To find out more about CMD.EXE, Process ID 0001E, enter the command `PSTAT /P:001E`. The `/P` option tells `PSTAT` to display information about a given Process ID. The results are shown in Figure 16.4.

This view shows all of the runtime link libraries, typically DLLs, associated with CMD.EXE. How is this information useful? First, these reports help the user become familiar with what is running in the system. Such familiarity helps the user feel at ease with the operating system. Concepts like DLLs and Processes are no longer something alien and they take on concrete meanings.

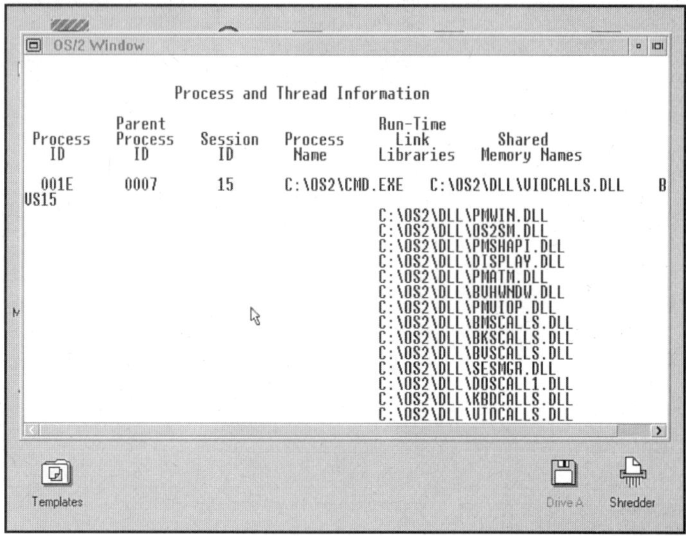

Figure 16.4. The results of PSTAT /P:001E.

Second, some IBM problem reports say that a program like SYSLEVEL will not work correctly if the PMSEEK.EXE program is running. The best way to find out if PMSEEK.EXE is running is to run `PSTAT` and capture the output to file via the syntax `PSTAT > RESULTS.TXT`. The RESULTS.TXT file can be viewed or printed. If PMSEEK.EXE is running, it shows up in RESULTS.TXT.

Finally, IBM periodically releases fixes, and sometimes these fixes take the shape of a specific module such as PMSPL.DLL. The user may not know if that fix is useful, so the user can invoke `PSTAT > RESULTS.TXT` periodically to see if PMSPL.DLL is loaded. If it is, applying the fix may be worthwhile.

Speaking of DLLs, `PSTAT` supports another command-line option to show just DLLs sorted by the Process Name the DLLs are associated with. Issuing `PSTAT /L` shows a screen similar to the one in Figure 16.5.

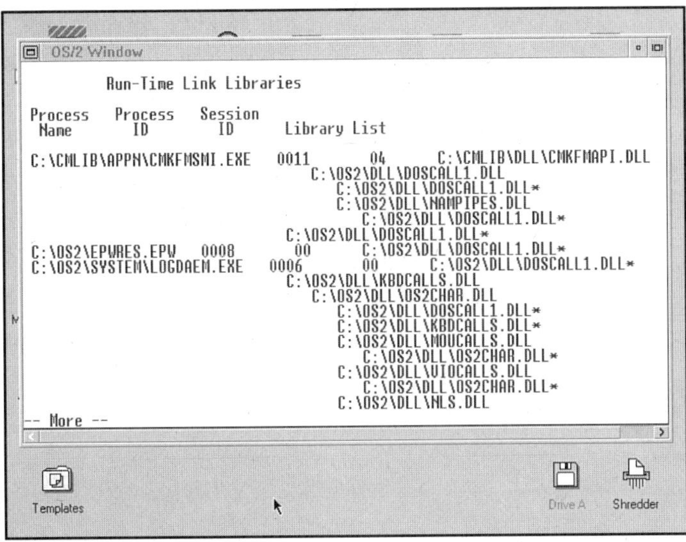

Figure 16.5. *The results of PSTAT /L.*

If the user has to involve OS/2 support personnel, whether they be IBM employees, CompuServe users or sysops, or corporate support staff, having a PSTAT capture just after an application failure could provide information helpful to solving the problem.

The LOG.SYS and SNA Format

One of the most sophisticated error-tracking components of OS/2 2.1 is the system error-logging facility. This tool traps system-level errors and logs them. Along with the error, it also logs a probable cause and probable solution.

The inconvenient part of this tool is that the user must order the *Systems Network Architecture Formats*, a massive volume from IBM (GA27-3136-12), to interpret the information. The user should contact the local IBM branch office to try to obtain a copy. If that does not work, the user should get onto

CompuServe and ask for help. *Systems Network Architecture Formats* is an essential reference to anyone who is serious about supporting OS/2 2.1. (The book is absolutely massive: about four inches thick. Fortunately, only a subset is relevant to supporting OS/2 2.1, and that part is the OS/2 SNA alerts in the SNA/MS Encodings chapter.)

Adding the two lines shown in Listing 16.7 to the OS/2 CONFIG.SYS and rebooting enables OS/2 event logging. Note, however, that adding these lines has a negative impact on system performance, so logging should only be done on systems with persistent and difficult-to-trace problems.

Listing 16.7. The CONFIG.SYS error-logging commands.

```
DEVICE=C:\OS2\LOG.SYS
RUN=C:\OS2\SYSTEM\LOGDAEM.EXE
```

By default, logging output is stored in C:\OS2\SYSTEM\LOG0001.DAT. The contents can be viewed by issuing the `SYSLOG` command in an OS/2 session. An alert generated by trying to print with no printer connected produces a log entry like the one shown in Figure 16.6.

The Qualifier field shows the code level (in this case, GA). The Originator shows that OS/2 itself generated the error. Note that applications can also be written to take advantage of the error-logging service. The Release Level, 200, indicates that OS/2 2.1 issued the error. In fact, the Software Name shows that it was OS/2's base operating system that generated the error.

The Generic Alert Subvector information can be found in the *SNA Formats* manual, pages 9-16, under "Basic Alert (X'92') Alert MS Subvector." Basically, 0000 breaks down as shown in Table 16.4.

Table 16.4. Elements of the Basic Alert Alert MS Subvector.

Place in Basic Alert MS Subvector	*Description*
00	Ignore

Place in Basic Alert MS Subvector	*Description*
0	Indicates that this is an alert that was not caused directly by a user. (1 means that it was a user's action that directly triggered the error.)
0	This is the held-alert indicator. 0 means the alert was generated immediately. (1 means that the alert had to wait for a session to act as a receiver for the alert.)

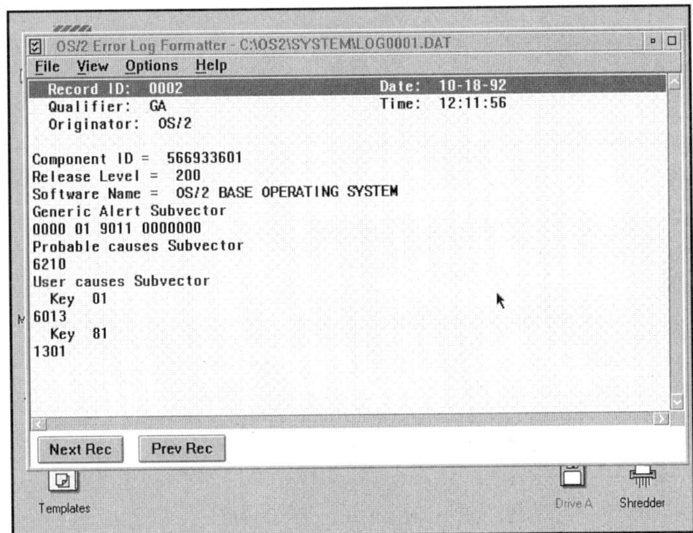

***Figure 16.6.** The printer error log screen.*

The next number, 01, indicates a permanent loss of availability. This field is called the Alert type. Table 16.5 lists some of the Alert Types.

Table 16.5. Alert Types.

Alert Type	*Description*
01	Permanent loss of availability until external intervention corrects the problem.
02	A temporary loss of availability that is corrected automatically, although the user may notice an interruption in service.
03	The system detected a reduction in performance based on preset guidelines.
10	The alert's originator is reporting that a target resource is available through the fault of something other than the target.
11	Something dreadful is about to happen!
12	Unknown.
14	An error has been bypassed, but the error still exists and may or may not have a noticeable impact on the user.
15	A redundant piece of hardware or software has been lost.

The next number, 9011, is called the Alert Description Code (see Table 16.6).

In this case, 9011 is an Intervention Required error—the printer is not ready. The full text (see pages 9 through 28) is "A printer has indicated that it is not ready for use, due to an unspecified intervention-required condition."

Because this is a printer problem, the user can assume immediately that turning it on or connecting it will probably correct the situation. However, OS/2 itself provides that corrective information, which will be of more value in other, less-obvious situations.

Table 16.6. Alert Description Codes.

Alert Description Code	Description
1xxx	Hardware
2xxx	Software
3xxx	Communications
4xxx	Performance
5xxx	Congestion
6xxx	Microcode
7xxx	Operator
8xxx	Specification
9xxx	Intervention Required
Bxxx	Notification
Cxxx	Security
Fxxx	Undetermined

The Probable Causes Subvector is the next piece of information. In the previous example, the Subvector is 6210. Probable Causes begins on page 9, "Probable Causes (X'93') Alert MS Subvector." There are several general categories, shown in Table 16.7.

Table 16.7. General Probable Causes Categories.

Category	Description
0000	Processor
0100	Storage
0200	Power Subsystem

continues

Table 16.7. continued

Category	*Description*
0300	Cooling or Heating Subsystem
0400	Subsystem Controller
0500	Subsystem
1000	Software Program
1100	Operating System
2000	Communications
2100	Communications/Remote Node
2200	Remote Node
2300	Connection Not Established
2600	Electrical Interference
3000	Channel
3100	Controller
3200	Communications Interface
3300	Adapter
3400	Cable
3500	Communications Equipment
3600	Modem
3700	LAN Component
4000	Performance Degraded
5000	Media
6000	Device
6100	Input Device
6200	Output Device
6300	Input/Output Device

Category	Description
6400	Depository
6500	Dispenser
6600	Self-service Terminal
6700	Security Problem
7000	Personnel
8000	Configuration
FE00	Undetermined

In the preceding table, Probable Causes Subvector 6210, falls into the Output Device category. On pages 9-51, the description for 6210 is "PRINTER: An output device that produces durable and optically viewable output in the form of characters (and optionally graphics) by a means other than by drawing with one or more pens."

This sounds odd—what other kind of output device does a microcomputer use? However, the user should remember that these codes cover a much broader range of equipment than just microcomputers. The output device could have been attached to a minicomputer or a mainframe, and it could have produced microfilm, which is not "optically viewable," or an optical/camera output.

Two more numbers remain: the User Causes Subvector Keys 01 and 81. Key 01 begins on page 9, "User Causes (X'01') User Causes Subfield." Like the fields before it, Key 01 has a number of categories that are shown in Table 16.8.

Table 16.8. Key 01 User Causes Subvector Categories.

Category	Description
0100	Storage Capacity Exceeded
0200	Power Off

continues

Table 16.8. continued

Category	*Description*
2200	Remote Node
2300	Connection Not Established
2400	Busy
2500	Line Not Enabled
3300	Adapter Not Ready
3400	Cable Not Connected
3800	LPDA DCE
4000	Performance Degraded
5100	Media Defective
5200	Media Jam
5300	Media Supply Exhausted
5400	Out of Supplies
5500	Media Supply Low
5600	Low on Supplies
6000	Device Not Ready
6400	Depository
7000	Operator
7100	Incorrect Procedure
7200	Dump Requested
7300	File Full
7400	Contamination
F000	Additional message data

On pages 9-63, the user will find 6013, which is the error in the example. The 6000s in general are Device Not Ready Messages. Message 6013 reads, "Printer Not Ready." So far, OS/2 has been able to tell the user precisely what is wrong. The final item, key 81, should tell the user what to do to correct the problem.

Key 81 begins on page 9, "Recommended Actions (X'81') Network Alert Common Subfield." It, too, is divided into multiple categories, shown in Table 16.9.

Table 16.9. Recommended Action Categories.

Category	*Description*
0000	Perform Problem Determination Procedures
0100	Verify
0200	Check Power
0300	Check for Damage
0400	Run Appropriate Test
0500	Run Appropriate Trace
0600	Obtain Dump
0700	No Action Necessary
1000	Perform Problem Recovery Procedures
1100	Vary Offline
1200	Retry
1300	Correct, Then Retry
1400	Restart
1500	Correct Installation Problem
1600	Replace Media

continues

Table 16.9. continued

Category	*Description*
1700	Replenish Supplies
1800	Replace Defective Equipment
1900	Perform Problem Bypass Procedures
1A00	Remove Media
1B00	Prepare
2000	Review Detailed Data
2100	Review Recent Alerts for This Resource
2200	Review Data Logs
3000	Contact Appropriate Service Representative
3100	Contact Administrative Personnel
3200	Report the Following
3300	If Problem Reoccurs Then Do the Following
3400	Wait for Additional Message Before Taking Action
3500	Refer to Product Documentation for Additional Information
F000	Additional Message Data

Key 81, 1301, falls under Correct, Then Retry. The precise message is "Ready the Device, then Retry." OS/2 2.1 has not only logged the problem, it has determined what the failing component was, what the cause of the failure was, and what to do to correct the problem.

Before the user lobbies to have the corporate help desk disbanded, however, it is important to understand the limitations of this tool. LOG.SYS will not record application errors unless the application itself is written to make use of LOG.SYS. It may not record routine errors like failed accesses to floppy drives or failing network connections, which the operating system will trap and handle at a higher level. An example of this is an application-related TRAP 000D, which opens an error panel of its own. However, it is one more tool that the sophisticated user can use to track down problems.

Author Bio

Terrance Crow began working in the microcomputer support and consulting department of a major insurance company in July 1986. He worked on the roll-out and support team for IBM OS/2 Extended Edition 1.0, and he has worked on every version since then. Crow is now responsible for the deployment and support strategy for IBM OS/2 2.1.

17

Networking

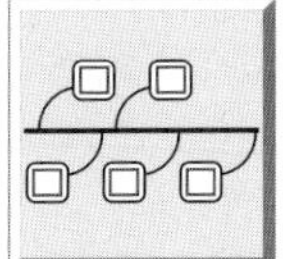

In This Chapter

One computer working alone is limited in capacity and resources. There are many benefits to linking multiple computers together to share work or peripheral devices. This is the basic premise of networking. The computer offering a service to other network members is called a server. The user of this service is typically called a client or workstation. OS/2 systems can share in many network environments, both as a server and a workstation.

Personal computers can be linked to mainframe hosts or minicomputers to access large databases and critical corporate data. Many UNIX-based minicomputers and government installations use a communications protocol called TCP/IP. There is a separate OS/2 product for this called, appropriately, TCP/IP for OS/2.

This chapter focuses on the issues and capabilities of linked multiple personal computers in a local area network (LAN). OS/2 2.1 is an excellent choice for a server operating system because of its preemptive multitasking and advanced disk access. It is a better network client than DOS or Windows because the controlling software runs in protected mode. The IBM LAN product is called LAN Server (currently, Version 3.0). Microsoft produces a workstation product based on similar technology called LAN Manager. The leading network vendor is Novell, which supplies NetWare Requester for OS/2.

LAN Components: Wiring and Adapters

Networked computers are attached with some type of wiring scheme. The most popular are Ethernet and Token Ring. Ethernet runs at 10 MHz and comes in thick, thin, and twisted-pair varieties. Thick wiring is shielded for use in difficult environments (factories, hospitals, and so on). Twisted-pair wiring uses data-grade phone wire and hubs for easy maintenance and low cost. This solution is referred to as 10BaseT. High speed 100 MHz Ethernet is in development and shows promise as a future standard. Ethernet transmissions are handled on a first come, first serve basis on a wire segment and collisions are rebroadcast until successful. The more users on a wire, the more collisions are

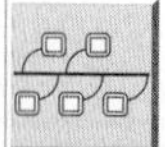

likely to occur, which can limit overall performance. Large Ethernet LANs are built by connecting many segments with intelligent hubs called repeaters. Monitoring and administrating the flow of data on the wire can be a full-time job.

Token Ring runs at 4 or 16 MHz and controls use of the wire by passing a "token." This scheme reduces collisions but requires more processing on the adapter side. For this reason, Token Ring is more expensive than Ethernet but larger networks are more maintainable. IBM supports Token Ring on many larger systems, which makes it a good choice when host connectivity is essential. Although there are several wiring options for Token Ring, twisted-pair wiring is the most prevalent.

The wiring scheme is somewhat transparent to a LAN workstation. The wire is attached to a network adapter in each machine. Adapters vary greatly in price and performance. All adapters have a memory buffer area to transmit and receive packets of data to and from the wire. The size of the buffer area is an important purchase decision. Some adapters have their own processors to facilitate data transfer to and from the wire. This bus-mastering technique is very useful for servers and multitasking workstations.

CONFIG.SYS software device drivers are loaded to link the adapter hardware to the operating environment. These drivers are provided by the network software vendor or the adapter manufacturer. There are many standards for this media access control (MAC) driver layer. LAN Server and LAN Manager now use the Network Device Interface Specification (NDIS) developed by 3-Com and Microsoft. LAN Server versions prior to 2.0 use proprietary IBM drivers, which limit the number of supported adapters. NDIS is supported by most vendors and drivers are readily available. You must use the OS/2 NDIS drivers that are different from their DOS counterparts. NetWare has its own standard called Open Device Interconnect (ODI). It is possible to connect to a NetWare server and NDIS with the ODINSUP protocol option.

Protocols

There is another device driver layer between the application software and the adapter drivers. Protocols are what the programmer sees when writing

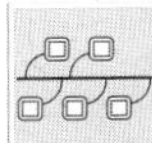

applications to communicate with the network. Protocols talk to NDIS or ODI, which packages the data stream and transmits it through the wire. Sharing data between a server and workstation requires that both run the same protocol. LAN Server uses the IEEE standard 802.2 or NETBIOS. LAN Manager has a similar version called NetBeui. NetWare uses the IPX protocol that is popular in DOS networking. TCP/IP is a universal protocol offered by LAN Server, LAN Manager, and NetWare. TCP/IP is prevalent on UNIX systems and government installations and is often used as a backbone to connect several LANs through communication links.

Certain applications may require a specific protocol (NETBIOS or 802.2, for example). This is especially true with electronic mail and remote boots. Keep this in mind when selecting a protocol.

It is often necessary to load multiple protocols on one machine to attach to disparate systems. NDIS can support multiple protocols on one adapter—this is very useful in larger sites. The alternative to loading multiple protocols on one machine is to install multiple network adapters, each with its own protocol. There are limits, however, to the number of adapter cards allowed in one system.

Another important element is the loopback driver, which is used for development and testing of network applications when no adapter or wire is available. Certain network operations fail if there is no response from the LAN. The loopback driver ensures that a proper response is returned. This is also used to demonstrate client/server applications on a single machine.

Workstation Software

The workstation or requester software is loaded on top of the protocol layer to control access to network resources. A device driver and an installable file system (IFS) in CONFIG.SYS are usually involved. The driver interacts with the protocol layer to handle network operations. The file system processes requests for files on shared network drives. In addition to these components,

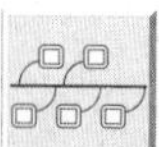

several detached processes are started. LAN Server and LAN Manager issue a `NET START` command in STARTUP.CMD to load these processes. The specifics of the processes are listed in the IBMLAN.INI or LANMAN.INI configuration files. NetWare Requester uses the `RUN` statement in CONFIG.SYS to start several daemon processes.

Utility programs are included to access specific network features. Some utility programs enumerate available resources and provide connection to them. Others control security or maintain user accounts. Messaging is another popular utility. LAN Server and Manager install these utilities on each workstation. Although this takes more disk space, it reduces network traffic. NetWare copies the utilities to a file server for shared access by all OS/2 Requesters.

Separate network utilities are required for protected-mode operation. The DOS versions often have the same name and automatically start a DOS session when invoked in OS/2. Be aware of paths and the session type. Many DOS network utilities do not work in OS/2, the protected-mode versions are used instead.

The workstation software also provides connectivity for MVDM sessions. Because OS/2 drivers are loaded in protected mode, they do not conflict with available DOS memory. Applications see 640K of RAM and extended and expanded memory. This (combined with fast disk caching on the local drive) often makes DOS applications run faster under OS/2 than in memory-constrained DOS environments. Several virtual DOS sessions can access the LAN simultaneously while OS/2 multitasks the network requests for a smooth ride. The only disappointment with MVDM support is the lack of network utility support. Drive and printer connections must be made in protected mode. DOS sessions see the shared resources but cannot manage them.

If strict DOS compatibility is needed, a boot image with DOS network support can be built from a working floppy or boot partition. Special drivers must be loaded for multiple boot images to share the same adapter. Connections made in a boot image are limited to that session. DOS network utilities work as advertised, including named pipe support.

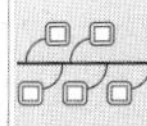

One last feature of workstation support is the remote boot. With LAN Server 2.0 and later releases, OS/2 workstations can boot off the file server. This approach eliminates the expense of local hard drives, but it requires a boot floppy or prom on the adapter card. The traffic load on the network wiring limits usefulness to small or very fast LANs. Security is one advantage of this technique. A properly configured workstation can boot without a floppy or hard drive. The boot image is maintained by the LAN administrator and can be tailored to individual stations. Each adapter card has a unique address that makes this possible.

Server Software

The final piece of the puzzle is the server software, which loads on top of the requester and device drivers. Because most of the work is handled at the driver level, server applications require only one or two floppies. The file service is the most popular application, and it provides shared access to disk devices. It is usually coupled with print queue management. User security and domain management are critical components of this package. LAN Server is the only product that currently offers a file server for OS/2 2.1.

Special-purpose servers are very popular in OS/2 networking and comprise the bulk of current installations. Database servers take advantage of the multitasking/threading capabilities to combine excellent performance with rigid security and reliability—Microsoft SQL Server, Oracle, and IBM Database Manager are the top sellers. They install over the requester and require either named pipes or NETBIOS support for client connectivity.

Mail servers are becoming quite popular and provide workgroup automation enhancements like the Lotus Notes product. Fax servers are used to manage shared fax lines and route incoming documents. Communications servers pool modems or expensive mainframe links for use by multiple clients. The modular design of OS/2 networking provides a rich platform to develop these services.

Several of these special services can run on a single system depending on memory and processor requirements. Adding mail to a file server usually involves loading two or three floppies and setting up user access. Several costly,

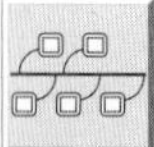

dedicated servers can be replaced by a single well-tuned unit. Now that OS/2 2.1 can access more than 16M of memory, the processor and bus speed are the limiting factors. With the Intel Pentium processor, reduced instruction set computer (RISC), local bus, and other technologies around the corner, the opportunities for flexible OS/2 networking are unlimited. (Table17.1 provides a comparison of the leading OS/2 networking products.)

Table17.1. Networking product comparison.

Product	*LAN Server*	*LAN Manager*	*NetWare Requester*
Version	3.0	2.1A	2.0
Adapter Layer	NDIS	NDIS	ODI
Protocol Layer	NetBios	NetBeui	IPX
Drivers	\IBMCOM\MACS	\LANMAN\DRIVERS	\NETWARE
Protocols	\IBMCOM\PROTOCOL	DRIVERS\PROTOCOL	\NETWARE
Configuration	IBMLAN.INI	LANMAN.INI	NET.CFG
Installation	Graphical	Character	Graphical
OS/2 Utilities	\IBMLAN\NETPROG	\LANMAN\NETPROG	File Server
MVDM Utilities	No	No	Yes
File Server	Yes	OS/2 1.x only	No
Named Pipes	Yes	OS/2 1.x only	Yes
Peer Server	Yes	OS/2 1.x only	No
UNC Support	Yes	Yes	No
Message Help	Yes	Yes	No
Reference Help	Yes	No	No
Remote Printer	Peer only	No	Yes
Remote Boot	Yes	No	Soon
Requester Price	$75 each	included	$30 site

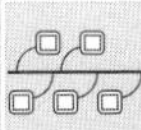

LAN Server

IBM released Version 3.0 of LAN Server in November of 1992. To date, it is the only file server software available for OS/2 2.1. Both the Entry and Advanced versions support unlimited workstations and have the same basic feature set. Advanced adds server fault tolerance and a high performance 32-bit network transport. There is a licensing fee per server and for each workstation. The server fee is modest in comparison to other vendors. The workstation fee approach is more economical in larger sites where each workstation is connected to many special-purpose servers.

Three major components are needed to build an OS/2 LAN Server system. The NDIS adapter and protocol drivers are installed with Network Transport Services/2 (NTS/2). The requester is then loaded with three floppies. The server software and utilities take another two floppies. The requester and server disks are loaded in one step when a new server is installed. In addition, the package contains several floppies for the DOS LAN requester function.

Adapter/Protocol Installation

NTS/2 and LAN Server have graphical installation programs. The first step loads the drivers into the \IBMCOM directory. There are several dynamic link libraries for adapter support and the \IBMCOM\DLL directory must be set in LIBPATH. Adapter files are in \IBMCOM\MACS and protocols are in \IBMCOM\PROTOCOL. The LAN Adapter and Protocol Support (LAPS.EXE) utility in Figure17.1 manages the adapters and drivers.

Supported adapters and protocols each have two corresponding files. The *.OS2 file is the actual driver. The network information file (*.NIF) is text explaining the options and parameters. Each section of the file has a header surrounded with brackets. Within each section are parameters that are interpreted by LAPS. Listing 17.1 contains the NIF for the 3-Com Etherlink II adapter.

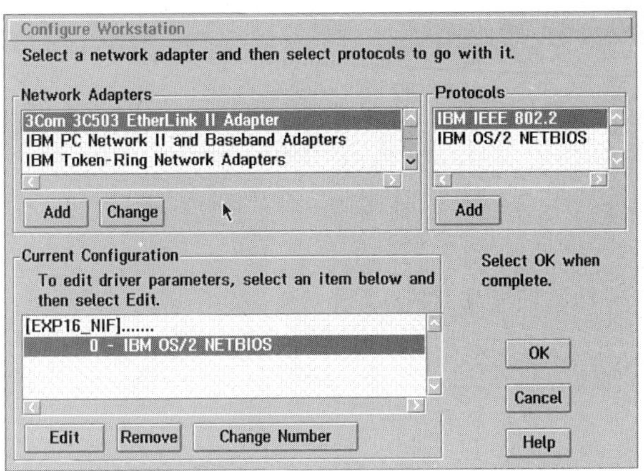

Figure 17.1. LAN Adapter and Protocol Support.

Listing 17.1. A sample adapter network information file.

```
[ELNKII]
Type = NDIS
Title = "3Com 3C503 EtherLink II Adapter"
Version = 1.1
Drivername = ELNKII$
Xports = NETBEUI LANDD
[FILE]
Name = ELNKII.OS2
Path = @lanroot\DRIVERS\ETHERNET\ELNKII
; Parameter start
[netaddress]
tag = NETADDRESS
display = "Network adapter address"
type = Hexstring
Strlength = 12
optional = YES
editable = YES
help = "This parameter overrides the network address of the network
 adapter card.  The value of this parameter is a hexadecimal string of
 12 digits, as in 020001020304.  The address must be unique among all
 other network adapter addresses on the network."
[interrupt]
tag = INTERRUPT
```

continues

Listing 17.1. continued

```
display = "Interrupt level"
type = decimal
range = 2 - 5
default = 3
optional = YES
editable = YES
help = "This parameter specifies the interrupt level used for
 notifications between the workstation and the network adapter card.
 Ensure that no conflicts exist between the various system components in
 their use of interrupts.  For an 80286, 80386, or 80486 workstation, the
 specified interrupt level will be redirected to interrupt level 9
 because the cascaded PIC is already using interrupt level 2."
[ioaddress]
tag = IOAddress
display = "I/O base address"
type = Hexadecimal
set = 250, 280, 2A0, 2E0, 300, 310, 330, 350
default = 300
optional = YES
editable = YES
help = "This parameter specifies the starting address of the
 input/output port for the network adapter card.  The defined value
 must be based on the jumper configuration of the network adapter card.
 If the value of this parameter does not match the network adapter card
 jumper configuration, the network adapter driver reports an error."
[transceiver]
tag = TRANSCEIVER
display = "Transceiver"
type = string
Strlength = 8
Set = EXTERNAL, ONBOARD
default = ONBOARD
optional = YES
editable = YES
help = "This parameter specifies the transceiver configuration of the
 network adapter card.  The specification of this parameter depends
 on the specific hardware configuration.  This parameter is used only
 for the EtherLink II adapter for Personal Computer AT workstations.
 Use 'ONBOARD' if you have a Coax or thin Ethernet connector and use
 'EXTERNAL' if you have a DIX or thick Ethernet connector."
[maxtransmits]
tag = MAXTRANSMITS
display = "Maximum number of queued transmits"
type = decimal
range = 8 - 50
default = 8
optional = YES
```

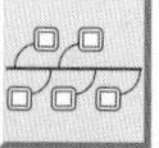

```
editable = YES
help = "This parameter specifies the maximum number of transmit queue
 entries for the network adapter driver.  For a server workstation or
 gateway workstation, set this parameter to 40."
[xmitbufs]
tag = XMITBUFS
display = "Number of adapter transmit buffers"
type = decimal
range = 1 - 2
default = 2
optional = YES
editable = YES
help = "This parameter specifies the number of 146-byte transmit
 buffers to allocate on the network adapter card.  Allocating a second
 transmit buffer may improve transmission performance but it also
 reduces the amount of memory available for storing received packets."
```

The NIF file is read by LAPS and managed in a series of dialog boxes. The adapter or protocol in the Current Configuration list box in Figure17.1 can be edited by selecting the Edit button, which presents the dialog shown in Figure 17.2.

The final product of the driver installation is a text file in \IBMCOM called PROTOCOL.INI and several entries in CONFIG.SYS. The INI file in Listing 17.2 defines the adapter relationships and parameters selected in LAPS. The `NETBEUI` section defines the protocol driver, `EXP16` is the adapter driver, and `PROT_MAN` is the protocol manager. This file can be edited manually if desired.

Listing 17.2. A sample PROTOCOL.INI file.

```
[PROT_MAN]
   DRIVERNAME = PROTMAN$
[IBMLXCFG]
   EXP16_nif = EXP16.nif
   NETBEUI_nif = NETBEUI.NIF
[NETBEUI_nif]
   DriverName = netbeui$
   Bindings = EXP16_nif
   ETHERAND_TYPE = "I"
   USEADDRREV = "YES"
   OS2TRACEMASK = 0xe7ff
   SESSIONS = 40
```

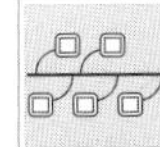

continues

Listing 17.2. continued

```
   NCBS = 95
   NAMES = 21
   SELECTORS = 5
   USEMAXDATAGRAM = "NO"
   ADAPTRATE = 1000
   WINDOWERRORS = 0
   MAXDATARCV = 4168
   TI = 30000
   T1 = 500
   T2 = 200
   MAXIN = 1
   MAXOUT = 1
   NETBIOSTIMEOUT = 500
   NETBIOSRETRIES = 8
   NAMECACHE = 0
   PIGGYBACKACKS = 1
   DATAGRAMPACKETS = 2
   PACKETS = 350
   LOOPPACKETS = 1
   PIPELINE = 5
   MAXTRANSMITS = 6
   MINTRANSMITS = 2
   DLCRETRIES = 5
[EXP16_nif]
   DriverName = EXP16$
   ioaddress = 0x300
```

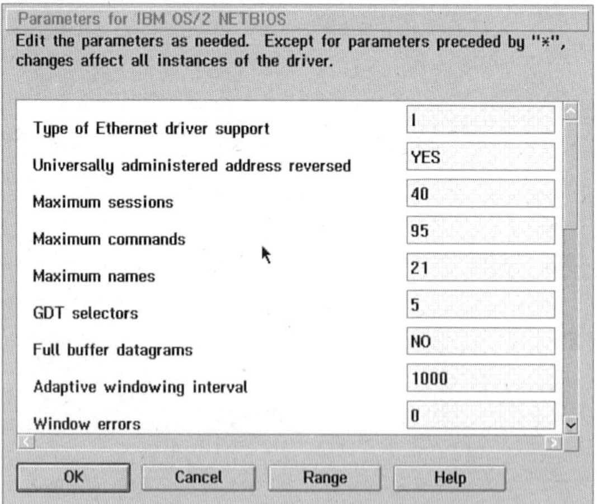

Figure 17.2. Editing a protocol in LAPS.

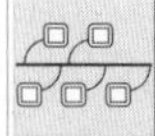

The CONFIG.SYS entries include PATH additions and device driver statements. The PROTMAN.OS2 driver is the protocol manager that links the adapter layer to the protocol interface. When it loads, it reads the /I parameter to find the directory location for PROTOCOL.INI. The NETBIND.EXE utility actually does the protocol binding.

```
DEVICE=C:\IBMCOM\PROTOCOL\LANPDD.OS2
DEVICE=C:\IBMCOM\PROTOCOL\LANVDD.OS2
DEVICE=C:\IBMCOM\LANMSGDD.OS2 /I:C:\IBMCOM
DEVICE=C:\IBMCOM\PROTMAN.OS2 /I:C:\IBMCOM
DEVICE=C:\IBMCOM\PROTOCOL\NETBEUI.OS2
DEVICE=C:\IBMCOM\PROTOCOL\NETBIOS.OS2
DEVICE=C:\IBMCOM\MACS\EXP16.OS2
RUN=C:\IBMCOM\PROTOCOL\NETBIND.EXE
RUN=C:\IBMCOM\LANMSGEX.EXE
```

Requester/Server Installation

The requester and server installations use the same graphical LANINST.EXE program. Advanced options are provided for building custom disk and response files for campus-wide installations. LAN Server can also be installed or upgraded over the LAN with a special boot floppy. Some of these tasks are presented in Figure 17.3.

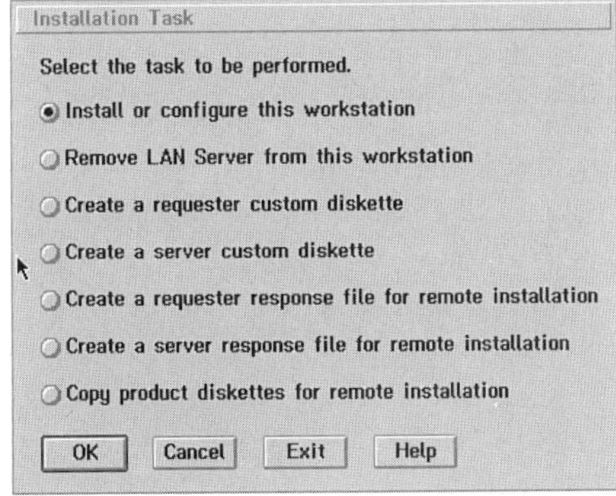

Figure 17.3. Installation tasks.

The install process optionally adds, removes, or configures various LAN Server modules, which are presented in the list box shown in Figure 17.4.

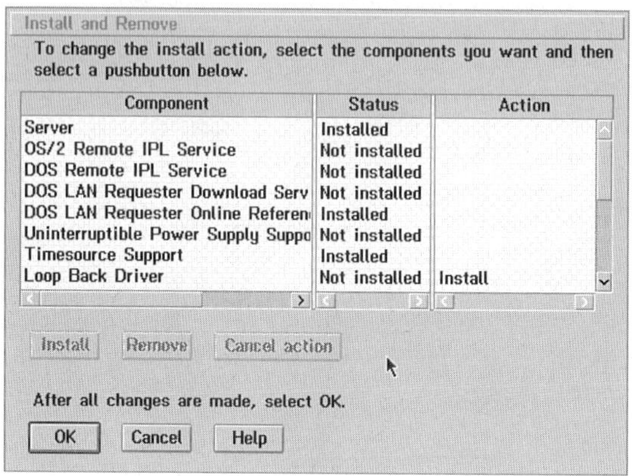

Figure 17.4. Selecting LAN Server components.

Once the components are selected, they must be configured (see Figure 17.5).

Each component has several parameters. Two of the most important options are the server name and domain. A domain is a logical grouping of servers, and it determines the location of the user account database. A server may be a primary domain controller that stores this database, an additional server, or a peer that is a server with limited sharing capabilities. The server name and domain are specified in Figure 17.6.

Once all of the components are configured, you must apply the changes. This creates a file called IBMLAN.INI in the \IBMLAN directory. This directory is the root for all LAN Server utilities and also includes the version information files for the SYSLEVEL utility. Several subdirectories are listed in Table 17.2.

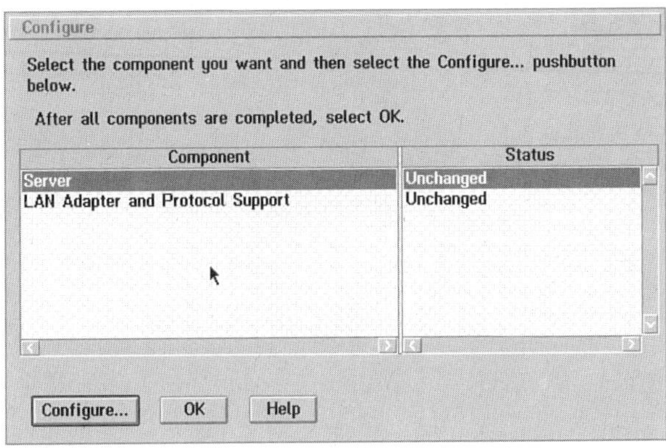

Figure 17.5. Configuring a component.

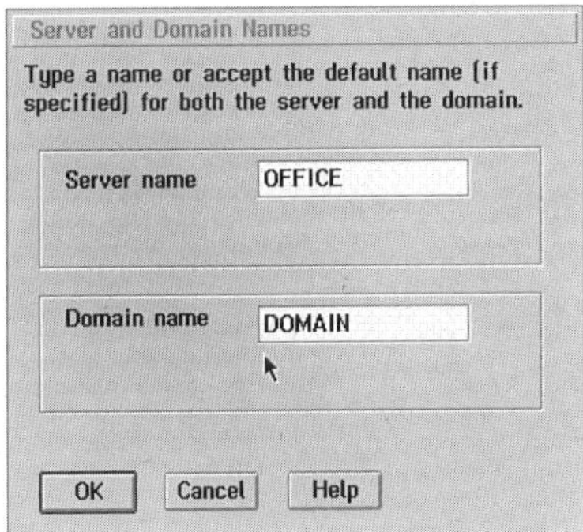

Figure 17.6. Entering the server name and domain.

Table17.2. LAN Server installation directories.

\IBMLAN\	root level, has IBMLAN.INI file
\IBMLAN\ACCOUNTS	user account database NET.ACC, scripts
\IBMLAN\BACKUP	archive copies of LANMAN.INI and CONFIG.SYS
\IBMLAN\BOOK	help files in INF format

continues

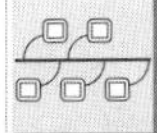

Table 17.2. continued

\IBMLAN\DCDB	domain control database
\IBMLAN\DOSLAN	files for installation of DOS requesters
\IBMLAN\INSTALL	installation and configuration utilities
\IBMLAN\LOGS	error and message logs
\IBMLAN\NETLIB	dynamic link libraries (set in `LIBPATH`)
\IBMLAN\NETPROG	utility programs (set in `PATH`)
\IBMLAN\NETSRC	header and source samples for API programming
\IBMLAN\REPL	default directories for replication service
\IBMLAN\SERVICES	service utilities (messenger, netpopup)
\IBMLAN\USERS	user files

IBMLAN.INI is an ASCII text file with sections and parameters, much like PROTOCOL.INI. There are sections for the network, requester, server, and each additional service. A service is an optional program that can be linked to LAN Server (it appears as part of the network operating system). This modular design provides great flexibility and encourages third-party vendors to add functionality.

The server and requester are also configured as optional services. Any service can be started, paused, and stopped as needed.

Listing 17.3 shows an IBMLAN.INI file with several service sections. Each section has configuration parameters. All of these are installed by LAN Server with the exception of Microsoft SQL Server, which is indicated in bold type. Third-party installation routines often add their own sections and an entry in the service section for the executable.

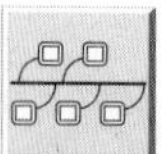

Listing 17.3. A LAN Server IBMLAN.INI file.

```
; OS/2 LAN Server initialization file
[networks]
; This information is read by the redirector at device initialization
time.
  net1=netbeui$,0,LM10, 32, 50, 14

[requester]
  COMPUTERNAME =WDS
  DOMAIN =DOMAIN

; The following parameters generally do not need to be
; changed by the user.
  charcount = 16
  chartime = 250
  charwait = 3600
  keepconn = 600
  keepsearch = 600
  maxcmds = 16
  maxerrorlog = 100
  maxthreads = 10
  maxwrkcache = 64
  numalerts = 12
  numcharbuf = 10
  numservices = 12
  numworkbuf = 15
  numdgrambuf = 14
  othdomains =
  printbuftime = 90
  sesstimeout = 45
  sizcharbuf  = 512
  sizerror = 1024
  sizworkbuf = 4096
; The next lines help you to locate bits in the wrkheuristics entry.
;                            1         2         3
;                  0123456789012345678901234567890123
  wrkheuristics = 1111110121311111110001011120111221
  wrknets =net1
  WRKSERVICES = lsclient,messenger
[messenger]
  logfile = messages.log
  sizmessbuf = 4096
[lsclient]
  multilogon = no
[netlogon]
  SCRIPTS = C:\IBMLAN\REPL\IMPORT\SCRIPTS
   pulse = 60
```

continues

Listing 17.3. continued

```
   update = yes
[replicator]
  replicate = IMPORT
  IMPORTPATH = C:\IBMLAN\REPL\IMPORT
  tryuser = yes
  password =
  interval = 5
  guardtime = 2
  pulse = 3
  random = 60
[server]
  alertnames =
  auditing = no
  autodisconnect = 120
  maxusers = 32
; The following parameters generally do not need to be
; changed by the user.  NOTE:  srvnets= is represented in
; the server info struct as a 16-bit lan mask.  Srvnet names
; are converted to indexes within [networks] for the named nets.
  guestacct = guest
  accessalert = 5
  alertsched = 5
  diskalert = 5000
  erroralert = 5
  logonalert = 5
  maxauditlog = 100
  maxchdevjob = 6
  maxchdevq = 2
  maxchdevs = 2
  maxconnections = 128
  maxlocks = 64
  maxopens = 250
  maxsearches = 50
  maxsessopens = 80
  maxsessreqs = 50
  maxsessvcs = 1
  maxshares = 16
  netioalert = 5
  numbigbuf = 12
  numfiletasks = 1
  numreqbuf = 36
  sizreqbuf = 4096
  srvanndelta = 3000
  srvannounce = 60
; The next lines help you to locate bits in the srvheuristics entry.
;                           1
;                 0123456789012345678
```

```
  srvheuristics = 1111014111131100133
  srvnets =net1
  SRVSERVICES = lsserver,netlogon,timesource
[alerter]
  sizalertbuf = 3072
[netrun]
  maxruns = 3
  runpath = C:\
[lsserver]
  srvpipes = 3
  cleanup = yes
[sqlserver]
  database = d:\dbms\sql\data\master.dat
  errorlog = d:\dbms\sql\errorlog
  executable = d:\dbms\sql\binp\sqlservr.exe
[ups]
[services]
  DLRINST = SERVICES\DLRINST.EXE
; Correlates name of service to pathname of service program.
; The pathname must be either
;       1) an absolute path (including the drive specification)
;                       OR
;       2) a path relative to the IBMLAN root
  requester = services\wksta.exe
  messenger = services\msrvinit.exe
  netpopup = services\netpopup.exe
  server = services\netsvini.exe
  alerter = services\alerter.exe
  netlogon = services\netlogon.exe
  replicator = services\replicat.exe
  netrun = services\runservr.exe
  lsclient = services\lsclient.exe
  lsserver = services\lsserver.exe
  remoteboot=services\rplservr.exe
  ups=services\ups.exe
  timesource=services\timesrc.exe
  genalert=services\genalert.exe
  sqlserver = d:\dbms\sql\binp\startsql.exe
```

Several changes are made to CONFIG.SYS during server installation. Appropriate entries are made in `PATH`, `LIBPATH`, and `BOOKSHELF`. The redirector is loaded as a device driver, installable file system, and a daemon program.

```
DEVICE=C:\IBMLAN\NETPROG\RDRHELP.200
IFS=C:\IBMLAN\NETPROG\NETWKSTA.200 /I:C:\IBMLAN /N
RUN=C:\IBMLAN\NETPROG\LSDAEMON.EXE
```

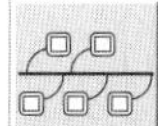

The /I in the IFS line indicates the location of the IBMLAN.INI file. This file is then read to start other services as needed.

Changes to the configuration can be made at a later time by running the LANINST program from the command line or the Workplace Shell Network folder. The same graphical interface is used to add, remove, or change selected services. Some operations require the installation disks and others need a system reboot to take effect.

It is good practice to keep copies of the CONFIG.SYS and INI files for disaster recovery. These text files are locked during LAN Server installation but can be freely copied any other time.

Operating LAN Server

The drivers and programs loaded by CONFIG.SYS set the stage for server operation. However, additional commands are needed to start the server. The command-line utility NET.EXE provides this capability. When combined with the proper parameters, NET can control and administer both requester and server operations. The following subsections define the NET options and syntax. Table 17.3 defines the NET options and syntax.

Table 17.3. LAN Server NET utility options and syntax.

`NET ACCESS [resource]`
`NET ACCESS resource`
`[/ADD [rights] ¦ /DELETE]`
`[/GRANT [rights] ¦ /CHANGE [rights] ¦`
`/REVOKE name [...]]`
`[/TRAIL:[YES ¦ NO]]`
`/FAILURE:{ALL ¦ NONE}]`
`[/FAILURE:{[OPEN];[WRITE];`
	`NET ACCESS` lists, creates, changes, and revokes permissions set for resources at the server. Permissions assigned to a directory automatically become the permissions for files within the directory unless specific

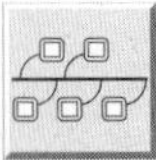

```
[DELETE];[ACL];[...]}
[/SUCCESS:{ALL ¦ NONE}]
[/SUCCESS:{[OPEN];[WRITE];
[DELETE];[ACL];[...]}
[/TREE]
```

permissions are assigned. Then the specific permissions override directory permissions.

```
NET ACCOUNTS [/ROLE:{PRIMARY ¦
   BACKUP ¦ MEMBER ¦ STANDALONE}]
   [/FORCELOGOFF:{minutes ¦ NO}]
   [/MINPWLEN:length]
   [/MAXPWAGE:{days ¦ UNLIMITED}]
   [/MINPWAGE:days]
   [/UNIQUEPW:number]
```

The `NET ACCOUNTS` command displays and modifies password and logon requirements for all accounts in the user accounts system (stored in the \IBMLAN\ACCOUNTS\NET.ACC file). This command is also necessary for setting server roles for the accounts database. Several conditions are required for options used with `NET ACCOUNTS` to take effect:

- The Netlogon service must be running on all servers in the domain that verify logon
- All requesters and servers that log on in the domain must have the same domain entry in the IBMLAN.INI file

```
NET ADMIN \\machineID [password ¦ *]
   /COMMAND [command]
```

The `NET ADMIN` command is used to run a command or start a command processor from the local server to manage a remote server.

continues

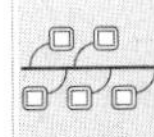

Table 17.3. continued

NET ALIAS aliasname [\\servername resource] [/WHEN:{STARTUP ¦ REQUESTED ¦ ADMIN}] [/REMARK:"text"] [/USERS:number ¦ /UNLIMITED] [/PRINT ¦ /COMM] [/PRIORITY:number] [/DELETE] [/DOMAIN:name]	The NET ALIAS command creates, deletes, changes, and displays information about aliases
NET AUDIT [/COUNT:number] [/REVERSE] [/DELETE]	NET AUDIT displays and clears the audit log for a server. The display includes the user ID of the person who used a resource, the type of resource, the date and time of its use, and the amount of time it was used. This command only works on servers.
For a requester: NET COMM {\\servername[\netname] ¦ device} {\\servername\netname ¦ device} [/PURGE]	NET COMM lists information about the queues for shared serial devices, and allows you to prioritize a queue or clear requests from a queue.
For a server: NET COMM [device] netname [/PURGE] [/PRIORITY:number] [/ROUTE:device[...]] [/OPTIONS]]	NET COMM lists information about the queues for shared serial devices, and allows you to prioritize or reroute a queue or clear requests from a queue.

Command	Description
`NET CONFIG [REQUESTER ¦ SERVER ¦ PEER [options]]`	`NET CONFIG` changes the configuration of a requester, a server, or the Peer service and displays configuration information.
`NET CONTINUE` service	`NET CONTINUE` continues Requester or Server services suspended by the `NET PAUSE` command.
`NET COPY [source[+source...]] [/A ¦ /B] [destination [/A ¦ /B] [/V]]`	`NET COPY` copies files from a source to a destination.
`NET DEVICE [device [/DELETE ]]`	`NET DEVICE` lists the status of shared serial devices. When used without options, `NET DEVICE` displays the status of the serial devices (com ports) shared by the local server. This command only works on servers.
`NET ERROR [/COUNT:number] [/REVERSE] [/DELETE]`	`NET ERROR` displays or clears the error messages stored in the error log file.
`NET FILE [id [/CLOSE]]`	`NET FILE` displays the names of all open shared files and the number of locks, if any, on each file. It also closes shared files and removes file locks. The listing includes the identification number assigned to an open file, the pathname of the file, the user ID, and the number of locks on the file.

continues

Table 17.3. continued

`NET FORWARD msgname fwdname` `msgname /DELETE`	`NET FORWARD` reroutes incoming messages for one user's messaging name to another messaging, or cancels forwarding.

`NET GROUP [groupID [/COMMENT:"text"]]`
`groupID {/ADD [/COMMENT:"text"]`
`¦ /DELETE}`
`groupID userID [...] {/ADD ¦ /DELETE}`
	`NET GROUP` displays the names of groups and their members and updates the group list for the domain when run at a server. The list of groups and group members is in the \IBMLAN\ACCOUNTS\NET.ACC database file.

`NET HELP [command [/OPTIONS]]`
`NET HELP topic`
`NET command [/HELP ¦ /?]`
	Help is available on server utilities and `NET` commands.

`NET LOG [[drive:\path]filename ¦ device]` `[/ON ¦ /OFF]`	`NET LOG` starts or stops sending messages to a file or printer, or displays information about message logging.
`NET MOVE source [destination]`	`NET MOVE` moves files between any two directories on the local area network you have permission to use. Moving relocates the file. The file remains unchanged during a move, but if the source and destination are

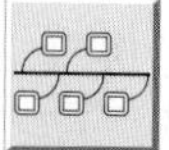

on different machines, the file is given the creation date and time when the move occurred. You don't need to connect to shared directories to use NET MOVE. The source or destination can include a network path instead of a devicename.

```
NET NAME [messagename
   [/ADD ¦ /DELETE]]
```

NET NAME displays, adds, or deletes the message names defined in a requester's list of message names. A requester can have three kinds of message names, each receiving messages:

- A machine ID, which is added as a message name with NET START REQUESTER when the Requester service is started
- A user ID, which is added as a message name when you log on
- Message names for sending messages, which are added with NET NAME or forwarded from another computer with NET FORWARD

continues

Table 17.3. continued

NET PASSWORD [[\\machineID ¦ /DOMAIN[:name] userID oldpassword newpassword	NET PASSWORD changes the password for your user account on a server or in a domain. Typing NET PASSWORD without options results in prompts asking you to type the machine ID or domain, your user ID, old password, and new password.
NET PAUSE service	NET PAUSE suspends a server or requester service. Pausing a service puts it on hold. Users who already have a connection to the server's resources are able to finish their tasks, but new connections to the resources are prevented.
For a requester: NET PRINT {\\machineID[\netname] ¦ device} NET PRINT {\\machineID ¦ device} job# [/HOLD ¦ /RELEASE ¦ /DELETE] *For a server:* NET PRINT netname [/PURGE ¦ /OPTIONS] NET PRINT job# [/HOLD ¦ /RELEASE ¦ /FIRST ¦ /DELETE] NET PRINT [netname ¦ device]	NET PRINT displays or controls single print jobs on a printer queue, displays or controls the shared queue, and sets or modifies options for the printer queue. When used without options, NET PRINT displays information about printer queues on the server. For each queue, the display lists job numbers of queued requests, the size of each job (in bytes), and the status of the printer queue.

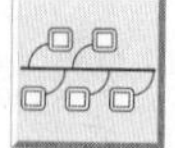

	The status of a print job can be Waiting, Pause, Held, Out of paper, Printing, Error.
`NET RUN` command	`NET RUN` runs a program or command on a server.

For a requester:
`NET SEND {messagename ¦ * ¦ /DOMAIN[:name] ¦ /BROADCAST} {message ¦ <pathname}`
For a server:
`NET SEND /USERS {message ¦ <pathname} {messagename ¦ * ¦ /DOMAIN[:name] ¦ /BROADCAST} {message ¦ <pathname}`
	`NET SEND` sends messages or short files to other computers or users on the local area network. You can only send a message to a message name that is active on the net work. If the message is addressed to a user ID, that user must be logged on. The Messenger service must be running on the receiving requester for that requester to receive the message. The size of the message is limited by the `sizmessbuff=` entry in IBMLAN.INI, which can be changed to accommodate messages as large as 62 kilobytes.

`NET SESSION [\\machineID] [/DELETE] [/PEER]`	`NET SESSION` lists or disconnects sessions between a server and other computers on the local area network.

continues

Table 17.3. continued

Command	Description

`NET SHARE [netname]`
`netname=device [password]`
`[/COMM]`
`[/USERS:number ¦ /UNLIMITED]`
`[/REMARK:text]`
`[/PERMISSIONS:XRWCDA]`
`[/PERMISSIONS:XRWCDA]`
`netname [password]`
`[/PRINT]`
`[/USERS:number ¦ /UNLIMITED]`
`[/REMARK:text]`
`[/PERMISSIONS:XRWCDA]`
`NET SHARE`
`netname=drive:\path [password]`
`[/USERS:number ¦ /UNLIMITED]`
`[/REMARK:text]`
`[/PERMISSIONS:XRWCDA]`
`NET SHARE [netname ¦ device ¦ drive:\path]`
`[/USERS:number ¦ /UNLIMITED]`
`[/REMARK:text]`
`[/DELETE]`
`[/PERMISSIONS:XRWCDA]`
	`NET SHARE` makes a server's resource available to local area network users. When used without options, `NET SHARE` lists information about all resources shared on the server. For each resource, LAN Server reports the device(s) or pathname associated with it and a descriptive comment.

`NET START [service [options]]`	`NET START` starts various services or displays a list of started services. When used without options, `NET START` lists running services. If none is started, the user is prompted to start the requester service.

Syntax	Description

For a requester:
`NET STATISTICS [REQUESTER [/CLEAR]]`
For a server:
`NET STATISTICS`
`[REQUESTER ¦ SERVER [/CLEAR]]`
For a requester running the Peer service:
`NET STATISTICS`
`[REQUESTER ¦ PEER [/CLEAR]]`
	`NET STATISTICS` displays and clears a list of statistics for requester or server functions on a computer. When used without options, it displays a list of services for which statistics are available.

`NET STATUS`	`NET STATUS` displays configuration settings and shared resources for the local server.
`NET STOP` service	`NET STOP` stops services. Stopping a service cancels any network connections the service is using. Some services are dependent on others. Stopping one service can stop others.
`NET TIME [\\machineID ¦ /DOMAIN[:name]]` `[/SET [/YES ¦ /NO]]`	`NET TIME` synchronizes the requester's clock with that of a server or domain or displays the time for a server or domain.

`NET USE [device ¦ \\machineID\netname]`
`NET USE device {\\machineID\netname ¦`
`alias} [password] [/COMM]`
`NET USE {device ¦ \\machineID\netname}`
`/DELETE`
	`NET USE` connects a requester to shared resources, disconnects a requester from shared resources, or displays information about network connections.

continues

Table 17.3. continued

`NET USER [userID] [password] [options]`
`NET USER [userID] [password]`
`[/ADD] [options]`
`NET USER userID [/DELETE]`
	`NET USER` lists, adds, removes, and modifies user accounts on servers with user-level security. The `NET USER` command sets up part of the user accounts system database for domains with user-level security. The database is stored in the IBMLAN\ACCOUNTS\NET.ACC file.

`NET VIEW [\\machineID]`	`NET VIEW` displays a list of servers or a list of resources shared by a server. Typing `NET VIEW` without options displays a list of servers in your startup domain, logon domain and other domains specified in the `/OTHDOMAINS=` entry of the IBMLAN.INI file.
`NET WHO [/DOMAIN:name ¦` `\\machineID ¦ userID]`	`NET WHO` displays user IDs logged on to a domain, a server, or a requester.

Many of the NET options are administrative tools. They are used from the command line, batch files, or REXX programs. A `NET START` command is usually entered in STARTUP.CMD to start the requester, server, or both. `NET START REQUESTER` loads the services necessary for requester operation. The `NET` command looks in the IBMLAN.INI [Services] section to find the executable for the requester. The program is started and it refers to the [Requester] section for configuration parameters. The `WRKSERVICES` line is a list of additional services to load with the requester. Each of these are launched in succession and

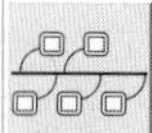

the corresponding IBMLAN.INI sections read. The LSCLIENT and MESSENGER services are usually included here.

Starting the server requires the requester. If it is not loaded, the `NET START SERVER` command starts the requester and loads the server code. The same startup procedure applies to the server with the `SRVSERVICES` line in the [Server] section listing additional services. The LSSERVER and NETLOGON services are often entered here. NETLOGON is the domain controller that provides user management and log on verification. Only one server in each domain needs to run NETLOGON.

If the requester and server load properly, the "Command completed successfully" message appears. Errors print a message number that can be read with the OS/2 help system. This message and error scheme applies to all NET commands.

The user must log on to the server domain controller before doing additional work. The LOGON command-line utility provides this function. A password is required at installation time but can be set as optional. LOGON username `/P:password` works from the command line or a batch file. LOGON is also offered in the User Profile Management folder on the Workplace Shell. The graphical version shown in Figure 17.7 prompts for the username and password. The defaults for these are read from IBMLAN.INI.

Logon

Note: The password will not display.

User ID USERID

Password

OK Cancel Help

Figure 17.7. *The User Profile Management log on dialog.*

Logging onto a domain gives access to all server resources on that domain. This may be one or a number of servers. Security for these resources is controlled at the domain level with permissions assigned by username and group

membership. The `NET USER`, `NET GROUP`, `NET SHARE`, and `NET ACCESS` commands control these operations.

The User Profile Management (UPM) utility can also be used to add user and group entries. This program shares this responsibility with the LAN Server NET commands and additionally provides access control for Extended Services. The User Profile Management is the graphical application pictured in Figure 17.8.

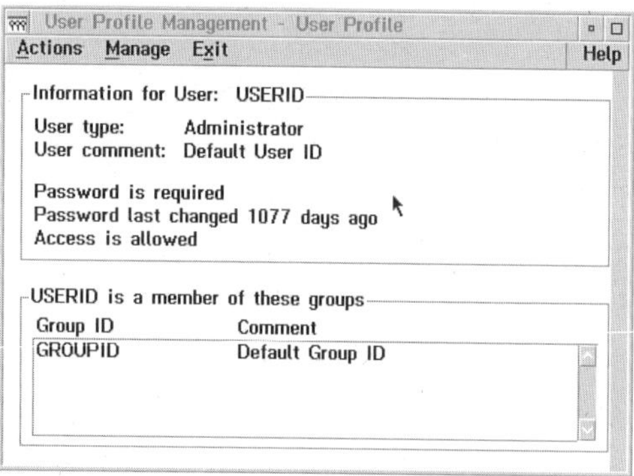

Figure 17.8. *The User Profile Management utility.*

Users are added and passwords maintained with the dialog shown in Figure 17.9.

Groups consist of one or more users. Groups cannot include other groups. It is more efficient to restrict access to domain resources by group rather than user. If a new user is added to a group, all access rights for that group are in effect. This avoids the painstaking entry of individual access rights for each user. Exceptions can be entered per user because user rights override group privileges. The group definition dialog is pictured in Figure 17.10.

The group called servers has special meaning for domain security. It lists each server in the domain by name. The role of each server is set with `NET ACCOUNTS`.

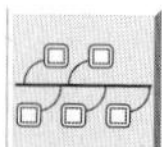

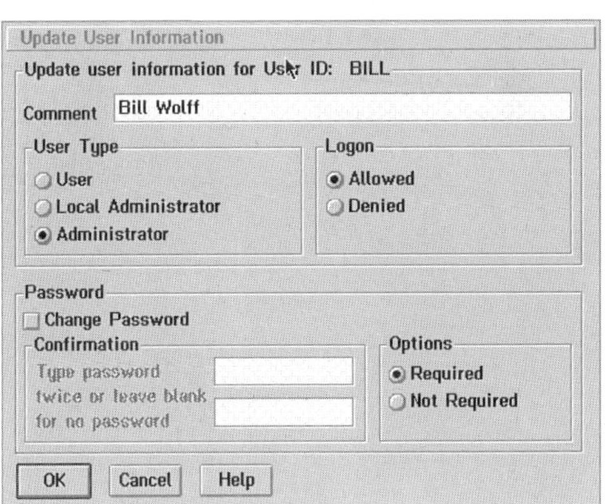

Figure 17.9. The User Profile Management user dialog.

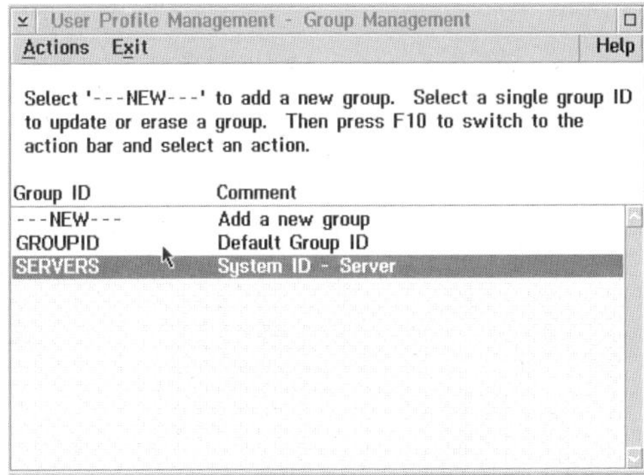

Figure 17.10. The User Profile Management group dialog.

The domain log-off function is also included in the UPM folder. A list box shows all domains that the user is connected to. Figure 17.11 shows the log-off dialog.

Command-Line Utilities

The NET commands listed in Table 17.3 are available for users and administrators. Learning and using them ensures that you have a solid understanding of

OS/2 networking. Many of these commands are also used on DOS workstations including DOS LAN Requester, LAN Manager, and Windows for Workgroups. Each command starts with the word *NET* followed by some action. Parameters often follow the action and refer to some network server, device, directory, or user. The naming conventions for these entities appear in Table 17.4.

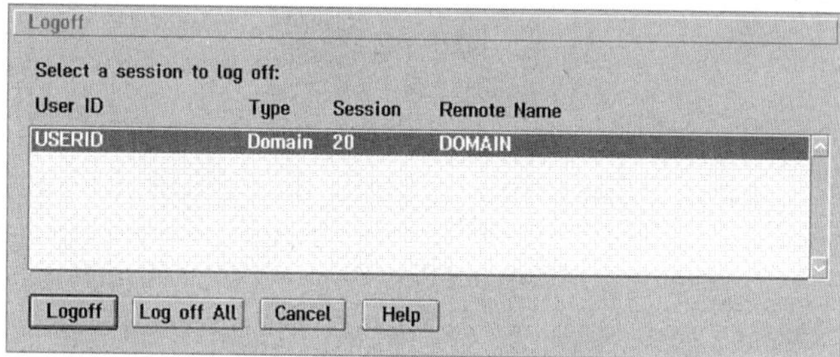

Figure 17.11. The User Profile Management log off dialog.

Table 17.4. Network naming conventions.

MESSAGE NAME	A name used to receive messages. This is not the same as a user ID.
MACHINE ID	The name of a server or a requester on a local area network. In a UNC name, a server's machine ID is preceded by two backslashes (as in \\SERVER\RESOURCE).
DEVICE	The identifier of a disk, printer, or other device physically connected to your computer, or the name assigned to a shared resource that you are using. These include disk drive letters (A:, B:, . . . Z:), serial ports (COMx), and parallel ports (LPTx).

FILENAME	A unique name for a file that can be from one to eight characters in length and may be followed by a filename extension consisting of a period (.) and one to three characters.
UNC NAME	A server's machine ID followed by the netname of a resource (as in \\SERVER1\PRINTQ). UNC is the abbreviation for Universal Naming Convention.
PATH	This includes the name of one or more directories, where each directory name is preceded by a backslash (\). \CUSTOMER\CORP\ACCT, for example, is a path.
PATHNAME	This includes the name of one or more directories followed by a filename. Each directory name and filename within the pathname is preceded by a backslash (\). The pathname \PROJECT\MONTHLY.RPT, for example, points to a file named MONTHLY.RPT in the project directory.
NETNAME	The name by which a shared resource is known to LAN Server.
USER ID	The name a user types when logging on to the local area network.

Most network operating systems share file resources by mapping a local drive letter to a network directory. The resource must be explicitly shared. The `NET SHARE` command is used on the service to establish the resource list. This operation names the resource and assigns permissions. `NET ALIAS` is similar to `NET SHARE` and defines share names global to a domain. These do not need a server name for qualification. The requester then does a `NET USE` to access the resource. The R: drive letter, for example, can be mapped to a database directory on the server:

```
NET USE R: \\SERVER\DATABASE
```

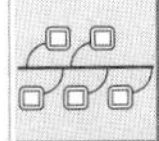

The requester can then use this drive letter as if it were a local drive. However, OS/2 requesters can act on resources directly without mapping a drive letter. The UNC is used to indicate network paths (this eliminates the trouble of explicit mapping and consumes less network resources):

```
NET COPY \\SERVER1\DATABASE\FILE \\SERVER2\PRINTQ
```

File and printer sharing is standard with LAN Server and this works with OS/2 and DOS stations. Print queue control is handled with `NET PRINT`. OS/2 requesters have the added advantage of sharing serial communications ports. This makes a handy modem sharing facility, although operation at high speeds is unreliable. Several NET commands (`COMM`, `DEVICE`) apply to serial port sharing.

Browsing users and resources on the network are the job of `NET VIEW` and `NET WHO`. `VIEW` lists all servers in a domain and optionally the shares for each servers. `WHO` is a list of active users and their descriptive names. This is often used with `NET SEND` to relay simple text messages. If users don't want to be disturbed they can use `NET LOG` to store their messages to a file.

The `NET SEND` messages are not a store and forward mail system. Users must be logged on to receive a message.

Administrators have several commands for user and resource management. All of these functions are mimicked in the following menu descriptions. The use of command-line functions is often quicker, works in a command file or REXX program, and operates well over slow, remote communications lines.

The `NET ADMIN` command is the key to remote management. This command enables a privileged administrator to take console control of a server. A single command or an interactive session can be started. The following example reads the statistics from a remote server:

```
NET ADMIN \\SERVER /C NET STATISTICS SERVER
```

Using the server name and `/C` (command) alone begins an interactive session. In this case, the command-line prompt changes to the remote server

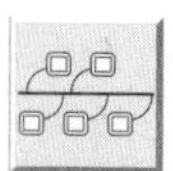

name in brackets [SERVER]. Several commands can be entered and the results scroll on the command screen. Type `EXIT` to return to the requester.

Remote administration sessions are limited in scope. Use CD to track the current directory and only run utilities that require standard input. Graphical applications are not operative. The `START` command (described in Chapter 7, "Command-Line Interface") is helpful here.

Other useful NET tricks are performed with `MOVE` and `COPY`, extended versions of their local counterparts. `MOVE` moves files from one directory to another, and `COPY` performs a copy. The advantage is evident when the source and target directories are on the same machine. In this case, the move or copy is done at the directory level and no data actually moves. This is very fast compared to the transmission of each file from server to workstation and back again.

`NET COPY` and `NET MOVE` work on only one directory at a time.

Help for all NET options is provided by the `NET HELP` command. Any option can be studied in detail by typing `NET HELP` followed by the task name. `NET HELP` alone displays a list of available topics.

Workplace Shell Operations

The Workplace Shell does a good job of hiding complex command syntax. Knowledge of the NET commands is not required if all work is handled through the shell. LAN Server uses shell objects to present shared file resources, printers, comm devices, and network configuration options. The network tools are separated into three folders at installation time. Combining these into one folder is simple and convenient (see Figure 17.12).

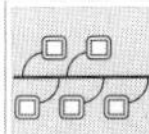

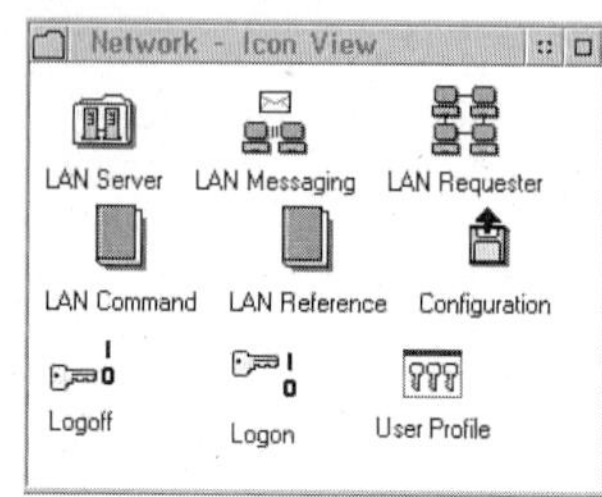

Figure 17.12. The Network folder including UPM and LAN services.

The network management services include the configuration/installation program (LANINST.EXE), the Requester full-screen interface, and the Messaging facility. User Profile Management handles user and group definitions and provides the Logon and Logoff dialogs previously described. The online reference materials are included and rely on the graphical VIEW utility.

The other object of interest is the LAN Server folder. One server object is created for each visible server in the log-on domain. This folder can be opened to view the available servers. The Alias folder depicts any alias definitions, which may also exist in server folders. Figure 17.13 shows a tree view of a LAN Server domain object.

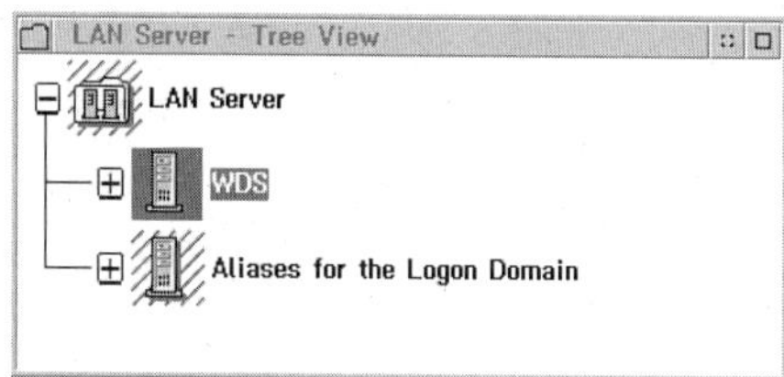

Figure 17.13. A tree view of network resources.

Each server folder can be opened to reveal available shared resources. Icons are used to differentiate file, communications, and printer objects. These objects respond to drag and drop and have pop-up menus and settings. Opening an object shows the contents in the form of a disk directory or print queue. Figure 17.14 contains the pop-up menu that is open for a printer object. The menu has options to set various queue parameters (including default printer).

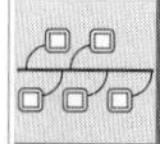

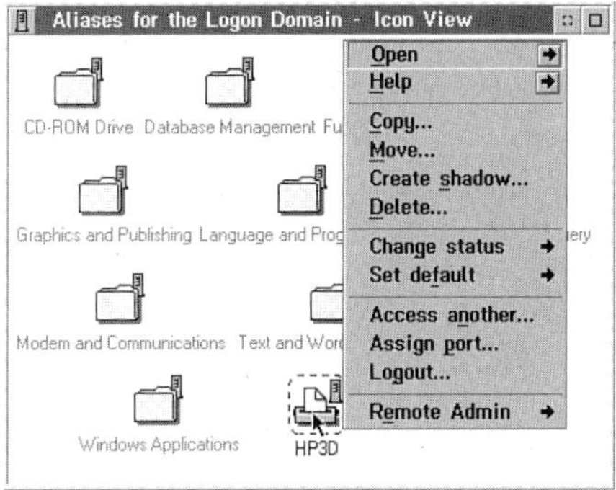

Figure 17.14. A Network folder with shared objects.

The settings notebook for each object has a Network page. Use this to review and set drive mappings and other information. Figure 17.15 shows the Settings for a shared drive. Use the pop-up menu option to disconnect a drive.

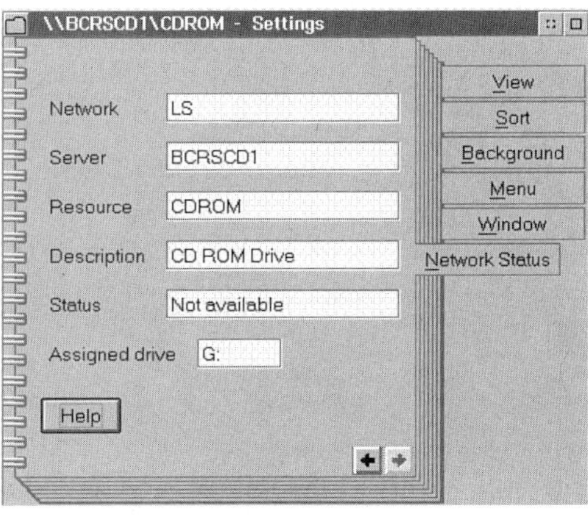

Figure 17.15. Network folder shared object settings.

The online help is plentiful in the Workplace Shell. LAN Server provides two documents. The first document is the command-line reference shown in Figure 17.16. Many of the administrative commands are documented with examples.

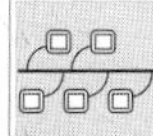

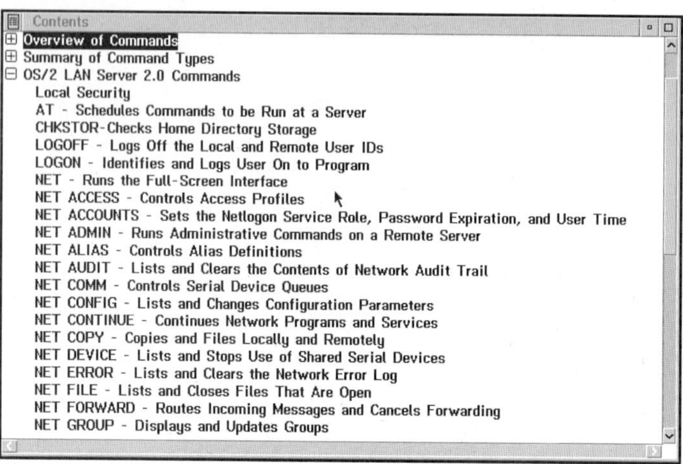

Figure 17.16. The LAN Server command reference.

The online reference is more general in nature and better describes network techniques. Use this in conjunction with the Master Help Index and the Glossary to master the Workplace Shell approach to networking.

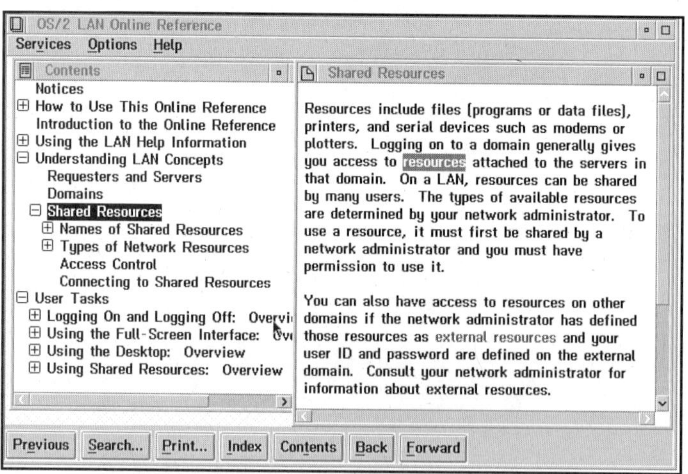

Figure 17.17. The LAN Server online reference.

Requester Menus

Most of the NET command functionality is combined into the full-screen menu interface called the Requester. Use the Network folder object or type `NET` by itself in a command session. The opening screen lists the date, time, username, domain, and machine ID. Press F10 to access the menus shown in Figure 17.18.

```
Actions  Definitions  Utilities  Exit                          F1=Help
                             Main Panel


Date . . . . . . . . . . . . . . . . . . :  12-22-92
Time . . . . . . . . . . . . . . . . . . :  05:44

Machine ID . . . . . . . . . . . . . . . :  OFFICE
User ID. . . . . . . . . . . . . . . . . :  BILL
User type. . . . . . . . . . . . . . . . :  Administrator

Domain name. . . . . . . . . . . . . . . :  DOMAIN
Preselected server . . . . . . . . . . . :  --None--
```

Figure 17.18. The Requester full-screen interface.

Users can be assigned drive letters that connect automatically at log-on time (see Figure 17.19). This requires the use of alias names. This is very convenient and hides the complexity of server and share names from the user.

In addition to alias drives and printers, applications can be defined for a domain and assigned to users at log on time. These applications appear in their Workplace folders and on the Requester menus. Figure 17.20 lists the three types of network applications.

The Access Profile is a set of permissions assigned to a share or alias. Users and groups can be permitted as needed. Figure 17.21 shows the Access Profile menu options.

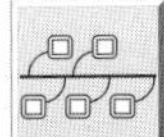

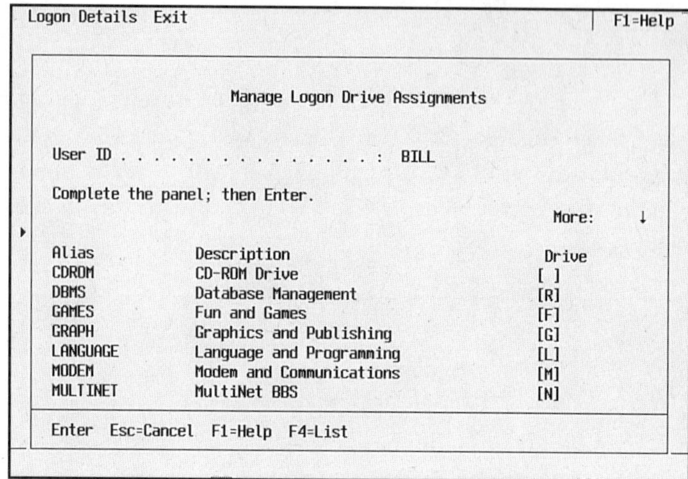

Figure 17.19. User Logon Drive Assignments.

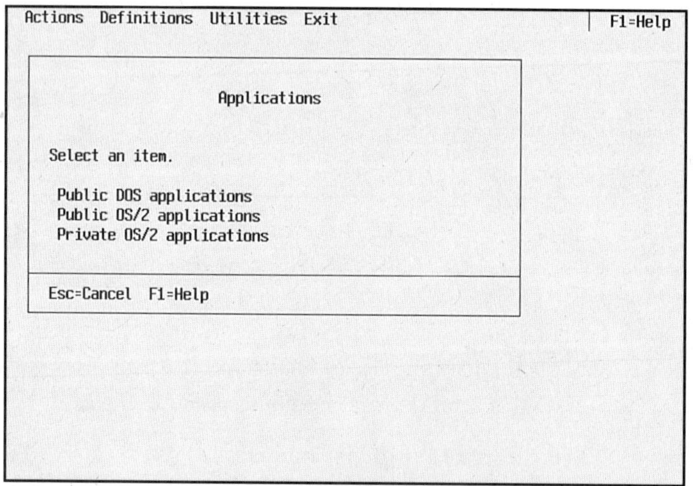

Figure 17.20. Domain application assignments.

Each share or alias has a detailed description. The number of concurrent users can also be limited as shown in Figure 17.22.

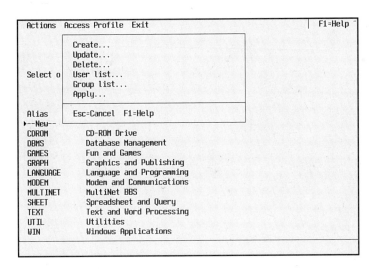

```
Actions  Access Profile  Exit                                        F1=Help

         Create...
         Update...
         Delete...
Select o User list...
         Group list...
         Apply...

Alias    Esc=Cancel  F1=Help
▸--New--
CDROM         CD-ROM Drive
DBMS          Database Management
GAMES         Fun and Games
GRAPH         Graphics and Publishing
LANGUAGE      Language and Programming
MODEM         Modem and Communications
MULTINET      MultiNet BBS
SHEET         Spreadsheet and Query
TEXT          Text and Word Processing
UTIL          Utilities
WIN           Windows Applications
```

Figure 17.21. Alias assignments.

```
Actions  Servers  Exit                                              F1=Help

                    Change Sharing Details - Files

  Change details; then Enter.

  Netname. . . . . . . . . . . . . . . . . . :  CDROM
▸ Alias. . . . . . . . . . . . . . . . . . . :  CDROM
  Server name. . . . . . . . . . . . . . . . :  WDS

  Description. . . . . . . . . . . . . . . .    [CD-ROM Drive              >
  Maximum number of users. . . . . . . . . .    [     ]

  Enter  Esc=Cancel  F1=Help
UTIL      Files                      Utilities                Shared
WIN       Files                      Windows Applications     Shared
HP3D      Printer                    Hewlett Packard IIID     Shared
```

Figure 17.22. Sharing details dialog.

Server services are available to administrators. They can be started, paused, and stopped as needed. Stopping the requester logs you off and closes the menu session. Figure 17.23 lists some server services and their statuses.

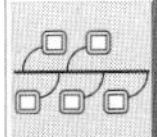

```
Actions  Exit                                                  | F1=Help

                         Manage Network Services

Select one or more services with the spacebar; then use F10 to
switch to the action bar above and select an option.

Machine ID . . . . . . . . . . . :  WDS

                                                        More:     ↓

Service                 Status
DLRINST                 Not Started
REQUESTER               Started                     Active
MESSENGER               Started                     Active
NETPOPUP                Not Started
SERVER                  Started                     Active
ALERTER                 Not Started
NETLOGON                Started                     Active
REPLICATOR              Not Started
NETRUN                  Not Started

Esc=Cancel  F6=All
```

Figure 17.23. Managing server services.

Configuration parameters for a server are stored in the IBMLAN.INI file. Several of these can be modified at runtime (see Figure 17.24).

```
Actions  Exit                                                  | F1=Help

                           Server Parameters

Server name . . . . . . . . . . . . . . . . . . . . . :  WDS
Domain name . . . . . . . . . . . . . . . . . . . . . :  DOMAIN
Current user. . . . . . . . . . . . . . . . . . . . . :  BILL

Description . . . . . . . . . . . . . . . . . . . . . :  Wolff Data Systems →
Autodisconnect timeout (mins) . . . . . . . . . . . . :  120
Alert recipients. . . . . . . . . . . . . . . . . . . :                    →
Alert counting interval (mins). . . . . . . . . . . . :  5
Thresholds:
   Error logs . . . . . . . . . . . . . . . . . . . . :  5
   Logon violations . . . . . . . . . . . . . . . . . :  5
   Access violations. . . . . . . . . . . . . . . . . :  5
   Low disk space (Kbytes). . . . . . . . . . . . . . :  5000
   Net I/O error. . . . . . . . . . . . . . . . . . . :  5

Maximum audit trail size (Kbytes) . . . . . . . . . . :  100

Esc=Cancel
```

Figure 17.24. The Server Parameter dialog.

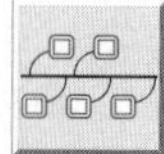

User permissions for shared files and directories contain the eight options shown in Figure 17.24. These are combined as needed and applied to users and groups. User permissions always take precedence over groups. A user can also be assigned to the administrative level, which has full permissions.

```
Actions  Servers  Exit                                        F1=Help

                                        trol Profile
              Permissions

   Select one or more permissions;
   then Enter.

    Letter           Description        S
     N               No access
     X               Execute
     R               Read                ]
     W               Write
     C               Create
     D               Delete             cesses
     A               Attributes          accesses
     P               Permissions

   Enter  Esc=Cancel  F1=Help  F6=All
```

Figure 17.25. Assigning access permissions.

MVDM Sessions

Multiple DOS session support is one of the finer benefits of OS/2 2.1. LAN Server extends this to network sessions. Several DOS applications can run concurrently while the virtual adapter code handles the traffic in protected mode. This yields maximum memory for large DOS programs and allows efficient multitasking. Combined with local disk caching, this allows some DOS applications to run faster than they can on a stand-alone DOS machine.

The downside of DOS session support is the lack of network utilities. The DOS version of the `NET` command does not work in a DOS session. Useful operations like `NET COPY` and `NET ADMIN` are not allowed. Instead, connections must be made in an OS/2 session or from the Workplace Shell. This is not a serious inconvenience in a structured environment where the drive mappings

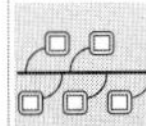

are static. For network support and application development, however, this can be annoying.

To its credit, OS/2 2.1 has a simple solution for these types of problems. A DOS boot image can be created to run a specific version of DOS. If this image includes LAN drivers and a path to the DOS network utilities, full support is possible. This works just like a dedicated DOS workstation. Remember to log on from the command line and set the connections with the `NET USE` command.

Some adapters are limited to the number of sessions on the card. LAN Server provides a virtual device utility to negotiate multiple images contending for the same adapter. If this is not used, only one DOS session can work at a time.

Advanced Server Options

LAN Server is unique in that it offers server support on OS/2 2.1. The server is an extension of the requester and requires only a few additional floppies. A machine can be switched from a requester to a server and back again by using the `NET START SERVER` and `NET STOP SERVER` commands. This is a useful feature for research and development.

Several advanced features are provided for performance, security, and reliability. OS/2 has built-in disk caching, which is used by the Entry Level LAN Server. The more cache the better. Adding more memory, well over 16M (some systems do not support more than 16M), gives ample cache, which comfortably supports more users.

The Advanced version includes HPFS386, which is a fast 32-bit network transport combined with cached disk access. The file permissions are stored directly in the file extended attributes instead of a separate table. This makes for fast user verification and gets the file out on the wire quickly. HPFS386 can also be used for local security, which password protects entire volumes. Even an

OS/2 boot floppy cannot access the hard drive data in this scenario. Several commands in Table17.5 are used to work with HPFS386.

The user account database is stored in a file called NET.ACC. This file is always open on a busy server. The BACKACC utility can make a backup copy of this file while the server is running. RESTACC puts it back. This is also used in conversions and reinstallation of damaged servers.

Four utilities that start with FT provide fault tolerance. Disk drives can be mirrored (two drives on one controller) or duplexed (separate controllers). If one drive fails, the other takes over and the administrator is notified. The drives do not have to be identical because the option is set up on a partition basis.

Another interesting feature in LAN Server is the remote boot option. A boot prom on the network adapter or a properly configured boot floppy can load OS/2 from a server to a workstation. This saves the cost of a local hard drive and provides stricter security in sensitive installations. Each adapter has a unique address that is used to define a boot image stored on the server. Each station can have its own image or they can be shared by several machines. This puts a lot of stress (due to excessive reads and writes to the server-based swap file, executables, and DLLs) on the network wiring and should be used with care. Remote boot is popular with DOS stations that require less resources. Table17.5 lists the advanced server utilities.

Table 17.5. Advanced server commands.

`AT [id] [/DELETE] time [/EVERY:date[,...] ¦ /NEXT:date[,...]] command`	AT schedules a program or command to run at a later date or time on a server. When used without options, it displays a list of programs and commands scheduled to run. The programs and commands are stored in the server's IBMLAN\LOGS\ SCHED.LOG file, so scheduled tasks are not lost if you restart the server.

continues

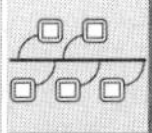

Table 17.5. continued

BACKACC [[drive:]pathname [/F:[drive:]target] [/L1:[drive:][path][filename]][/A] [/S]]	BACKACC backs up permissions on the 386 HPFS volumes, the user accounts database (NET.ACC), and the audit log (NET.AUD) while LAN Server is running. When used without options, BACKACC backs up the user accounts data-base and the audit log.
CACHE [/BUFFERIDLE:[drive:]time] [/LAZY:[drive:]{ON ¦ OFF}] [/MAXAGE:[drive:]time] [/OPTIONS[drive:]] [/STATS: [CLEAR ¦ DYNAMIC]]	CACHE establishes file system caching for a 386 HPFS volume. When used without options, it displays caching statistics. CACHE is placed in the operating system configuration file at installation.
CHGSRVR currentsrvname newsrvname	CHGSRVR changes the server name of a domain controller or the name of an additional server and updates the domain control database and user information with the new name. CHGSRVR does not change the names in the IBMLAN.INI file.
CHKSTOR [\\computername ¦ /DOMAIN[:name]] [name [...]] [/ALERTS:{YES ¦ NO}] [/ALL]	CHKSTOR checks the storage remaining in home directories on a server. When used without options, it displays a report of used disk space for the local server. Only those users who are over their storage limit are

	included in the report, unless the `/ALL` parameter is used. For each home directory on the server that is over the storage limit, CHKSTOR reports the user ID, disk space allowed, disk space used, and the home directory's path. The `NET USER` command must have /MAXSTORAGE set to a number to use the CHKSTOR utility. This command only works on servers.
`FIXACC`	`FIXACC` restores a damaged user accounts database (NET.ACC). The old NET.ACC is renamed to NETACC.BAD. This command requires that the Requester service and UPM are stopped.
`FTADMIN [\\computername] [/MONO]`	FTADMIN starts the FTADMIN fault-tolerance utility. It is an OS/2 application that runs in a Presentation Manager window. When used without options, FTADMIN starts the fault-tolerance utility on the local computer.
`FTMONIT [/ALERT:{YES ¦ NO}] [/COMPARE:{YES ¦ NO}] [/QUIET:{YES ¦ NO}] [/CLEAR:{YES ¦ NO}]`	FTMONIT starts the fault-tolerance utility's error-monitoring feature or clears statistics about error monitoring. When used without options, it displays statistics.

continues

Table 17.5. continued

`FTREMOTE [/R:responsefile] [/L1:statusfile] [/L2:historyfile]`	The FTREMOTE utility is a response-file-driven version of FTADMIN and FTSETUP that activates fault tolerance, configures the drives to use fault tolerance in an unattended state, verifies mirrored drives, and corrects errors. Running FTREMOTE activates fault tolerance, unless the command `DEACTIVATE` is contained in the response file.
`FTSETUP`	FTSETUP installs the Disk Fault Tolerance system and prompts for information needed to configure drive mirroring and drive duplexing.
`GETRPL`	The GETRPL utility is run on remote IPL servers after installation or reinstallation of LAN Server. GETRPL migrates RPL.MAP workstation and server records from previous levels of LAN Server into the RPL.MAP on the current remote IPL server. DOS remote IPL users are moved from previous levels of LAN Server into a group called RPLGROUP and an access control profile for RPLGROUP is created, granting all privileges to the users in that group. GETRPL ensures that new OS/2 remote IPL and DOS remote IPL users added with LAN Server 3.0 are added to the group. It installs all the OS/2 device drivers and display support routines.

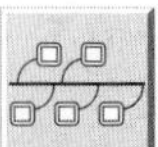

`HDCON` `[d:]\>HDCON[-o] ¦ [-n] [*] ¦ [userx]`	The HDCON utility allows you users' home directory aliases to migrate from LAN Server Version 1.3 into the format used by the current version. When this is accomplished, the old aliases are deleted. Another use of the utility is to create aliases for home directories created in LAN Server Version 3.0 for those users who are accustomed to using or need to use the old format. HDCON can convert all users in a domain at one time or convert a list of users provided at the OS/2 command prompt. Only an administrator can use HDCON to migrate users' home directories.
`MAKEDISK [/BOOTDRIVE:k]`	The MAKEDISK utility can be used to create a 386 HPFS boot disk for the workstation after installing OS/2 2.1 and LAN Server 3.0 on a workstation. Use the `DISKCOPY` command to make copies of the OS/2 2.1 installation disk and the OS/2 2.1 Installation/Disk 1 before using this utility. When MAKEDISK is run, certain files on the backup copy of the OS/2 2.1 Installation/Disk 1 are altered. Other files are deleted to make room for the 386 HPFS system-related files. The disk device drivers and 386 HPFS system files are copied from the workstation's root directory on the boot drive.

continues

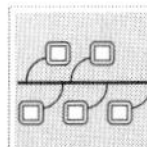

Table 17.5. continued

`MAKEIMG [[d:outfile] ¦ [infile]] [/Ssss] [/Fxxx]`	The MAKEIMG utility packages the system programs required for a remote IPL requester into an image file. If you want to make an image that does not contain DOS LAN Requester, use a model definition file that does not attempt to start DOS LAN Requester instead of using the standard definition files. All files must exist on the domain controller in the IBMLAN\DCDB\IMAGES subdirectory.
`MKRDPM`	The MKRDPM utility allows the user to create remote IPL disks. The user can select the network adapter type from a list displayed on the main panel. A remote IPL disk is created that initializes the network adapter and starts the remote IPL boot process.
`PREPACL /P [/FL:filename ¦ /DL:filename ¦ /D:dirname] /B:filename ¦ /N [/L1:filename] [/L2:filename] [/O]`	The PREPACL utility removes access control profiles from subdirectories and files on 386 HPFS drives required by the OS/2 program. Run PREPACL prior to installing OS/2.
`PRIV command [values]`	PRIV ensures that a background process started by an administrator on a 386 HPFS server with local security remains privileged after the administrator logs off. A privileged process is a background process that has the equivalent of administrative privilege.

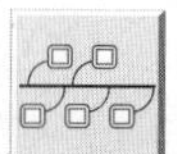

	A privileged process can access all files on the server for as long as it runs, no matter who logs on or off locally at the server. This command only works on servers.
`RESTACC [drive:]pathname [[drive:]newname] [/F:[drive:]source] [/L1:[drive:][path][filename]] [/S]`	RESTACC restores the permissions for 386 HPFS volumes, the user accounts database, and the audit file stored with BACKACC.
`RPLENABL`	RPLENABL enables the Remote IPL service at a workstation that has a hard disk. It configures the hard disk so that the workstation can be started from a server that is running the Remote IPL service. This does not prevent access to the hard disk after the workstation is booted remotely.
`RPLDSABL`	RPLDSABL disables the Remote IPL service at a workstation that has a hard disk. Use RPLDSABL at a workstation that is no longer going to be started remotely. After running RPLDSABL, the workstation boots from its own hard disk rather than from a server running the Remote IPL service.
`THIN386 /B:d: /T:d:path [/L1:d:\path\filename] [/L2:d:\path\filename]`	The THIN386 utility creates a temporary 386 HPFS file system that can be used by the LAN Server 3.0 installation/configuration program.

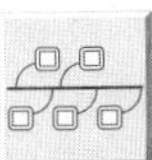

LAN Manager

LAN Manager is the Microsoft version of OS/2-based networking. The foundation and file structures are very similar to LAN Server. At the API level, you can hardly tell them apart. In fact, the two products were rumored to converge in function, but with the merger of NT and LAN Manager, that promise is just a memory. The installation and administration interfaces are the most striking differences.

Microsoft offers only workstation (requester) software for OS/2 2.1 and includes it with the purchase of a LAN Manager server package. Their server product still relies on OS/2 1.3, which is robust but limited to 16M of memory with the old Program Manager menu interface. NDIS provides the adapter and protocol management. LAN Manager workstations can administer LAN Server domains and provide client named pipe support. There is little Workplace Shell interaction, but the DOS session capabilities are on a par with LAN Server Requester. The simplicity of the workstation software makes this a quicker requester.

One-Step Installation

The installation utility is called SETUP and loads from several floppies. A full-screen character interface with drop menus provides the basic functions. The adapter and protocol are selected from list boxes (see Figure 17.26).

Several other dialogs collect the required information. The domain and machine names follow the same rules as LAN Server. The MESSENGER and NETPOPUP services allow simple messaging and audit warnings. The default username is also entered in Figure 17.27.

The install copies the necessary files, modifies CONFIG.SYS, and builds LANMAN.INI and PROTOCOL.INI. There are less directories than with LAN Server because the server and the API code are missing. \LANMAN is the default root listed in Table 17.6.

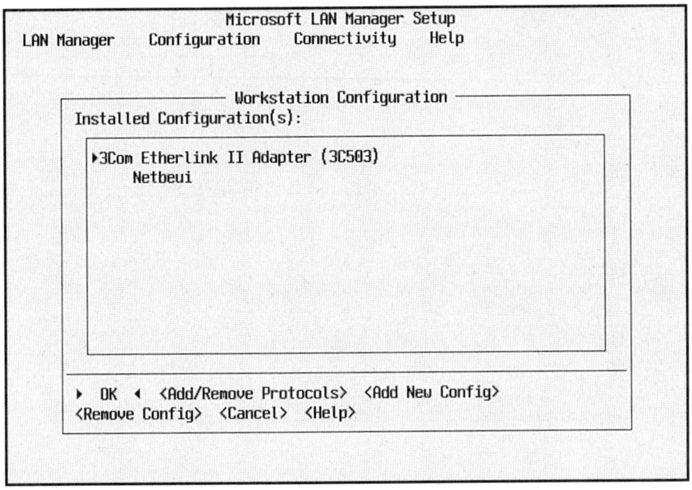

```
                    Microsoft LAN Manager Setup
LAN Manager    Configuration    Connectivity    Help

        ┌──────────── Workstation Configuration ────────────┐
        Installed Configuration(s):

          ▸3Com Etherlink II Adapter (3C503)
              Netbeui

        ▸ OK ◂  <Add/Remove Protocols>  <Add New Config>
        <Remove Config>  <Cancel>  <Help>
```

Figure 17.26. Adapter and protocol configuration.

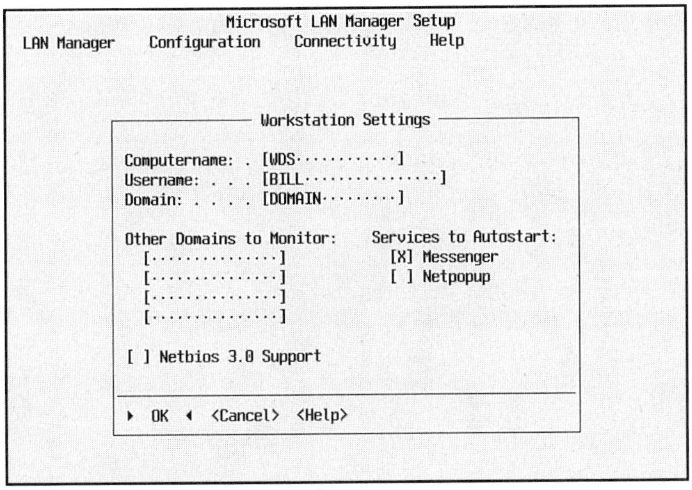

```
                    Microsoft LAN Manager Setup
LAN Manager    Configuration    Connectivity    Help

              ──────── Workstation Settings ────────

              Computername: . [WDS············]
              Username: . . . [BILL················]
              Domain: . . . . [DOMAIN·········]

              Other Domains to Monitor:    Services to Autostart:
                [···············]            [X] Messenger
                [···············]            [ ] Netpopup
                [···············]
                [···············]

              [ ] Netbios 3.0 Support

              ▸ OK ◂  <Cancel>  <Help>
```

Figure 17.27. Workstation settings.

Table 17.6. LAN Manager installation directories.

\LANMAN\	root directory, INI files, setup, version
\LANMAN\DRIVERS	adapter drivers and protocols
\LANMAN\LOGS	message and error logs
\LANMAN\NETLIB	dynamic link libraries
\LANMAN\NETPROG	utilities and device drivers
\LANMAN\PROFILES	user log-on profiles
\LANMAN\SERVICES	workstation services

CONFIG.SYS entries load the protocol manager, adapter driver, and protocol driver. The workstation redirector is loaded as a device driver, an installable file system, and the NETVDD (virtual device) driver. LAN Manager marks the lines with comments. The `PATH` and `LIBPATH` variables are adjusted for the proper directories.

```
REM ==== LANMAN 2.1a === DO NOT MODIFY BETWEEN THESE LINES === LANMAN
2.1a ===
DEVICE=C:\LANMAN\DRIVERS\PROTMAN\PROTMAN.OS2 /i:C:\LANMAN
DEVICE=C:\LANMAN\DRIVERS\ETHERNET\ELNKII\ELNKII.OS2
DEVICE=C:\LANMAN\DRIVERS\PROTOCOL\NETBEUI\NETBEUI.OS2
DEVICE=C:\LANMAN\NETPROG\RDRHELP.SYS
IFS=C:\LANMAN\NETPROG\NETWKSTA.SYS /i:C:\LANMAN
DEVICE=C:\LANMAN\NETPROG\NETVDD.SYS
REM ==== LANMAN 2.1a === DO NOT MODIFY BETWEEN THESE LINES === LANMAN
2.1a ===
```

The LANMAN.INI file in Listing 17.4 is very similar to IBMLAN.INI. There are fewer services and only a handful of parameters. Microsoft relies on automatic tuning to set the configuration values. These can be overridden by explicit entries in this file. Few optional services are available because the server function is not supported. This means that named pipe applications such as SQL Server will not run on the workstation.

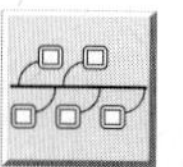

LAN Manager includes TCP/IP support in their workstation product.

Listing 17.4. LAN Manager LANMAN.INI file.

```
;**************************************************************;
;**                    Microsoft LAN Manager                 **;
;**             Copyright(c) Microsoft Corp., 1992           **;
;**************************************************************;
;  LAN Manager initialization file, for workstation configuration.
[networks]
; This info is read by redir at device init time.  It is available to
; apps via NetBiosEnum.
  net1 = netbeui$,0

[workstation]
  computername = WDS
  domain = DOMAIN
  othdomains =
  wrkservices = messenger
  wrknets = net1
[messenger]
[netshell]
  refresh = 15
  remote =
  username = BILL
[version]
  lan_manager = 2.1a.0
[tcpip_node]
  Hub =
  HubIPAddr =
  Domains =
  DoUAS = yes
  DoView = yes
  DoLogon = yes
  DoWho = no
  DoSend = no
  DoRepl = yes
  DoUser1 = no
  DoUser2 = no
  DoUser3 = no
  UserMailSlot1 =
  UserMailSlot2 =
  UserMailSlot3 =
[services]
; Correlates name of service to pathname of service program.
; The pathname must be either
;    1) an absolute path (including the drive specification)
;             OR
;       2) a path relative to the LanMan root
```

continues

Listing 17.4. continued

```
  workstation = services\wksta.exe
  tcpip_node = services\node.exe
  messenger = services\msrvinit.exe
  netpopup = services\netpopup.exe
```

The basic structure of PROTOCOL.INI in Listing 17.5 is the same as LAN Server. The addition of help text is valuable when editing the ASCII file. This file is kept in the \LANMAN directory instead of the separate \IBMCOM area used by NTS/2.

Listing 17.5. The LAN Manager PROTOCOL.INI file.

```
[PROTMAN]
  DRIVERNAME = PROTMAN$
[NETBEUI_XIF]
  Drivername = netbeui$
  SESSIONS = 40
  NCBS = 85
  BINDINGS = "ELNKII_NIF"
[ELNKII_NIF]
;
;    3c503 3Com EtherLink II adapter
;
    DRIVERNAME = ELNKII$
;        2nd driver name = ELNKII2$
    INTERRUPT = 3
;        interrupt channel number (required, default = 3)
;        Use 2,3,4,5   Software selectable
    IOADDRESS = 0x300
;        adapter base address (required, default = 0x300)
;        Must match the I/O base address jumper setting on the adapter
;        Use 0x250, 0x280, 0x2A0, 0x2E0, 0x300, 0x310, 0x330, 0x350
    DMACHANNEL = 1
;        DMA channel number (optional, default = 1)
;        Use 1 or 3, software selectable
;    DATATRANSFER = SINGLE_DMA     ;Single mode dma, slow, but compatible
;    DATATRANSFER = BLOCK_DMA      ;Block mode dma, faster DMA method
;    DATATRANSFER = DEMAND_DMA     ;Demand mode dma, fastest DMA method
;          If DMA does not work in your computer,
;          or there's no DMA channel available
;          or your running MicroSoft Windows 3.0, use
```

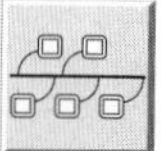

```
;    DATATRANSFER = PIO_WORD
;          Programmed I/O word mode xfer (use on 286, 386 machines)
;    DATATRANSFER = PIO_BYTE
;          Programmed I/O byte mode xfer (use on very fast 386, 486
           ➥machines)
     MAXTRANSMITS = 40
;        number of transmit queue elements (optional, default = 8)
;        Min = 8, Max = 50
;        Use the default for DOS and normal OS/2 clients
;        Set MAXTRANSMITS = 40 for OS/2 servers
;    XMITBUFS = 2
;        number of adapter resident xmit buffers (optional, default =
         ➥2)
;        Min = 1, Max = 2
;    NETADDRESS = "02608C123456"
;        network address (optional, default = network address PROM
         ➥value)
;        the network address is 12 hex digits enclosed in quotes
;    TRANSCEIVER = EXTERNAL
;        Ethernet connection method (optional, default = onboard)
;        EXTERNAL specifies the AUI (DIX) connector
```

The completed setup can be edited at any time with the SETUP utility kept in the \LANMAN directory. A SETUP.INI file and help screens make this a simple chore. The installation can also be detached as needed. This keeps the files on disk but removes and saves the pertinent CONFIG.SYS entries. This is useful for part-time networking or demonstration equipment. The attach menu item puts everything back in place.

Command-Line Operation

The workstation is started from STARTUP.CMD or the command line with `NET START WORKSTATION`. Most of the NET commands previously listed work the same with the notable exception of `ALIAS`. LAN Manager does not support the LAN Server alias concept and cannot automatically use resources or catalog applications at log on. Instead, a profile is saved with the desired connections. The LMUSER.INF file in the \LANMAN directory stores the connections from the last session and automatically restores them.

User Profile Management and the graphical log-on dialogs are not included. The command line `NET LOGON Username Password` operation does the log-on chores. `NET LOGOFF` is the counterpart.

Remote administration of LAN Manager or LAN Server domains is offered by the `NET ADMIN` command. This is recommended over the menu interface for LAN Server so that aliases and the other features unique to IBM are available. Full support of the Universal Naming Convention and hidden shares make LAN Manager a useful administrative tool.

Mastering the command-line tools in LAN Manager is important because Workplace Shell support is limited. There are no network folders, shared drives, or printer icons. The user can set up network-aware objects on their own, although this requires a bit of work. The usual file and print Workplace operations can handle the basics. Message help is available from the command line but there are no INF files for reference.

DOS session operation is limited to whatever resources are set up in protected mode. LAN Manager DOS network utilities will not work. Memory management is excellent and named pipes work well.

Full-Screen Menu Interface

A full-screen character interface provides user and administrative access to basic LAN functions. This is similar to the LAN Server requester screen and mimics the command-line utilities. A user session is started with the `NET` command. Administrators use the `NET ADMIN` option (see Figure 17.28).

A list box in the center of the screen displays the local station and any servers in the monitored domains. Move up and down with the arrows and press Enter to focus on a particular server. The Current Focus message changes at the top of the screen as shown in Figure 17.29.

The View menu panel has options for listing shared or used resources, printers, and serial devices. Option buttons on the bottom of each dialog perform actions or provide more information. Figure 17.30 lists some shared resources.

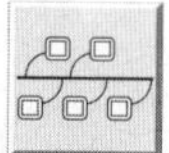

View Message Config Status Accounts Help
Current focus : \\WDS
Your username . . : BILL
Your computername : \\WDS
Your domain . . . : DOMAIN
Set current focus on [\\MIM]
Server nam
Local
MIM
You have administrative privileges at \\MIM.
You may receive detailed help at any time
by pressing the F1 key.
< OK >

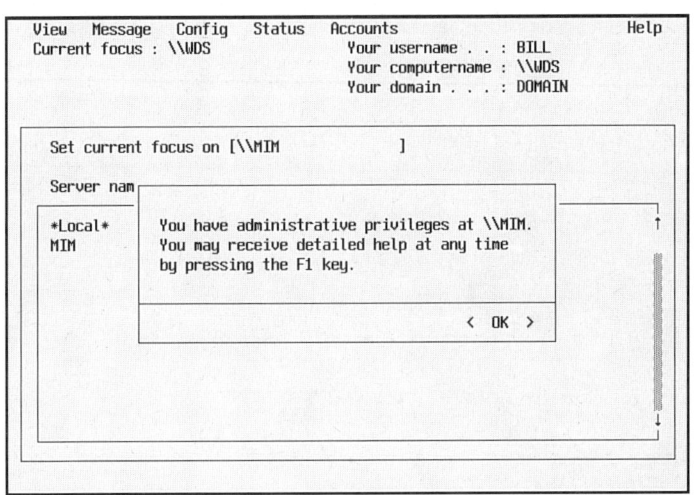

Figure 17.28. Administrative privileges message.

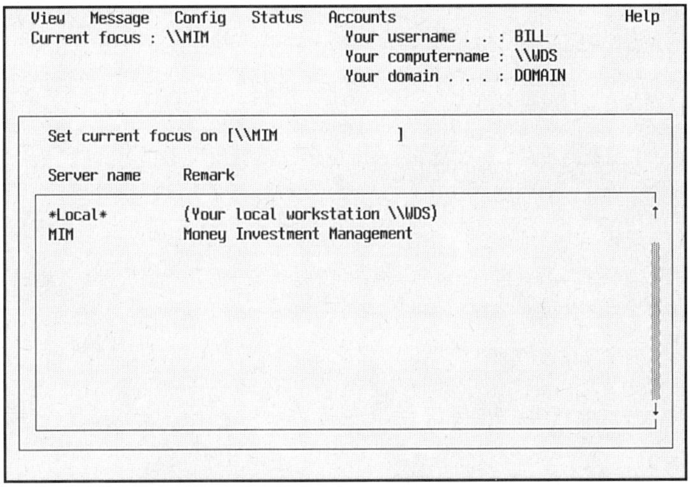

View Message Config Status Accounts Help
Current focus : \\MIM
Your username . . : BILL
Your computername : \\WDS
Your domain . . . : DOMAIN
Set current focus on [\\MIM]
Server name Remark
Local (Your local workstation \\WDS)
MIM Money Investment Management

Figure 17.29. Setting the focus on a server name.

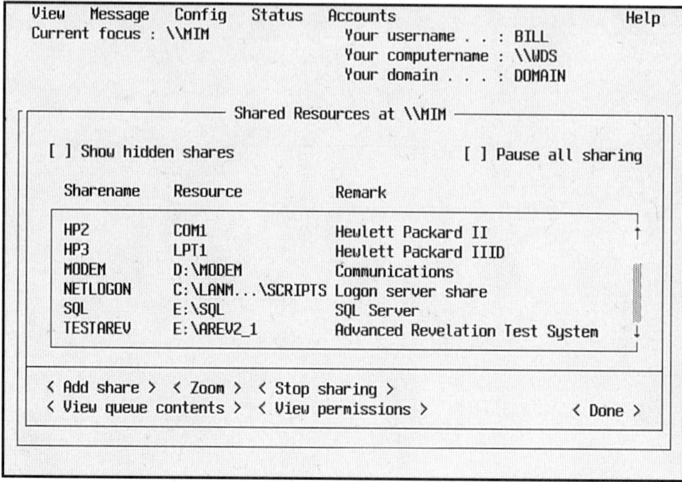

Figure 17.30. The Shared Resources list box.

Resources in use can include hidden shares denoted by a trailing $. These are usually restricted to administrative use. Figure 17.31 shows two server disk drives in use by a workstation.

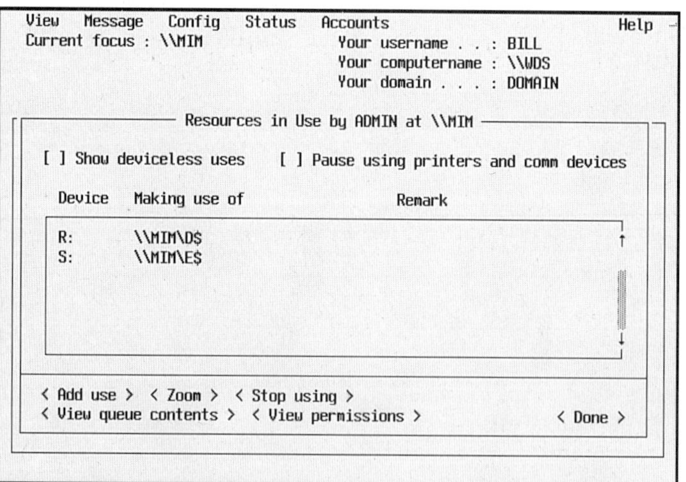

Figure 17.31. Resources in use.

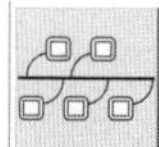

The list of services includes server options if the focus is on a LAN Manager server. These can be started, paused, and stopped remotely. The familiar list box dialog is used in Figure 17.32.

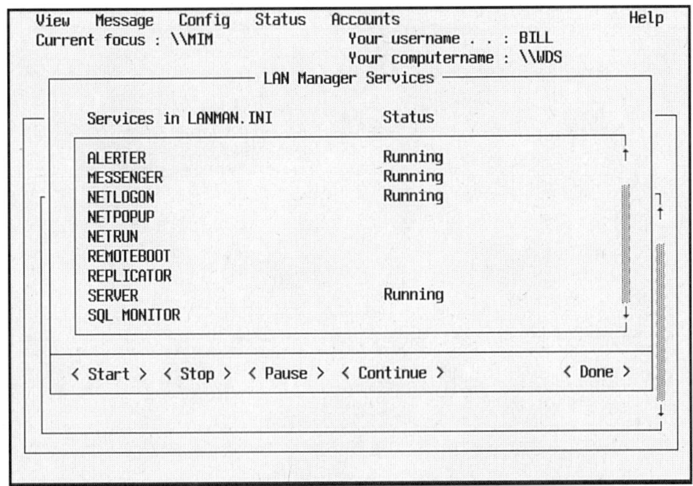

Figure 17.32. Managing server services.

Server configuration settings are available for LAN Manager networks. Figure 17.33 shows a domain controller (NETLOGON) running SQL Server (SQL Database).

The workstation and server statistics are summarized in a read-only dialog. Monitor the information shown in Figure 17.34 to track server performance.

The active users or files can be listed and controlled. Figure 17.35 displays the full user name and configuration details.

Users and groups are maintained directly in the `NET ADMIN` utility instead of User Profile Management. The domain controller has a group called SERVERS that tracks member server names. The default groups of ADMINS and USERS shown in Figure 17.36 are also present in LAN Server.

The server role is important in domain management. This and other security settings are grouped together in Figure 17.37.

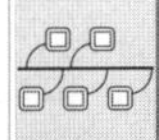

```
View   Message   Config   Status   Accounts                                  Help
Current focus : \\MIM                      Your username . . : BILL
                                           Your computername : \\WDS
                                           Your domain . . . : DOMAIN
          Set Configuration for Server \\MIM

  Server's remark . . . . . [Wolff Data Systems·····················]
  Send alerts to  . . . . . [·······································]

  Server options:                              Start server services:
    [X] User security                            [X] Server
                                                 [X] Admin alerter
                                                 [ ] Netrun service
                                                 [X] Netlogon
                                                 [ ] Remote boot
                                                 [ ] File replicator
                                                 [X] SQL database

  < Auditing >                                     <  OK  >  <Cancel>
```

Figure 17.33. Setting server configuration.

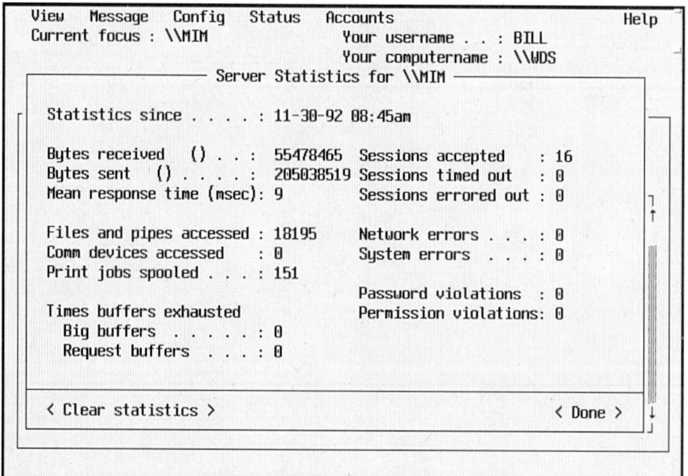

Figure 17.34. Monitoring server statistics.

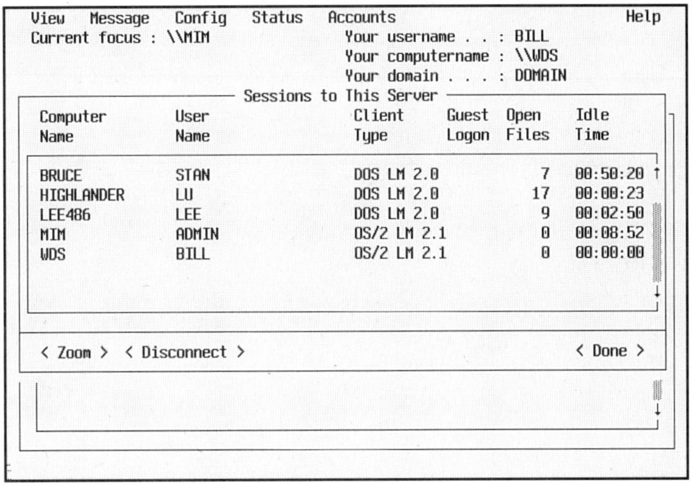

```
View   Message   Config   Status   Accounts                                Help
Current focus : \\MIM                Your username . . : BILL
                                     Your computername : \\WDS
                                     Your domain . . . : DOMAIN
                         Sessions to This Server
 Computer        User                 Client      Guest  Open    Idle
 Name            Name                 Type        Logon  Files   Time

 BRUCE           STAN                 DOS LM 2.0              7  00:50:20
 HIGHLANDER      LU                   DOS LM 2.0             17  00:00:23
 LEE486          LEE                  DOS LM 2.0              9  00:02:50
 MIM             ADMIN                OS/2 LM 2.1             0  00:08:52
 WDS             BILL                 OS/2 LM 2.1             0  00:00:00

 < Zoom >  < Disconnect >                                  < Done >
```

Figure 17.35. Monitoring session status.

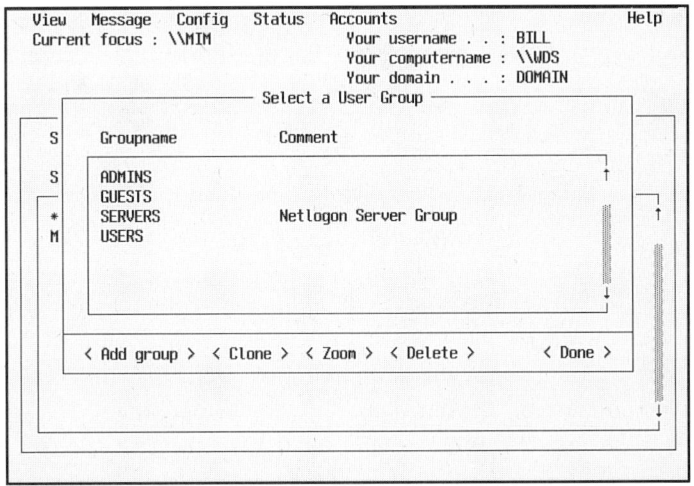

Figure 17.36. Group and user administration.

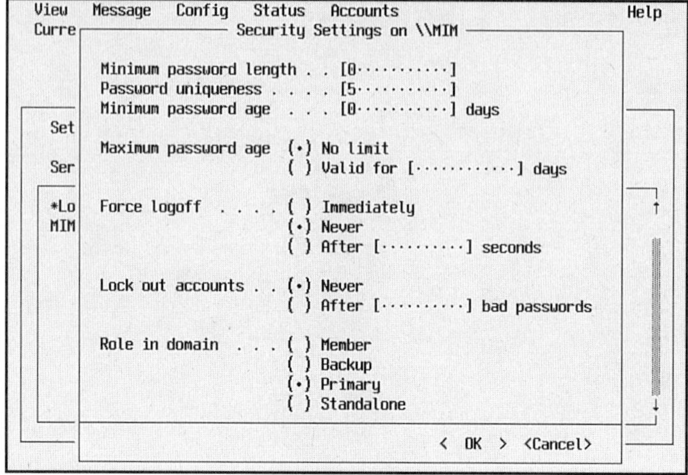

Figure 17.37. Setting the server security parameters.

Novell NetWare Requester for OS/2

Novell NetWare is the most popular server operating system on the market. For OS/2 to be successful in corporate environments, strong NetWare support is essential. Novell delivered a reasonable Requester for OS/2 1.x. The 2.0 version with interesting new features was released several months after OS/2 2.0. There is some support for the Workplace Shell and good DOS session management. Named pipe server capability is important in OS/2-bound client/server products like Microsoft SQL Server and Lotus Notes. This is still improving but far from perfect. Several patches are posted on CompuServe (NetWire) to handle these deficiencies.

Graphical Installation

The graphical Requester installation program copies the necessary files and creates a Novell folder on the desktop. The single disk is shown in Figure 17.38.

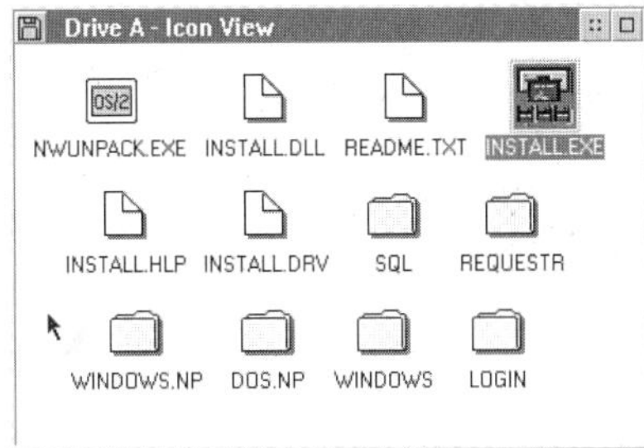

Figure 17.38. NetWare Requester installation disk.

The INSTALL.EXE program contains drop menus to install and later reconfigure the Requester. Figure 17.39 shown the base installation window.

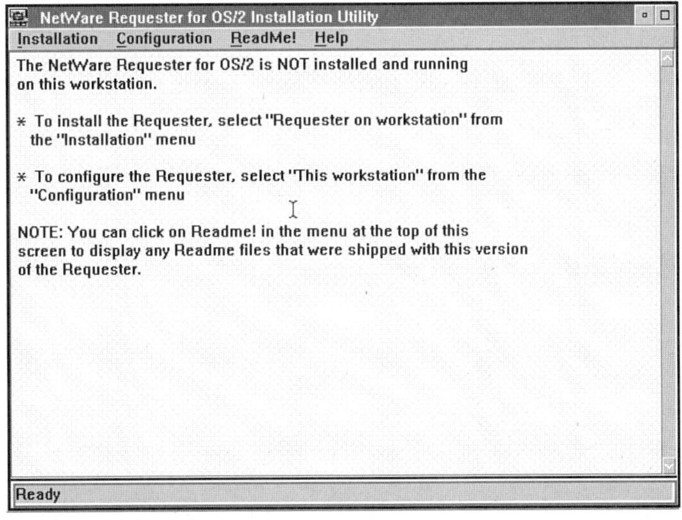

Figure 17.39. The main installation screen.

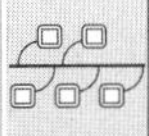

The ReadMe! option in Figure 17.40 scrolls the latest text information on the disk. This is recommended reading because it contains significant details on adapter and protocol support.

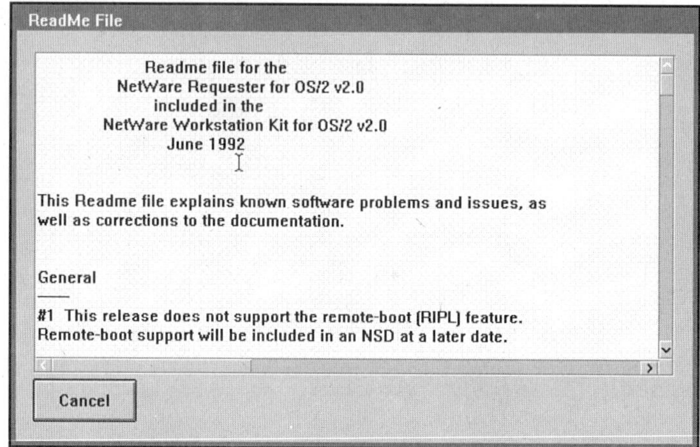

Figure 17.40. Installation ReadMe utility.

The \NETWARE directory stores all of the installed files including drivers, dynamic link libraries, utilities, and configuration files. In contrast to LAN Server, the primary network utilities are installed on a shared directory on the server instead of each workstation. An option is provided in the install program to do this, but you must first log in to the target server. This saves disk space and is easier to upgrade on a large LAN. These files are stored in \PUBLIC\OS2, \SYSTEM\OS2, and \LOGIN\OS2.

The CONFIG.SYS file `PATH` statement is modified and the following lines are added:

```
REM — NetWare Requester statements BEGIN —
DEVICE=C:\NETWARE\LSL.SYS
RUN=C:\NETWARE\DDAEMON.EXE
DEVICE=C:\NETWARE\TOKEN.SYS
rem DEVICE=C:\NETWARE\ROUTE.SYS
DEVICE=C:\NETWARE\IPX.SYS
DEVICE=C:\NETWARE\SPX.SYS
RUN=C:\NETWARE\SPDAEMON.EXE
rem DEVICE=C:\NETWARE\NMPIPE.SYS
rem DEVICE=C:\NETWARE\NPSERVER.SYS
```

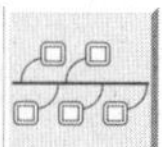

```
rem RUN=C:\NETWARE\NPDAEMON.EXE NP_COMPUTERNAME
DEVICE=C:\NETWARE\NWREQ.SYS
IFS=C:\NETWARE\NWIFS.IFS
RUN=C:\NETWARE\NWDAEMON.EXE
rem DEVICE=C:\NETWARE\NETBIOS.SYS
rem RUN=C:\NETWARE\NBDAEMON.EXE
DEVICE=C:\NETWARE\VIPX.SYS
DEVICE=C:\NETWARE\VSHELL.SYS
REM — NetWare Requester statements END —
```

Several drivers and daemon processes are loaded. Special features like named pipes and source routing are included as comment lines. The manual instructs you to edit these lines to add the desired functionality.

The NMPIPE and NPSERVER drivers and the NPDAEMON program provide server side named pipes for products like Microsoft SQL Server. Replace the NP_COMPUTERNAME token with the desired database server name.

The install Configure option creates a file called NET.CFG in the \NETWARE directory. This file is optional and contains parameters similar to those in IBMLAN.INI and PROTOCOL.INI. Figure17.41 shows the install edit utility for NET.CFG. (The section is displayed in outline format on the left with descriptions and examples on the bottom. Any entries are recorded in the list box on the right.) The NET.CFG file can also be edited by hand.

Once installation is complete, reboot the system to load the drivers. Each driver posts a status message in colors, which is both helpful and amusing.

Operating the Requester

The Novell folder shown in Figure17.42 installs on the Workplace Shell. There are three utilities provided including installation, remote printing, and NetWare Tools.

The Tools object is most important and acts as a control center for most network activities including log in and log out. Drive mappings, printer

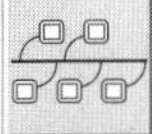

redirection, server status, user lists, and other options are presented in a windowed interface. Figure 17.43 shows five windows open on one server.

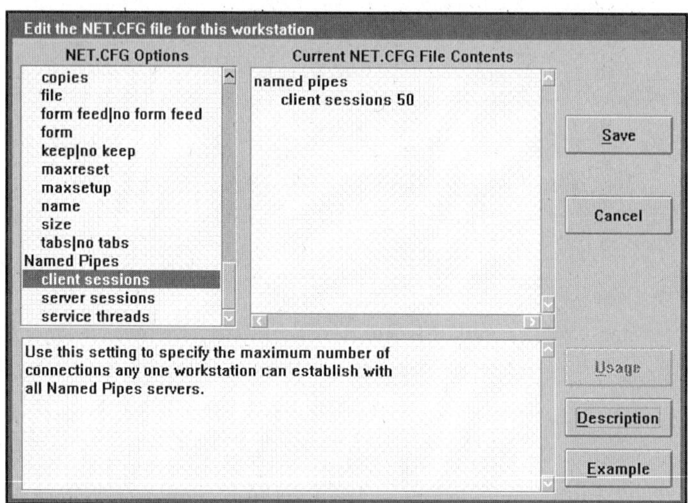

Figure 17.41. Editing the NET.CFG file.

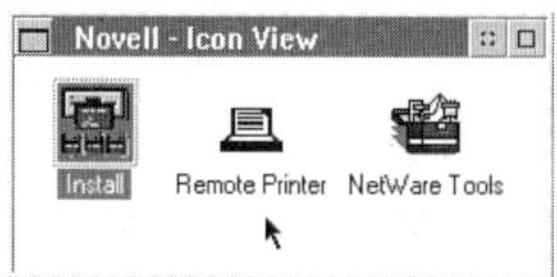

Figure 17.42. The NetWare Requester tools folder.

Dialogs are provided for most NetWare utilities like Capture. Figure 17.44 sets the printer port to a file server print queue. This does not integrate as well as the LAN Server pop-up menus and Workplace objects, but at least it is graphical.

You can also use the familiar command-line utilities in NetWare. Most administrative tasks, like SYSCON shown in Figure 17.45, use a point-and-shoot character interface that works in a windowed or full-screen session. These utilities lack mouse support but are well known to network support personnel.

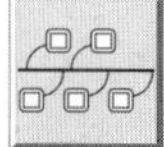

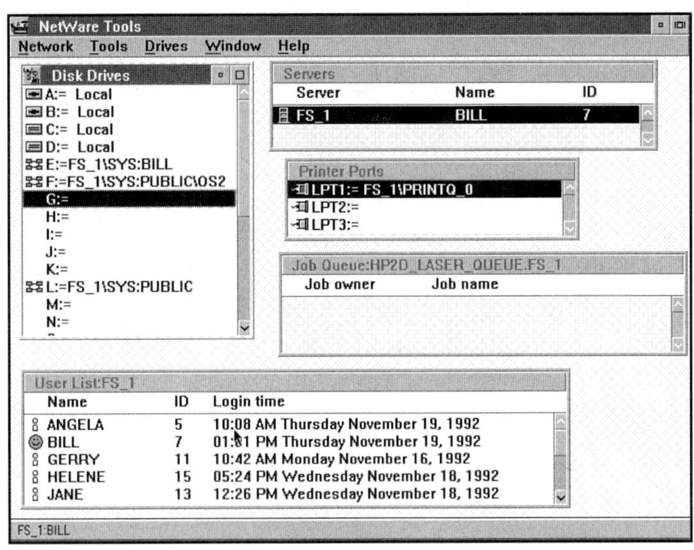

Figure 17.43. NetWare tools with several open windows.

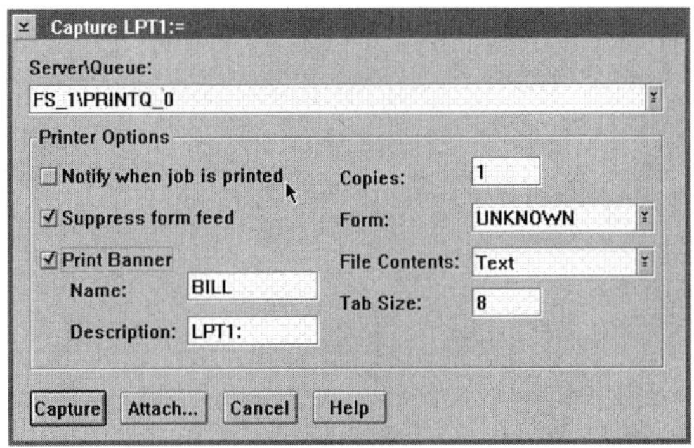

Figure 17.44. Setting the print destination with Capture.

NetWare has its own help system. There are no OS/2 message or reference files. Table 17.7 lists some common NetWare utilities.

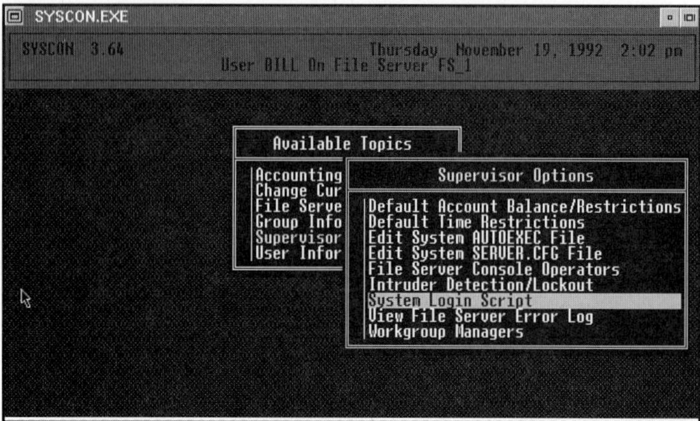

Figure 17.45. Managing a server with SYSCON.

Table 17.7. NetWare Utilities

CAPTURE	Traps printer data for a network queue
CASTOFF	Refuses display of network messages
CASTON	Allows display of network messages
CHKVOL	Checks the size and space on a disk volume
DSPACE	Shows available disk space
ENDCAP	Ends a print capture and returns to local mode
FILER	File management utility
FLAG	Flags a file or directory with user rights
FLAGDIR	Flags a directory with user rights
GRANT	Grants user trustee rights
LISTDIR	Expanded network directory list
LOGIN	Logs in to an attached server
LOGOUT	Logs off from a server session

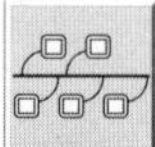

MAKEUSER	Makes a user account from a template
MAP	Assigns drive letters to shared resources
NCOPY	Copies files directly on the server
NDIR	Expanded network directory listing
NPRINT	Prints files to a network printer
NVER	Network version levels
PCONSOLE	Manages printer queue
PRINTCON	Prints console
PRINTDEF	Defines printers
PURGE	Completely removes deleted files
REVOKE	Revokes user trustee rights
RIGHTS	Displays active trustee rights
RPRINTER	Sets up and runs a remote printer
SALVAGE	Salvage deleted files
SEND	Sends a message
SETPASS	Sets password
SETTTS	Sets up a transaction tracking system
SYSCON	System console, setup accounts, setup scripts
SYSTIME	Sets the workstation time/date from the server
TLIST	Lists trustee rights per file
USERDEF	Defines user accounts for supervisors
USERLIST	List of active users
VERSION	A particular version
VOLINFO	Monitors disk activity and available space
WHOAMI	Information on user name and connection time

OS/2 versions of the NetWare utilities are included. Be sure these are in your path (not their DOS counterparts). Both have the same names and reside on the same server!

Permissions for shared resources are set by the supervisor with the SYSCON utility. Log-in scripts are used to establish connections are log-in time. These are also managed by SYSCON.

The RPRINTER utility is used to set up a remote print server. This is popular on NetWare DOS workstations and works more efficiently with multitasking OS/2. The NetWare folder has an object for RPRINTER. Run the program to configure the attached printers. Drag this object to the Startup folder to start the print server automatically.

DOS Sessions

Novell put extra effort into DOS session management. There are five basic methods: global log in, private log in, IPX only, single session, and boot image. Each has merits depending on the intended use.

All DOS, Windows, and OS/2 sessions set up for global log in share a single log-in connection. Drives mapped in one session appear in all others. In contrast to LAN Server, the mapping and printer redirection works from DOS and OS/2 sessions. This minimizes the number of server connections on a busy LAN. Set the `NETWARE_RESOURCES` option in the DOS settings page of the session to Global.

Private log in sets the `NETWARE_RESOURCES` option to Private. In this case, NETX.COM must be loaded and each session must log in separately. Connections made in one session do not effect others. This method is preferred for certain DOS applications that require specific mappings and port redirection. \OS2\MDOS\LPTDD.SYS also needs to be loaded if you want to use CAPTURE in a Private DOS session.

Private and Global sessions can be mixed on one system. Just make separate DOS session objects with different settings. There is a third setting on

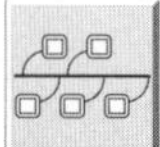

NETWARE_RESOURCES called None. This disables log in but provides support for applications that directly use SPX and IPX for network communications.

Setting NETWARE_RESOURCES to None and VIPX_ENABLED to Off disables all network support. Use this for local DOS sessions.

Novell includes utilities for DOS named pipe clients and full WINOS2 support. These items were overlooked by LAN Server and LAN Manager. There is also a NETBIOS TSR for that popular network protocol.

The single session method uses the DOS_DEVICE feature of MVDM shown in Figure 17.46. LAN device drivers are loaded directly in a DOS session. IPX and NETX are run to attach to a file server. Log in is for that session only.

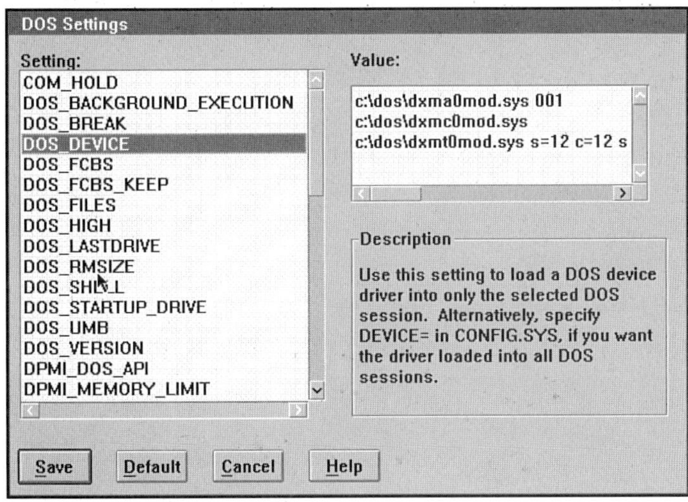

Figure 17.46. Setting the DOS device parameters.

The boot image approach is similar to this. A DOS boot floppy is prepared with the necessary adapter drivers, IPX, and NETX. The OS/2 boot image utility builds a file with this information. This file is specified as the boot device. Log in is restricted to that session only. Figure 17.47 shows a successful

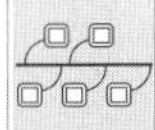

single session log in. Any DOS application or network utility can be run from that point.

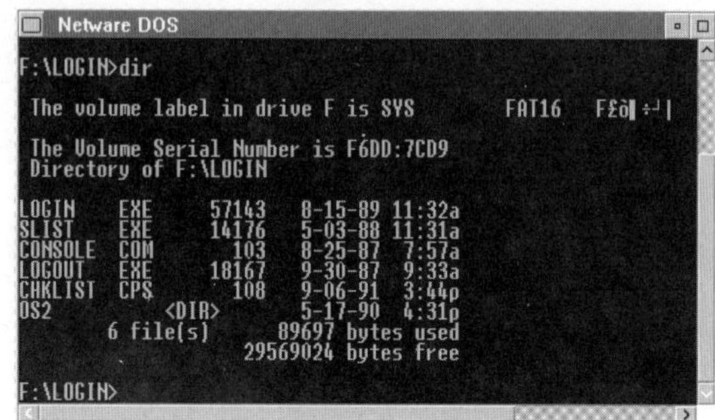

Figure 17.47. NetWare DOS log in in a private session.

Author Bio

Bill Wolff is founder and president of Wolff Data Systems, a client/server database consulting firm in the Delaware Valley. His development and training focus primarily on OS/2 LANs and database servers. Wolff is Vice President of the Delaware Valley SQL Server Users Group.

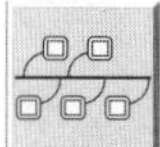

18

Multimedia

In This Chapter

Because the OS/2 operating system is able to coordinate many things simultaneously, it may just be the best platform for PC multimedia. However, OS/2 seems to have entered the multimedia game late; few products are available that actually utilize the vast capability of OS/2. That could change rather quickly, however, as IBM releases development tools, along with the release of OS/2 2.1 that includes the Windows 3.1 multimedia capability.

What Is Multimedia?

Multimedia is a term that often confuses both experienced and novice computer users. Some consider anything available on CD-ROM as multimedia, and others define not the storage medium, but the presentation technology. Especially with OS/2, what is sold to the consumer as "multimedia" is typically raw hardware. In other cases, games with sound and graphics are considered to be multimedia.

CD-ROM

CD-ROM is merely a software distribution media, and this in itself does not guarantee multimedia. However, it is an important enabling technology for multimedia. To be more specific, it is important to understand that digitized audio and video consume a tremendous amount of computer storage. A 70-minute musical compact disc (CD) holds the equivalent of more than 600M of uncompressed computer data. Video data is even worse—600M holds a few minutes worth of uncompressed television-quality video. Now you know why those video laser discs are so much larger than CDs.

CD-ROM is quickly gaining importance in the computer industry. CD-ROM is becoming a popular medium for large software products, including OS/2 2.1 development tools. CD-ROM, in the form of the Kodak Photo-CD, is also gaining a lot of consumer interest. Kodak's Photo-CD format allows more than one hundred high-quality photograph scans to be placed on a single disc. These discs can be attached to special players and viewed on a color

television. CD-ROM XA-compatible drives, however, can import these pictures into computer applications.

Audio and Sound Effects

Some consider programs that present visual and sound information at the same time as multimedia. Using this definition, almost any game would be classified as multimedia. Technically this is true, as more than one form of media (presentation) is being used. However, defining what makes a game "multimedia" is truly a gray area; usually, games that use speech and extensive high-quality animation are considered multimedia.

Figure 18.1. *King's Quest V.*

Figure 18.1 shows Sierra's King's Quest V CD-ROM game. The CD-ROM version of this game includes digitized speech. The characters actually move their mouths in sync with the speech. This disc contains more than 115 megabytes of game and sound data.

With business applications, voice annotation tends to make a program multimedia. Many Windows programs (and hopefully soon, OS/2 programs) now support "voice notes" that you can attach to a document. Lotus actually ships a version of 1-2-3 for Windows on CD-ROM with support for this type of activity. Wavefrom audio (WAVE) files have also become a common way to make everyday computer work a bit more entertaining. Even screen savers such as After Dark for Windows support audio!

Animation and Graphics

Graphic animation is another area that relates to multimedia. Video capture and playback, graphic animation, and presentation programs are all examples of computer-controlled visual presentation aspects. Video animation typically comes in two forms: software-based and hardware-based animation. Later in this chapter, the IBM ActionMedia II hardware board is outlined. As it stands now, it is not possible to import and export video data as easily as text or graphics. Although there are currently no well-established standards for software-only video presentations, IBM is working on such a solution.

Overall

Multimedia can be defined to mean programs that use nontraditional ways of communication. In some cases, this may mean using sounds. In the past, most sounds on a personal computer were used for entertainment. Now sounds can be used to add voice notes to spreadsheets and word-processing documents. Even with business applications, much of the multimedia sounds are intended for entertainment purposes.

In other instances, these nontraditional ways of communicating employ graphics. Consider that graphics are already used to express ideas in OS/2—you may or may not consider this multimedia. What if the graphics are animated or fluid-motion like television? The hardware technology is heading in this direction, as is OS/2.

As this fledgling technology matures, multimedia will come to mean all of these things combined. Programs that employ sound and animation (such as video) and control will be truly interactive multimedia. Some of this, however, is available today, and OS/2 can tap these products.

OS/2 as a Multimedia Platform

OS/2 has several strengths relative to multimedia development and usage:

- Preemptive multitasking allows multiple methods of output, such as sound and video at the same time (it also simplifies design issues for developers wanting to create such applications).
- OS/2 can prioritize multitasking for time-critical activities such as video and audio capture.
- Large memory resources can handle the huge data sets commonly associated with digital sound and video.
- Graphical interface can facilitate user-friendly interfaces using sliders, knobs, and pushbuttons.
- Well-developed programming interfaces standardize development of all aspects of multimedia software.
- Support for existing DOS and Windows multimedia products.

These are part of the reason that IBM has selected OS/2 as its premier Multimedia platform. IBM refers to its Multimedia products as Ultimedia.

IBM Ultimedia

At this time, IBM's Ultimedia products are the best-supported hardware devices under OS/2. Hopefully this will change as OS/2 gains more popularity. IBM's Ultimedia product line is quite extensive, including several PS/2 machines that carry the Ultimedia name. The PS/2 Ultimedia workstations

include XGA graphics capability, an internal CD-ROM drive, an M-Audio Capture and Playback adapter, and a high-speed SCSI controller (used for CD-ROM and fixed disks). These PS/2 Ultimedia systems represent the best of IBM's "ready-to-run" multimedia workstations.

As well integrated as the Ultimedia workstations are, they may not be for everyone. In respect to multimedia, IBM does not intend to leave previous computer owners in the past. It is important to understand that IBM has gone to considerable lengths to ensure that much of this technology is available in stand-alone cards and modules. In fact, IBM has done quite well in support of ISA systems. Obviously IBM would rather have you use their own PS/2 systems, but they will support you as an equal using competitors' systems. The OS/2 operating system is another good example of this type of previously unprecedented IBM support.

The following list contains a summary of OS/2-supported IBM Ultimedia hardware devices:

PS/2 TV: an external device that enables you to receive and display television channels on your VGA or XGA monitor. PS/2 TV allows "picture-in-a-picture" viewing of video source on VGA and full-screen viewing on VGA and XGA. This unit has a built-in 181-channel cable-ready TV tuner, and it also supports base-band signals (VCR, video camera, laser disk, game machine, and so on). Although it is external, and can function with any system using VGA or XGA, it does interface with and requires a PS/2-style keyboard. The hardware operates independently of the computer, requiring no CPU attention. The device does not support any type of computer video capturing.

ActionMedia II Display Adapter: an ISA or Microchannel board for complete digital video and sound. This device includes a SCSI interface for a CD-ROM drive. Intel/IBM developed Digital Video Interactive (DVI) standard playback (hardware-assisted compression and playback). It can playback pictures and digital audio simultaneously (30 frames per second, television quality). It includes a direct interface for base-band and S-VHS.

ActionMedia II capture option: this can be added to the base board for capture purposes, and it supports real-time motion capture and super-quality, 24-bit, single-frame snapshots.

M-Audio Capture and Playback adapter: an ISA or Microchannel board for capture and playback of digital audio with 8- or 16-bit sampling.

8516 Touch Display: IBM's XGA-class monitor designed for touch-based control. IBM has drivers available for both OS/2 and Windows environments. This can be used in place of a mouse.

As mentioned, some of the PS/2 Ultimedia models ship with these options or they can be installed in other ISA or PS/2 machines. OS/2 currently supports all of these multimedia devices, along with some third-party boards such as the Creative Labs Sound Blaster and Sound Blaster Pro.

OS/2 Support for Multimedia Devices

There are two ways of approaching the question of what devices are supported under OS/2: the base operating system includes support for SCSI-based CD-ROM drives; and individual device drivers are available for specific devices. Some of these devices are intended to interface with the MultiMedia Presentation Manager/2 (MMPM/2) package that IBM offers.

Base OS/2 CD-ROM Support

If you have a SCSI CD-ROM drive that is usable under OS/2 2.1, you can run existing DOS and Windows Multimedia products such as Compton's MultiMedia Encyclopedia for Windows. Using third-party programs or MMPM/2 you can play CD-Audio (music discs) on CD-ROM drives. With the release of OS/2 2.1, almost all SCSI CD-ROM drives will enjoy native support, including CD-Audio.

Even with the improved support of OS/2 2.1, few non-SCSI CD-ROM drives will have native support. For nonsupported CD-ROM drives, it is possible to use DOS drivers under OS/2 to create a single session capable of running DOS or Windows multimedia programs. This is outlined later in this chapter.

Windows 3.1 Multimedia

OS/2 2.1 includes support for Windows 3.1 applications. This subsystem, WIN-OS/2, includes the WAV and musical instrument digital interface (MIDI) support that is now included with Windows 3.1. Several programs are already available to take advantage of this capability, including ones you might not normally expect. Lotus offers 1-2-3 for Windows Version 1.1 on CD-ROM that includes a multimedia tutorial called SmartHelp.

Any WAVE and MIDI files designed for Windows 3.1 should work fine under OS/2 MMPM/2. However, Windows 3.1 multimedia applications do not require the MMPM/2 because the Windows 3.1 subsystem includes a self-contained multimedia capability.

Multimedia Sampler

To date, most of the multimedia attention has been placed on CD-ROM titles. As mentioned earlier, a CD-ROM does not necessarily ensure that a product is truly multimedia. The following sections review just a few of the many CD-ROMs that are truly multimedia.

Compton's MultiMedia Encyclopedia

Compton's MultiMedia Encyclopedia for Windows is perhaps one of the best examples of CD-ROM-based multimedia. Not only does it contain text for an entire encyclopedia, it also contains several still pictures, animation, and sound. The mass-storage strengths of CD-ROM shine in this data-intensive application, which includes the following features:

- sound samples of famous speeches such as Martin Luther King's "I Have a Dream" speech
- graphics snapshots of items described in the text (sample X-rays in the medical section, for example)
- charts and graphs representing statistical data
- maps

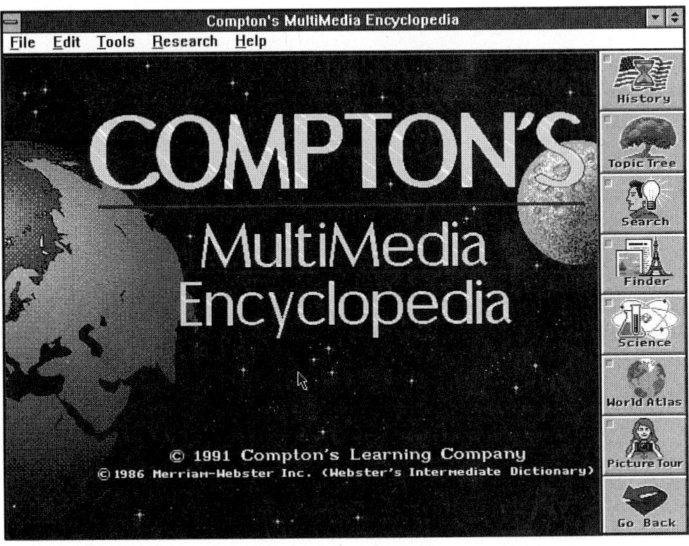

Figure 18.2. Compton's MultiMedia Encyclopedia.

Obviously the uses of multimedia for an encyclopedia are almost endless. Compton's is quite impressive but is just a sample of what will be available in the future. CD-ROM enables inexpensive duplication of the hundreds of megabytes required to store the large data sets for sound and graphics, let alone an entire encyclopedia!

The graphical nature of Compton's MultiMedia Encyclopedia also helps in the location of information. Instead of traditional text-based searches, Compton's supports a graphics history line, among other organizations. See Figure 18.3 for an example of this search method.

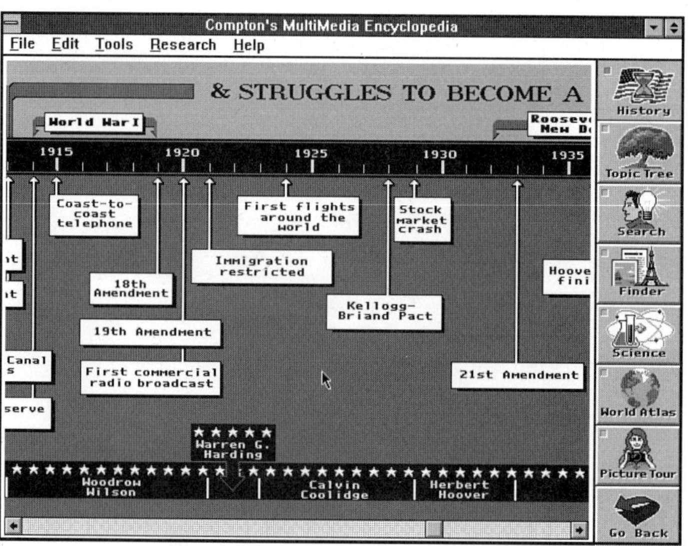

Figure 18.3. Compton's time line search.

Text from within the encyclopedia can be cut and pasted into other OS/2 or Windows programs. Figure 18.4 shows a portion of the text on "Radio," including icons used to display pictures. You should also note the "see Television 'Technology'" and its associated icon (to jump to that location in the encyclopedia).

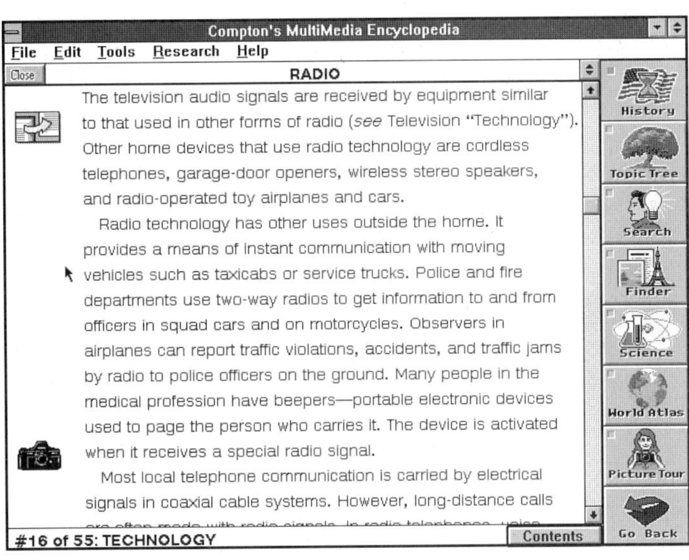

Figure 18.4. Compton's text sample.

National Geographic Multimedia Mammals

This disc is sort of a specialty encyclopedia. It serves as a good multimedia sampler (it makes extensive use of software-based video motion and CD-Audio playback). The software-based animation, which requires no special playback hardware, is quite impressive. Figure 18.5 shows the opening screen for the Mammals program.

Figure 18.5. National Geographic's Mammals.

The disc also features captured photographs of mammals, typically five or more for each mammal. The photographs are full-screen at 320x200x8 (x8 equals 256 colors) resolution. A simple identification game is also included in this package.

TIP

Compton's MultiMedia Encyclopedia for Windows does not include a print option. To print from this program, copy the current text or screen image to the clipboard and then copy it to another program to print. This method can also be used to transfer encyclopedia contents to your Windows or OS/2 word processor.

MMPM/2 in Detail

Multimedia Presentation Manager/2 (MMPM/2) is an add-on to the base OS/2 operating system that provides facilities for sound and video support. MMPM/2 has a fully graphical installation program, and it enables you to customize the installation to your specific needs. Figure 18.6 shows the installation program (you can select or unselect each individual module from the list).

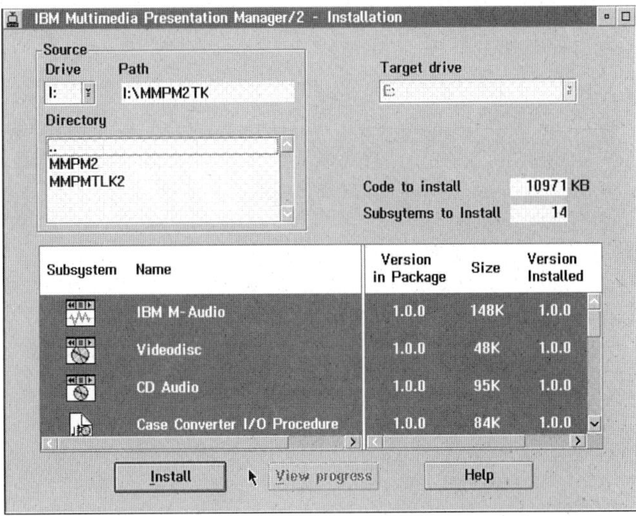

Figure 18.6. The MMPM/2 - Installation screen.

Sound Support

The base MMPM/2 product includes support for two types of sound:

- WAV: digital audio files (in the same format as Microsoft Windows)
- MIDI: synthesized audio files

MMPM/2 includes a recorder and playback module for WAV and MIDI files. See Figure 18.7 for a view of the record and playback module. IBM has made the multimedia relatively device-independent; the same media player is used to control WAV, MIDI, and ActionMedia II video. With respect to sound, MMPM/2 currently has drivers for the IBM M-Audio adapter, Creative Labs Sound Blaster, Creative Labs Sound Blaster Pro, and the MediaVision Pro AudioSpectrum.

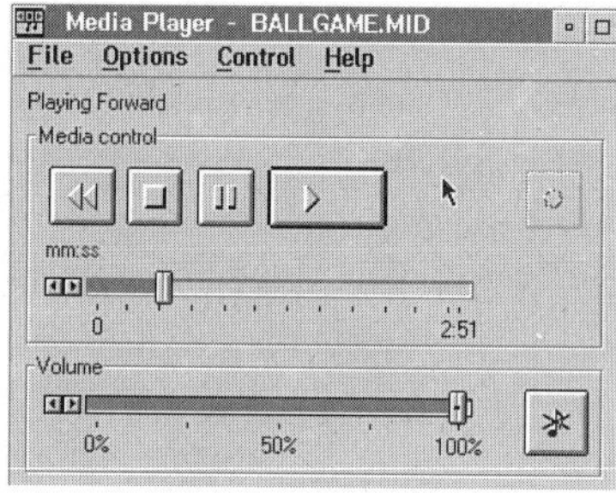

Figure 18.7. The Media Player for MIDI.

Using Creative Labs Sound Blaster Pro, I recorded 60 seconds of music using the MMPM/2 Digital Audio Recorder. It was quite impressive to use two modems (both active at 14,400bps) and sample sound through a microphone at the same time. Using Pulse, OS/2 showed less than 30 percent CPU utilization on a 80486DX-33 ISA system. Uncompressed digital audio takes a considerable amount of storage—the 60-second sample took 1.3M of disk space.

CD-Audio Support

OS/2 Multimedia Presentation Manager/2 includes a program to play CD music (CD-Audio in computer terms) discs. IBM also offers an employee-written multimedia explorer program that achieves the same results. This explorer program is distributed under the EWS (employee-written software) program; it is available on the OS/2 Professional Developers Kit CD-ROM, along with several OS/2 BBS systems and CompuServe.

MM

Video Playback/Capture

IBM's all-digital ActionMedia II adapter is nothing less than state-of-the-art, hardware-based video playback. The quality of the captured images is superb—it's equal to live television. Given the powerful digital video interactive (DVI) hardware compression, a normal fixed disk (or even a slower optical disk) can keep up with a 30-frame-per-second (fps) video signal. Even with extensive hardware compression, a 60-second video session took 9.3M of disks space.

IBM has OS/2 drivers for this SCSI port, and it achieves the same thing as any OS/2-supported SCSI adapter. When using this port and the appropriate drivers, your SCSI CD-ROM functions as a native OS/2 device—accessible to all program sessions.

The ActionMedia II base board has only playback capability; you must add a capture board for authoring. This board is capable of capturing and playing both digital video and audio at the same time.

Creative Labs, perhaps the leader in low-cost multimedia products, has released a still-frame ISA video capture and windowing board: the Video Blaster. Although it does not allow motion video capture or sport the quality of the ActionMedia II, it is less than one third of the price. Be careful when considering this board, however, as it does not currently function under OS/2 (including WIN-OS/2). The current ISA version of the board is also designed to work with systems with less than 15M of RAM; OS/2 users often have 16M or more. If you had 16M or more of system RAM, you would actually have to remove some to utilize the board. As an OS/2 user, it may be best to look at other boards or contact Creative Labs for information on future boards with better OS/2 support. In any case, always research your needs carefully before assuming that a board is supported by the software you intend to use.

Computer-Controlled Laser Disc

OS/2's Multimedia Presentation Manager/2 includes drivers necessary to control the video display of a Pioneer video disk player. One of your system's serial ports is used to synchronize actual video presentations with user commands and computer information. The video disk player is controlled through a serial port.

Installation of MMPM/2

IBM's MMPM/2 product is quite easy to install (see Chapter 1, "Installation," for specific installation details). First, you want to be sure you have a supported device that is properly configured. The following sections summarize the requirements for some of the devices.

IBM M-Audio

This is a sound board accessible through the MMPM/2 WAV and MIDI players. Drivers for this device ship with MMPM/2, and hardware configuration is accomplished with the reference disk included with the hardware.

Pioneer Video Disk

MMPM/2 has the ability to control the operations of a video disk player; in most cases, this is used to play video in sequence with computer events (such as a menu selection). The video itself is processed within the video disk player; the computer is merely instructing the player which tracks to access and when to play and stop. This control is accomplished through a serial port, which is required for the player to be used with MMPM/2.

CD-Audio

MMPM/2's CD-Audio player utilizes the SCSI command sequences to control the CD-Audio. OS/2 2.1 includes drivers capable of controlling these

functions. The CD-Audio player works by instructing the CD-ROM drive to play an audio disk at the specified track. Fundamentally, all of the sound processing is performed by the CD-ROM, which is almost identical to a traditional non-computer CD music player. With external CD-ROM drives, there are typical RCA-type phono jacks for connection to an amplifier. Both internal and external drives have an 1/8-inch audio adapter (identical to those found on hand-held portable radios) for a set of headphones or tabletop speakers. Unless your sound board has specific provisions, it may be important to note that CD-Audio is not played through your sound board; two sets of speakers or additional routing cables may be required. With the correct routing cables, some of the sound boards will play both types of sound through one set of speakers.

Sound Blaster/Sound Blaster Pro

Configuration of these boards is somewhat more complicated because you must know the IRQ and base address of your hardware adapter. Assuming you know these, the selection within MMPM/2 is quite simple because a list box is provided for each parameter. Typically, the Creative Labs sound boards come configured for IRQ 7 and base address 220. Once installed, these boards allow MMPM/2 to play MIDI and WAV files. Current releases of the drivers do not support external MIDI devices or MIDI recording. Checking with Creative Labs is advised to get the latest status on these features.

MediaVision Pro AudioSpectrum

Drivers for this device are included with OS/2 2.1 MMPM/2 to support its audio features. MediaVision has also made drivers available to control the Trantor-based SCSI function on the SCSI Pro AudioSpectrum boards. You install these as any other OS/2 SCSI driver, and they also support fixed disk and other supported SCSI devices. Some of the Pro Audiospectrum boards are based on a SonyBus CD-ROM interface, for which CD-ROM drivers do not yet exist.

When working with the Creative Labs Sound Blaster or MediaVision Pro Audiospectrum, especially the ISA versions, it is important to consider proper IRQ placement. For example, the Sound Blaster comes pre-configured for IRQ7, which is required under OS/2 to access the LPT1 printer port. IRQ5 is also supported, which is the LPT2 printer port; more likely, IRQ5 will be free on your system. The MediaVision Pro AudioSpectrum 16 requires two IRQs, one for the Sound Blaster compatibility (IRQ5 is the default), and a software-assignable IRQ for the advanced capability. One of the higher, typically unused, IRQs such as 10, 11, or 12 are recommended for this second IRQ. Parameters on the Pro AudioSpectrum device driver are used to assign this second IRQ.

Using Unsupported CD-ROM Drives

It might be possible to use an unsupported CD-ROM drive if the manufacturer supplies an OS/2 device driver. If that support is not available, you may still be able to use your CD-ROM drive in a VDM with the DOS device driver. Finally, you can create a DOS boot image that includes your CD-ROM device driver. See Chapter 8 for complete details. For a list of supported CD-ROM drives see Chapter 1.

Other SCSI CD-ROM Drives

It might be possible to use your non-supported SCSI CD-ROM under OS/2 if you are willing to experiment a little. You must have a SCSI host

adapter that has OS/2 devices drivers. Any SCSI controller that is forced to use the INT13 driver will not support a CD-ROM device under OS/2 2.1. See Chapter 1 for a list of supported SCSI controllers.

Drivers for Adaptec, DPT, Future Domain, and IBM are included with the OS/2 2.1 packagc (view the README file for installation instructions). Trantor drivers must be acquired from CompuServe or Trantor. Ultra store, Bustek, and other vendors have also started to distribute OS/2 SCSI drivers.

Is it possible to add a SCSI adapter to a system that already has an MFM, RLL, or IDE disk controller? Yes, it is possible. SCSI adapters are designed to coexist with your existing controller, and most also operate without one (assuming you have ALL-SCSI fixed disks).

Assuming that you have a supported disk controller, you must properly install and configure the device driver. This usually involves locating the appropriate driver file and adding a `BASEDEV` line to your CONFIG.SYS. If you are already using it to control a fixed disk, this step should have been completed for you.

If you are using your SCSI adapter to control your fixed disk, be sure that you are using the actual adapter device driver and not the INT13 device driver.

If you have just installed the SCSI adapter device driver, it is recommended that you reboot to ensure that it is properly configured. If it is installed correctly, your system should boot with no errors. However, if you encounter an error loading that particular device driver, your board is probably not properly configured.

With the board properly installed, you need to ensure that the base OS/2 2.1 SCSI drivers and CDROM.IFS file system are on your system. These files should be in your \OS2 system directory. If they are not, you can use the

selective install to ensure that they are properly installed. See Chapter 1 for information on installing CD-ROM support.

When you are sure you have CDROM.SYS and CDROM.IFS on your system, you need to verify that they are properly activated in your CONFIG.SYS file. The following lines need to appear in CONFIG.SYS:

```
IFS=D:\OS2\CDFS.IFS
BASEDEV=FD16-700.ADD
BASEDEV=OS2SCSI.DMD
DEVICE=D:\OS2\CDROM.SYS /N:4
DEVICE=D:\OS2\MDOS\VCDROM.SYS /I
```

1. `IFS=` installs the file system driver for CD-ROM devices. When your CONFIG.SYS is loaded, several information lines appear when this file is activated. You can place a `/Q` parameter after the line to eliminate this display.

2. `BASEDEV=FD16-700.ADD` is for a Future Domain 1670 SCSI host adapter. This may be different for your system, depending on the brand and model of SCSI adapter.

3. `BASEDEV=OS2SCSI.DMD` is activated to load the base SCSI support for OS/2.

4. The fourth line (with `CDROM.SYS`) actually initiates contact with the CD-ROM device. Using unsupported drives, this one presents the most problems.

5. The last line is used to load DOS virtual device support for the CD-ROM drive.

It is not likely that these lines will all appear in this same order (or in the same place). If your OS/2 is installed with a partition other than D:, you need to place the appropriate letter for the file references.

When using a non-supported CD-ROM device, the CDROM.SYS file usually reports that an "unsupported manufacture" is being used when booting the system. There are a couple of ways around this. There is an `/I` parameter that you can add to the CDROM.SYS device line instructing it to bypass some of the compatibility checks. However, most users have found that this still generates the same error.

Assuming that does not work, you should attempt to locate a (newer) version of the CDROM.SYS file that does not have the brand consistency check. If that is not possible, or if it fails to work, one last resort is to make a copy of the CDROM.SYS file and manually alter the contents with a binary file editor.

Unless you have tried this type of binary file editing before, it is not recommend that you attempt this. The instruction given here is merely a conceptual overview, and it is assumed that you are experienced with binary file editors.

To edit this binary file, you need to have experience with a sector editor, such as those included with Norton Utilities or PC Tools. It is also required that you run these programs on native DOS, not OS/2. Assuming that all other attempts have failed and you are working with a backup copy of the file, search the file for the string `TOSHIBA`. This can be replaced with the string that your CD-ROM manufacturer uses, such as `NEC`. It is important to pad any leftover characters with spaces so that previous letters do not remain. In the case of this example, the `TOSHIBA` should be changed to `NECHIBA` (you need to place spaces over `HIBA`).

If you get a patched version of the CDROM.SYS, you should be able to utilize your CD-ROM. If you are still unable to get access, check with your computer dealer, a local users group, or CompuServe users.

Even with successful access to unsupported SCSI CD-ROM drivers, it is possible that OS/2 CD-Audio support will not function. For OS/2's MMPM/2, there is no known workaround. For DOS programs, you may want to review the next section concerning MS-DOS drivers.

Using DOS CD-ROM Drivers

There are certain CD-ROM drives that do not adhere to the SCSI hardware interface, and they require a special interface board. In most cases, the vendors do not yet support OS/2. However, it might be possible that you can access a non-supported CD-ROM using OS/2's capability to run DOS programs—assuming that you have a CD-ROM drive configured and properly functioning under native DOS. If this is the case, it may be possible to access your CD-ROM under a single OS/2 DOS session, which enables you to run DOS and WIN-OS/2 programs.

The easiest way to experiment with this capability is to set up a DOS disk for your A: drive. To keep space available, it is recommend that you put the minimal complement of DOS files on this disk (hidden system files, and COMMAND.COM). It is also recommended that you start with a simple CONFIG.SYS as follows:

The following example uses the DOS driver for the Future Domain controller and MSCDEX drivers. Both are supported by OS/2 2.1; however, if you have a non-supported CD-ROM drive or an older version of MSCDEX, this example provides a model that may be helpful.

```
FILES=50
BUFFERS=16
LASTDRIVE=Z
```

```
DEVICE=A:\FDCD.SYS /D:MSCD000
DEVICE=A:\FSFILTER.SYS
DEVICE=A:\HIMEM.SYS
```

It is important to understand that many of OS/2's DOS settings are not available when you boot a special DOS kernel. Examples include the `DEVICE`, `BUFFERS`, and `FILES` lines—these need to be put in the actual CONFIG.SYS on drive A. However, other parameters such as the amount of DPMI and XMS memory are important.

> `FILES=50`: this line configures the DOS session for the appropriate number of files. As with a standard DOS 5.0 system, be sure you have enough to run Windows.
>
> `BUFFERS=16`: internal file buffers for the DOS session (identical function as to the value under DOS 5.0).
>
> `LASTDRIVE=Z`: this line is used to ensure that all letters are available to the CD-ROM. The MSCDEX.EXE program (in the following AUTOEXEC.BAT) is used to specify to which drive letter the CD-ROM is assigned.
>
> `DEVICE=FDCD.SYS`: this line is the Future Domain SCSI CD-ROM driver. You need to install the appropriate DOS CD-ROM driver for your controller.
>
> `DEVICE=FSFILTER.SYS`: the file FSFILTER.SYS is provided with OS/2 2.1, resides in the \OS2\MDOS subdirectory, and should be copied to your A: disk. This file allows the DOS 5.0 session to fully access OS/2 partitions when running under OS/2.
>
> `DEVICE=HIMEM.SYS`: this is the HIMEM.SYS file taken from OS/2 2.1, and it resides in the \OS2\MDOS subdirectory. This gives the DOS 5.0 session access to OS/2-provided XMS memory.

TIP The FSFILTER.SYS and HIMEM.SYS files must be from the \OS2\MDOS directory, otherwise the bootable DOS image might not work.

You now need to configure an appropriate AUTOEXEC.BAT for this DOS session:

```
SET PROMPT=$p$g
SET PATH=A:\;
A:\MOUSE.COM
A:\DOSKEY.COM
A:\MSCDEX.EXE /D:MSCD000 /M:10 /L:G
```

As you can see, the AUTOEXEC.BAT has nothing different than what regular DOS 5.0 requires. `MOUSE.COM` should be the one taken from the \OS2\MDOS directory; using a DOS version of the mouse driver may render your mouse unusable under your OS/2 sessions.

You may notice that DOS 5.0 SETVER.EXE was not included in the CONFIG.SYS. This was not required for the test machine, as the latest version of MSCDEX.EXE, v2.21, does not require that SETVER command for compatibility with DOS 5.0. Older versions of MSCDEX may require you to use DOS 5.0 SETVER. The newest MSCDEX should be available from your dealer, Microsoft, or CompuServe.

Now that you have your floppy disk properly configured, you can select the "DOS from Drive A:" option on the Command Prompts folder. This initiates the loading of this DOS 5.0 session from your newly configured floppy disk. During troubleshooting, you may want to make a copy of this program reference (the "DOS from Drive A:"), and change it to run in a window.

A booted DOS session can not be exited in the normal manner. You must switch to the Window List and close it. IBM produces a tiny program that you can run to self-terminate the session (such as EXIT would in a normal OS/2 DOS session).

TIP

If you find that you frequently use a DOS 5.0 boot session, you may want to configure your C: partition for FAT and DOS 5.0. This assumes that you use the Boot Manager. If you configure it this way, you can tell OS/2 to boot this DOS session from the C: partition instead of from an image file or a floppy disk. This is the quickest method of booting, and it allows the most flexibility.

NOTE

Even if you have a SCSI CD-ROM that is mounted as a native OS/2 device (available to all sessions), you may find that certain DOS programs require the actual MSCDEX to be loaded. Even when OS/2 is talking to the SCSI controller, the DOS boot session may still work! In fact, at least with some controllers, OS/2 allows both the OS/2 and DOS device drivers to control the SCSI card. (This has been tested on a Future Domain controller.) Obviously, care should be taken. It is advised that this not be attempted on a SCSI controller that is also controlling writable storage devices—data corruption may occur. This method can also be used to gain CD-Audio capability for DOS and WIN-OS/2 programs.

Figure 18.8 shows a DOS 5.0 windowed session, with CD-ROM drivers loaded, booted from the C: partition. Note that CONFIG.SYS and AUTOEXEC.BAT contain additional entries not necessarily shown in the preceding listing. It is possible to start WIN-OS/2 by issuing the command `WINOS2`. This requires that the DOS 5.0 session path be properly configured to point to the WIN-OS/2 directory. Starting WIN-OS/2 allows you to run Windows-based multimedia programs. To run WIN-OS/2 on top of this session, it is recommended that you switch it to a full-screen mode.

MM

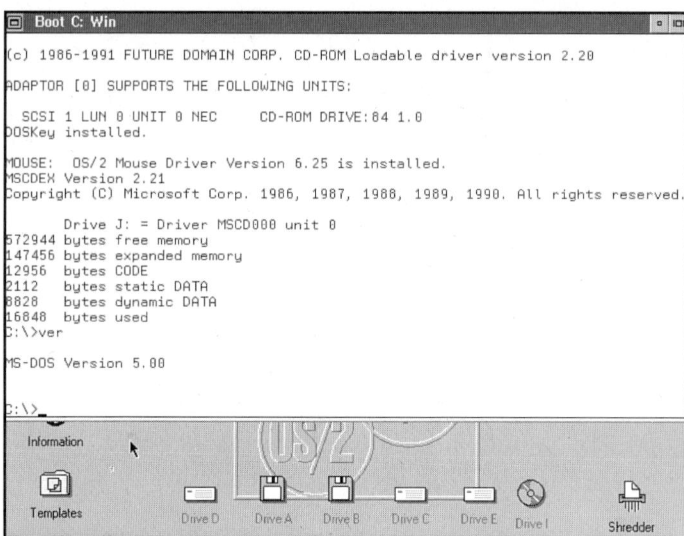

Figure 18.8. A DOS 5.0 session with CD-ROM.

Managing DOS Configuration

You may find that you have a number of DOS programs that require drivers for a sound board or CD-ROM. Although DOS sessions can use the same AUTOEXEC.BAT file, the CONFIG.SYS portion is unique for each program reference. Particularly when you want to set up multiple programs, or for multiple systems, you may wish to use REXX calls to create program references (menu icons). For example, the following REXX program creates a program reference for DOS game Wing Commander:

```
/*Wing Commander Test*/
/*Create program reference on OS/2 Workplace Shell*/

Call RxFuncAdd 'SysLoadFuncs','REXXUTIL','SysLoadFuncs';
Call SysLoadFuncs;
```

```
reply='UpdateIfExists'
rc=SysCreateObject('WPProgram','Wing Commander','<WP_DOSGROUP>',,
  'EXENAME=C:\WING\WC.BAT;'¦¦,
  'PROGTYPE=VDM;'¦¦,
  'STARTUPDIR=E:\WING;'¦¦,
  'SET DOS_FILES=40;'¦¦,
  'SET DOS_BREAK=1;'¦¦,
  'SET DOS_HIGH=1;'¦¦,
  'SET DOS_DEVICE=c:\proaudio\mvsound.sys d:7 q:15 j:0;'¦¦,
  'SET INT_DURING_IO=1;'¦¦,
  'SET DOS_BACKGROUND_EXECUTION=0;'¦¦,
  'SET HW_TIMER=1;'¦¦,
  'SET IDLE_SENSITIVITY=100;'¦¦,
  'SET KBD_BUFFER_EXTEND=0;'¦¦,
  'SET KBD_ALTHOME_BYPASS=1;'¦¦,
  '', reply);

If rc<>1 Then
   Say 'Program: Wing Commander could not be created/updated !'
```

In the preceding example, it is assumed that Wing Commander is called by a DOS batch file named WC.BAT that resides in a subdirectory called C:\WING. You will also see that a line is included to activate a device driver C:\PROAUDIO\MVSOUND.SYS. This example would be used for a MediaVision Pro AudioSpectrum board, with the drivers in the C:\PROADUIO subdirectory. In this example, the program is added to `WP_DOSGROUP` (the Dos Programs folder on the desktop). Other sound boards, such as Creative Labs, do not require a DOS device driver to be used with DOS programs.

> **TIP** When creating a REXX program command file, the file must begin with a REXX comment, such as `/* Test */`. This must be on the first line of the command file for OS/2 to recognize this as a REXX program. See Chapter 15, "REXX Programming," for more information on REXX programs.

NOTE

The example use of the MVSOUND.SYS file deserves some clarification. The driver is for a MediaVision Pro AudioSpectrum sound board and was designed to be used in a "pure DOS" environment. DOS programs, typically games, may require this driver to access the Pro AudioSpectrum for sound effects and speech. However, it is important to understand that this DOS driver will directly access the hardware of the sound board, and does not virtualize the resource. Multiple programs should not be run at the same time that would utilize this driver. It is also significant that this driver runs entirely independent of MMPM/2; in fact, MMPM/2 is not required to use your sound board in this fashion (for DOS programs). Also watch out for conflicts between a true MMPM/2 driver and a DOS driver. The January 1993 beta of MediaVision Pro AudioSpectrum MMPM/2 driver recommends that you not use the MVSOUND.SYS file for DOS programs.

TIP

The line that begins with `rc=SysCreateObject` may have to change if you upgrded to OS/2 2.1 from OS/2 2.0. Change `<WP_DOSGROUP>` to `<DOS Programs>` if the file doesn't work. The name of the object changed between OS/2 2.0 and 2.1. Look for the resulting object in the DOS Programs folder.

WIN-OS/2 Multimedia

OS/2 2.1 includes the capabilities of Windows 3.1 in the form of WIN-OS/2. Because OS/2 2.0 did not have the multimedia capabilities, the OS/2 2.1 upgrade has been greatly anticipated. Under true Windows 3.1 (without OS/2), Windows depends on DOS for the CD-ROM drivers, so there is a

clear distinction between sound boards and CD-ROM. WAV and MIDI files depend on the sound board, whereas CD-Audio and program loading use the CD-ROM device driver. For this reason, sound board drivers for WIN-OS/2 are configured and function the same way as under true Windows 3.1, although the installation and access of the CD-ROM under WIN-OS/2 can be entirely different.

WIN-OS/2 MultiMedia includes a Media Player and Sound Recorder application. WIN-OS/2 also supports sound effects that are tied to specific events, such as when WIN-OS/2 is opened and closed. To activate and configure these events, use the WIN-OS/2 control panel.

When working with a sound driver for WIN-OS/2, it is important to understand that the performance of these drivers is sometimes limited by the virtual 86 mode of the Intel Processors (which OS/2 uses to run DOS and Windows programs). In particular, interrupts are sometimes delayed, and this results in distorted sound. Some of the drivers supplied with WIN-OS/2 are more optimized for the OS/2 environment. When possible, use the drivers supplied with WIN-OS/2. Check with your hardware vendor for the latest release.

Multimedia Development Environment

The OS/2 operating system has always been well received by developers because it facilitates many of the multitasking aspects of programming. Although OS/2 2.1 is somewhat behind in multimedia development tools, IBM is working hard with others to catch up.

IBM includes the MMPM/2 and MMPM/2 Toolkit with the OS/2 Professional Developers Kit CD-ROM. Even non-multimedia developers have been attracted to this package because it contains many types of controls (such as turning knobs) that are not in the base operating system.

Future Multimedia

Much of multimedia's capability lies in the future. At this point, no hardware platform dominates software-vendor attention; several systems have a variety of "raw capability" but few affordable applications. IBM obviously considers multimedia an important part of its future, and it backs their products with solid OS/2 2.1 support. However, the "consumer grade" products are just beginning to garner interest, and only the most common devices are currently included in packages.

CD-ROM is already a proven media for distribution of sound and computer data. As standards take hold for video playback, it will also serve as a tool for video playback. Writable CD-ROM devices are still quite expensive, but they have generated a lot of user interest. Other forms of optical storage are also promising, but CD-ROM is destined to stay.

IBM seems to have already covered the high-end of the PC hardware, and it has done an excellent job of supporting both ISA and Microchannel users under OS/2 2.1. As time progresses, these boards will become more powerful and affordable. However, at least for the time being, they seem destined for business users who can afford the high price of good-quality video capture and playback. Because Intel was a key player in the development of DVI, it is rumored that a specialized version of the 80486 will be offered with some type of DVI playback capability. For now, however, systems with built-in video playback are nothing but a rumor. Of course, it is pretty safe to assume that this capability will someday be standard on a desktop PC, although it is anyone's guess as to how long it will take for this to happen.

Conclusion

Although OS/2 2.1 has yet to offer substantial multimedia titles, it does not preclude the use of existing DOS and Windows multimedia software. OS/2 2.1 is also a very appealing environment for developers because it is a well-defined modern environment. There is also another factor to consider: the

OS/2 operating system has attracted the majority of the "power users" that are interested in CD-ROM and multimedia applications. As they say, it can only get better.

Author Bio

Stephen A. Gutknecht is a systems engineer with experience in both corporate support and retail. He is employed at Slator Steel of Fort Wayne, Indiana. Most recently, he was the general manager for a computer reseller, also located in Fort Wayne. Previous corporate positions include information systems coordinator for a company in the insurance industry. Having been in the computer industry for seven years, Gutknecht values his ability to combine hardware and software knowledge into practical business solutions.

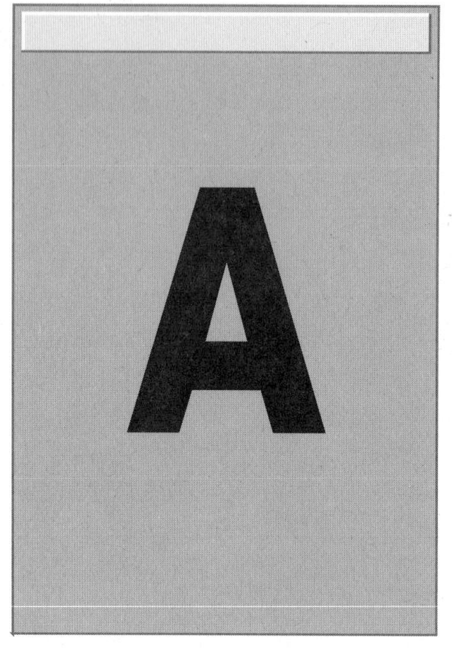

Freeware, Public Domain Software, and Shareware

There are essentially three kinds of software available to users that can be legally distributed via bulletin board systems and freely copied: freeware, public domain, and shareware. The differences between the first two are sometimes difficult to see. Neither freeware nor public domain software carry charges to the user. Anyone can use them for as long as they like without payment.

Public domain software means that the author has given up ownership rights, allowing users to do anything they like with the software, including modifying the code or incorporating it into their own software. Freeware generally means the software is still available at no charge, but copyright ownership is maintained by the author. Any modifications or use of the code for other applications usually require authorization from the copyright owner.

Shareware, on the other hand, is commercial software. The only difference between shareware and the software you see in your local computer store is the distribution method. Shareware allows you to try the product, at your own pace, on your own equipment, and relies on the honor system for purchase if you decide to keep it and continue to use it. Retail channels require that you purchase the product sight unseen, without a testing period.

Shareware authors sometimes gain enough revenue from sales of their products to devote more time to development, which in turn produces a better product. Sometimes sales are so good the authors can devote all of their time to development. In most cases, shareware authors are very open to suggestions for features. Because of the lack of retail distribution and marketing requirements, shareware programs can have a very short development cycle and new versions loaded with new features can appear quite often.

With freeware, public domain software, and shareware, you benefit by getting good software that only gets better over time. In the case of shareware, however, professional programmers count on registration fees to support their efforts. Regardless of the means by which you acquire shareware, you're still obliged to pay for it if you find it valuable and continue to use it. Unless you honorably send in registration fees after deciding to keep the products, shareware authors won't have incentive to continue with development or support.

The Association of Shareware Professionals (ASP) is an organization that promotes and sets standards for shareware products. They developed a code of ethics for members that greatly benefits shareware users. For instance, ASP member developers cannot distribute a product with a limited feature set and require payment for a fully functional version. They also have to provide at least 90 days of free support after registration. ASP developers include notice of their membership in their documentation.

Finding Shareware

OS/2 shareware can be found on public bulletin board systems (BBSs), large commercial information systems, Internet FTP sites, and even at user group meetings. You can also purchase CD-ROMs with hundreds of titles from companies such as Walnut Creek.

Bulletin board systems, such as Fernwood or Pete Norloff's OS/2 Shareware, have become huge repositories of OS/2 shareware and information. You probably have others in your local dialing area as well. Commercial systems, such as CompuServe, have many areas where you can find OS/2 shareware—most notably in IBM's OS/2 forums. A favorite Internet FTP site is ftp-os2.nmsu.edu, formerly known as hobbes.nmsu.edu. A large list of current BBS systems is available in Appendix B of this book.

User group meetings are excellent sources for shareware. One of the best things about them is that you have immediate access to the person supplying the shareware. This is nice if you have questions about how it's installed or used, or if it's worth trying. A small sampling of user groups is contained in Table A.1.

Table A.1. OS/2 user groups

User Group	*City, State*	*Phone*
OS/2 User Group	Ft. Wayne, IN	219-484-0062
New Orleans PC Club	Metairie, LA	504-866-2577

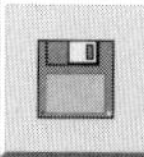

User Group	*City, State*	*Phone*
Acadiana Microcomputer Users Group	Lafayette, LA	318-235-6701
Cajun Clickers Computer Club	Baton Rouge, LA	504-275-9413
PC Club of Western LA	Leesville, LA	318-206-5439
Chalmette COmputer Users' Group	Chalmette, LA	504-279-8606
Pioneer Valley PC Users Group	North Amherst, MA	413-547-4856
Boston Computer Society	Cambridge, MA	617-967-2547
BCS - IBM-PC Users' Group	Newton, MA	614-964-2547
Pioneer Valley Computer Club	Westfield, MA	413-568-1366
ZI/TEL Users Group of BCSWest	Newton, MA	617-965-6343
Saginaw Valley Computer Assoc.	Saginaw, MI	517-792-6874
South Eastern Michigan Computer Organization	Bloomfield Hills, MI	313-398-7560
Midland Computer Club	Midland, MI	517-631-7162
The Users' Personal Computer Organization	Lansing, MI	517-627-7609

continues

Table A.1. continued

User Group	*City, State*	*Phone*
Hudson Valley PC Club	Kingston, NY	914-657-6354
Buffalo IBM PC User Group	Amherst, NY	716-695-2593
Central NY PC Users Group	Syracuse, NY	315-455-6817
PC UG of Rockland County	New City, NY	914-634-6618
FROG Computer Society	Rochester, NY	716-244-4038
Picture City PC Programmers Club	Rochester, NY	716-328-6686
Catskill Power Users	Monticello, NY	914-794-7111
Dresser-Rand Computer Club	Olean, NY	716-375-3392
Poughkeepsie IBM Club Micro Computer Club	Hyde Park, NY	914-229-8939
Cincinnati PC User Group	Cincinnati, OH	513-745-9992
Columbus Computer Society	Columbus, OH	614-878-8925
Greater Cleveland PC Users Group	Cleveland, OH	216-781-4131
Western Reserve IBM & Compatible PC Assoc.	Warren, OH	216-539-4858
Lake-Ashtabula IBM PC Users Group	Madison, OH	216-428-6163

User Group	City, State	Phone
Akron Canton PC Users Group	Akron, OH	216-499-5623
Newark Area Computer Club	Granville, OH	614-344-2323
Philadelphia Area Computer Society OS/2 SIG	Philadelphia, PA	215-657-2124

OS/2 Unleashed Companion Disk

The companion disk included with this book contains a number of files with the LZH (Lempel-Ziv-Huffman) extension:

```
4os2.lzh        228226      1-31-93     18:09
deskman.lzh     155738      2-01-93      9:29
diskstat.lzh     33015      1-28-93     20:10
galleria.lzh    191173      4-20-93     14:28
inimaint.lzh    269483      4-21-93     14:35
install.cmd       2017      1-31-93     18:54
lh.exe           49153      3-30-92      2:12
lh2.lzh          34513      1-25-93     18:28
pmscrpbk.lzh     91418      4-20-93     14:29
readme.doc        1830      4-19-93     17:10
te2.lzh         359765      1-28-93     18:16
         1,416,331 bytes in 11 file(s)
```

The following sections contain brief descriptions of the functionality you can expect from the utilities contained on the companion disk.

4OS2

4OS2 was developed to bring the power and convenience of the popular 4DOS program to users of the OS/2 operating system. Whether you are a computer

novice or an experienced user, 4OS2 helps you get the most out of your OS/2 system.

4OS2, like its cousin 4DOS, is a command interpreter or "shell" (see Figure A.1). 4OS2 was designed to be compatible with both 4DOS and OS/2's normal command-line shell program, CMD.EXE.

```
4OS2 32
To return to BRIEF, type "exit".
4OS2/32 1.11 (RC11)   OS/2 Version is 2.10
Copyright 1988-1993  Rex Conn & JP Software Inc.  All Rights Reserved
4OS2 S/N 200711, registered to Productivity Solutions Incorporated
for use on up to 3 computers.  May not be distributed to others.

1 d:\unleash>start collage

1 d:\unleash>?
?            ALIAS        ATTRIB       BEEP         CALL         CANCEL
CD           CDD          CHCP         CHDIR        CLS          COLOR
COPY         DATE         DEL          DELAY        DESCRIBE     DETACH
DIR          DIRS         DPATH        DRAWBOX      DRAWHLINE    DRAWVLINE
ECHO         ECHOS        ENDLOCAL     ERASE        ESET         EXCEPT
EXIT         FOR          FREE         GLOBAL       GOSUB        GOTO
HELP         HISTORY      IF           IFF          INKEY        INPUT
KEYS         LIST         LOADBTM      LOG          MD           MEMORY
MKDIR        MOVE         PATH         PAUSE        POPD         PROMPT
PUSHD        QUIT         RD           REBOOT       REM          REN
RENAME       RETURN       RMDIR        SCREEN       SCRPUT       SELECT
SET          SETDOS       SETLOCAL     SHIFT        START        TEE
TEXT         TIME         TIMER        TYPE         UNALIAS      UNSET
VER          VERIFY       VOL          VSCRPUT      WINDOW       Y

1 d:\unleash>
```

Figure A.1. The 4OS2 command window.

If you are familiar with 4DOS or with the OS/2 command prompt, you won't have to change your computing habits or unlearn anything to use 4OS2. If you know how to use commands to display a directory, copy a file, or start an application program, you already know how to use 4OS2.

Functionality

The rich 4OS2 feature set complements the standard OS/2 commands and is a valuable addition for novice and advanced users. Ease-of-use and customization are strong points of 40S2. The command-line editing keys are improved and include tricks like the completion of a filespec with a single keystroke. The command history can be loaded and saved from a file. The Page Up key displays the scrolling command history.

Aliases are named macros that abbreviate commands. They can also be loaded from a file. Additional help is provided, especially with the `/?` command-line option. The OS/2 *Command Reference* and 4OS2 reference books are loaded when F1 is pressed or `HELP` is entered at the prompt. The

environment has several additional variables and can be global to all sessions using the SHRALIAS utility. Environment strings can be edited with ESET instead of the usual retyping required by CMD.EXE.

Video customization includes line drawing, text placement, boxes, menus, and named color controls. The `COLOR` command sets the text color and uses names rather than numbers:

```
COLOR BRI WHITE ON BLUE
```

The command screen and major utilities can have separate color schemes. Many of these settings can be stored in the 4OS2.INI text file. One of the most popular features is the colorized directory listing. Color names can be assigned to directories and various file extensions. Any use of the `DIR` command displays a colorful barrage with .EXEs in one color, .DOCs in another, and .BAK files blinking wildly.

Several new commands are added that should be part of OS/2 and DOS. `FREE` shows the amount of disk space available on a drive. `MEMORY` shows RAM usage in DOS and the largest block of memory in OS/2. `DESCRIBE` adds useful comments to filenames and stores them in a hidden text file. These are automatically displayed when the user does a `DIR`. Many other options are provided for `DIR`, including `/2` and `/4` for two- and four-column lists, `/F` for full path names, `/L` for lowercase, and `/T` for attributes.

TIMER is a utility that clocks execution time. It is very useful for performance testing and works well in command files. `LIST` displays files in a scrolling window with a handy find option. `SELECT` is combined with other commands for picklist input. The following statement displays a full-screen multiple selection list (`*.SYS`):

```
SELECT DEL (*.SYS)
```

Batch processing enhancements offer the advanced user unlimited control of command procedures. Internal variables provide the program with system information such as process number, screen position, and application type. Functions include mathematics, date and filename formatting, and string handling. Blocks of text can be displayed with the `TEXT` and `ENDTEXT` operators. These can be combined with screen controls and input commands to create powerful menu-driven utilities.

The batch files can be stored in the traditional .CMD text format or in a .BTM file. The latter process is much quicker, because the file is kept in memory instead of individual lines being read off the disk. Two special command files are used by 4OS2 sessions: 4START is processed whenever a new command-line session is started; 4EXIT runs whenever a session is closed or exited. Of course, 4OS2 is also compatible with the REXX language. If you use the command line, give this program a try.

Files Included

```
4dosa.ico          888   6-08-92  1:00a
4dosb.ico          888   6-08-92  1:00a
4os2.doc        170305   6-08-92  1:00a
4os2.exe         99680   9-30-92  1:00a
4os2.inf        138303   6-08-92  1:00a
4os2a.ico          888   6-08-92  1:00a
4os2b.ico          888   6-08-92  1:00a
4os2h.msg        22409   6-08-92  1:00a
license.doc      12225   6-08-92  1:00a
order.frm         5251   6-08-92  1:00a
orderinf.doc     30352   6-08-92  1:00a
readme.doc       14849   1-31-93  5:40p
shralias.exe      3015   6-08-92  1:00a
support.bbs       1318   6-08-92  1:00a
sysop.doc         3770   6-08-92  1:00a
vendor.doc        4724   6-08-92  1:00a
     509,753 bytes in 16 file(s)
```

Registration Information

When you register 4OS2, you will receive the complete manual and some additional utilities.

To save paper and time, the order form is included separately in the file ORDER.FRM. This allows you to view the information in this file on the screen and print only the actual order form.

For convenient phone ordering, call JP Software between 9 a.m. and 5 p.m. Eastern Standard Time (United States) at (800) 368-8777 (U.S. only; orders only please!) or (617) 646-3975, or transmit your order form by fax to (617)

646-0904. You can also order via CompuServe (75020,244), BIX (mail to "jpsoft"), or Internet (75020.244@compuserve.com). Please include all information on the order form with your electronic order, preferably in the same format.

Please read the ordering information contained in the file ORDERINF.DOC before placing your order. This file explains order and payment policies. If you don't read over the policies before ordering, you may leave out important information, send payment that can't be accepted, and so on. This can delay your order and result in additional costs to you.

JP Software, Inc.
P.O. Box 1470
East Arlington, MA 02174
Phone: (617) 646-3975
Fax: (617) 646-0904
BBS: (617) 354-8873 Channel 1
CIS: [75300,210]
Version: 1.1
Price: $69; $89 with the DOS version

TE/2—Terminal Emulator/2

TE/2, pictured in Figure A.2, is a general-purpose, character-based (VIO) telecommunications program. TE/2 includes most features found in commercial software, including multiple dialing directories of up to 200 entries each, call logging, chat mode with split-screen support, user-definable protocols, 5 file transfer protocols, and seven terminal emulations. Users have the option to use TE/2's own comprehensive internal script language or REXX scripts.

Functionality

TE/2 is a communications program for OS/2 protected mode. It is a full-screen application (not a Presentation Manager application) that runs in either a full-screen session or a VIO windowed session. Because TE/2 is multithreaded, it cannot be made into a bound application.

Figure A.2. The TE/2 opening screen.

The shareware version of TE/2 is a fully functional communications program. There is no "expiration date" on which it self-destructs or otherwise becomes inoperable. The features that this version has in common with the full, registered version are complete and not "crippled" in any way. These features include:

- Five terminal emulation modes: raw TTY, standard ANSI-BBS, an extended ANSI mode called ANSI-TE/2, VT100, and IBM 3101 emulation.
- Six upload/download protocols: standard Xmodem-CRC with Checksum fall-back, XModem-1K, which supports 1024-byte packets and automatic fall-back to standard XModem, YModem batch protocol, YModem-G variant of the YModem protocol for MNP modems, ZModem batch protocol, and straight ASCII text-file uploads and log file capture ability for text-file "downloads."
- Multiple 200-entry dialing directories.
- Default line parameters, terminal emulation, and transfer protocol assignable to each directory entry.
- Time and date of last connection and number of connections to date saved for each directory entry.

- Auto redialing, manual dialing, and round-robin "queue-dialing."
- Alternate keyboard setups for use with remote host programs such as OS2You or Doorway.
- Split-screen "chat" mode with access to nearly all of the program functions normally available in standard terminal mode.
- Unlimited number of user-definable external programs with robust command-line handling. External programs may be executed in the foreground or background as a child process or as a separate session.
- All 48 function keys fully programmable as text macros.
- Shell to operating system.
- "Scroll-back" redisplay buffer, user-definable to nearly any desired size. The scroll-back buffer may be searched for text, and the entire buffer or a subset may be written to disk or retransmitted as an ASCII upload with optional "quoting."

Included Files

```
commpak2.dll    203192  12-22-92  7:10p
cpk2_102.doc     12088   9-10-92  1:02a
cpk2_191.doc      2380   2-22-92  7:10p
kermit.lzh       13420   1-28-93  6:05p
modem.inc         1023   6-15-92  1:20a
modems.lzh       36457   1-28-93  6:06p
oberon.doc        5092   2-10-92  1:02a
order.frm         5239   6-15-92  1:20a
read.me           5752   6-15-92  1:20a
script.doc      104679   6-15-92  1:20a
te2.dir            687  11-14-92  5:00a
te2.doc         169850   6-15-92  1:20a
te2.exe         198008   6-15-92  1:20a
te2.fnk            157   6-15-92  1:20a
te2.ico           3192   6-15-92  1:20a
te2.ini           5874   6-15-92  1:20a
te2.xex            458   6-15-92  1:20a
te2color.exe     19514   6-15-92  1:20a
te2inp.xlt         256   6-15-92  1:20a
te2out.xlt         256   6-15-92  1:20a
whats.new        15332   6-15-92  1:20a
     802,906 bytes in 21 file(s)
```

Registration Information

Oberon Software is not an ASP member, so the shareware version is not the same as the one that registered users are given. Specifically, registered users gain the following functionality:

- Complete script language capability, including user-definable dynamic string and 32-bit integer variables, file-handling functions for opening, closing, reading, and writing any number of files, asynchronous event watches that can launch another script or just toggle a variable, and low- and high-level interface into most of TE/2's.
- A command-line interface for executing single statements.
- The capability to write your TE/2 scripts in the REXX Procedure language. All built-in functions available to the built-in script language are also available to the REXX script, plus you have access to all of the built-in OS/2 system functions that you normally use with REXX command files.
- The CompuServe B+ protocol and an enhanced ZModem, which includes the ability to fine-tune several internal ZModem settings and the ability to resume aborted downloads.

Oberon Software
518 Blue Earth Street
Mankato, MN 56001-2142
Phone: (507) 388-7001
Fax: (507) 388-7568
BBS: (507) 388-1154
CIS: [72510,3500]
Version: 1.20
Price: $65

DiskStat

DiskStat is a 32-bit utility that displays drive statistics including specified drive letter, volume label, installed file system, disk size, available bytes, and percent of disk used. If the system swapper file will also on the drive, its size will also be displayed (see Figure A.3). DiskStat displays the percentage of disk space used on its icon when reduced.

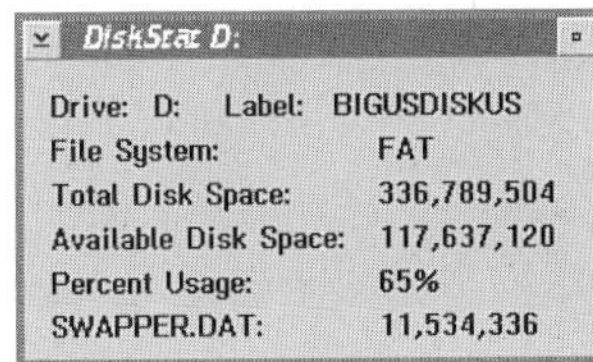

Figure A.3. The DiskStat information window.

Functionality

DiskStat provides a continually updated display of certain statistics for a specified disk drive:

- The drive letter and volume label.
- The installed file system for the disk.
- The size of the disk in bytes.
- The number of bytes currently available on the disk.
- The current disk space usage as a percent.
- The current size of the swapper file if the specified disk contains the system swapper file.
- When DiskStat is minimized, the percent usage is displayed in its icon.

A dialog that displays the time DiskStat began execution, the current time, and the largest and smallest values for available disk space on the target drive during the current DiskStat session may be invoked with an Overall item on DiskStat's System Menu.

When any of DiskStat's windows or dialogs have the input focus, the F1 key provides help and information on DiskStat and Oberon Software.

Included Files

```
diskstat.doc      4591  12-10-92  1:02a
diskstat.exe     33354  12-10-92  1:02a
diskstat.hlp     16333  12-10-92  1:02a
oberon.doc        5092  12-10-92  1:02a
      59,370 bytes in 4 file(s)
```

Registration Information

Oberon Software
518 Blue Earth Street
Mankato, MN 56001-2142
Phone: (507) 388-7001
Fax: (507) 388-7568
BBS: (507) 388-1154
CIS: [72510,3500]
Version: 1.01
Price: Free

LH2

LH2 is an OS/2 clone of the DOS program LHARC. It is based on the source code the author previously released as "LH-ANSIC.LZH," the ANSI-C version of a simplified LHARC-compatible compressor/decompressor. File extended attributes and long file names are supported. The help screen for LH2 is shown in the following listing.

```
Lh2         (Compress files)    Peter Fitzsimmons 89/09/19
                                              Version 2.14
Usage:     LH <cmd> <archive> [file1 file2 ...] [options]
Purpose:   Collect and compress files.
Commands:  A - Add files to archive.
           M - Move files to archive (erases files).
           L - List files in archive.
           X - Extract files from archive.
           T - Test - Extract files to NUL.
           D - Delete files from archive.
Options (may appear anywhere on the command line):
          /v - verbose                    (L command)
          /a - maintain file attributes.  (A, M or X)
```

```
/s - collect/extract subdirs.   (A, M or X)
/o - no prompts.                (L or X)
     (When used with X, /o will overwrite
     existing files without prompting)
/i - ignore EAs.                (A, M or X)
/c - compatibility mode (-lh1-) (A or M)
/m - store modified files only  (A or M)
/h - additional information.
```

Examples

1. `LH2 A PROGRAMS \usr\*.c D:\*.h /s`

   Collect all *.c files from \usr (and children of \usr), as well as all of the *.h files from every directory on drive D:.

2. `LH2 X PROG*`

   Extract all archives matching prog*.lzh into the current directory. Any path information in the archives is ignored.

3. `LH2 X PROG* e:\home *.c`

   Follow Example 2, but extract files into e:\home (directory must exist). Only extract files matching *.c.

4. `LH2 X PROG* e:\home *.c /s`

   Follow Example 3, although path information is kept. Directories are created off of e:\home as needed.

Included Files

```
lh.doc            8539   3-30-92  2:10a
lh.exe           49153   3-30-92  2:12a
      57,692 bytes in 2 file(s)
```

Registration Information

This program is based on the LZH compression method developed by Haruhiko Okumura and Haruyasu Yoshizaki. The compression routines were derived from the uncopyrighted LZHUF.C, posted by Haruhiko Okumura.

The file format (*.lzh) is compatible with LHARC, the DOS archiver by Haruyasu Yoshizaki. The format of LHARC files was learned from the public domain LHX.H (LHX is a *.lzh file-repair utility) by Mark Armbrust.

Peter Fitzsimmons
A:WARE Inc.
P.O. Box 670
Adelaide St Postal Stn.
Toronto, Canada M5C 2J8.
Phone: (416) 858-3222
BBS: (416) 867-9663
Version: 2.14
Price: Free

Deskman/2

The Workplace Shell, first offered with OS/2 2.0, heralds a new day in the arena of mass market operating systems. It, and the underlying System Object Model (SOM), mark the first time that objects, not data files and programs, are key figures for both users and programmers. These objects are key to proper use and enjoyment of OS/2.

However, the problem is that unlike files, objects are not easy to copy between machines, exchange with other users, or (lacking the right kind of tools) even back up. DeskMan/2 (shown in Figure A.4) addresses these needs. Unlike some technologies, DeskMan/2 does not use internal knowledge of the Workplace Shell's data structures to do a mass backup of the shell's current state. Instead, DeskMan/2 is a citizen of the shell, interacting with other objects using documented interfaces in order to uncover the necessary information for reconstructing them.

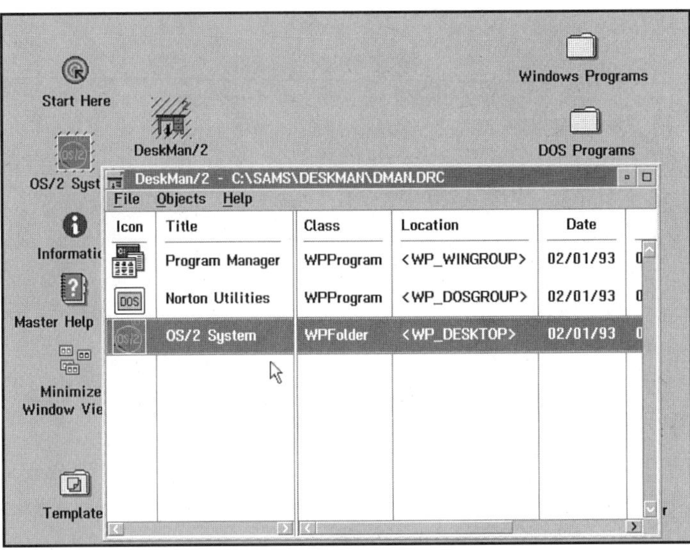

Figure A.4. DeskMan/2.

Functionality

With DeskMan/2, you can selectively build a database of object information by dragging objects onto DeskMan/2. Later, you can use DeskMan/2 to reconstruct those objects, or even generate a REXX script to generate those objects. Not only can DeskMan/2 selectively reconstruct objects from its database on the original machine, but it can also reconstruct them on other DeskMan/2-enabled machines, even mapping drive references! In addition, to exchange objects with people who don't have DeskMan/2, you can generate REXX scripts that will reconstruct objects when run.

Optionally, DeskMan/2 can even migrate the desktop icons from one machine to another! Thus, you can use DeskMan/2 to do the following things:

- Selectively back up and restore your desktop using a drag and drop interface. Alternatively, one command can back up the entire desktop.
- Create a database of standard objects and selectively restore them on multiple machines (e.g., on a corporate network).

- Create REXX scripts that can perform restore activities on non-DeskMan/2-enabled machines. Imagine now much easier it would be to create installation scripts from an already installed system.
- And more!

By using the defined interfaces for querying information about Workplace Shell objects, rather than blindly copying data, DeskMan/2 even catches some inconsistency errors that occasionally crop up when migrating between releases of the Workplace Shell.

Developers and beta testers never have to dread the "Please reformat the drive before installing" warning that often accompanied prerelease versions of the OS/2 operating system. Because it rebuilds objects from their descriptions, using defined interfaces, DeskMan/2 can continue to work even when the Workplace Shell's data structures change (as they have in the past, and will continue to do in the future).

Included Files

```
dman.dll       260953    1-23-93 10:57p
dman.inf        52624    1-23-93 11:03p
dman.txt         4887    1-22-93  1:40p
dman2.ico        2910    1-01-93 12:18p
dmanshar.cmd    10995    2-01-93  9:28a
     332,369 bytes in 5 file(s)
```

Registration Information

At the ColoradOS/2! conference in January 1993, the authors of DeskMan/2 and *OS/2 2.1 Unleashed* became aware of each other's projects. Impressed with the scope of *OS/2 2.1 Unleashed*, the Deskman/2 authors wanted to contribute a special version of the DeskMan/2 application to the cause. With the deadline for the companion disk nearing, and with DeskMan/2 still in development, we froze the code and started on a strict diet of debugging, which resulted in this version. This special limited release lacks some of the features of the full package, which includes the following:

- Handling of folder contents, including folders within folders. The limited release versions of DeskMan/2 require you to separately back up folders

and their contents (although multiple objects may be dragged at one time).

- Generation of REXX scripts.
- Restore Missing Only; see the online manual for details.
- Online help. An early version of the online manual is provided; type VIEW DMAN to see it.

If you find DeskMan/2 to be of value, you can order the full version:

Development Technologies, Inc.
Dept. 3716
8329 High School Road
Elkins Park, PA 19117-2027
Technical Support, Phone: (803) 790-9230
Price: $49

Galleria

Galleria is a general-purpose program for the display, editing, and conversion of bitmap files. Galleria also supports file search operations, concurrent operation of most tasks (such as display, save, and print), and multilevel undo of edits. An example Galleria screen is shown in Figure A.5.

Functionality

- Displays images at varying magnifications.
- Converts images to monochrome, grayscale (16 shades) or color (16 colors), using nearest colors or error-diffusion dither.
- Performs a number of edits, including cropping and resizing.
- Loads images from disk in a number of formats, or copies from the Clipboard.
- Saves images to disk in a number of formats, or copies to the Clipboard.
- Prints images on any supported printer at varying resolutions.

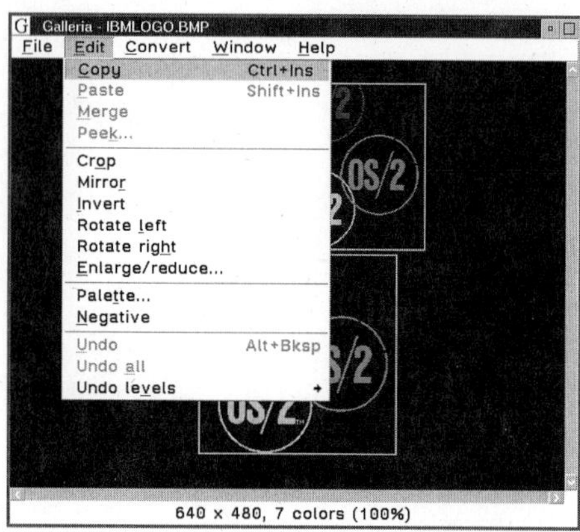

Figure A.5. The Galleria main window.

Included Files

```
BITWARE0 DLL     45414  04-13-93   1:40a
BITWARE1 DLL     39648  04-13-93   1:40a
BITWARE2 DLL     67600  04-13-93   1:40a
GALLERCM EXE     28401  04-13-93   1:40a
GALLERCM HLP     13214  04-13-93   1:40a
GALLERIA INF     13214  04-13-93   1:40a
GALLERIA EA       6543  04-13-93   1:40a
GALLERIA EXE     88834  04-13-93   1:40a
GALLERIA FIX        54  04-13-93   1:40a
GALLERIA HLP     34740  04-13-93   1:40a
GALLERIA INF     34740  04-13-93   1:40a
ORDER    DOC      2112  04-13-93   1:40a
README   DOC     13070  04-13-93   1:40a
```

Registration Information

This version of Galleria is provided with a limited evaluation license not exceeding 21 days in duration from first use. Unregistered use beyond this evaluation period is in violation of this license.

If you find this program useful and would like to license your copy, a fee of $75 (Australian dollars) or approximately $53 United States dollars for individual use, or $295 (Australian dollars) or approximately $207 United States dollars for corporate use is payable. This entitles you (or your corporation) to full use of current and subsequent releases of the product plus support via CompuServe.

A software key made out in the name of an individual (or corporation) is returned when the program is registered. The license type and name must be specified when the software is registered.

- Send a mail message to CompuServe 100033,340 with your Mastercard/Visa details (card number, full name as shown on the card, and expiration date). A software key for enablement of unlimited use will be returned to your CompuServe ID.
- Send a fax to +61-6-2810175 with Mastercard/Visa information. The current version plus software key will be sent on 3.5-inch floppy to the address you specify. Delivery (by airmail) normally takes 2 weeks from receipt of order. Add $10 (Australian dollars) or approximately $7 United States dollars for shipping and handling.
- Post either Mastercard/Visa information or a check for the appropriate registration fee (in Australian currency or converted equivalent) to the following address:

  Bitware, Software & Services
  P.O. Box 3097
  Manuka A.C.T. 2603
  Australia
  CIS: [100033,340]
  FAX: +61-6-2810175
  Price: $53 (individual), $207 (corporate license), plus $7 shipping and handling

The current version plus software key will be sent on a 3.5-inch floppy to the address you specify. Delivery (by airmail) normally takes 2 weeks from receipt of order. Add $10 Australian dollars or $7 United States for shipping and handling. (See the enclosed file ORDER.DOC for pricing details and special offers with Nikon II, Bitware's screen capture utility.)

PMScrapbook

PM Scrapbook is an OS/2 32-bit application for the storage and organization of files, notes, and personal information. The organization of this information

is stored and graphically displayed in a hierarchical "tree" format. Each piece of information consists of an entry in the tree window, its title, and detail (see Figure A.6).

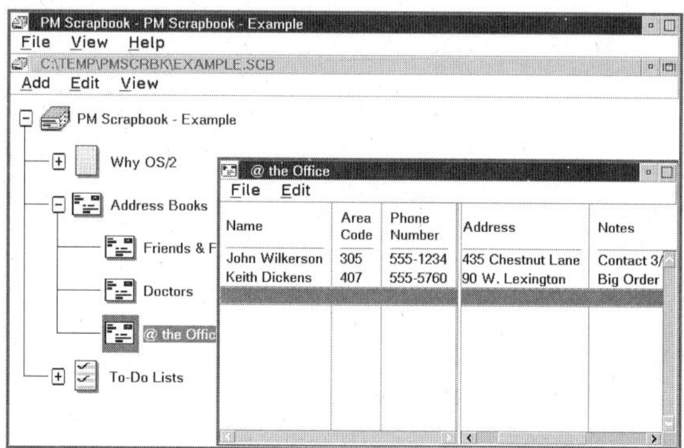

Figure A.6. The PM Scrapbook tree window.

PM Scrapbook contains a text editor for textual data as well as specialized editors for some internal data types. PM Scrapbook also keeps track of the dates associated with these entries for occasional housecleaning.

Functionality

PM Scrapbook uses the following data formats/types:

- Text: free format text typed in or imported from text files.
- Address: internal address book format consisting of name, area code, phone number, extension, address, and notes.
- To-Do: internal to-do list format consisting of event, date entered, target date, and completion date.
- List: internal general list format consisting of two columns of data with user-definable column headings.

All data type editors allow you to select the font for that instance of the editor. Each editor instance also remembers its final windows size and position when last saved. All editors (except the text editor) and the tree view use the

OS/2 method of text entry: hold down the Alt key on the keyboard and click mouse button 1 over the text area to be edited. Keyboard shortcuts are also provided.

Included Files

```
EXAMPLE  SCB    86101   03-05-93  1:39p
PMSCRPBK EXE    88064   03-05-93  1:39p
PMSCRPBK HLP    36766   02-23-93 10:42a
READ     ME      3066   02-17-93  4:01p
REGISTER DOC     1843   02-23-92  1:01p
```

Registration Information

You are free to use PM Scrapbook for only a short period of time. This demo version is limited in that it allows only 7 entries to be made in each scrapbook.

If, after 30 days, you find PM Scrapbook useful, you should register it. The registration fee for individuals is $35 (United States dollars). The registered version imposes no limits on the number of entries per scrapbook.

Dan Holt
P.O. Box 18863
Atlanta, GA 30326
CIS: [76500,2557]
Price: $35 (per copy)

See Register.doc or the registration section in the online help for registration details. Comments, suggestions, and bug reports may be submitted through CIS Mail ID 76500,2557, by name (Dan Holt) on some of the major OS/2 BBSs, or through the address listed in Register.doc. These comments will be answered on a "best effort" basis.

INIMaint

INIMAINT is an OS/2 PM program used to display and manage OS/2 INI files (see Figure A.7). Unlike the Windows environment, OS/2's INI files are

binary files. This is both good and bad. The good part is that users can't change the INI file settings, thus introducing potential errors. The fact that the user can't view or edit these files is the bad part. Because the user can't read these files, they can't modify them, even for applications they have installed themselves.

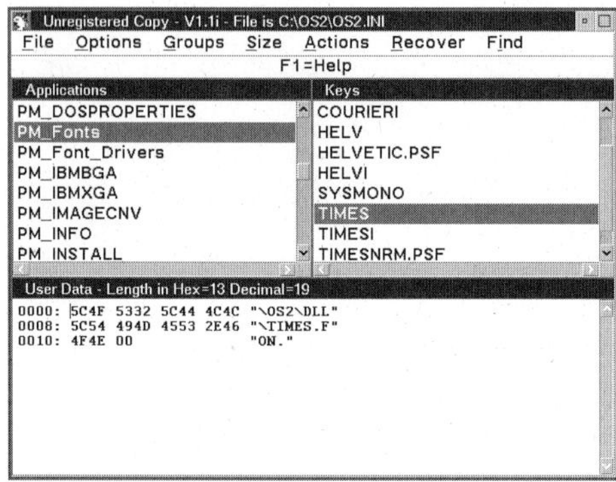

Figure A.7. The INIMAINT window.

INIMAINT gives you the capability to make virtually any change you want to any of the INI files in your OS/2 environment. Making changes to these files must be done with care. You can do serious and unpredictable damage to your environment. It is strongly suggested that you ensure that you have a usable backup of any INI file that you modify in any way.

Functionality

1. File gives the user the ability to change INI files, refresh the current INI file, dump the contents of the INIMAINT variables, compare two INI files, and exit from INIMAINT. The Compare option allows the user to compare two INI files on any one of three different levels:

A. List applications that are in one INI file, but not the other.

B. Level A plus any key names that are in one file, but not the other.

C. Levels A and B plus any key values that are in both files, but are not equal. The differences are displayed in a list box within a dialog that allows the user to print or write a listing of the list box contents and/or create an INI file with some or all of the applications or keys that have differences.

2. Options displays a dialog that gives you the capability to do the following things:

   A. Turn off the display of the opening INIMAINT dialog.

   B. Turn off the dialogs that ask for confirmation before deleting or modifying the contents of the current INI file.

3. Groups displays a dialog that allows you to define and manage the various groups for this INI file. INIMAINT gives the user the capability to group applications in an INI file. These groups are used in a number of different INIMAINT operations and ease the problems of handling an INI file with a large number of applications. The Groups dialog gives the user the ability to define new groups, to add and delete applications, and delete groups.

   To establish a new group, select Groups in the Group dialog, select New Group, and supply a name. Add applications to the group by selecting them in the list box.

   A single application can be a member of up to 5 different groups at any one time, so it is possible to define overlapping groups.

4. Size calculates the minimum amount of disk space that would be required for an INI file that contained a selected set of applications in the current INI file. When this item is selected, you will be asked what you want to size. There will always be several choices: the various standard INI files, the current file, and the currently selected application. If there are any groups defined, they will be included among the selections. If there is more than one group defined, there will be an All Groups selection.

5. Actions gives the user the capability to do a number of things:

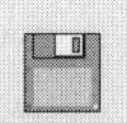

A. Update Current Key writes any changes that have been made to the data in the MLE into the current INI file.

B. Delete Application and Delete Key do the obvious.

C. Add Application, Add Key, and Replace Key Value are similar functions entered at different points. Add Application asks for the name of a new application to add to the current INI file. The Add Key asks for the name of the new key.

D. Rename and Duplicate Key gives you the capability to change the name of an existing key or to make a duplicate copy of the key using a different key name.

E. Copy and Move prompts you for a target file for the copy/move. The selected Applications then move or copy to the target INI file, which will be created, if it does not exist.

F. Backup allows for an easy backup of the System INI file, User INI file, or both the System and User INI files.

6. Recover contains a list of capabilities designed to give you the capability to recover from corrupted INI files:

   A. Change User and/or System INI files allows the user to change the INI files that OS/2 is using. Great care must be exercised when doing this, but it is sometimes the only way that problem entries can be removed from an INI File.

   B. Repair inconsistencies between the INI file and the desktop.

   C. Condense the current INI file, the System INI file, the User INI File, or both. Condensing the System or User INI files is not a simple task. They cannot be copied or erased while they are being used by OS/2. This item switches the files to the copies long enough to erase the old files and copy a condensed backup to the original names.

7. Find allows the user to search the Application Listbox, the Key Name Listbox, the Key Value MLE, all of the key names in the currrent INI file, all of the Key Values for the current Application or all of the key values in the current INI file for either an ASCII string or a hex value.

Included Files

```
INISHARE TXT     18365  03-13-93   1:15p
INICHNGE TXT     38809  03-17-93  10:40a
INIFILE  TXT      4588  08-13-92   5:23p
INIGROUP TXT      4038  08-13-92   4:00p
INIREPAR TXT      3182  10-18-92  11:15a
INIMAINT EXE    266752  03-17-93  10:52a
INICOPY  EXE     27126  03-17-93  10:51a
INIMTAPI DLL    173264  02-20-93  10:20a
INIMAINT HLP     65961  03-03-93   5:36p
```

Registration Information

The version of INIMAINT that accompanys this documentation is a shareware version of the program that must be registered with Carry Associates if you intend to use it, except for a brief test. This is not a free program and has been copyrighted by Carry Associates. It is a violation of the copyright laws to use the program without registering and paying for it. The purpose of the unregistered version is only to give users an opportunity to try the program so they can determine whether they feel the program is worth the cost.

Unregistered copies of INIMAINT display an initial dialog that notes the unregistered condition. This dialog stays on the screen for 15 seconds, unless dismissed by clicking on the OK button. The dialog cannot be dismissed until it has been visible for 3 seconds. In addition, the title bar contains a note that this is an unregistered version of INIMAINT.

To obtain your registration identifier, send a check for $29.95 per license for single licenses, or $299 for an unlimited copies license, made payable to:

Carry Associates
990 Ironwood Court
Marco Island, FL 33937
Phone: 813-642-9126
Fax: 813-642-1007
CIS: [71435,470]

After you have your registration identifier, you can register your copy of INIMAINT by selecting Register Your Copy.

Bulletin Board Systems

Bulletin boards are a great resource for ideas, opinions, shareware, and file updates. CompuServe and Internet are available throughout the world. They are explained in detail with sample commands and forum lists in this appendix. Multi-Net is presented as an example of OS/2-based BBS software. Popular bulletin boards that favor OS/2 are also listed with descriptions.

CompuServe

One of the online services IBM supports OS/2 users and developers is CompuServe Information Systems (CIS). CompuServe is a worldwide system with local access numbers in most areas and hundreds of thousands of subscribers.

There are more than 1,700 services on CompuServe, a large percentage of which are forums. A forum is an area for support for a given special interest. Each service has an associated page name that you use to access it. Each forum has a message base, a file library, and an online conference area.

The message bases are the most active areas, and in some forums hundreds of messages are posted every day. Because a forum is allotted a finite number of message slots, older messages are scrolled off to make room for new messages. The time it takes for messages to scroll off (the scroll rate) can be more than a week for forums with light message traffic, or a matter of a day or two for heavy message traffic.

Messages are contained in a linked tree format. Messages and their replies form message "threads" that can be read in order. Whenever possible, you should be sure to leave a reply rather than a new message in response to a current message. This makes reading and tracking messages simple and logical.

You can leave private messages in some forums, but many sysops elect to turn the feature off so all messages are public. If you wish to leave a private reply to a message in a forum, you can send it via CompuServe Mail directly from the forum message read prompt.

In the file libraries you can upload and download files. Updates, patches, informational files, and utilities are some of the things to look for here. Connect time charges are suspended during uploads, but all other actions in a forum are charged at standard rates.

Online conference areas are areas where users "chat," sending real-time messages to one another. Sometimes there are scheduled conferences with specific topics or special guests. Most of the time, however, any user who just wants to chat can enter a conference. Because higher baud rates cost more, many users log on at 300 baud for conferencing.

Each area on a forum is made up of up to 18 sections (0 through 17). It's up to the forum administrators to decide how many there are and their purpose. You can choose to view only those sections that you find interesting—this, of course, saves you time and money. To learn more about working in a forum without generating connect time charges, use the Practice forum. Use the command `GO PRACTICE` to enter the forum. Table B.1 contains an overview of some of the commonly used commands.

Table B.1. Basic CompuServe commands.

Command	*Argument*	*Result*
`GO`	`<pagename>`	Move to specified CIS page
	`INDEX`	Move to an area where you can search for other areas
`OPT`		Get menu for changing forum options
	`NAME`	Option to store your name as seen on messages
`ANN`		Get a menu of announcement topics
`MESS`		Enter message area
	`SCAN`	Scan message headers
	`QSN`	Quick scan for headers since last read
	`READ`	Read messages

Command	*Argument*	*Result*
	RTN	Read new messages in thread order
	RI <message nnn>	Read individual message number nnn
	L(EAVE)	Compose a new message
	POST	Send the composed message publicly
	POST PRI	Send the composed message privately
	POST UNF	Send the composed message with no CIS reformatting
LIB		Enter file library
	SCA	Scan library
	SCA SHO	Condensed scan
(Browse)	/LIB:nn	Look in library number nn
	/ALL	Look in all libraries
	/AGE:nn	Look for files up to nn days old
	/KEY:xxx	Look for files with keyword xxx
	BRO	Browse library (shows long description)
	DOW	Download file
	UPL	Upload file
CON		Enter conference area
	/HELP	Gets list of available conference commands
UST		User Status to see who else is online in forum
SEN	nn text	Send one line text to user on channel nn
WEA		Check your local weather report (no kidding!)

It's a good idea to use CompuServe-specific communications software or a standard communications package with specialized scripts to allow you to perform most actions off-line. Because you are charged for online connect time, you can really run up the charges if you type or read slowly! At this time there is only one Presentation Manager-based CompuServe access package: Golden CommPass from Creative Systems Programming Corp., which can be reached at (609) 234-1500.

Most of the leading industry software developers and hardware manufacturers have support forums, or at least support sections on "vendor" forums. IBM has four forums for OS/2 support (see Table B.2).

Table B.2. CompuServe OS/2 forums/sections.

Page	*Forum Name*	*Section*	
OS2USER	OS/2 User Forum	1	OS/2 Public Image
		2	1.x General Q & A
		3	OS/2 & Hardware
		4	Application Quest.
		5	Documentation
		6	New User Questions
		7	Suggestions
		8	Ask IBM
		9	TEAM OS/2
		13	*Golden CommPass
		15	Open Forum [USER]
		16	Fun & Games
		17	IBM Files [USER]
OS2SUPPORT	OS/2 Support Forum	1	General Questions
		2	Install Questions

Page	Forum Name	Section
		3 H/W - I/O Media
		4 H/W - Platform
		5 H/W - Displays
		6 H/W - Printers
		7 H/W - Miscellaneous
		8 WPS / SOM Questions
		9 ES / LS Questions
		10 REXX / Lang. Quest.
		11 DOS Appl. Questions
		12 Windows Appl. Ques.
		13 OS/2 Appl. Quest.
		14 COMM Appl. Quest.
		15 OPEN Forum [SUP]
		16 Beta Program '92
		17 IBM Files [SUP]
OS2DF1	OS/2 Developer Forum 1	1 Base OS API's
		2 PM API's
		3 Object Technology
		4 IBM C SET/2, IPMD
		6 REXX/Other Language
		7 Development Tools
		8 Debugging
		9 Thunking 16 <-> 32
		10 OS Migration

continues

Table B.2. continued

Page	*Forum Name*	*Section*
		11 Device Driver Dev.
		12 MMPM/2 - Multimedia
		13 DMK/2 - Mirrors
		15 Open Forum [DF1]
		16 Product Suggestions
		17 IBM Files [DF1]
S2DF2	OS/2 Developer Forum 2	1 Communications Mgr.
		2 Database Manager
		3 LAN Server
		4 NTS/2 - Transport
		5 TCP/IP
		6 CID Enablement
		7 PEN Software
		9 SPM/2 - Performance
		12 Developer CD-ROM
		13 OS/2 Developer Mag.
		15 Open Forum [DF2]
		16 Product Suggestions
		17 IBM Files [DF2]

There is also a special page, OS2SERV, where users can download current service packs. There used to be only one IBM OS/2-related forum, IBMOS2, but IBM expanded support because interest in OS/2 grew to a large extent after the release of Version 2.0. Other developers with OS/2 product support on CompuServe are listed in Table B.3.

Table B.3. Developer support forums.

Page	*Developer*	*Products*	*Support ID*
ADOBE	Adobe	ATM Fonts	76704,21
SBALDU	Aldus	PageMaker	72647,1464
BDEVTOOLS	Borland International	ObjectVision	76702,1575
BCPPWIN	Borland International	C++	76711,534
BORAPP	Borland International	Sidekick	75300,1730
COREL	Corel Software	CorelDRAW!	72350,2233
DIGITALK	Digitalk	SmallTalk/PM	76711,366
IBMPRO	Comeau Computing	C++ with Templates	72331,3421
LOTUSA	Lotus Development Corp.	1-2-3	75300,1157
LOTUSB	Lotus Development Corp.	Freelance, Notes	76004,3375 76702,1357
PCVENA	DeScribe Corporation	DeScribe	71333,154
PCVENB	J.P. Software	4OS2	75300,210
PCVENC	PKWare	PKZIP2/PKUNZIP2	75300,730
PCVENE	SemWare	QEDIT	75300,2710
PCVENF	Hillgraeve	HyperACCESS/5	75300,3402
WINAPA	Micrographx	Draw	76702,1034

continues

Table B.3. continued

Page	*Developer*	*Products*	*Support ID*
WINAPC	Matesys	CommonView /ObjectView	76702,1605
WINAPD	Pioneer Software	Q+E	71333,125
MSNETWORK	Microsoft Corp.	SQL Server	76704,61
ORACLE	Oracle Corporation	Oracle Server	76702,456
REVELATION	Revelation Technologies	Advanced Revelation	76711,104
VENTURA	Ventura Software	Ventura Publisher	76702,646

Internet

This section consists of an overview of Internet and how to get files using it. If you would like more information, it can be obtained through Internet from the NSF Network Service Center (NNSC). *The Internet Resource Guide* (IRG) can be obtained via "anonymous FTP" from `nnsc.nsf.net`. The guide is in the `pub/resource-guide` directory.

Internet started life as an experiment by the United States Department of Defense and was originally called ARPAnet. As other regional networks were added, it became larger and eventually was known as Internet. It has grown to include sites in almost every country in the world. All these regional networks are hooked together using the TCP/IP protocol. The most popular connections used are 56kb leased lines. Some connections are 1mbs T1 links, and the heavily used backbones are made up of 45mbs T3 links.

The great speed of the Internet (as a real-time connection) allows people to communicate or participate in research with colleagues from all parts of the world. Most of this work is very important to the individuals involved. They rely on Internet to be available to them at all times. For this reason you should always keep in mind that Internet should not be used as an electronic playground. Be responsible for what you do and remember that although it may be the middle of the night where you are, it may be midday at the site you are connected with—they may be in the midst of great activity. This responsible behavior is simply known as *netiquette.*

Transferring Files

File transfer is accomplished using file transfer protocol (FTP). This is both a protocol as well as the program that is used to transfer the files regardless of the operating system used for storage and retrieval. FTP allows you to connect to a remote machine and upload/download files. The convention `UPLOAD` is a transfer from your machine to the remote machine, and `DOWNLOAD` is a transfer from the remote machine to your machine. The way FTP connects to a remote machine is through the use of an Internet address (IP). Each machine on Internet has a unique address that is made up of four sets of numbers. There are usually aliases for these numbers to make it easier for you to remember. For example, the Internet address of one of IBM's machines is 129.34.139.5, but most people use the name software.watson.ibm.com. This means that the person using the textual address has a name server available to associate the two. If a name server is not available, you must use the (numeric) IP address. This machine holds some very useful files such as the latest EWS software. You could connect to this machine by using the actual numeric address or the machine name; however, it is probably easier to use the English machine name.

Once you connect to the remote machine, you have to log into it. Because you probably don't have an actual log-in ID on IBM's machine, you can use the ID anonymous. This is known as "anonymous FTP," and it was set up so people could transfer files between sites without having to go through the trouble of getting a log-in ID on each and every machine on Internet. Not every machine supports anonymous log in for security reasons. Listing B.1

shows the results of connecting to this IBM machine (the commands you enter are in bold type).

Listing B.1. A sample FTP session.

```
local.machine> ftp software.watson.ibm.com
Connected to software.watson.ibm.com.
220 software.watson.ibm.com FTP server (IBM RT) ready.
Name (software.watson.ibm.com:rdk): anonymous
331-Software on this FTP server is furnished by the terms
331-and conditions put forth in the README.FTP file in the
331-pub directory. By continuing, you agree to get
331-the above mentioned file and agree to these conditions with
331-respect to the software here. Otherwise, disconnect now.
331 Guest login ok, send ident as password.
Password:
230 Guest login ok, access restrictions apply.
```

You are now connected to the IBM machine software.watson.ibm.com. You should enter your mail address as the password. Some sites like to monitor usage of their machines and they can use the mail address as a means to accomplish this. At some sites, nothing is accepted except your mail address as a password. If you don't enter it correctly, you are denied access to the machines.

FTP Commands

Now that you are logged into the remote machine, you have to have some way to navigate. The five most important commands you need are `CD`, `DIR`, `GET`, `PUT`, and `BYE`.

`CD` is used to change directory. It has a syntax similar to OS/2 or DOS. The major difference is that you should use the slash (/) instead of the backslash (\) between directory names. In the next example, the directory is changed from the current directory to the **pub/os2** directory.

```
ftp> cd pub/os2
250 CWD command successful.
```

In this example, the directory changes from the current directory (**pub/os2**) to the **ews** directory. Both these commands could have been put on one line (i.e., cd pub/os2/ews), but they were separated for demonstration purposes.

```
ftp> cd ews
250 CWD command successful.
```

The DIR command works like the DIR command in OS/2 or DOS. The display differs depending on the operating system of the machine that you are connected to, so don't be surprised when the output format looks odd. Wildcard characters such as * or ? are supported. Listing B.2 lists a UNIX-style directory:

Listing B.2. A sample Internet directory.

```
ftp> dir
200 PORT command successful.
150 Opening data connection for /bin/ls (129.32.1.21,4531) (0 bytes).
total 2572
-r—r—r— 1 system    1219  Aug 5 14:19  aping.package
-r—r—r— 1 system  102159  Aug 5 14:20  aping.zip
    .    .    .    .    .    .    .    .    .    .
    .    .    .    .    .    .    .    .    .    .
    .    .    .    .    .    .    .    .    .    .
-r—r—r— 1 system    1250  Sep 24 14:39  vrexx2.package
-r—r—r— 1 system  202532  Sep 24 14:39  vrexx2.zip
226 Transfer complete.
2367 bytes received in 0.47 seconds (4.89 Kbytes/s)
```

In the previous example of DIR you can see that the output shows information such as date, time, and size of the files. The information on the far left of the display is similar to information displayed using the ATTRIB OS/2 command. The last line tells you how fast the directory listing was transferred across Internet to your local machine.

Now that you can see the files you would probably like to transfer them to your local machine. The way to transfer files is with the GET or MGET commands. GET transfers one file at a time; MGET transfers multiple files. The syntax for each command is similar, although MGET accepts more that one filename and it allows the use of wildcard characters. MGET also prompts you to confirm each file as it is about to transfer it. You can avoid being prompted by using the

PROMPT command. PROMPT is a toggle—issue it once and interactive mode is turned off; issue it again and interactive mode is turned on:

```
ftp> prompt
Interactive mode off.
```

Now that interactive mode is turned off, you can get some files without being bothered to confirm each one. Listing B.3 transfers the two PMGlobe files to the local machine. Note the use of the * as a wildcard.

Listing B.3. The *MGET* command.

```
ftp> mget pmgb32.*
200 PORT command successful.
150 Opening data connection for pmgb32.package (129.32.1.21,4533)
(1363 bytes).
226 Transfer complete.
local: pmgb32.package remote: pmgb32.package
1391 bytes received in 0.03 seconds (42.21 Kbytes/s)
200 PORT command successful.
150 Opening data connection for pmgb32.zip (129.32.1.21,4534) (106146
bytes).
226 Transfer complete.
local: pmgb32.zip remote: pmgb32.zip
106604 bytes received in 7.92 seconds (13.15 Kbytes/s)
```

FTP tries to keep you informed as to what it is doing as it goes along. It lets you know that it is opening a data connection and tells you the amount of data being transferred. The name of the local file and the rate of transfer is also displayed. The speed at which Internet transfers files depends on how much traffic is on the net and by how much work the remote system is doing. The Internet connection usually has a low priority to avoid slowing down legitimate users.

Usually, you need to transfer a file in binary mode. Binary mode prevents the receiving machine from doing any translations on characters. For the most part, ZIP and text files come across Internet fine (without resorting to specifying binary mode). If you experience problems extracting files, usually manifested as CRC errors, get the files again but specifying binary mode first. The opposite of BINARY is ASCII. Most sites are set for ASCII mode by default. The BINARY and ASCII commands are not toggles. Therefore, if you issue that

BINARY command twice in succession, the response will be the same both times and you will still be in binary mode.

```
ftp> binary
200 Type set to I.
ftp> ascii
200 Type set to A.
```

The BYE command closes the connection and returns you to your local machine:

```
ftp> bye
221 Goodbye.
local.machine>
```

File Extensions

Most files on Internet are stored in a compressed (or archived) format. Compressing (or archiving) files accomplishes two things: it makes the files smaller and it allows programs, documentation, and support files to be stored as one file. This cuts down on transfer and connect time. The extensions of the files should tell you how to uncompress the files. For instance, in the example I downloaded a file with the ZIP extension. Most people who have worked with micros know to use Phil Katz's PKUNZIP program to extract the files. You may find files that have extensions that are unknown to you. Table B.4 should help you get at the programs you download.

Table B.4. Typical file extensions.

ZIP	PKUNZIP
ZOO	ZOO
Z	UNCOMPRESS
TAR	UNIX TAR utility

These utilities all have sufficient documentation that explains how to extract files. It is not uncommon to find that someone has done more than one type of compression on a file. Many times you will see a file with a name like

94-9
ftp-os2.nmsu.edu gets new uploads first and has easiest access.
It and ftp-os2.cdrom.com are mirrored with each other.

…press the file then process it with TAR to

Anonymous FTP Sites

…he directories specified here may not … l Internet sites are subject to change … are included in case your machine cannot resolve the remote machine name. The following section contains a brief list of OS/2 locations available via anonymous FTP.

software.watson.ibm.com (129.34.139.5)

This site contains many of the IBM programs/files. Directories include the following:

EPM	latest version of the enhanced editor
EWS	IBM employee shareware
INFO	INF formatted files including the redbooks
SERVPAK	the latest service pack to OS/2

ftp-os2.nmsu.edu (128.123.35.151)

This is probably the largest location of OS/2 software on Internet that is available via anonymous FTP. There is a mirror directory of **software.watson.ibm.com** at this site, along with directories for GNU software, OS/2 2.0-specific, OS/2 1.3-specific, and general OS/2 software.

ftp.cica.indiana.edu (129.79.20.84)

This site contains many ATM and TrueType fonts along with software that works in WIN-OS/2.

This section contained a peek into the possibilities on Internet. There are many more commands, sites, and resources including BBSs, forums, and lists that can be reached through your modem. Don't forget that there are also human resources available through the net, so ask questions—you are bound to get at least one answer. Finally, remember that when you connect to a remote site, you are a guest on that machine—don't wear out your welcome.

Multi-Net BBS

Multi-Net is a commercial bulletin board package compatible with OS/2 1.x and above. It supports multiple lines and multinode network systems. IBM uses it extensively at the National Support Center in Georgia. Multi-Net is written by Paul Breedlove who also publishes PM-Comm. Magnum and Maximus are the two other bulletin board systems popular under OS/2. Contact a related BBS listed in "Bulletin Board Listing," for more information on these products.

Multi-Net takes advantage of several OS/2 features to provide trouble-free background communications. Threads are used for modem handling, which requires less resources than a polling DOS application. Separate full-screen sessions are used for each node and can be controlled with the Workplace Shell window list. A folder can be created to hold objects for each node, which facilitates starting and stopping sessions. Local log-on and several sysop utilities are provided from the full-screen session.

The setup program is a menu-driven Presentation Manager application with simple dialog boxes. Each node has a separate setup file that is stored in binary format. This makes for quick loading and allows customization per node. Modem support is good with built-in protocols including ZModem. The session status screen displays the communication messages during log on and log off. File transfer status is displayed in a text box. Several local sysop commands are available while a user is online to monitor status, chat, and terminate sessions.

A special sysop menu is provided for online administration. Security is based on individual passwords and levels. The user base is indexed but awkward to update. Up to 40 conferences and file areas are supported. This is somewhat limiting and forces the sysop to crowd the file areas. Each file area has a description file with 40-character short comments and optional 5-line detail records. All file areas are indexed together, which makes file searches quick, although all filenames must be unique. Files can be added online and uploaded from a local or network directory during local log on.

Most commands are single letter and the menus are easily customized. Help messages and colors are not as flexible as with other systems. There is a full-screen editor with WordStar-type cursor control and a standard line editor.

One interesting feature is the user Notepad, which stores comments and ideas from one session to the next. File lists can be marked for later download. Questionnaires, voting booths, and simple text databases add to the user experience.

The sysop menu includes a shell to OS/2 function. This is good for simple file commands, but is not meant to run console OS/2 applications. Creative use of the START command allows powerful background processing. An event manager adds some flexibility to overnight operations. A sample file list application is included to Zip the master file list for download. Macros are supported for recurring message text.

Perhaps the best feature of Multi-Net is the programmability. Each menu choice can be replaced by a program. Specific security levels can display different menus and run appropriate programs. New programs and menu choices can be added as needed. These are written in C or REXX. Dynamic link libraries and sample source code are included to help with this interface. The speed of REXX under OS/2 2.1 makes this extremely useful.

Bulletin Board Systems

There are a large number of bulletin board systems (BBS) that are available to the general public. You can access these with your modem simply by dialing the access phone number and logging on to each system. OS/2 2.1 provides the PM Terminal program, which is usually sufficient to connect with any BBS. Chapter 13, "Productivity Applets," describes this application. Most BBS locations have a guest account that you can log in to if you have never connected to them before.

The remainder of this appendix lists a number of BBS locations that may be of interest to you as a user of the OS/2 operating system. The list is sorted by states within the United States, so you can locate one nearest to you and avoid large long-distance telephone charges.

This is by no means a complete list, and does not contain any BBSs outside of the United States. If you want to track down other BBS locations, CompuServe forums are usually a good place to start. If you live outside the

United States, one of the CompuServe forums that is dedicated to your country may be the best place to ask for assistance.

Bulletin Board Systems: Arizona

Analog Gate, The

Sysop: Mike McGuire
Phone/Node/Modem: (602) 458-0451, 1:309/9, USR HST DS 16.8 V.32b/V.42b
Location: Sierra Vista, Arizona
Primary Focus: OS/2
Comments: Carries OS2DOS, OS2BBS, and OS2HW Fidonet echos and has first-time access and file request. A Fernwood File Distributor.

Emerald Isle, The

Sysop: Mike Mahoney
Phone/Node/Modem: (602) 749-8638, 1:300/14.0, USR HST DS 14.4 V.32b/V.42b
Location: Tuscon, Arizona
Primary Focus: OS/2 Conferences from Fidonet, ibmNET, and Usenet
Comments: OS/2 Version 2.0, BinkleyTerm 2.56, Maximus 2.01. Internet Gateway for Network 300. A little bit of Ireland in the desert.

ORAC/2

Sysop: Eugene Grover
Phone/Node/Modem: (602) 864-8862, 1:114/12, USR HST DS 14.4 V.32b/V.42b
Phone/Node/Modem: (602) 864-8862, 5602/12 (EchoNet), USR HST DS 14.4 V.32b/V.42b
Phone/Node/Modem: (602) 864-8862, 81:301/1 (OS2NET), USR HST DS 14.4 V.32b/V.42b

Location: Phoenix, Arizona
Primary Focus: OS/2
Comments: Carries OS/2 message and file areas.

Bulletin Board Systems: California

AsmLang and OS/2

Sysop: Patrick O'Riva
Phone/Node/Modem: (408) 259-2223, 1:143/37, USR HST 14.4 V.42
Location: San Jose, California
Primary Focus: OS/2 and Assembly Language programming
Comments: 60+M files (no games or GIF's). Open Access policy.

Computer Education Services

Sysop: Rollin White
Phone/Node/Modem: (714) 965-9963, 1:103/132, ZyXEL 14.4 V.32b/V.42b
Location: Huntington Beach, California
Primary Focus: OS/2 and Programming
Comments: ProgNet and Sourcenet Regional, OS2NET NC, WildNet Hub,Calnet QWK gateway, ibmNET, Fidonet, and RaNet node. Dedicated to the distribution of programming and OS/2-related information and files.

Magnum BBS

Sysop: Chuck Gilmore
Phone/Node/Modem: (805) 582-9306, n/a, USR HST DS 9600 V.32b/V.42b
Location: California
Primary Focus: OS/2
Comments: Support BBS for Magnum BBS software.

OS/2 Connection

Sysop: Craig Swanson
Phone/Node/Modem: (619) 558-9475, 1:202/514, ZyXEL 14.4 V.32b/V.42b
Location: La Jolla, California
Primary Focus: OS/2
Comments: Our open access download areas have more than 2,100 OS/2 files totalling more than 150MB, including the complete Fernwood collection as of January, 1992, plus many new files received over OS2NEW and Usernet's comp.binaries.os2. We carry all OS/2-related Fidonet, Usenet, and OS/2 shareware message areas, plus many other technical areas covering topics such as hard disk drives, CD-ROM, SCSI, and modems. No upload/download ratios are enforced, but bonus time is given for those who upload OS/2 files. Contributors receive additional time (90 minutes per call, 100 minutes per day) and have access to a second BBS line for contributors only (which will be starting up soon).

Omega-Point BBS

Sysop: Unknown
Phone/Node/Modem: (714) 963-8517, n/a, 2400
Location: California
Comments: Home of Omega-Point BBS software.

PCAware OS/2

Sysop: David Lents/Sue Lin Poh
Phone/Node/Modem: (619) 291-9791, 1:202/918, USR HST DS 14.4 V.32b/V.42b
Phone/Node/Modem: (619) 291-2963, n/a, ZyXEL 14.4 V.32b/V.42b
Phone/Node/Modem: (619) 291-9792, n/a, 2400 (*6* Lines)
Location: San Diego, California
Primary Focus: OS/2, political discussions, hardware sales and support
Comments: Our 8-node Maximus/2 system is unique among OS/2 boards. First-time callers can download from our library of more than 1,500 files. We have more than 500M of HPFS drive space, so uploaders

are generously rewarded. New files are received each day from Fernwood, SDSOS, PDNOS2, as well as many other file echos. We carry more than 80 FidoNet areas, including all OS/2 topics. Registration brings increased access, and all contributors can choose to increase privileges up to 3 hours and 10M per day, or even unlimited time/DLing! Users can check out PCAware's great products and low prices and obtain online quotes for all computer equipment not listed in our online catalog. Mail order is available for LD callers.

SeaHunt BBS

Sysop: Michael Nelson
Phone/Node/Modem: (415) 431-0473, 1:125/20, USR HST DS 14.4 V.32b/V.42b
Phone/Node/Modem: (415) 431-0473, 8:914/501 (Rbbs-Net), USR HST DS 14.4 V.32b/V.42b
Phone/Node/Modem: (415) 431-0227, No mailer, BBS Only, USR HST 14.4
Location: San Fransisco, California
Primary Focus: OS/2, programming, echos
Comments: Several Internet conferences, including several that are OS/2-specific. A growing collection of OS/2 files. Running on an i486/33, 650MB, under OS/2 2.0. Maximus/2OS/2 BBS software, and BinkleyTerm 2.55 OS/2 Mailer.

T.E.L. Net Systems #2

Sysop: Chris A. Epler
Phone/Node/Modem: (714) 597-7858, 1:207/107, USR HST 14.4
Location: Chino Hills, California
Primary Focus: OS/2, HAM radio support
Comments: Several OS/2 and HAM radio-related discussion and file areas. Fidonet, RBBSNet, CalNet, and UserNet message areas. Running Maximus under OS/2. The area code (714) will be soon changing to (909).

Zzyzx Road OS/2 BBS

Sysop: Michael Cummings
Phone/Node/Modem: (619) 579-0135, 1:202/338, ZyXEL 14.4 V.32b/ V.42b
Location: El Cajon, county of San Diego, California
Primary Focus: OS/2 message bases and files with some business echos
Comments: This BBS is online 24 hours daily, 7 days a week, and is a member of FidoNet (1:202/338) and BizyNet (70:1/15). Our file areas are devoted to OS/2 shareware of all sorts, and we carry a few business echos for those interested in conducting real business in a network environment.

Bulletin Board Systems: Colorado

Canadian Connection, The

Sysop: Preston Smith
Phone/Node/Modem: (719) 599-4568, 1:128/77, USR HST DS 14.4 V.32b/V.42b
Phone/Node/Modem: (719) 599-4568, 81:300/1, USR HST DS 14.4 V.32b/V.42b
Location: Colorado Springs, Colorado
Primary Focus: OS/2, C/C++ programming, Canadian Echos
Comments: First-time access to downloads, no ratios.

Cuerna Verde

Sysop: William Herrera
Phone/Node/Modem: (719) 545-8572, 1:307/18 aka 1:307/1, 9600 V.32/ V.42b
Location: Pueblo, Colorado
Primary Focus: OS/2 and conferences/files support for helping professions
Comments: Running Binkley/2 and Maximus/2 in the background on an OPTI 486-25 with 8M RAM, 600 MEB on 2 IDE drives (Maxtor80,

Fijitsu 520). Both formatted HPFS. Specializes in OS/2 conferences and files, and also carries most health/wellness-type message areas on the backbone.

Socialism OnLine!

Sysop: Randy Edwards
Phone/Node/Modem: (719) 392-7781, 1:128/105, USR HST 9600 V.42b/MNP
Location: Colorado Springs, Colorado
Primary Focus: OS/2
Comments: Carrying a full line of OS/2 files, along with the OS/2'OS2NEW' file-echo, and more than a dozen OS/2 echo-mail conferences.

Bulletin Board Systems: Connecticut

Ascii Neighborhood I & II

Sysop: Bob Morris
Phone/Node/Modem: (203) 934-9852, 1:141/332, 9600 PEP
Phone/Node/Modem: (203) 932-6236, 1:141/333, USR HST DS 9600 V.32b/V.42b
Location: West Haven, Connecticut
Primary Focus: General-purpose OS/2 and MS-DOS file areas
Comments: Contains "Fernwood Collection" OS/2 files. Running BinkleyTerm and Maximus. Many OS/2-related echos available.

Bullet BBS

Sysop: Steve Lesner
Phone/Node/Modem: (203) 329-2972, 1:141/260, USR HST 9600 V.32
Phone/Node/Modem: (203) 322-4135, 1:141/261, USR HST 9600 V.32
Location: Stamford, Connecticut

Primary Focus: OS/2, LANs, programming
Comments: These boards focus on OS/2 and narrow in on running OS/2 Novell network software. Both nodes are running Maximus and have the ability to spawn a copy of Simplex. Lots of PD files for DOS, Windows, and OS/2, as well as Novell software (much of it acquired from the CIS NOV forums).

Caladan

Sysop: Rob Schmaling
Phone/Node/Modem: (203) 622-4740, 1:141/243, USR HST 14.4 V.42b
Location: Greenwich, Connecticut
Primary Focus: OS/2
Comments: Running under OS/2 and Maximus 2.01.

Excelsior, The

Sysop: Felix Tang
Phone/Node/Modem: (203) 466-1826, 1:141/222, USR HST DS 14.4 V.32b/V.42b
Phone/Node/Modem: (203) 466-1892, n/a, 2400
Location: New Haven, Connecticut
Primary Focus: OS/2, Amiga, Virtual Reality, DOS, and Windows (in that order of importance)
Comments: 820M online capacity. OS2NEW (Fernwood) distribution. Running Maximus 2.01wb under OS/2 1.3 SE.

Fernwood

Sysop: Emmitt Dove
Phone/Node/Modem: (203) 483-0348, 1:141/109, USR HST DS 9600 V.32b/V.42b
Phone/Node/Modem: (203) 481-7934, 1:141/209, USR HST 14.4 V.42b
Location: Branford, Connecticut
Primary Focus: OS/2

Comments: Origin of the Fernwood Collection. All first-time callers have full access and 90 minutes per call. All files are file-requestable—request OS2FILES for a listing of all OS/2-related files, or FWOS2INF.ZIP for a VIEWable listing.

Storm Front - OS/2, The

Sysop: Chris Regan
Phone/Node/Modem: (203) 234-0824, 1:141/600, USR HST 9600
Phone/Node/Modem: (203) 234-0824, 1:141/565, USR HST 9600
Location: North Haven, Connecticut
Primary Focus: OS/2

Treasure Island

Sysop: Don Dawson
Phone/Node/Modem: (203) 791-8532, 1:141/730, USR HST DS 14.4 V.32b/V.42b
Location: Danbury, Connecticut
Primary Focus: Something for everyone
Comments: 400+M of files, including BBS, ANSI, OS/2, DV, Windows, SDS/SDN/PDN/WinNet/UtilNet. 200+ Fidonet echos. Running BinkleyTerm/Maximus/OS/2 under two phone lines.

Bulletin Board Systems: Delaware

Singer Bear BBS

Sysop: John Tarbox
Phone/Node/Modem: (302) 984-2238, 1:150/130, USR HST 9600
Location: Wilmington, Delaware
Primary Focus: Technical, including OS/2, Client/Server, and programming

Comments: System has more than 1,700 files available for download by first-time callers. Running BinkleyTerm and Maximus under OS/2. Online since 1988. (Will soon be using a USR Dual Standardmodem.)

Space Station Alpha

Sysop: Scott Street
Phone/Node/Modem: (302) 653-1458, 1:2600/135, USR HST DS 14.4 V.32b/V.42b
Location: Smyrna, Delaware
Primary Focus: OS/2 and programming OS/2
Comments: Primary focus on OS/2 FidoNet echos. Fernwood files are available.

Bulletin Board Systems: Florida

OS2 Exchange

Sysop: Don Bauer
Phone/Node/Modem: (904) 739-2445, 1:112/37, ZYXEL 14.4 V.32b/V.42b
Location: Jacksonville, Florida
Primary Focus: OS/2
Comments: More than 40M of OS/2 shareware, articles, and technical information. Open access policy. Request FILES via mailer or OS2EXCH.LST via BBS for complete files listing. Automated file retrieval from comp.binaries.os2 in addition to all FTP sites carrying OS/2 shareware. We keep up with the latest drivers/fixes.

Other World, The

Sysop: Troy Kraser
Phone/Node/Modem: (904) 893-2404, 1:3605/56, Cardinal 9600 V.32
Location: Tallahassee, Florida

Primary Focus: DOS and OS/2
Comments: Have file areas for both DOS and OS/2, hoping to focus on the OS/2 sections by collecting new OS/2 shareware. No registration requirements (except real names).

SandDollar, The

Sysop: Mark Wheeler
Phone/Node/Modem: (407) 784-4507, 1:374/95, USR HST 9600
Location: Cape Canaveral, Florida
Primary Focus: OS/2 and Windows 3.0
Comments: Carries a lot of OS/2 and Window programs.

Bulletin Board Systems: Georgia

IBM National Support Center

Sysop: IBM
Phone/Node/Modem: (404) 835-6600, n/a, 2400
Phone/Node/Modem: (404) 835-5300, n/a, USR HST DS 9600 V.32b/V.42b
Location: Atlanta, Georgia
Comments: Very active OS/2 conference areas. Helpful IBM'ers doing an outstanding job.

Information Overload

Sysop: Ed June
Phone/Node/Modem: (404) 471-1549, 1:133/308, USR HST 9600
Location: Riverdale, Georgia
Primary Focus: OS/2
Comments: Atlanta's OS/2 Users Group BBS. First-time callers have full access, 90 minutes per day. Carries all OS/2 FidoNet echos, along with

the comp.os2... newsgroups from Internet. Receives the Fernwood File Distribution. No DOS files, please!

Bulletin Board Systems: Hawaii

Ghostcomm Image Gallery

Sysop: Craig Oshiro
Phone/Node/Modem: (808) 456-8510, 1:345/14, USR HST DS 14.4 V.32b/V.42b
Phone/Node/Modem: (808) 456-8510, 8:908/23 (RbbsNet), USR HST DS 14.4 V.32b/V.42b
Location: Pearl City, Hawaii
Primary Focus: Imaging and graphics, OS/2, some Macintosh, and MSDOS
Comments: Free access to OS/2 Fidonet conferences and OS/2 file areas. File retrievals from Internet ftp archives such as ftp-os2.nmsu.edu are performed on a daily basis. Latest patches and fixes from software.watson.ibm.com as they are made available. OS2NEW retrievals from zues.ieee.org. Currently running in a DOS 5.0 boot image.

Bulletin Board Systems: Illinois

GREATER CHICAGO Online!! BBS

Sysop: Bill Cook
Phone/Node/Modem: (708) 895-4042, n/a, 9600
Location: Chicago, Illinois
Primary Focus: OS/2
Comments: Supporting OS/2 in the Chicago metropolitan area. Home of the Chicago OS/2 User Group. Approximately 400 OS/2 files, and around 200 active users.

I CAN! BBS

Sysop: Bogie Bugsalewicz
Phone/Node/Modem: (312) 736-7434, 1:115/738, USR HST DS 14.4 V.32/V.42b
Phone/Node/Modem: (312) 736-7388, n/a, PP 2400SA MNP
Location: Chicago, Illinois
Primary Focus: Disability topics, Max/Squish support, OS/2
Comments: ADAnet Regional Hub (94:107/0). Large collection of message bases (150) on assorted topics, including technical forums. Nominally disability oriented, but extremely eclectic. Other network address: 96:207/738.

Bulletin Board Systems: Indiana

Catacombs, The

Sysop: Mike Phillips
Phone/Node/Modem: (317) 525-7164, 1:231/380, USR HST 9600
Phone/Node/Modem: (317) 525-7164, 8:74/1, USR HST 9600
Location: Waldron, Indiana
Primary Focus: DOS, OS/2, programming, technical
Comments: Full access to first-time callers, no fee. Open 24 hours, file requests honored 24 hours a day.

Fortress BBS

Sysop: Stephen Gutknecht
Phone/Node/Modem: (219) 471-3918, n/a, 14.4 V.32b/V.42b
Phone/Node/Modem: (219) 471-4016, n/a, Unknown
Location: Indiana
Primary Focus: OS/2
Comments: Running two lines 24-hours per day, 7 days per week.

Play Board, The

Sysop: Jay Tipton
Phone/Node/Modem: (219) 744-4908, 1:236/20, USR HST 9600
Phone/Node/Modem: (219) 744-4908, 60:4800/1, USR HST 9600
Phone/Node/Modem: (219) 744-4908, 60:3/220, USR HST 9600
Location: Fort Wayne, Indiana
Primary Focus: OS/2
Comments: OS/2 support for Fort Wayne and contact point for Fort Wayne's OS/2 users group. We carry most of the FidoNet OS/2echos and voyager echos.

Bulletin Board Systems: Kansas

Byte Bus, The

Sysop: Troy Majors
Phone/Node/Modem: (316) 683-1433, 1:291/13, USR HST DS 16.8 V.32b/V.42b
Location: Wichita, Kansas
Primary Focus: OS/2 files, messages, information
Comments: More than 150M of OS/2 files. Member of Fernwood OS/2Distribution Network, OS2NET, and ibmNET Echo and File Distribution Networks.

Bulletin Board Systems: Louisiana

HelpNet of Baton Rouge

Sysop: Stan Brohn
Phone/Node/Modem: (504) 273-3116, 1:3800/1, USR HST DS 9600 V.32b/V.42b

Phone/Node/Modem: (504) 275-7389, 1:3800/2, USR HST 9600
Location: Baton Rouge, Louisiana
Comments: Carry OS/2 files and downloadable programs. The second line is echos only.

Padded Cell BBS, The

Sysop: Jim Sterrett
Phone/Node/Modem: (504) 340-7027, 1:396/51, USR HST DS 14.4 V.32b/V.42b
Location: Marrero (New Orleans), Louisiana
Primary Focus: OS/2, sysop support
Comments: OS/2 shareware, FileBone File Echo Hub, SDS. Open access policy. Request files for complete listing.

Simple Board, The

Sysop: Rick Ferguson
Phone/Node/Modem: (504) 664-2524, 1:3800/24, PPI 14400FXSA V.32b/V.42b
Location: Denham Springs, Louisiana
Primary Focus: OS/2, Programming, Messages
Comments: Dedicated to the support of OS/2. It is running on Binkley 2.56, Maximus/2 2.01. A member of OS2NET (81:206/1).

Bulletin Board Systems: Massachusetts

Polish Home, The

Sysop: Vladek Komorek
Phone/Node/Modem: (617) 332-9739, 1:101/316, SUPRA 14.4 V.32b/V.42b

Location: Newton, Massachusetts
Primary Focus: Polish-related echomail/lists, OS/2, Fido/Internet gate programs.
Comments: I am trying to support the metro-Boston community with OS/2-related files and information.

Bulletin Board Systems: Maryland

Last Relay, The

Sysop: James Chance
Phone/Node/Modem: (410) 793-3829, 1:261/1120, 14.4 V.32b/V.42b
Phone/Node/Modem: (410) 793-3829, 100:904/0, 14.4 V.32b/V.42b
Phone/Node/Modem: (410) 793-3829, 100:904/1, 14.4 V.32b/V.42b
Location: Crofton, Maryland
Primary Focus: OS/2, Windows, and desktop publishing
Comments: More than 100M of OS/2 and Windows files, complete SDSload.

Bulletin Board Systems: Michigan

Cornerstone BBS, The

Sysop: Dave Shoff
Phone/Node/Modem: (616) 465-4611, 1:2340/110, 14.4 V.32b/V.42b
Location: Bridgman, Michigan
Primary Focus: OS/2
Comments: Carries all OS/2 echos (except OS2PROG). Member of OS2NEW(Fernwood) File Distribution.

Bulletin Board Systems: Minnesota

Oberon Software

Sysop: Brady Flowers
Phone/Node/Modem: (507) 388-1154, 1:292/60, USR HST 14.4
Location: Mankato, Minnesota
Primary Focus: OS/2
Comments: User support BBS for Oberon Software products (TE/2, fshl, and so on). Everyone is welcome.

Bulletin Board Systems: Missouri

Gateway/2 OS/2 BBS

Sysop: Ron Gines
Phone/Node/Modem: (314) 554-9313, 1:100/220, 9600 V.32/V.42b
Phone/Node/Modem: (314) 554-9313, 81:200/1 (OS2NET), 9600 V.32/V.42b
Location: St. Louis, Missouri
Primary Focus: OS/2

Multitasking Systems

Sysop: Bill Hirt
Phone/Node/Modem: (816) 587-5360, 1:280/304, 14.4 V.32b/V.42b
Location: Kansas City, Missouri
Primary Focus: OS/2
Comments: Both Fidonet and Usernet message areas. Internet private mail available to registered users. Full access requires mail-in registration. No fee.

OS/2 Woodmeister, The

Sysop: Woody Sturges
Phone/Node/Modem: (314) 446-0016, 1:289/27, USR HST DS 14.4 V.32b/V.42b
Location: Columbia, Missouri
Primary Focus: OS/2
Comments: Carries all the major OS/2 echos and files areas. Free access, no ratios.

Bulletin Board Systems: North Carolina

Backdoor BBS

Sysop: Thomas Bradford
Phone/Node/Modem: (919) 799-0923, 1:3628/11, Hayes Optima 14.4 V.32b/V.42b
Phone/Node/Modem: (919) 350-0180, n/a, Hayes Optima 2400
Location: Wilmington, North Carolina
Primary Focus: OS/2
Comments: An OS/2-oriented BBS that only carries OS/2 libraries and the FidoNet OS/2 echos, as well as some smaller ones that aren't on the Backbone. The OS/2 Fernwood File Distribution Network is the latest addition and ensures that we stay on top of new programs, revisions, and fixes. All files FREQable from 5 a.m. to 6 a.m.

Programmer's Oasis BBS, The

Sysop: Chris Laforet
Phone/Node/Modem: (919) 226-6984, 1:3644/1, USR HST DS 14.4 V.32b/V.42b
Phone/Node/Modem: (919) 226-7136, 1:3644/2, USR HST DS 14.4 V.32b/V.42b
Location: Graham, North Carolina

Primary Focus: OS/2 and programming (C, Pascal, Assembler)
Comments: Hooked into Fernwood OS/2 file distribution.

Psychotronic BBS

Sysop: Richard Lee
Phone/Node/Modem: (919) 286-7738, 1:3641/1, USR HST DS 9600 V.32b/V.32b
Phone/Node/Modem: (919) 286-4542, 1:3641/224, USR HST 9600 V.32
Location: Durham, North Carolina
Primary Focus: Echomail
Comments: We carry almost every FidoNet technical conference and support the XRS, QWK, and Blue Wave off-line readers. Member of the Fernwood, Programmer's Distribution Net, HamNet, and several other file distribution networks. PCPursuitable(NCRTP), Starlinkable. Always 100 percent free.

Bulletin Board Systems: New Jersey

Capital City BBS

Sysop: Bob Germer
Phone/Node/Modem: (609) 386-1989, 1:266/21, USR HST DS 14.4 V.32b/V.42b
Phone/Node/Modem: (609) 386-1989, 8:950/10, USR HST DS 14.4 V.32b/V.42b
Location: Burlington, New Jersey
Primary Focus: OS/2, Word Perfect, Disabilities
Comments: Users who answer a 10-question registration form get download privileges on first call. QWK format message download supported.

Dog's Breakfast, The

Sysop: Mike Fuchs

Phone/Node/Modem: (908) 506-0472, 1:266/71, USR HST DS 14.4 V.32b/V.42b
Phone/Node/Modem: (908) 506-6293, n/a, Intel 2400 MNP-5
Location: Toms River, New Jersey
Primary Focus: Business and professional microcomputer users
Comments: More than 50 networked Echomail conferences, and participation in numerous file distrubution networks, including OS2NEW, WinNet, PDN, SDN, SDS, bringing in a continuous flow of the latest in OS/2, Windows, program development tools and code, and high-quality shareware. No fees. First-time callers get full read-only access to EchoMail and all file areas.

MACnetics BBS, The

Sysop: Ralph Merritt
Phone/Node/Modem: (908) 469-4603, 1:2605/611, USR HST DS 14.4 V.32b/V.42b
Location: Bound Brook, New Jersey
Primary Focus: Machintosh, OS/2, and Windows
Comments: All backbone/non-backbone OS2* echos plus gated InternetNewsGroups (COMP.OS.OS2.*). Member of Fernwood OS/2 File Distribution Network. Open Access. File-request OS2FILES for a list of OS/2-specific files for download/FREQ. Originally Macintosh focus, we have expanded to include OS/2 and Windows.

Monster BBS, The

Sysop: Bob Hatton
Phone/Node/Modem: (908) 382-5671, n/a, USR HST 9600
Location: Rahway, New Jersey
Primary Focus: OS/2
Comments: Running Magnum BBS software with drive storage of 1.1G (not counting the system drive). The BBS is free, limited access on node 1. All that is required to be a regular user is an introduction message. Background tasks include file list creation, message list creation (for off-line editing, replying, and so on), and soon-to-be-added online fax

send/receive capability. The BBS is OS/2-based running a BETA 2.0, but DOS users, as well as Apple, Amiga, CoCo, and Commie users, are welcome. Few games, lots of files, and the original HotRod/Musclecar message base, as well as tech topics and others.

Sorcery Board BBS, The

Sysop: B.J. Weschke
Phone/Node/Modem: (908) 722-2231, 1:2606/403, USR HST DS 9600 V.32b/V.42b
Phone/Node/Modem: (908) 704-1108, 1:2606/407, USR HST DS 9600 V.32b/V.42b
Location: Bridgewater, New Jersey
Primary Focus: File echos
Comments: Carries file echos catering to any type of user up to and including OS/2. They have echos available on OS/2 BBSing.

Bulletin Board Systems: Nevada

Caddis OS/2 BBS

Sysop: Kerry Flint
Phone/Node/Modem: (702) 453-6981, 1:209/705, USR HST DS 16.8 V.32b/V.42b
Location: Las Vegas, Nevada
Primary Focus: OS/2 files and echos
Comments: Carries all available OS/2 file and message echos. Running BinkleyTerm and Maximus under OS/2. Full file access on first call. Freq FILES for file listings (except during ZMH).

Choice BBS, The

Sysop: Mark Woolworth

Phone/Node/Modem: (702) 253-6527, 1:209/710, USR HST DS 16.8 V.32b/V.42b
Phone/Node/Modem: (702) 253-6274, n/a, 9600 V.32/MNP
Location: Las Vegas, Nevada
Primary Focus: files and messages
Comments: Added 6 more lines in January 1993. 702-253-6527 will expand to a 4-line USR HST DS 16.8k baud rotary. 702-253-6274 number will change to a 5-line rotary with 2400 baud modems. This BBS has hundreds of file areas available, some of which include the Fernwood OS/2 file echos, SDN, PDN, SDS, WinNet, SkyNet, DDS. In all, we have several thousand files online. We have 750M online now, and will be expanding that to several gigabytes during the first quarter of 1993. We also have dozens of message echos online. Everything from programming to languages to general interest echos. There is no registration process. Call in and you have full access, plus a full hour to browse the system.

Communitel OS/2 BBS

Sysop: Dennis Conley
Phone/Node/Modem: (702) 399-0486, 1:209/210, USR HST DS 14.4 V.32b/V.42b
Location: Las Vegas, Nevada
Primary Focus: OS/2 (files, messages, and information)
Comments: FREQ "FILES" for list of available list of files to download or from BBS download "F209-210.ZIP".

Bulletin Board Systems: New York

BlueDog BBS

Sysop: Philip Perlman
Phone/Node/Modem: (212) 594-4425, 1:278/709, USR HST DS 9600 V.32/V.42b

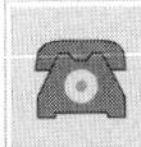

Location: New York, New York
Primary Focus: OS/2, programming, FidoNet, USENET
Comments: New York's FileBone hub.

Kind Diamond's Realm

Sysop: Mikel Beck
Phone/Node/Modem: (516) 736-3403, 1:107/218, USR HST DS 14.4 V.32b/V.42b
Location: Coram, Long Island, New York
Primary Focus: OS/2 and VAX/VMS
Comments: Carrying the following Fidonet conferences: OS2, OS2BBS, OS2DOS, OS2HW, OS2PROG, OS2LAN, and the following Usenet newsgroups: comp.os.os2.misc, comp.os.os2.programmer.

Bulletin Board Systems: Oklahoma

Asylum BBS, The

Sysop: Bill Schnell
Phone/Node/Modem: (918) 832-1462, 1:170/200, USR HST 14.4 V.42b
Location: Tulsa, Oklahoma
Primary Focus: OS/2 and Windows support

BBS/2

Sysop: Scott Dickason
Phone/Node/Modem: (918) 743-1562, 1:170/101, 2400
Location: Tulsa, Oklahoma
Primary Focus: OS/2, Windows 3.x, music and sound
Comments: More than 150M of shareware, including many Windows 3.x, Sound MIDI & Music, Cheats and Unprotects, and a growing OS/2 collection. Many FidoNet echos. Open access policy.

Distortion

Sysop: Jeremy Lakey
Phone/Node/Modem: (918) 459-0597, n/a, GVC 9600 V.32/V.42b
Location: Tulsa, Oklahoma
Primary Focus: Drivers
Comments: Call this BBS for drivers for anything. I'll get it if I haven't got it.

H*A*L

Sysop: Lloyd Hatley
Phone/Node/Modem: (918) 682-7337, 1:3813/304, 14.4 V.32b/V.42b
Location: Muskogee, Oklahoma
Primary Focus: OS/2, programming, technical support
Comments: The Human Access Link is devoted to support. We encourage both system and human support of computer-related tasks. Active member of FidoNet 1:3813/0 (HC) and1:3813/304, RFnet 73:102/0 (REGHUB), 73:102/1,DoorNet 75:7918/205, and OS2NET 81:202/301.

LiveNet

Sysop: Dave Fisher
Phone/Node/Modem: (918) 481-5715, 1:170/110, USR HST DS 16.8 V.32b/V.42b
Location: Tulsa, Oklahoma
Primary Focus: OS/2
Comments: More than 250M (3,000+ files) of OS/2 shareware, articles, and technical information. Request FILES via network mailer, or ALLFILES.ZIP via BBS for a complete file listing. Many OS/2 echos are archived weekly and available for downloading. Open access policy. Contributors receive greatly increased online time and download ability. Regional manager for the Fernwood OS/2 Network, South USHost for ibmNET, and member of OS2NET.The OS/2 World BBS List is distributed from LiveNet. Network addresses: 1:170/110@fidonet, 40:4372/0 (ibmNET), and 81:202/201 (OS2NET).

The SNAKE PIT!

Sysop: Rad Craig
Phone/Node/Modem: (918) 494-5624, 1:170/813, ZyXEL 14.4 V.32b/V.42b/MNP3-5
Location: Tulsa, Oklahoma
Primary Focus: Yale BBS beta site and midwestern U.S. headquarters
Comments: Avid interest in OS/2, programming, LAN's, files, echos, and development of utilities for Yale BBS.

Bulletin Board Systems: Oregon

Integrated Media Services

Sysop: Bill Taylor
Phone/Node/Modem: (503) 296-8192, 1:105/507, ZyXEL U1496E 14.4 V.32b/V.42b
Location: The Dalles, Oregon
Primary Focus: General-purpose BBS
Comments: Carries FidoNet backbone OS/2 echos, SDSOS2, OS2NEW file echo, plus Windows, DV, and DOS files. Runs under BinkleyTerm and Maximus for OS/2. Access to all but adult areas for first-time callers.

Multi-Net

Sysop: Paul Breedlove
Phone/Node/Modem: (503) 883-8197, n/a, USR HST DS 9600 V.32b/V.42b
Location: Lakeside, Oregon
Primary Focus: OS/2
Comments: Support BBS for Multi-Net BBS software and PM Comm communications software.

Bulletin Board Systems: Pennsylvania

U.S. Telematics

Sysop: Richard A. Press
Phone/Node/Modem: (215) 493-5242, 1:273/201, USR HST 9600 V.32/V.42b
Location: Yardley, Pennsylvania
Primary Focus: Medical, handicap, and transportation issues; OS/2 echos/files
Comments: Regional outlet for ADAnet. Running TBBS, TIMS, TDBS, and BinkleyTerm.

Bulletin Board Systems: South Carolina

PMSC OnLine Resource

Sysop: Paul Beverly
Phone/Node/Modem: (803) 735-6101, 1:376/32, 2400
Location: Columbia, South Carolina
Primary Focus: OS/2
Comments: First-time callers have very limited access. You must follow the directions when you first call to gain access. Fairly large OS/2 file collection that is growing rapidly. File requests welcome. No file ratios. Carries major OS/2 echos and USENET.

Bulletin Board Systems: Tennessee

Lonnie Wall

Sysop: Operand BBS
Phone/Node/Modem: (901) 753-3738, n/a, 2400

Phone/Node/Modem: (901) 753-7858, 1:123/58, Galaxy UFO 14.4 V.32b/V.42b
Location: Germantown, Tennessee
Primary Focus: OS/2, DOS, Windows 3.1, Adult GIFs and animations
Comments: Running Maximus 2.01wb under OS/2 2.0.

Looking Glass, The

Sysop: Edward Owens
Phone/Node/Modem: (901) 872-4386, 1:123/81, SupraFax 14.4 V.32b/V.42b
Location: Millington, Tennessee
Primary Focus: OS/2 and C, C++, and Pascal programming and OS/2 DN files
Comments: Software running is BinkleyTerm and Maximus under OS/2. I have lots of OS/2 files for downloads. I am working on door games that will run under OS/2, so you don't have to interface to DOS and other utilities. Carries programming echos and files of all kinds. Will be putting in second node that will hunt from first line to keep up with traffic.

Strictly OS/2

Sysop: Stan Gammons
Phone/Node/Modem: (615) 449-3579, 1:116/66, USR HST 9600
Location: Lebanon, Tennessee
Primary Focus: OS/2, programming, echos, OS/2 files
Comments: Echos carried: OS2, OS2BBS, OS2HW, and OS2PROG.

Talkin' Ring Network, The

Sysop: Charlie Coffman
Phone/Node/Modem: (615) 385-2316, 1:116/17, 2400
Location: Nashville, Tennessee
Primary Focus: OS/2
Comments: Intended to be a support BBS for users of OS/2 and for professionals who support OS/2. Running all software under OS/2

Version 2.00. OS/2 shareware, OS/2 echos, and other international echos of interest to computer professionals. 14.4k bps V.32bis/V.42bis.

Bulletin Board Systems: Texas

Alternate Escape (I and II)

Sysop: Bob Fudge
Phone/Node/Modem: (903) 883-4441, 1:19/26, USR HST DS 9600 V.32/V.42b
Phone/Node/Modem: (903) 883-4444, 1:19/27, USR HST 9600
Location: Greenville, Texas
Primary Focus: OS/2

COMM Port One

Sysop: Bob Juge
Phone/Node/Modem: (713) 980-9671, 1:106/2000, USR HST DS 14.4 V.32b/V.42b
Location: Houston, Texas
Primary Focus: OS/2, DOS communications
Comments: SDS Region 19 coordinator, OPUSarchive.

Cache Flow

Sysop: Kevin Cook
Phone/Node/Modem: (817) 483-2283, 1:130/403, 14.4 V.32b/V.42b
Location: Arlington, Texas
Primary Focus: Windows, OS/2, Motif, X-Windows, GUIs in general
Comments: Carries most TIC areas related to GUIs and all the Fidonet message areas also related.

DOOGER'S Place OS/2

Sysop: Jim Dailey
Phone/Node/Modem: (713) 469-3689, 1:106/202, ZyXEL 14.4 V.32b/V.42b
Location: Houston, Texas
Primary Focus: OS/2, OS/2-related echos
Comments: The BBS is dedicated to the usage of OS/2. More than 1,500 OS/2 files available.

Dugout BBS, The

Sysop: Shawn Haverly
Phone/Node/Modem: (817) 773-9138, 1:396/12, USR HST DS 16.8 V.32b/V.42b
Phone/Node/Modem: (817) 773-9140, n/a, 2400
Location: Temple, Texas
Primary Focus: DOS and OS/2
Comments: Running under OS/2 2.0 and Maximus/2 on a 340M drive. Still supporting DOS heavily with OS/2 support up and coming on strong.

Nibbles & Bytes

Sysop: Ron Bemis
Phone/Node/Modem: (214) 231-3841, 1:124/1113, USR HST 9600
Location: Dallas, Texas
Comments: Carries a number of BBS-related OS/2 utilities.

Roach Coach, The

Sysop: David Dozier
Phone/Node/Modem: (713) 343-0942, 1:106/3333, USR HST DS 14.4 V.32b/V.42b
Location: Richmond, Texas
Primary Focus: OS/2, echos, cooking

Comments: We carry FidoNet and Internet OS/2 echos. OS/2 files all available for file request or first-time download; everyone is welcome.

Rock BBS, The

Sysop: Doug Palmer
Phone/Node/Modem: (512) 654-9792, 1:387/31, ZyXEL 1496E
Phone/Node/Modem: (512) 654-9793, n/a, Boca M2400E
Location: San Antonio, Texas
Primary Focus: Religion, debate, literature, and technical issues
Comments: Two nodes, one high speed, one 2400/ARQ. More than 100 echos from all over the United States. Multiline chat available, some files. Focus is on message traffic and religious issues. Equipment: i486/33 20Meg RAM 428Meg HD, OS/2. Specializes in point support, too.

RucK's Place/2

Sysop: Ken Rucker
Phone/Node/Modem: (817) 485-8042, 1:130/65, USR HST DS 14.4 V.32b/V.42b
Location: Fort Worth, Texas
Primary Focus: OS/2
Comments: All first-time callers have full access and 60 minutes per call. All files are files-requestable; request 130-65.ZIP for a listing of all files, or RucK2BBS.ZIP for a VIEWable listing.

Soldier's Bored, The

Sysop: Art Fellner
Phone/Node/Modem: (713) 437-2859, 1:106/437, USR HST DS 9600 V.32/V.42b
Location: Missouri City (Houston), Texas
Primary Focus: OS/2
Comments: First-time callers have full access.

Stadium Club OS/2, The

Sysop: Ed Baldwin
Phone/Node/Modem: (713) 458-2037, 1:106/1028, USR HST DS 14.4 V.32/V.42b
Location: Houston, Texas
Primary Focus: OS/2, echos
Comments: Member of Fidonet and OS2NET (81:202/2). Running BinkleyTerm/2 and Maximus/2 under OS/2 2.01.

Bulletin Board Systems: Virginia

Max's Doghouse

Sysop: Joe Salemi
Phone/Node/Modem: (703) 548-7849, 1:109/136, 2400 MNP
Location: Alexandria, Virginia
Primary Focus: OS/2
Comments: Also supports LANs.

OS/2 Shareware

Sysop: Pete Norloff
Phone/Node/Modem: (703) 385-4325, 1:109/347, USR HST DS 14.4 V.32b/V.42b
Phone/Node/Modem: (703) 385-4325, n/a, USR HST DS 14.4 V.32b/V.42b
Location: Fairfax, Virginia
Primary Focus: OS/2
Comments: Collection of more than 3,400 OS/2-specific files totaling more than 250M in 20 file areas. 2,700 callers from 20 countries, 8 phone lines; currently taking more than 10,000 calls a month. Connected to four computer networks. Carrying 36 OS/2-related message conferences. Open access policy on public nodes; subscriber lines available. Online since March 1990.

Systems Exchange, The

Sysop: Bill Andrus
Phone/Node/Modem: (703) 323-7654, 1:109/301, USR HST 9600
Location: Fairfax, Virginia
Primary Focus: OS/2
Comments: OS/2 ASYNC Comm software, with source. Also features graphics conversion software and OS/2 games, most with source.

OS/2@Manassas

Sysop: David Bannister
Phone/Node/Modem: (703) 369-0672, 1:265/101, 14.4 V.32b/V.42b
Location: Manassas, Virginia
Primary Focus: All facets of OS/2
Comments: More than 3,000 files totaling 220M online. All Fido and ibmNETOS/2-related conferences. Also a member ofibmNET (40:4370/101).

Bulletin Board Systems: Washington

Alternate Reality

Sysop: Todd Riches
Phone/Node/Modem: (206) 557-9258, 1:343/118, Smart One 2400 MNP 2-7
Location: Issaquah, Washington
Primary Focus: DOS, OS/2, and Windows utilities, games, and music
Comments: DOS, OS/2, and Windows file areas.

Sno-Valley Software Exchange

Sysop: LeRoy DeVries
Phone/Node/Modem: (206) 880-6575, 1:343/108, USR HST DS 9600 V.32b/V.42b

Location: North Bend, Washington
Primary Focus: Files and messages for OS/2
Comments: Hub distribution for FidoNet Backbone files.

Interlink Data Services

Sysop: Dana Laude
Phone/Node/Modem: (414) 233-5926, 1:139/710, USR HST DS 9600 V.32/V.42b
Phone/Node/Modem: (414) 233-3181, 1:139/711, Viva 2496if (2400)
Location: Oshkosh, Wisconsin
Primary Focus: IBM's OS/2 operating system support
Comments: Originally brought online in 1986 under the name AppleMeadow BBS. We now specialize in support for IBM's OS/2 operating system; a member of ibmNET and the Developer's Assistance Program. We also carry a wide selection of DOS, UNIX, and Amiga files online.

OS/2 System Messages

Critical errors in OS/2 are processed by a central error handler. Any action that results in a serious error, such as a drive that is not ready, produces a system modal dialog box with a message number and descriptive text. This system error dialog has three choices (see Figure C.1).

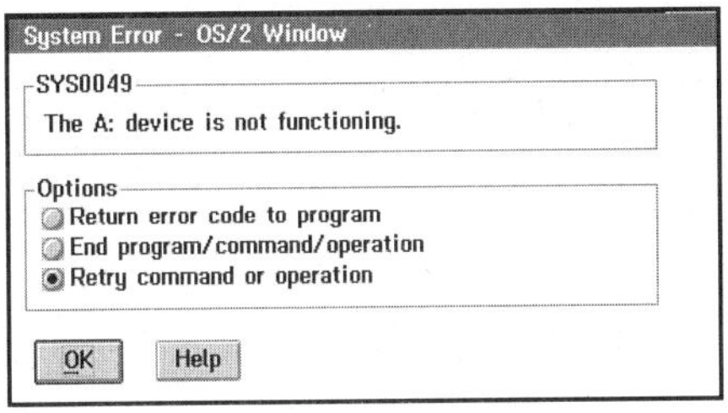

Figure C.1. A drive not ready error from OS/2 2.1.

This dialog is similar to the popular DOS "Abort, Retry, Ignore" message. Select the first option when the application stopped by the error can handle it. For example, issuing the `DIR` command on a drive that does not exist results in error message 36. Returning the error to the program allows the session to continue, and the command processor displays text from message 21.

The third option can be used after a corrective operation. If the `DIR` command is issued on a drive with the door open, the system error message shown in Figure C.1 appears. Retry works once the door is closed.

The second option is a last resort that closes the offending session. If this does not work, the system is in serious trouble and probably needs a warm or cold reboot.

If you are using your application in a full-screen session, the critical error handler displays the error in a full screen. The entire screen blanks and displays only the error message.

If you are using an application on the Workplace Shell desktop, the critical error handler displays the message in a Presentation Manager window (without erasing the entire screen). OS/2 2.1 uses this method for OS/2 and DOS applications that you run in a windowed command line, as well as Presentation Manager applications.

When OS/2 2.1 displays the critical error in a Presentation Manager window, you can usually use the Print Screen key to send a copy of it to the printer. This is useful to capture all the processor's register information for fatal protection violation errors.

For fatal errors from which OS/2 2.1 cannot recover, you have the option to display further information that is useful for an application developer to debug the problem. You can request that the OS/2 operating system display the processor register contents. Memory protection violation errors produce the SYS3175 error, and you can select to display the register information similar to that shown in Figure C.2.

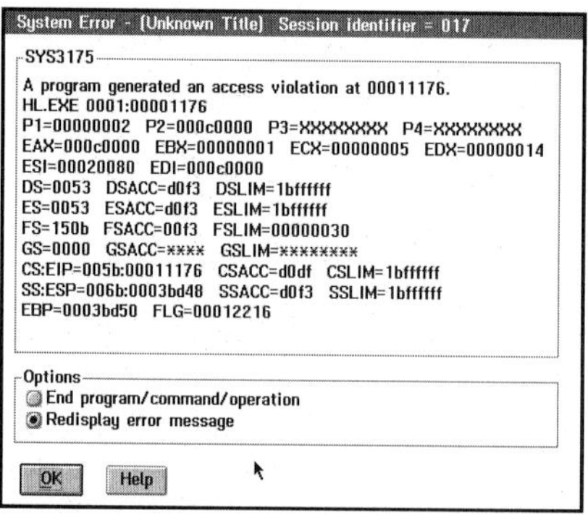

Figure C.2. *Register contents after a fatal protection violation error in an application program.*

If you ever see an error message like this, it is a good idea to write down the information that appears in this message. The developers of your application may need this information for debugging assistance. Again, you can usually press the Print Screen key to capture the information.

> **TIP** The important information is the name of the failing program (on the second line of the error message) and the CS:EIP register contents. This is usually enough to determine the location of the error. The system error dialogs also have a help button. When this is selected, the dialog expands to display additional information. This usually has two parts: an explanation and an action. This text is also accessible from the command line. Note the error number and type `HELP SYS####`.

The error messages are stored in several files in the OS2\SYSTEM directory. They have the extension MSG and work in header/detail pairs. Error message numbers have a three-character code followed by a four-digit number. OSO001.MSG contains the default system messages and uses the code SYS. Other codes include REX for REXX errors and SPL for the print spooler. Some applications install their messages in other directories. LAN Server messages have the code NET and are stored in \IBMLAN\NETPROG. The system error handler can find them if the directory is set in `DPATH`.

The following listing is an example of an OS/2 error message (SYS0002). The entry contains the following information: the error code, the message, the explanation, and the recommended action. Use the command line Help utility for more information.

Message: The system cannot find the file specified.

Explanation: The file named in the command does not exist in the current directory or specified search path, or the filename was entered incorrectly.

Action: Retry the command using the correct file name.

You can generate a full listing of OS/2 error messages with the following REXX command file:

```
/* Sample REXX command file to dump error messages */
   Do i = 2 to 3400
     help i
   End
```

Index

Symbols

A

B

C

D

E

F

G

H

I

J

K

L

M

N

O

P

Q

R

T

U

V

W

X-Z

What's on the Disk

- 4OS2—a powerful replacement for the OS/2 command processor (based on the award-winning 4DOS program)
- INIMaint—a Presentation Manager program for displaying and managing your *.INI files
- Terminal Emulator 2—a protected-mode communications program
- LH2—an archive and compression utility
- Galleria—this utility allows you to display, edit, and convert bitmap graphic files
- Presentation Manager Scrapbook—a 32-bit Presentation Manager application for organizing files and information
- DeskMan/2—a utility that backs up folders and objects in the Workplace Shell
- DiskStat—this utility provides a continually updated display of statistics for any disk drive

Installing the Disk

The software on the disk is stored in a compressed form. You cannot use the software without first installing it on your hard drive. To automatically install all the files to your hard drive, use the following procedure:

> From the OS/2 command line, type `drive:INSTALL` and press Enter (`drive:` is the letter of the drive that contains the disk).

This installs all the programs to your hard drive, and each program is installed in its own subdirectory. Please read the README.DOC file on the disk for more information. To install all the files, you need at least 3 megabytes of free space on your hard drive.